American Law and the Constitutional Order

American Law
and the Constitutional Order

Historical Perspectives

Edited by
Lawrence M. Friedman
and
Harry N. Scheiber

Harvard University Press
Cambridge, Massachusetts, and London, England

Library of Congress Cataloging in Publication Data
Main entry under title:

American law and the constitutional order.

   1. Law — United States — History and criticism — Addresses, essays, lectures. 2. United States — Constitutional history — Addresses, essays, lectures. I. Friedman, Lawrence Meir, 1930-   II. Scheiber, Harry N. KF352.A79   340'.0973   77-16640
ISBN 0-674-02525-3 (cloth)
ISBN 0-674-02526-1 (paper)

To Willard Hurst

Preface

The last fifteen years have witnessed a vigorous resurgence of interest in American legal and constitutional history in the nation's universities. For many years previously, legal history, when it was taught at all, was in most law schools restricted to tracing the rise of the common law — which meant British legal history roughly from the Norman Conquest to the death of Henry VIII. Modern British law and most of American law (especially in the national period) were strangely neglected. Outside the law schools as well, university curricula ignored a significant portion of American legal history. To be sure, there was a vigorous tradition of research and teaching in constitutional history; but courses and seminars rarely gave systematic attention to the history of law in the states — or indeed to some of the larger issues relating to American legal culture and institutions.

Now, as a result of several important lines of inquiry by students of law, history, and social science, the tide has shifted. It is becoming well recognized that law has had a significant place in American development that reaches far beyond the federal Supreme Court. Law has played its role on many stages—state, local, and national, in lawyer's offices, at the desks of registers and receivers of the federal and state land offices, in corporation boardrooms and legislative cloak-rooms, in the daily transactions of people in the marketplace and in their voting on election days. For much of the history of this country, law at the federal level has been only one element (and not, by any means, uniformly the most important) in a much broader process by which Americans have ordered their lives, their business, and their social relations.

Rediscovery and analysis of law in the full richness of its historical complexity have their counterparts in historical scholarship more generally. Economic historians have been reappraising the institutional structure of the "market." They have been reexamining assumptions about the rationality of market behavior and the alleged "autonomy" of market forces in light of formal legal institutions and informal social behavior that reveal social mores and behavioral norms regarding law. Social historians have been examining American communities more closely, and they have sought to define the meaning of the full range of "ordinary transactions" in a society whose functioning cannot be well enough illuminated by exclusive attention to the great lightning flashes that emanate from Washington.

The tendency of Americans to use (or overuse) formal legal institutions was noticed in the 1830s by Tocqueville, and the tendency has not lessened with the years. When a society lacks certain functional equivalents for law, it will make heavy use of formally structured legal institutions. Every society requires tools of social control — in other words, authority. No one has improved upon Max Weber's well-known threefold classification of types of legitimate authority: the charismatic, the traditional, and the rational-legal. In America, "charisma," as Weber defined it, has always been in short supply. One can certainly find charismatic authority in American history (Brigham Young is a good example), but we can safely discount its general importance. Traditional authority, too, has been weaker in the United States than in other societies. The early colonial theocracies tried to minimize the use of formal law, or to take the law into their hands and rule in their own discretion under the cover of divine authority. Their attempts, in the long run, failed.

In general, the United States has been so heterogeneous, so large and loosely populated, that the traditional patterns of authority and stratification, brought over from European society, lost their magic and their power. No doubt an abundance of land and a high degree of social mobility also helped undermine traditional authority. Under these circumstances Americans turned to law, sometimes perhaps unconsciously, for want of a better glue to keep society cohesive. Hence, the story of law and legal institutions is at the center of American development in a way that it is not in China or even in France.

For two hundred years, moreover, the United States has been a federal republic; and for a hundred and fifty years before that, it was a collection of colonies that owed some sort of common allegiance to the British crown, but almost none to one another. Under these circumstances, an inherited legal language split into a babel of dialects, just as the Latin of the Roman Empire disintegrated into the various Romance tongues. For most of our history the states have been able to go their own ways, fashioning legal systems to suit their needs and tastes, though within a single legal culture (and bound together to a certain extent by the similarity of their people and the common background of lawyers and judges). Local autonomy is hard pressed to maintain itself in the twentieth century. Curiously, the constitutional regime itself is now one of its enemies: it is the vehicle through which some kind of common basis of order is imposed on the states and the cities. To an astonishing degree, in the last generation constitutional law has been extending its reach into other parts of the legal tradition. Almost no field of law today is untouched by national rules and interests; almost no field is exempt from standards forced on it through the use of one or more of the lapidary phrases of the federal Constitution, vigorously and imaginatively interpreted by the federal courts. What was more local a century ago than selling wheat, or going to school, or arresting a drunk? Yet federal rules and standards are now intruders in all of these areas.

The history of law is a vital field, a growing field, and a field that has much to offer the student, despite the technicality and jargon that lawyers have traditionally used as wrappings for their packages. Once the hurdles of language are overcome, the inherent drama of the subject is bound to engage the student. These readings are offered toward that end.

In this volume we have sought to present a sample of useful and stimulating work in legal and constitutional history. We say "sample," because obviously we have had to make hard choices, and while we include among our authors many who have been leaders in this field, others who have made important contributions are not represented. The choices were made with the aim of striking a balance between the history of constitutional law and the larger history of American legal institutions. The selection may help to redress what has been mentioned as a deep-seated imbalance in teaching and scholarship— the excessive, almost exclusive, attention given to federal constitutional history. It is indicative of the great interest in law that prevails at the frontiers of scholarship today that we can include not only works from history and law but also exemplary studies from sociology, political science, and economic history. We are grateful to the authors, publishers, and journal editors who have extended permission to include the studies in this collection.

Lawrence M. Friedman

Harry N. Scheiber

Contents

American Law and the Constitutional Order

Part One

American Legal Culture

Chapters 1 and 2 introduce the reader in a general way to what is distinctive in the American legal tradition. Willard Hurst considers the rule of law and its role in the development of American society, with particular emphasis on how law served the economy. He tries to catalog the various functions of law in the society of the United States, particularly its impact on the marketplace. His conclusions incline him to find previous research in legal history to be wanting, one-sided in many regards, and skewed in the direction of the dramatic and the overtly political. It has overlooked or neglected the richness of legal data. What, for example, is the relationship between the very distinctive use of law in the United States and the distinctiveness of American society? This is the kind of question that Hurst believes should be at the very heart of legal history.

Hurst's influence on American legal historiography has been great. He has insisted on rejecting legal history that is written in terms of "topics defined by legal categories." He is not concerned with the great "consitutional debates" so much as with less obviously dramatic topics, the "relation of tax policy to the

fortunes of agriculture and other extractive industries," for example. Such topics illuminate how law works its influence in every corner of social life in ways that prove, in the long run, decisive. Hurst warns us against the "bias toward themes of conflict," themes "which emphasize conscious and debated decisions." The most important events in legal history may not be dramatic events at all, but the cumulative effects of tiny acts — buying and selling land, cutting timber, and making out promissory notes. These bits of behavior in the aggregate may transform the economy and revolutionize the society. Historians should study every nook and cranny of the legal system, examining "social inertia and social drift," as well as "conscious contrivance." The reader should consider what is gained — and what is lost — through this perspective and this approach to legal history.

Lawrence Friedman's essay stresses the role of law as an instrument of social control; his major focus is on criminal justice and the relationship between the moral ideas of the community and its patterns of law enforcement. Friedman looks on various trends — the shifting public attitudes toward victimless crimes, for exam-

American Legal Culture

ple — and speculates about the currents of thought and patterns of behavior in the larger society that produced them.

The two essays share one common point of view: they find the prime source of legal change *outside* the law and within society itself.

Further Reading

Bloomfield, Maxwell. *American Lawyers in a Changing Society, 1776-1876.* Cambridge, Mass.: Harvard University Press, 1976.

Fleming, Donald, and Bernard Bailyn, eds. *Law in American History.* Boston: Little, Brown, and Co., 1971.

Friedman, Lawrence M. *A History of American Law.* New York: Simon & Schuster, 1973.

Hurst, Willard. *The Growth of American Law: The Law Makers.* Boston: Little, Brown, and Co., 1950.

————. *Law and Social Process in United States History.* Ann Arbor: University of Michigan Law School, 1960.

White, G. Edward. *The American Judicial Tradition.* New York: Oxford University Press, 1976.

1

Willard Hurst

The Law in United States History

Not only the man in the street but also professional students of society hold very limited images of what "law" means. Most often they take it to mean simply the drama of criminal trials: Perry Mason on Saturday-night television, the lurid promise of the murder yarns on drugstore racks. If they think of law in a little broader reference, probably it will be in terms of a remembered picture in a high school history text of portly gentlemen in frock coats striking attitudes: Webster replies to Hayne. If one presses them, the social scientists at least may concede there is more to law than this. Law, they will grant, states a great many doctrines which provide much of the vocabulary of public-policy discussion. But this is, after all, largely formal stuff; sophisticated students know that reality lies in the substance, in operations, in getting behind the law's formalism to the hard facts of interest and practical maneuver. So much for law — and little wonder, then, if neither the man in the street nor the student of society shows much curiosity to learn what aspects of social events or social processes might be better illumined by

Reprinted with minor editorial changes, from *Proceedings of the American Philosophical Society*, vol. 104, no. 5 (October 1960), pp. 518-526, by permission.

knowing more about the law's contribution.

Criminal trials and constitutional debates are important. Important, too, in ways which to a distressing degree are not understood even by well-educated men, is the formality of legal process. But these aspects of legal order, however important, fall far short altogether of representing the significance of legal process in this society. A more adequate definition of the attributes of our legal order suggests that study of law in these terms — and in particular study of legal history in these terms — should contribute more to the understanding of the society than the lay stereotypes would indicate.

For studying social process, the most useful definitions of law are made in terms of social functions of law. What are the most distinctive and most important jobs we have asked the law to do in this society? This asks for a modest definition: not what is "law" anywhere, anytime, but what has law been in the development of this particular society. This modesty is appropriate to the limits of what we know about the social functions of legal order. It is appropriate also to a definition of law looked at historically, because history regards events, that is, looks at processes always in particular context. Moreover, this relativist definition of law is peculiarly appropriate to our situation. For we have taken as a central value the idea that legal order should find its warrant in serving men as they strive to realize the larger potential of being — which means that law must find its warrant in relation to particular experience.

Four functions have been especially important to defining law's roles in the growth of this society. (1) To law we assigned the legitimate monopoly of violence; normally only the policeman goes armed. As a corollary, to law we assigned ultimate scrutiny of the legitimacy of all forms of secular power developed within the society — that is, of all means by which some men may exercise over the wills of other men. Modes of competition and forms of private association thus exist subject to legal regulation to protect the public interest. (2) We used law to define and to implement an idea of constitutionalism as the norm of all secular power. This is an idea which with us had reference to all forms of secular power, not merely to official power. It meant, first, that we believed there should be no center of secular power which was not in some way subject to review by another center of such power. If there seems something paradoxical in this notion, the historic record nonetheless shows that we lived by it; for example, we used law to foster and protect the growth of private (that is, nonofficial) associations like the business corporation or religious, political, and social associations, to build centers of energy and opinion which might provide counterweights to official power. Thus we sought to make all secular power responsible to power outside itself, for ends which it alone did not define. But responsibility means nothing until we know, responsibility for what? The second and most distinctive aspect of our insistence that all secular power be responsible (constitutional) power was that we held the final measure of responsibility to be in serving individual life. (3) We used law to promote formal definition of values and of appropriate means to implement values.

In other words, this legal order was characterized by strong insistence on procedural regularity. (4) Finally, we assigned to legal process important roles in allocating scarce resources — of manpower and human talent, as well as of nonhuman sources of energy — for shaping the general course of economic development. This was an especially important use of law, in a society which believed that in economic creativity it held the means to fashion new standards of human dignity. At the outset government here held the unique asset of the public domain, which we spent to help build turnpikes, canals, and railroads and to create in the Mississippi Valley a republic of family farms. Likewise, we made bold use of taxing and spending powers of national, state, and local governments to help create the framework of economic growth. Resource allocation by law was the more striking in our history because we placed great reliance on broad dispersion of economic decision making into private hands through the market, implemented through the law of property and contract. We supplemented private energies in the market by important delegations to nonofficial persons of powers of public concern. We gave railroads the right of eminent domain; we granted franchises to enterprisers to conduct public utilities and to charge toll for their services; by grant of limited liability to corporation stockholders and by contract, property, and tort doctrines which in effect favored venture, we encouraged men to take the risks of action, letting losses lie where they fell unless someone who had been hurt showed compelling reason why the law should help shift the burden.

These uses of law mean that law wove itself into the organization and processes of this society in ways which should make the study of legal process — and in particular of legal history — important to social science. (1) Because it held the legitimate monopoly of force, and incident thereto the authority to call to account all other forms of secular power, law bore some relation to all types of association and all means for mustering collective will and feeling. The obverse of free religious association here, for example, was the legally embodied policy of separation of church and state. (2) Because North American legal order sought to give content to the idea that all power must be constitutional (responsible) power, law entered into the practical meaning that individuality had in this society. The constitutional character of this legal order likewise meant that law was actually or potentially part of the social structure and social process; there was no pattern of social organization, no procedure of social interaction whose significance could be appraised without taking into account the demands which an ideal of constitutional order either did in fact make on it, or should make on it. Thus, for example, we cannot tell the story of the status and roles of women in the United States without including the meaning which the movements for married women's property legislation and equal suffrage had for defining the condition of woman as an effective member of the society. Again, we cannot understand the social history of the business corporation without including the search for acceptable definitions in law of the gounds on which, first, the practical power of corporate owners and, more recently, of corporate management may establish legitimacy. (3) Because this legal order emphasized procedural regularity — providing diverse organized means for bringing choices to definition and mustering evidence and reasoned argument for their resolution — law entered significantly into the process by which men created social goals and mobilized energies of mind and feeling to move toward their goals. Of course we must not exaggerate the rationality of the law, any more than that of other insitutions. Regard for procedures tends to create inertia or complacency with familiar ways; passion and prejudice color legal operations as they color any human operations where men feel deep concern about the stakes. Moreover, how men feel is at least as valid a part of their experience as what they achieve by reason; indeed, reason probably finds justification ultimately only as an instrument by which men achieve more subtle, more varied, and more shared emotion. So qualified, however, and always within the framework of a constitutional ordering of power, the increase in men's rational competence and the extension of more rationalized processes of human relations ranked high among the organizing values of this society. Legal process ranked with industrial technology and with organized science as a major means for enlarging the scope of rationalized behavior. In the second half of the twentieth century the trend of events seemed likely to give larger importance to the law's rationalizing role, in the interests of maintaining a vital constitutional tradition. The pressure of scientific and technical rationalization of social processes increased the scale and intricacy of social organization, the demands made in the name of organizational integrity and efficiency, and the inertia created by organizational mass. Legal procedures in part had served and would continue to serve to provide a framework of reasonably assured expectations, backed by the force of the state, within which a complex social division of labor could work. More important, however, in our tradition legal procedure had the ultimate function of implementing the constitutional idea — that choices, and the costs as well as gains of choices, be brought to definition, that power holders be made to account for their use of power, and in the last analysis that power be used to serve individual life. That growth proceeded along these lines was witnessed by the painful efforts to hammer out a law of labor relations within which management and labor might create a kind of due process and equal protection of law to govern the discipline of the modern factory. (4) Because we used law boldly as a means of resource allocation — with at least as great effect as we used the market — the history of legal process was woven closely into the general growth of the economy and of key relations of social and eco-

Willard Hurst

nomic power in the United States. The terms on which we disposed of the public domain in the Mississippi Valley, for example, materially affected the development of a tradition of agrarian political revolt on the one hand, and on the other the growth of the political as well as business and social power of big corporations, of which the first models were the land-grant railroads. The public domain no longer offers government the unique leverage it afforded for nineteenth-century social planning — though current controversy over franchises for use of the airwaves reminds us that social growth may bring new areas of public domain into policy significance. However, through its fiscal powers twentieth-century government plays as large a role in affecting the directions and content of the commonwealth as did nineteenth-century government through the public lands. Demands upon the resources-allocation functions of law continue to involve law in the main processes of social change and stability.

This essay seeks to appraise United States legal history as a field of scholarship, in its promise and in its development to date. I need not, nor could I within this span, take stock of the whole reach of research in law. However, what can be said of the discipline of legal history applies in large measure to other types of legal research.

Four limitations of the general product attest the want of philosophy in the study of North American legal history. (1) Historians have exaggerated the work of courts and legal activity immediately related to litigation. (2) They have paid too little attention to the social functions of law. (3) They have not distributed their effort with adequate response to the facts of timing and the reality of major discontinuities in the country's growth in relation to the uses of law. (4) They have exaggerated areas of conscious conflict and deliberated action, at the expense of realistic account of the weight of social inertia and the momentum of social drift.

Anglo-American law men are by tradition and training biased toward equating law with what judges do, to the neglect not only of legislative, executive, and administrative activity, but also to the neglect even of the out-of-court impact of the work of lawyers, let alone the additions or subtractions made in legal order by lay attitudes and practices affecting legal norms. We early trained lawyers by apprenticeship which taught them court pleadings and client caretaking. When the principal revolution in legal education arrived in the 1870s, it was organized about the case method of instruction, which again emphasized the work of courts. Most of the business of the bar through the nineteenth century had to do with the property and contract affairs of clients, and most of the law of these fields was common (that is, judge-made) law, so that through the formative period of our main legal tradition the focus remained on the judicial process. Thus, first our treatise writing and later the writing done for legal journals dealt mainly with public policy as declared by courts. This bias of professional thinking was not affected by the fact that through the nineteenth century Congress and the state legislatures churned out large quantities of important legislation, or by the fact that in great areas of policy which did not lend themselves easily to common-law development the framework of the law was erected mainly in statutes (as in the law of the public lands, public education, public utilities, highways, health and sanitation, or the organization of local government). From limited beginnings in the late nineteenth century, executive and administrative lawmaking grew to great proportions alongside the statute law. Judicial lawmaking was never as exclusively important as the concentration of legal writing might seem to show. From the 1870s on, legislative, executive, and administrative processes definitely became the principal sources of formed policy. The course offerings of even the better law schools were slow to reflect this reality. But legal research was even slower, with legal historians badly lagging the field. Of course the work of the courts continues to be of great importance. In our time legal and nonlegal institutions take on increasing size, and there is growing readiness to accept demands made on individuals in the name of the security and operating efficiency of large social aggregates. In this context more than ever before the availability of independent courts and an independent class of professional advocates supported not by grace of the state but by private fees, represent basic elements of civil liberty. In the second half of the twentieth century the courts have distinctive importance because they are the forum in which individuals and small groups, of their own resources, can best call organized power to account. To recognize this, however, in no measure justifies the extent to which legal-history writing, along with legal philosophy and other legal research, has treated the judicial process as if it were the whole of legal order. Symbolic is the fact, for example, that while twentieth-century scholarship has given us at least four large-scale treatises, a dozen substantial monographs, and scores of essays in the law journals on the history of constitutional doctrine as it has been made by the Supreme Court of the United States, we lack a single first-rate modern work on the history of constitutional doctrine as it has been formed in the Congress.

The bulk of legal-history writing has been about topics defined by legal categories. We have much writing about commerce-clause doctrine, but little about the meaning of commerce-clause doctrine for the development or operation of sectional or nationwide marketing organization, or about the impress which such business history may have made on constitutional principles. There is some rather formal history of property law, but little history of the significance of fee-simple title for types of land use, for the private and social accounting of income and costs of alternative land uses, or for the political and social balance of power.

There are some essays on the history of contract law, but little or no effort to define or appraise the meaning that contract law had for the functioning of the market, the provision of credit, or the allocation of gains and costs of business venture. There are scattered writings about the history of the mortgage, the corporate indenture, the receivership and tax law, but we lack the good studies we should have of the historic relations of law to the growth and channeling of investment capital. There is a good deal in print about various aspects of the Bill of Rights, but no connected story of the implications of civil-rights doctrines for the shifting balance of power among various kinds of groups and between the individual and official and private group power at different stages of the country's growth. Though better than a generation has gone by since we heard the call for a sociological jurisprudence, legal-history writing has made little response, but continues content on the whole to let the formal headings of the law fix its subject matter. It is an ironic course of affairs, in a society whose tradition is so strongly constitutional, insisting that legal order is not an end in itself but gains legitimate meaning only in terms of its service to ends of life outside law.

In the total distribution of effort, there has been a disproportionate attention in legal-history writing to beginnings — and to beginnings in their most obvious sense — at the expense of proper development of hypotheses concerning the main lines of growth through to our own time. Much attention has focused on colonial origins, on the period of constitutional experiment from 1776 to 1790, and on the successive frontier phases of national expansion. I do not quarrel with the worth of attending to such formative periods taken in themselves, but only with the tendency to fasten onto origins without equal curiosity to follow through, and with failure to see that in terms of law's relation to gathering issues of power and social function there were other less obvious periods of beginnings

Willard Hurst

which should also be studied. First, as an example of the want of follow-through, it is odd that for so many states we have writing which, with care sometimes verging on antiquarian enthusiasm, traces the beginnings of territorial and state courts (once again, the excessive preoccupation with judicial process), but little good writing on such basic themes as law's relation to the creation of transportation networks, the law's response to the business cycle, or the relation of tax policy to the fortunes of agriculture and other extractive industries. These omissions are, of course, part of the neglect of the social-function history of law which I have already noted. But they also represent a neglect of a familiar and important time sequence characteristic of the growth of these states, whose people normally established their basic legal institutions in the nineteenth century with some obvious impatience to get on to their central care, which was the expansion of their economy.

Second, on the neglect of the less obvious beginnings, the most notable example is the relative inattention to the sharp changes in direction and pace of social movement which came about in the 1830s, the 1870s, and the 1930s. The 1830s saw rapid development of markets and marketing emphasis in the public policy making of one state after another, with reflection especially in the statute books, as we passed from relatively simple agrarian to more commercial and credit-centered economies. The 1870s saw the rapid cumulation of forces channeled or given new impetus by the new scale of organization of men and capital and the new techniques of public and private finance generated out of the North's war effort. Change here was far more drastic than in the 1830s and amounted to a major break in continuity. Due mainly to the shifts in the size of private industrial and financial organization and in the reach of markets which gathered force in the seventies, by the late nineties the United States was a qualitatively different society from what it had

been before the Civil War. The strains and conflicts, the gains and losses attendant upon this rapid and major alteration of the country's power structure and modes of operation provide main themes for legal history which we have hardly begun to explore. The 1930s saw the cumulate impact of trends in social and economic interdependence which had been gathering force since World War I. The challenge of these themes is so large, indeed, that one may wonder whether more essays on territorial beginnings represent contributions to knowledge so much as refuges from more exacting studies.

Legal-history research may be especially subject to a bias toward themes of conflict, or at least toward themes which emphasize conscious and debated decisions. Such a bias is favored by the emphasis of our legal order on formal procedures. Insofar as they are efficient, regular procedures for framing, deliberating, and adopting constitutions, statutes, executive orders, and administrative rules work toward bringing choices to definition, aligning interested parties, promoting expression, and energizing will. Lawsuits and court decisions work even more dramatically to these ends. Hence, insofar as legal-history research has tended toward exaggerated emphasis upon the judicial process, it has particularly strengthened a bias toward equating men's history with the record of their more or less conscious strivings. Yet, the broader the reach of our hypotheses and the deeper our concern to study the social functions of legal order, the more we will learn to respect the relative influence of inertia and drift in affairs. The most realistic view of all aspects of man's history leads to the conclusion that most of what has happened to men has happened without their wanting it or striving for it or opposing it or — more important — without their being aware of the meaning of trends until patterns of structure and force have developed past points of revoking. This general judgment seems no less true of legal history in this country. There is peculiar irony in the fact, since it is the business of constitutional legal order to promote responsible control of events. No example is more instructive than the history of antitrust law, whose development both reflected and persistently lagged behind the imperious course of revolutions in industrial and financial organization. Aside from some efforts either to expound or refute Marxian styles of hypothesis — and even here the institutional cast of language only thinly disguises villains or heroes felt to be working in the background — the writing of North American legal history has paid little attention to putting legal phenomena in due perspective relative to the massive weight of inertia or to the implacable movement of decisions taken by drift and default.

If legal-history research and writing in this country have moved within too narrow limits, the criticisms point to some positive prescriptions. (1) We need to allocate more effort to studying legislative, executive, and administrative processes as well as the bar's contributions to these formal processes and to the informal social regulation that goes on through the market and through private association. Likewise we need more attention to ways in which lay attitudes toward law (including laymen's disregard of law or their mistaken images of it) have affected the creation of institutions of social order other than formal legal institutions. (2) Legal history should begin to contribute more to develop fact-based, fact-tested theories of social structure and social process. For example, we should have more legal history written in terms of law's operational significance for the institution of the market, studied in as wide a range of interplay of law and market as the wit and devotion of legal scholarship can compass. (3) Legal-history writing should come to bear with greater emphasis upon the past one hundred years in the United States. Especially should there be substantial scholarly investment in study of

the profound shifts in structure, process, and attitudes that occurred in the generations beginning about 1820 and 1861, and in the depression 1930s. Legal history has not been made only by quill pen and candlelight. (4) Not with despair but with realistic estimate of the odds against man's conscious contrivance and out of conviction that his distinctive quality lies in rebellion against the odds, legal history should treat as critical themes the impact of social inertia and social drift. Nor can we afford to take this direction with any moral complacency, weighing our own shrewdness against the blunders of our ancestors. If the more significant decisions regarding natural-resources use were made by default in the nineteenth century, no less by default have been the twentieth-century decisions on metropolitan growth; if the nineteenth century allowed market demands for rail transport unduly to determine the course of public policy, no less has the twentieth century allowed the immediate conveniences, comforts, and social-status markings of the automobile to determine a fantastic range of matters of public concern, from the safety of life to the location of commerce and industry. The physical size of this country, the invitations to large-scale economic effort posed by its natural resources and population growth, as well as deep-rooted, but little-calculated, faith in the self-evident values of growth and movement and change (in intangible senses of status and accomplishment as well as by tangible measures of product and location) — such factors contributed to make provision of transport an element of uncommon influence on our public policy, and a good example in both nineteenth- and twentieth-century settings of the type of unplanned and largely undirected cumulation of events which had basic shaping effect upon what law was asked to do and how it did it.

There are many profitable directions in which a broader conception of legal history might take us. I have drawn specific prescriptions from four criticisms of limitations implicit in the bulk of work so far done. In addition let me note some more general developments that would be useful. Two concern the more effective study of legal institutions themselves. Two concern particularly critical kinds of meaning which the study of legal history might have for better understanding the general course of this society.

First, as to legal institutions: (1) In times when social change moves fast, wide, and deep amid peril to the prized values of a constitutionally ordered community, we need more sophisticated knowledge of the potentials and the limits of the major agencies of lawmaking. If no other currents of events enforced this need, it would gain enough urgency because of the extent to which we depend upon public finance to sustain the momentum of the economy and upon foreign policy to maintain the national security. On the whole the organization, procedures, and working traditions of the legislative and executive branches represent responses to conditions which the fast pace of events has put far behind us. If there need be less concern for the adequacy of judicial organization, this is not because it lacks serious defects. However, the most important job for the courts in this highly organized modern society is not that of general policymaking but of insuring some minimum of decent procedural protection for individuals and small groups confronting large organized power. On the whole this is a task simpler enough than general policymaking so that it can be handled with what we have, if bench and bar apply their traditions with intelligence and courage. The situation is quite different as to the sufficiency of the legislature and executive before the daunting challenges of the times; the difference is reflected, for example, in contemporary controversies over the proper roles of legislative investigation and over functions of the National Security Council or the Joint Chiefs of Staff, or in hearings and debates of the Congressional Joint Committee on the Economic Report

of the President's Council of Economic Advisors. Types of public problems vary in distinctive character and challenge; types of public agency vary in distinctive capacities, whether born of formal structure and process or of tradition. Legal history should lend us more insight into the working character, promise, and limitations of formal agencies for making public decisions. (2) There is no more badly neglected area of legal research than that of sanctions, the comparative study of methods of implementing policy. Given life's infinite variety and the hard limits of social science research techniques so far available, the study of sanctions is an area in which we now stand to gain most from history. Nor should we view it as the study of factors of secondary importance. The more difficult the basic policy choices, the more surely must judgments of the promise and costs of implementation enter into the basic decisions. Moreover, we grow into some basic decisions out of experience of what we can expect to do. Sophisticated study of experience in enforcing public policy will require overleaping the limitations which have marked the bulk of legal historical writing — appraising the interplay of legislative and executive with judicial processes, relating law to the functional character of other social institutions on which it impinges, putting legal decisions and procedures into the proper perspective of the times in which they are made, weighing the positive investment of resources which the law must provide or direct to obtain desired results. It is a commentary on the failure of scholarship thus far to tackle many major problems, that, for example, in the 1960s when we confront the difficulties of building equal protection of the laws for Negroes in voting and schooling we have no studied body of experience for guidance in handling problems of large-scale hostility to public policy. If legal historians will set themselves to significant problems in legal sanctions, they will lack no longer for a more searching philosophy of their discipline; their problems will push them into philosophy.

Second, consider two respects in which a broader approach to legal history might yield insights of two types especially important to understanding the general life of society.

(1) Because of the four key functions we have assigned to law — its scrutiny of all types of secular power, its constitutionalism, its emphasis on procedural regularity, and its role in resource allocation — but especially because of law's formality (its attention to regular procedures for examining and taking decisions), law offers peculiarly important evidence of the values which give this society coherence and vitality. Of course this is not true in equal measure of all we find recorded in law; inertia and drift play their roles here, too, so that a prime job for legal history is to distinguish what has living force from what is dead or dying, deceptive or hypocritical. Granted this need for making distinctions, legal history, just because of its relative formality, offers unusual evidence of the development of the values our people have held. Thus, study of legal history can make special contribution to the general history of ideas. The study of a people's values has basic importance to understanding a society, for it is the sharing of values that provides the bond of lasting human relations, even where (as with the value we put on the competitive processes of market) the shared values may express themselves in secondary conflict. Study of the growth of shared values has special importance not only for understanding this particular society, but for contributing to its strength. We have grown fast amid a great bustle of events and subject to major discontinuities in the emergence of new relations of power and process. We need to know ourselves in our strengths and failings much better than we do. There is evidence of this need in the uncertain allegiance which common opinion has shown under stress even to such traditional values as those of the Bill of Rights. A broader concern with legal history as an avenue to the study of ideas will bring this discipline into relation to the most fundamental kinds of social analysis as well as into relation with the most critical living problems of our generation.

(2) Because legal processes and legal records bulk large among ways in which we bring values to definition, a broadly conceived legal history could help us come to terms with the good and the bad features of the pragmatic attitudes that are so central in this culture. Our actions show that we have believed that within a framework of generalized values men must make meaning for themselves in a universe whose baffling detail and sweep favor drift and inertia as the norm of men's experience. In this light the main theme of man's history is the cultivation of his awareness and of his capacities of mind and will to act upon his greater awareness of his situation. We need to strive to see, and to learn what our creative possibilities are by striving to act upon what we see. The experimental and activist bias of our culture rests upon these valid insights. On the other hand, our preoccupation with directed effort and what it teaches has led us also into a bias toward exalting the immediately practical — in the sense of knowledge which can be translated into immediate operations — at the expense of understanding larger causes and more remote chains of effects. Thus a valid pragmatism is constantly at war with an illegitimate pragmatism in our way of life. Because it brings so much focused effort to bear upon making choices and counting gains and costs, legal process offers rich tangible evidence of these warring brands of pragmatism in our common life. For example, the history of our worship of the fee-simple title to land — in its fruitful relation to the development of civil liberty, on the one hand, and its unfortunate relation to the waste of natural resources, on the other — could be told in ways that would show how legal history might illuminate the sound

growth and also the distortion of pragmatic values in this society. If the cultivation of awareness is the basic theme which expounds man's most distinctive life role, the most characteristic functions of our legal order — its scrutiny of the arrangements of power, its insistence on the responsibility (constitutional status) of legitimate power, and on procedural regularity, and its uses for resource allocation — point to the intimate relation which the imaginative study of legal history should have to the study of general history.

Implicit in what I have said in appraising some approaches to legal history is the notion that we should study history to learn more about realizing life's possibilities. History itself will teach us not to hold a naive faith that men readily learn from history. Moreover, the view I take of man means that there is no need to apologize for studying history partly because there is pleasure in the effort; the enjoyment lies precisely in man's nature, for his life consists most distinctively in his consciousness. But writing and reading history are more than aesthetic experiences. They are themselves kinds of activity that constitute man's distinctive being, which consists in his response to and rebellion against the challenges of an impersonal universe. It is in this sense that legal-history research and writing stand under the functional command to serve the growth of our philosophy.

2

Lawrence M. Friedman

Notes Toward a History of American Justice

In Kent County, Delaware, in 1703, Adam Latham, a laborer, and Joan Mills, wife of a laborer named Andrew Mills, were brought before the county court. The grand jury presented Joan Mills for adultery. She pleaded guilty to the charge. For punishment, the court ordered her to be publicly whipped — twenty-one lashes on her bare back, well applied; she was also sentenced to prison, at hard labor, for one year. Adam Latham was convicted of fornication. He was sentenced to receive twenty lashes on his bare back, well laid on, in full public view. He was also accused of stealing Isaac Freeland's dark brown gelding, worth two pounds, ten shillings. Adam pleaded guilty; for this crime he was sentenced to another four lashes, and was further required to pay for the gelding. Adam had been in trouble over Joan Mills before, charged with "the Sin of Incontinency and fornication." At that time, he was acquitted, but the court ordered him to post bond guaranteeing "good behavior." He had broken his word. Now he was ordered to "weare a Roman T on his left arme on the Outside of his uppermost garment ... for the space of six months next."[1] These were typical crimes and punishments in colo-nial America. Published colonial records show hundreds of similar examples.[2]

We note the tremendous stress on visibility. The whipping post, pillory, and stocks stood in the public square. They did not gather dust. Countless men and women felt the whip, or stood in the stocks. When Christopher Lawson, of York County, Maine, came into court "unsevelly," with a "turbilent behea-viouer," in July 1669, he was forthwith "comited to sitt on ower in the stockes."[3] In the same volume of records we read about Sarah Morgan, who struck her husband, horror of horrors, and was given the choice of paying a fine or standing for a half-hour at Kittery, at a public town met-ting, with a gag in her mouth and "the cause of her offence writt upon her for-head."[4] The law made common use of brands and badges of shame. A burglar, under the Laws and Liberties of Massa-chusetts (1648), was to be "branded on the forehead with the letter (B)." A second offender would be "branded as before," and whipped. The third offender would be "put to death, as being incorrigible."[5] Colonies made liberal use of devices such as the bilbo, the cucking stool, and, for military offenders, the wooden horse — all of which carried stigma and shame.

It is a commonplace that social forces produce law, directly and indirectly. It follows that different cultures will make

Reprinted from *Buffalo Law Review*, vol. 24 (1974), p. 111-134 by permission. Copyright, 1974 by *Buffalo Law Review*.

Lawrence M. Friedman

law in different ways. In every society there are the rulers and the ruled: some individuals, groups, and strata have more power or influence than others; the law that any society makes will reflect the interests of those on top to the extent of their superior might. But power and influence do not directly act on law. Law — statutes, doctrines, legal behavior in general — comes about only when individuals and groups make *demands* on the system. *Demands*, then, rather than interests, are the proximate causes of law. The structure of demands is a cultural factor; no doubt its shape always reveals the powerful pull of long-term pressures, deriving from those with influence and power. But one cannot deduce the catalog of demands current in society directly from a knowledge of the real, objective needs of those with power — actual and potential. Every society rests on a set of implicit bargains about the legitimate limits of law; in every society a set of important attitudes supports these bargains.

For every era we want to ask: what forces had power, real and potential; what were their interests; and what were their demands? These demands need not be solely economic in nature. Power is not solely economic. Distinct and important are the demands for the maintenance of *moral* hegemony — demands for a monopoly of respectability — in short, for legitimacy.

We will analyze, in a much oversimplified scheme, three periods of American history in terms of these simple propositions. The three periods are: colonial America, the first two-thirds of the nineteenth century, and the period from about 1870 to the present. There is nothing neat about these "periods." They do seem, however, to reflect differences in prevailing frames of mind.

We began with colonial America. We cannot sum this period up, of course, in a single glib formula. There were more than a dozen separate "colonies," and the colonial "era" spanned a century and a half. But for much of this period the rulers, par-

ticularly in New England, had a clear idea of what crime meant. Crime was a kind of sin. Society's leaders did not easily abandon hope for the sinner. These were, in the main, small societies; they believed, rightly or wrongly, in repentence and rehabilitation. Except for the most hardened and abandoned cases, it was thought that men could respond to pressure and improve their way of life if they were instructed in proper behavior, punished for wrong conduct, subjected to shame and derision from their neighbors, and stigmatized when they strayed from the straight and narrow path. This is the reason why punishment was so open, so public. The man who was whipped in view of everyone was receiving physical punishment; but far more important, perhaps, he felt on his back the invisible whip of public opinion. Colonial society hoped to reform the sinner by invoking the mockery and scorn of his neighbors. Of course, everyone knew that a certain hard core would not respond. These people were, first, clearly labeled as the damned and then, in the most aggravated cases, banished or put to death. Kai Erickson has pointed out that branding marked a person "with the permanent emblem of his station in life." Branding thus made it difficult to restore the offender to a normal social role.[6] Only serious offenders, then, or repeaters suffered this penalty. The death penalty was infrequently used, but it was also an instrument of education. Hanging was as public as whipping. The world could observe the wages of sin.

The records of Kent County, Delaware, identified Andrew Mills and Adam Latham as laborers. Colonial society was nowhere democratic; indeed, no colonial society even pretended to such an ideal. Society was stratified and hierarchical. To be sure, compared to England, great numbers of people owned property and, therefore, made use of common-law institutions and the political process. James A. Henretta, in a study of colonial Boston, found 1,036 individuals in 1687 who paid taxes on real estate or on their income from trade.[7] The population of Boston was then roughly 6,000. Since children could hardly be expected to own property and most wives were effectively outside the economic system, landowners and tradesmen clearly constituted a sizable percentage of the people of colonial Boston and therefore were customers for the tools and techniques of formal law.

At the bottom of the social pyramid were the landless laborers, indentured servants, and, in the South, the mass of blacks held in slavery. What the records make clear is that the weight of colonial social control bore down most heavily upon this underclass. It was not the merchant, landowner, or minister who was whipped in public, branded, and set in the stocks. These were punishments for servants, laborers, and apprentices. The people who owned property, the leaders, and their willing followers defined what was the correct morality. The criminal law enforced this code, upholding a moral regime that the upper classes no doubt considered universal, but that strained the human nature of their servant. Whatever its ethical base, the code had a cold-blooded function. It aimed to maintain control over a work force on whose labor and obedience the community depended.

From the standpoint of the twentieth century, the law of crime and punishment in the American colonies is remarkable because of its emphasis on crime against morality — particularly what we would now call victimless crimes. But to the colonists every crime had a victim: society. In colonial Massachusetts, the man who blasphemed God, who was idle, who failed to attend church, or who slept with a servant girl was a criminal — and a sinner. He had to be punished in order to preserve the moral order. The argument that these acts hurt nobody would have puzzled and annoyed the good citizens of Massachusetts Bay. The moral order *was* society; injury to one was injury to both.

Colonial social control was by no means unique in this regard. Law and order take a similar form in small, face-to-face communities which have clear lines of authority—explicit notions of who is on top and who is on the bottom. Discipline in Massachusetts Bay was not unlike discipline among schoolchildren. We note, for example, Lawrence Wylie's study of a village in France where the usual way to punish a school-child was through shame — isolating him, and pitting the rest of society against him. Teachers in the village consistently used "mocking criticism" to bring children into line. Sometimes they made a child kneel at the wall, pressing his forehead against it, his hands folded on top of his head. Or they made a child spend recess walking in a circle in the schoolground, hands folded on his head, while other children mocked him.[8] Derision, of course, is a common form of punishment and, in stateless societies, an almost inevitable one.[9] The criminal law of colonial society used a common technique, then, when it invoked public opinion to enforce the rules of moral order. These rules were a paramount concern of that small closely knit community.

The civil side of the law in colonial society also fit the needs and demands of that particular social order. Colonial justice was open and cheap. People did not hesitate to bring disputes to court, even for rather petty claims. In 1639-40, in the Pynchon Court Record of Western Massachusetts, we read of an "action of the Case for 3 boards";[10] and an action of debt for 2s 6d.[11] In these small communities everyone knew who the judges were and where they could be found. In colonial records we find thousands of small wills processed, thousands of petty complaints filed, and thousands of local disputes adjudicated. These show how low the threshold of access to court was, at least in some colonies and in some periods of time. In this regard, too, colonial courts were like the courts of preliterate societies or, in some ways, like the neighborhood courts of Cuba and other socialist countries.[12] In colonial society courts were inexpensive and at everybody's doorstep. No affair was too petty for scrutiny. It was a gossipy, ingrown society. People regularly brought disputes before the courts.

Lawerence M. Friedman

The courts settled them — admonishing, governing, and teaching. These traits differed, of course, from colony to colony. They were probably most pronounced in the early period and in the theocratic Puritan colonies. In these, law was bossy, parental, and moralistic; but (on the civil side) it was also cheap and open of access.

In the nineteenth century the legal system changed dramatically. To be sure, much of the *formal* criminal law was carried over from colonial days. The statute books kept the old moral laws. Fornication, adultery, and blasphemy were still crimes after the Revolution, as they had been before. But this is only the surface; in reality, these laws soon fell out of use. William E. Nelson studied criminal prosecutions in seven Massachusetts counties between 1760 and 1774, the very end of the colonial period. He counted 2,784 prosecutions; no less than 38 percent of these (an astonishing percentage) charged sexual offenses, mostly fornication. Another 13 percent, 359 in all, were for religious offenses — blasphemy, profanity, and nonattendance at church.[13] These figures confirm that the statutes were part of the living law of the colony. But in the early nineteenth century, without major change in the statutory base, the rate of prosecution for these crimes declined almost to nothing. Criminal justice turned its attention to crimes against property: to crimes such as burglary and theft.

There is evidence that this lack of interest in crimes against morality was generally felt. Francis Laurent carefully sifted the court records of Chippewa County, Wisconsin. Between 1855 and 1894 he found a total of five cases of incest, nine of adultery, four of fornication, and one of lewd and lascivious behavior — not much of a harvest of sin.[14] Jack Williams studied crime and punishment in pre–Civil War South Carolina, hardly a society without sinners; he found few prosecutions for crimes against morality. Indictments for bastardy ran to about 2 percent of the total, but many of them were really cases of nonsupport. Incest, bigamy, sodomy, and adultery hardly appeared in the court records.[15]

One is welcome to believe, of course, that actual rates of fornication and blasphemy declined in this country in the nineteenth century. This may be; but such dramatic declines are unlikely. What changed, then, must have been a social factor, which affected the demand for prosecution of victimless crimes and which altered the system of criminal justice. The secular, instrumental men of the nineteenth century were less interested in the moral code as such, so long as infractions wore a low profile. Colonial magistrates had wanted to build an ideal, godly society. But in the nineteenth century wealth and opportunity were recurrent themes in the writings (and presumably the thoughts) of the elite and articulate. The task of law was to foster what J. Willard Hurst has called "the release of individual creative energy."[16] People had "sighted the promise of a steeply rising curve of material productivity as the dynamic of a new kind of society";[17] they had a "deep faith in the social benefits to flow from a rapid increase in productivity."[18] Consequently, the main emphasis of the law shifted to the encouragement of economic activity, rather than the enforcement of the ideal moral code.

In any event the cozy colonial system of social control was no longer possible. Society was larger, more mobile, and transient; it was busy with commercial affairs; rapid technological growth brought constant novelty and complexity. Society was less able to entrust its safety to stigma, shame, and the opinon of neighbors, particularly in the industrial North. Hence, reformers of the nineteenth century no longer saw society as cleansing and educating, as a hammer of reform and retribution, or as the teacher and parent of men. Rather, as David Rothman has argued, they saw society in a much more questionable role. The peer group was, if anything, corrupting. Bad company, idleness, and vice were ever present in society. A rotten environment was ruinous to man. Everyone was "under seige . . . . Once, observers believed, neighbors had disciplined neighbors. Now, it seemed that rowdies corrupted rowdies."[19]

This was the age in which a new institution, the penitentiary, was devised. In it, the deviant would be *removed* from society to be reshaped in a monastic, protected environment. Of course, the whipping post did not vanish overnight. It continued to be used, particularly in the South. Many states, such as South Carolina, still hung incorrigibles in public, and people flocked on foot, on horseback, sometimes even on special trains, to see the spectacle.[20] But more and more, imprisonment became the standard punishment for serious crimes.

The old-style jails had been dirty, insecure, and loosely run. The new prison was radically different. To work reform, prisons had to be redesigned. The two most famous of the early penitentiaries, Auburn in New York and Cherry Hill in Pennsylvania, were both based on the principles of solitude and silence. In Auburn (1821), the prisoners slept alone at night in their cells. During the daytime they worked together in a workshop, but were not allowed to talk to each other, or even to look at their fellow inmates. Cherry Hill (1829) tried to achieve even more radical isolation. Prisoners ate, worked, and slept in individual cells. Sometimes they wore masks. They listened to religious services through peepholes. They were utterly silent, utterly alone.

The new penology burst like a bombshell in the world of social thought. Foreign visitors, such as Beaumont and Tocqueville, came to study the penitentiary in its native habitat. On the whole, the two Frenchmen were impressed by its rigor, its efficiency.[21] Charles Dickens, who came a bit later, visited Cherry Hill and found it horrible: the prisoners seemed to him like men who were buried alive. Isolation, he felt, was a mental torture worse than any "torture of the body."[22] Apparently few of his peers saw things his way. Certainly contemporaries endlessly argued the merits of the two systems, which to us today are as alike as Tweedledum and Tweedledee. But all over the country legislatures eagerly copied the one or the other.[23]

In its pure state, the silent system could not and did not last. To keep one man to a cell, in solitude, cost a good deal of money; and the money was simply not forthcoming. Penitentiaries gradually became mere prisons; the solitude and silence were surrendered except as a special punishment for troublemakers. By the time of the Civil War even the famous penitentiaries that had led the way often slept more than one man to a cell, and only a handful of wardens still made a serious effort to enforce the regulations of silence.[24]

But the basic idea of the penitentiary flourished. Reformers believed that strict regimens, sermons, piety, loneliness, and quiet would regenerate a shattered soul. The average man probably rejected the advanced views of the reformers, while agreeing that hard work, regimentation, a spartan life, and long sentences were appropriate punishments for crime. Criminals were dangerous to society. They could not be cured through stigma and shame. They, therefore, had to be removed from normal life. Those who were not to be hung or imprisoned forever would, it was hoped, be cured of their tendencies. If not, the prisoner was at least out of harm's way.

Victorian society has a reputation for prudery and sexual intolerance. American society was as prudish in language and official behavior as the corresponding circles in England. Yet, apparently nowhere did the law take seriously the job of enforcing the sexual code. The law of divorce also illustrates the complex interaction between official morals and unofficial behavior. Divorce had always been difficult to get, rare and expensive. Absolute divorce was not available at all in England except through act of Parliament;[25] and in some southern states before the Civil War divorce was equally difficult and uncommon.[26] Yet in the North, a group of states had dramatically relaxed their divorce laws. In Maine, by a law of 1849, any justice of the supreme judicial court could grant a divorce if he felt it was "reasonable and proper, conducive to domestic harmony and peace,

Lawrence M. Friedman

and consistent with the peace and morality of society." Connecticut, too, had an easy divorce law.[27] The divorce rate was very low by modern standards, but some contemporaries still found it alarming that there should be divorce at all or that divorce rates should rise.

Divorce, however, unlike adultery or blasphemy, could not be allowed to exist in a kind of moral underworld. There was a genuine demand for it for social and economic reasons. For the sake of the legitimacy of children, for security of property rights, for the right to live *legally* with a second consort, divorce was an absolute necessity. Hence, the attack on easy divorce ultimately failed. But the easy *laws* were repealed. They were replaced with tougher, more "moral" laws — laws with a strong, healthy ethical surface — but the collusive divorce and the Nevada divorce mills made the situation one of extreme and blatant hypocrisy.[28]

Yet the nineteenth-century seemed to prefer, even to welcome, this hypocrisy. By all accounts, throughout the century, particularly after the first quarter of the century, there was a great deal of crime, brawling, drunkenness, gambling, and general hell-raising, just as one would expect from normal human flesh. But a rather sharp line was drawn between that which was officially allowed and that which was unofficially tolerated. This is the key, perhaps, to the strange fact already noted that the state stopped punishing fornication and other crimes against morality, but never repealed the laws against these acts. This may be the very heart of Victorian attitudes toward moral behavior. What had to be preserved at all costs was the *official* code of strict morality. What went on underneath was deplorable, but inevitable, and in a curious way almost acceptable.

Evidence of the dark underbelly of Victorian life[29] throws this hypocrisy into high relief. Victorians on both sides of the Atlantic published and read dirty books, cavorted with prostitutes, engaged in buggery and every form of vice. They drank and gambled to excess. But they seemed to take care not to sin in such a way as to threaten the moral norms publically. A society can tolerate a great deal of deviance so long as the deviants do not attack the norms themselves, but remain hidden in the woodwork. When deviants become what Joseph Gusfield has called "enemy deviants,"[30] that is, when they attack the norms themselves and try to overthrow them, they represent a greater (or at any rate a different) danger, and those who benefit from the normative status quo, economically or spiritually, will react repressively.

One such group of enemy deviants was the body of the Mormon faithful, who insisted on practicing polygamy. Many people all over the country were polygamists in fact, if not in law. Yet, the Mormons were open, defiant polygamists. A crusade against polygamy followed, the savagery and shrillness of which can barely be imagined today.[31]

A kind of Victorian hypocrisy also characterized the whole of the criminal law. On paper every man was entitled to elaborate procedural safeguards. He came to trial wearing the armor of the Bill of Rights; he had claims to a fair and speedy trial before a jury of his peers and scrupulous observance of the rules of the game. But during the century, the sheer volume of trials overwhelmed these rights. Society became more serious about catching and trying thieves and murderers. Instead of amateur, haphazard methods of patrolling cities, after 1830 many cities turned to full-time professional police.[32] The police themselves often ignored formal law and fought violence with their own weapons. Masses of people were arrested and treated routinely, almost cavalierly, in court. Rights were never *formally* relaxed. Upper courts zealously combed the records of lower courts looking for errors. The state renounced terror and torture as means for controlling the lower classes. But, as far as we can tell, the lower courts and the enforcers, particularly in the cities, ignored many of the formal rights. The population never accepted as an absolute good the official legal code. The vigilantes in the West, lynch mobs in the South, and police brutality in the cities all demonstrated over and over that, when the chips were down and the situation serious enough, men inside and outside the system were willing to take the law into their hands.

There was a similar hypocrisy in the civil part of law. American law affected the work and welfare of great masses of people. In the United States, land law was not a remote, aristocratic concern; millions dealt in the market, buying and selling land, moving about, getting and giving deeds, using mortgages, drawing up wills. Many borrowed money, or lent it out at interest; it was common to make, endorse, or accept bills and notes. Perhaps, compared to old Massachusetts, a rather lower percentage of the people directly confronted the law. But, if commercial and land laws did not touch the life and interest of everyone, they did affect the life and interest of the vast middle class.

To accommodate this mob of "consumers," to release latent economic energy, to maximize opportunity, society developed its law in such a way as to make transactions both safe and efficient, that is, routine. The documents in use were redesigned to become simple, streamlined, and standard. Deeds shrank in size. Businessmen developed form contracts to sell goods on the installment plan. These forms depended, in a way, on the courts. The courts ratified the devices that businessmen developed — devices such as conditional sales, garnishments, and chattel mortgages — and began to process them swiftly and efficiently. At the same time, society seemed to feel that in a market economy the legal system could not both promote efficiency and do strict, careful justice between individual parties. Courts turned their back on what in most societies is their primary and ordinary function — the settlement of disputes. They abandoned people to their own institutions and

devices. The law of a mass economy avoids individualization. It reduces transactions to the typical, to the routine; it slices up some small segment of reality and handles it in a standardized way. Behaviors are converted to legally relevant forms. A person pays his debts by check — a piece of paper fixed in form and in legal meaning. Routinization makes a good deal of sense. The work of society could not proceed if judges had to stop to examine each little dispute in a compulsive thoroughgoing way.

It is dangerous, of course, to attempt to read the minds of past generations and generalize about what "society" thought. Yet one senses in the nineteenth century a widely held belief that it would be best if people stayed out of court and tended to their own affairs. Through law, society established a basic framework, ensuring security to property and contract. Inside this framework people were to do their jobs, getting and spending, making the wealth of the country grow. In American law and, so far as we can tell, in Western law in general, courts gradually withdrew from the basic task of settling everyday disputes. One bit of evidence is the startling fact, suggested by data from a number of countries, that formal litigation tends not to keep pace with population growth in the industrial nations. During an initial period of expansion (perhaps because of the removal of restrictions left over from the medieval past), the caseload rises; but with mature industrialization, the number of cases per 1,000 population turns static or even declines. In England, where judicial statistics after 1850 are relatively good, the number of cases filed in court rose throughout the nineteenth century — perhaps less, however, than one might expect. In the twentieth century, the trend reversed itself.[33]

In the long run, cost was an important monitor of the case loads of the courts. Litigation seems to have become more and more expensive. High costs raise the threshold at which it makes sense for a person to funnel disputes into court.

Lawrence M. Friedman

Colonials litigated over pennies. Many matters got to court or were appealed that could appear today, if at all, only in a small-claims court.

Costs of litigation defy precise measurement, especially in the past. The largest element, for example, is the lawyer's fee; but this does not show on the face of the record. This fact itself is an interesting historical footnote. American courts do not award attorney's fees to the winner of a lawsuit, as do the English. The American rule seems to date from around 1850.[34] Supposedly, this rule was a historical accident, but if so, it was a suspiciously convenient one. What the rule does, of course, is raise the threshold of suit. Even a winning party loses, unless damages cover the attorney's fee and then some. The natural result of the American rule is to discourage small claims and noneconomic causes of action.

Delays and overcrowding also raise the price of a lawsuit. Colonial courts did their business quickly. They had no backlogs. Of course these were not mass societies. Great delays occur when judges and staffs are inundated by great numbers of cases. This happens in a society with a huge population. But when one considers how economical it is to run a system of justice compared to schools, hospitals, highways, or armies, one wonders why society was never willing to spend a few dollars more in order to expand the system and meet growing needs. One senses a feeling, implicit no doubt, that a logjam in court is not all to the bad. It discourages litigation. Then, too, the country has allowed its lawyers to unionize (as it were), raising standards and fees; it has refused to subsidize litigation, and it has made, until recently, only feeble attempts to provide cheap justice for the poor.[35]

Most important of all, perhaps, is the nature of law itself. Legal rules and procedures are impersonal and remote, dryly technical, forbidding. Law in the urban, industrial countries is very different from law in small societies; everybody knows a lot of law since it is nothing special to know.[36] Colonial law had some smattering of this aspect. The law was technical in detail, but in broad outline it spoke an everyday language.[37] A high degree of technicality will inevitably discourage litigation. If justice is mysterious, if law resembles a lottery, people will be unwilling to take a chance even if they feel morally secure in their cause. An unpredictable outcome is a high-cost, high-risk result.

All these factors create a zone of behavior which one might call a "zone of reciprocal immunity."[38] Landlord and tenant sign a lease agreement. The tenant promises not to play his radio loudly or late at night. The landlord promises to keep the outside stairway in repair. Each violates a little. Because litigation is costly, because there is no neighborhood court, because justice is risky, far off, and expensive, each is in a way immune from legal attack, at least for these minor infractions. They must settle the matter themselves.

On the whole, a system of reciprocal immunities may be quite functional in a society of our type. We do not want people running to court at the drop of a hat. But this sort of system produces severe and dangerous side effects. Compared with other societies and other periods, Western legal systems have removed the bulk of the population from any voluntary contact with the courts. The system of immunities on the whole favored business over private citizens; it was therefore, itself a device of allocation. The nineteenth century, practically speaking, denied justice to the poor and the powerless. Redress of grievances through law was distinctly abnormal. There may have been, in absolute terms, a tremendous volume of litigation. But the man in the street did not use courts to adjust his problems or settle his disputes. The average man was left alone, separated from whatever wisdom, understanding, and justice may inhere in the formal principles of law.

Nor was the situation of the lower middle class much better. The courts did not and could not reach out for the business of the common man even if he were an entrepreneur of sorts. It may be that courts in urban, market societies simply cannot play the role that a tribal or village court plays. American courts, however, never tried, though a certain number of schemes helped patch the system up, helped mitigate some of the most severe defects of justice.

Many scholars, looking at the legal system in the first part of the nineteenth century, have come away impressed with a sense of economic optimism. Obviously, many things were palpably wrong with the country. A gigantic failure to solve problems of region and race brought on the great Civil War. Cycles of boom and bust destroyed thousands of homes, businesses, farms, and fortunes. Yet overall, people believed that America was a land of opportunity, that in the long run economic horizons would constantly expand, that the stock of national wealth would grow larger and larger. Here, then was a second period of American justice — a period of rapid growth in society and rapid change in law. Criminal justice and civil justice alike ceased to be concerned with the individual as such. Rather, they became responsive to the socioeconomic needs of the society (as courts and legislatures interpreted these) through routinization of transactions, on the civil side, and through routinization and professionalization of law enforcement, the penitentiary system, and the stressing of the protection of property rather than morality, on the criminal side.

The age of optimism did not last forever. By the end of the nineteenth century it seemed to have come to an end, and a new, third period can be said to have begun. A sense of crisis, a kind of darkening of mood, seemed to seize the country. Concrete social change underlay this shift in the climate of opinion. Much of the population lived in big cities, which seemed more and more rotten, filthy, crime ridden, ugly, crowded and corrupt. People deserted the wholesome

life of farms and small towns for the dreary life of factories and slums. New inventions and techniques made life healthier, but somehow complicated it beyond the grasp of the average man. The frontier passed away. There was no more free land at the end of the rainbow. Never mind the question of how real the frontier had been, how much of an outlet it was for American energies. It was the symbol of unlimited opportunity, and by 1890 to 1900 it was gone. By this time many in the middle class felt that something vital had disappeared from American life. There was no longer room in the economy for everyone; social life was a struggle for survival. What one gained, another lost. The economy could not expand forever. The specter of class struggle hung over the nation. Interest groups jockeyed for power and position more blatantly than before.[39]

A certain paranoia set in on the subject of race. This was the period of lynch law and the furor over the so-called yellow peril. At one time the country had welcomed immigrants. The country wanted settlers and workers. Immigrants would create a demand for land and commodities; land values would rise and the economy would gain. Of course, people had in mind only a certain kind of immigrant. When others took the welcome sign too literally, nativist reaction set in. The debates over the Chinese at the California Convention of 1878-79 make hair-raising reading: one speaker denounced the Chinese as "moon-eyed lepers"; speaker after speaker expressed fear of cheap coolie labor. The Chinese would destroy white civilization and pauperize the people of California: "If clover and hay be planted upon the same soil, the clover will ruin the hay, because clover lives upon less than the hay; and so it is in this struggle between the races. The Mongolian race will live and run the Caucasian race out."[40] John R. Commons felt that immigrants from northwestern Europe — Germans and Scandinavians — were from the start the model farmers of America; they had qualities of thrift and self-reliance and pursued intensive agriculture.[41] The Jewish immigrant, on the other hand, was "unfitted for the life of a pioneer."[42] Commons drew a line between the "thrifty, hard-working and intelligent American or Teutonic farmer" and the "backward, thriftless and unintelligent races", who worked best "in gangs in large estates".[43] "Races wholly incompetent as pioneers and independent proprietors are able to find a place when once manufactures, mines and railroads have sprung into being, with their captains of industry to guide and supervise their semi-intelligent work."[44] Attitudes such as these helped mold a body of immigration law that became more and more restrictive and complex. The first step was to exclude the Chinese. Ultimately, the federal government put sharp limits on entry and adopted a quota system in 1924. The quotas discriminated, of course, against the "incompetent races."[45]

It is particularly interesting to note in the history of immigration law how fear of the effect of immigrants on the economy is mingled with moral or cultural horror. Both motives were behind the movement to exclude the less-favored immigrants. Perhaps the economic mood caused the moral mood; perhaps the lines of causality ran the other way around. At any rate, by the turn of the century millions were displeased with the national prospects. Industrialism was a monster that had run amuck. The mobs of "incompetent races" who flooded the country only stimulated the growth of this monster and, in the process, drove down the wage rate. Tremendous industrial combines were forming. Small businessmen, farmers, and merchants trembled in fear of their power. Today fear of the "trusts" seems as overwrought as fear of Chinese workers. But in the days of the Sherman Act, passed in 1890,[46] the fears were certainly real and in deadly earnest.[47]

Naturally each major concern bred a mass of new law. In the struggle for existence, the power of the state was one of the most useful of weapons. In the late nineteenth century, economic interest groups multiplied in number. The urge to organize stemmed, at least in part, from the natural feeling that in union there was additional strength, and strength was sorely needed in difficult times. The interest groups fought each other in the marketplace and occasionally on the streets, but primarily in the halls of the legislatures. Unions, for example, wanted legitimacy for their tactics, and when those tactics failed, they wanted to win through law what they could not gain through bargaining and fighting with management.

This was only one instance of the use of law to achieve organizational aims. Occupational licensing was another. Doctors, lawyers, barbers, plumbers, nurses, and accountants lobbied for licensing laws. Licensing was a way to give control of a trade group to itself, along with the power to keep out the marginals and support the prices and prestige of the members. A whole array of occupations, ministering to human wants from cradle to grave (from midwives to morticians and embalmers) asked for and got the right to be licensed. Even coal miners were briefly licensed in Illinois.[48] The form was novel, the concept was not. In general, workers joined unions, farmers joined farm organizations, businesses belonged to trade associations and formed combines. The middle-class trades licensed themselves.[49]

Along with the economic struggle raged a fight for normative domination. The Victorian solution slowly broke down. Deviant minorities burst into public view, bringing uneasiness and pain to the moral majorities. The process was, and is, slow and complex. Frequently, the moral majorities fought back. When deviants openly defied them, they had no choice but to repress — or else surrender their claims to moral superiority. Consequently, after a long period of relative quiet, a number of dead moral laws seemed to spring back to life, and new laws on similar subjects were passed. Sometimes the motives seemed mainly economic. Toward the end of the century, the Sunday laws were the focus of enforcement campaigns in many cities. Labor strongly supported these laws. They wanted to win a shorter work week for their members, and Sunday laws were a useful means to that end.[50] But ministers and preachers were their willing accomplices; labor and religion formed an odd but understandable coalition. Arguably, Sunday laws were all show and hypocrisy — economic laws masquerading as moral legislation. But probably the moral disguise which the economic motives wore was not wholly lacking in meaning. If the concept of a Sunday full of harmony and rest had had no power of persuasion, the unions could not have put together a coalition with the religious.

Many other signs of a resurgent moral militancy appeared at the end of the nineteenth century. The federal government crushed interstate traffic in lotteries in 1895.[51] The temperance movement became stronger and ultimately achieved a disastrous success. Joseph Gusfield, for one, interprets the temperance struggle as a struggle for normative dominance, a struggle to show the "superior power and prestige of the old middle class in American society."[52] In the early twentieth century, some states even tried to ban the cigarette. One of these states was Arkansas, which in 1907 made it a crime to make, sell, or give away cigarettes or cigarette papers to anyone, child or adult.[53] In the same year, Arkansas prohibited betting on horse races[54] and passed a law against malicious disturbance of church congregations by "profanely swearing, or using indecent gestures," violence, or any "language" or act which would "disquiet, insult or interrupt said congregation."[55] This period, too, had the honor of ushering in a crusade against drugs and addiction. Arthur Conan Doyle described how Sherlock Holmes, as one author has put it, "relaxed at the Baker Street flat after his bouts with Professor Moriarty by summoning Dr. Watson to prepare him a needle."[56] There was little or no opprobrium attached. Troy Duster has written that in

1900 "anyone could go to his corner druggist and buy grams of morphine or heroin for just a few pennies. There was no need to have a prescription . . . No moral stigma attached to such narcotics use."[57] Within twenty years, the law savagely proscribed the addict, who was now labeled a dope fiend; severe federal and state sanctions were imposed, and the country embarked on the dubious adventure of trying to stamp out drug use through repressive measures. Finally, in 1910, another nightmare or fantasy of a beleagured moral majority gave rise to the Mann Act, which outlawed "white slavery."[58]

We are paying a heavy price for some of these nightmares. Arguably prohibition created a generation of lawbreakers, unwittingly vested immense power in gangsters, corrupted officials, and distorted the administration of justice.[59] Similar charges are leveled at the modern enforcement of drug laws.

More hopeful and productive was another breach of the Victorian compromise. This was the revolt of the underdogs themselves — the refusal of the downtrodden to accept their labels. It included the insistence of moral minorities on the right to their own view of life, not secretly, but de jure, right up front. This revolution is quite recent. It has been influenced strongly by the example of the civil rights movement, which is in one sense as old as slavery, but in another sense distinctly a product of the twentieth century. Some might think that to put under one roof the civil rights movement and the revolt against moral taboos (obscenity, blasphemy, and non-biblical behavior in bed) trivializes the struggle for racial equality. But this much is held in common: unwillingness to abide by Victorian arrangements. These were arrangements made with the expectation that the lower orders — "lower" in the social, economic, and also the moral sense — would more or less stay in their place.

Numerous devices fastened down the Victorian arrangements, and convenient ideologies and myths buttressed them. It

Lawrence M. Friedman

is not the purpose of this paper to examine this subject in detail. However, some of the myths of ideologies might be mentioned. One was equality before the law. Obviously inequality, not to mention curruption, was rife, but a system of beliefs justified or excused inequalities. Among these was the belief that the United States was a country of great social mobility. Most influential was the notion that nothing much could be done to redistribute power and wealth without ruining the country — that is, nothing which was radical or required active state action. Economists and their popular spokesmen told the country that only disaster could result from interference with natural laws. No one believed this entirely, but enough people believed it enough to keep the country politically calm — at least for a while. But faith in the invisible hand lasted only as long as the optimism of the formative period. When the hand dealt bad cards, the players began to cheat. This ushered in the age of the pressure groups.

Whatever the causes, twentieth-centruy man seems less inclined to accept the social order as a given and his place within it as fixed. He demands for himself, his interests, and his aspirations, recognition and legitimacy, as well as practical achievement. There is, consequently, a massive demand to close the gap between the official surface of the law and the reality. Already in the late nineteenth century, devices to improve the administration of justice and access to the law had developed; the pace of these changes quickened in the twentieth century.

The law of obscenity provides us an excellent example. Pornography itself was centuries old. The First Amendment to the Constitution — and a rather strong national tradition — protects freedom of speech. Yet no one in the nineteenth century imagined for a moment that "free speech" included hard-core pornography. Pictures and descriptions of sex were taboo, except for medical and scientfic purposes, or behind a screen of euphemism. Nudity on the stage or in live sex shows was out of the question. There was no demand for these entertainments, no test cases; the idea was simply unthinkable. The United States Supreme Court did not decide an obscenity case until after the Second World War.[60] This first case dealth with Edmund Wilson's novel, *Memoirs of Hecate County*. The Court divided equally. Not even a Bible-Belt schoolmarm would blink at the book today, with the *Kama-Sutra* and *Lady Chatterley* in every drug store, to mention only the mildest examples. Since 1948 the law has amazingly expanded the public zone of sexual expression — what can be said, seen, touched, felt, and done in the open. Whether there is a similar explosion of sexual behavior is much less clear. No doubt behavior has changed and will change further, but the initial and more dramatic change is in the balance between licit and illicit, between what is flaunted and what is hidden. Indeed, one of the best examples of the new permissiveness is John Cleland's book, *Memoirs of a Lady of Pleasure*, commonly called *Fanny Hill*, written in the late eighteenth century but safely underground until about ten years ago. The question whether *Fanny Hill* is obscene has been adjudicated by the United States Supreme Court itself;[61] it goes without saying that never before in its two hundred years would this book have dared show its face in public. Yet a market for pornography existed in 1800, 1850, and 1900. There were people who wanted to read *Fanny Hill* and who were willing to pay for a copy. What was lacking was an appreciable demand on the law to legitimate that market. People were content to remain underground in their lechery, or were resigned to that fate. There were deviants, but not enemy deviants.

What does this history suggest? Law, we have said, is a kind of map of interests and demands. Its structure and substance betray current conceptions of law and current concepts of the legitimate limits of law. Law reflects the agenda of controversy — the things that are in actual dispute. It also gives strong negative evidence about which issues are *not* in dispute, the things that nobody questions. The issues in dispute are demands and counterdemands. When we speak of a crisis in law, civil or criminal, we mean a crisis in demands. Clearly in the third and present period, which began roughly a century ago, two distinct pressures on law have produced such a "crisis." First, the oppressed and the deviant have demanded legitimization; second, counterpressure has developed from the old majorities whose moral and economic dominance has been threatened.

The current agitation about law and order — crime in the streets — is a meeting ground or battlefield of these two armies, pushing against the legal structure from opposite sides. Most people assume that crime is rampant in the cities; a walk in the streets after dark is perilous. Also widespread is the idea that life in the cities is rotten and corrupt and getting worse. This, of course, is not a new idea. The bad reputation of the cities is centuries old. But there seems to be an increase now, a stridency in the fears and demands of broad masses of people.

Yet in the face of this clamor some scholars flatly proclaim that the crime wave is a myth. Over the long haul, they say, violent crime has, if anything, declined in the cities.[62] Urban crime may have jumped, but only in the last few years, and even that is disputed. New York and other big cities, it is argued, were hotbeds of crime in 1870 to a much greater extent than they are today.

If so, then what is the crisis in crime? First of all, it is possible that something real *has* happened to the crime rate. People care less about raw numbers of crimes than about the kinds of crime, who commits what acts, in what places, how, and to whom. It is one thing for crime to run rampant where the middle class never penetrates, in places it cares nothing about; but it is quite another thing for those same crimes to be committed in a city in which everyone is interdependent and within striking distance of one another. This is the condition of a mass society, with mass mobility, and in which slums gird the core of the city. The "dangerous classes"[63] once lived in tight districts, out of sight and almost out of mind. Now no place is safe. The paths of those who live in the slums cross the paths of the rich on their way to work, theaters, restaurants, and banks.[64]

Much violence in the past took place outside the cities. In a raw frontier community a Dodge City let us say, grown men committed violent crimes — many of them on other grown men. What horrifies people today is violence committed on the helpless and the innocent. When an addict murders an eighty-year-old widow, the statistic is the same as when one gunfighter shoots down another. Socially, however, the two crimes are quite different. In one case victim and killer stand on an equal footing. Both entered a violent world more or less of their own free will. In the other case, the relationship is involuntary — a relationship of predator and prey.

Even so, the crisis in law is a crisis of demand. Whether or not conditions have gotten worse in the outside world, the tolerance level has certainly declined and, correlatively, the level of demand that something be done has risen. The demand for an attack on crime is a demand for sterner police measures, tougher prisons, less "permissiveness." It is tied — not logically but emotionally — to fear and hatred of the moral minorities and of the unruly and political factions of the underprivileged. The demands of *these* people have brought about great improvements in access to law and in the administration of justice. Demand now meets counterdemand of equal or almost equal strength. There is no obvious short-run solution to the clash of these sets of demands.

The third period, then — our period — is a period of conflict and struggle in the two specific areas we have stressed. There has always been conflict and strug-

Lawrence M. Friedman

gle, but the current forms seem particularly nasty and sharp. This is because the moral world appears to have lost some of its classical shock absorbers. The unshakeable faith of the colonial elites is gone. The nineteenth century was fortified by faith in economic growth and a basic stock of moral principles. Now old compromises and accommodations have lost much of their strength. Opposing forces are struggling, not only for power, but also for legitimacy; and legitimacy is not easy to share. No doubt there will be new accommodations and new compromises; but their shapes and sizes, at least for now, are not visible to the naked eye.

Part Two

Studies in Colonial Law

There is a relatively rich literature on the law of the colonial period, thanks in part to the large body of records that have survived. The legal and social tradition the colonists brought with them from England was tested and modified in the New World in ways that provide for scholars evidence of what amounted to a social experiment on the interactions of law, geography, and culture. Out of the many studies on colonial law that have resulted, we have selected three: the first explores the social and intellectual roots of the law of the colonies; the second deals with the influence and spread of colonial law; and the third looks in detail at a particular controversy in the eighteenth century that concealed a struggle for power and control under its legal trappings.

The article by the late Julius Goebel, "King's Law and Local Custom in Seventeenth-Century New England," examines the law in the tiny colony founded at Plymouth. When Goebel wrote, many American legal historians were still debating whether the common law had been "received" in the colonies — that is, whether it did or did not prevail during the colonial period. Goebel reminded scholars that they were comparing something real (American legal practices) with something abstract (a stiff, static conception of the common law as the "King's Law," derived exclusively from the rulings of the royal central courts). The source of American law, Goebel argued, was not the lawyer's law of the London courts; it was local legal custom. The legal institutions of Plymouth were not duplications of a specific model, but "crude imitation(s) of inaccurately remembered things." The "things" inaccurately remembered were institutions of local law. Religion, too, had a significant influence on colonial practice; the colonists, in Goebel's nice phrase, had two dominant identities: they were at the same time "English commoners and religious zealots."

George Haskins picks up the Plymouth colony where Goebel leaves off. Goebel traces, for example, the roots of the impulse to codify the law that was so striking a feature of legal life in Plymouth; Haskins tells how the Plymouth codes influenced law and legal institutions in other colonies as well. The law of Plymouth mirrored the life of the community, its needs and habits; as a result, it also sheds much light on the "problem of

Studies in Colonial Law

cultural transplantation." But the number of legal innovations that can be traced to this tiny colony is truly remarkable.

Stanley Katz's essay on the chancery courts focuses on legal life in the eighteenth century, a period which has been sorely neglected except insofar as its movements and events can be treated as leading to the Revolution. His essay is a model of careful exploration of sources. The English courts of chancery were not easily transferred to this side of the Atlantic: Massachusetts and Pennsylvania rejected them outright; elsewhere, they were the subject of controversy. Katz finds, however, that criticism of chancery did not relate to its work with "mundane private law," but rather to the political implications of control of chancery under colonial conditions. His essay helps us understand how this much attacked institution survived independence so well; it is an important study of the relationship of legal structures to society.

This relationship is also the theme of David Flaherty's essay on the enforcement of morals in the colonial period. The Puritanism of the New England colonies has been the subject of furious discussion; this essay documents the ways in which theories of the good and godly society were translated into concrete legal manifestations. The essay is particularly useful in showing that the movement was pan-colonial; Flaherty draws in data from the southern and middle colonies as well as from New England. How crime, morals, and law interrelate is a recurrent theme in American legal historiography and is also explored elsewhere in this book in essays by Friedman and William Nelson.

Further Reading

Flaherty, David H., ed., *Essays in the History of Early American Law*. Chapel Hill: University of North Carolina Press, 1969.

Goebel, Julius, Jr., and T. Raymond Naughton. *Law Enforcement in Colonial New York: A Study in Criminal Procedure (1664-1776)*. New York: The Commonwealth Fund, 1944.

Greenberg, Douglas. *Crime and Law Enforcement in the Colony of New York, 1691-1776*. Ithaca: Cornell University Press, 1976.

Haskins, George L. *Law and Authority in Early Massachusetts: A Study in Tradition and Design*. New York: Macmillian, 1960.

Morris, Richard B. *Studies in the History of American Law, with Special Reference to the 17th and 18th Centuries*. 2d. ed. Philadelphia: J.M. Mitchell Co., 1959.

Smith, Joseph H., ed. *Colonial Justice in Western Massachusetts, 1639-1702: The Pynchon Court Record*. Cambridge, Mass.: Harvard University Press, 1961.

3

Julius Goebel, Jr.

King's Law and Local Custom in Seventeenth-Century New England

The first century and three-quarters of American legal development is bounded by two landmarks which have served as monuments to those historians who have attempted to survey the field of colonial law. The first of these is the royal charter; the second is the so-called reception statute. The former, with its mandate that the law in the lands granted should be agreeable or not repugnant to the law of England, is commonly regarded as a forecast of what was to transpire. The latter — with its declaration that the common law of England, insofar as it had been adopted at a particular date, was the law of a state — is held to have marked the consummation of the forecast. With these landmarks before them and acting upon an assumption that I think wholly unwarranted, our historians have taken as a measure the common law of England: Coke for the outset, Hale for the turn of the century, and Blackstone for the latter years of colonial America. A technique has been established no more recondite than the process of matching colors by which Chief Judge Cardozo has so bitingly characterized the inept use of precedents. At the basis of this naive and uninspired method, for

Reprinted, with footnotes abridged and minor editorial changes from *Columbia Law Review*, 31 (1931), 416-448, by permission.

which we may not unjustly blame the low estate of colonial legal history, lies the fallacy that the sum of the law of England was the law of the king's courts — the common law.

So accustomed are we to focus our attention upon the expansion of the king's law that we have closed our eyes to the fact that at the outset of the seventeenth century local custom and local courts were still immensely important parts of the law administration in England. True, these local institutions were marked for eventual doom, but they had resisted over centuries successive assaults by *quo warranto*; they were yet a part of the fabric of law and government. No one who ventures into the forbidding welter of contemporary charters can fail to be appalled by the multitude and extent of franchises, the tenacity with which they were clung to, and the astounding picture of jurisdictional diversities they disclose. This, then, is the fact to which we must cleave: the law of England was something greater and more multiform than that of the courts at Westminster.

It is not necessary to enter upon a discussion of whether or not the provisions in the first colonial charters had reference to the statutes and the common law alone, or whether they contemplated including that part of the law of England with which

Julius Goebel, Jr.

the courts at Westminster rarely occupied themselves. In the last analysis the charter provisions are significant only as to the relations of a particular colony with the homeland[1] and cannot be regarded as constituting a reliable guide to what in fact transpired in America. While in thus casting away the charter it would appear that we had abandoned the last beacon by which to lay our course, we nevertheless retain one important light — that the colonist will avail himself of his cultural heritage whether this has to do with religion, with law, or with methods of farming. In accepting as valid this premise we must, of course, rely upon work that has been done by lay historians in fields other than the law, but I see no good reason for traversing their conclusions. At the same time it should be noted that the acceptance of this premise necessarily involves the rejection of what I have already described as the technique employed in existing studies in American law. Instead of comparing the English common law with the legal monuments in the colonies, our task now becomes more complex. It is necessary for us to determine what was the cultural heritage of the first settlers, and in what form this heritage first expressed itself in the new land.

It is my purpose to single out for study one colony, not only because it was the first important English settlement north of the fortieth parallel, but because the achievements of this colony were imitated by succeeding groups which settled in New England.[2] This is the colony at Plymouth, whose legal history over a period of three decades we shall examine.

If we regard the personnel of this first settlement, the picture presented to us seems relatively simple. The group was divided into two parts: those persons who were Separatists from the English Church, a large number of whom had settled at Leyden, but many of whom came directly from England to America; and a number of persons who appeared to have had no religious connection with the Separatists, but who, probably for economic reasons, desired to move to the new settlement.

There is very little evidence that the bulk of the settlers had any intellectual contacts beyond those which their religion had given them. In other words, with the exception of a few leaders it seems unlikely that the colonists were aware of any of the literary movements of the time, of the law, or even of the politics of the royal court. Most of them were small farmers or artisans. Their leaders were exiles because of their beliefs. They were in respect of law and government footloose, maintaining with the homeland no more than a commercial relation with the group which financed them. Among their number were none who had been initiated into the mysteries fostered by the Inns of Court. To suppose that they would introduce a system as complex and esoteric as that which prevailed in the king's courts is as absurd as to expect that they would establish a religious system on the principles of the Anglican Church. Unless we are willing to resort to the frontier theory (that *pons asinorum* of American historiography)[3] we can make but one assumption: for the purpose of civil order in the colony, resort was had to the law with which the colonists had grown up.

It was inevitable that the local courts and the customary law would assume a position of transcendent importance in the life of the ordinary man. It was to these courts that the farmer or artisan would turn if he wished to replevy his cows or to collect a bill, and that turned upon him if his hogs were unringed or if he put his garbage in the street. Except what these humble men may have known of the ecclesiastical courts, with their sompnours spying upon their amours, and the apparitors to take them to jail if they worshiped heretically, the workings of the county, manorial, or borough tribunals were the length and breadth of their knowledge of the administration of justice, the local customs the sum of their law. Since it was men from these walks of life by which the Plymouth Colony was established, we must seek the secular source from which their legislative inspiration flowed in the local institutions of their native land. Historians have not failed to observe that in respect to the machinery of government the local institution was that which was first duplicated in America. Only a profound and abysmal disregard for the character of English law in the seventeenth century could have made them blind to the fact that in respect to the law conditions were no different.

The premise that colonists recruited from the lower strata of English society would put into action overseas the aspects of law and law administration which formed a part of their experience extended further than to the point of mere duplication. Much that was familiar to the settlers in New England was distasteful to them. Some things they objected to on the grounds of economic expediency. Some things were despised because they ran counter to their religious beliefs. For these they had definite notions of reform long before the idea of emigration had been ventilated. The adoption of English local customs in America is to be studied consequently in the light of these reservations.

The intellectual background of the Plymouth men, as I have stated, was determined largely by their intense concern with religion. The basis of their ideas is to some extent to be found in the theological literature of the reformed religion, transmitted to them directly or through the medium of their teachers. In addition to these sources we must likewise take into account what may be termed the popular literature of the dissentients, the vast flood of pamphlets, many of them openly polemic, by which the anti-Anglican movement gained headway among the commoners. It is in this type of writing that we find the abstractions of Calvin's *Institutes of Christian Religion* translated in terms of English institutions. Here, if anywhere, will be the rudimentary program of law reform leveled at local conditions. Here are the roots of those elements in the laws of the early New England colonists that we may describe as the results of idealism.

For our purpose we must direct attention to certain manifestations of Calvinism such as the growth of biblicism and

the exaltation of the Mosiac law, the embracing of Calvin's conception of the law of nature, and particularly a quickening of social-ethical ideals. These things become articulate not merely in religious issues, dogmatic and disciplinary, but in definite ideas for law reform among the radical dissenting groups in England. They are the inspiration for the demands that the law of Moses be a part of the law of the land, for the violence with which the church jurisdiction over morality is attacked, and for the assaults upon oaths of purgation. In America we shall observe their florescence in many details.

In outlining the extent to which the law was swept into the purification activities of English dissentients, it has not been my intention to imply that here were objectives consciously before the emigrants, or that anything as pretentious as a program existed. Their ideas mark at best the limits of what we might expect would emerge in their legislation as a result of religious idealism. Moreover, these notions would normally be slow in finding expression. Foremost in the settlers' minds was their primary purpose of propagating the gospel of the Kingdom of Christ. Except as practical necessity or unplanned action intervened, legal institutions and organizations were necessarily ancillary to this.

I think the growth of the law in Plymouth can be best understood if we keep before us the fact that here was a group settling on lands to which they had initially no grant and no governmental powers derived from or authorized by the crown.[4] Whatever legislative powers were assumed depended therefore upon some view of the inherent capacity of the group. A necessary consequence of the Separatists' ideas of church forming was that a certain corporate quality attached to the congregation formed by covenant.[5] The free use by Separatist writers from Browne to Robinson of analogies drawn from English borough constitutions, to fortify their conception of the corporate nature of their church, lends color to this theory. Thus, we know that before the Pilgrims left Holland, they formed by covenant a church, and that their pastor conceived this to have been simultaneously equivalent to the formation of a "civil body politick." This would doubtless have been sufficient to their needs except for the presence of persons not members of the church. The Mayflower Compact was executed, as Bradford states, to keep these non-Separatists in order. Since the power to legislate was the consequence of corporate character implicit in the Separatist or Congregational Church, the compact was no more than a reiteration and confirmation of this corporate association, plus an announcement of a design to "enact and frame just and equal laws."[6]

It is obvious that a group which believed it could create corporate capacity on the civil side by complying with its own formalities of ecclesiastical association, and which looked primarily to the Bible for substantive norms of conduct, was in no immediate need of comprehensive legislation. This indeed seems to be borne out by the records. Not until 1636 was there an attempt at a farreaching establishment of laws. That year was signaled by the establishment of a code intended to be a complete statement of law. Since this code was the first of a series of similar codes in New England and as I am of the opinion that the subsequent codifications in those regions were all of them influenced by this first attempt at a concise and compact statement of the law, it is necessary to inquire why such a code should have been enacted.

Nowhere do the religious and experiential elements in the legal development of Plymouth merge more closely than in relation to the colonists' idea as to the form in which law was to be expressed, in their seemingly unprecedented enthusiasm for the *lex scripta*, for codification. This notion was by no means new to English law, but codification was not an idea favored by the common lawyers. The code idea as it had taken form in England was expressive of a particularistic conception of law and government utterly opposed to the centralizing tendencies of the king's courts. Insofar as codes had survived in seventeenth-century England, they were the vestiges of medieval conditions, the depositories of ancient law.

I have already made reference to the diversity of franchises in England at the opening of the seventeenth century. The existence of these franchises, many of them dating back to the Norman Conquest, had favored the development of local law and customs. The latter were not universally reduced to record, but as a rule the more important the jurisdiction, the more surely were its local customs committed to writing. These custumals varied from the relatively complete statements of local law, arranged in an approximately systematic way and fully deserving the name of codes, to the more primitive recordings of manorial ordinances. In all cases the active principle behind the reduction to writing was the desire to achieve certainty, to preserve the franchise, and to aid the local courts which enforced the custom. These codes existed as living law, despite the fact that they belonged to the past and not to the future. So widely diffused were they that it is difficult to avoid the conclusion that they exercised some influence upon the Plymouth planters in their choice of a code as a medium of expressing their will. This was due in part to undoubted familiarity with local conditions and in part to the fact that the intense biblicism of the past century had given to the code idea a new vigor.

We have seen how the so-called Mosaic law had been seized upon and exploited by the radical religious elements in England as the true guide of men's ethical behavior. There can be no doubt that the great things which had been accomplished at Geneva, supposedly on the basis of Old Testament jurisprudence, had stimulated this enthusiasm. For it was a cardinal point of Calvin's propaganda that God's Kingdom could be realized on earth only by the adaptation of Israelite models. There was but one law in the Kingdom and that was the law of God as revealed in the Old Testament.

In addition to this more articulate aspect of biblicism a major characteristic was the insistence upon a literal use of the Book and an irrefragable confidence in the written word. It is here that we shall find at least a partial explanation of the desire strikingly manifested throughout New England to have the rule of law reduced to written form, the absence of judicial interpretation, the requirements for recordation of titles, and the preservation in writing of evidence. In England we see how this tendency had already been expressed in the Puritans' demands for explicit church canons that would leave no doubt as to what the law was. In the later days it is exemplified in the vicious attacks upon the amorphous nature of equity jurisprudence. In Massachusetts Bay the prevalence of this point of view even operated to defeat the purpose of the projectors of theocracy to have the law a growth of custom along biblical lines, so that the charter's injunction that their law be "not contrarie or repugnant" to the law of England could be avoided.

It is not to be expected that the result of this curious union of religious objectives and lay experience would resemble except vaguely the English prototypes, particularly as these draftsmen had before them no copy of any local custumals. On the other hand, I find persuasive of my theory, that English custumals motivated the use of a code, the fact that the commencement of the Plymouth code resembles generally many of the English custumals.[7] It opens with a recital of authority and a specification of powers. Then follow sections relating to the election of officers and the oaths to be taken by them. Precisely the same arrangement was followed in the beginning of a great many English custumals. This presents itself as evidence worth considering, for

men are prone to remember how things begin, be they constitutions or laws or poems, however far they may stray from their models before they are through.

I have tried to make clear my view that in the growth of legal institutions at Plymouth we are dealing not with an exact duplication of a definite model, but with the crude imitation of inaccurately remembered things. This explains the use of the code form. It likewise explains certain aspects of law administration to which I desire briefly to advert. Thus the absence of clear-cut lines between the legislative and judicial function,[8] and the failure to distinguish entirely between civil and criminal[9] jurisdiction are characteristics of Plymouth and of the country courts in England. No one who has read the records of the local courts of seventeenth-century England can fail to be stuck with the remarkable resemblance between the two. The eventual abandonment of what appears to have been an initial imitation in Plymouth of suit of court with judgment by the suitors, in favor of an elected and representative magistracy, tended to emphasize what I call the essentially leet court character of jurisdiction. Similarly the earliest Plymouth statute of 1623 required a jury trial in all civil actions, including debt. This was a characteristic of the undifferentiated manor courts, where civil and police jurisdictions were intermingled. In county courts and local courts exercising untarnished civil jurisdiction, wager of law was prevalent. The Plymouth statute, a reflection of the dissentients' antipathy to purgation, tended to fix procedure along the indicated lines.

For our guides to pleading in English local courts we are cast upon seventeenth-century handbooks like those of Dalton, Kitchin, or Greenwood. Except perhaps in the county court no such uniformity existed, as these writers would have us believe. We do know, however, that the primitive methods of complaint and answer were usual, and this seems to

have obtained in the earlier decades of
Plymouth history. On the other hand,
until 1636 there was in that colony no
clear conception of forms of action, at
least if we may judge from the fact that
only twice in the records does the clerk
append a name to the action. Thereafter,
however, we find designation to be
usual, a fact which leads me to think that
a book like Kitchin's *Jurisdictions of
Courts Leet* may have reached these
shores. There is, moreover, a remarkable
preponderance of actions on the case, a
characteristic of all early American procedure in the North. For this phenomenon no satisfactory explanation has ever
been offered, but I venture to suggest that
it was a contemporaneous condition in
England. In the king's courts, case had
been on the rise. The indications are that
the same thing was true in the local
courts. Perhaps the emasculated action of
trespass in the county courts — the trespass without allegation of force — may
have had something to do with this. The
formal distinctions between trespass and
case were here totally lacking. The substantive characteristics which the form of
the writ imparted to the two actions
being absent, one naturally wonders
whether or not, within the scope of the
county court's jurisdiction, the form of
action had any significance. Until more
is known of the English county court we
shall not have an answer, but the early
American records are highly suggestive.

Before we turn to criminal procedure it
is necessary that the substantive law be
briefly characterized. It mirrors in the
first instance the colonists' biblicism and
the enormous concern of the English dissentients with morality. The robber is not
mentioned, but the fornicator was left
few loopholes. The expression "felony"
used occasionally in the court records
does not appear in the statutes, but "misdemeanor," at that time not yet established as a word of classification in the
common law, is used to describe conduct
the criminal character of which the magistrate was to determine. This was

thoroughly Calvinistic and entirely in
line with the Puritans' notion of wide
judicial discretion in penal matters.

Genevan rather than English the Plymouth criminal law indeed was, but
nonetheless it was enforced by very
English machinery — a strange hybrid
compounded of leet and quarter-session
practice. Jury trial in all criminal causes
was provided,[10] but this was not significant, since the magistrate was given virtually an ordinance power in respect to
specifying misdemeanors.[11] The indications in the records are that a petty jury
was drawn as a matter of course only in
case of a major crime. Where an offender
was presented, the court apparently proceeded to sentence without further trial,
the findings of the grand jury being
deemed sufficient inquest.[12] In the
English leets unanimous presentment
except in cases where the freehold was
involved operated as a conviction, and
this may have been the source of Plymouth practice. Occasionally the accused
as well as witnesses were examined in
open court, but apparently a jury was
impaneled for small offenses only if the
presentment was formally traversed.
Since the bulk of offenses — drunkenness, sexual transgressions, and uncivil
carriage — far outnumbered more serious
infractions of public order, this quasi-
summary method of procedure was workable, and having religious and customary
precedents behind it, was not regarded as
subversive of individual rights.[13]

It is not alone in the field of law
administration that the experience of the
planters at home is perceptible, but in the
problem most vital to their existence —
the land. Here the custom of England
held only bitter memories, and here we
shall find attempts to right those things
for which at home there had been no
remedies.

The Pilgrims generally came from
those regions of England where the
effects of the agrarian revolution of the
sixteenth century had been most profoundly experienced. The bulk of the ten-
ancies in northern and eastern England

were copyholds, and upon these had descended the full brunt of the movement for enclosure. The copyholders, as tenants at will by copy of court roll according to the custom of the manor, were roughly divisible into two groups: those who held copies of the roll establishing their tenancy, and those who relied upon oral proof of the custom. Their remedy against landlord encroachment lay in the first instance in the manor court, but as enclosure was usually begun by the lord, this was an illusory protection. Chancery had first taken the copyholder under its wing. Late in Edward IV's reign King's Bench had intimated he would have an action on the case against the evicting landlord, and finally, upon the accession of the Tudors, the Court of Requests became his protector. These courts, however, were at best available to the richer copyholder or to a group financing an action. In actual fact the copyholder was usually at the mercy of his lord.

We cannot enter here into the details of the agrarian problem. I can emphasize only the wholesale character of the process of enclosure, the widespread misery which induced a succession of revolts as late as 1607, and the crowding of the town by hordes of wretched beings without funds or means of livelihood. Fumbling efforts by the crown to investigate and to control matters by statute were unavailing.

To the English peasant the effect of all this was to create a deep and abiding distrust of the ancient tenure; a noticeable distaste for the new economic, as against the old customary, rents; a suspicion of leases by which the new system was put into effect; a great solicitude for the recorded title or written evidence of right in the land; and finally a nostalgia for the one type of landholding, the freehold, where the risks of tenure were slight. What transpired in Plymouth was a reflection of peasant psychosis after decades of unrest.

Even before removal to America the Pilgrims were involved in acrid discussion with the adventurers who financed them over the problem of landholding. The latter demanded that all lands be held in common, to be divided at the end of seven years. They wanted security. The planters wanted homes of their own that could not be taken away at the end of a term. Since no agreement was reached before departure, the first division of land was made without reference to the adventurers' demands. Corn growing was undertaken in common on the open-field cultivation system, but this was not successful. In 1623 the governor assigned to each family land in proportion to its members (from one to ten acres) for purposes of tillage, a portion of the produce to be deposited in the common stock.

If we attempt to describe this tenure in current legal terminology we shall have difficulty. The agreement with the adventurers had been finally executed. In 1621 Pierce, an adventurer, secured from the New England Council a grant to the lands. Title was vested in him and his associates; but the Plymouth allotees were not tenants at will, as they had a joint claim arising out of their contract, not to specific lands but to an assignment of undetermined lands to be made at the end of a term. Five years later the adventurers sold out, and the debt was assumed by a few leading colonists. To liquidate the debt, all heads of families and young men were made into a company and a share allotted to each, and for each member of the family. The land assignments of 1623 were confirmed. The remaining land was then divided by lot, and each share received twenty acres, besides the acres already held. This was tillable land abutting the bay. The rest was designated waste and common land. The meadows were not laid out, but each year a share was allotted for mowing, based on the number of cattle each man owned.

The meager record of this transaction does not tell much. The Pierce grant had not been assigned and a direct grant was not gotten until 1629. Since the adventurers had sold out all interest and claims including lands, this purchase seems to have been regarded as having conferred title to the soil. The right acquired by each shareholder was equivalent to a fee interest, although allotment was conditional upon possession of a share, which required payment in kind toward debt liquidation.

The earliest deeds, crude in form, indicate that landholding was conceived in the image of the English freehold. There is evidence, moreover, that a form of Yorkshire freehold, the so-called meerstead freehold, was known to the settlers. This type of land tenure obtained at Royston, near the home of Bradford, and was one in which the seignorial element was almost indiscernable. Certainly it is a striking coincidence that meerstead is used for messuage in Plymouth, and that the term so far as I can ascertain was not used elsewhere in England.

An essential aspect of the land problem in Plymouth was the provision in the Code of 1636 requiring the recordation of all sales, gifts, mortgages, and other conveyances of houses and lands. It went far beyond the limited scope of the Statute of Enrollments, with the terms of which the settlers were probably unacquainted. It was motivated in part by certain borough customs and in part by the colonists' recollections of the importance of the written word as proof of the copyholder's custom, and the desire to have a means of remembrancing which would forestall the mean and petty tricks by which unscrupulous landlords had in England cheated the tenant of his property. It is to this feeling, of which great evidence abounds in contemporary English writing on enclosure, that we may attribute the early and widespread enactment of registration statues in colonial America, for property rights had not become so involved as to make recording an economic necessity.

I desire to point out but one further aspect of the Plymouth land system that deserves attention. This was the notion of economic use expressed in laws which required the occupation of land or the consequent devolution to the government.[14] This rule had its origin in the fact that a share of produce had for a period of years to be paid to the company which had assumed the debt from the adventurers. The same object could have been attained by leasing, but I have mentioned that the lease was an abhorred incident of English enclosure, and furthermore, where civil status depended upon freeholding, leaseholds would have threatened the stability and growth of the colony.

The picture just outlined of the law's growth in Plymouth over the early decades of the colony's existence has many flaws. It is difficult to get into proper perspective things the outlines of which have been dimmed by the preconceptions of writers and by the erasures of time. But as I have said before, if we remember that these men were English commoners and religious zealots, the records of civilization in their motherland will enable us to effect that meticulous and microscopic reconstruction essential to the true depiction of transplantation of any culture. Local custom, substantive as the Winchester measure, pretentious as the notion of the code, ineradicable as the methods of law administration, fortuitous as a form of tenure; bitter experience at the hands of a zealous bishop and his pursuivants, or a stony-hearted evicting landlord; hope and salvation in the Word of God preached by word or pamphlet, these things are the materials that went with settlers to Plymouth and out of which their law was fashioned.

The curious melange of religious ideas and remnants of English local customs and practices which pervaded the Plymouth legal institutions is not without parallel, for her neighbors in Massachusetts, Connecticut, and Long Island exhibited similar procilivities. Each colony had, of course, its peculiar characteristics, but in the seventeenth century before the Leviathan common law had been set in motion, the basic factor was the transplantation of local institutions and customary law. Regarded from this standpoint the first century of American law no longer seems chaotic and absurd; on the contrary, the frontier theory, as I have intimated, becomes an artificial and labored explanation. We cannot brush this century aside as meaningless; neither should we invest it with greater importance for the future than it actually possesses. Yet the fact that it gave us legal institutions which the common law never succeeded in smothering is sufficient reason for devoting to it some scientific attention.

4

George L. Haskins

The Legal Heritage of Plymouth Colony

More than one legal historian has more than once drawn attention to the contributions that Plymouth Colony made to American law in the seventeenth century.[1] Yet recent general studies continue to insist that Plymouth made few permanent contributions of any kind to the American heritage. Thus Samuel Eliot Morison, dean of American colonial historians, writes that nearly all American historians are now agreed upon "the insignificance of the Plymouth Colony in the colonial era."[2] "By any quantitative standard," he says, "it was one of the smallest, weakest, and least important of the English colonies."[3] "Massachusetts Bay, rather than Plymouth Colony, was the seedbed of New England. There and in Connecticut and New Haven the distinctive New England institutions of church and state, culture and commerce were developed."[4]

To this majority opinion of the court of history these pages are filed as a partial dissent. In the light of the known evidence it is impossible to disagree with much that Professor Morison has concluded with respect to Plymouth. The Pilgrims who founded the colony were simple folk, drawn principally from a class that, in Governor Bradford's words, "followed the inocente trade of husbandrey."[5] They had little familiarity with any intellectual currents of the day except those pertaining to religion. They were not and did not become great shipbuilders, successful fishermen, or traders. They did not establish or live under democracy in any modern sense. Indeed, much that they accomplished was done after annexation to Massachusetts in 1691. In large measure, their importance lies in the example they continue to afford of courage in the face of danger, resourcefulness in the face of difficulty, and fortitude in the face of adversity.[6] In spiritual quality, the Pilgrim leaders were second to none in the New World, and in many respects, as Henry Adams said of the great Virginians at the close of the eighteenth-century, they were "equal to any standard of excellence known to history. Their range was narrow, but within it they were supreme."[7]

At the same time, it must be recognized that Plymouth Colony made several important contributions to American legal institutions, not the least of which was an early articulation of the ideal that

Reprinted from *University of Pennsylvania Law Review*, 110 (1962), 847-859, by permission.

finds expression in the famous language of the constitution of Massachusetts — "a government of laws and not of men."[8] At the outset, the colonists succeeded in establishing a self-governing community without benefit of a royal charter, royal proprietor, or corporate overlord, and in this respect they evinced an early political maturity which was not matched in any other American colony. They also succeeded in establishing a system of law suited to the situation and conditions in which they found themselves and to the religious purposes for which the colony had been established.

The Code of 1636

In assessing Plymouth's contribution to the American legal heritage, it should first be pointed out that to that colony belongs the credit of having established what may fairly be described as the first American constitution. At a meeting of the General Court in October 1636, the laws of the colony were read, and some "were found worthy the reforming — others the rejecting and others fitt to be instituted and made."[9] In consequence, a committee was appointed to "sertefie and prepare such as should be thought most convenient, that if approved they may be put in force at the next general court."[10] The work was accomplished within a few weeks, and the laws were drawn up in the form of a code dated November 15, 1636.[11]

Two things are remarkable about this code, which turned out to be something more than a mere compilation and revision of existing laws. In the first place, the code sets forth the general scheme or frame of government of the colony: the source of legislative power, the duties and authority of the several officers of the colony, qualifications for the franchise, provision for the holding of courts, and the source of authority to declare war. Second, it contains a rudimentary bill of rights, certainly the first in America, antedating by five years that adopted by Massachusetts Bay in the Body of Liberties of 1641.[12] These two features alone justify

the statement that the 1636 code established a constitution of the type that was to become familiar in America after the Revolution. Nothing that was attempted earlier in Virginia was of the same scope; there the so-called constitution was chiefly composed of orders and instructions directed at, but not established by, the colonists, and certainly it included nothing that might be termed a general bill of rights.[13]

Significance of the 1636 Code

The 1636 code, with its revision of the colony's laws and enactment of constitutional provisions, is significant from four standpoints: first, because this codification — quite apart from its constitutional significance — was the first code of laws in any modern sense in North America; second, because it reveals much of the social organization of the colony; third, because it preserved and gave vitality to English legal institutions which otherwise might not have survived; fourth, because it contains laws, first introduced at Plymouth, that made lasting contributions to the present-day law of Massachusetts and, ultimately, to the modern law of the United States.

THE FIRST MODERN CODE IN AMERICA

In the history of world jurisprudence, codification of law may be said to have taken two forms, roughly described by the terms "ancient" and "modern". Of the former type are the Code of Hammurabi, the Twelve Tables at Rome, and the primitive Anglo-Saxon compilations which antedate the Norman Conquest. Of the latter or "modern" type, the Code Napoléon is among the most famous. The distinction between these two types of codes is essentially that the ancient code sought to reduce traditional law to writing, often as a defense against autocratic rulers, whereas "modern" codes have had as their object — beyond the necessary compilation — the revision of existing law in the light of accepted ideals for the purpose of elaborating the law and providing fresh starting points for legal development.[14] Judged by this test, and particularly in the light of its bill of rights, the first Plymouth code is modern — not so modern as the more mature and developed code adopted by the Bay Colony in 1648,[15] but a first step in that direction and certainly antecedent to it. The earlier collection of Virginia laws, enacted in 1619, cannot properly be termed a code, for it manifests no effort in the direction of either revision or completeness.[16] In any event, the later Plymouth revisions, embodied in compilations of 1658, 1671, and 1684,[17] fully justify characterization as a developed and detailed modern code. All these codes, along with that of Massachusetts Bay, provided examples that were looked to and borrowed from by other colonies in establishing their legal systems, including notably Connecticut and, later, New York under the Duke of York's laws.[18]

A Sociological Document

Although much neglected as source material,[19] the Plymouth laws constitute a valuable group of contemporary documents for the understanding of Plymouth's history, and they shed important and broadly diffused light upon social, economic, and institutional developments; for, whether one looks to the seventeenth or to the twentieth century, law in its broad sense is much more than a complex of rules for settling disputes between litigants in court. Law is a command of the state, but it is also a social product and an agency of social control, a regime for prescribing countless aspects of the relations of men in organized society and for adjusting their desires and claims with respect to each other and to things. Although particular legal rules may be the outcome of legislation, executive order, or judicial decision, by and large those rules reflect contemporary pressures caused by the needs and interests of the community or of groups within the community. At the same time legal rules reflect ethical elements — the sense of justice and injustice and the ideals of

the society within which they operate. Hence, in its operation, law is both an anchor to tradition and a vehicle for change — a pressure upon social organization and a device for accommodating new and emerging forces.[20]

Viewed in this perspective, the legal records of Plymouth, as of any society, merit study as a reflection of social organization and social purpose. They aid in the identification of the groups — formal and informal — that make up the anatomy of social organization and in the delineation of the functions of those groups. They help us to assess, for example, the situation of debtors and creditors, the importance of the family unit, the extent to which environment affects the group and the individuals within the group. They shed light on the sentiments and understandings that make for stability or the lack of it. Hence, whether one looks to rules which prescribe that swine shall be ringed[21] or to those which prescribe the economic use of land,[22] the law is revealed as a highly specialized form of social control, regulating competing interests between individuals and groups in organized society.

The enacted laws also shed light on the problem of cultural transplantation to the extent that they were imitative or adoptive of those portions of the English legal system with which the colonists were familiar. At the same time, their conscious rejection of other portions of that system reflects, for example, their dissatisfaction with the English land law and with English criminal law and procedure and their urgent wish to effect reforms in those areas. Reliance upon and literal use of biblical texts in framing provisions relating to crime provides, in another area, evidence not only of tradition and design, but of the continuing importance of the religious ideals which had inspired the founding of the colony.

The earliest Plymouth laws reflect concern about basic problems common to all communities: landholding, the inheritance of property, marriage, crime, court proceedings, and the like. As time went on and the colony grew, the laws reflected not only the maturing social organization, but local problems and conditions, such as those involved in legislation about bridges and ferries, highways, fairs, weights and measures, price and wage control, licensing of innkeepers, the quality of exports, and provision for the poor.

One of the most striking features of several provisions is the typically Puritan concern about the regulation of personal conduct and behavior. In the course of the seventeenth century, Plymouth enacted numerous laws punishing and providing specified fines for drinking, gaming, idleness, lying, swearing, and the like. They were not general prohibitions, but for the most part detailed provisions describing the offense. The tests of drunkenness, for example, are set forth with a degree of specificity which would astound many a modern police court.[23]

The significance of such provisions lies not only in their exemplification of Puritan ideas about right living but in what they reveal about the Pilgrims' views of law. To them law was conceived of in large measure as a restraint on individual action in the interest of the whole group. At Plymouth, as in the Bay Colony, the individual was essentially a member of the community, so that there was no aspect of his life, not even his private conduct, which was free of the control of the law insofar as the law was designed to further effective organization and good order in the community. To us today such intrusions upon privacy may appear as unwarranted invasions of personal liberty, but to the Puritans such regulation seemed both proper and necessary.[24]

Lest it be thought, however, that the legal system of Plymouth was entirely an indigenous product of local conditions and of Puritan religious beliefs, it should be emphasized that the colonists drew extensively on their English legal inheritance and even on their Dutch experience.[25] There are several references to the common law of England, by which to a substantial degree they felt bound. But there are other provisions that reflect local

English customs of the districts from which they had come. The terms and the forms which appear in the records are in great part the forms and procedures of manor and borough courts rather than those of the king's courts that developed the common law.[26] That this should be so is not surprising, for in the seventeenth century the legal center of gravity for the average Englishman was the local court of the neighborhood — the borough court, the court leet, and the county court.[27] There he would turn to collect a debt, replevy a cow, or abate a nuisance, and it is a matter of no small interest that the early Plymouth court records bear a striking resemblance of those of the English manorial courts of this period.[28] Moreover, the Code of 1636 is reminiscent of many fifteenth and sixteenth century English borough custumals, which probably furnish the models on which the colonists consciously framed this and later compilations. In them, for example, are the same recitals of authority, the specifications of power, the election of officers, the oaths to be taken, that are found in the English custumals.[29]

PRESERVATION OF ENGLISH INSTITUTIONS

In adopting local customs and other practices of the borough and manor courts, the Plymouth colonists preserved and helped to transmit legal institutions which in the seventeenth century still had enormous tenacity as well as vitality. In time, those customs were to be smothered by the gradual but inexorable encroachments of the common law of the king's courts. Few of the Pilgrim settlers, however, had much familiarity with that law save on the criminal side, and the customary law of the local courts assumed "a position of transcendent importance in the life of the ordinary man."[30] Hence, it was entirely natural that the colonists should have availed themselves of their cultural inheritance in customary law, just as they did in religion and methods of farming. Their introduction of a code, of a recording system, and of a scheme of partible inheritance, to give but three

George L. Haskins

instances, appears to have derived in substantial measure from English customs. The idea of a code, for example, although stemming in part from the Pilgrims' reverence for the Mosaic code of the Old Testament, was well known in the English boroughs as a device which helped to assure certainty in the application and enforcement of local law and which became increasingly popular for similar purposes in the New England colonies.[31] The example of the procedures of the English local courts, untechnical compared with those followed in the common-law courts, offered a flexibility that was advantageous to litigants untrained and largely unacquainted with the complexities of the forms of action. Thus, the introduction of half-remembered English customs at Plymouth brought into the stream of American law institutions which would otherwise have perished and which, instead, furnished in several areas a foundation on which that law would build. From another standpoint, those transplantations shed further light on the problem of survival and adaptation of patterns of thought and habits of life; at the same time they reflect, as in a glass darkly, much of the image of local England that was shortly to disappear from view.

SUBSTANTIVE PROVISIONS

The fourth distinctive contribution of the 1636 code and of other laws which were in force but not expressly incorporated therein was in the development of new laws which have since had a permanent influence on the American legal system. This contribution was in two directions.

A Bill of Rights. First, the code gave expression to the idea of fundamental law embodied in a bill of rights and written constitution. That idea had already made an appearance in Massachusetts Bay in the preceding year when it was agreed to frame a body of laws "in resemblance to a Magna Charta."[32] However, except for the draft of fundamental laws prepared in 1636 by John Cotton, which was never adopted, nothing was done about the project until the Body of Liberties was enacted in 1641.[33] Thus, the Plymouth declaration of rights, rudimentary though it was, was certainly the first enactment of its kind in America. The preamble promptly claims for the colonists the rights and liberties of Englishmen, stating that they had come "as free borne subjects of the state of Engl ... endewed [with] all and singular the priviledges belong to such ..."[34] Then, at intervals between other provisions of the code, come the following:

[N]o imposiĉon law or ordnance be made or imposed upon or by ourselves or others at present or to come but such as shall be made or imposed by consent according to the free liberties of the state and Kingdome of Engl. and no otherwise.[35]

That all trialls whether capitall or between man & man be tryed by Jewryes according to the presidents of the law of Engl. as neer as may be.[36]

That the lawes and ordnances of the Colony & for the government of the same be made onely by the freemen of the Corporaĉon and no other, provided that in such rates & taxaĉons as are or shall be laid upon the whole they be without partiality so as the freeman be not spared for his freedome, but the levy be equall. And in case any man finde himselfe aggrieved, that his complaint may be heard & redressed if there be due cause.[37]

As time went on, these fundamentals were elaborated and enlarged, so that by 1671 they were expressed in much more sophisticated terms and in recognizably modern form, occupying nearly three full printed pages.[38] It is not without interest that at least six provisions of that later code appear in equivalent form in the present-day constitution of Massachusetts.[39]

Innovations. The other direction in which Plymouth made a distinctive contribution to the American legal heritage was in the formulation of certain provisions of new substantive law: civil marriage, equality of descent among children, provision for widows, and recording of deeds. All these were marked advances on English law.

The introduction of civil marriage is undoubtedly the best known of Plymouth's innovations. Whereas Anglican doctrine in contemporary England, conforming to that of the Roman Catholic Church, prescribed that marriage should be solemnized in church, at Plymouth the colonists introduced marriage by officers of the civil government. Bradford speaks of the practice as having been founded on the "laudable custome of the Low-cuntries,"[40] and it appears therefore to have been one of the fruits of the Pilgrims' sojourn in Holland. The practice was also followed in Massachusetts Bay when that colony was established, and its acceptance there can fairly be attributed to Plymouth influence.[41] Civil marriage is not expressly dealt with in the first Plymouth code, but it appears to have been universally practiced. The general recognition of civil marriages in the United States today is too well known to require comment, but the practice can be traced at least in part to seventeenth-century Plymouth.

Among the notable advances of Plymouth law over that of contemporary England was the provision for the descent of land to all children rather than to the eldest son, as under the English rule of primogeniture.[42] As early as 1627, Isaak de Rasieres, then acting secretary of New Netherland, visited Plymouth and observed that "in inheritances they place all the children in one degree, only the eldest son has an acknowledgement for his seniority of birth."[43] The reference to seniority was to the practice of giving a double portion to the eldest son, pursuant to the precept of Deuteronomy 21:17, upon which it was ostensibly based. The rule of partible descent was expressly recognized in 1641 in the Massachusetts Body of Liberties, which apparently adopted the Plymouth practice.[44] From

there it spread to Connecticut, Rhode Island, and even to Pennsylvania and thus antedated by many generations Thomas Jefferson's attack on primogeniture in 1776. In the ultimate abolition of primogeniture throughout the United States, the influence of the early practice at Plymouth can hardly be ignored.

The provision for the widow was also novel.[45] Generally speaking, the common law of England at this time assured a widow a life estate in one-third of all the lands of which her husband had been seized during marriage. Plymouth also recognized a similar general right,[46] but went far beyond English law in assuring to her an absolute interest in one-third of his goods and chattels as well. In England, only by exceptional local custom could the widow share in personal property, as opposed to freehold lands, unless the husband left a will which expressly gave her such property.[47] The Plymouth law as to personal property was also followed in Massachusetts Bay, presumptively by adoption. With modifications it ultimately became the law of the Commonwealth. In time, the Statute of Distribution in England[48] and its counterparts in America were to assure the widow of an intestate share in her husband's personal estate, but these provisions came long after the early Plymouth law.

Of even greater significance was the introduction at Plymouth of a system of recording sales, gifts, mortgages, and other conveyances of houses and lands.[49] Stemming in part from a peasant psychosis bred of years of misery brought on by the enclosure movements, yet influenced by recording practices in the English boroughs and probably by Dutch example as well, the recording system furnished basic guarantees of security of land titles. As early as 1636 two features of the modern recording system were in force at Plymouth, namely, the entry of the entire deed on an official record and prior acknowledgment of the deed before a government official. These two features, subsequently adopted by Massachusetts Bay and supplemented by two

George L. Haskins

further features introduced in that colony in 1640, provided the basis for modern systems not only in Massachusetts but in the United States generally.[50] Indeed, it is worthy of note that, in spite of more than twelve revisions, the present-day Massachusetts recording statute[51] goes back, substantially unchanged in form, to the Bay Colony act of 1640, which appears to have stemmed from the earlier enactment at Plymouth.

The Rule of Law

Each of these contributions of Plymouth — to its own laws, to the law of the Bay Colony, and, ultimately, to modern American law — is impressive. If Massachusetts Bay was to receive much of the credit as the vehicle of transmission, the fact illustrates the old saying that the Pilgrim saddle is always on the Bay horse. What is particularly impressive, however, is the evidence which appears early and persistently in the Plymouth enactments and court records, that the colonists were governed by and lived under a rule of law.[52] Few ideas have had so profound or so pervasive an influence in Anglo-American jurisprudence as has the idea that no man is above the law. It has crystallized in the doctrine of the "rule" or "supremacy" of law, which has long been regarded as one of the central and most characteristic features of the Western legal tradition. The doctrine first found expression in medieval England in the course of struggles to check the threatened usurpations of kings. It also is evident in the numerous borough codes that expressly guarded the customs and franchises of townsfolk from the encroachments of the king's officers and the king's courts. In the seventeenth century the idea rose to central prominence both as a weapon of attack upon the royal prerogative courts and as a means of protecting the established rights of individuals from the jurisdiction of such tribunals as the High Commission and the Star Chamber, which claimed not be be bound by the accepted procedures of the ordinary courts.[53]

The rule of law was thus much more than a doctrine of lawyers and political theorists. Few had suffered more at the hands of the prerogative courts than the Pilgrims, and all Puritans were united in a belief in the overriding force of temporal law that reflected moral law. As early as the Mayflower Compact in 1620, the signatories convenanted and combined into a body politic and declared by virtue thereof that they did "enact, constitute and frame such just and equal laws, ordinances, acts, [and] constitutions . . . as shall be thought most meet and covenient [sic] for the general good of the colony."[54] Note that those laws, acts, and constitutions were to be "just and equal"; note, also, that the signatories themselves covenanted to give "all due submission and obedience" thereto.[55] Later, in the Code of 1636, the idea of a government of laws is reflected more explicitly in provisions such as that which prescribed that "no imposicōn law or ordnance be made or imposed upon or by ourselves or others at present or to come but such as shall be made or imposed by consent according to the free liberties of the state and Kingdome of Engl. and no otherwise."[56] By 1671, when the Plymouth "Generall Fundamentals" had been elaborated into a recognizably modern bill of rights, it was ordered and declared in language echoing Magna Carta, and later to be repeated in so many American state constitutions:

That Justice and Right be equally and impartially Administered unto all, not sold, denied or causelesly deferred unto any.

[T]hat no person in this Government shall be endamaged in respect of Life, Limb, Liberty, Good name or Estate, under colour of Law, or countenance of Authority, but by virtue or equity of some express Law of the General Court of this Colony, the known Law of God, or the good and equitable Laws of our Nation suitable for us, being brought to Answer by due process thereof.[57]

Not only the provisions of the first and later Plymouth codes, but the numerous orders, fines, and judgments recorded in the court records of the colony attest to the persistent conviction that the laws must be enforced and obeyed. The conscious adoption of laws for the expressed good of the community, together with the numerous examples of restraint on individual action, reflects an overriding concern with the interest of the order of the whole group to which the law applied. As in ancient Greece, where the promotion of good order in the community was believed to give individuals a wider freedom, so in Plymouth the community was believed to thrive on the right living of its members. Indeed, there is more than a casual relation between Plymouth ideals and the recurrent statements throughout Greek literature that to obey the law is to be free. That idea was echoed and given wide currency by Cicero, and later was reinforced by Puritan doctrine which prescribed obedience to the law as a religious duty.[58] Hence it has become a priceless legacy of Western civilization that we are slaves of the law as the condition of our freedom.[59]

5

Stanley N. Katz

The Politics of Law in Colonial America: Controversies over Chancery Courts and Equity Law in the Eighteenth Century

In a variety of ways, each of the colonies adopted portions of the law and (especially) the procedure of the High Court of Chancery in the years following the Glorious Revolution. They also inherited the seventeenth-century English tradition of antagonism to their courts of chancery and maintained it during an era in which chancery had long since been quietly accepted as a part of the legal system of England. Roscoe Pound long ago suggested that "Equity has never been popular in America," but he was imprecise. In the colonial period, at least, Americans objected to chancery courts rather than to equity law. The problem is to determine why there was such a radical disparity of attitudes toward, on the one hand, the institution and, on the other, the type of justice it dispensed.

Most of the colonies south of Connecticut experienced episodes of bitter opposition to their chancery courts. In New Jersey the issue flared up twice, the result of the Elizabethtown Bill in Chancery in the 1740s and of Governor William Franklin's efforts to reestablish the court in

Reprinted, in abridged form, from *Law in American History*, ed. Donald Fleming and Bernard Bailyn, (Boston: Little, Brown and Company, 1971), pp. 265-266, pp. 273-284, by permission.

1768. In North Carolina grave difficulties arose when Governor Gabriel Johnston attempted to establish an exchequer court to facilitate the collection of quitrents. In South Carolina one of the results of the "revolution" of 1719 was the elimination of the colonial chancery court, though it soon reappeared in a slightly different form. Nowhere, however, was the question of chancery courts more divisive than in New York.

The initial designation of a chancery court in New York was by the act of the colonial legislature in 1683 (reaffirmed in 1691 and 1692), which established the court in the governor and council. The origin of the functioning chancery is found later, however, in the subsequent gubernatorial ordinances of Nanfan and Cornbury (1701 and 1704). The court operated sporadically for a few years until, in 1711, Governor Robert Hunter determined to provide an efficient equity court for the colony.[1]

Hunter hoped that he could persuade the royal authorities in England to order the establishment of an independent court, and he reported to the board of trade that he had been "pelted with Petitions" for the court both in New York and New Jersey. He argued that there was a

46

need for relief from the vagaries of the common law, citing in particular an excessive judgment in an action for debt, and he also stressed his own inability, as a nonlawyer, to provide adequate judgment in chancery.[2] The home government cautiously assured Hunter that he had authority to act as chancellor by virtue of his royal commission, and he proclaimed the court open for business merely on the advice of his council in 1711.[3]

From 1711 until the American Revolution a gubernatorial chancery court was maintained almost continuously in New York. A few governors, especially in the late 1720s and early 1730s, hesitated to exercise the chancellor's powers, but the framework of the court survived to be perpetuated by their successors. Its business grew quite rapidly after 1750, and by the time of the American Revolution the New York chancery was a respected and ordinary court of justice which transacted much of the same sort of work as its counterpart in England.[4]

To reject "losers" is risky historical technique, though, and to ignore the thirty years of opposition to New York chancery is especially misleading, despite the fact that the court emerged apparently unchanged by the attacks upon it. The first chancery controversy was coincidental with Hunter's opening of the "modern" court, and it appears to have been a classical legislative objection to the establishment of a prerogative court. On November 24, 1711, the assembly resolved that "the erecting of a court of chancery without consent in general assembly, is contrary to law, without precedent, and of dangerous consequence to the liberty and property of the subject." To which the council made the traditional retort: "It is not without precedent that a Court of Chancery has been erected in this Province without consent in General Assembly, and if the erecting of it without their consent be lawfull, we are very well assured that it will not be attended with any dangerous consequences."[5] Governor Hunter described the "angry mood" of the assemblymen, attributed their opposition

to the court to their determination to disclaim "all powers not immediately derived from themselves," and maintained that the court must be kept open as a demonstration of the rights of the Crown.[6] The intensity of the conflict can probably better be understood by Hunter's boast to the board of trade in 1717 that prior to 1711 it had been impossible to collect quitrents in New York, but that subsequently "Deliquents were subpoen'd" to the chancery, the arrears "were immediately brought in and have ever since been regularly paid into the King's Receiver."[7]

Governor William Burnet, one of the few legally trained New York chancellors, vigerously exerted his chancery powers in order collect quitrents. He also proclaimed a Chancery Fee Ordinance designed to regularize practice in the court and to avoid the excessively high fees charged by lawyers for equity litigation. Chancellor Burnet's zeal was finally rewarded on November 25, 1727, with a series of assembly resolutions against his exercise of judicial power. The preamble to the resolves asserted that "by the violent Measures taken in and allowed by it [the chancery court], some have been ruined, others obliged to abandon the Colony, and many restrained in it, either by Imprisonment, or by excessive Bail exacted from them, not to depart even when no Manner of Suits are depending against them" The first resolve stated that, without legislative consent, the chancery court "is unwarrantable, and contrary to the Laws of *England*, a manifest Oppression and Grievance to the Subjects, and of a pernicious Consequence to their Liberties and Properties," and two additional resolutions promised an inquiry into the proper basis of an equity court in New York, and an act declaring "all Orders, Ordinances, Decrees and Proceedings" of the court "to be illegal, null and void, as by Law and Right they ought to be."[8]

The council responded with the standard gubernatorial defense of the chancery: it had been established pursuant to the powers granted in the royal comissions to Governors Hunter and Burnet. The councillors pointed out that the 1711 assembly resolution had been rejected by the board of trade and asserted that "a Court of Equity is necessarily supposed in our Constitution, and that Justice cannot be obtained in all Cases without the Aid of such a Court, and therefore that the King has undoubtedly a Right of erecting the same in the Plantations." Admittedly, some reforms should be made, and the council advised the governor to review the Chancery Fee Ordinance with an eye to changes which would prevent lawyers from augmenting bills of costs and which would end the traditional delay in chancery proceedings. More important, they argued that the motives of the assemblymen were suspect: "The Design of these Resolves was not to redress Grievances," but "to show the People, what Influence the Assembly doth assume over the other Branches of the Legislature here, as well as to alienate the Peoples Affections from His Majesty's Government, by making them believe that illegal and arbitary Powers were and are given to the Governours of this Province."[9]

Burnet and his supporters were in no doubt as to the true reasons for the outburst against the chancery court: the governor had sealed a decree "only two days before" which ran against Adolph Philipse, the speaker of the assembly and the leader of its antigubernatorial faction. William Smith and Cadwallader Colden explained in detail how Philipse and his associates had rammed the resolves through in the closing hours of the last session of the 1727 legislature, which Burnet as quickly dissolved in retaliation. Burnet seemed to acknowledge that the opposition to chancery was based on something more than Philipse's spite, however, for he reported to the board of trade: "One great reason why the Country People are prejudiced against the Court of Chancery has been that several Bills have been brought to ascertain and recover large sums due to the King for Quit Rents on which I have generally given Decrees in favour of the King ... but this rais'd a pretty general clamour, because it fell

heavy on several Patentees."[10] The 1727 incident constituted a major political crisis in New York, and although Peter Zenger's New York Weekly Journal was reminding colonists of Philipse's self-interest in the matter a decade later, it seems clear that the attack on the court struck a genuinely sensitive spot in the government of the province.[11]

The repercussions of the assembly resolves of 1727 were so profound that Governor John Montgomerie, who held office from 1728 to 1731, refused to act as chancellor. Montgomerie reported to the board of trade that the chancery controversy had divided the province into three parties: one, based in the council, supported the court as reformed by Burnet's fee ordinance; another party opposed "this or any other Court of Equity that is not Established by an Act of General Assembly, and they particularly insist upon the Governors being by law incapable of being Sole Judge"; the third, "not so violent as the last but yet desirous of some alteration," perferred to reform the court by establishing the equity power in both the governor and council.[12] Montgomerie confessed to Newcastle that he himself thought the court ought to be reformed, but there would seem to be a good deal of truth in the charge made by Lewis Morris, Jr., that the governor's unwillingness to open the chancery was due to his fear of economic retaliation by the assembly, which bitterly opposed the court.[13] The board of trade directed Montgomerie to hold courts of chancery ("when there shall be occasion, as former Governors have done"), but to no avail. Montgomerie, it would appear, simply refused to endanger his relations with the Philipse faction.[14] The board also urged the council president, Rip Van Dam, who succeeded to the government upon Montgomerie's death in 1731, and the next governor, William Cosby, to hold the court in order to facilitate the collection of royal quitrents in New York.[15]

The most dramatic, but by no means the last, act in the history of the chancery court in New York was played out during the Cosby administration. The script was more or less the same as it had been previously in New York — the argument turned on the necessity for legislative consent in the establishment of a chancery court — but, confusingly, the characters switched roles. The former defenders of the gubernatorial court became the leading protagonists of the prerogative of the assembly, while Philipse and other antichancery men of 1727 took up the governor-chancellor's defense. The reason for the exchange was that with the change in governors, from Burnet to Montgomerie and Cosby, the former political "ins" had become "outs" and one of the time-tested techniques of early-eighteenth-century "outs" was to attack the structure of chancery courts.

The details of the controversy of 1733-1737 can only be sketched hurriedly here, but the essential point is that two concurrent problems were involved. The first was Cosby's attempt to establish an equity jurisdiction in the exchequer branch of the New York Supreme Court, and the second was the governor's use of his personal chancery powers in determining the validity of conflicting titles to the "Oblong" land graft.

The exchequer episode is the better known. It arose from Governor Cosby's need to find a legal forum in which he might sue Council President Van Dam for half his income as lieutenant governor in the brief period between Montgomerie's death and Cosby's arrival. A common-law action was the ordinary procedure, but it had the twin disadvantages that it permitted trial by jury (between a newly appointed royal official and a respected local merchant) and "set-off" (which could reduce Cosby's recovery by the amount of income he had received from the New York post prior to his coming to America).[16] Neither could Cosby proceed in the chancery, where he would be sole judge in his own case, and therefore he prosecuted his suit on the equity side of the exchequer division of the provincial supreme court. There was a rather vague tradition of such an equity jurisdiction in the supreme court, but the council's ordinance of December 4, 1732, establishing the court provoked an immediate outcry by Cosby's opponents that such an establishment threatened their liberties and properties.[17] The governor and council defended the exchequer court on the ground that it was simply a better means of affording an equity jurisdiction in New York, especially since the governor was not a lawyer and he was so frequently away from New York City that sessions of the chancery could not be held regularly.[18]

When the governor pressed forward with the suit against Van Dam, Chief Justice Lewis Morris denied that his court had jurisdiction to entertain the case, affirming his belief in the necessity for legislative consent in the establishment of new courts, and Cosby dismissed him from his judgeship. The case was never brought to a conclusion, but the controversy was deemed of such importance that, at the instance of the Morrisite opposition, the question of the exchequer jurisdiction was debated before the assembly on June 7, 1734, by William Smith (against) and Joseph Murray (for the court). Perhaps, as Smith's son uncharitably concluded, "the Senators were confounded by the long arguments they had heard," or, more likely, their differences had in reality little to do with equity courts, but the assembly took no action to alter the structure of the court system.[19]

The second part of the equity controversy took place in Governor Cosby's court, which was otherwise not a very busy institution. Cosby, like Montgomerie, was allied with those who had opposed Governor Burnet (and his chancery court) and he too was reluctant to hold the court. Vincent Matthews, a leading member of the anti-Cosby group, complained that the attorney general was bringing chancery bills for the collection of quitrents against Cosby's opponents in Orange County, but the minute book of the chancery court indicates that few bills were actually heard by Cosby.[20] The governor knowingly provoked the wrath of his opponents in 1734, however, by entertaining a bill alleging that the local holders of a Montgomerie patent to the huge

Stanley N. Katz

Oblong tract located along the New York–Connecticut border had acquired their title by fraud. The suit was initiated by Francis Harison, an associate of the governor who was acting on behalf of a group of complainants who had a later English patent to the land. The importance of the suit was not only that it threw into question most of the existing titles to land in New York, but also that the Montgomerie patentees were without exception political opponents of Governor Cosby who did not scruple to interpret the attack on their grant in the most extreme light: "If a Governour can set aside patents without a tryal at Law, a Governour can soon make himself master of any mans Landed Estate in the province that he pleases, & if the practice be once Established the whole people will in consequence soon become tenants at will and slaves to Governours."[21]

In October 1735, fifty-nine of the New York patentees petitioned the assembly to intervene in the chancery proceeding against them, requesting the legislators "to take such Steps as may secure the Liberties and Properties of [the petitioners] ... from being at the Disposal and meer Will and Pleasure of a single Man, without any reasonable Check or Appeal for Relief within this Province." They pointed out that the assembly had twice previously spoken out against the governor's chancery court, and yet had neglected "to give these Resolves their full Force, by bringing in of Bills ... or making proper Remonstrances thereupon." The case for action was now clear, since the equitable challenge to their patent had no precedent since the era of James II, when Chancellor Jeffries abetted the royal scheme to vacate English corporate charters in order to establish "a despotick Power in the King over the Rights and Liberties of the Subject." The threat to New Yorkers was serious, since most landowners held such technically imperfect title that "there is not one patent in the whole Country for the setting aside of which a cunning Lawyer may not find a Pretence." Furthermore, costs in a chancery suit are high; the only appeal is to the crown in council ("no Costs are to be recovered [as it is said] when the Suit is brought in the King's Name"); and, worst of all, the chancellor is by definition an interested party since as governor he has the right to regrant forfeited lands. Lewis Morris, Jr., defended the petitioners and the pro-Morris assembly on November 6 passed the by now traditional resolution that a gubernatorial chancery court, without legislative consent, was "contrary to law" and "of dangerous Consequence to the Liberties and Properties of the People."[22]

Like the exchequer incident, the Oblong suit provoked a loud and intense public debate in New York over the rights of the people and the prerogatives of the crown. In both cases the defenders of legislative consent in 1735 were the defenders of prerogative courts in 1727. In both cases the antigubernatorial lawyers offered exceptions to the equity jurisdiction contended for by government officials, and the exceptions were overruled. Neither case ever came to a final decision. The issue was as clear as it was narrow, for even former Chief Justice Morris admitted that New York required a court of equity. It was put precisely by Cadwallader Colden: "The Question must be reduced to this Whether all the Courts of Equity as well as Law are & ought to be erected by the Governour & Councils Authority along or by the Concurrent Authority of the Assembly for as to what the King can do by his Prerogative comes not into the present debate." Colden did not deny that New Yorkers had a "birthright" to a court of equity, but he argued that the court could not constitutionally exist "without any positive law determining it but in the Representative of the whole Community or in the Legislature."[23]

These prolegislative sentiments were echoed by the assembly in its September 7, 1737, address to Lieutenant Governor George Clarke, asserting the impropriety of a gubernatorial chancery court founded on the commission of the governor. In what would prove to be the last of the assembly's protests against the chancery, the legislators reminded Clarke of their previous resolutions on the subject: "Though these Resolves, have been as often as made, treated by the Governors, with an unreasonable Disregard and Comtempt of them; yet to Men of Prudence, they might have been effectual to have made them decline persisting in a Procedure so illegal and so generally dissatisfactory; and which (as they managed it) proved of no use to the Publick, or benefit to themselves."[24] Clarke did not discuss the chancery question in his answer to the Assembly, but neither was he an active chancellor. In effect, however, the controversy over the New York chancery court ended with the death of William Cosby in 1736 and the dispersion of the Morrisite political faction in the Clarke administration. The chancery was henceforth removed from politics and freed for its dramatic legal development after mid-century.

Even this rapid survey suggests certain conclusions about the colonial chancery controversies. Equity law was accepted by all concerned — the dispute was over the constitution of the courts that dispensed equity. The crown and the proprietors insisted upon a narrow, prerogative authority for chancery courts, while most colonists were equally insistent upon the need for legislative consent. The occurrence of political attack upon chancery courts was closely related to their use as forums for the collection of quitrents and, more important, to their convenience as rallying points for the "out" or "country" factions in colonial politics. Objections were seldom to the kinds of mundane private law which occupied most chancellors and equity courts. Finally, the controversies had pretty well ceased by 1750, when the generally recognized need for equity as part of the Anglo-American legal system had resulted either in viable chancery courts or in alternative devices in the existing common-law system. Polit-

ical criticism of chancery courts had lost even its rhetorical usefulness.

Two very general conclusions about eighteenth-century America can also be suggested. In the first place, the period from 1700 to 1750 can be seen as one of unexpected importance in constitutional and ideological development. The attack on chancery courts and the elaboration of the arguments for legislative consent appear as an important form of an emerging political maturity which operated to lend prestige and dignity to what seem to have been basically mean-spirited political disputes. The attack may also be a token of a growing intellectual awareness of American peculiarities — in particular, a probing toward the gradually-realized incongruity in the location of sovereignty in the colonies. The very existence of chancery courts, with their long tradition in English history, made it apparent that, in America, if the conscience of the king was not the source of equity jursdiction, then a more popular legislative source must be identified. Power without an attributable source caused unease, and the legislatures rushed in to assert the prerogatives of the people. At the same time, the whole question of the relative functions of the different branches of government began to be explored, although the inquiry was not pressed home.

Second, one is struck by the tenuous connection between ideology and political action in the early eighteenth century, as compared to the radical intensity of their interconnection in the Revolutionary era. To cite only the most obvious example, it was Lewis Morris who defended Governor Burnet's exercise of equity power in New York and New Jersey in 1727 but who opposed both chancery and exchequer equity jurisdiction in New York in 1733–1737, and yet himself served as an apparently untroubled chancellor in New Jersey after 1738. His inconsistency is typical of the era, and it indicates the ephemeral character of so many of the seemingly profound constitutional struggles of the first half of the

Stanley N. Katz

century. Like so many others, the problem of the chancery courts arose fitfully, ran close to the surface of politics and ideology, and did not really have to be solved. In the first half of the century ideas were brittle and discontinuous, contrasting dramatically with the more radical character of constitutional rethinking which developed after mid-century.

6

David Flaherty

Law and the Enforcement of Morals in Early America

The Relationship of Law and Morals

The moral law was the offical guideline for the enforcement of morals in the American colonies and the basis of the civil law itself. Sin and crime, divine law and secular law, the moral law and the criminal law were all closely intertwined. The preamble to the famous Massachusetts Code of 1648 took specific notice of attempts to distinguish between the laws of God and the laws of men. When the administration of civil authority "is according to deductions, and rules gathered from the word of God, and the clear light of nature in civil nations, surely there is no humane law that tendeth to common good (according to those principles) but the same is mediately a law of God, and that in way of an Ordinance which all are to submit unto and that for conscience sake."[1] In theory it was not possible for the divine and secular laws to contradict one another. According to Governor John Winthrop and his associates, "we have no laws diametrically opposite to those of England, for then they must be

contrary to the law of God and of right reason, which the learned in those laws have anciently and still do hold forth as the fundamental basis of their laws, and that if anything hath been otherwise established, it was an errour, and not a law, being against the intent of the lawmakers."[2] All secular laws, especially in the realm of morality, tended toward the same end of pronouncing punishment "against those crimes which God's eternal law has condemned." An earthly power could neither dispense with nor ignore those divine stipulations.

The Puritans were accused of attempting to legislate the Mosaic code into practice, since to them the Bible was a model for the organization of God's community on earth. In both England and America in the sixteenth and seventeenth centuries it was fashionable to cite the Bible as authority in particular legal cases. The New England colonists specifically listed biblical authority for statutes in their law codes and firmly believed that the English common law was grounded on the law of God.[3] Yet the insistence that the criminal statutes must be inspired by the moral law did not result in the simple enactment of biblical precepts into law. In 1636 the Massachusetts General Court instructed

Reprinted, in abridged form, from *Law in American History*, ed. Donald Fleming and Bernard Bailyn (Boston: Little, Brown and Company, 1971), pp. 203-253, by permission.

the governor and certain of his associates to draft a code of laws agreeable to the word of God and to decide cases in current litigation "according to the lawes nowe established, and where there is noe law, then as neere the lawe of God as they can."[4] The code was not to be drawn directly from the word of God. A draft by John Cotton entitled "Moses His Judicialls" purported to do just that and was not enacted into law by the authorities.[5] The colonists conceived of the Bible as a source of basic wisdom in law as in morality; it was a general preceptor, not a technical guide to those who defined and enforced the ordinary laws. The laws of God were the ideals to be approached in human affairs.

The essential contribution of the moral law to the secular law was the equation of sin and crime. In all but a literal sense, what was a sin was also a crime:[6] thus the reference to fornication in a Massachusetts law of 1665 as "a particular Crime, a shameful Sin, much increasing amongst us, to the great dishonour of God, and our Profession of his Holy Name."[7] The precepts of moral law furnished the initial reasons for punishing a crime. If God had branded certain actions as seriously immoral and sinful, these normally became crimes by statute in every American colony, for the authorities were bound to inhibit such behavior.

In a society where law and morals were so closely identified, the nature and extent of the parallel relationship between church and state becomes significant. The universal acceptance of Christianity in the American colonies inevitably made for a close association between church and state, but the accompanying harmoniousness of moral outlook made an official interlocking unnecessary. Modern commentators have recognized that a high degree of homogeneity in a society is an essential prerequisite to the legal enforcement of morality. Such a precondition existed in colonial society. On this basis it was possible in some colonies to have a close association of law and morals without an accompanying intermingling of church and state.

Despite their common commitment to the support of the moral law, the church and the state in early America had separate goals and roles. While the Massachusetts Code of 1648 lauded the advantages of church and state joined in the covenant of grace growing up together, "whereby each do help and strengthen other (the Churches the civil Authoritie, and the civil Authoritie the Churches)," the Cambridge Platform of Church Discipline of the same year asserted that "as it is unlawfull for church-officers to meddle with the sword of the magistrate, so it is unlawfull to meddle with the work proper to church-officers."[8] In general terms the Code of 1648 asserted the primacy of secular control over society as a whole. In England the established church shared this supervision over society through the system of ecclesiastical courts which paid particular attention to personal behavior. No American colony joined church and state together in this fashion for the enforcement of morals. In sixteenth- and seventeenth-century England it was also not unusual for various levels of ecclesiastical officials to serve as justices of the peace and preside with lay magistrates at the court of quarter sessions.[9] Such a practice was never followed in New England and only rarely in any other American colony. The primary responsibility for the enforcement of morals was in the hands of the colonial state, and all of its officials were laymen.[10]

The enforcement of the moral law became one of the primary obligations of colonial governments. The goal of colonial authorities was to translate the divine moral law into criminal statutes in the interests of popular morality. The civil authorities in every colony made a regular effort to establish and uphold high standards of conduct in society as an integral part of what they were expected to do.[11] Solomon Stoddard told the assembled rulers of Massachusetts in 1703 that "rulers have Opportunity many ways to discountenance sin; and thereby to give a check to mens corruptions: the holding the reins of Government strait, bridles men in and restrains them from much evil."[12] The magistrates had an essential role to play in the suppression of vice in society. The threat of the judgment of God hung over a society where vice was not discouraged.

The Regulation of Morals

The intimate association of law and morality in early America resulted in the enactment of legislation tending toward the establishment and maintenance of high moral standards. As Cotton Mather stated, "Good laws are important machines, to keep very much evil out of the world." The institutionalization of the regulation of morals primarily occured in the first decades of the settlement of a colony, when authorities were forced to give substantial consideration to the formulation of a criminal code. Such statutes initially set forth standards of personal conduct that reflected the community's general opinion. Legislation played a part in sustaining the conviction that some types of personal conduct were morally unacceptable. The secretary to the General Court of Massachusetts reported that the Code of 1648 was a response to the pleas of the populace for a printed book of laws, "wherein (upon every occasion) you might readily see the rule which you ought to walke by."[13] And there were similar pleas elsewhere. There is hardly a specified moral offense in New England that did not have its counterpart in the criminal code of Virginia in the seventeenth century. The formulation of laws for the regulation of morals did not even require a vigorous established church for the initial impetus, as in the case of Virginia and Maryland.

The statute books of the various American colonies reveal a series of laws designed to regulate public morals. The concerns of Virginia and Maryland with drunkenness, fornication, adultery, blasphemy, bastardy, swearing, rape, and the like, were typical. In Virginia, as in the other colonies, "the Assembly passed many more laws dealing with public morals than with offenses against the

state, or religion, or the person, or property."[14] Devising suitable sanctions for "the effectual suppression" of such offenses was a common problem that repeatedly came up for reconsideration.[15]

The laws regulating morals in most of New England and in New York were particularly distinguished by their initial severity. The Massachusetts Code of 1648 made adultery a capital offense.[16] Both parties to the adultery were to be put to death, according to the Mosaic prescription. In fact this punishment was rarely inflicted on anyone in New England.[17] Although the death penalty for adultery was not abolished until after the Charter of 1691,[18] there is evidence of some earlier doubts. In 1642 Governor William Bradford of Plymouth Colony wrote to the authorities in Massachusetts that it was not clear to some of his associates that adultery should be punished with death.[19] The Code of 1648 further stated that fornication should be punished by the requirement of marriage, by a fine, by corporal punishment, or by all three, as the judges will decide "is most agreeable to the word of God.[20] The recognition by secular authorities in each colony that some types of fornication were more serious than others indicated that in many significant ways the colonists were not as strict as they might have been concerning the extent to which law and morals should be identical. Any prosecution associated with an impending or currently existing marriage reduced the significance and punishment of the act of fornication. Colonial authorities also considered copulation between a married man and a single woman as an act of fornication. Such an offense by a married woman was adultery.[21] The sexual code, reflecting the early existence of a double standard in America, was rarely very harsh on males.

In Pennsylvania William Penn's Great Law of 1682 contained elaborate provisions that were extremely enlightened in the sense that rape, sodomy, bigamy, incest, and adultery were not made capital offenses. Most were punished by some combination of whipping, forfeiture,

David Flaherty

fines, and imprisonment. The failure of these lighter sanctions resulted in an unusual, short-term trend toward increasing severity after 1700, culminating in the wholesale adoption of the English penal code in 1718.[22] Adultery remained a noncapital offense. In the eighteenth century the penalty for the third adultery conviction was twenty-one lashes, seven years in jail, and marking with an "A" on the forehead.[23] Fitzroy noted that fornication was punished more severely after an act of 1700 with a choice of whipping or a fine, but "before that there was considerable confusion, and, though the offence was of a moral nature, it was treated quite mildly with punishments of a few lashes or light fines."[24]

In the view of the long traditions of the English common law, there was little originality in the colonial criminal laws regulating morals. Most statutes reflected those enforced by the civil and ecclesiastical jurisdictions in England. The criminal law was one area where the charter provisions requiring the colonists to fashion statutes as similar as possible to the laws of England made a good deal of sense. For serious criminal offenses a colony like Virginia or Maryland either enforced the English statute without question or formally adopted it into its own jurisprudence. In the late 1650s a Virginia statute simply stated that the English law against bigamy was to be in force.[25] Even in New England the criminal laws enacted by the colonists were not particularly reformist in character, except for a general reduction in the number of capital offenses. Wolford concluded that in the Code of 1648, many of the criminal offenses, "while founded on Mosaic law, were in considerable conformity with the common law of England."[26]

The motivation for the enactment of moral regulations did not remain uncontaminated by baser considerations. Although the exact array of motives was rarely evident, many moral offenses were punished not simply because they were immoral but because they caused social problems and disturbances as well. Even

as the religious motive weakened among some individuals in the course of the seventeenth century, a wide variety of political, economic, and social justifications for the enforcement of morals appeared in its place. The prosecution of moral offenders allegedly helped to avert various social and economic ills. Blackstone's explanation of why bigamy was more than an offense against the ecclesiastical law illustrated this: "The legislature has thought it just to make it felony, by reason of its being so great a violation of the public economy and decency of a well ordered state."[27] Such mundane considerations were never far from the surface in colonial lawmaking and law enforcement.

The upper classes in colonial society considered it a part of their moral responsibility to impose appropriate forms of morality on the lower orders. This was a common phenomenon in preindustrial England. Such legislation also served as a handy instrument of social control. In fact, a student of Virginia society has suggested that gradually "the more severe injunctions against immorality were directed in support of a stabilized class system."[28] This was evident in Virginia legislation prohibiting ten specific games to persons of the lower classes, including artificers, fishermen, husbandmen, laborers, mariners, apprentices, and servants.[29] In the area of sexual offenses in Virginia, free persons were less frequently prosecuted for fornication or adultery than servants, who were regularly brought to justice.[30]

Modern authorities on criminal law advocate distinctions between public and private offenses and between acts of duress and relations between consenting adults. Could the American colonists make such distinctions in theory? In the first place the colonists did not conceive of themselves as using the power of the state to enforce purely moral or religious standards. Since the moral law was the basis of the criminal law, the secular and spiritual interests of society were intertwined. Private immoral acts might not be specifically harmful to others, while remaining injurious to the spiritual interests of the offender, offensive to God, and calculated to call down his vengeance upon society as a whole. Any immoral act could thus be construed as a threat to the public safety and welfare. "The well-ordering of this plantation," which was the goal of the Massachusetts General Court in 1635 in establishing a committee to draft laws, automatically included the enforcement of morals in every area of existence.

Practical limitations on the ability of the state to interfere in private lives and concern for the privacy and freedom of individual citizens sometimes combined to restrict severely the capacities of the state in the realm of private relations. There is surely some relevance to the issue of immoralities committed in private in the fascinating provision in the Massachusetts Code of 1648 that "no Magistrate, Juror, Officer or other man shall be bound to inform, present or reveal any private crime or offence wherein there is no perill or danger to this Colonie, or any member thereof, when any necessarie tye of conscience, grounded on the word of God bindes him to secresie."[31] To some extent a sense of the rights and liberties of the inhabitants discouraged active interference in the private lives of subjects in the area of moral regulation. More frequently such limitations were a consequence of law-enforcement practices rather than of legislative decisions.

The enactment of statutes was, of course, only the first step in the implementation of the moral law. In establishing an adequate law-enforcement apparatus, colonial officials sought to outdistance their English brethren. The Puritans in particular believed that they could successfully enforce the moral laws. By their standards, everyone else had failed. In other colonies expectations concerning the implementation of these laws were probably no more ambitious than in England.

The framers of the Massachusetts Code of 1648 were well aware that law enforce-ment was the Achilles heel of moral regulation: "You have called us from amongst the rest of our Bretheren and given us power to make these lawes: we must now call upon you to see them executed· remembring that old and true proverb. The execution of the law is the life of the law."[32]

In fashioning law-enforcement apparatus in the New World the colonists faced an interesting structural problem. In England the enforcement of morals was the primary responsibility of the established Anglican Church through its ancient system of ecclesiastical courts. These were organized from the parish and diocesan level of archdeacon's and consistory courts to the provincial court that supervised a region. A separate system of ecclesiastical courts helped to maintain some formal degree of separation between the secular law and the enforcement of morals. English civil authorities had not yet played a substantial role in the moral sphere since the church had almost exclusive jurisdiction over marriage, divorce, illegitimacy, incest, and adultery. The justices of the peace had some limited involvement in cases of sexual immorality, when, for example, they might handle a case of bastardy, while the church courts punished the offender for fornication. But, in general, adultery and fornication were not secular crimes before 1650.[33] The regular ecclesiastical courts continued to supervise the sexual morals of the local English population. Cases of incontinence in all its forms were by far the most common presentments before the archdeacon's courts. A recent analysis of selected English courts in four different counties from 1590 to 1633 revealed that presentments for sexual immorality averaged from one to four cases per parish annually, with the earlier period showing the larger number of such indictments. Such prosecutions often constituted more than 50 percent of the total presentments for ecclesiastical offenses from a parish.[34]

The most important fact about English ecclesiastical courts from the colonial point of view is that they became unpopular and were abolished in the 1640's. The first settlers of America welcomed this abolition because of the activity of these courts against religious noncomformity and their lax enforcement of morals. The Root and Branch Petition submitted in December 1640 to the House of Commons blamed the ecclesiastical jurisdiction for "the great increase and frequency of whoredoms and adulteries, occasioned by the prelates' corrupt administration of justice in such cases, who taking upon them the punishment of it, do turn all into monies for the filling of their purses."[35]

Whatever the justice of these complaints, many of the early colonists considered ecclesiastical courts undesirable on these shores, and none were established in America.[36] Outside of New England, the effective removal of ecclesiastical responsibility for the supervision of morals was an unintended by-product of antipathy to their jurisdiction on other grounds. Secular courts became responsible for the enforcement of morals. The Puritans believed that the enforcement of morals belonged in the hands of the civil authorities in any event. No colony seems to have anticipated that secular courts might not be effective in the regulation of morals.

A serious attempt in Virginia to establish a system of ecclesiastical courts illustrated their continuing unpopularity in a colony not notable for intense religious fervor. The Reverend James Blair, who had come to a parish in Virginia from England in 1685, was appointed the Bishop of London's commissary in 1689. In 1690 a convention of ministers that met at his request approved a plan to set up ecclesiastical courts for the reform of abuses against the moral law. In the summer of 1690 Blair proclaimed his intention "to revive and put in execution the Ecclesiastical laws against all cursers Swearers and blasphemers, all whoremongers fornicators and Adulterers, all drunkards ranters and profaners of the Lords day . . . and against all Scandalous persons, whether of the Clergy or Laity within this dominion and Colony of Vir-

ginia."[37] The governor and the Council of State were said to have initially supported Blair. Yet his plan never went into full operation and soon became a dead letter. By 1691 one of his surrogates had attempted to set up an ecclesiastical court and had cited a civil-court clerk to answer allegations. The lieutenant governor summoned Blair and his associate to apologize for this attempt. The records of the House of Burgesses simply noted that the legislators decided to proceed no further against the pair. Virginians were obviously content with their own modest secular efforts at the reformation of morals, however inadequate these may have seemed to certain of the clergy.

A secular court system structured in a simple, streamlined, and efficient fashion was the colonists' first line of attack in the enforcement of morals. There was to be local and swift justice for criminal offenders. The hierarchy of courts was similar from colony to colony despite minor differences in titles and functions. The courts held by individual magistrates or justices of the peace to dispense speedy justice or bind over an offender to the county court operated at the most immediate and local level of a New England town or a Virginia county. Justices of the peace themselves played a considerable role in setting the moral tone of the comminity. Their enthusiasm or lack of interest in the enforcement of morals was a crucial point in the system. Most cases of incontinence were too serious for disposition by a single justice and were held over to the next regular meeting of a county court or its specific criminal arm, sometimes termed the general sessions of the peace. Most criminal cases involving the enforcement of morals were disposed of at this level of justice. It was unusual for a criminal prosecution of this sort to reach a superior court or other appellate court. The few capital offenses against morals were notable exceptions.

The secular courts and the ecclesiastical systems of discipline established by such groups as the Puritans and Quakers should not be confused. In the Congregational churches ecclesiastical discipline applied only to testified regenerate members, more easily referred to as full church members, and, after the Half-Way Covenant of 1662, those sons and daughters of full church members who had become covenanted members of the church. The role of the Congregational church was to secure a declaration of repentance from the offender before or after his secular conviction. In their totality full church members were rarely a majority of the adult population in a New England town. These members could be punished for the same offense — especially when the charge was incontinence — both in church disciplinary proceedings and before the secular courts. Dual prosecution by the church and secular authorities was probably more typical of the early years of settlement, although there are no studies on this subject to date. For those Puritans and Quakers who aspired to the higher levels of saintliness, such double jeopardy was at most a minor irritant. The Quakers, who soon became a minority in their own colony, organized their membership in local meetings, monthly gatherings of the individual meetings in a township, quarterly assemblies of the meetings in a county, and then a yearly meeting. The close disciplining of individual Quakers occurred at the lower levels of this hierarchy. In the sphere of personal morals the list of Quaker concerns paralleled those in the secular courts. Whatever the official irrelevance of Puritan or Quaker proceedings to the civil court's activities in a case, the system of ecclesiastical justice could not help reinforcing the secular moral order in areas where it operated.

The secular authorities generally appointed the traditional English law-enforcement officers and charged them with varying degrees of responsibility for the apprehension of moral offenders. The list in a town or a county included the important offices of constables, sheriffs and grand jurors. Sometimes nightwatchmen in towns and such temporary phenomena as the Massachusetts tythingmen

played a role in this matter. Some authorities continued to encourage informers to earn fees by reporting offenders.

Churchwardens presented abuses against the moral code in Virginia, Maryland, and New York.[38] In Virginia the housekeepers in a parish chose a vestry of twelve leading men, who annually in association with the minister selected two of the vestrymen to be churchwardens. The latter then made presentments of moral offenders directly to the civil courts, which created a formal tie between church and state such as the Puritans would never have permitted. The scope included "persons not coming to Church; those who prophane the Sabbath, by Working, Traveling, Tippling at Ordinaries, Drunkenness, Swearing, Cursing, and all Persons who shall transgress any Penal Laws, made for the Restraint of Vice and Immorality."[39] Directives relating to fornication and adultery made explicit that the churchwardens, with a significant assist from grand jurors, were the primary authorities charged with reporting such transgressions to the secular courts. In 1785 the new overseers of the poor took over this obligation.

The Enforcement of Morality

There is substantial historical discussion of the prevalence of sexual offenses in New England, perhaps because such information is so much at odds with the popular conception of the Puritan life-style. Practically every scholar who has studied this subject has commented on the existence of widespread sexual irregularities.[40] A random examination of county court records in any of the New England colonies would illustrate this situation. New England legal machinery prosecuted many breaches of the moral laws, but the violations remained numerous. Legislative repression of sexual misbehavior did not succeed, despite the continued experiments with types of laws and punishments. Perhaps the most startling evidence comes from the disciplinary records of the Congregational churches, where prosecutions

David Flaherty

for incontinence were routine. The author of the leading study of this subject simply concluded that "the suggestion that Puritanism was sexually ascetic . . . is not supported by the evidence."[41] By the eighteenth century the secular courts treated cases of fornication and bastardy with considerable leniency and often did not prosecute the men involved.

The situation with respect to the enforcement of morals was not very different in Pennsylvania. The Quakers' apparent goal was to stamp out breaches of the moral law by strict enforcement. By the beginning of the eighteenth century the court records were already full of cases of bastardy, fornication, and adultery.[42] Fornication was common in the select Society of Friends: it followed marriages that breached certain prohibitions in the order of most common offenses. Yet the vigorous prosecution of Quakers for fornication did not improve the situation. "During the colonial period fornication and illegitimate births increased while membership remained stable. By the disownments it produced, prosecution of fornication decimated the membership of Friends."

In Virginia there were many complaints that the laws against immorality were not being enforced. General Assemblies, vestries, and county courts joined the lament at recurrent intervals. Sex offenders were among the most common criminal offenders before the county courts. Although adultery and fornication were punished only occasionally, "prosecutions for bastardy form the most important single group of cases which came before the county courts."[43] Far more women than men were prosecuted. Commissary Blair would not have initiated his ill-fated plan for the establishement of ecclesiastical courts in 1690 had the state of the enforcement of morals in Virginia been satisfactory.

In Maryland in the seventeenth century, calls for the enforcement of the moral laws became a regular feature of the political landscape. In 1658 officials, alarmed at the number of unmarried servants who were becoming pregnant, instituted more severe punishment of bastardy.[44] The offense remained a common one in the county-court records. The governor closed the 1696 session of the Maryland legislature by reminding his listeners "that the making of good lawes was altogether ineffectuall unless they were duly put into Execution. Therefore since most parte of the house were Magistrates in their Severall Countys he Straitly charged them to put in Execution all the good lawes against Sabbath-breaking, Prophane Cursing and Swearing, Adultery, and fornication, etc."[45] There is no evidence that this or any other colonial governor was ever very successful in such endeavors.

Despite their good intentions about upholding public morality, the colonists were duplicating English experience — immorality had been and continued to be a significant problem. Sexual offenses were exceedingly common in the English ecclesiastical courts prior to the Civil War.[46] Immorality had become such a problem in the early Stuart era that in 1650 the Civil War Parliament passed an act making adultery and fornication secular offenses. Adultery became a capital offense, while fornication was punishable with three months' imprisonment. Yet even amidst the revolutionary fervor of the 1650s any initial rigor in the enforcement of this act was soon relaxed. As public opinion proved increasingly unsympathetic, it became difficult to obtain convictions, especially for adultery.[47] Cromwell himself failed in his efforts to stimulate the act's enforcement. It lapsed at the Restoration, when jurisdiction was restored to the ecclesiastical courts. By the early eighteenth century many of the English laws regulating morality, especially those against adultery, had fallen into desuetude.[48] Thereafter the English abandoned the legal regulation of adultery and fornication.

Yet most colonial authorities did not consider their enactments on moral matters to be mere ideals for the edification of the weak. In many ways they never gave up the enforcement of morals as a lost cause. Prosecutions for fornication continued into the late eighteenth century in one form or another. The authorities did not abandon the search for better laws that might actually improve public behavior or at least reduce the economic burden. As Arthur Scott noted in studying moral offenses in Virginia, "the great number of laws and amendments which the Assembly found it necessary to pass bear eloquent testimony to the perplexities encountered in devising suitable penalties and an adequate machinery of law enforcement." As early as 1658 Virginia sought to encourage the enforcement of laws to suppress odious sins by declaring those convicted of adultery or fornication incapable of being a witness or of holding any public office. This applied to "persons of what degree or qualitie soever." Later acts against vice did not repeat this provision. A Virginia enactment in 1727 illustrates another problem in the enforcement of the moral law. It imposed fines on householders who did not report bastards born in their homes to the authorities. Scott concluded that the gradual diminution in prosecutions for such moral offenses as adultery and fornication "was more probably due to an increasing indifference on the part of the public, or at least to a growing hopelessness of dealing with such offenses by coercive measures, rather than to an actual diminution in the frequency of these moral lapses."[49] Perhaps there was a sense that to stop enforcing the laws on sexual morality completely would be to countenance such misbehavior.

Some of the reluctance to enforce certain statutes and some of the effective limits to the implementation of legislation concerning morals also helped to maintain a livable situation for the inhabitants of the colonies. The Massachusetts magistrates seem never to have carried out the explicit threat in the fornication law of 1665 to disfranchise a freeman for fornication.[50] Persons convicted of capital sexual offenses such as adultery in early New England did not suffer capital punishment. The early New England courts demonstrated appropriate leniency in fornication cases that eventuated in a marriage. The growing leniency in punishments for fornication in all of the colonies as the seventeenth century progressed bore testimony to the increasing tolerance for sexual deviance in the New World and the slackening commitment to the strict enforcement of a moral code. The goals of the colonial criminal law were not stated with the sophistication of a twentieth-century *Model Penal Code*, but in practice some of the basic aims were similar. The maintenance of law and order in the local setting and the prevention and punishment of acts that hurt other persons were the primary goals of colonial magistrates. Sexual acts that were illegal and immoral but not harmful to anyone did not have a high priority among the tasks of most persons charged with law enforcement. This did not, however, prevent periodic enforcement to reassert the moral condemnation of the community.

One has a sense of an increasing offical tolerance of private immoralities, if only on the ground that little could be done about them anyway. Legislatures did not create a law enforcement apparatus that could effectively prosecute private immoral conduct. In 1731 the monthly meeting of Philadelphia Quakers in voicing its long-standing suspicions that one of the brethern was engaging in fornication, lamented that since "such secret works are often difficult to prove, nothing more could be done for a long time, but frequent admonitions." In practice private illicit behavior was almost untouchable by the available means of enforcement. As a magistrate in the town of Boston in 1714, Samuel Sewall asked a crowd drinking in a tavern on a Saturday evening after the Sabbath had begun to leave such public premises, but he did not intervene when someone invited the group to move to the privacy of his house.[51] The concept of the home as a castle provided privacy for individuals. In practice the authorities followed a policy of noninterference in the personal and private affairs of others that were not publicly recognized as seriously harmful or that required extensive surveillance for prosecution. Public offenses that challenged the honor and reputation of the

society demanded prosecution, but unde-
tected behavior that avoided scandal in the
community was felt to be less pressing.

Another motive that operated in the
selective enforcement of moral legislation
by colonial authorities was much less idealistic than concern for personal privacy.
Especially in Virginia, where the trend
was much in evidence, economic considerations came significantly into play in
prosecutions for sexual offenses. Moral
offenses had a low rating among the priorities of concern of the Virginia gentry
except when their interests were at stake.
This accounts for the frequency of bastardy
prosecutions alone without an accompanying presentment for fornication or adultery. In any colony a bastard child
represented a significant drain on the
parish poor funds unless the authorities
discovered a source of financial support.
This was particularly true in cases of pregnant servants in Virginia. Their terms were
extended to the benefit of the master, and
efforts were made to apprehend the
responsible male. Out of 490 York County
criminal cases studied by Scott, 73
involved servant women having illegitimate children, 8 of men for fornication
with servants, 9 adultery cases, and only
35 cases of fornication.[52] Virginia did not
prosecute the reputed father of a bastard if
he tendered security to a churchwarden. In
addition, the law stated that "a Bastard of a
Person able to keep it, and not likely to be
chargeable to the Parish, is not within the
Statute of 18 Eliz. cap. 3."[53] Scott concluded that in Virginia "the relentlessness
of the prosecutions for bastardy indicates
that it was the birth of the child rather than
the breach of the moral code involved
which was the real offense in the eyes of
the ruling classes."[54]

Such an economic motive also figured
prominently in cases in other colonies,
since the need to find support for the illegitimate child was always a major consideration. Massachusetts introduced a
bastardy law in 1672 to relieve the economic burden of a town where bastards
were born of poverty-stricken persons. In
future a man accused by the female during
labor would be legally responsible for the
support of the child, however much he
himself might deny paternity, unless he
had excellent proof. Although laws
against fornication were already in existence, this was the only punishment to
which the male was liable under this statute. Gentlemen normally received more
lenient treatment at the hands of the law.[55]
Although South Carolina did not enact
statutes forbidding fornication and adultery, it did formulate an act against bastardy in 1703. The sequence of motives in
the preamble was revealing: "Whereas
great Charges ariseth upon many Places in
this Province by Reason of Bastardy,
besides the great Dishonour to Almighty
God, and the evil Encouragement of lewd
life."[56] The punishments inflicted were
purely of an economic nature.

The association of law and the regulation of morals in the hands of the state in
America considerably weakened the entire
relationship. The abolition of ecclesiastical courts had broader consequences than
anyone had anticipated as the state took
over from the church almost complete control of the enactment and enforcement of
statutes. An English cleric who had been
living in Virginia commented that, as a
consequence of the absence of an ecclesiastical court there, "Vice, Prophaneness,
and Immorality are not suppressed as
much as might be: The People hate the
very name of the Bishop's Court."[57] His
suggestion that an ecclesiastical court
might perform better struck close to an
important point. The state lacked the
essential long-term moral commitment to
the enforcement of the sexual code that the
church possessed. The gradual process of
secularization of society that began in
America in the latter half of the seventeenth century made the infusion of the
state with moral fervor less and less likely.
The secular aims of government took permanent procedence over more noble but
less relevant ones.

Popular attitudes made a substantial
contribution to the failure of the attempt to
associate law and morals in the interests of
high moral standards in society. The toler-

ance of moderate immorality, the lack of proper zeal for the enforcement of morals, and the opportunities for immorality in a rural environment constituted elements of this picture. The twentieth century has forgotten that the colonists were pre-Victorian in their attitudes to sexual matters. They did not attempt to hide the reality of sexual urges or of nature. The actualities of houses of prostitution and sexual lapses were much in their traditional and current experiences.[58] An agricultural society that was close to nature and marked by serious violence in many forms did not view the offense of premarital sexual involvement or illicit activity generally with much alarm. Americans seem to have been informally tolerant of women who gave birth out of wedlock.[59] There are innumerable examples of notable individuals who engaged in illicit sexual activities. Benjamin Franklin was also afflicted by "that hard-to-be-governed passion of youth," but allowed it to lead him into sexual adventures in both Philadelphia and London. He sired an illegitimate son who in turn imitated his father.[60] The heroic sexual exploits of William Byrd II (1674-1744) of Virginia are much better known than those of any other colonist because of his explicit shorthand record. His Virginia diary from 1709 to 1712 records his illicit inclinations and attempted seductions.[61] In London after the death of his wife, Byrd kept a succession of mistresses and cavorted with streetwalkers.[62]

The presence of the well-known madam, Alice Thomas, in seventeenth-century Boston makes clear that Puritan New England was not immune to the pleasures of the flesh.[63] In 1712 and 1713 Cotton Mather sought a "list" of all whorehouses in Boston and a "catalogue" of men who patronized them: "I am informed of serval Houses in this Town, where there are young Women of a very debauched character . . .; unto whom there is a very great Resort of young men." His resolutions to extinguish the mischief through his Societies for the Suppression of Disorders do not seem to have matured.[64] A British officer visiting Newport at later date made a comment about his encounter with a local prostitute that was most revealing of local attitudes: "She keeps a house of pleasure and has done so for a good many years past in a more decent and reputable manner than common, and is Spoke of by everybody in Town in a favourable manner for one of her Profession . . . This place must have arrived to a tollerable degree of modern luxury when houses of that kind were publickly allowed of, and the Manners of the People by no means rigid when subjects of that sort become family conversation."[65]

Many colonists were not deeply disturbed or surprised when someone infringed on the moral code in sexual matters, expecially if the offense was fornication or bastardy. Prosecutions for such offenses were so common that they could not long remain shocking to the average citizen. Many residents viewed the usual offender against the moral code with a mixture of tolerance, amusement, and titillation. Such episodes temporarily fueled the local fires of gossip. Although the majority of the population formally discountenanced immorality, the general moral climate, the prevalence of gaming and drinking, for example, created a situation where a person could not do much more than discourage sexual vices officially and in his family. In 1698 the young minister of a rural Massachusetts town blamed the "prevailing, growing evil" of fornication on parents who allowed their children and servants to roam at night and on common inducements: "Such are, over costly, light garish attire, filthy communications, idleness, intemperance, by which the body is inflamed, and modesty banished."[66]

The total situation in the colonies was of a type to discourage the successful association of law and morality. Incidents of illicit behavior occurred, especially among younger persons and the lower classes, including servants and slaves. Custom permitted courting couples to bundle in some regions. Some colonists blamed the arrival of various European immigrant groups in the eighteenth century for an increase in vice and immorality. The levels of adherence to asceticism of these groups of newcomers surely differed. In actual fact the flow of British immigrants was a more constant source of moral standards and patterns of behavior somewhat at odds with the expectations of the founders of the colonies. Many colonists themselves held liberal views with respect to some of life's pleasures. Sexual immorality in moderate doses was not the great offense to the residents of colonial New England that it became for some of their descendants.[67]

A zeal for successful implementation of moral legislation was not pervasive in colonial society. The colonists recognized moral standards, just as they were not startled by deviations from the norm. They expected known breaches of the moral order to be punished, as in the inevitable situation of a woman who had a child out of wedlock, or soon after her wedding day. But the colonists were not attuned to involving themselves in the search for moral offenders. The process of informing never attracted popular support. Virginia hardly encouraged the practice by making the informer pay the court costs if the verdict was for the defendant.[68] In small communities few private individuals actively concerned themselves in the prosecution of offenses against morality. This was a major source of frustration to a New England minister like Solomon Stoddard, despite his excellent grasp of the sociological reasons for this situation.[69]

The frequent opportunities for sexual irregularities helped weaken the impulse to moral reform. The presence of unmarried white servants and black slaves in small communities provided a regular source of, and outlet for, sexual immorality. Indentured servants who were not free to marry accounted for the bulk of the incontinence cases that appeared in the Virginia courts. An overwhelming percentage of these white immigrants to the southern colonies were males, while in New England the proportion of male immigrants was about 60 percent. The economic motive at work in the prosecution of servants should not be discounted, since their terms of service were extended for such offenses. Masters not infrequently seduced their female servants. While the evidence for the explicit use of slaves as sexual objects by the white population is not prominent in the existing records, the possibilities are fairly evident.[70] Slaves were in a permanently debased condition and lacked substantial exposure to the Christian moral code. Whites of any class enjoyed some degree of authority over the slaves by reason of their own color. Younger males found some black females ready prey for their earliest sexual adventures. The practice of allowing younger slaves to walk about naked, the sexual attractiveness of some slave women to the white male, and the relatively defenseless position of female slaves contributed to this situation. In Charleston whites openly kept slaves as mistresses. The statutory responses of some legislatures suggested that interracial sexual activity was common by the eighteenth century. The authorities threatened drastic punishments as a terror tactic to discourage such relationships. In 1715 Maryland decided that any free white man or woman who had a child by a Negro should be reduced to servitude for a seven-year period. White servants had their term extended by seven years. Free Negroes involved in such episodes with whites also were subject to servitude for a seven-year period. Pennsylvania adopted the latter provision in 1726.[71] It is doubtful that such harsh measures were actually implemented.

The lack of popular enthusiasm for participation in the enforcement of morals infected those officially charged with this task. Governors, reformers, and clerical leaders frequently blamed responsible officials for their unwillingness to enforce the laws. Since legislators were often also justices of the peace in their home community, such accusations evidenced their own guilty feelings. But lack of zeal extended to grand jurors, petty jurors, churchwardens, constables, and deputy sheriffs as well. They exercised a potential veto power over the extent to which morals were to be enforced in any locality. In the eighteenth century this veto reached heights of absurdity when an individual agreed to pay child support in a bastardy case, but a jury refused to convict him of fornication.

Indifference, inefficiency, fear, corruption, the burden of office, and an unwillingness to prosecute friends contributed to the laxity of law enforcement in the area of personal morals.[72] There was no professional force operating in this area. Agents of the law were satisfied if they were able to maintain elementary law and order in an unruly society. The routineness of incontinence cases and the routinized response of the courts in punishing them did not encourage any colonial official to unusual zeal in the prosecution of offenses that did not come readily to his attention. Even ministers of religion were loath to outdistance their flock in the zealous enforcement of morals. Ministers in the predominant churches of New England and Virginia, for example, were employees of their congregations. Well-informed commentators in Virginia around 1700 remarked on a minister's usual subservience to vestries that frequently entered into annual agreements for his services: "He must have a speciall Care how he preach'd against the Vices that any great Man of the Vestry was guilty of; for if he did, he might expect a Faction would be made in the Vestry, to be against renewing the Agreement with him for another year."[73]

The most striking evidence of the failure of colonial authorities in the enforcement of morals occurred in seventeenth-century Massachusetts. It was fitting in the face of previous failures that the Puritans should have made one last effort to support the moral law by instituting the new office of tythingman in the mid-1670s. Each neighborhood in each town was to appoint a tythingman to oversee the morals of ten neighboring families. The tythingman was to be the universal, all-purpose censor of morals and to remedy all previous deficiencies in law enforcement. The system did not fail immediately; in fact it began auspiciously with the magistrates of some county courts openly welcoming this needed assistance. In some instances presentments for offenses against the moral law dramatically increased for a short period of time. But basically the original system died a gradual death in response to its unpopularity, in particular the unwillingness of neighbors to undertake such a burdensome and potentially quarrelsome task.[74] By the early eighteenth century at the latest the office of tythingman was either a dead letter or had been turned into an informing system for liquor offenses. If the Puritans could not enforce the rigors of the moral law successfully, no other group of colonists could.

The thrust of this essay has been to demonstrate the relative failure in terms of original expectations of laws concerning the enforcement of morals in a setting where law and morals were consciously intertwined. The upholding and enforcement of morality by extralegal means was by contrast relatively successful. The failure of laws and law enforcement did not result in promiscuity or a particularly low level of morality in the colonies. Alternative methods of social control existed and have always prevailed in Western society to make up for deficiencies in official legal processes. While this study cannot explore the extralegal modes of social control in great detail, several can at least be mentioned. Particularly in the realm of sexual morals, communities developed a self-generating form of control over the behavior of the populace. Small population units living in relative intimacy and collective isolation from other villages induced conformity of behavior in the majority and discouraged conscious imitation of deviant behavior. The force of public opinion, the prevailing concept of conventional behavior, the threat of becoming a subject of gossip, the difficulties of shielding from neighbors such unconventional conditions as pregnancy out of wedlock, and continued acceptance of the sinfulness of immorality all served to uphold the moral law much more effectively than secular laws and law enforcement. Libertinism was not widespread in the colonies, especially in comparison with London and its environs in the eighteenth century. Whatever their status as pre-Victorians, most colonists had a sense of modesty and even prudery in moral matters that helped maintain standards of behavior. Virginity remained the ideal for unmarried women. Most colonists avoided illicit sexual activity not because it was illegal but because it was sinful.[75]

Part Three

The Revolution and the New Constitutional Order

The history of formal institutions and the development of legal doctrines were important elements of the colonial American legal heritage. Also central to the colonial experience, however, was the popular attitude toward law — and especially toward efforts by the British to impose "law and order" in North America. Beginning in the mid-seventeenth century, efforts by the English to enforce trade restrictions met with periodic outbreaks of mob violence as well as with formal resistance from the American legislatures. In the later years of the seventeenth century, widespread popular resistance appeared; civil disobedience and, indeed, what one scholar has termed "a veritable anarchy" seemed to prevail. This crisis passed, but even with the return of greater stability in the eighteenth century British officials remained sensitive to the possibility of popular uprisings. Unwilling to put to too severe a test the loyalty of the colonists, the British adopted their policy of "salutary neglect," deliberately ignoring evasions of their trade laws in order to avert crises. After 1763 salutary neglect was abandoned as the British determined that they would impose their authority in its full measure.

Thus the colonies were impelled toward rebellion and independence, for, as one member of the House of Lords declared in a 1775 debate, the Americans proved to be fully as "obstinate, undutiful and ungovernable" then as they had been "from the beginning."

In her article on popular uprisings and civil authority, the historian Pauline Maier probes this aspect of colonial legal culture and popular behavior. Finding parallels in the history of European mob action, Maier argues that mob force had a certain legitimacy, indicating "willingness among many Americans to act outside the bounds of law." Some analysts have contended that mobs reflected the frustrations of angry, dispossessed groups that represented a democratic counterforce to elite rule. In Maier's view, however, the apparently widespread tolerance of mobs was not necessarily "anti-authoritarian in any general sense."

The Revolution and the establishment of republican government placed all such issues on a new basis, and the Constitutional Convention of 1787 introduced centralized government. The essay by Harry N. Scheiber concerns the nature of the "original understanding" of 1787,

67

The Revolution and the New Constitutional Order

dealing especially with the character of the new "federal" structure and its compatibility with republican ideals.

The Federalist era of the 1790s witnessed a series of intense political crises triggered by the "centralizing policies" of Alexander Hamilton and the Federalist Party under Washington and John Adams. Many political leaders viewed with deepest misgivings the formation of an institutionalized opposition party, which came in the form of the Jeffersonian Republicans and whose emergence gave a new dimension to the working political system beyond the formal bounds of the constitutional order mandated in 1787. As party conflict intensified and grew bitter — under the pressure of differences over foreign policy and the threat of war with France no less than differences over domestic affairs — the Federalists controlling Congress finally resorted to stringent laws to bar "dangerous" aliens from immigration and to place strict limits on dissent. To the hard-line Federalists, dissent and opposition were evidence of treason and sedition. And like the British in the 1760s and 1770s, they decided that the time had come to draw the line — this time, against what they viewed as slander, subversion, and treason in the political dialogue of the stump and the press. In his essay on liberty and the First Amendment, Leonard W. Levy reexamines the First Amendment crisis triggered by the Sedition Act of 1798 and places the issue in the context of the history of libertarian thought.

Further Reading

Conkin, Paul. *Self-Evident Truths: . . . Origins and Development of the First Principles of American Government.* Bloomington: Indiana University Press, 1974.

Jensen, Merrill. *The Founding of a Nation: A History of the American Revolution, 1763-1776.* New York: Oxford University Press, 1968.

Maier, Pauline. *From Resistance to Revolution: Colonial Radicals and the Development of American Opposition to Britain, 1765-1776.* New York: Alfred A. Knopf, 1972.

Mason, Alpheus T. *The States Rights Debate: Antifederalism and the Constitution.* 2d ed. New York: Oxford University Press, 1972.

Smith, James Morton, ed. *The Constitution.* New York: Harper & Row, 1971.

Smith, James Morton. *Freedom's Fetters: The Alien and Sedition Laws and American Civil Liberties.* Ithaca: Cornell University Press, 1956.

Wood, Gordon S. *The Creation of the American Republic, 1776-1787.* Chapel Hill: University of North Carolina Press, 1969.

Wright, Benjamin F. *Consensus and Continuity, 1776-1787.* Boston: Boston University Press, 1958.

7

Pauline Maier

Popular Uprisings and Civil Authority in Eighteenth-Century America

It is only natural that the riots and civil turbulence of the past decade and a half have awakened a new interest in the history of American mobs. It should be emphasized, however, that scholarly attention to the subject has roots independent of contemporary events and founded in long-developing historiographical trends. George Rudé's studies of preindustrial crowds in France and England, E.J. Hobsbawm's discussion of "archaic" social movements, and recent works linking eighteenth-century American thought with English revolutionary tradition have all, in different ways, inspired a new concern among historians with colonial uprisings.[1] This discovery of the early American mob promises to have a significant effect upon historical interpretation. Particularly affected are the revolutionary struggle and the early decades of the new nation, when events often turned upon well-known popular insurrections.

Eighteenth-century uprisings were in some important ways different from those of today — different in themselves, but even more in the political context within which they occurred. As a result they car-

ried different connotations for the American revolutionaries than they do today. Not all eighteenth-century mobs simply defied the law: some used extralegal means to implement official demands or to enforce laws not otherwise enforceable, others in effect extended the law in urgent situations beyond its technical limits. Since leading eighteenth-century Americans had known many occasions on which mobs took over the defense of the public welfare — which was, after all, the stated purpose of government — they were less likely to deny popular upheavals all legitimacy than are modern leaders. While not advocating popular uprisings, they could still grant such incidents an established and necessary role in free societies, one that made them an integral and even respected element of the political order. These attitudes, and the tradition of colonial insurrections on which they drew, not only shaped political events of the Revolutionary era, but also lay behind many laws and civil procedures that were framed during the 1780s and 1790s, some of which still have a place in the American legal system.

Not all colonial uprisings were identical in character or significance. Some

Reprinted from *William and Mary Quarterly*, 3d ser. 27 (1970), 3-35, by permission.

involved no more than disorderly vandalism or traditional brawls such as those that annually marked Pope's Day on November 5, particularly in New England. Occasional insurrections defied established laws and authorities in the name of isolated private interests alone — a set of Hartford County, Connecicut, landowners arose in 1722, for example, after a court decision imperiled their particular land titles. Still others — which are of interest here — took on a broader purpose, and defended the interests of their community in general where established authorities failed to act.[2] This common characteristic linked otherwise diverse rural uprisings in New Jersey and the Carolinas. The insurrectionists' punishment of outlaws, their interposition to secure land titles or prevent abuses at the hands of legal officials followed a frustration with established institutions and a belief that justice and even security had to be imposed by the people directly.[3] The earlier Virginia tobacco insurrection also illustrates this common pattern well: Virginians began tearing up young tobacco plants in 1682 only after Governor Thomas Culpeper forced the quick adjournment of their assembly, which had been called to curtail tobacco planting during an economic crisis. The insurrections in Massachusetts a little over a century later represent a variation on this theme. The insurgents in Worcester, Berkshire, Hampshire, Middlesex, and Bristol counties — often linked together as members of "Shays's Rebellion" — forced the closing of civil courts, which threatened to send a major portion of the local population to debtors' prison, only until a new legislature could remedy their pressing needs.[4]

This role of the mob as extralegal arm of the community's interest emerged, too, in repeated uprisings that occurred within the more densely settled coastal areas. The history of Boston, where by the mid-eighteenth century "public order ... prevailed to a greater degree than anywhere else in England or America," is full of such incidents. During the food shortage of 1710, after the governor rejected a petition from the Boston selectmen calling for a temporary embargo on the exportation of foodstuffs, one heavily laden ship found its rudder cut away, and fifty men sought to haul another outward-bound vessel back to shore. Under similar circumstances Boston mobs again intervened to keep foodstuffs in the colony in 1713 and 1729. When there was some doubt a few years later whether or not the selectmen had the authority to seize a barn lying in the path of a proposed street, a group of townsmen, their faces blackened, leveled the structure, and the road went through. Houses of ill fame were attacked by Boston mobs in 1734, 1737, and 1771; and in the late 1760s the *New York Gazette* claimed that mobs in Providence and Newport had taken on responsibility for "disciplining" unfaithful husbands. Meanwhile in New London, Connecticut, another mob prevented a radical religious sect, the Rogerenes, from disturbing normal Sunday services, "a practice they ... [had] followed more or less for many years past; and which all the laws made in that government, and executed in the most judicious manner could not put a stop to."[5]

Threats of epidemic inspired particularly dramatic instances of this community-oriented role of the mob. One revealing episode occurred in Massachusetts in 1773-74. A smallpox hospital had been built on Essex Island near Marblehead "much against the will of the multitude" according to John Adams. "The patients were careless, some of them wantonly so; and others were suspected of designing to spread the smallpox in the town, which was full of people who had not passed through the distemper." In January 1774 patients from the hospital who tried to enter the town from unauthorized landing places were forcefully prevented from doing so; a hospital boat was burned; and four men suspected of stealing infected clothes from the hospital were tarred and feathered, then carted from Marblehead to Salem in a long cortege. The Marblehead town meeting finally won the proprietors' agreement to shut down the hospital; but after some twenty-two new cases of smallpox broke out in the town within a few days "apprehension became general," and some "Ruffians" in disguise hastened the hospital's demise by burning the nearly evacuted building. A military watch of forty men was needed for several nights to keep the peace in Marblehead.[6]

A similar episode occurred in Norfolk, Virginia, when a group of wealthy residents decided to have their families inoculated for smallpox. Fears arose that the lesser disease brought on by the inoculations would spread and necessitate a general inoculation, which would cost "more money than is circulating in Norfolk" and ruin trade and commerce such that "the whole colony would feel the effects." Local magistrates said they could not interfere because "the law was silent in the matter." Public and private meetings then sought to negotiate the issue. Despite a hard-won agreement, however, the proinoculation faction persisted in its original plan. Then finally a mob drove the newly inoculated women and children on a five-mile forced march in darkness and rain to the common Pest House, a three-year-old institution designed to isolate seamen and others, particularly Negroes, infected with smallpox.[7]

These local incidents indicate a willingness among many Americans to act outside the bounds of law, but they cannot be described as antiauthoritarian in any general sense. Sometimes in fact — as in the Boston bawdy-house riot of 1734, or the Norfolk smallpox incident — local magistrates openly countenanced or participated in the mob's activities. Far from opposing established institutions, many supporters of Shays's Rebellion honored their leaders "by no less decisive marks of popular favor than elections to local offices of trust and authority."[8] It was, above all, the existence of such elections that forced local magistrates to reflect community feelings and so prevented their becoming the targets of insurrections. Certainly in New England, where

the town meeting ruled, and to some extent in New York, where aldermen and councilmen were annually elected, this was true; yet even in Philadelphia, with its lethargic closed corporation, or Charleston, which lacked municipal institutions, authority was normally exerted by residents who had an immediate sense of local sentiment. Provincial governments were also for the most part kept alert to local feelings by their elected assemblies. Sometimes, of course, uprisings turned against domestic American institutions — as in Pennsylvania in 1764, when the "Paxton Boys" complained that the colony's Quaker assembly had failed to provide adequately for their defense against the Indians. But uprisings over local issues proved *extra-institutional* in character more often than they were antiinstitutional; they served the community where no law existed, or intervened beyond what magistrates thought they could do officially to cope with a local problem.

The case was different when imperial authority was involved. There legal authority emanated from a capital an ocean away, where the colonists had no integral voice in the formation of policy, where governmental decisions were based largely upon the reports of "king's men" and sought above all to promote the king's interests. When London's legal authority and local interest conflicted, efforts to implement the edicts of royal officials were often answered by uprisings, and it was not unusual in these cases for local magistrates to participate or openly sympathize with the insurgents. The colonial response to the White Pines Acts of 1722 and 1729 is one example. Enforcement of the acts was difficult in general because "the various elements of colonial society ... seemed inclined to violate the pine laws — legislatures, lumbermen, and merchants were against them, and even the royal governors were divided." At Exeter, New Hampshire, in 1734 about thirty men prevented royal officials from putting the king's broad arrow on some seized boards; efforts to

Pauline Maier

enforce the acts in Connecticut during the 1750s ended after a deputy of the surveyor-general was thrown in a pond and nearly drowned; five years later logs seized in Massachusetts and New Hampshire were either "rescued" or destroyed.[9] Two other imperial issues that provoked local American uprisings long before 1765 and continued to do so during the revolutionary period were impressment and customs enforcement.

As early as 1743 the colonists' violent opposition to impressment was said to indicate a "Contempt of Government." Some captains had been mobbed, the Admiralty complained, "others emprisioned, and afterwards held to exorbitant Bail, and are now under Prosecutions carried on by Combination, and by joint Subscription towards the expense." Colonial governors, despite their offers, furnished captains with little real aid either to procure seamen or "even to protect them from the Rage and Insults of the People." Two days of severe rioting answered Commodore Charles Knowles's efforts to sweep Boston harbor for able-bodied men in November 1747. Again in 1764 when Rear Admiral Lord Alexander Colville sent out orders to "procure" men in principal harbors between Casco Bay and Cape Henlopen, mobs met the ships at every turn. When the *St. John* sent out a boat to seize a recently impressed deserter from a Newport wharf, a mob protected him, captured the boat's officer, and hurled stones at the crew; later fifty Newporters joined the colony's gunner at Fort George in opening fire on the king's ship itself. Under threat to her master the *Chaleur* was forced to release four fishermen seized off Long Island, and when that ship's captain went ashore at New York a mob seized his boat and burned it in the Fields. In the spring of 1765 after the *Maidstone* capped a six-month seige of Newport harbor by seizing "all the Men" out of a brigantine from Africa, a mob of about five hundred men similarly seized a ship's officer and burned one of her boats on the common. Impressment also met mass resistance at Norfolk in 1767 and

was a major cause of the famous *Liberty* riot at Boston in 1768.[10]

Like the impressment uprisings, which in most instances sought to protect or rescue men from the "press," customs incidents were aimed at impeding the customs service in enforcing British laws. Tactics varied, and although incidents occurred long before 1764 — in 1719, for example, Caleb Heathcote reported a "riotous and tumultuous" rescue of seized claret by Newporters — their frequency, like those of the impressment "riots," apparently increased after the Sugar Act was passed and customs-enforcement efforts were tightened. The 1764 rescue of the *Rhoda* in Rhode Island preceded a theft in Dighton, Massachusetts, of the cargo from a newly seized vessel, the *Polly*, by a mob of some forty men with blackened faces. In 1766 again a mob stoned a customs official's home in Falmouth (Portland), Maine, while "Persons unknown and disguised" stole sugar and rum that had been impounded that morning. The intimidation of customs officials and of the particularly despised customs informers also enjoyed a long history. In 1701 the South Carolina attorney general publicly attacked an informer "and struck him several times, crying out, this is the Informer, this is he that will ruin the country." Similar assaults occurred decades later, in New Haven in 1766 and 1769, and New London in 1769, and were then often distinguished by their brutality. In 1771 a Providence tidesman, Jesse Saville, was seized, stripped, bound hand and foot, tarred and feathered, had dirt thrown in his face, then was beaten and "almost strangled." Even more thorough assaults upon two other Rhode Island tidesmen followed in July 1770 and upon Collector Charles Dudley in April 1771. Finally, customs vessels came under attack: the *St. John* was shelled at Newport in 1764 where the customs ship *Liberty* was sunk in 1769 — both episodes that served as prelude to the destruction of the *Gaspée* outside Providence in 1772.[11]

Such incidents were not confined to New England. Philadelphia witnessed some of the most savage attacks, and even the surveyor of Sassafras and Bohemia in Maryland — an office long a sinecure, since no ships entered or cleared in Sassafras or Bohemia — met with violence when he tried to execute his office in March 1775. After seizing two wagons of goods being carried overland from Maryland toward Duck Creek, Delaware, the officer was overpowered by a "licentious mob" that kept shouting "Liberty and Duck Creek forever" as it went through the hours-long rituals of tarring and feathering him and threatening his life. And at Norfolk, Virginia, in the spring of 1766 an accused customs informer was tarred and feathered, pelted with stones and rotten eggs, and finally thrown in the sea where he nearly drowned. Even Georgia saw customs violence before independence, and one of the rare deaths resulting from a colonial riot occurred there in 1775.[12]

White Pines, impressment, and customs uprisings have attracted historians' attention because they opposed British authority and so seemed to presage the Revolution. In fact, however, they had much in common with many exclusively local uprisings. In each of the incidents violence was directed not so much against the "rich and powerful"[13] as against men who — as it was said after the Norfolk smallpox incident — "in every part of their conduct . . . acted very inconsistently as good neighbors or citizens." The effort remained one of safeguarding, not the interests of isolated groups alone, but the community's safety and welfare. The White Pines Acts need not have provoked this opposition had they applied only to trees of potential use to the navy, and had they been framed and executed with concern for colonial rights. But instead the acts reserved to the crown all white-pine trees including those "utterly unfit for masts, yards, or bowsprits," and prevented colonists from using them for building materials or lumber exportation even in regions where white pine constituted the principal forest growth. As a

result the acts "operated so much against the convenience and even necessities of the inhabitants," Surveyor John Wentworth explained, that "it became almost a general interest of the country" to frustrate the acts' execution. Impressment offered a more immediate effect, since the "press" could quickly cripple whole towns. Merchants and masters were affected as immediately as seamen: the targeted port, as Massachusetts' Governor William Shirley explained in 1747, was drained of mariners by both impressment itself and the flight of navigation to safer provinces, driving the wages for any remaining seamen upward. When the press was of long duration, moreover, or when it took place during a normally busy season, it could mean serious shortages of food and firewood for winter, and a general attrition of the commercial life that sustained all strata of society in trading towns. Commerce seemed even more directly attacked by British trade regulations, particularly by the proliferation of customs procedures in the mid-1760s that seemed to be in no American's interest, and by the Sugar Act with its virtual prohibition of the trade with the foreign West Indies that sustained the economies of colonies like Rhode Island. As a result even when only a limited contingent of sailors participated in a customs incident, officials could suspect — as did the deputy collector at Philadelphia in 1770 — that the mass of citizens "in their Hearts" approved it.[14]

Because the various uprisings discussed here grew out of concerns essential to wide sections of the community, the "rioters" were not necessarily confined to the seamen, servants, Negroes, and boys generally described as the staple components of the colonial mob. The uprising of Exeter, New Hampshire, townsmen against the king's surveyor of the woods in 1754 was organized by a member of the prominent Gillman family who was a mill owner and a militia officer. Members of the upper classes participated in Norfolk's smallpox uprising, and Cornelius Calvert, who was later attacked in a related incident, protested that leading members of the community, doctors and magistrates, had posted securities for the good behavior of the "Villains" convicted of mobbing him. Captain Jeremiah Morgan complained about the virtually universal participation of Norfolkers in an impressment incident of 1767, and "all the principal Gentlemen in Town" were supposedly present when a customs informer was tarred and feathered there in 1766. Merchant Benedict Arnold admitted leading a New Haven mob against an informer in 1766; New London merchants Joseph Packwood and Nathaniel Shaw commanded the mob that first accosted Captain William Reid the night the *Liberty* was destroyed at Newport in 1769, just as John Brown, a leading Providence merchant, led that against the *Gaspée*. Charles Dudley reported in April 1771 that the men who beat him in Newport "did not come from the ... lowest class of Men," but were "stiled Merchants and the Masters of their Vessels"; and again in 1775 Robert Stratford Byrne said many of his Maryland and Pennsylvania attackers were "from Appearance ... Men of Property." It is interesting, too, that during Shays's Rebellion — so often considered a class uprising — "men who were of good property and owed not a shilling" were said to be "involved in the train of desperado's to suppress the courts."[15]

Opposition to impressment and customs enforcement in itself was not, moreover, the only cause of the so-called impressment or customs "riots." The complete narratives of these incidents indicate not only that the crowd acted to support local interests, but that it sometimes enforced the will of local magistrates by extralegal means. Although British officials blamed the *St. John* incident upon that ship's customs and impressment activities, colonists insisted that the confrontation began when some sailors stole a few pigs and chickens from a local miller and the ship's crew refused to surrender the thieves to Newport officials. Two members of the Rhode Island council then ordered the gunner at Fort George to detain the schooner until the accused seamen were delivered to the sheriff, and "many People went over the Fort to assist the Gunner in the Discharge of his Duty." Only after this uprising did the ship's officers surrender the accused men.[16] Similarly, the 1747 Knowles impressment riot in Boston and the 1765 *Maidstone* impressment riot in Newport broke out after the governors' requests for the release of impressed seamen had gone unanswered, and only after the outbreaks of violence were the governors' requests honored. The crowd that first assembled on the night the *Liberty* was destroyed in Newport also began by demanding the allegedly drunken sailors who that afternoon had abused and shot at a colonial captain, Joseph Packwood, so they could be bound over to local magistrates for prosecution.[17]

In circumstances such as these, the "mob" often appeared only after the legal channels of redress had proved inadequate. The main thrust of the colonists' resistance to the White Pines Acts had always been made in their courts and legislatures. Violence broke out only in local situations where no alternative was available. Even the burning of the *Gaspée* in June 1772 was a last resort. Three months before the incident a group of prominent Providence citizens complained about the ship's wanton severity with all vessels along the coast, and the colony's governor pressed their case with the fleet's admiral. The admiral, however, supported the *Gaspée*'s commander, Lieutenant William Dudingston; and thereafter, the *Providence Gazette* reported, Dudingston became "more haughty, insolent and intolerable, ... personally ill treating every master and merchant of the vessels he boarded, stealing sheep, hogs, poultry, etc. from farmers round the bay, and cutting down their fruit and other trees for firewood." Redress from London was possible but time-consuming, and in the meantime Rhode Island was approaching what its governor called "the deepest calamity" as supplies of food and fuel were curtailed and prices, especially in Newport, rose steeply. It was significant that merchant John Brown finally led the Providence "mob" that seized the moment in June when the *Gaspée* ran aground near Warwick, for it was he who had spearheaded the effort in March 1772 to win redress through the normal channels of government.[18]

There was little that was distinctively American about the colonial insurrections. The uprisings over grain exportations during times of dearth, the attacks on brothels, press gangs, royal forest officials, and customsmen all had their counterparts in seventeenth and eighteenth-century England. Even the Americans' hatred of the customs establishment mirrored the Englishman's traditional loathing of excise men. Like the customsmen in the colonies, they seemed to descend into localities armed with extraordinary prerogative powers. Often, too, English excisemen were "thugs and brutes who beat up their victims without compunction or stole or wrecked their property" and against whose extravagances little redress was possible through the law.[19] Charges of an identical character were made in the colonies against customsmen and naval officials as well, particularly after 1763 when officers of the Royal Navy were commissioned as deputy members of the customs service,[20] and a history of such accusations lay behind many of the best-known waterfront insurrections. The Americans' complaints took on particular significance only because in the colonies those officials embodied the authority of a "foreign" power. Their arrogance and arbitrariness helped effect "an estrangement of the Affections of the People from the Authority under which they act," and eventually added an emotional element of anger against the Crown to a revolutionary conflict otherwise carried on in the language of law and right.[21]

The focused character of colonial uprisings also resembled those in England and even France where, Rudé has pointed out, crowds were remarkably single-minded and discriminating.[22] Targets were characteristically related to grievances: the Knowles rioters sought only the release of the impressed men; they set free a captured officer when assured he had nothing to do with the press, and refrained from burning a boat near Province House for fear the fire would spread. The Norfolk rioters, driven by fear of smallpox, forcefully isolated the inoculated persons where they would be least dangerous. Even the customs rioters vented their brutality on customs officers and informers alone, and the Shaysite "mobs" dispersed after closing the courts which promised most immediately to effect their ruin. So domesticated and controlled was the Boston mob that it refused to riot on Saturday and Sunday nights, which were considered holy by New Englanders.[23]

When colonists compared their mobs with those in the Mother Country they were struck only with the greater degree of restraint among Americans. "These People bear no Resemblance to an English Mob," John Jay wrote of the Shaysites in December 1786, "they are more temperate, cool and regular in their Conduct — they have hitherto abstained from Plunder, nor have they that I know of committed any outrages but such as the accomplishment of their Purpose made necessary." Similar comparisons were often repeated during the revolutionary conflict and were at least partially grounded in fact. When Londoners set out to "pull down" houses of ill fame in 1688, for example, the affair spread, prisons were opened, and disorder ended only when troops were called out. But when eighteenth-century Bostonians set out on the same task, there is no record that their destruction extended beyond the bordellos themselves. Even the violence of the customs riots — which contrast in that regard to other American incidents — can sometimes be explained by the presence of volatile foreign seamen. The attack on the son of customsman John Hatton, who was nearly killed in a Philadelphia riot, occurred, for example, when the city was crowded by over a thousand seamen. His attackers were apparently Irish crew members of a vessel he and his father had tried to seize off Cape May, and they were "set on," the Philadelphia collector speculated, by an Irish merchant in Philadelphia to whom the vessel was consigned. One of the most lethal riots in the history of colonial America, in which rioters killed five people, occurred in a small town near Norfolk, Virginia, and was significantly perpetrated entirely by British seamen who resisted the local inhibitants' efforts to reinstitute peace.[24] During and immediately after the Revolutionary War some incidents occurred in which deaths were recorded; but contemporaries felt these were historical aberrations caused by the "brutalizing" effect of the war itself. "Our citizens, from a habit of putting . . . [the British] to death, have reconciled their minds to the killing of each other," South Carolina Judge Aedanus Burke explained.[25]

To a large extent the pervasive restraint and virtual absence of bloodshed in American incidents can best be understood in terms of social and military circumstance. There was no large amorphous city in America comparable to London, where England's worst incidents occurred. More important, the casualties even in eighteenth-century British riots were rarely the work of rioters. No deaths were inflicted by the Wilkes, anti-Irish, or "No Popery" mobs, and only single fatalities resulted from other upheavals such as the Porteous riots of 1736. "It was authority rather than the crowd that was conspicuous for its violence to life and limb"; all 285 casualties of the Gordon riots, for example, were rioters.[26] Since a regular army was less at the ready for use against colonial mobs, casualty figures for American uprisings were naturally much reduced.

To some extent the general tendency toward a discriminating purposefulness was shared by mobs throughout Western Europe, but within the British Empire the focused character of popular uprisings and also their persistence can be explained in part by the character of law-enforcement procedures. There were no professional police forces in the eighteenth century. Instead the power of government depended traditionally upon institutions like the "hue and cry," by which the community in general rose to apprehend felons. In its original medieval form the "hue and cry" was a form of summary justice that resembled modern lynch law. More commonly by the eighteenth century, magistrates turned to the posse comitatus, literally the "power of the country," and in practice all able-bodied men a sheriff might call upon to assist him. Where greater and more organized support was needed, magistrates could call out the militia.[27] Both the posse and the militia drew upon local men, including many of the same persons who made up the mob. This was particularly clear where these traditional mechanisms failed to function effectively. At Boston in September 1766 when customsmen contemplated breaking into the house of merchant Daniel Malcom to search for contraband goods, Sheriff Stephen Greenleaf threatened to call for support from members of the very crowd suspected of an intent to riot; when someone suggested during the Stamp Act riots that the militia be raised Greenleaf was told it had already risen. This situation meant that mobs could naturally assume the manner of a lawful institution, acting by habit with relative restraint and responsibility. On the other hand, the militia institutionalized the practice of forcible popular coercion and so made the formation of extralegal mobs more natural that J. R. Western has called the militia "a relic of the bad old days," and hailed its passing as "a step towards . . . bringing civilization and humanity into our [English] political life."[28]

These law-enforcement mechanisms left magistrates virtually helpless whenever a large segment of the population was immediately involved in the disorder, or when the community had a strong sympathy for the rioters. The Boston militia's failure to act in the Stamp Act riots, which was repeated in nearly all the North American colonies, recapitulated a similar refusal during the Knowles riot of 1747.[29] If the mob's sympathizers were confined to a single locality, the governor could try to call out the militias of surrounding areas, as Massachusetts Governor William Shirley began to do in 1747, and as, to some extent, Governor Francis Bernard attempted after the rescue of the *Polly* in 1765.[30] In the case of sudden uprisings, however, these peace-keeping mechanisms were at best only partially effective since they required time to assemble strength, which often made the effort wholly pointless.

When the disorder continued and the militia either failed to appear or proved insufficient, there was, of course, the army, which was used periodically in the eighteenth century against rioters in England and Scotland. Even in America peacetime garrisons tended to be placed where they might serve to maintain law and order. But since all Englishmen shared a fear of standing armies the deployment of troops had always to be a sensitive and carefully limited recourse. Military and civil spheres of authority were rigidly separated, as was clear to Lord Jeffery Amherst, who refused to use soldiers against antimilitary rioters during the Seven Years' War because that function was "entirely foreign to their command and belongs of right to none but the civil power." In fact troops could be used against British subjects, as in the suppression of civil disorder, only upon the request of local magistrates. This institutional inhibition carried, if anything, more weight in the colonies. There royal governors had quickly lost their right to declare martial law without the consent of the provincial councils that were, again, usually filled with local men.[31]

For all practical purposes, then, when a large political unit such as an entire town or colony condoned an act of mass force, problems were raised "almost insoluble without rending the whole fabric of English law." Nor was the situation confined to the colonies. After describing England's institutions for keeping the peace under the later Stuarts, Max Beloff suggested that no technique for maintaining order was found until nineteenth-century reformers took on the task of reshaping urban government. Certainly by the 1770s no acceptable solution had been found — neither by any colonists, nor "anyone in London, Paris, or Rome, either," as Carl Bridenbaugh has put it. To even farsighted contemporaries like John Adams the weakness of authority was a fact of the social order that necessarily conditioned the way rulers could act. "It is vain to expect or hope to carry on government against the universal bent and genius of the people," he wrote, "we may whimper and whine as much as we will, but nature made it impossible when she made man."[32]

The mechanisms of enforcing public order were rendered even more fragile since the difference between legal and illegal applications of mass force was distinct in theory, but sometimes indistinguishable in practice. The English common law prohibited riot, defined as an uprising of three or more persons who performed what Blackstone called an "unlawful act of violence" for a private purpose. If the act was never carried out or attempted, the offense became unlawful assembly; if some effort was made toward its execution, rout; and if the purpose of the uprising was public rather than private — tearing down whorehouses, for example, or destroying all enclosures rather than just those personally affecting the insurgents — the offense became treason since it constituted a usurpation of the king's function, a "levying war against the King." The precise legal offense lay not so much in the purpose of the uprising as in its use of force and violence "wherein the Law does not allow the Use of such Force." Such unlawful assumptions of force were carefully distinguished by commentators upon the common law from other occasions on which the law authorized a use of force. It was, for example, legal for force to be used by a sheriff, constable, "or perhaps even . . . a private Person" who assembled "a competent Number of People, in Order with Force to suppress Rebels, or Enemies, or Rioters"; for a justice of the peace to raise the posse when opposed in detaining lands, or for crown officers to raise "a Power as may effectually enable them to over-power any . . . Resistance" in the execution of the King's writs.[33]

In certain situations these distinctions offered at best a very uncertain guide as to who did or did not exert force lawfully. Should a posse employ more force than was necessary to overcome overt resistance, for example, its members acted illegally and were indictable for riot. And where established officials supported both sides in a confrontation, or where the legality of an act that officials were attempting to enforce was itself disputed, the decision as to who were or were not rioters seemed to depend upon the observer's point of view. Impressment is a good example. The colonists claimed that impressment was unlawful in North America under an act of 1708, while British authorities and some — but not all — spokesmen for the government held that the law had lapsed in 1713. The question was settled only in 1775, when Parliament finally repealed the "Sixth of Anne." Moreover, supposing impressment could indeed be carried on, were press warrants from provincial authorities still necessary? Royal instructions of 1697 had given royal governors the "sole power of impressing seamen in any of our plantations in America or in sight of them." Admittedly that clause was dropped in 1708, and a subsequent parliamentary act of 1746, which required the full consent of the governor and council before impressment could be carried on within their province, applied only to the West Indies. Nonetheless it seems that in 1764 the Lords of the

Admiralty thought the requirement held throughout North America.[34] With the legality of impressment efforts so uncertain, especially when opposed by local authorities, it was possible to see the press gangs as "rioters" for trying en masse to perpetrate an unlawful act of violence. In that case the local townsmen who opposed them might be considered lawful defenders of the public welfare, acting much as they would in a posse. In 1770 John Adams cited opposition to press gangs who acted without warrants as an example of the lawful use of force, and when the sloop of war *Hornet* swept into Norfolk, Virginia, in September 1767 with a "bloody riotous plan . . . to impress seamen, without consulting the Mayor, or any other magistrate," the offense was charged to the pressmen. Roused by the watchman, who called out a "riot by man of war's men," the inhabitants rose to back the magistrates, and not only secured the release of the impressed men but also imprisoned ten members of the press gang. The ship's captain, on the other hand, condemned the townsmen as "Rioters." Ambiguity was present, too, in Newport's *St. John* clash, which involved both impressment and criminal action on the part of royal seamen and culminated with Newporters firing on the king's ship. The Privy Council in England promptly classified the incident as a riot, but the Rhode Island governor's report boldly maintained that "the people meant nothing but to assist [the magistrates] in apprehending the Offenders" on the vessel, and even suggested that "their Conduct be honored with his Majesty's royal Approbation."[35]

The enforcement of the White Pines Acts was similarly open to legal dispute. The acts seemed to violate both the Massachusetts and Connecticut charters; the meaning of provisions exempting trees growing within townships (act of 1722) and those which were "the property of private persons" (act of 1729) was contested, and royal officials tended to work on the basis of interpretations of the laws that Bernhard Knollenberg has called far-fetched and, in one case, "utterly untenable." The Exeter, New Hampshire, "riot" of 1734, for example, answered an attempt of the surveyor to seize boards on the argument that the authorization to seize logs from allegedly illegally felled white-pine trees in the act of 1722 included an authorization to seize processed lumber. As a result, Knollenberg concluded, although the surveyors' reports "give the impression that the New Englanders were an utterly lawless lot, . . . in many if not most cases they were standing for what they believed, with reason, were their legal and equitable rights in trees growing on their own lands."[36]

Occasions open to such conflicting interpretations were rare. Most often even those who sympathized with the mobs' motives condemned their use of force as illegal and unjustifiable. That ambiguous cases did arise, however, indicates that legitimacy and illegitimacy, posses and rioters, represented but poles of the same spectrum. And where a mob took upon itself the defense of the community, it benefited from a certain popular legitimacy even when the strict legality of its action was in doubt, particularly among a people taught that the legitimacy of law itself depended upon its defense of the public welfare.

Whatever quasi-legal status mobs were accorded by local communities was reinforced, moreover, by formal political thought. "Riots and rebellions" were often calmly accepted as a constant and even necessary element of free government. This acceptance depended, however, upon certain essential assumptions about popular uprisings. With words that could be drawn almost verbatim from John Locke or any other English author of similar convictions, colonial writers posited a continuing moderation and purposefulness on the part of the mob. "Tho' innocent Persons may sometimes suffer in popular Tumults," observed a 1768 writer in the *New York Journal,* "yet the general Resentment of the People is principally directed according to

Justice, and the greatest Delinquent feels it most." Moreover, upheavals constituted only occasional interruptions in well-governed societies. "Good Laws and good Rulers will always be obey'd and respected"; "the Experience of all Ages proves, that Mankind are much more likely to submit to bad Laws and wicked Rulers, than to resist good ones." "Mobs and Tumults," it was often said, "never happen but thro' Oppression and a scandalous Abuse of Power."[37]

In the hands of Locke such remarks constituted relatively inert statements of fact. Colonial writers, however, often turned these pronouncements on their heads such that observed instances of popular disorder became prima facie indictments of authority. In 1747, for example, New Jersey land rioters argued that "from their Numbers, Violences, and unlawful Actions" it was to be "inferred that . . . they are wronged and oppressed, or else they would never *rebell agt. the Laws.*" Always, a New York writer said in 1770, when "the People of any Government" become "turbulent and uneasy," it was above all "a certain Sign of Maladministration." Even when disorders were not directly leveled against government they provided "strong proofs that something is much amiss in the state" as William Samuel Johnson put it; that — in Samuel Adam's words — the "wheels of good government" were "somewhat clogged." Americans who used this argument against Britain in the 1760s continued to depend upon it two decades later when they reacted to Shays's Rebellion by seeking out the public "Disease" in their own independent governments that was indicated by the "Spirit of Licentiousness" in Massachusetts.[38]

Popular turbulence seemed to follow so naturally from inadequacies of government that uprisings were often described with similes from the physical world. In 1770 John Adams said that there were "Church-quakes and state-quakes in the moral and political world, as well as earthquakes, storms and tempests in the physical." Two years earlier a writer in the *New York Journal* likened popular tumults to "Thunder Gusts" which "commonly do more Good than Harm." Thomas Jefferson continued the imagery in the 1780s particularly with his famous statement that he liked "a little rebellion now and then" for it was "like a storm in the atmosphere." It was, moreover, because of the "imperfection of all things in this world," including government, that Adams found it "vain to seek a government in all points free from a possibility of civil wars, tumults and seditions." That was "a blessing denied to this life and preserved to complete the felicity of the next."[39]

If popular uprisings occurred "in all governments at all times," they were nonetheless most able to break out in free governments. Tyrants imposed order and submission upon their subjects by force, thus dividing society, as Jefferson said, into wolves and sheep. Only under free governments were the people "nervous," spirited, jealous of their rights, ready to react against unjust provocations; and this being the case, popular disorders could be interpreted as "Symptoms of a strong and healthy Constitution" even while they indicated some lesser shortcoming in administration. It would be futile, Josiah Quincy, Jr., said in 1770, to expect "that pacific, timid, obsequious, and servile temper, so predominant in more despotic governments" from those who lived under free British institutions. From "our happy constitution," he claimed, there resulted as "very natural Effects" an "impatience of injuries, and a strong resentment of insults."[40]

This popular impatience constituted an essential force in the maintenance of free institutions. "What country can preserve it's [sic] liberties if their rulers are not warned from time to time that their people preserve the spirit of resistance?" Jefferson asked in 1787. Occasional insurrections were thus "an evil ... productive of good": even those founded on popular error tended to hold rulers "to the true principles of their institu-

tion" and generally provided "a medecine necessary for the sound health of government." This meant that an aroused people had a role not only in extreme situations, where revolution was requisite, but in the normal course of free government. For that reason members of the House of Lords could seriously argue — as A. J. P. Taylor has pointed out — that "rioting is an essential part of our constitution"; for that reason, too, even Massachusetts's conservative Lieutenant Governor Thomas Hutchinson could remark in 1768 that "mobs a sort of them at least are constitutional."[41]

It was, finally, the interaction of this constitutional role of the mob with the written law that makes the story of eighteenth-century popular uprisings complexity itself.[42] It mobs were appreciated because they provided a check on power, it was always understood that, insofar as upheavals threatened "running to such excesses, as will overturn the whole system of government," "strong discouragements" had to be provided against them. For eighteenth-century Americans, like the English writers they admired, liberty demanded the rule of law. In extreme situations where the rulers had clearly chosen arbitrary power over the limits of law, men like John Adams could prefer the risk of anarchy to continued submission because "anarchy can never last long, and tyranny may be perpetual," but only when "there was any hope that the fair order of liberty and a free constitution would arise out of it." This desire to maintain the orderly rule of law led legislatures in England and the colonies to pass antiriot statutes and to make strong efforts — in the words of a 1753 Massachusetts law — to discountenance "a mobbish temper and spirit in ... the inhabitants" that would oppose "all government and order."[43]

The problem of limiting mass violence was dealt with most intensely over a sustained period by the American revolutionary leadership, which has perhaps suffered most from historians' earlier inattention to the history of colonial uprisings. So long as it could be maintained — as it was only fifteen years ago — that political mobs were "rare or unknown in America" before the 1760s, the revolutionaries were implicitly credited with their creation. American patriots, Charles McLean Andrews wrote, were often "lawless men who were nothing more than agitators and demagogues" and who attracted a following from the riffraff of colonial society. It now seems clear that the mob drew on all elements of the population. More important, the revolutionary leaders had no need to create mob support. Instead they were forced to work with a "permanent entity," a traditional crowd that exerted itself before, after, and even during the revolutionary struggle over issues unrelated to the conflict with Britain and that, as Hobsbawm has noted, characteristically aided the revolutionary cause in the opening phases of conflict but was hard to discipline thereafter.[44]

In focusing popular exuberance the American leaders could work with long-established tendencies in the mob toward purposefulness and responsibility. In doing so they could, moreover, draw heavily upon the guidelines for direct action that had been defined by English radical writers since the seventeenth century. Extralegal action was justified only when all established avenues to redress had failed. It could not answer casual errors or private failings on the part of the magistrates, but had to await fundamental public abuses so egregious that the "whole people" turned against their rulers. Even then, it was held, opposition had to be measured so that no more force was exerted than was necessary for the public good. Following these principles colonial leaders sought by careful organization to avoid the excesses that first greeted the Stamp Act. Hutchinson's query after a crowd in Connecticut had forced the resignation of stampman Jared Ingersoll — whether "such a public regular assembly can be called a mob" — could with equal appropriateness have

been repeated during the tea resistance, or in 1774 when Massachusetts mandamus councillors were forced to resign.

From the first appearance of an organized resistance movement in 1765, moreover, efforts were made to support the legal magistrates such that, as John Adams said in 1774, government would have "as much vigor then as ever" except where its authority was specifically under dispute. This concern for the maintenance of order and the general framework of law explains why the American Revolution was largely free from the "universal tumults and all the irregularities and violence of mobbish factions [that] naturally arise when legal authority ceases." It explains, too, why old revolutionaries like Samuel Adams or Christopher Gadsden disapproved of those popular conventions and committes that persisted after regular independent state governments were established in the 1770s. "Decency and Respect [are] due to Constitutional Authority," Samuel Adams said in 1784, "and those Men, who under any Pretence or by any Means whatever, would lessen the Weight of Government lawfully exercised must be Enemies to our happy Revolution and the Common Liberty."[46]

In normal circumstances the "strong discouragements" to dangerous disorder were provided by established legislatures. The measures enacted by them to deal with insurrections were shaped by the eighteenth-century understanding of civil uprisings. Since turbulence indicated above all some shortcoming in government, it was never to be met by increasing the authorities' power of suppression. The "weakness of authority" that was a function of its dependence upon popular support appeared to contemporary Americans as a continuing virtue of British institutions, as one reason why rulers could not simply dictate to their subjects and why Britain had for so long been hailed as one of the freest nations in Europe. It was "far less dangerous to the Freedom of a State" to allow "the laws to be trampled upon, by

Pauline Maier

the licence among the rabble ... than to dispence with their force by an act of power.'' Insurrections were to be answered by reform, by attacking the "Disease" — to use John Jay's term of 1786 — that lay behind them rather than by suppressing its "Symptoms." And ultimately, as William Samuel Johnson observed in 1768, "the only effectual way to prevent them is to govern with wisdom, justice, and moderation."[47]

In immediate crises, however, legislatures in both England and America resorted to special legislation that supplemented the common law prohibition of riot. The English Riot Act of 1714 was passed when disorder threatened to disrupt the accession of George I; a Connecticut act of 1722 followed a rash of incidents over land titles in Hartford County; the Massachusetts act of 1751 answered "several tumultuous assemblies" over the currency issue and another of 1786 was enacted at the time of Shays's Rebellion. The New Jersey legislature passed an act in 1747 during that colony's protracted land riots; Pennsylvania's Riot Act of 1764 was inspired by the Paxton Boys; North Carolina's of 1771 by the Regulators; New York's of 1774 by the "land wars" in Charlotte and Albany Counties.[48] Always the acts specified that the magistrates were to depend upon the posse in enforcing their provisions, and in North Carolina on the militia as well. They differed over the number of people who had to remain "unlawfully, riotously, and tumultuously assembled together, to the Disturbance of the Publick Peace" for one hour after the reading of a prescribed riot proclamation before becoming judicable under the act. Some colonies specified lesser punishments than the death penalty provided for in the English act, but the American statutes were not in general more "liberal" than the British. Two of them so violated elementary judicial rights that they were subsequently condemned — North Carolina's by Britain, and New York's act of 1774 by a later, revolutionary, state legislature.[49]

In one important respect, however, the English Riot Act was reformed. Each colonial riot law, except that of Connecticut, was enacted for only one to three years, whereas the British law was perpetual. By this provision colonial legislators avoided the shortcoming which, it was said, was "more likely to introduce *arbitrary Power* than even an *Army* itself," because a perpetual riot act meant that "in all future time" by "reading a Proclamation" the crown had the power "of hanging up their Subject wholesale, or of picking out Those, to whom they have the greatest Dislike." If the death penalty was removed, the danger was less. When, therefore, riot acts without limit of time were finally enacted — as Connecticut had done in 1722, Massachusetts in 1786, New Jersey in 1797 — the punishments were considerably milder, providing, for example, for imprisonment not exceeding six months in Connecticut, one year in Massachusetts, and three years in New Jersey.[50]

Riot legislation, it is true, was not the only recourse against insurgents, who throughout the eighteenth century could also be prosecuted for treason. The colonial and state riot acts suggest, nonetheless, that American legislators recognized the participants in civil insurrections as guilty of a crime peculiarly complicated because it had social benefits as well as damages. To some degree, it appears, they shared the idea expressed well by Jefferson in 1787 that "honest republican governors" should be "so mild in their punishments of rebellions, as not to discourage them too much."[51] Even in countering riots the legislators seemed as intent upon preventing any perversion of the forces of law and order by established authorities as with chastising the insurgents. Reform of the English Riot Act thus paralleled the abolition of constituent treasons — a traditional recourse against enemies of the crown — in American state treason acts of the revolutionary period and finally in Article III of the federal Constitution.[52] From the same preoccupation, too, sprang the limitations placed upon the regular army provided for in the Constitution in part to assure the continuation of republican government guaranteed to the states by Article IV, section 4. Just as the riot acts were for so long limited in duration, appropriations for the army were never to extend beyond two years (Article I, section 8, clause 12), and the army could be used within a state against domestic violence only after application by the legislature or governor, if the legislature could not be convened (Article IV, section 4).

A continuing desire to control authority through popular action also underlay the declaration in the Second Amendment that "a well regulated Militia being necessary to the security of a free State," citizens were assured the "right . . . to keep and bear Arms." The militia was meant above all "to prevent the establishment of a standing army, the bane of liberty"; and the right to bear arms — taken in part from the English Bill of Rights of 1689 — was considered a standing threat to would-be tyrants. It embodied "a public allowance, under due restrictions, of the *natural right of resistance and self preservation*, when the sanctions of society and laws are found *insufficent* to restrain the *violence of oppression*." And on the basis of their eighteenth-century experience, Americans could consider that right to be "perfectly harmless . . . If the government be equitable; if it be reasonable in its exactions; if proper attention be paid to the education of children in knowledge, and religion," Timothy Dwight declared "few men will be disposed to use arms, unless for their amusement, and for the defence of themselves and their country."[53]

The need felt to continue the eighteenth-century militia as a counterweight to government and the efforts to outlaw rioting and to provide for the use of a standing army against domestic insurrections under carefully defined circumstances together illustrate the complex attitude toward peacekeeping that prevailed among the nation's founders. The rule of law had to be maintained, yet complete order was neither expected nor even desired when it could be purchased, it seemed, only at the cost of forcefully suppressing the spirit of a free people. The constant possibility of insurrection — as institutionalized in the militia — was to remain an element of the United States Constitution, just as it had played an essential role in Great Britain's.

This readiness to accept some degree of tumultuousness depended to a large degree upon the lawmakers' own experience with insurrections in the eighteenth century, when "disorder" was seldom anarchic and "rioters" often acted to defend law and justice rather than to oppose them. In the years after independence this toleration declined, in part because mass action took on new dimensions. Nineteenth-century mobs often resembled in outward form those of the previous century, but a new violence was added. Moreover, the literal assumption of popular rule in the years after Lexington taught many thoughtful revolutionary partisans what was for them as unexpected lesson — that the people were "as capable of despotism as any prince," that "public liberty was no guarantee after all of private liberty."[54] With home rule secured, attention focused more exclusively upon minority rights, which mob action had always to some extent imperiled. And the danger that uprisings carried for individual freedom became ever more egregious as mobs shed their former restraint and burned Catholic convents, attacked nativist speakers, lynched Mormons, or destroyed the presses and threatened the lives of abolitionists.

Ultimately, however, changing attitudes toward popular uprisings turned upon fundamental transformations in the political perspective of Americans after 1776. Throughout the eighteenth century political institutions had been viewed as in a constant evolution: the colonies' relationship with Britain and with each other, even the balance of power within the governments of various colonies, remained unsettled. Under such circumstances the imputation of governmental shortcoming that uprisings carried could easily be accepted and absorbed. But after independence, when the form and conduct of the Americans' governments were under their exclusive control, and when those governments represented, moreover, an experiment in republicanism on which depended their own happiness and "that of generations unborn," Americans became less ready to endure domestic turbulence or accept its disturbing implications. Some continued to argue that "distrust and dissatisfaction" on the part of the multitude were "always the consequence of tyranny or corruption." Others, however, began to see domestic turbulence not as indictments but as insults to government that were likely to discredit American republicanism in the eyes of European observers. "Mobs are a reproach to Free Governments," where all grievances could be legally redressed through the courts or the ballot box, it was argued in 1783. They originated there "not in Oppression, but in Licentiousness," an "ungovernable spirit" among the people. Under republican governments even that distrust of power colonists had found so necessary for liberty, and which uprisings seemed to manifest, could appear outmoded. "There is some consistency in being jealous of power in the hands of those who assume it by birth . . . and over whom we have no control . . . as was the case with the Crown of England over America," another writer suggested. "But to be jealous of those whom we chuse, the instant we have chosen them" was absurd: perhaps in the transition from monarchy to republic Americans had "bastardized" their ideas by placing jealousy where confidence was more appropriate.[55] In short, the assumptions behind

the Americans' earlier toleration of the mob were corroded in republican America. Old and new attitudes coexisted in the 1780s and even later. But the appropriateness of popular uprisings in the United States became increasingly in doubt after the federal Constitution came to be seen as the final product of long-term institutional experimentation, "a momentous contribution to the history of politics" that rendered even that most glorious exertion of popular force, revolution itself, an obsolete resort for Americans.[56]

Yet this change must not be viewed exclusively as a product of America's distinctive revolutionary achievement. J.H. Plumb has pointed out that a century earlier, when England passed beyond her revolutionary era and progressed toward political "stability," radical ideology with its talk of resistance and revolution was gradually left behind. A commitment to peace and permanence emerged from decades of fundamental change. In America as in England this stability demanded that operative sovereignty, including the right finally to decide what was and was not in the community's interest, and which laws were and were not constitutional, be entrusted to establish governmental institutions. The result was to minimize the role of the people at large, who had been the ultimate arbiters of those questions in English and American revolutionary thought. Even law enforcement was to become the task primarily of professional agencies. As a result, in time all popular unheavals alike became manacing efforts to "pluck up law and justice by the roots," and riot itself gradually became defined as a purposeless act of anarchy, "a blind and misguided outburst of popular fury," of "undirected violence with no articulated goals."[57]

8

Harry N. Scheiber

Federalism and the Constitution: The Original Understanding

"The result of the deliberations of all collective bodies," wrote Alexander Hamilton in *The Federalist*, "must necessarily be a compound as well of the errors and prejudices, as of the good sense and wisdom, of the individuals of whom they are composed." The Constitution, he admitted, was no exception: it was "necessarily . . . a compromise of [thirteen] dissimilar interests and inclinations."[1]

Historians' extensive research on the Constitutional Convention's "inside history" has suggested no reason to dispute Hamilton's characterization of what happened behind closed doors at Philadelphia in 1787. These historical studies remind us that while the delegates innovated brilliantly in political theory, they also were political men in a relationship of barter, bargain, threat, and counterthreat. The written records that survive of the convention's deliberations, the private correspondence of delegates, and the ratification debates in the states all offer indications of how the pursuit of special interests helped shape the Constitution.[2]

Undue fascination with the intrigues and compromises of the convention, how-

ever, may serve to obscure some of the basic elements of the founders' original understanding. What follows here is an effort to reconstruct that understanding, concentrating attention not on the motivations of bargaining and the interplay of interests, but rather upon the principal issues of federalism as embodied in the Constitution and debated at the time.

The Great Purposes of Government

The great purposes of a national government were placed before the convention as early as May 31, only a few days after the first meeting, by Edmund Randolph of Virginia. He proposed, first, that the prospective national legislature be empowered "to enjoy the legislative rights vested in Congress by the confederation; and moreover to legislate in all cases, to which the separate States are incompetent." This was accepted by a vote of nine to zero. Also accepted without significant dissent was a further proposal by Randolph that the national legislature enjoy full authority to act in all cases "in which the harmony of the United States may be interrupted by the exercise of individual legislation" of the

This article is published for the first time in this volume.

states authority as well "to negative all laws passed by the several States contravening . . . the articles of union or any treaty under the Union."[3]

Such ideas bespoke a great chasm between the consensus of the nine delegations represented in May and the ideas that were popularly shared in the nation at large. For it was widely believed that the states were the only legitimate repositories of supreme power. The nation was still lively with memories of rhetoric in Parliament about the "harmony" of the Empire, employed to justify incursions on the liberties of the colonials; and conflicting concepts of what the colonial legislatures legitimately were "competent" to do had precipitated the taking up of arms. Randolph's proposals and the ensuing debate in the convention's early phase were dramatic indications, as one historian has written, that "the delegates spoke and acted as if the question before them was *what kind* of national government would be created." Yet the real issue outside the closed doors of the meeting and, ultimately, inside as well "was whether there would be a national government — and therefore a nation — at all."[4]

One cannot understand the compromises and bargains that went into the final drafts of the Constitution without asking first why the delegates were so receptive to Randolph's thoroughgoing centralism. The answer lies simply in this: they were willing to confront an inevitably powerful opposition to ratification based on the popular fear of centralized government, even at the risk of losing all, precisely because they thought all had been nearly lost already. National government under the Articles of Confederation, they thought, was a nullity, incapable of pursuing the great purposes of nationhood.[5]

Under the Articles, each state had retained "its sovereignty, freedom, and independence." Congress had been delegated the authority essential to national government, but not the means by which to exercise power. The revenues of the central government depended entirely upon voluntary cooperation by the states, and yet in practice one state after another had turned its back on congressional requests for funds. Paralysis of government had been the result: indeed, by 1786 Congress often lacked even nine state delegations, the minimum necessary to conduct its business. There was no national control over representation in Congress itself: the states sent or recalled their representatives at will. "In 1775 there was more patriotism in a village than there is now in the thirteen States," David Ramsey complained in early 1786. In a poignant appeal to the states to send representatives so that Congress could act, he warned that "the remissness of the States . . . naturally tends to annihilate our Confederation."[6] Thus had occurred what Alexander Hamilton later called "almost the last stage of national humiliation." The ambassadors of the nation abroad, he wrote, "are the mere pageants of a mimic sovereignty . . . We have neither troops nor treasury nor government."[7]

Gradually the states had drifted apart, so that definition of national purposes even on theoretical terms became nearly impossible. One state levied tariffs against another; inspection laws were employed to discriminate against products of other states; and there was a prolonged struggle throughout the 1780s over the question of how disputed western territories of the various states would be managed and governed. Negotiations with Great Britain toward a final settlement of the Revolution were nearly impossible; the credit of the government was practically nil; and the disintegration of even the formalities of union was a possibility. For the most part, the men who gathered at Philadelphia in 1787 shared a deep concern for what they saw as a nearly fatal loss of national prestige and national power. They viewed continual disunity as intolerable, not only because of its unfavorable impact upon commercial interests but also because it stripped the nation of the instruments vital to asserting itself in the arena of world politics.[8] Thus Gouverneur Morris struck a responsive chord when he objected that his colleagues appeared to give their exclusive attention in the debates to considerations of states' rights and of individual rights. He urged the need to consider "the aggregate interest of the whole," to build a government capable of "supporting the dignity and splendor of the American Empire."[9]

To those who defended the status quo and who later took up the Antifederalist cause against ratification of the Constitution, such language smacked of autocratic beliefs. The Antifederalists asserted that the splendor of the American nation depended instead on state sovereignty: for on the control by each state electorate of its own government, on the ability of each distinct people within the union to defend its own liberties through the instrumentality of government close at hand, rested the success of America's experiment in republicanism. As Luther Martin contended in the convention, the rights of the people were "already secured by their guardians, the state governments. The general government is therefore intended only to protect and guard the rights of states as states."[10]

In sharp contrast to this view, most of the framers of the Constitution consistently denied that the states had demonstrated their ability to protect the rights and happiness of free men. The ills that beset America, as Madison averred, included not only "a constant tendency in the States to encroach on the federal authority [and] to violate national Treaties," but also a pattern of manifest infringement of "the rights and interests of each other" and oppression of "the weaker party within their respective jurisdictions."[11] Because Madison expressed the sense of the convention, the delegates agreed that some of their main concerns must be to assure more effectual government, "the security of private rights, and the steady dispensation of justice."[12] They deplored the tendency in the states to resort to violence — indeed, the memory of Shays's Rebellion, the previous year, was still vivid in their minds. They viewed such instability as doubly danger-

ous: not only did violent settlement of political disputes reveal the internal weakness of the states, but it also threatened the ability of the states collectively to assert the national interest, the "dignity and splendor of the American Empire" in the arena of world affairs.

The "Compound Principle" of American Federalism

Some delegates to the convention were persuaded that the only viable solution was abolition of the states. Thus George Read of Delaware asserted that if the states were to continue as political entities, jealousies among them inevitably would undermine any central government; therefore, he contended, the states "must be done away with." Butler of South Carolina was similarly "content" with the prospect of abolishing state legislatures "and becoming one Nation instead of a confederation of Republics." Predictably enough Alexander Hamilton stood with this group: he viewed the states as unimportant "for any of the great purposes of commerce, revenue, or agriculture." James Madison — whose ambiguous views of states' rights would become for historians one of the great perplexities of this period — said on June 21 that he believed no fundamental liberties would be lost if the States were abolished or died a natural death. At the very least, he wanted the national legislature to be vested with absolute power to veto state legislation.[13]

Thus the first great issue before the convention, inclined as it was to accept Randolph's broad principles, was whether or not to construct a government in which the states would continue to function. (This issue was even more fundamental than the much-remarked debate over whether the national government's laws should operate "directly" on individuals or should be enforced instead through the states and by coercing state governments that refused to collaborate with the national government.) The decision of the convention was finally to adopt a "compound" principle of government without precedent in the annals of ancient or modern history — a system that we have come to call "federal," in which the national government (as Morris said) has power to exert "compleat and *compulsive* operation" upon individual citizens so far as its allocated sphere of authority was concerned, but in which the states could exert sovereign powers in the sphere marked out for them. Such a concept, as Madison later wrote, was then "a novelty and a compound"; indeed the convention lacked for "technical terms or phrases appropriate to it."[14]

Here, then, was "a system hitherto unknown," as James Wilson declared — a plan for "a perfect confederation of independent states."[15] This compound system of government was founded on two principal features. The first was structural: it involved "engrafting" the system of national government onto the existing system of states by giving the states as such a direct representation in Congress and by leaving with the states major powers in controlling the process of elections. The second feature was operational: it involved a formal division of powers between the states and the national government, with government at both levels operating on individual citizens in pursuit of the common interest.

The structural features were the first to be settled by the Convention. Once it was agreed (informally at least) that the states would not be abolished, it was decided to create a national congress composed of two houses, with representation in each to be based on different principles. In the Senate, the states were to be represented on an equal basis — this, the product of the so-called Great Compromise, when representatives of the large states backed down and accepted what Madison and others had previously regarded as a principle that could not be squared with republican ideology. With characteristic bluntness, Alexander Hamilton said that the great debate over representation in the Senate, though interlaced with the rhetoric of "liberty" and "equality," was in

truth "a contest for power, not for liberty."[16] He was correct, of course: the realities of power did prevail in this case, for if a compromise on representation had failed the convention would have been deadlocked. The compromise also represented a theoretical commitment to the precept that "the States have their interests as such," so that they must be given the power to defend their interests from within the very core of the national government's structure. As one of the men who framed the Great Compromise asserted, the effect of the dualistic representation in Congress, with state equality in the upper house, was "to make the general government *partly federal* [that is, confederative] and *partly national.*"[17]

In a sense, every succeeding decision of the convention flowed from this decision on representation. For instance, as the delegates elaborated the structure of the national government, they also left to the states major powers in controlling the franchise in the election of national officers. Furthermore, the president was to be named by the electoral college, with a significant weighting of the scales in favor of states' rights, so that it was possible for a minority of the national population to elect a president.[18]

The other main feature of the Constitution that lent to the new government its "compound" character was the division of formal authority between the states and the national government. "A general principle readily occurred," James Wilson later said, "that whatever object was confined in its nature and operation to a particular State ought to be subject to the separate government of the States; but whatever in its nature and operation extended beyond a particular State, ought to be comprehended within the federal jurisdiction."[19] Here, in more elaborate language, was the essence of Randolph's original proposal that Congress should be vested with authority in all matters to which the states individually were "not competent"; here one can find, too, a problem bearing upon what Randolph termed "the harmony of the United

States," since any object of policy not confined "in its nature and operation to a particular State" was apt to become a source of friction among the states.

The general distinction they made between national and local questions contained two inherent problems for the framers. First, there remained the need to establish bounds beyond which neither the national government nor the states could act. Second, there needed to be some federal "umpire," to rule in cases of disputed jurisdiction between the states and Congress. On the matter of boundaries, the Constitution finally struck a balance between grants of authority and express limitations. In the Congress they vested the power to levy taxes and duties, to maintain an army and navy, to borrow money, to regulate commerce, award patents on inventions, control admiralty matters, establish federal courts, and the like. But prescribed bounds were set, too, in the interests of personal liberty and of property rights: no ex post facto laws, bills of attainder, or suspension of habeas corpus would be permitted. Similar restrictions were placed on the states: all must give full faith and credit to the laws of each, no duties might be levied without approval of Congress, no coinage of money was permitted, titles of nobility were prohibited, ex post facto legislation was barred. The national power was pledged to the protection of the states against invasion or insurrection; and finally, a republican form of government was guaranteed to each state.[20]

Obviously, the language of the Constitution, both as it granted and as it limited authority, left ample room for conflicting interpretation. In whom the power was vested to decide in cases of jurisdictional conflict would therefore be crucial. During the convention's early weeks, most of the delegates appeared to agree that Congress must be given power to decide: in fact, not until late August, only a month before the convention concluded its work, did the delegates finally vote (and then by a margin of only a single state's vote) to discard a provision for congressional veto

power over any and all state legislation.[21] Instead, the convention inserted the important clause declaring acts of Congress and treaties concluded under constitutional processes to be the supreme law of the land. In ambiguous phrases, the Supreme Court of the national government was given power to subject cases involving constitutionality to judicial review. And finally, in what would become the storm center of constitutional controversy for a century and a half, the Constitution conferred upon Congress the power to act for "the general welfare" and to enact all legislation "necessary and proper" for implementation of its delegated powers.

But in the last analysis the settlement of conflicts between the states and Congress would have to be decided by the informal political process. When the framers took up the defense of the Constitution against Antifederalist critics during the ratification controversy, repeatedly they rested their case upon an estimate of how the political process would actually work.

The Balance of Power: The View of *The Federalist*

The brilliant collaborative defense of the Constitution by Jay, Hamilton, and Madison in *The Federalist* essays must be understood in the context of the ratification debate. The Antifederalists had condemned the system proposed in the Constitution as "a perfect medley of confederated and national government." That it was "without example and without precedent" (in this they agreed with its defenders) was no recommendation, for this "strange hotch-potch" of political institutions would tend to one end only — the destruction of states' rights and sovereignty, and with them the people's liberties. Such minor concessions as they had made to the states, it was said, were included by the framers only to confuse "the unsuspecting multitude."[22] Moreover, the Antifederalists questioned the legitimacy of the convention's proposal for a new government and its call for ratification directly by the people acting through state conventions. "The people have no right to do this without the consent of those to whom they have delegated their power," it was argued; through the voice only of the state legislatures the people can speak, "through their ears, only, can hear."[23] That the convention had arrogantly assumed unwonted authority was bad enough; but now it was foisting on the people a monstrous hybrid of federative and centralist government which in fact would become an instrument for oppression. The means for such oppression were ready at hand in the Constitution: its supremacy clause would support nearly any attack on state sovereignty; the necessary-and-proper and general-welfare clauses comprised practically unlimited writs of authority; and, in any case, such issues would become moot soon enough, for the power to raise an army by conscription (thus subjecting thousands of citizens to loss of liberty by subjecting them to military law) would become the power to suppress popular elections and finally to enthrone a monarch.[24] Even in the hands of men of unimpeachable republican principles, such authority as the Constitution proposed to vest in the president and Congress could not be responsibly exercised: the country was geographically too extensive for a national government on truly republican principles — "you might as well attempt to rule Hell by prayer."[25]

The authors of The Federalist replied first to the criticism that the Constitution lacked meaningful safeguards for states' rights. In No. 45, Madison admitted that he put "the happiness of the people" above state sovereignty whenever the two could not be reconciled. But he could see no potential danger in the formal powers of the national government granted in the Constitution: "Its jurisdiction extends to certain enumerated objects only," he declared. "It leaves to the several States a residuary and inviolable sovereignty over all other objects."[26] In No. 14, he had written: "The general government is not to be charged with the whole power of making

and administering laws. Its jurisdiction is limited to certain enumerated objects, which concern all the members of the republic, but which are not to be attained by the separate provisions of any. The subordinate governments which can extend their care to all those other objects, which can be separately provided for, will retain their due authority and activity." He reiterated in No. 45 that the powers delegated to the national government would be "few and defined; those which are to remain in the State Governments are numerous and indefinite."

In addition to a division of power that favored the states, Madison argued, the compound nature of representation in the national government would assure the states of their legal rights and afford them an ample opportunity to pursue local interests. Without the states, the national government could not be set into operation: they were to be "constituent and essential parts" of the federal system, whereas the national government was "nowise essential to the operation or organization" of the states. With the president's election dependent upon voting by states, with Senate elections left to the legislatures, and even the House of Representatives left exposed to the influence of state legislatures, both Congress and the executive would much more likely be "too obsequious," rather than "overbearing," toward the states.[27] Similarly, in his private correspondence, Madison wrote that the national government would derive its powers "entirely from the subordinate authorities," a fact that would "effectually ... guard the latter against any danger of encroachments."[28]

Though Madison denied the Antifederalists' contention that the national government and the states would always be "mutual rivals and enemies," he was willing to explore the probable course of events should rivalry occur. All the weight of traditional popular loyalties lay on the side of the states, he wrote; and so, if the issue at stake was one of immense importance to a state, the state could put powerful obstructions in the way of national authorities by means of legislation, outright civil disobedience, or even a resort to arms. Moreover, "ambitious encroachments" by the government on the authority of one state would be perceived immediately as a threat to all the states — and so "every [state] Government would espouse the common cause. A correspondence would be opened . . . One spirit would animate and conduct the whole."[29]

Alexander Hamilton, in his contributions to *The Federalist,* began with premises different from Madison's, but he came to much the same conclusions. In contrast to Madison's stress on the formal division of sovereignty that favored the states and his emphasis on the limited extent of the enumerated national powers, Hamilton placed his greatest emphasis on the importance of a single sovereign. Those who wished to have the states retain all their existing powers, Hamilton said, "seem to cherish with blind devotion the political monster of *imperium in imperio.*"[30] Whereas Madison repeatedly underlined the importance of the states to the operations and structure of the national government, Hamilton insisted that "the majesty of the national authority" could not be compromised — "it must stand in need of no intermediate legislations."[31] Similarly, Madison wrote in No. 45 that the new Constitution would invigorate the powers vested in Congress by the Articles, rather than instituting new powers; whereas Hamilton adduced "the absolute necessity for an entire change in the first principles of the system."[32] The leaders of the Revolution had "formed the design of a great confederacy," Hamilton wrote, but "they erred most in the structure of the union" — and the union had now been *"new-modelled"* by the act of your Convention."[33]

"Your Convention" — these words were addressed directly to the people, not the states. Uncompromisingly Hamilton insisted on the common status of all the people of the states as "fellow citizens of one great respectable and flourishing empire." Though he did make passing reference in the ninth essay to "certain exclusive and very important portions of sovereign power" to be left with the states, his basic premise was that the pursuit of paramount national purposes required "the most ample authority" for the national government.[34]

Yet when Hamilton considered the possibility of conflict on some intensely felt issue between a state and the national government, he rested his argument on much the same basis as Madison had done: all the natural loyalities of the people would be on the side of the state. This would be especially true among common men; for unlike "speculative men" they could not be expected to understand the national interest or to put their highest loyalty in the national government. Again like Madison, Hamilton predicted that localistic pressures from thirteen separate state interests "will . . . constantly *impose* on the national rulers the *necessity* of a spirit of accommodation."[35] But here, too, there was a subtle difference of viewpoint. Whereas Madison admitted that "numerous, indefinite" powers would remain "exclusively" with the states, Hamilton indicated no sense of such broad state powers. He spoke instead in the future-conditional tense, in tentative, pragmatic terms, of "those residuary authorities, which it might be judged proper to leave with the States for local purposes." Becoming more specific, he went only so far as to cite "the administration of private justice between citizens of the same State, the supervision of agriculture, and . . . other concerns of a similar nature, all those things in short which are proper to be provided for by local legislation." He could foresee no incentive for the "national rulers" to make incursions on the states' powers, considering that such powers "would contribute nothing to the dignity, to the importance, or to the spendour of the national government."[36] Then, turning the argument around, Hamilton insisted in No. 17 that the common man's almost blind, unthinking devotion to the states was the best reason for giving to the federal government "all the force which is compatible with the principles of liberty."

But what amount of centralization was in fact compatible with libertarian principles? And what remedies were at hand for the people if, as the Antifederalist critics of the Constitution warned, the central government were to become the instrument of an unscrupulous monarchical or aristocratic faction? Here the authors of *The Federalist* took a common stand in opposition to their critics. The cornerstone of their argument was a theory of American pluralism formulated first in the convention and then more elaborately in *The Federalist* essays, particularly in No. 10, by James Madison.

Pluralism and the Requirements of Union

Speaking in the convention on June 6, during the debate on representation in Congress, Madison expounded on the basic dilemma of representative government that once a majority forms, it might exercise tyrannous control over the minority. It was inevitable, he said, that "civilized Societies would be divided into different Sects, Factions, & interests, as they happen to consist of the rich & poor, debtors & creditors, the landed, the manufacturing, the commercial interests, the inhabitants of this district, or that district, the followers of this political leader or that political leader, the disciples of this religious sect or that religious sect. In all cases where a majority are united by a common interest or passion, the rights of the minority are in danger." Madison contended that the results of the American experiment in republican government since the Revolution had been twofold. On the one hand, in the name of "the real or supposed interest of the major number," arbitrary state laws infringing rights of creditors had been enacted, "the landed interest" had pushed through legislation at the expense of "the mercantile interest," and personal liberties generally had been

trampled in the states. On the other hand, as Madison and most of the Federalists repeatedly asserted, the local interests of thirteen separate states — and worse still, in many cases, the interests of transient and tyrannous majorities in the individual states — had been pursued under the flag of sovereign states' rights, at the expense of the nation's common interests, such as provision of effective self-defense and conduct of a vigorous foreign policy.[37]

"The only remedy," Madison asserted, "is to enlarge the sphere, and thereby divide the community into so great a number of interests and parties, that in the first place a majority will not be likely at the same moment to have a common interest separate from that of the whole or of the minority; and in the second place, that in case they should have such an interest, they may not be apt to unite in the pursuit of it."[38] Because the lower house of Congress was to be apportioned on a district system, it would assure the necessary division of the community into fragmented parts that would make majority coalitions on a monolithic basis all but impossible. Factions, parties formed around individual leaders, self-interested men or groups seeking power "adverse to the rights of other citizens" — all such threats to liberty would need to confront a representative government extending over the scale of the nation and as diverse as the nation was diverse.[39] In this manner, Madison departed from the prevailing political theory of the day that republican governments could operate effectively only over a relatively small territory.[40]

In *The Federalist*, No. 10, he expounded the principle further, asserting that the ability of the union under the Constitution "to break and control the violence of faction" would be among its greatest strengths. To destroy the liberty on which faction breeds would be unthinkable. Instead, the Constitution would vest important powers in the central government (thus assuring, it may be added, that no significant faction would fail to struggle for influence in its decisions); it would provide for election of representatives who would "refine and enlarge the public views," in themselves moderating the effects of faction; and finally it would enlarge the polity so as to reduce the possibility that factious leaders could obtain control of all the government's various instruments of power. For with a government of three branches at the national level, including one branch elected by the people themselves divided into relatively small districts, and with thirteen or more state governments, it would be unlikely that men of evil intent would find it possible "to spread a general conflagration" through states outside their own. The character and enlarged views of such men as were likely to be elected to the majesty of national office; the "greater security afforded by a greater variety of parties" against domination by any one; and "the greater obstacles" to coordination of efforts to form a majority were all arguments for forming the national government.[41]

The essence of Madison's formula was the idea that the system would work in a complex relationship of continual tension. Just as the national government under the Constitution would consist of three branches (including a divided, bicameral legislature) working in a system of checks and balances, so too would the states and the national government be jealous of one another's prerogatives, and so too would legitimate local or factional interests be free to struggle for primacy in the many seats of power into which the government was fractionalized. In Madison's scheme, as in the model of working government postulated by most of the Federalist spokesmen, there would be numerous centers of energy in the system, and also multiple repositories of power.[42]

But we would misjudge the Federalists if we assumed that all of them put their faith entirely in Madison's finespun theory of the different governments controlling one another by separation of powers, each controlling itself by checks and balances, and all controlling factions, in a system of elaborate tension. For Federalist leaders advanced two other important arguments in favor of the Constitution that rested on considerations of brute power. One was articulated most explicitly by Hamilton, who betrayed his basic differences with Madison when he said in the New York convention: "We are attempting by this constitution to abolish factions and to unite all parties for the general welfare."[43] By his own confession Hamilton was in "the habit of using strong language," and particularly now on the subject of the Constitution, for on no matter had he known "stronger emotion, or more anxious concern."[44] We need not attribute to the heat of debate alone, however, his strenuous language, for Hamilton's rhetoric reflected accurately enough his belief that only a powerful central government could "energize" the nation, or act with the dignity and majesty that must mark the actions of a great empire.

Hamilton was even willing to contemplate the use of naked force when the stability of the government or the national interest was at stake. Thus in *The Federalist*, No. 9, he argued for "the utility of a confederacy, as well to suppress faction and to guard the internal tranquillity of States, as to increase their external force and security." He expressed contempt for the idea of a nation composed "of little jealous, clashing, tumultuous commonwealths, the wretched nurseries of unceasing discord"; under the Constitution, he went on (quoting Montesquieu on combining the advantages of monarchy with those of republicanism in a strong federation of republican states), the central government could put down insurrections wherever they might occur. Similarly, in the last article of *The Federalist*, a summary argument for the Constitution, Hamilton invoked the ability of a strong union to impose "restraints . . . on local factions and insurrections."[45]

The second deviation from Madison's theory of factions appeared in the Feder-

Harry N. Scheiber

alists' arguments regarding the possibility of majoritarian solutions in situations of intense political conflict. From reading Madison in No. 10 of *The Federalist*, it is easy to conclude that he respected so completely the salutary force of tensions in a pluralistic situation that his theory left no room for majoritarianism. And yet we find Madison and Hamilton agreed, elsewhere, that even though the federal system might hamper majority domination — and even though the use of central authority might be a deterrent to local insurrections or tumult — still, forthright majoritarian action was not foreclosed by the Constitution. Thus in No. 85, Hamilton pointed out that when there was a genuine popular will for change — whether to curb excessive centralization *or for any other purpose* — the states and the people could force a change virtually overnight by the amendment process. "Whenever nine states concur," Hamilton pointed out, "the national rulers . . . will have no option on the subject."

In a remarkable passage, Hamilton indicated his expectation that the ordinary course of political process in the United States would involve the pluralistic organization of interests, as had occurred in the convention itself: "Many of those who form the majority on one question," he wrote, "may become the minority on a second, and an association dissimilar to either may constitute the majority on a third." Hamilton went on to argue, however, that when the people feel so intensely on some issue that pluralistic coalitions should break down or prove inadequate, then the majority could organize itself and push through a constitutional amendment on that single issue. "There would then be no necessity for management or compromise, . . . no giving nor taking. The will of the requisite number would at once bring the matter to a decisive issue."[46] Implicit in the argument, it is worth pointing out, is the corollary view that because intensely felt issues could be isolated as constitutional-amendment questions, the ordinary pro-

cesses of politics on a pluralistic basis could better hope to survive great crises.

The basic difference, then, between the Federalist argument and the Antifederalist view on the great question of majoritarianism was this: Hamilton and other Federalists regarded a majoritarian solution as a remedy *appropriate only for extraordinary issues* evoking extreme divisions, while the Antifederalists regarded the majoritarian resolution of conflict as *appropriate to all issues,* indeed the only political process that they deemed legitimate by republican standards. Majorities in each state, in the Antifederalist view, were better trusted with defense of personal and property rights than some remote but powerful (potentially dominant) national authority. They simply did not share Madison's faith in checks and balances or in the extension of republic institutions over a large territory as guarantees of American pluralism, any more than they shared Hamilton's faith in the majesty of the nation as an overriding objective of political organization justifying the powerful centralization of authority.

Manifold Legacies of the Original Understanding

In the brilliant debates during the convention, in the pamphlets of the ratification controversy, and, most notably, in *The Federalist* essays, the champions of the Constitution provided not only a rationale for their innovative theory of federalism but also a coherent basis for the forging of an American political ideology. But to venerate the work of the founders is not enough: for despite the telling accuracy of many of their broad political insights and their specific predictions, they were on some points divided in their own counsels, and so their legacy was at least to that extent ambiguous.

One major ambiguity of the Federalists' defense of the Constitution has vexed constitutional debate in this country ever since their times: it can be found in their conception of federal-state relationships in the compound system of government that they formulated. On the one hand, the Founders argued that they had assimilated the national government into the existing system of states, or, as one of them phrased it, they had "engrafted" one upon the other. On the other hand, they argued that the resulting division of authority had created two separate and distinct spheres of sovereignty, in which the central government would be supreme but the states would retain exclusive sovereign jurisdiction over their "domestic" concerns. Thus even Hamilton, the most candid centralist of them all, conceded that the states would retain certain exclusive attributes of sovereignty; yet he used indefinite and pragmatic terms — saying that the states' authority would reach as far as the states were "competent," leaving the impression that states' rights would be defined pragmatically according to circumstances.[47] Although Madison, too, argued that changing conditions in a growing nation required the "necessary and proper" clause, he took a different tack: "The Federal and State Governments," he wrote in *The Federalist*, No. 46, were "instituted with different powers, and designated for different purposes." In subsequent years the Madisonian-Hamiltonian division over the meaning of "different powers" would emerge as the great focus of division of American politics, pitting the broad-constructionist Federalists against the Jeffersonian party, which became dedicated to a strict interpretation of the enumerated powers granted Congress by the Constitution — but the seed of controversy had already been planted by 1789.

When Madison attempted to blend his theory of separate, distinct powers with the concept of assimilation in a compound system, his argument foundered on sterile abstractions. For his construct raised more new perplexities than it resolved: "The States," he argued, were "constituent and essential parts of the Federal Government, whilst the latter is nowise essential to the operation and organization of the former."[48] On its face this notion lacked credibility: that the national government would somehow be dependent on the states, but without reciprocal dependence, in the system's practical operation, was an idea credible only if one accepted Madison's highly abstracted view of what the words "organization" and "operation" would mean. Whatever its logical merits, Madison's postulate reflected a more serious failure of vision: for clearly, he badly underestimated the possibility that the national government's operations might become so pervasive in the society at large and in the federal system per se that the autonomy of the states would become severely attenuated. Evidence of this failure was Madison's assertions in No. 45 of *The Federalist* that the central government's civil establishment "will be much smaller" than the comparable civil service in the states; that the national government would seldom, if ever, resort to direct internal taxation; and that even if military might should become a measure of comparative strength, the states would command more strength in their militias than the national government could assert through use of a standing army.

Hamilton's view was more realistic: at least he granted the theoretical possibility that the central government might become more essential to the states' continued operation than the reverse. He argued in No. 17 that this might occur if the states lost the localistic loyalties of their citizens by dint of "a much better administration" of the federal government.

The most accurate predictions, however, actually came from the Antifederalists. It was they who foresaw that the "general welfare" and "necessary and proper" clauses in the Constitution could readily legitimize sweeping changes in the balance of national versus state powers.[49] By contrast with Madison's tortured construct of an "assimilated" system in which the lines of dependence ran only one way, the Antifederalists predicted accurately that the national government might eventually, or even immediately, become the instrument for massive centralization of power — indeed, potentially of nearly all power. Of course, the accuracy of the Antifederalist view can only be demonstrated from the perspective of the twentieth century, when modern industrialization and a succession of major wars have imposed basic changes of power distribution. The massive centralization predicted by the Antifederalists did not occur as the result of a "monarchist" conspiracy as they had imagined — unless one wants to read the legislative record of the Washington and Adams administrations through Antifederalist-Jeffersonian lenses.

On still another great issue, the framers offered only implicit theory, susceptible to varied interpretation: it concerned their conception of the "common good" and the relationship between that concept and "majority rule." As we have seen, notions of an overarching common interest were invoked repeatedly in the arguments of *The Federalist*, as in No. 45 when Madison argued that the Revolution had been fought not for state sovereignty but for "the public good, the real welfare of the great body of the people." Similarly, Madison's famous model of factions was based on the assumption, common in that day, that special interests would work for self-interested aims in politics to the detriment of the public good.[50]

Neither Madison nor Hamilton, nor indeed any of the other pro-Constitution spokesmen, was ready to contend that in all instances the will of the majority would be consistent with (or a definition of) the common good. Thus while Madison stressed the importance of counterpoised factions, others in the convention emphasized the need for a small upper house of Congress that could exert a meliorating influence on the popularly elected House of Representatives which, as the voice of the democracy, was cap-

able of passionate and capricious politics. In No. 78 of *The Federalist*, Hamilton asserted the importance of the judiciary as a first line of defense against "those ill humours which the arts of designing men, or the influence of particular conjunctures, sometimes disseminate among the people themselves."

Nowhere in *The Federalist*, however, is there an explicit definition of the differences between the common good and the will of transient majorities.[51] Instead we must deduce a definition from what was implicit in the convention debates and in the literature of the ratification controversy. Part of their definition of common good was negative in approach; that is, the Federalists clearly defined majority will as contrary to the public interest when it imposed its will on minorities and capriciously assaulted property or personal liberties. The preamble to the Constitution asserted the people's determination to "secure the Blessings of Liberty to ourselves and our posterity." This phrase was drawn from the rhetoric of libertarian thought expressed in the Declaration of Independence, where it spoke of "life, liberty, and the pursuit of happiness." Obviously the Federalist view of majorities involved a fear that they might jeopardize the blessings of liberty insofar as they imposed "serious oppressions of the minor party in the community."[52]

But the Federalist definition of the common good had its positive aspect as well, and, as Louis B. Wright has reminded us, it was an advanced democratic view. For though modern analysts of the framers always cite Madison's view of factions counterpoised one against the other within a framework of governmental checks and balances, seldom remembered is Madison's own admission that "in the last resort, a remedy must be obtained from the people, who can by the election of more faithful representatives, annul the acts of . . . usurpers." Elsewhere he defined the essence of the ratification issue in similar terms: "Either the mode in which the

Federal Government is to be constructed will render it sufficiently dependent on the people, or it will not.''[53] If a conflict should arise, pitting the central government against the states, the ultimate consideration was that both were "agents and trustees of the people''; and so "the ultimate authority, wherever the derivative may be found, resides in the people alone,'' and the outcome of such conflict would "depend on the sentiments and sanction of their common constituents.'' Madison was even willing to modify his view of inevitably self-interested factions to this degree: that in an extensive nation founded on republican principles, and embracing heterogeneous interest groups, majorities could seldom form "on any other principles than those of justice and the general good.''[54]

In the end, then, Madison did not trust transient majorities, but he did, perforce, trust *the people*. What "animates every votary of freedom,'' he wrote, was an "honorable determination . . . to rest all our political experiments on the capacity of mankind for self-government.''[55] It was a similar faith in the republican "genius'' (or "spirit'') of the people of America that led George Mason of Virginia to argue in the convention that the people's representatives in Congress "should think as they think, and feel as they feel.'' An identical belief supported James Wilson's view that government must not only possess the power adequate to govern but also possess "the mind and sense of the people at large.''[56] Even Alexander Hamilton, who was more disposed than many to stress "the passions we see, of avarice, ambition, interest, which govern most individuals, and all public bodies,''[57] admitted in No. 78 of *The Federalist* that all issues must rest in the end on "that fundamental principle of republican government, which admits the right of the people to alter or abolish the established constitution whenever they find it inconsistent with their happiness.'' The same faith in the people's capacity to govern themselves was reflected in the Constitution's provisions regarding suf-

frage: unlike most of the state constitutions, it established no property or religious qualifications for officeholding, and it left the door open for progressive expansion of the suffrage in the states.[58]

It was a curious kind of confidence, this belief of the Federalists in the mind and spirit of the people, for it was not a blind faith in the people's capacity for self-government forever and under all conditions. Rather it was a realistic belief that so long as the republican spirit — the desire for self-government and the willingness of men to make representative institutions work — endured, the new federal republic would endure. Here, too, the seeds of future political division were evident. For, on the one hand, Hamilton, within two years after the new nation was formed, would lead the new Federalist party toward a program for economic development using heavily centralized instruments of policy. During the late 1790s he would champion such repressive laws as the Alien and Sedition Acts and argue for a standing army sufficiently large to ensure the nation's safety against both subversion and invasion. On the other hand, Madison would join with Thomas Jefferson to champion diversity as an instrument superior to imposed national unity for the pursuit of the "common good,'' and he would seize upon a strict construction of constitutional grants of power to Congress as the bulwark of liberty in the face of what he viewed as outrageous transgressions.

As Madison came to view it, a national republican government must be built, in the last analysis, as "one paramount Empire of reason, benevolence, and brotherly affection.'' The "public mind'' must be the first line of defense against incursions on liberty; "the sense of the people'' must be understood as the principal operative check against a dangerous concentration of power in any one center.[59] As Hamilton's prescriptions for public policy were spelled out in his monumental papers on credit, banking, and manufacturing, it became evident

Harry N. Scheiber

that, as John Miller has written, he "saw nothing to be gained by appealing to patriotism, altruism or magnanimity."[60] Hamilton thus insisted that a forceful and energetic national government must lead, and not merely moderate and foster coalition by consent at the points of least resistance. In his emergent definition of "common good," though power to overturn the existing order still remained with the people, the national government must harness the ambitions of men to itself by holding out incentives — that is, by offering a "payoff" that in time would buy the loyalty of the private centers of power that counted most of all. As Professor Miller has argued: "While he spoke the language of conservatism, Hamilton in fact undertook to revolutionize the economic and political life of the United States. His dream was the transformation of the republic into a highly centralized nation in which manufacturing, commerce and agriculture were made to serve the purposes of an overriding nationalism."[61]

Both the new Federalist Party's concept of "overriding nationalism," together with the uses of governmental power that such a goal implied, and the Jeffersonian Republicans' vision of a "paramount Empire of reason, benevolence, and brotherly affection" were logically consistent with the concepts of "common good" variously implied in the Federalists' formulation and defense of the Constitution. Just as with the limits of enumerated powers and broad construction and with the meaning and potential shape of an "assimilated" and "compound" government, the Federalists' ambiguous concept of public good contained the basis of controversy. Within the ideological consensus in favor of self-government on libertarian, republican principles that marked Federalist and Antifederalist thought alike, there had been ample room for controversy over

means for their attainment in the ratification controversy of 1788, and these became the basis for division that resulted in the formation of national political parties in the 1790s.[62]

Similar differences of persuasion are evident in today's controversies on the future of American federalism. The wisdom of *The Federalist* — that in the end the people must rule — is still highly relevant to our present-day concerns, but we cannot derive all the help we might ideally like from the content of the original understanding. For both the Constitution itself and the conditions under which it operates are fundamentally different from the document and conditions of the past. The issues of responsible government have been recast in a context beyond the vision of the framers as a result of the Civil War–Reconstruction-period amendments. The Constitution has been restructured to square political practice with egalitarian ideals: individuals as well as states have now been guaranteed equality of legal standing in the nation. The Senate, which is elected directly by the people now, no longer has precisely the basis of representation conceived by the founders. And by dint of the Sixteenth Amendment, the national government has preempted virtual control over the most productive and flexible source of revenues, the income tax. Moreover, accretions of power have formed in the private sector that pose challenges to responsible government in a manner unforeseen in 1787; the national government, by regulation of industry, by vesting of special representative powers in labor unions, by subsidies and defense spending, and the like, is intertwined and mixed with private-sector interests.[63] The resulting structural complexity of public and private power renders it difficult even to identify where power actually lies, let alone how it can be made responsible.

9

Leonard W. Levy

Liberty and the First Amendment: 1790–1800

In 1798 there was a sudden break-through in American libertarian thought on freedom of speech and press — sudden, radical, and transforming, like an underwater volcano erupting its lava upward from the ocean floor to form a new island. The Sedition Act, which was a thrust in the direction of a single-party press and a monolithic party system, triggered the Republican surge. The result was the emergence of a new promontory of libertarian thought jutting out of a stagnant Blackstonian sea.

To appreciate the Republican achievement requires an understanding of American libertarian[1] thought on the meaning and scope of freedom of political discourse. Contrary to the accepted view,[2] neither the Revolution nor the First Amendment superseded the common law by repudiating the Blackstonian concept that freedom of the press meant merely freedom from prior restraint. There had been no rejection of the concept that government may be criminally assaulted, that is, seditiously libeled, simply by the expression of critical opinions that tended to lower it in the public's esteem.

Reprinted from *American Historical Review*, 58 (1962), 22-37, by permission. Copyright © 1962 by Leonard W. Levy.

To be sure, the principle of a free press, like flag, home, and mother, had no enemies. Only seditious libels, licentious opinions, and malicious falsehoods were condemned. The question, therefore, is not whether freedom of the press was favored, but what it meant and whether its advocates would extend it to a political opponent whose criticism cut to the bone on issues that counted. Jefferson once remarked that he did not care whether his neighbor said that there are twenty gods or no God, because "it neither picks my pocket nor breaks my leg."[3] But in drafting a constitution for Virginia in 1776 he proposed that freedom of religion "shall not be held to justify any seditious preaching or conversation against the authority of the civil government."[4] And in the same year he helped frame a statute on treasonable crimes, punishing anyone who "by any word" or deed defended the cause of Great Britian.[5] Apparently political opinions could break his leg or pick his pocket, thus raising the question of what he meant by freedom of the press. We can say that he and his contemporaries supported an unrestricted public duscussion of issues if we understand that "unrestricted" meant merely the absence of censorship in advance of publication: no one needed a government license to

Leonard W. Levy

express himself, but he was accountable under the criminal law for abuse of his right to speak or publish freely.[6]

Before 1798 the avant-garde among American libertarians staked everything on the principles of the Zenger case,[7] which they thought beyond improvement. No greater liberty could be conceived than the right to publish without restriction if only the defendant might plead truth as a defense in a criminal prosecution for seditious, blasphemous, obscene, or personal libel, and if the criminality of his words might be determined by a jury of his peers rather than by a judge. The substantive law of criminal libels was unquestioned.

Zengerian principles, however, were a frail prop for a broad freedom of the press. Granted, a defendant representing a popular cause against the administration in power might be acquitted, but if his views were unpopular, God help him — for a jury would not, nor would his plea of truth as a defense. A jury, then as today, was essentially a court of public opinion, often synonymous with public prejudice. Moreover, the opinions of men notoriously differ: one man's truth is another's falsehood. Indeed political opinions may be neither true nor false and are usually not capable of being proved by the rules of evidence, even if true. An indictment for seditious libel based on a defendant's accusation of bribery or corruption by a public official can be judged by a jury. But the history of sedition trials indicates that indictments are founded on accusations of a different order, namely, that the government, or one of its measures or officials, is unjust, tyrannical, or contrary to the public interest. Libertarians who accepted Zengerian principles painted themselves into a corner. If a jury returned a verdict of guilty despite a defense of truth, due process had been accorded and protests were groundless, for the substance of the law that made the trial possible had not been challenged.

American acquiescence in the British or common-law definition of a free press was so widespread that even the frail Zen-

gerian principles seemed daring, novel, and had few adherents. It was not until 1790, after the framing, but before the ratification, of the First Amendment, that the first state, Pennsylvania, took the then radical step of adopting the Zengerian principles[8] which left the common law of seditious libel intact. The Pennsylvania provision was drafted by James Wilson, who (in the state convention that ratified the Constitution) declared, without challenge by any of the ardent proponents of a bill of rights: "What is meant by the liberty of the press is that there should be no antecedent restraint upon it; but that every author is responsible when he attacks the security or welfare of the government." The mode of proceeding, Wilson added, should by by prosecution.[9] The state constitutional provision of 1790 reflected this proposition, as did state trials before and after 1790.[10]

Delaware and Kentucky followed Pennsylvania's lead in 1792,[11] but elsewhere the status quo prevailed. In 1789 William Cushing and John Adams worried about whether the guarantee of a free press in Massachusetts ought to mean that truth was a good defense to a charge of criminal libel, but they agreed that false publications against the government were punishable.[12] In 1791, when a Massachusetts editor was prosecuted for a criminal libel against a state official, the Supreme Judicial Court divided on the question of truth as a defense, but, like the Pennsylvania judges,[13] agreed that the state constitutional guarantee of a free press was merely declaratory of the common law in simply prohibiting a licensing system.[14]

The opinions of Jefferson, the acknowledged libertarian leader in America, and of Madison, the father of the Bill of Rights, are especially significant. Jefferson, in 1783, when proposing a new constitution for Virginia, exempted the press from prior restraints, but carefully provided for prosecution — a state criminal trial — in cases of false publication.[15] In 1788, when urging Madison to support a bill of rights to the new federal Constitution, Jefferson made the same recommendation.[16]

Madison construed it in its most favorable light, observing: "The Exemption of the press from liability in every case for *true facts* is . . . an innovation and as such ought to be well considered."[17] On consideration, however, he did not add truth as a defense to the amendment that he offered on the press when proposing a bill of rights to Congress.[18] Yet his phrasing appeared too broad for Jefferson, who stated that he would be pleased if the press provision were altered to exclude freedom to publish "false facts . . . affecting the peace of the confederacy with foreign nations,"[19] a clause whose suppressive possibilities can be imagined in the context of a foreign-policy controversy such as the one on Jay's Treaty.

Madison fortunately ignored Jefferson's proposal, but there is no evidence warranting the belief that he dissented from the universal American acceptance of the Blackstonian definition of a free press. At the Virginia ratifying convention in 1788 Madison remained silent when George Nicholas, one of his closest supporters, declared that the liberty of the press was secure because there was no power to license the press.[20] Again Madison was silent when John Marshall rose to say that Congress would never make a law punishing men of different political opinions "unless it be such a case as must satisfy the people at large."[21] In October 1788, when replying to Jefferson's argument that powers of the national government should be restricted by a bill of rights,[22] Madison declared: "absolute restrictions in cases that are doubtful, or where emergencies may overrule them, ought to be avoided."[23]

When Madison proposed an amendment in Congress guaranteeing freedom of the press, he did not employ the emphatic language of the Virginia ratifying convention's recommendation that the press cannot be abridged "by any authority of the United States."[24] The amendment, in the form in which Madison introduced it, omitted the important clause "by any authority of the United States,"[25] which would have cov-

ered the executive and the judiciary as well as Congress. The omitted clause would have prohibited the federal courts from exercising any common-law jurisdiction over criminal libels. As ratified, the First Amendment declared only that Congress should make no law abridging the freedom of speech or press.

What did the amendment mean at the time of its adoption? More complex than it appears, it meant several things, and it did not necessarily mean what it said or say what it was intended to mean. First, as is shown by an examination of the phrase "the freedom of the press," the amendment was merely an assurance that Congress was powerless to authorize restraints in advance of publication. On this point the evidence for the period from 1787 to 1791 is uniform and nonpartisan. For example, Hugh Williamson of North Carolina, a Federalist signatory of the Constitution, used freedom of the press in Blackstonian or common-law terms,[26] as did Melancthon Smith of New York, an Antifederalist. Demanding a free-press guarantee in the new federal Constitution, despite the fact that New York's constitution lacked that guarantee, Smith argued that freedom of the press was "fully defined and secured" in New York by "the common and statute law of England" and that a state constitutional provision was therefore unnecessary.[27] No other definition of freedom of the press by anyone anywhere in America before 1798 has been discovered. Apparently there was, before that time, no dissent from the proposition that the punishment of a seditious libeler did not abridge the proper or lawful freedom of the press.[28]

That freedom was so narrowly understood that its constitutional protection did not, per se, preclude the enactment of a sedition law. The security of the state against libelous attack was always and everywhere regarded as outweighing any social interest in completely unfettered discussion. The thought and experience of a lifetime, indeed the taught traditions of law and politics extending back many generations, supplied an unquestioned assumption that freedom of political discourse, however broadly conceived, stopped short of seditious libel.

The injunction of the First Amendment, nevertheless, was not intended to imply that a sedition act might be enacted without abridging "the freedom of the press." A sedition act would not be an abridgment, but that was not the point of the amendment. To understand its framers' intentions, the amendment should not be read with the focus on the meaning of "the freedom of the press." It should not, in other words, be read merely to mean that Congress could impose no prior restraints. It should be read, rather, with the stress on the opening clause: "Congress shall make no law . . ." The injunction was intended and understood to prohibit any congressional regulation of the press, whether by means of a licensing law, a tax, or a sedition act. The framers meant Congress to be totally without power to enact legislation respecting the press. They intended a federal system in which the central government could exercise only such powers as were specifically enumerated or were necessary and proper to carry out the enumerated ones. Thus James Wilson declared that, because the national government had "no power whatsoever" concerning the press, "no law . . . can possibly be enacted" against it. Thus Hamilton, referring to the demand for a free-press guarantee, asked, "Why declare that things shall not be done which there is no power to do?"[29] The illustrations may be multiplied fiftyfold. In other words, no matter what was meant or understood by freedom of speech and press, the national government, *even in the absence of the First Amendment*, could not make speech or press a legitimate subject of restrictive legislation. The amendment itself was superfluous. To quiet public apprehension, it offered an added assurance that Congress would be limited to the exercise of its delegated powers. The phrasing was intended to prohibit the possibility that those powers might be used to abridge speech and press. From this viewpoint, the Sedition Act of 1798 was unconstitutional.

That act was also unnecessary as a matter of law, however necessary as a matter of Federalist party policy. It was unnecessary because the federal courts exercised jurisdiction over nonstatutory or common-law crimes against the United States. At the Pennsylvania ratifying convention James Wilson declared that, while Congress could enact no law against the press, a libel against the United States might be prosecuted in the state where the offense was committed, under Article III, section 2, of the Constitution which refers to the judicial power of the United States.[30] A variety of common-law crimes against the United States were, in fact, tried in the federal courts during the first decade of their existence.[31] There were, in the federal courts, even a couple of common-law indictments for the crime of seditious libel.[32] All the early Supreme Court judges, including several who had been influential in the Philadelphia Convention, or in the state ratifying conventions, or in the Congress that passed the Judiciary Act of 1789, assumed the existence of a federal common law of crimes.[33] Ironically, it was a case originating as a federal prosecution of Connecticut editors for seditious libels against President Jefferson that finally resulted in a ruling by a divided Supreme Court in 1812 that there was no federal common law of crimes.[34]

There was unquestionably a federal common law of crimes at the time of the Sedition Act. Why then was the act passed if it was not legally needed? Even in England, where the criminal courts exercised an unquestioned jurisdiction over seditious libels, it was politically advisable in the 1790s to declare public policy in unmistakable terms by the enactment of sedition statues.[35] Legislation helped ensure effective enforcement of the law and stirred public opinion against its intended victims. The Federalists, hoping to control public opinion and elections, emulated the British model. A federal statute was expedient also because the Republicans insisted that libels against the United States might be tried only by the state courts.

This suggests another original purpose of the First Amendment. It has been said that a constitutional guarantee of a free press did not, in itself, preclude a sedition act, but that the prohibition on Congress did, though leaving the federal courts free to try cases of seditious libel. It now appears that the prohibition on Congress was motivated far less by a desire to give immunity to political expression than by a solicitude for states' rights and the federal principle. The primary purpose of the First Amendment was to reserve to the states an exclusive legislative authority in the field of speech and press.

This is clear enough from the countless states' rights arguments advanced by the Antifederalists during the ratification controversy, and it is explicit in the Republican arguments during the controversy over the Sedition Act. In the House debates on the bill, Albert Gallatin, Edward Livingston, John Nicholas, and Nathaniel Macon all agreed — to quote Macon on the subject of liberty of the press: "The States have complete power on the subject ... "[36] Jefferson's Kentucky Resolutions of 1798 expressed the same proposition,[37] as did Madison's "Address of the General Assembly to the People of the Commonwealth of Virginia" in 1799.[38]

It is possible that the opponents of the Sedition Act did not want or believe in state prosecutions, but argued for an exclusive state power over political libels because such an argument was tactically useful as a means of denying national jurisdiction, judical or legislative. If so, how shall we explain the Republican prosecution in New York in 1803 against Harry Croswell, a Federalist editor, for a seditious libel against President Jefferson?[39] How shall we explain the Blackstonian opinions of the Republican judges in that case?[40] How shall we explain Jefferson's letter to the governor of Pennsylvania in the same year? The President, enclosing a newspaper piece that unmercifully attacked him, urged a "few prosecutions" because they "would have a wholesome effect in restoring the integrity of the presses."[41] How shall we explain Jefferson's letter to Abigail Adams in 1804 in which he said: "While we deny that Congress have a right to controul the freedom of the press, we have ever asserted the right of the states, and their exclusive right to do so."[42] And if exclusive state power was advanced not as a principle but as a tactic for denying federal jurisdiction, how shall we explain what Jefferson's opponents called his "reign of terror":[43] the common-law indictments in 1806 in the United States Circuit Court in Connecticut against six men charged with seditious libel of the president?[44] How shall we explain his letter of 1807 in which he said of the "prosecutions in the Court of the U S" that they could "not lessen the useful freedom of the press," if truth were admitted as a defense?[45]

Earlier, in 1798, the Federalists had also felt that the true freedom of the press would benefit if truth — their truth — were the measure of freedom. Their infamous Sedition Act, in the phrase of Gilbert and Sullivan, was the true embodiment of everything excellent. It was, that is, the very epitome of libertarian thought since the time of Zenger's case, proving that American libertarianism went from Zengerian principles to the Sedition Act in a single degeneration. Everything that the libertarians had ever demanded was, however, incorporated in the Sedition Act: a requirement that criminal intent be shown; the power of the jury to decide whether the accused's statement was libelous as a matter of law as well as of fact; and truth as a defense — an innovation not accepted in England until 1843.[46] By every standard the Sedition Act was a great victory for libertarian principles of freedom of the press—except that libertarian standards abruptly changed because the Republicans immediately recognized a Pyrrhic victory.

The Sedition Act provoked them to develop a new libertarian theory. It began

Leonard W. Levy

to emerge when Congressmen Albert Gallatin, John Nicholas, Nathaniel Macon, and Edward Livingston argued against the enactment of the sedition bill.[47] It was further developed by defense counsel, most notably George Blake, in Sedition Act prosecutions.[48] It reached its most reflective and systematic expression in tracts and books which are now unfortunately rare and little known even by historians. The main body of original Republican thought on the scope, meaning, and rationale of the First Amendment is to be found in George Hay's tract, *An Essay on the Liberty of the Press;*[49] in Madison's *Report* on the Virginia Resolutions for the Virginia House of Delegates;[50] in the book, *A Treatise Concerning Political Enquiry, and the Liberty of the Press*, by Tunis Wortman of New York;[51] in John Thomson's book, *An Enquiry, Concerning the Liberty, and Licentiousness of the Press;*[52] and in St. George Tucker's appendix to his edition of Blackstone's *Commentaries*,[53] a most significant place for the repudiation of Blackstone on the liberty of the press. Of these works, Wortman's philosophical book is preeminent; it is an American masterpiece, the only equivalent on this side of the Atlantic to Milton and Mill.

The new libertarians abandoned the strait-jacketing doctrines of Blackstone and the common law, including the recent concept of a federal common law of crimes. They scornfully denounced the no-prior-restraints definition. Said Madison: "This idea of the freedom of the press can never be admitted to be the American idea of it" because a law inflicting penalties would have the same effect as a law authorizing a prior restraint. "It would seem a mockery to say that no laws shall be passed preventing publications from being made, but that laws might be passed for punishing them in case they should be made."[54] As Hay put it, the "British definition" meant that a man might be jailed or even put to death for what he published provided that no notice was taken of him before he published.[55]

The old calculus for measuring the scope of freedom was also rejected by the new libertarians. "Liberty" of the press, for example, had always been differentiated from "licentiousness," which was the object of the criminal law's sanctions. "Truth" and "facts" had always divided the realm of lawfulness from "falsehoods," and a similar distinction had been made between "good motives" and "criminal intent." All such distinctions were now discarded on grounds that they did not distinguish and, therefore, were not meaningful standards that might guide a jury or a court in judging an alleged verbal crime. The term "licentiousness," said Thomson, "is destitute of any meaning" and is used by those who wish "nobody to enjoy the liberty of the Press but such as were of their own opinion."[56] The term "malice," Wortman wrote, is invariably confused with mistaken zeal or prejudice.[57] It is merely an inference drawn from the supposed evil tendency of the publication itself, just a further means of punishing the excitement of unfavorable sentiments against the government even when the people's contempt of it was richly deserved. Punishment of "malice" or intent to defame the government, concluded Madison, necessarily strikes at the right of free discussion, because critics intend to excite unfavorable sentiments.[58] Finding criminality in the tendency of words was merely an attempt to erect public "tranquility ... upon the ruins of Civil Liberty," said Wortman.[59]

Wholesale abandonment of the common law's limitations on the press was accompanied by a withering onslaught against the constrictions and subjectivity of Zengerian principles. The Sedition Act, Hay charged, "appears to be directed against falsehood and malice only; in fact ... there are many truths, important to society, which are not susceptible of that full, direct, and positive evidence, which alone can be exhibited before a court and a jury."[60] If, argued Gallatin, the administration prosecuted a citizen for his opinion that the Sedition Act itself was unconstitutional, would not a jury, composed of the friends of that administration, find the opinion "ungrounded, or, in other words, false and scandalous, and its publication malicious? And by what kind of argument or evidence, in the present temper of parties, could the accused convince them that his opinions were true?"[61] The truth of opinions, the new libertarians concluded, could not be proved. Allowing "truth" as a defense and thinking it to be a protection for freedom, Thomson declared, made as much sense as letting a jury decide which was "the most palatable food, agreeable drink, or beautiful color."[62] A jury, he asserted, cannot give an impartial verdict in political trials. The result, agreed Madison, is that the "baleful tendency" of prosecutions for seditious libel "is little diminished by the privilege of giving in evidence the truth of the matter contained in political writings."[63]

The renunciation of traditional concepts reached its climax in the assult on the very idea that there was a crime of seditious libel. That crime, Wortman concluded, could "never be reconciled to the genius and constitution of a Representative Commonwealth."[64] He and the others constructed a new libertarianism that was genuinely radical because it broke sharply with the past and advocated an absolute freedom of political expression. One of their major tenets was that a free government cannot be criminally attacked by the opinions of its citizens. Hay, for example, insisted that freedom of the press, like chastity, was either "absolute"[65] or did not exist. Abhorring the idea of verbal political crimes, he declared that a citizen should have a right to "say everything which his passions suggest; he may employ all his time, and all his talents, if he is wicked enough to do so, in speaking against the government matters that are false, scandalous and malicious."[66] He should be "safe within the sanctuary of the press" even if he "condemns the principle of republican institutions . . . If hc censures the measures of our government, and

every department and officer hereof, and ascribes the measures of the former, however salutary, and the conduct of the latter, however upright, to the basest motives; even if he ascribes to them measures and acts, which never had existence; thus violating at once, every principle of decency and truth."[67]

In brief the new libertarians advocated that only "injurious conduct," as manifested by "overt acts" or deeds, rather than words, might be criminally redressable.[68] They did not refine this proposition except to recognize that the law of libel should continue to protect private reputations against malicious falsehoods. They did not even recognize that under certain circumstances words may immediately and directly incite criminal acts.

This absolutist interpretation of the First Amendment was based on the now familiar but then novel and democratic theory that free government depends for its existence and security on freedom of political discourse. According to this theory, the scope of the amendment is determined by the nature of the government and its relationship to the people. Since the government is their servant, exists by their consent and for their benefit, and is constitutionally limited, responsible, and elective, it cannot, said Thomson, tell the citizen, "You shall not think this, or that upon certain subjects; or if you do, it is at your peril."[69] The concept of seditiousness, it was argued, could exist only in a relationship based on inferiority, when people are subjects rather than sovereigns and their criticism implies contempt of their master. "In the United States," Madison declared, "the case is altogether different."[70] Coercion or abridgment of unlimited political opinion, Wortman explained, would violate the very "principles of the social state," by which he meant a government of the people.[71] Because such a government depended upon popular elections, all the new libertarians agreed that the wildest possible latitude must be maintained to keep the electorate free, informed, and capable of making intelligent choices. The citizen's freedom of political expression had the same scope as the legislator's, and for the same reasons.[72] That freedom might be dangerously abused, but the people would decide men and measures wisely if exposed to every opinion.

This brief summary of the new libertarianism scarcely does justice to its complexity, but it suggests its boldness, originality, and democratic character.[73] It developed, to be sure, as an expediency of self-defense on the part of a besieged political minority struggling to maintain its existence and right to function unfettered. But it established virtually all at once and in nearly perfect form a theory justifying the rights of individual expression and of opposition parties. That the Jeffersonians in power did not always adhere to their new principles does not diminish the enduring nobility and rightness of those principles. It proves only that the Jeffersonians set the highest standards of freedom for themselves and posterity to be measured against. Their legacy was the idea that there is an indispensable condition for the development of free men in a free society; the state must be bitted and bridled by a bill of rights which is to be construed in the most generous terms and whose protections are not be be the playthings of momentary majorities.

Part Four

Law and the Economy in Ante-bellum America

Recent studies on the relationship between law and the economy in pre–Civil War America have produced a rich harvest of significant reinterpretations bearing on governmental institutions, the substance of law and public policy, and the legal norms that animated a society dedicated to rapid economic growth and expansion. Preeminent among the scholars who have developed these new lines of inquiry have been the lawyer Willard Hurst and the historian Paul W. Gates. In the selection that follows Hurst explores how the law established a framework for "the market" in which both individual and collective entrepreneurial energies could operate in the quest for economic growth. Hurst is critical of wastefulness and lack of direction — what he terms "drift and default" — in nineteenth-century law. He also condemns what he views as a pervasive lack of concern with long-run social costs. But Hurst does recognize that there was nonetheless considerable purposeful intervention by government to shape economic change, and he seeks to analyze as well what he terms a broad popular consensus concerning the proper role of law.

Gates, in his article on American land policy, takes a very different scholarly vantage point: the policy area that he examines is one in which governmental action was continuous, explicit, and generally formulated by policy makers who articulated premises concerning long-term social and economic consequences. Gates's analysis may be viewed as a case study of the interaction between government and private interests. The reader will want to examine closely the history that Gates presents to inquire why significant (if episodic and weak) efforts at social planning were so readily overwhelmed by private pressures, in the framework of nineteenth-century institutions.

The essays by Harry N. Scheiber and Morton Horwitz deal with two areas of the law in which the courts initiated major doctrinal changes with far-reaching consequences for the development of capitalist institutions and for economic growth. In Horwitz's study, the focus is on the transformation of property rights, which he illustrates by the change in water rights (riparian law) "from a static agrarian conception ... to a dynamic, instrumental, and more abstract view of property" better suited to a society committed to rapid economic development. Scheiber's study deals with a parallel and

107

Law and the Economy in Ante-bellum America

comparable movement in the law: how the power of eminent domain was used to take land away from private owners when it was needed for purposes deemed to be of major social importance. In both riparian law and the law of eminent domain, the legislatures and courts abridged vested rights, established priorities for the society, and changed basic rules concerning the privileges and immunities that pertained to private ownership. The portrait of nineteenth-century law in action provided by Horwitz and Scheiber runs counter to the long-standard view that American law always honored, above all, the sanctity of vested rights in property; but it is a portrait entirely consistent with what Gates and Hurst portray as the pattern of deference and support that nineteenth-century government extended to entrepreneurial interests.

Leonard W. Levy's contribution here is a summary analysis of the work of the Massachusetts Supreme Court under Chief Justice Lemuel Shaw, one of the giants of ante-bellum American law. Massachusetts judges led in many of the movements in legal doctrine discussed in these pages. But that state's court, and Shaw in particular, also developed powerful legal doctrines in support of state power. How Shaw balanced the powerful claims of individualism against the legitimate needs of the state to maintain order, to shape social relationships, and to main-tain the vitality of the "Commonwealth" concept that bespoke collective goals and the common welfare is closely analyzed in Levy's study.

Further Reading

Friedman, Lawrence M. *A History of American Law*. New York: Simon and Schuster, 1973. Pt. II, chaps. 3-6.

Handlin, Oscar, and Mary F. Handlin. *Commonwealth: A Study of the Role of Government in the American Economy: Massachusetts, 1774-1861*. Cambridge: Harvard University Press, 1947; rev. ed. 1969.

Hartz, Louis. *Economic Policy and Democratic Thought: Pennsylvania, 1776-1860* (Cambridge: Harvard University Press, 1948).

Horwitz, Morton J. *The Transformation of American Law, 1780-1860*. Cambridge: Harvard University Press, 1977.

Hurst, James Willard. *Law and Social Process in United States History*. Ann Arbor: University of Michigan Law School, 1960.

Kutler, Stanley I. *Privilege and Creative Destruction: The Charles River Bridge Case*. Philadelphia: Lippincott, 1971.

Levy, Leonard W. *The Law of the Commonwealth and Chief Justice Shaw*. Cambridge: Harvard University Press, 1957.

Scheiber, Harry N. *Ohio Canal Era: A Case Study of Government and the Economy, 1820-1861*. Athens: Ohio University Press, 1969.

10

Willard Hurst

The Release of Energy

One day in February of 1836, in the scarce-born village of Pike Creek on the southeastern Wisconsin shore of Lake Michigan, Jason Lothrop — Baptist minister, schoolteacher, boardinghouse proprietor, and civic leader — set up on a stump a rude press of his own construction and with ink which he had made himself printed a handbill setting forth the record of the organizational meeting of "the Pike River Claimants Union . . . for the attainment and security of titles to claims on Government lands."

The settlers whose union this was had begun to move into the lands about Pike Creek beginning in the summer of 1835. They were squatters; put less sympathetically, they were trespassers. They might not lawfully come upon the lands before the federal survey was made, and this was not completed in this area until about February 1, 1836; they might not make formal entry and buy until the president proclaimed a sale day, and Presidents Jackson and Van Buren withheld proclaiming these newly surveyed lands

Reprinted in abridged form with permission of the copyright holder, Northwestern University, and of the author, from James Willard Hurst, *Law and the Conditions of Freedom in the Nineteenth-Century United States*, 1956, the University of Wisconsin Press, pp. 1-39.

until 1839; they might not establish claims by preemption, for the existing preemption law expired by limitation in June 1836, and was not immediately renewed because of objections to speculators' abuses. These were formidable legal obstacles. The settlers' reaction tells us some basic things about the working legal philosophy of our nineteenth-century ancestors. Jason Lothrop recalled twenty years later:

Much conflicting interest was manifest between the settlers, from the first, in making their claims. Some were greedy in securing at least one section of 640 acres for themselves, and some as much for all their friends whom they expected to settle in the country. Before the lands were surveyed, this often brought confusion and disputes with reference to boundary lines, and still greater confusion followed when the Government surveys were made in the winter of 1835-36. These contentions often led to bitter quarrels and even bloodshed.

The settlers met several times to discuss the need of a more orderly framework within which growth might go on. Finally their discussions produced a meeting at Bullen's store in Pike Creek on February 13, 1836, where they adopted the constitution of their Claimants Union. They created the office of clerk and set the terms on which claims might be recorded with him, and they established a board of censors to adjudicate claims disputes. Through the turgid grandiloquence of their constitution's preamble shows a pattern of attitudes and values which explains much about nineteenth-century law in the United States, reaching to concerns far greater than those of the tiny frontier village.

> Whereas, a union and co-operation of all the inhabitants will be indispensably necessary, in case the pre-emption law should not pass, for the securing and protecting of our claims;
>
> And whereas, we duly appreciate the benefit which may result from such an association, not only in regulating the manner of making and sustaining claims, and settling differences in regard to them, but in securing the same to the holders thereof against speculators at the land sale; and being well aware that consequences the most dangerous to the interests of settlers will follow, if such a union be not formed; and as Government has heretofore encouraged emigration by granting pre-emption to actual settlers, we are assured that our settling and cultivating the public lands is in accordance with the best wishes of Government; and knowing that in some instances our neighbors have been dealt with in an unfeeling manner, driven from their homes, their property destroyed, their persons attacked, and their lives jeopardized, to satisfy the malignant disposition of unprincipled and avaricious men; and looking upon such proceedings as unjust, calculated to produce anarchy, confusion and the like among us, destroy our fair prospects, subvert the good order of society, and render our homes the habitations of terror and distrust — those homes, to obtain which we left our friends, deprived ourselves of the many blessing and privileges of society, have borne the expenses, and encountered the hardships of a perilous journey, advancing into a space beyond the bounds of civilization, and having the many diffculties and obstructions of a state of nature to overcome, and on the peaceable

> possession of which our all is depending;
>
> We, therefore, as well meaning inhabitants, having in view the promotion of the interest of our settlement, and knowing the many advantages derived from unity of feeling and action, do come forward this day, and solemnly pledge ourselves to render each other our mutual assistance, in the protection of our just rights . . . [1]

Frontier communities have often been described as "lawless" or at least careless of law. It is too glib a characterization. True, the Pike Creek story was typical of many in the settlement of the Mississippi Valley. From the survey Ordinance of 1785 on, squatters settled large areas of the public lands in defiance of law, ahead of official survey, without color of title other than that created by the impact of a popular feeling that would not be denied. At government auctions, they assembled in force unlawfully to frighten off free outside bidding and prevent competition from forcing any of their company to pay the public land office more than the legal minimum to regularize his holdings. But, as at Pike Creek, while they waited for the public sale day, these settlers all over the central and midwestern states set up local governments in the form of "claims associations," elected officers with whom to record their land claims and from whom to obtain decisions of conflicts, and then generally abided among themselves by these records and decisions. Often unlawful in origin, settlement nevertheless quickly brought effective demand for law.

The preamble of the Pike Creek Claimants Union reflects in miniature two working principles by which we organized the relations of legal order and social order in the nineteenth-century United States. I speak particularly of "working" principles, principles defined and expressed primarily by action. It is in this aspect that the Pike Creek document is most relevant to our purpose. For this essay seeks to understand the law not so much as it may appear to philosophers, but more as it had meaning for workaday people and was shaped by them to their wants and vision. Of course, this is not the only viewpoint from which to appraise the legal order. Nor is law that is formed largely by the imperatives of action necessarily the best law. We are simply trying one angle of vision provided by history for the distinctive reality it may disclose. Whatever its limitations, it is a point of view warranted by the central principle of our legal order, that law exists for the benefit of people and not people for the benefit of law. Such a legal order cannot in the long run be true to itself and at the same time be better than the values or vision of its beneficiaries. Moreover, emphasis on "working" principles seems peculiarly in point when we are trying to understand ourselves. Our history amply validates Tocqueville's observation that we have been a people not given to general theory. One senses that he is closer to apprehending the decisive faiths and beliefs of our nineteenth-century ancestors when he reads these out of what they did and said as they acted, rather than out of their self-conscious philosophizing.

The base lines of nineteenth-century public policy implicit in the Pike Creek document are three. (1) Human nature is creative, and its meaning lies largely in the expression of its creative capacity; hence it is socially desirable that there be broad opportunity for the release of creative human energy. (2) Corollary to the creative competence which characterizes human nature, the meaning of life for men rests also in their possessing liberty, which means basically possessing a wide practical range of options or choices as to what they do and how they are affected by circumstances. (3) These propositions have special significance for the future of mankind as they apply in the place and time of the adventure of the United States. Here unclaimed natural abundance together with the promise of new technical command of nature dictates that men should realize their creative energy and exercise their liberty peculiarly in the realm of the economy to the enhancement of other human values.

From these premises we drew two working principles concerning the uses of law. (1) The legal order should protect and promote the release of individual creative energy to the greatest extent compatible with the broad sharing of opportunity for such expression. In pursuit of this end, law might be used both (a) to secure a man a chance to be let alone, free of arbitrary public or private interference, while he showed what he could do, and (b) to provide instruments or procedures to lend the support of the organized community to the effecting of man's creative talents, even where this involved using the law's compulsion to enforce individual arrangements. (2) The legal order should mobilize the resources of the community to help shape an environment which would give men more liberty by increasing the practical range of choices open to them and minimizing the limiting force of circumstances. The people at Pike Creek wanted the community to guarantee their claims to be let alone in working their land and to lend its force to support their dealings with the land, that they might realize their "fair prospects." They also wanted the general government to use its resources positively to enlarge their opportunities as they sought to "overcome" "the many difficulties and obstructions of a state of nature"; to this end they wanted a preemption law or at least some affirmative legal preference of settlers over speculators.

If one took at face value some judicial expositions of doctrines of "vested rights," or those economic propositions which Henry Carey set forth as axioms of nature, one might believe that law played a minimum positive role in shaping our nineteenth-century society. It has been common to label nineteenth-century legal policy as simple laissez faire, and political debate of the last sixty years has propagated a myth of a Golden Age in which our ancestors — sturdier than we — got along well enough if the legislature provided schools, the sheriff ran down horse thieves, the court tried farmers' title disputes, and otherwise the law left men to take care of themselves.

The record is different. Not the jealous limitation of the power of the state, but the release of individual creative energy was the dominant value. Where legal regulation or compulsion might promote the greater release of individual or group energies, we had no hesitancy in making affirmative use of law. Relative to the greater simplicity of structure in the Wisconsin community of 1836-1870, for example, there was hardly less readiness to use the positive power of the state than one sees in 1905-1915 as we usher in the twentieth century of administrative regulation.

However, there is likely to be some basis in experience for every myth. The myth of our laissez faire past rests on two important aspects of our eighteenth- and nineteenth-century development: (1) the central place of the modern institution of private property in our politics as well as in our economic organization; (2) the extent to which the challenge of the unopened continent dominated our imagination until the last quarter of the last century.

Nineteenth-century preoccupation with the market as a key social institution led men to think of private property as an idea almost solely economic in its significance. But to the men whose bid for power formed the working institution of modern private property in the seventeenth and eighteenth centuries, property was chiefly a political idea. To them the heart of the matter was that law should define and guarantee a wider dispersion of the powers of decision in the community; this it did by committing to private hands legally protected control over the bulk of economic resources. Before the full tide of the disturbing forces we call the commercial and industrial revolutions, power was tightly held in England. In various combinations at different times, it lay within a close circle of the crown and its friends, the established church, the military and the greater and lesser landed men. Commerce and industry put new means of influence into the hands of new men; these consolidated their opportunities by achieving a legal order which gave them large autonomy in commanding the economic resources on which their influence was founded.

Regarded thus as a political institution affecting the distribution of power, private property involved three central ideas in its English development, to which we have added a fourth. (1) Since a high value was put on men's right to be let alone — to be "private" — there must be a reasonable public interest to justify imposing the public force on individuals' activities. This is the substance of what in the United States we eventually called "due process of law." (2) Such limits as government imposed on private freedom of decision must be declared according to a legitimate, public procedure, designed to keep law responsive to some influential nonofficial opinion. In our seventeenth-century inheritance this meant that an elected assembly should be the chief policy maker, its supremacy residing in its control of the public purse and its authority to ask questions about how the executive spent the public money. The original relation of this principle to the rise of the middle class was underlined by the property qualifications set upon the right to vote or hold legislative office, as well as by a traditional distrust of the executive as the historic source of arbitrary intrusions on privacy. (3) The legal order must provide every man with means to make formal insistence that law be applied to him fairly and impartially. Otherwise crown grants of monopolies to court favorites or discriminatory taxes might soon make a sham of private freedom of action. In modern terms, there must be a guarantee of the equal protection of the laws for that framework of reasonable expectations within which alone private property would be meaningful. (4) Nineteenth-century United States legal growth added the elements of a judiciary given constitutionally guaranteed tenure during good behavior and authority to refuse effect to legislation found by the judges to be unconstitutional. Ready access to courts so armed added a factor that made itself deeply felt in our further definition of the property principle.

These doctrines defined private property in terms of a legally assured measure of autonomy for private decision makers as against the public power. Of course, others than officials could threaten the security of private property; very old rules of criminal and tort law remind us that property is also the creation of the law's protection against the intrusions of arbitrary private force. But this latter role of the law was so taken for granted in early nineteenth-century policy as not to contribute much that is distinctive; as I have noted, despite easy generalizations about the "lawless" frontier, nothing is plainer than that settlement quickly brought demand for this kind of legal order. Some developments in nineteenth-century tort and criminal law promoted the release-of-energy policy. Otherwise, concern about the threat of private power to private property does not bring a fresh element into our legal history until the late-century interest in railroad and antitrust regulation.

The order of events in time thus emphasized for the early nineteenth century the constitutional aspect of private property. In this context property was primarily a bundle of legal limits on the intrusion of official power into nonofficial decision making; the seventeenth-century drama of conflict with the crown had given a purely negative aspect to the institution. However, there was nothing merely negative about the tone of life in the nineteenth-century United States. This obvious fact alone casts doubt on the adequacy of an exposition of nineteenth-century public policy which describes it solely in terms of negative propositions. We were a people going places in a hurry. Men in that frame of mind are not likely to be thinking only of the condition of their brakes. Thus, as we examine further we find that prevailing nineteenth-century attitudes in fact made private property preeminently a dynamic, not a static institution. Our situation was inappropriate to

the growth of a dominant *rentier* interest, merely sitting on its possessions. We did not devote the prime energies of our legal growth to protecting those who sought the law's shelter simply for what they had; our enthusiasm ran rather to those who wanted the law's help positively to bring things about. The sign of this was the overwhelming predominance of the law of contract in all its ramifications in the legal growth of the first seventy-five years of the nineteenth century.

The challenge of the unexploited continent was the second factor in disguising the actual extent of positive resort to law in shaping our society. This was what gripped our imagination and what has dominated our retrospect upon the century. The generally superficial and haphazard constitutional debates in the new states, the early established pattern of wholesale borrowing of statutes from older states, the fumbling, trial-and-error method by which new legislation evolved all testify that we were conscious that we needed a legal framework, but were impatient of the time and effort it took to provide it. After the extraordinary generation of political activity that accompanied and followed the Revolution, for most of the nineteenth century we put little of our creative talent into making the basic framework of law except in areas which we saw most directly contributing to the release of private energy and the increase of private options. Politics in the grand sense had been the focus of our creative energy from 1765 to 1800, when first the impact of imperial policy and then the novelty of new governments forced us to attend to problems of the organization of power. With these matters apparently settled, and confronting the challenge of the continent, the nineteenth century was prepared to treat law more casually, as an instrument to be used wherever it looked as if it would be useful. This instrumentalist view tended to put aside consideration of the larger problems of the organization or limitation of power and to take for granted the law's framework-setting function to an extent that did not do justice to its actual importance.

The substance of what business wanted from law was the provision for ordinary use of an organization through which entrepreneurs could better mobilize and release economic energy. Partly this business demand was to get rid of a limiting governmental policy; it sought release of the law's jealously restrictive control over this type of association. But it is characteristic of the nineteenth century that there was here also a demand for positive help from the law. Merely to be let alone to combine capital was not the substance of the entrepreneurs' desire. Here, as so often, a lively and pervasive sense of capital scarcity, relative to our opportunities, supplied the dynamic of public policy. One did not mobilize and discipline scattered resources merely by exhorting government to keep its hands off. Entrepreneurs wanted the positive prestige of the sanction of the state implicit in the charter grant. They wanted the aid of an orderly capital-subscription procedure under which capital could be fed into the enterprise on a defined installment plan, with provisions for periodic assessments of stockholders and forfeitures to enforce the assessments. The influence of provisions for the limited liability of corporate stockholders for the debts of the business has perhaps been exaggerated as a source of the pressure for incorporation. But, whatever the relative weight of this element, there is no doubt that the grant of the limited-liability privilege was sought as a positive aid by law to the enlistment of capital. Entrepreneurs wanted, too, a form of organization which firmly and broadly delegated power over mobilized capital to managers and directors.

We identify no legal development more sharply with the nineteenth century than the judicial protection of "vested rights." The modern concept of private property began with the tradition of the Parliamentary Revolution, involving reliance upon a legislative assembly responsive to propertied interests and armed with powers of purse and inquiry to curb the arbitrary

intrusions of the executive. But legislatures in the United States did not rest on such well-defined and limited class interest as did the seventeenth- and eighteenth-century House of Commons. Soon repenting of the broad authority given the legislative branch in our earliest state constitutions, substantial interests pressed successfully for limitations written into constitutional form and supported the courts' authority to enforce the superiority of constitution over statute. A realistic understanding of the nineteenth century's faith in release of energy involves relating this to the vested-rights doctrine.

"Vested rights" sounds like pure standpattism, as if it connoted merely protection of what is because it is, because nothing is valued more than stability. But on the whole, the nineteenth-century United States valued change more than stability and valued stability most often where it helped create a framework for change. The century so highly valued change because imagination could scarcely conceive that it could be other than for the better. We may look somewhat wryly on this faith, but we must acknowledge it as a prime fact in our nineteenth-century public policy making. Thus, the more one looks at the lines along which the vested rights doctrine grew, the less satisfied is he to appraise it as a simple expression in favor of the status quo. Dynamic rather than static property, property in motion or at risk rather than property secure and at rest, engaged our principal interest.

We were concerned with protecting private property chiefly for what it could do; as one looks at the facts of cases and pays somewhat less attention to the sonorous language of judicial opinions, he is impressed that what we did in the name of vested rights had less to do with protecting holdings than it had to do with protecting ventures. There is no key instance where vested-rights doctrine protected a simple *rentier* interest. We abolished primogeniture and entail, disestablished the few established churches we had, and gave married women control of their property, all without serious barrier from vested-rights doctrine. The federal Constitution forbade the nation or the states to grant any title of nobility. The Northwest Ordinance and the consistent policy of Congress under its constitutional authority to admit new states together foreclosed development of a privileged old-state class by providing for entry of new states out of our western lands and fixing the policy that these be admitted on terms of political equality with the old. The bulk of the nineteen-century cases which developed vested-rights doctrine involved the conduct of business or capital venture, including land speculation. The later decisions which protected freedom of contract, or entrepreneurs' freedom, as a "liberty" guaranteed by the Fourteenth Amendment were only the most explicit indicators of the main current of our concern for vested rights. Looking back from a mid-twentieth-century United States characterized by steady expansion of one form or another of securities holdings among the upper middle class, one might see the Income-tax Decision (1895) as an expression of *rentier* interest. But in its contemporary context the major significance of the decision was for large-scale capital formation and the shape of big business. The principal nineteenth-century vested-rights cases, which protect property simply as a claim to hold onto what one has, are those concerning the valuation of property in eminent-domain proceedings. Even these rest less on protection of vested rights as such than on a kind of insistence on equal protection of the laws — that a particular individual should not be made to bear out of his own resources the cost of a community benefit.[2]

Nineteenth-century vested-rights doctrine developed chiefly in relation to protection of venture capital and the limited autonomy of business because through most of the century we were scarce of capital and of necessity were preoccupied with opening up the continent. We had neither the means nor the time for an important *rentier* class. Circumstances through the first three-quarters of the century thus never called for a major test of attitudes toward protecting the status quo simply as such, unless one counts the issue of slavery as an instance. No single neat formula can contain the whole of the tension between North and South or the whole of the moral problem presented by property in human beings. One element in northern support for confiscating the property in slaves was the conviction that slavery had proved to be a system which did not fulfill the proper property function of generating a constantly expanding reach of human creative power. Nor should we forget that Lincoln drew the ultimate issue as the preservation of Union, whether any particular form of private property stood or fell.[3]

Of course, there were decisions, and there was much judicial language, looking to the protection of property considered simply as a claim to the maintenance of what someone had or the situation he was in. But it is important to note that the main current ran to the protection of property in action, for otherwise we may be surprised by some of the limits the nineteenth century put on protection of vested rights. A Wisconsin Supreme Court opinion of 1860 expresses the period's central concern with the safeguarding of venture capital. Asked to overrule an 1849 decision which had sustained the constitutionality of the mill-dam act, the court refused, though it indicated that as an original matter it would not now sanction the statute, which in effect delegated the power of eminent domain to waterpower developers who wished to flow others' land. Since the 1849 case, said Justice Cole, it was fair to assume that large amounts of capital had been invested in reliance on it.

And, although the period has been comparatively brief since the (1849) case ... was decided, yet we all know that within that time enterprising towns and flourishing villages have grown up, whose wealth and prosperity are mainly dependent upon their hydraulic power, and whose business relations and industrial resources would be seriously affected, if we were now to overrule that case . . . The rule *stare decisis,* has great force in such a state of things, and emphatically applies.[4]

Because it most valued private property for its productive potential, the nineteenth century was prepared to make strong, positive use of law to maintain such conditions as it thought essential to the main flow of private activity. Bankruptcy law began mainly as a protection to creditors against the dishonesty of debtors. But by the mid-nineteenth century, both in national bankruptcy laws and in state insolvency legislation, the trend of policy was as much to provide means by which debtors might be saved from irretrievable ruin and salvaged as venturers who might yet again contribute productively to the market. "The discharge of the debtor has come to be an object of no less concern than the distribution of his property" under federal bankruptcy policy.[5] The contract clause of the federal Constitution prevented state insolvency laws from discharging debts contracted before their enactment. But no contract clause limited the federal bankruptcy power. The Fifth Amendment might bar destruction of a creditor's security interest in specific property acquired before passage of a bankruptcy law, but there was no taking of property without due process of law in employing a bankruptcy act to discharge debts contracted before the law went on the books.

In no just sense do such governmental regulations deprive a person of his property without due process of law. They simply require each individual to so conduct himself for the general good as not unnecessarily to injure another . . . Every member of a political community must necessarily part with some of the rights which, as an individual, not affected by his relation to others, he might have retained. Such concessions make up the consideration he gives for the obligation of the body politic to protect him

in life, liberty, and property. Bankrupt laws, whatever may be the form they assume, are of that character.[6]

Likewise valid, if they were not too drastic, were laws which stayed a creditor's remedies to afford the debtor a breathing spell in which he might regather his strength. Again a test was whether the regulation would tend reasonably to preserve the general course of dealing. Mr. Chief Justice Dixon put it so for the Wisconsin court in sustaining an 1858 statute extending the time in foreclosures:

Although such changes are in general exceedingly unwise and unjust, yet if from sudden and unlooked-for reverses or misfortune, or any other cause, the existing remedies become so stringent in all or a particular class of actions that great and extensive sacrifices of property will ensue, without benefit to the creditor or relief to the debtor, a relaxation of the remedies becomes a positive duty which the State owes to its citizens.[7]

Of broader but analogous policy import were other familiar nineteenth-century rulings that vested rights must yield before government action to maintain the general framework of dealings. The community might take for a public highway a bridge owned by a private corporation under a legislative franchise given long before the applicable eminent-domain statute was passed; here was no impairment of the obligation of contract, for every contract is made subject to exercise of the framework-setting powers of government.[8] Likewise the contracts clause was held not to limit the general power to tax or the police power.[9] Most drastic in application to existing commitments and expectations was the holding that Congress might provide for the issue of paper money and make it legal tender for debts previously incurred.[10]

It was natural to its buoyant optimism and its confidence in the release of energy that nineteenth-century law coupled concern for vested rights with a high regard for keeping open the channels of change. This was one aspect of the bankruptcy and insolvency laws. It is a viewpoint implicit in the type of decisions just noted, in which judges were alert to protect the community's authority to deal with shifting conditions affecting the functional integrity of the whole system. The classical statement of policy in favor of freedom for creative change as against unyielding protection for existing commitments was Taney's opinion in the *Charles River Bridge* case. Public grants should be strictly construed in favor of the public; nothing should pass by implication; hence the legislative grant of a franchise to build and operate a toll bridge should not be held by implication to give the grantees an exclusive charter, so that they might prevent the building of a nearby competing bridge under a later grant.

> In a country like ours, free, active, and enterprising, continually advancing in numbers and wealth, new channels of communication are daily found necessary, both for travel and trade; and are essential to the comfort, convenience, and prosperity of the people. A State ought never to be presumed to surrender this power [of promoting the happiness and prosperity of the community], because, like the taxing power, the whole community have an interest in preserving it undiminished ... No one will question that the interests of the great body of the people of the State, would, in this instance, be affected by the surrender of this great line of travel to a single corporation, with the right to exact toll, and exclude competition for seventy years. While the rights of private property are sacredly guarded, we must not forget that the community also have rights, and that the happiness and well being of every citizen depends on their faithful preservation.

The preference for dynamic rather than static property, or for property put to creative new use rather than property content with what it is, emerges in Taney's further description of the policy choices implicit in the case:

> If this court should establish the principles now contended for, what is to become of the numerous railroads established on the same line of travel with turnpike companies; and which have rendered the franchises of the turnpike corporations of no value? Let it once be understood that such charters carry with them these implied contracts, and give this unknown and undefined property in a line of travelling, and you will soon find the old turnpike corporations awakening from their sleep, and calling upon this court to put down the improvements which have taken their place. The millions of property which have been invested in railroads and canals, upon lines of travel which had been before occupied by turnpike corporations, will be put in jeopardy. We shall be thrown back to the improvements of the last century, and obliged to stand still, until the claims of the old turnpike corporations shall be satisfied, and they shall consent to permit these States to avail themselves of the lights of modern science, and to partake of the benefit of those improvements which are now adding to the wealth and prosperity, and the convenience and comfort of every other part of the civilized world.[11]

The uniform legislative reaction to the *Dartmouth College* case made it clear that Taney expressed the dominant mid-century preference for property as an institution of growth rather than merely of security. With little question or exception, in the very act of providing franchises for private capital development, state constitution makers and legislators developed the practice of including in their grants a standard reservation of legislative authority to amend or repeal what they gave. Governors' vetoes enforcing this policy made explicit its preference for retaining maneuverability in the face of an always evolving situation. Thus, in 1882 Wisconsin's Governor Rusk vetoed a dam franchise given to named individuals because the statute did not include a reserved power of repeal or amendment analogous to the reservation which the state constitution made as to all grants to corporations. His message

Willard Hurst

mingles characteristic policy tones of the century: law must provide a framework within which many may venture, rather than a favored few, and it must take care that future release of creative energy is not barred by the rigidity of old concessions:

> The improvement may be for the public good, the tolls fixed may be fair and reasonable, but nearly all such measures affect the interests of many who know nothing of their pendency and are unheard as to their effect. In the nature of things it is impracticable for the legislature to make thorough and exhaustive investigation in each case, and to know the precise effect upon all interests of the measures asked for. Moreover, what may be an improvement in the situation of affairs to-day, may be very far from an improvement a few years hence; and what may be fair compensation for maintaining dams and other public improvements to-day, may not be fair or reasonable after the lapse of time. So that the public interest would seem seriously to demand that the legislature in all such grants should reserve to itself the right, should the public interest require it, to revoke the same, or to continue them upon new terms and subject to additional restrictions.[12]

To this point, I have sketched the release-of-energy policy almost entirely in terms of the relation of law to the economy. This accords with the emphasis which the times gave this policy. It was a century which put all the energy and attention it could into economic interests, Politicians might concern themselves with the sectional balance of power and humanitarians with slavery and drink and the rights of women. From time to time the zealous minority interested in these matters could whip up a general, emotional reaction to them. But in most affairs one senses that men turned to noneconomic issues grudgingly or as a form of diversion and excitement or in spurts of bad conscience over neglected problems. The law of the first half

of the century particularly reflects this; in the latter half, simple social mechanics, the force of stubborn facts, began to bring law into contact with a wider range of concerns that those immediately economic.

General policy, expressed in practice more often than in formal declaration, favored the release of individual creativity in areas of life apart from the market. But the law played a quite indirect role in this. So far as colonial laws set limits on men's freedom to choose their religion or to gather with their fellows in sociable groups or to set their personal patterns of expenditure and their personal choices of pleasure, these were largely repealed or fallen into disuse amounting to practical repeal by the end of the first quarter of the nineteenth century. Where there was formal legal action to remove old limitations, as in the disestablishment of churches, it is difficult to believe that law brought about the change, rather than ratifying changes produced by social facts — by our fluid class structure, our abundance of land, our growing population with its recurrent waves of immigration.

The most important nineteenth-century uses of law in relation to social problems involved the control of the general environment. So far as it concerned the simple release of individual energy in social affairs, law had its principal influence in the tolerance, protection, and sometimes fostering, of associations of all kinds. Legally assured freedom of religious association was in the background of one of the most dynamic elements of the first half of the century: the evangelical Protestant movement in the rural areas, especially on the frontier, whose credo of individual dignity generated much of the emotional fervor of agrarian politics. Freedom of association let loose another dynamic factor for individualism in the abolitionist societies. Liquor control became a fighting issue because there could be temperance societies; liquor and suffrage both came into the arena because women could organize groups on such public issues before they were able to vote or to manage property. Outside the economic area religion was involved in the most serious conflicts over free association, in controversies over Masonic lodges, Catholic convents and schools, and Mormon communities. These figured in local and national politics in rather sporadic bursts of attention. Some legislation went on the books regulating secret societies; some additions were made to that pragmatic store of precedents which constitutes our policy of "separation of church and state"; some serious violence reminded us that effective civil liberty requires the positive protection of law. In the first half of the century these matters have significance primarily as parts of our history of middle-class morals and values, and of population growth and immigration; they involve legal history only indirectly.

Freedom in political activity expressed a number of important public policies, besides promoting release of the individual's creative energies. Political participation is relevant to social interest in human dignity, in the legitimacy and distribution of power, and in the simple administrative necessity of getting questions settled. But, among these other objectives, a continuing inheritance from Jefferson was the faith that broad popular political activity would multiply fruitful thought, insight, invention in public affairs to the general benefit.

The removal of property qualifications on voting or holding office was the outstanding action in law to set free men's political energies. The current set firmly in this direction as early as the New York constitutional convention of 1821, where the aged Kent futilely opposed it. In the newer states white male suffrage was not a serious issue, but the vote for free Negroes, for immigrants, and for women stirred controversies throughout the century. Emancipation of the slaves brought problems which called for positive implementation in law, if political freedom were to be real, and which remained as unresolved civil liberties issues of the nineteenth century.

Political freedom for individuals involves other civil liberties besides the right to vote: rights of free speech, press, assembly, and petition, and of access to and enjoyment of the proper procedures of the civilian courts. The Alien and Sedition Acts, the Civil War and Reconstruction, and the conflicts over labor organization late in the century produced the notable problems on these fronts. The enforced lapse of the Alien and Sedition Acts was the clearest substantial victory of the century for the release-of-energy principle in these fields. The great civil liberties decision arising out of the Civil War — *Ex parte Milligan* — came after the crisis that produced the issue had abated. The transfer of political leadership from Radical Republicans to men whose prime interest was in economic growth, and the acquiescence of the Supreme Court in this direction of policy, ended for the nineteenth century any aggressive program in law to implement the liberty granted the Negroes in the South. No firm precedent for individual liberty emerged from the labor difficulties of the end of the century except insofar as Altgeld's courageous pardon of the Haymarket anarchists asserted the fundamental importance of a fair and temperate trial process. More typical of the indecisiveness of the law's role in civil liberties in those years was the flamboyant resurrection of an obsolete theory of "treason" to indict leaders of the Homestead strike, followed after a time by a quiet dropping of the charges.[13]

The nineteenth century produced some important issues for individual civil liberties, but showed no impressive record of grappling with them. It is symbolic that the most decisive eposide, the controversy leading to the nonrenewal of the Alien and Sedition Acts, came at the opening of the century, in our classic generation of high politics. There is little that happens after 1800, until the Holmes-Brandeis dissents begin to build a supporting body of opinion in the 1920s, to suggest the presence of a really substantial public opinion interested in, and prepared to pay the costs of, supporting individual civil liberties. It would distort the view of our nineteenth-century life to say that it embodied any substantial, defined hostility to individual political freedoms; the accepted and revered political generalities all exalted individual liberty. But the century was so market-focused as to be politically naïve. Its prevailing attitudes tended to range from indifference to impatience with matters that distracted attention from "progress," defined as increase of capital and consumable wealth. Toward the end of the century the right of association took on high importance in practice, but this was felt then more as a matter of redressing the general balance of power in the society than as an issue of individualism. All this is part of our inheritance, along with the Bill of Rights. One could not be certain how different was the alignment of working belief on the value of individual civil liberty in the mid-twentieth century, except that in the later time we were more impatient with what distracted from attention to "security" than we were with interruptions to "progress." At least in the 1950s, however, the weight to be placed on individual civil liberties was recognized as a major political issue; in that respect, the situation stood in marked contrast to that of most of the nineteenth century.

Belief in the release of private individual and group energies thus furnished one of the working principles which give the coherence of character to our early-nineteenth-century public policy. This principle found expression in no simple removal of legal restrictions or staying of the regulatory hand. Limitations on official power were very important elements of this pattern of policy. But so, too, was a complicated affirmative use of law to furnish instruments and procedures and to impose as well as enforce patterns of dealing. In this aspect, our nineteenth-century policy involved a good deal less of simple laissez faire than has often been claimed for it. Joseph Spengler has properly cautioned against exaggerating the extent of legal intervention in the economy by way of regulatory laws: such government operations tend to leave a larger residue of records, especially in comparison with the relatively simple, non-bureaucratized business of the early part of the century; moreover, in their nature such intervention and the advocacy of such intervention are more likely to leave positive records of initiatives taken or proposed than is the advocacy of a negative position.[14] It it true, however, that we made considerable use of legal compulsion to meet the challenge of our environment and that by no means did we always treat the release of energy as wholly beneficial. When these regulatory uses of law are taken together with the framework of legal compulsion within which the regime of contract operated, it is plain that while the enlargement of men's freedom was the objective, it was, indeed, freedom under law.

11

Paul W. Gates

An Overview of American Land Policy

In attempting to present an overview of American land policy I propose to discuss in the most general terms the acquisition of the public domain, the fundamental constitutional questions relating to it, the divergent points of view of the older states and the newly developing West, the double effect of the various policies adopted, and the prevailing belief, at least until fairly recently, that the federal government should divest itself of the ownership of public land and get it into private hands. Finally I hope to show that many of the old disputes about our public-land policies are still unresolved and that we are, in a sense, back to square one.

Philadelphia, the center of government in 1787, was host to the Constitutional Convention which met in Independence Hall while, simultaneously, the Congress of the Articles of Confederation was meeting in Carpenters' Hall writing the Northwest Ordinance to provide government for the territory north of the Ohio. After many disputes and petty jealousies had been composed, Virginia, Massachusetts, and Connecticut had surrendered to the national government all or parts of western land claims and the Congress had pro-

vided in the Land Ordinance of 1785 a plan for the management and sale of the land. Though the power to own, manage, grant, and otherwise dispose of the public lands was to be one of the most nationalizing factors in the life of the federal republic, that power received slight attention in the new Constitution of 1787. It is confined to twenty-six words in Article IV, section 3: "The Congress shall have Power to dispose of and make all needful Rules and Regulations respecting the Territory or other property belonging to the United States . . ."[1] But more detailed powers and restrictions had previously been agreed to during the period of the Confederation.

Virginia had ceded her western-land claims in order to secure Maryland's accession to the Articles of Confederation. But Virginia had imposed two restrictions. First, the lands were to be "considered as a *common* fund for the use and benefit of such of the United States as have become, or shall become members of the confederation or federal alliance of the said States, Virginia included, according to their usual respective proportions in the general charge and expenditure, and shall be . . . disposed of for the purpose, and for no other purpose whatsoever . . ." Second, the ceded territory should be divided into states and admitted into the

Reprinted from *Agricultural History*, vol. 50, no. 1 (January 1976), 213-229, by permission. Copyright © 1976 by the Agricultural History Society.

Union with "the same rights of sovereignty, freedom and independence as the other States." In accepting Virginia's act of cession, Congress resolved that it should be "recorded and enrolled among the acts of the United States in Congress assembled."[2] Thus it was established that the public lands were the sole property of the United States, that any income derived therefrom was to be shared by all the states in proportion to their representation in Congress, and that the new states were to have the same rights as the original states.

In the Northwest Ordinance of 1787 Congress declared: "The legislatures of these districts or new States, shall never interfere with the primary disposal of the soil by the United States . . . nor with any regulations Congress may find necessary, for securing the title in such soil, to the *bona fide* purchasers. No tax shall be imposed on lands . . . of the United States; and in no case shall non-resident proprietors be taxed higher than residents." Despite these limitations upon the sovereignty of the new states, and the greater one which barred slavery, Congress stated in that same ordinance that the new states should be admitted into the Union "on an equal footing with the original States, in all respects whatever . . ."[3] These and other inconsistencies and ambivalent positions respecting the public lands were to have a major bearing on the question, Whose public lands?

The Congress of the Confederation had found it difficult to resolve questions relating to the public lands over which it had thus obtained jurisdiction because each of the thirteen original states had retained such ungranted or forfeited lands as remained within their boundaries as they exist today. In addition, Massachusetts had retained ownership of present-day Maine and still held a large portion of western New York; Connecticut retained its western reserve in northeastern Ohio; New York still had many ungranted lands; Virginia retained, until 1792, public land in present-day Kentucky; and Georgia had the greatest amount of ungranted land within its present boundaries and did not cede its western-land claims until 1802.[4] Sovereignty was associated with the ownership of ungranted lands within a state's boundaries, yet this right was to be denied to new states created out of the public lands. The public-land states were never to forget this limitation upon their sovereignty, and their representatives were to devote themselves to rectifying the situation while the original states continued to maneuver to induce Congress to carry out the pledge it had made to Virginia that the benefits arriving from the public domain should be shared by all the states in proportion to their federal ratio.

Notwithstanding the restrictions imposed by the Virginia Act of Cession, Congress had provided in the Land Ordinance of 1785 that section sixteen in each township, or one thirty-sixth of the land, should be reserved for schools.[5] It thereby established a precedent for the continued violation of the principle that the public lands were being held for the benefit of all the states. When, subsequently, Congress made one grant after another to the western states, resentment in the older states intensified. The Virginia Act of Cession was not the only basis for their claim that the benefits of the public domain should be shared by all. Equally important was the fact that the Revolution had been won by all thirteen original states at much cost to themselves and that the cession of territory made by Great Britain had been made to the United States.

Thus there developed two major divisions of opinion on public-land questions. The one concerned with the sharing of the land or its benefits among the states became essentially an East-West conflict between the thirteen original states, who were supported after a time by some of the older public-land states. They were opposed by the newer public-land states who felt that the land should be theirs and as their resources produced income it should be reinvested within their boundaries. The second division was similarly sectional, and even more political, with the more conservative eastern states wishing to prevent the public-land states of the West from drawing population away from the East, thereby reducing its congressional representation and also affecting land values and employment costs in the older area.

How was the public domain to be disposed of? In considering this question the Congress of the Confederation and later Congresses had the experience of the mother country and of the thirteen colonies to draw upon. During this long period of 180 years, great estates of millions of acres had been granted to the Penn, Calvert, Fairfax, and Granville families and smaller holdings, ranging in size from a few thousand to several hundred thousand — even a million — acres had been bestowed on many more influential persons. These estates were farmed by tenants who paid their landlords both rents and services. By the close of the Revolution the largest of these estates had been forfeited or confiscated, and there had been a considerable division of properties into smaller holdings for sale, although these changes were far from revolutionary. Some proprietors who had either evaded taking a stand in the Revolution or who had wisely opted for rebellion, managed, like the Schuylers, Livingstons, and Van Rensselaers of New York, to retain their holdings. Despite the radicalism of the Declaration of Independence and the agrarian uprisings of the time, the period of the Confederation was marked by the establishment of additional large private holdings, by Massachusetts in its New York lands, by Virginia in Kentucky, and by Tennessee and Georgia, which all distributed their lands in the most profligate manner. However, estate making was paralleled in the southern colonies by the headright system, and in New England the proprietors' grants were soon divided. Consequently freemen in good standing with the authorities were able to acquire small tracts of land, and, generally speaking, the larger holdings were interspersed with small farms. The very liberality of the various land systems

had proved to be the principal attraction to settlers from the Old World.[6] By 1790 the population of the United States was already 40 percent of that of Great Britain.[7]

After the Revolution neither of these colonial precedents was at first to be followed. The egalitarian ideas of the time, the growing hostility between the owners of large estates and their tenants, and the financial needs of the federal republic sufficiently account for the fact that the United States did not make extensive *grants* of land to influential people (it did make large sales to two influential groups), but neither did it adopt the headright system with its free grants to free men. The public domain was needed for other purposes.

Alexander Hamilton was anxious that the public lands should provide revenues for the heavily indebted young nation. By an act of 1790 the income from land sales was pledged solely to payment of the nation's debts.[8] Hamilton expected that speculators and land companies would be the principal buyers and that they would then retail the land to actual settlers. At the outset, then, Congress created a wideopen land system with no limitation upon the amount of land individuals could buy. Not until the mid-nineteenth century were any limitations to be placed on purchases, and these proved quite ineffective.

Questions concerning the pricing of land, the speed at which it should be surveyed and opened for settlement, and the treatment to be meted out to squatters who had helped themselves to the public domain soon created that second fundamental division of opinion between East and West previously referred to. Hamilton had hoped for prompt sale of the public land in large blocks. Later, the conservative attitude toward the public lands, favored by Henry Clay and, during his early career, by Daniel Webster, was that the lands should be surveyed and opened to settlement only when older areas had been well taken up and improved and the land should be offered at prices that would not tend to draw farmers away from these older areas since their leaving might adversely affect land values and also the wages of labor. Moreover, slow extension of surveys and opening the land to settlement would facilitate compact growth, keep management costs down, and ensure the early introduction of roads, schools, churches, and local government, and mean good order. But western pressure groups advocated the speedy opening of new land, the conservative policy was breached, the thinly maintained barriers were broken. The frontier of settlement advanced from Florida to Louisiana, and up the Mississippi to Arkansas and Missouri, and from Ohio to Illinois to Michigan, and new territories and states were created. Soon population reached Utah territory, the Oregon country, and California. Before long the Superintendent of the Census was deploring, with a little less than accuracy, that the frontier was gone. The Webster-Hayne argument about what section had done more for the West was futile, for it was the new West, with its vigorous restless representatives, that had demanded the reduction of all barriers and the elimination of the Indians from any area attractive to whites, and they had been successful in wresting from reluctant representatives of the older states concessions in the price of land and in the terms of purchase. They obtained a general prospective Preemption Law for the protection of squatters and a Homestead Law, subsequently supplemented by additional legislation that made free homesteads of various sizes available to settlers who complied with specific requirements.

The sales policies that were in force everywhere up to 1862 and in areas previously declared open to sale until 1889, plus the government's practice of rewarding veterans with bonuses of land, not cash, had the dual effect of creating both small properties and numerous extensive speculator holdings, the latter often of choice land. The result was the development of a strong antimonopolist feeling in the West and a land reform movement in the East, initiated by men like George

Henry Evans and Horace Greeley who saw in the public lands the means of alleviating the lot of eastern workingmen. But not until 1866 was the principle of land limitation adopted, and then only for the five southern states of Arkansas, Alabama, Florida, Louisiana, and Mississippi. Some congressmen supported the act more as a punitive than a reform measure. George W. Julian, an Indiana congressman and the most realistic of the land reformers, hoped that by limiting the forty-six million acres of public lands remaining in these states to homestead entries of no more than eighty acres it would be possible to provide farms for the freedmen and landless whites. Unfortunately the lands available for entry under the Southern Homestead Act were covered with longleaf pine or were sandy barrens not well adapted to farming. The poorer class and the freedmen received little benefit from the act. Upon the insistence of southern congressmen, who felt that the measure was a shameful discrimination, it was repealed in 1876.[9]

Although the Homestead Act of 1862 was for a time an outstanding success in enabling many thousands of settlers with little capital to become farm owners, the development of large properties continued even after this fundamental change in policy. Its effectiveness in contributing to the creation of farms was limited by the abuse of the settler laws, the use of dummy entrymen, the continuation of the cash-sale system, and the extraordinarily generous sharing of the public lands with the railroads and the states which did not allow free homesteads on their part. Not unitl 1888-1891 did Congress get around to adopting a general limitation of 160 acres upon land entries, by which time 365,000,000 acres or an area ten times the size of Illinois were not open to homesteading and an additional 50,000,000 acres had passed into the hands of speculators waiting for the rise in the value of their holdings.[10]

The federal government's control of the public domain has been a major factor in shaping federal-state relations. From the outset the new states learned to respect the powers of the national government and to look to it for assistance. When a new state was admitted into the Union it was required to write into its fundamental law the famous clause, irrevocable without the consent of the United States, disclaiming all right and title to the unappropriated lands, including the right to tax them, and declaring that the public lands "shall be and remain at the sole and entire disposition of the United States," that nonresident-owned land should never be taxed higher than resident-owned land, and that public land, when sold, should be exempt from taxation for five years. This practice was begun with the admission of Ohio in 1803, made more explicit with the admission of Louisiana in 1812, and somewhat modified by the omission of the tax-exemption clause when Michigan was admitted in 1837.[11]

The western states detested these infringements on their sovereignty, which meant that they were not being admitted to the Union on the same basis as the original states, but, anxious for statehood, they accepted them.[12] Besides, what the federal government took away with one hand it began returning with the other. New states received the sixteenth section in each township for schools, as the Land Ordinance had provided, and also land for seminaries and a university, the salt springs, and 5 percent of the net proceeds from the sale of public lands within their borders for construction of roads. As time went on, increasingly generous grants were made to states on their admission or, subsequently, for education, for the drainage of wetlands, and for the construction of roads, canals, or railroads. Few factors had a greater influence on breaking down states-rights' parochialism than the federal government's practice of sharing the public lands and the income derived from them with the states. The West learned to look to Washington for assistance with projects it could not yet afford. Constitutional limitations on the power of the federal government to undertake them were evaded with the argument that these gifts

of public land to the states would increase the value and hasten the sale of the land that was retained. Yet, despite federal generosity, the attitude of the West on the public-land question remained ambivalent. The western states benefited from federal policy and resented it, because public land within their borders was not all their own to manage as they saw fit.

By sharing portions of the public land with the states the federal government obliged them to create their own land-administering agencies. At the outset the public-land states were under heavy pressure to make their lands available to settlers or other buyers as speedily as possible. They gave little attention to the possibiliy of withholding the lands for higher prices so that they would more adequately serve the purposes for which they had been granted. Later on, states were less prodigal in their management policies and were to obtain larger endowments for schools and universities. One could say that by the twentieth century most of the newer states were doing about as well with their lands as the federal government, some even better. Local control over portions of their resources did not always mean that the newer western states permitted self-seeking interest to dictate improvident management and sales policies. Indeed, in the twentieth century the great giveaway has been more characteristic of federal than of state policies.

At the outset the grants for railroads were made to states which either undertook construction of the lines themselves or conveyed the land to private corporations. In either case, the state had prime jurisdiction over them. When interstate transcontinentals were planned in the 1860s, Congress granted the land directly to the corporation, which meant that the states could not regulate these railroads, could not tax their lands until they had been sold and the title conveyed to individuals, and could not compel forfeiture of unearned grants so as to open the land to homesteaders. The railroad mileage of the country increased from 9,021 in 1850 to 123,320 by 1895. I have not tried to determine what proportion of this mileage was built with the aid of land grants. It included most of the main lines of the Union Pacific, the Southern Pacific, the Santa Fe, the Burlington Northern, the Rock Island, the Northwestern, the Milwaukee, the Illinois Central, and the Missouri Pacific. Six new states were admitted into the Union between 1850 and 1885. All the rest of the West was divided into rapidly growing territories, from which seven states had been admitted to the Union by 1896. The construction of the railroads and the colonization work they carrried on played a vital part in this rapid development.[13] Altogether an area about the size of Texas was granted for railroads. The Association of American Railroads has long devoted much time and energy to an attempt to convince the country that the grants were mostly of mediocre land.[14] They did include desert land, poor grazing land, and barren mountain tops. But they also included choice corn-belt land in Illinois, Missouri, Iowa, and Nebraska, and excellent wheat land in North Dakota, Montanta, and Colorado. Some of the richest and most heavily timbered lands in Washington and Oregon passed to railroads, as did oil- and coal-bearing lands today worth billions of dollars. Much of the latter they still retain (or at least the subsurface rights to such land), although the public transportation services these railroads were supposed to supply have dwindled away.[15]

Representatives of the original thirteen states became resentful of the liberality with which Congress was sharing the public domain with the western states, building them up with grants for roads, canals, and railroads which the older states had had to provide for themselves, and drawing their farmers and their labor away to the cheaper and more fertile lands of the West. The older states recalled that it had been agreed that the public domain should benefit all the states. It was theirs too, was it not? They were determined to get their share. In 1832 Henry Clay, a native Virginian, who regarded the terms of the Virginia cession as binding on the government, brought forth a bill to distribute the net proceeds from the sale of the public lands among the states in proportion to their federal ratio and with a special bonus allowed to the states in which the land was sold. Jackson vetoed it.[16] The older states then prepared an alternative to Clay's distribution plan. This was the act which directed that the federal surplus, largely derived from public-land sales, be deposited with the states, strictly in proportion to their federal ratio. It became law and was in operation only a short time before it was suspended.

A third effort of the older states to share in the proceeds from western-land sales reached enactment in the Distribution Act of 1841, but to win support for its adoption they had to accept features they detested: allowing general prospective preemption of settlers on public lands before the public sale and granting 500,000 acres of land to each public-land state for the building of internal improvements. Distribution lasted for but a moment, but the western gains were permanent.

In the 1850s, when Congress was granting lands lavishly to the western states for railroads and swampland drainage and was doubling its grants to new states for public schools, representatives from the non-public-land states came forth with proposals that they should share directly in the public lands. One measure, which passed the House but not the Senate, would have given 29,250,000 acres to the non-public-land states for public schools; the Dix bill, which easily passed Congress but was vetoed by President Pierce, would have given every state large grants in proportion to their size and population for the improvement in the case of indigent insane people; a third measure, the Morrill Land Grant College Act of 1862, gave 30,000 acres of land or scrip (land-office money) for each senator and representative to which it was entitled for the establishment of colleges of agriculture and mechanic arts. This marked the high tide of the movement for the older states to share in the public lands. Since it could not be argued that grants for agricultural colleges would increase the sales value of the remaining public lands, as the railroad grants had been expected to do, it is obvious that the Land Grant College Act was a practical recognition and application of the principle of the Virginia cession and a strong step toward a more liberal interpretation of the constitutional powers of the federal government.

Unfortunately, many of the new colleges were to find they had not the resources to support research in the newer agricultural sciences. Farm leaders, realizing the inadequacies of the new institutions, moved on a broad front to secure more federal aid for them. The agricultural-college scrip given to the landless states of the East had entitled them or their assignees to land in the public-domain states of the West, which strongly resented that fact, particularly as the scrip had been sold chiefly to speculators who thus acquired large holdings cheaply. This time, therefore, it was proposed to ask not for land but for income from public-land sales to subsidize research programs in the agricultural sciences. Since the revenues from public-land sales ranged from $4 million to $11 million annually between 1886 and 1891 some of it could easily be spared. Accordingly the Hatch Act of 1887 authorized appropriations of $15,000 to support agricultural experiment stations in every state and the Second Morrill Act of 1890 authorized a similar annual sum for the support of the land-grant colleges. (The 1890 Act permitted the establishment of more than one college in each state.) The latter sum was to be increased each succeeding year until the annual grant amounted to $25,000.

Westerners regarded as extremely dangerous to their interests an alternate proposal which Morrill of Vermont, Blaine of Maine, Hoar of Massachusetts, and other eastern senators had previously advanced. It would have required *all* the net proceeds from the public lands, after certain deductions, to be invested and the earnings to be distributed among all the states for education according to their federal ratio. In the end Morrill concluded that it was wiser to ask for half a loaf then to risk all. He therefore substituted for this proposal his second Morrill bill which Congress, in great relief, adopted. By 1890 Congress had moved far and broken down many barriers in supporting agricultural experiment stations and in instituting annual appropriations for state colleges. At the same time Congress had prevented the older states from tying up the entire revenue from public lands for which it was shortly to advocate a purely sectional use.

One of the aspects of past American land policies that is giving us trouble today is the manner in which land has been acquired from the Indians. Colonial and British governments were badgered by land promoters, with and without capital, and by frontier settlers to purchase additional land from Indian tribes. Often such persons, impatient for the land, induced the Indians to make private agreements with them and then tried to get their Indian deeds validated. The controversies that grew out of such negotiations, the terms of which were often unconscionable, and which often failed to recognize the claims of minor bands or other tribes to the territory in question, led the British government to insist that only properly accredited representatives of the government should have any part in negotiations with the Indians. Territory in which they were conceded to have rights was declared closed to white settlers, whose unauthorized intrusions had in the past led to Indian raids and warfare. The government of the United States adopted these same policies but did not succeed in preventing Indian wars. There was constant pressure from the South and West for the acquisition of reserves that had been solemnly guaranteed to the Indians. The fur trade brought

Paul W. Gates

white traders into the reservations. Soon the leading traders had the Indians, and particularly the chiefs, so indebted to them that they were able virtually to dominate the treaty negotiations and bring them to the conclusion desired by the whites. Lump-sum payments for the land surrendered by the Indians went to meet their obligations to the traders, who could also look forward to profiting from the annuities agreed upon. Choice sites, often reserved for the chiefs at the instance of the traders, were soon acquired by them. It was the traders who were responsible for the introduction of the individual allotment system into the treaties with the Miami, Potawatomie, Choctaw, Creek, and Chickasaw Indians made during the first third of the nineteenth century. Doubtless the traders contributed also to the Dawes Severalty Act of 1887.[17] Despite the restrictions on alienability, the allotments soon passed into the possession of whites, and those who were responsible for the Act ought to have been well aware what the results would be. Step by step the Indians were deprived of their land, forced or induced to sign treaties and accept terms of compensation which they now regard as unconscionable. By an act of 1946 they have been permitted to reopen their claims on the United States Treasury, and have won $524,000,000 in awards, one tenth of which has gone to predominantly white lawyers. But the Indians, having gained a bagatelle, now want to recover possession of lands they were once cheated out of.[18]

Well before 1890 the best of America's arable lands had passed into private ownership. There remained large areas of dry land east of the Rockies in the intermountain country and in the Pacific Coast states. Irrigation had been practiced on a small scale by Indians in the Southwest, and at the missions in California, and the Mormons had resorted to it from their first settlement in Utah. By the end of the century much private capital had been invested, particularly in the San Joaquin Valley of California, in reclaiming arid land. Overoptimistic esti-

mates of the amount of water available and inadequate appreciation of the soil problems of irrigated areas had resulted in large losses but had shown the possibilities in semiarid areas, if greater financial resources could be obtained for their development and if more careful planning were done. In 1899, 7,528,000 acres in the public-land states were irrigated to some extent.[19] Officials of the western railroads, the real estate interests, and boomer people joined together to win government aid — that is, federal aid for irrigation schemes. Three main proposals came under discussion. Outright cession of the remaining public lands to the states, which might then mortgage them to raise funds for irrigation projects accessible to water; grants to the states to enable them to experiment on a small scale, possibly on pilot projects that might lead to something bigger; finally, federal subvention of irrigation. Cession which had been raised over and over again by western states (and was to come up again in the twentieth century) seemed out of the question in view of the West's continued failure to win sufficient eastern support for this proposal. Small pilot plants were experimented with under the Carey Act of 1894, which promised as much as one million acres to any state containing desert lands that undertook irrigation projects. Little was accomplished. During the next eight years only 11,321 acres were patented, and all together less than a million acres of potentially irrigable land had been selected by the eleven eligible states.

Representative Francis G. Newlands, borrowing heavily from the past, including experience with distribution and the two Morrill Acts, won enactment of a bill to create a revolving fund into which should pour all but 5 percent of the proceeds from public-land sales in the sixteen western states and territories. The monies were to be used for the construction of irrigation works in the states from which they were derived

Estimates of the amount of land that could produce crops if water could be provided ranged as high as 120 to 540 million acres, the former figure being that of Major John W. Powell, though all were extremely optimistic, and based on no careful consideration. Newlands, at one point, estimated the possible irrigable area to be 70 million acres and later reduced the figure to 60 million. Actually, little more than 33 million acres are today irrigated, and this includes Texas which was not a public-land state.[20] The number of farms into which the irrigable lands might be divided ranged as high as three to six hundred thousand. Planners and dreamers — and propagandists of the time — presented the scheme as one outranked in significance only by the Homestead Act of 1862 in its potential for strengthening rural America. The generating of hydroelectric power was not at that time contemplated. However, it was soon apparent that few or no reclamation projects could be financed without attaching them to hydroelectric plants and selling the water and the power, for which there was a ready demand for industrial and domestic use. Willy-nilly then, the Newlands Act, the increasing demands of the West for power, and the fact that irrigated land could repay only a small fraction of the cost of the great dams being planned pushed the government into the development of public power on an immense scale. The planners and dreamers may have thought of establishing a rural Arcadia in the West, but today their accomplishments are more commonly judged by the great industrial development and vast urban sprawl on the once-desert lands of southern California and parts of Arizona and New Mexico.

By the late twenties the West was dissatisfied with the slow progress of water and power projects financed with the aid of the revolving fund of the Newlands Act.[21] Actually the fund failed to revolve, again because of poor planning of the projects. Soon western interests were urging that additional appropriations for reclamation and power projects be made out of general funds. The greater part of the more than seven billion dollars expended to date by the Bureau of Reclamation has been supplementary appropriations from general funds. Nothing comparable to this enormous expenditure of public funds, ostensibly for the irrigation of farmland but increasingly to provide at very low rates hydroelectric power and water for domestic and business uses in the West, has been made in any other section of the country. Even the subsidized Tennessee Valley Authority power development in the South is a small venture in comparison with public power in the West.

Despite the generous treatment the West received from the federal government, it remained dissatisfied. Western states continued to feel that the remaining public lands ought to be controlled and managed for their particular benefits. Limits on the alienation of the public domain should not be imposed, the public ranges should be thrown open to all users without limit, efforts to halt timber plundering from public lands should be resisted, and the growing conservationist sentiment of eastern men, whom the West at that time dubbed "sentimentalists," should be fought to the bitter end. What the West wanted was no restriction on growth. Only western men familiar with the needs of that section of the country should have responsibility for it. Hence the commissioners of the General Land Office, the registers and receivers of the local land offices, and the House and Senate Committees on the Public Lands, and later members of the Public Land Law Review Commissions should be from the West.[22]

With reluctance westerners had had to accept national parks and national forests and controlled grazing districts on the public range and administration by a bureaucracy centered in Washington, but they had the political clout to provide in legislation that the income of these agencies from the sale of products and services should be spent in the West. An act of 1905 appropriated the revenues from the national forests for "the protection, administration, improvement and extension" of the forest reserves, but two years later it was provided that 10 percent of

Paul W. Gates

such revenues, later increased to 25 percent, should be returned to the states or territories in which they were collected for the support of schools and roads. Step by step other provisions for returning to the states portions of the revenue from the public lands were adopted: 37.5 percent of the income from sales and royalties for coal, oil, and gas taken from the public lands was allocated to the states of origin and 52.5 percent of these revenues to the Reclamation Fund. Approximately the same distribution was made of the income from the enormously rich lands once granted to the Oregon and California Railroad but revested in the United States. Of the income from grazing leases 12.5 percent was allotted to the states and most of the balance was to be spent in improving the range.[23] Despite these generous allocations of funds from the public lands the West was dissatisfied. In its report to the president in 1970, the western-dominated Public Land Law Review Commission urged that, in addition, the federal government should make payments to the states in lieu of taxes for public land it still holds in the West, the amount ranging from 60 to 90 percent of taxes on privately owned lands.[24]

Western parochialism appeared in a new guise in 1953 when — inspired by powerful oil interests which found state ownership of natural resources superior for them to federal, combined with a little revived government-type philosophy — it overwhelmed the past vigorous nationalism of the section and induced Congress to convey the tidelands to public-land states and Texas.[25] Though this action greatly reduced the possible flow of money into the Reclamation Fund, that was not a serious matter for long, since Congress under western pressure had taken to voting it public funds from general revenue in great amounts.

The big questions about our national land policies raised at the outset and debated from that day to this are still unsettled. Whose public land is it? For whose benefit is it to be administered?

How should it be managed and by whom?[26] Easterners thought the public domain should benefit the entire Union with special regard to conservation, broadly speaking: westerners thought it should be administered for their benefit. Neither section won completely in the end. The West continues to resent the retention in federal ownership of any land within their boundaries. We seem to be back where we started.

The old debate continues, but there is not the same division of opinion between East and West. There are still elements in the West who feel that the federal government should divest itself of the public lands, if not to individuals as in the old days, at least to the states who, they believe, can manage it best. But there are other elements, both East and West, who feel that the federal government should retain what remains of the public domain, husband it carefully, not primarily for revenue purposes as in the old days, but for careful conservation of our national resources — soil, subsoil, water, trees, and minerals. They feel that the federal government will take the larger view and not allow itself to be pressured by exploitative interests to the same extent it has in the past. Others think that the states are more alert to these dangers. The old debate is still going on but in a larger frame of reference. We now take a broader view of the value of our public domain and have a more acute realization of all the ecological and human interests that must be safeguarded.

It may seem futile to try to decide with the benefit of hindsight whether American land policies have been at all times wise. Not one of the policies adopted worked out in accordance with its advocates' objectives (or what they publicly stated as their objectives); speculator accumulations were rarely contained, whatever the intent of the legislation. Adequate classification of the lands was not made before legislation, sometimes unsuited to it, was applied. Administration was not always efficient or even honest. Endless disputes occurred in some areas. Revenues were wasted. Our national decisions about our public domain were taken originally when the new nation had certain needs and was under certain pressures. Her people had already a hundred and seventy years of frontier experience that had permanently marked their attitude toward the land. As a nation we had had our revolutionary experience, and our forefathers, some of them at least, had certain ideological hopes for the future as a nation. Newcomers arrived, drawn hither by various hopes and experience in societies dominated by landlords. The techniques of agriculture and transportation and industry were at any moment at a given stage of development. All these factors influenced our land policies.

In conclusion, may I suggest that while the mangement of our remaining public domain is still a most serious and important problem, the management of that portion of our territory that has become private property is a more serious problem. In fact, the old distinction between public and private property is losing its sharpness, or is being eroded away, and for the sake of later generations it should be. Has a man a right to destroy good, irreplaceable agricultural land by covering it up with cement or by stripmining it? Can a man do what is most profitable for him with his own? But is it his own in an unlimited sense? Rather has he not received from society in the ownership of land a bundle of rights which society protects but which society may also limit or modify or even take over? Is not the public land that has passed into private hands a trust? Older and more crowded societies than ours have long since been obligated to take this stand, and we should come to this point of view also and soon.[27]

12

Harry N. Scheiber

Property Law, Expropriation, and Resource Allocation by Government, 1789-1910

Expropriation of private property by government is seldom found on the list of policies which have influenced the course of economic development in American history. To be sure, the once-vigorous myth of ante-bellum laissez faire has been discarded, and it is no longer taken as a startling proposition that governmental interventions to promote and regulate the economy occurred regularly throughout the nineteenth century.[1] But for two reasons, I think, expropriation as an instrument of conscious resource allocation has failed to receive from historians the attention it deserves.

In the first place, the whole notion of property takings on an involuntary basis by means of eminent-domain law — what Corwin termed that "most invidious branch of governmental authority" — runs against the broad tendency to stress the stability of property rights in the American legal order.[2] When the "institutional environment" of United States economic development is analyzed, the legal system is usually portrayed as one "in which property received extreme protection," and the doctrinal concern of law-

Reprinted from the *Journal of Economic History*, vol. 33, no. 1 (March 1973) 232-251, by permission. Copyright, 1973, Economic History Association.

makers for vested property rights is cited as "the basic doctrine of American constitutional law."[3] Even when historians examine the police power of government, it is often on the assumption (which I have argued elsewhere is flatly wrong) that only with the Supreme Court's decision of the Granger Cases in 1877 did the common-law doctrine of "property affected with a public interest" establish the "ground rules" necessary to validate far-reaching regulative interventions.[4] Presumably, up to that time the legal system had operated largely to strengthen the bulwarks of vested rights; the "liberty" rather than the "duties" or "public obligations" of property, as Commons asserted, was ascendent in the law. Entrepreneurs had to acquire the property they needed for their undertakings through market transactions, while vested-rights doctrines served to protect established interests in property.[5]

The second reason why expropriation gains little scholarly attention is that it lacked the visibility a policy issue of this sort would gain by its debate and definitive resolution in Congress. Simon Kuznets has written that each decade of nineteenth-century American growth "marked some decision by the [government] — on currency, on tariffs, on internal improvements, on land, on immigration — and each one was reached after explicit discussion in which its importance for the country's economic growth was realized."[6] Unlike the policy decisions on Kuznets's list, the law of eminent domain was the product of policy making at the state level, and there were striking differences of policy from one state to another. Moreover, many issues that centered on expropriation policy were resolved by the state courts, not constitutional conventions or even legislatures, and there was significant variation in the timing, as well as outcome, of decisions. Not until 1848 did the federal Supreme Court hand down a decision directly on the eminent-domain power of state governments. Both then and subsequently, its role was mainly a validating one, supportive of state autonomy and tolerant of substantial diversity.[7]

From what one scholar has termed the "massive body of case law, irreconcilable in its inconsistency, confusing in its detail and defiant of all attempts at classification,"[8] one can still identify some coherent policy patterns that indicate the place of expropriation in the larger fabric of "institutional environment," the "decision rules" of the legal system, and the spectrum of policy instruments by which government allocated resources.[9] The following discussion attempts to illuminate these themes and to offer both a conceptual and a narrative framework for historical study of expropriation in the United States to 1910. No measurements are offered concerning the redistributive effects of eminent-domain policies. But an effort is made to identify the directions in which expropriation was purposefully used to allocate resources, to influence the structure of entrepreneurial opportunity, and even to provide effective subsidies for favored types of business enterprise, often at high cost to "vested rights" in property.

In the colonial period, the provincial legislatures had authorized the taking of land for highways and other transport facilities, while milldam laws and, to some extent, fisheries regulations had "qualified" property rights in a manner that validated coercive takings.[10] Even so, few of the early state constitutions contained explicit definitions of the eminent-domain power or its limitations. It therefore fell largely to the courts to develop the fundamental doctrines of eminent-domain law.

The state judiciaries proved uniformly disposed to derive from natural law, civil law, and common law three basic concepts which by the early 1820s had become firmly engrafted onto the constitutional law of the states. These concepts were: (1) that the eminent-domain power was an inherent attribute of sovereignty, so that private property was held subject to takings by the state; (2) that this power could be legitimately exercised by the state only for a "public use" or "public purpose"; and (3) that when property was so taken, the injured private owner must be paid a "just" or "fair" compensation. Taken at face value, these three doctrines comprised a legal fortress behind which property would be secure from arbitrary or uncompensated expropriation. They expressed a theory that the cost of public undertakings would be "socialized" rather than left to fall upon those individual property owners who happened to stand directly in the path of improvements.[11]

The "public use" limitation did not arouse substantial controversy, so far as projects built and operated by government itself were concerned; a public road or a state canal project was clearly a public use. But the courts went further than mere validation of coercive property takings in such cases. They also formulated a series of *expediting doctrines* to complement the basic expropriation concepts. These doctrines found their justification in the extraordinary public importance of such projects (for example, the Erie Canal — termed by Chancellor Kent "a great public object, calculated to intimidate by its novelty, its expense, and its magni-

Harry N. Scheiber

tude"[12]); the expediting doctrines were designed to render the power of the state consistent with the magnitude of such undertakings. Hence the ante-bellum state courts generally ruled that a private property owner who wanted to challenge state officials engaged in eminent-domain takings was restricted exclusively to statutory remedies; he was foreclosed from resorting to the traditional equitable remedies, such as nuisance, trespass, and damage suits.[13]

Another important expediting doctrine limited the right to compensation only to property that was physically taken. Indirect or consequential damages were not deemed compensable. One landmark decision, by the Massachusetts court in 1823, ruled that a house owner had no right to compensation when the city regraded the street, exposing the house's foundations and destroying accessibility. "Every one who purchases a lot upon the summit or on the decline of a hill," the court declared, "is presumed to foresee the changes which public necessity or convenience may require."[14] One is left to ponder whether John Winthrop, when he announced the building of "a citty upon a hill," should have appended a *caveat emptor!* Pennsylvania's court, in a similar ruling, admitted that such a rule left an individual to "be made involuntarily to contribute much more than his proportion to the public conveniences" — precisely what eminent-domain law was designed to avert — but offered plaintiffs the solace that they had "at least the miserable good luck to know that they have companions in misfortune."[15] Finally the Supreme Court, in 1857, upheld this devastating interpretation of the compensation requirement on the broad grounds that "private interests must yield to public accommodation."[16]

A third expediting doctrine related to procedure. So long as a statute provided specific procedures by which damages were appraised, could be appealed, and would be paid, there was no constitutional requirement that a jury trial should be permitted, or the like.[17] Finally, most state courts permitted legislatures to mandate that benefits to the remaining property of an owner who lost only part of it under eminent-domain takings should be "offset" against the appraisal of damages. This offsetting doctrine held down the state's costs, and it provided the basis for a potentially large involuntary subsidy for the projects being undertaken. Though a precise quantitative estimate of that subsidy cannot be calculated,[18] the frequent references to the offsetting doctrine's effects in court records and other sources suggest that the subsidy was a considerable one.

To validate a set of cost-reducing doctrines, all in the name of great public works owned and operated by the government, was one thing. But the most important single development in early-nineteenth-century eminent-domain law probably was the wholesale transfer of these doctrines to the private sector, in aid of incorporated companies on which legislatures devolved the power of eminent domain. That was something else again.

Devolution of the eminent-domain power upon turnpike, bridge, canal, and railroad companies was done in every state.[19] Indeed, if such companies had lacked the power to take property coercively for rights of way, they would have been left at the mercy of any individual landowner disposed to be stubborn or extortionate. Once a state legislature decided to vest its eminent-domain power in a private corporation, the courts would generally rule that this carried with it all the expediting doctrines originally conceived to support the sovereign exercise of governmental power by the state itself. Hence in some states railroad companies were enabled to acquire land at virtually no cost, on grounds that the benefits to the landowners' remaining property entirely offset the value of property taken. In Ohio, for example, railroads were notoriously successful in obtaining appointment by the courts of friendly appraisers who would assess benefits as equal to all the damages, and in Illinois, railroad takings frequently resulted in assessment of damages of one dollar. In New York, Vermont, Massachusetts, and other states, subsidization of railroads through offsetting had become common by the 1850s.[20] Similarly, the courts afforded to both private transport-project promoters and milldam builders the same immunity to actions for nuisance, trespass, and torts as had been granted earlier to state officials. The property owner who dared seek a common-law injunction against such private promoters was put down with a heavy hand by the courts. And so long as some (almost any) procedure was specified in statutes for compensation of owners who lost land to companies exercising the eminent-domain power through devolution, equitable remedies were foreclosed.[21]

The courts also authorized a corporation, once vested with the eminent-domain power, to exercise that power repeatedly to expedite alterations or enlargements of the project within the broad terms of its state charter, and so abutting landowners stood in constant jeopardy. Justifying this interpretation of eminent-domain devolution, the Illinois court stated flatly that a railroad company must be able to lay its hands on whatever it might need "for its own convenience or the public accommodation." Similarly, in Massachusetts the high court validated property takings beyond what was originally expropriated by a railroad on grounds that "these works are comparatively new, and improvements are constantly making in the structure and management of the works, and thus companies may profit by their own experience and that of others." Besides, the corporation's own officials could best judge the extent of its needs, "and their decision therefore must be definitive"![22]

Judges spun a fine web of doctrine to justify such devolutions of power on private companies. One thread was theoretical: it was for the legislature, in its exercise of the majestic powers of sovereignty, to decide where to place the expropriation power and how to wield it,

"not only where the safety, but also where the interest or even the expediency of the state is concerned." Jurists who were reluctant to adopt so sweeping a formal validating doctrine might instead insist that the legislature had a free hand in devolving the eminent-domain power "for some necessary and useful purposes."[23] Another doctrinal thread was unwound from the common law: in many states, courts cited the common-law concept of riparian property that was not strictly private but rather *publici juris* — under special obligations, or a "servitude," to the public. Expropriation was justified for privately financed canals and railroads in these courts because like navigable rivers and highways they would have to be kept open to the public, or (like turnpikes) their proprietors were "compellable to permit the public to use them, on paying toll."[24]

Courts also drew upon long-standing legislative precedents afforded by the milldam acts. In many states, because of the importance of gristmills to a farming community the legislatures had extended special privileges to millers. Among these privileges was the power to overflow neighboring lands in order to create a millpond or reservoir for waterpower. To compensate owners of the land overflowed, the milldam statutes had provided for either annual assessment by commissioners of the income loss incurred, or else a once-for-all damage judgement.[25]

Beginning in the mid-1830s and continuing through the next three decades, numerous states greatly extended the milldam principle by devolving the expropriation power upon manufacturing firms in quest of water-power sites for purposes other than grinding grain. The New Jersey court was the first to adjudicate a case challenging this dramatic enlargement of eminent-domain doctrines. When that state's legislature authorized a private corporation to expropriate land for the development of some seventy mill sites along a six-mile stretch of the Delaware River, lawyers resisting the project termed it a blatant attempt to "take private property for private use" — a legal innovation that would render worthless the "public use" limitation on the eminent-domain power. But the court upheld the statute. Even though the corporation's primary purpose was private profit, the court said, "The ever varying condition of society is constantly presenting new objects of public importance and utility; and what shall be considered a public use or benefit, must depend somewhat on the situation and wants of the community for the time being."[26]

Massachusetts followed suit soon afterward, its high court ruling that a tide-dam corporation given the expropriation power, "although commenced with a view to the private advantage of the stockholders, promised to be of immense and certain utility to the state."[27] Although New York, Georgia, and Alabama courts refused to permit expansion of the "public use" concept to validate expropriation for general manufacturing purposes, the enthusiasm spread widely to other states. By 1870 such laws had been upheld in Main, Connecticut, New Hampshire, Wisconsin, Indiana, and Tennessee. The most pragmatic sort of validating doctrine was adopted in all these states: that if water-power development "would largely conduce to the prosperity of the state," as one critic phrased it, then expropriation of land at dam sites was constitutional.[28]

In effect these states gave to certain manufacturing firms the status of public utilities. But this was done only to justify arming them with power to expropriate some of America's choicest water-power sites, such as those on the Connecticut River, the Delaware, and the Merrimac. Needless to say, legislatures that were so anxious to attract manufacturing investment did not seek to *regulate* such enterprises as public-utilities doctrine might have justified. The manufacturers had the best of both worlds.

Before turning to the period after 1870, brief observations are warranted regarding three subsidiary questions that entered into the history prior to that time.

In the first place, there was substantial opposition by some lawyers, jurists, and political leaders who regarded the successive expansions of eminent-domain doctrines as dangerous. For many conservative figures, such as Daniel Webster and Joseph Story, the focus of their concern was a position taken by several state courts in the 1840s, holding that even corporation franchises could be taken under eminent domain. Such a doctrine, Webster contended, would destroy the climate of investment which had favored economic progress, and in the hands of "ultra" legislative radicals could lead to an "unlimited despotism."[29] But when the issue finally came before the Supreme Court in 1848, the Court found that a state could authorize the taking of a chartered company's bridge and its conversion to a public way, upon payment of compensation to the company. The eminent-domain power, the Court declared, was "paramount to all private rights vested under the government."[30]

Others who opposed the eminent-domain power's extension were men on the other side of the political spectrum. Suspicious of monopoly and privileged corporations, they denounced "offsetting" and other expediting techniques as instruments to exploit the "little man," the simple farmer or householder who was subjected to loss of property to a favored business enterprise without truly just compensation.[31] But this group obtained no more support from the Supreme Court than did the property-minded conservatives. For in 1850 the Court ruled that even if the facts showed that a governmental taking blatantly violated both the "public use" and "fair compensation" requirements of a state constitution, "it rests with the State legislatures and State courts to protect their citizens from injustice and oppression of this description."[32] Beginning in the 1850s, however, opponents of the extended eminent-domain power had begun to push through some reforms in state constitutional conventions. In language widely copied later by other state conventions, Ohio's constitution writers in 1851 wrote a provision that if a corporation took property under eminent domain, it must provide prior payment to the injured property owner, with compensation to be determined "irrespective of any benefit from any improvement proposed by such corporation, ... by a jury of twelve men." Iowa followed suit in 1857, and the 1859 Kansas constitution included a provision nearly identical. Over the next thirty years, other states adopted the Ohio model for constitutional reform on these lines.[33]

A second important feature of pre-1870 eminent-domain law was the wide application, in state courts, of the "fair compensation" requirement as a *negative check* on the police power. Courts invoked the compensation doctrine, in other words, to require government to indemnify property owners for some types of damage that resulted from regulatory statutes. Cases of this sort proved especially important as they influenced governmental efforts to allocate resources on internal waterways: they raised a host of questions about the legitimate reach of regulatory laws to protect public fishing rights, about milldam and log-boom franchises on rivers, and about the protection of navigational rights on streams deemed "under servitude to the public."[34]

Finally, it is noteworthy that by the 1850s the doctrine of "public use" developed in eminent-domain litigation was having major spillover affects in taxation law and in the law of nuisances. The extensive state aid and local assistance given private railroad corporations, beginning in the 1850s, was justified by the courts on the same grounds as had legitimated devolution of the eminent-domain power.[35] As to the law of nuisances, the doctrine that certain types of business enterprise were so vital as to justify eminent-domain devolution could also be turned to their advantage by immunizing such enterprises from nuisance-damage liability. Thus the courts afforded to railroads a sweeping immunity from common-law suits against smoke or noise pollution. And in Pennsylvania and other states where the importance of mining as a "leading industrial interest" had been invoked by the courts to validate takings of property to build strictly private roads into mines, the same courts held that mining companies were not liable for damages resulting to downstream proprietors from their pollution of streams. "The necessities of a great public industry, which although in the hands of a private corporation, subserves a great public interest," the Pennsylvania court declared, justified such "trifling inconveniences to particular persons" as the contamination of a house owner's domestic water supply! Thus, in nuisance law, as in the jurisprudence of expropriation, "the rough outline of natural right or natural liberty," as an Alabama judge averred, "must submit to the chisel of the mason, that it enter symmetrically into the social structure."[36]

The heyday of expropriation as an instrument of public policy designed to subsidize private enterprise can probably be dated as beginning in the 1870s and lasting until about 1910. During that era of alleged laissez faire (which in fact was a period of broad-ranging public subsidies for business), all the constitutional stops were pulled out.

No longer did judges or framers of state constitutions rely so much upon sophistries about "public use." Instead, they now merely paused to assert prescriptively that one private interest or another — mining, irrigation, lumbering, or manufacturing — was so vitally necessary to the commonweal as to be a public use by inference. In some of the western states, they went beyond that; without verbal evasion, they simply declared certain types of private enterprises to be "public" in their constitutions. All this was done, moreover, despite the availability of the Fourteenth Amendment — an instrument which the courts readily used when they decided to invalidate state laws to regulate private enterprise.[37]

By the time this period of eminent-domain law had begun, the legal doctrines forged in the East had already provided a sufficient foundation for

Harry N. Scheiber

newer states to break through the cake of legal custom. Indeed, two of the most frequently cited precedents in this period came from New England. One was the case of *Talbot* v. *Hudson*, a Massachusetts decision of 1860 which declared:

It has never been deemed essential that the entire community or any considerable portion of it should directly enjoy or participate in an improvement or enterprise, in order to constitute a public use ... [E]verything which tends to enlarge the resources, increase the energies, and promote the productive power of any considerable number of the inhabitants of a section of the State, or which leads to the growth of towns and the creation of new sources of private capital and labor, indirectly contributes to the general welfare and to the prosperity of the whole community.[38]

A New Hampshire case of 1867, *Great Falls Manufacturing Company* v. *Fernald*, stressed the need to adapt law to the realities of topography and climate. Validating as constitutional an act that authorized a general manufacturing firm to overflow neighboring lands to create a reservoir for water-power, the court stated: "Nature has denied us the fertile soil and genial climate of other lands, but by way of compensation has endowed us with unrivaled opportunities of turning our streams of water to practical account." It was legitimate, the court declared, to make the law bend to the dictates of nature and comport with "the character of our business and the natural productions and resources" of the state.[39]

Little wonder that these doctrines should have proved attractive to jurists in the far-western states in ensuing years. For there, the hardships of life in arid lands and mountain fastnesses, the nature of the resource base, vast distances, and, above all, men's impatience to force the pace of economic development, all seemed to overwhelm the remaining bulwarks of legal-constitutional structure.

Colorado blazed the path of eminent-domain law for the West. That state's constitutional convention of 1875-76 adopted a provision that private property might be taken for *private use* "for private ways of necessity, ... reservoirs, drains, flumes, or ditches on or across the lands of others, for mining, milling, domestic, or sanitary purposes."[40] Other Rocky Mountain states followed this model closely.[41] In the Idaho constitutional convention of 1889, the debate over expropriation produced a sharp clash of farming interests against miners. Neither interest group stood for an abstraction that can be termed "vested rights"; rather, each wanted the upper hand in the rivalry to exploit common resources. The bitter debate over what one delegate termed "a doctrine that is anti-republican in every respect, ... contrary to the right to hold property ... or to pursue happiness" ended in a compromise.[42] Idaho's constitution thus declared as a public use all uses of land for irrigation and drainage purposes, for the draining and working of mines including "the working thereof, by means of roads, railroads, tramways, cuts, tunnels, shafts, hoisting works, dumps or other necessary means to their complete development, or any other use necessary to the complete development of the material resources of the state." For these purposes might private property be expropriated upon payment of compensation.[43]

To the state courts that subsequently reviewed statutes enacted under these western constitutions, doctrinal support for such elevation of private uses to an exalted constitutional status derived as well from a landmark Nevada territorial decision of 1876. Upholding an act of 1875 authorizing expropriation of land, lumber, and other construction materials by mining companies, the court distinguished between two types of business enterprises. On the one hand, there were ordinary businesses that could be conducted without regard to a specific site location, and this type was ineligible for eminent-domain devolution. On the other hand, there were businesses such as mining which were tied to a particular resource site; for this type of enterprise, a clear necessity for eminent-domain devolution existed.[44] This Nevada decision was widely cited in other western states. But interestingly enough, it was almost always for its blanket declaration that "an interest of great public benefit to the community" warranted expropriation for private use. Emblematic of the spirit which prevailed in the western courts was the fact that the "site necessity" argument — a more impressive one by far — was left in the background.[45]

Given western terrain and the distribution of mineral resources, it was inescapable that the exigencies of site, or location, should often be controlling. This was highlighted in a Montana case of 1895, in which a railroad company sought to block the expropriation of part of its right of way (not actually in use for track) and repeated crossing of its tracks by a second railroad, then under construction, building into the Butte Hill mining area. The court ruled that if the Anaconda, the Wake Up Jim, the Buffalo, the Moscow, and other mines in this region were to be benefited by the second railroad, then the "publicity" (that is, "public use") of the enterprise was "too obvious to require more extended comment." For in that locality, mining was "the all-important pursuit" and so "benefits to the public" deriving from benefits to the mining companies could hardly be doubted.[46] In the scramble for development in this country where men dug ore out of mountains, the niceties of eminent-domain limitations — which even in the more genteel eastern states had been treated with some sophistry — thus gave way without "extended comment."

In Idaho the legislature enacted a law in 1887 for devolution of the eminent-domain power which, after revision in 1903, embraced the following: "wharves, docks, piers, chutes, booms, ferries; bridges, toll-roads, by-roads, plank and turnpike roads; steam, electric, and horse railroads; reservoirs, canals, ditches, flumes, aqueducts, and pipes; [projects] for public transportation, supplying mines and farming neighborhoods with water, and draining and reclaiming

lands," and for storing logs.[47] Reviewing this statute in 1906, the Idaho court found little in the state's constitution that could fault such a law, for unless the eminent-domain power was as broad as this, "a complete development of the material resources of our young state could not be made."[48] On similar grounds, the courts of Nevada, Montana, Colorado, Idaho, Washington, New Mexico, and Arizona upheld laws permitting expropriation of property when necessary for purposes of running an irrigation canal or ditch across private land. For, as the Arizona territorial court insisted, a legislature must be permitted to use (or devolve) the power of eminent domain so that local "advantages and resources may receive the fullest development for the general welfare."[49] Elsewhere the public-utilities doctrine was invoked to validate takings for private irrigated farming: so long as water companies could be regulated, they could be vested with eminent-domain power.[50]

A vital part of the constitutional context was, of course, the response of the Supreme Court when the western states' doctrines were challenged. In a word, the Supreme Court largely upheld local practices. As early as 1871 the Court had begun to tighten the requirements for "just compensation" by ruling that certain kinds of consequential, or indirect, damages constituted a "taking" of property.[51] And in 1897 the Court expressly ruled that the Fourteenth Amendment in effect applied the Fifth Amendment's "just compensation" requirement to all state-sanctioned eminent-domain proceedings.[52] But when the legitimacy of the broad expropriation power for explicitly "private use" in the western states came before the Court, there was no comparable will to intervene. California's laws permitting water companies to condemn private land for irrigation purposes were tested before the Court in 1896 and were upheld. Eight years later, in the case of *Clark* v. *Nash*, the Court validated a Utah statute authorizing an individual to condemn a neighbor's land in order to convey water to his own. If the taking "be essential or material for the prosperity of the community," the Court declared, it was valid.[53] Such statutes must be adjudged by a standard of constitutionality, said that Court, that takes account of "peculiar condition[s] of the soil or climate":

> The validity ... may sometimes depend upon many different facts, the existence of which would make a public use, even by an individual, where, in the absence of such facts, the use would clearly be private ... [The State's own courts] understand the situation which led to the demand for the enactment of the statute, and they also appreciate the results upon the growth and prosperity of the State ... The Court must recognize the difference of climate and soil, which render necessary these different laws in the States so situated.[54]

No doubt the Supreme Court may well have been moved to leave such broad discretion with the arid-land states out of sympathy, too, for efforts to prevent "water monopoly" from blocking new settlement or leaving latecomers at the mercy of men who had already established title to lands along the region's streams.[55] But its solicitude reached beyond the concerns of small farmers to embrace mining corporations, lumber companies, and railroad interests as well, and in 1907 the Court upheld an eastern railroad's taking of property to construct a spur track which would serve the factory warehouse of a large shipper and relieve congestion at the company's existing terminal and yards. The Court recalled that it had consistently upheld state courts' positions on what constituted a "public use" in expropriation cases, and it reaffirmed that it would give sympathetic consideration not only to evidence as to "the resources" and "the capacity of the soil" but also as to "the relative importance of industries to the general public welfare, and the long-established methods and habits of the people."[56]

By about 1910, the configuration of expropriation law had begun to change markedly in the United States. As mentioned earlier, many states adopted changes in their constitutions, such as requiring jury trials in cases of takings by private corporations, narrowing the range of permissible "offsetting" procedures, and requiring prior payment in cases of expropriation. In addition, numerous state constitutions were amended to require compensation not only when property was "taken" but also when "damaged."[57] By this time, moreover, eminent-domain powers were being employed as an instrument of city planning and improvement; and the practice of "excess condemnation" was becoming a central issue much debated in legislatures and in courtroom litigation.[58] Later in the twentieth century, especially with the beginnings of massive regional development in the Tennessee Valley and with dramatic expansion of the federal urban-renewal law and highway programs, the main focus of eminent-domain law has shifted to government projects and their social consequences. As the checkered history of the urban and highway programs amply attests, however, the interpenetration of private business interests and governmental programs justifying expropriation continues to be a central problem of public policy. Nor has the expropriation power proved to be a policy instrument less fearsome in the hands of governmental authorities than it had been in the heyday of "private use". Witness the uses of eminent domain in recent decades to obliterate black urban neighborhoods or to cut broad highways through treasured landscapes at such high cost to our ecological heritage.[59] Hence perhaps the most important continuity in public debate over expropriation, coming down to our own day, is the widely shared sense that the appalling technical complexities of eminent-domain law, troublesome enough in themselves, are but the surface manifestation of the serious social inequities associated with it. To be sure, there has lately been a radical cutback in sovereign tort immunities, so that many issues which in 1910 would have reached the courts as eminent-domain cases now do so instead as tort suits against the government.[60] But genuinely searching reappraisal and reform of expropriation law are probably only commencing.

To understand expropriation policy in the present era requires an appreciation of how that policy functioned in that earlier period of American economic history which has been our concern here. If nothing else, closer study of our own history may offer a perspective from which to appraise such policy documents as one issued by the White House and disarmingly entitled "Economic Assistance and Investment Security in Developing Nations." This fascinating contribution to the Pax Americana warns the developing nations that "the wisdom of any expropriation is questionable, even when adequate compensation is paid." It goes on to specify sanctions that the United States government will impose against nations that violate three American requirements in cases of expropriation: "That any taking of American property will be non-discriminatory; that it will be for a public purpose; and that [our] citizens will receive prompt, adequate compensation."[61] It would be a salutary thing, perhaps, to ponder that a doctrine of public use "depend[ing] somewhat on the situation and wants of the community for the time being" was expounded by a respected American court more than a century before Fidel Castro offered his own variant of it — or to consider what place "prompt, adequate compensation" has had in our own country's historic law of property taking.[62]

Another purpose to be served by reappraisal of expropriation as an American policy instrument is one more narrowly the profession's, concerned as we are with understanding the legal rules by which American capitalism flourished in the nineteenth century. It is to look anew at the standard notions of stability of property rights, and to reconsider the simplistic definitions of "vested rights" and interpretations of how those rights were treated in the law. In short, we ought to test through empirical study Willard Hurst's contention (so ably documented in his own pioneering scholarship) that how the nineteenth-century American legal system functioned "in the name of vested rights had less to do with protecting *holdings* than it had to do with protecting *ventures*."[63]

13

Morton J. Horwitz

The Transformation in the Conception of Property in American Law, 1780-1860

The productive development of land and natural resources at the beginning of the nineteenth century drew into question many legal doctrines formulated in an agrarian economy. In the eighteenth century the right to property had been the right to absolute dominion over land, and absolute dominion, it was assumed, conferred on an owner the power to prevent any use of his neighbor's land that conflicted with his own quiet enjoyment.[1] Blackstone, in fact, asserted that even an otherwise lawful use of one's property could be enjoined if it caused injury to the land of another, "for it is incumbent on a neighboring owner to find some other place to do that act, where it will be less offensive."[2] Not until the nineteenth century did it become clear that, because this conception of ownership necessarily circumscribed the rights of others to develop their land, it was, in fact, incompatible with a commitment to absolute dominion. Logical difficulties had been easily concealed by experience, since the prevailing ideal of absolute property rights arose in a society in which a low level of economic activity made conflicts over land use extremely rare. As the spirit of economic development began to take hold of American society in the early years of the nineteenth century, however, the idea of property underwent a fundamental transformation — from a static agrarian conception entitling an owner to undisturbed enjoyment, to a dynamic, instrumental, and more abstract view of property that emphasized the newly paramount virtues of productive use and development. By the time of the Civil War, the basic change in legal conceptions about property was completed. This article examines the process by which the change took place.

Property Rights in the Nineteenth Century: The General View

Two potentially contradictory theories of property rights underlay eighteenth-century legal doctrines for resolving conflicts over uses of property. The first, an explicitly antidevelopmental theory, limited property owners to what courts regarded as the "natural" uses of their land, and often "natural" was equated with "agrarian." For example, in cases involving the conflicting claims of two riparian owners, courts usually gave precedence to appropriation of water not only for domestic purposes but often for agriculture and husbandry as well.[3]

Abridged from *University of Chicago Law Review*, 40 (1973), 248-261, 290, by permission.

Natural uses of land were probably favored also by strict liability in tort: any interference with the property of another gave rise to liability; only the lowest common denominator of noninjurious activity could avoid a suit for damages. The frequency with which eighteenth-century courts solemnly invoked the maxim *sic utere tuo, ut alienum non laedas*[4] is a significant measure of their willingness to impose liability for injury caused by any but the most traditional activities.

The second theory of property rights on which courts drew in the eighteenth century, though it appeared in a variety of legal forms, amounted to a rule that priority of development conferred a right to arrest a future conflicting use. Sometimes this rule was simply stated by the long-standing maxim "first in time is first in right." More refined formulations required that the first user be engaged in his activity for a period of time sufficient to ripen into a prescriptive property right against interfering activities.

At first glance, the rule of priority seems more compatible with economic development, since it gives at least the first user freedom to develop his land as he wishes. By contrast, doctrines based on natural use confer on all landowners equal power to maintain the traditional order of things and thereby to impose a continuing pattern of nondevelopment. Before the nineteenth century, however, the theory of property was harnessed to the common antidevelopmental end. Where two neighboring parcels of land were underdeveloped, each owner could claim a right, based on priority, to prevent further development. Thus, depending on the level of economic development from which one begins to measure priority, the consequences of the theories of natural and prior use may be the same; since the lowest level of development is also the earliest, each party acquires a prior right to the land in its natural state.

Furthermore, just as the theory of priority could be reduced to one of natural use, so could the natural-use doctrine claim to enforce a rule of priority. If the starting point for judgment is not the first introduction of a new use on the land but rather the prior state of inactivity before the new use appears, then once again the doctrines of priority and natural use yield the same result. Indeed, when in the name of economic development the inevitable attack on eighteenth-century property doctrine begins, these two are regularly lumped together by their opponents as parts of one theory.

Though the two theories can be merged, they can also be made to have profoundly different consequences. If priority is measured not from a common denominator of natural use but from the time that a new technology appears, the theory of natural use coninues to enforce its antidevelopmental premises, but a rule of priority now confers an exclusive property right on the first developer.

The potential for conflict between the two theories first began to surface in the nineteenth century. There are, for example, no cases before then dealing with conflicts over use of water in which an English or American court acknowledges that different consequences follow from a rule of "natural flow" as opposed to one of "prior appropriation." Courts were induced to distinguish between the two rules in such cases only when the judges began trying to break away from the antidevelopmental consequences of common-law doctrine.

Once priority and natural use had taken on different operational meanings, the common law had moved into the utilitarian world of economic efficiency. Claims founded on natural use began to recede into a dim preindustrial past, and the newer "balancing test" of efficiency came into sharp focus. As priority came to take on a life of its own distinct from doctrines of natural use, it was put forth not as a defense against encroachments of modernity but as an offensive doctrine justified by its power to promote economic development. In a capital-scarce economy, its proponents urged, the first entrant takes the greatest risks; without the recognition of a property right in the first developer—and a concomitant power to exclude subsequent entrants—there

Morton J. Horwitz

cannot exist the legal and economic certainty necessary to induce investors into a high-risk enterprise.

Though the strength of its hold varied among particular areas of the law, in general, priority became the dominant doctrine of property in the early stages of American economic growth. Its development paralleled that of pervasive state-promoted mercantilism in the early-nineteenth-century American economies; while it was displaced almost immediately in some areas of the law, in others it continued to stand firm well into the century.

The attack on the rule of priority reveals the basic instability of utilitarian theories of property. As property rights came to be justified by their efficacy in promoting economic growth, they also became increasingly vulnerable to the efficiency claims of newer competing forms of property. Thus, the rule of priority, wearing the mantle of economic development, at first triumphed over natural use. In turn, those property rights acquired on the basis of priority were soon challenged under a balancing test or "reasonable use" doctrine that sought to define the extent to which newer forms of property might injure the old with impunity. Priority then claimed the status of natural right, but only rarely did it check the march of efficiency. Nor could a doctrine of reasonable use long protect those who advanced under its banner since its function was to clear the path for the new and the efficient. Some of its beneficiaries eventually reclaimed the doctrine of priority, this time asserting the efficiency of "natural monopoly" and the inevitability of a standard of priority.

Viewed retrospectively, one is tempted to see a Machiavellian hand in this process. How better to develop an economy than initially to provide the first developers with guarantees against future competitive injury? And once development has reached a certain level, can the claims of still greater efficiency through competition be denied? By changing the rules, and disguising the changes in the complexities of technical legal doctrine, the façade of economic security can be maintained even as new property is allowed to sweep away the old.

The plan that the historian sees in retrospect, however, is not what the participants in this process saw. They were simply guided by the conception of efficiency prevailing at the moment. Practical men, they may never have stopped to reflect on the changes they were bringing about, nor the vast differences between their own assumptions and those of their predecessors.

Water Rights and Economic Development

The extensive construction of mills and dams at the end of the eighteenth and beginning of the nineteenth centuries gave rise to the first important legal questions bearing on the relationship of property law to private economic development, and it was here that the antidevelopmental doctrines of the common law first clashed with the spirit of economic improvement.[5] As a result, the evolving law of water rights had a greater impact than any other branch of law on the effort to adapt private-law doctrines to the movement for economic growth.

Most of the legal controversies over water rights were of three types. The first, and by far the most important, involved an action by a downstream riparian landowner against his upstream neighbor, either for diverting the stream for agricultural purposes or for obstructing the natural flow of water in order to raise an upstream mill-dam. As dams grew larger, a second set of cases dealt with the suit of an upstream mill owner against the downstream mill owner for throwing the water back so far as to impede the wheels or impair the fall of the upper mill. In a third group of cases, arising under the mill acts passed by most states, a neighboring landowner sued the proprietor of a mill who had flooded his land by raising a dam. Since the far-reaching impact of the mill acts is discussed later in this article, the discussion here will focus on the widespread changes in the rules regulating the exploitation of water resources during the first half of the nineteenth century. This branch of law is important not only because of its direct influence on the course of early economic growth but also because the problems it was forced to confront and the legal categories developed for dealing with them reveal the basic structure of thought about all forms of property in the nineteenth century.

"WITHOUT DIMINUTION OR OBSTRUCTION"

Two basic assumptions determined the approach of the common law to conflicts over water rights. First, since the flow of water in its natural channel was part of nature's plan, any interference with this flow was an "artificial," and therefore impermissible, attempt to change the natural order of things. Second, since the right to the flow of a stream was derived from the ownership of adjacent land, any use of water that conflicted with the interests of any other proprietor on the stream was an unlawful invasion of his property. A late-eighteenth-century New Jersey case clearly expressed the prevailing conception:

> In general it may be observed, when a man purchases a piece of land through which a natural water-course flows, he has a right to make use of it in its natural state, but not to stop or divert it to the prejudice of another. *Aqua currit, et debet currere* is the language of the law. The water flows in its natural channel, and ought always to be permitted to run there, so that all through whose land it pursues its natural course, may continue to enjoy the privilege of using it for their own purposes. It cannot legally be diverted from its course without the consent of all who have an interest in it. . . . I should think a jury right in giving almost any valuation which the party thus injured should think proper to afix to it.[6]

The premise underlying the law as stated was that land was not essentially an instrumental good or a productive asset but rather a private estate to be enjoyed for its own sake. The great English gentry, who had played a cental role in shaping the common-law conception of land, regarded the right to quiet enjoyment as the basic attribute of dominion over property. Thus the New Jersey court regarded the legitimate uses of water as those that served domestic purposes and husbandry, requiring insignificant appropriations of the water's flow. All other interferences with the natural flow of water, including both diversion and obstruction, were illegal "without the consent of all who have an interest in it." Exploitation of water resources for irrigation or milldams, which necessarily required significant interference with the natural flow of water, was thus limited to the lowest common denominator of noninjurious development, just as conflicts over the use of land were invariably resolved in favor of economic inactivity.

When American judges first attempted to resolve the tension between the need for economic development and the fundamentally antidevelopmental premises of the common law, the whole system of traditional rules was threatened with disintegration. Some courts went so far as virtually to refuse to recognize any right to prevent interference with the flow of water to a mill. Connecticut courts, for example, for a while limited the lower proprietor to the rights to prevent waste and to receive enough water to satisfy "necessary purposes."[7] Even after discarding this doctrine in 1818, Connecticut jurists continued to disagree over whether a right to water was based on the common-law rule of natural flow or was gained only by a long-standing pattern of appropriations.[8] The Supreme Judicial Court of Massachusetts in *Shorey v. Gorrell* (1783)[9] held that without long usage sufficient to confer a prescriptive right, there was no legal basis for preventing a newcomer from obstructing a stream. As a result, there were Massachusetts cases that denied any relief against even the substantial diversion of a stream for the

Morton J. Horwitz

purpose of irrigation.[10] Although it appears that the Massachusetts courts soon succeeded in eroding the force of *Shorey* v. *Gorrell* by treating the plea in prescription as a mere matter of form, efforts to escape from the restrictive consequences of common-law doctrines continued into the early nineteenth century as claims for relief against obstruction by upstream dams became more common. Some judges maintained that the common-law action for diversion was simply not applicable to the temporary obstruction of water by upstream dams.[11] Others sought to modify the common-law definition of legal injury in order to permit extensive, uncompensated use of water for business purposes.

The most important challenge to the common-law doctrine was the so-called reasonable use or balancing test. Though it did not ultimately prevail until the second quarter of the nineteenth century, a handful of decisions early in the century had already laid the ground for its eventual triumph. In the earliest case, *Palmer* v. *Mulligan*,[12] a divided New York Supreme Court for the first time held that an upper riparian landowner could obstruct the flow of water for mill purposes. The common-law action for interference with the flow of water, Judge Brockholst Livingston said, "must be restrained within reasonable bounds so as not to deprive a man of the enjoyment of his property." Courts, Livingston argued, must be prepared to ignore "little inconveniences" to other riparian proprietors resulting from obstruction of the natural flow. Otherwise, he reasoned; "he who could first build a dam or mill on any public or navigable river, would acquire an exclusive right, at least for some distance, whether he owned the contiguous banks or not; for it would not be easy to build a second dam or mound in the same river on the same side, unless at a considerable distance, without producing some mischief or detriment to the owner of the first."[13]

Palmer v. *Mulligan* represents the beginning of a gradual acceptance of the idea that the ownership of property implies above all the right to develop that property for business purposes. Livingston understood that a rule making all injuries from obstruction of water compensable would, in effect, confer an exclusive right of development on the downstream property. The result, he concluded, would be that "the public, whose advantage is always to be regarded, would be deprived of the benefit which always attends competition and rivalry." Again, in *Platt* v. *Johnson*,[14] in which the court held in favor of an upstream mill owner whose dam occasionally detained the flow of water for a number of days, the court observed that the sacred common-law maxim *sic utere* "must be taken and construed with an eye to the natural rights of all." The court revealed a fundamentally new outlook on the question of conflicting rights to property: "Although some conflict may be produced in the use and enjoyment of such rights, it cannot be considered, in judgement of law, an infringement of right. If it becomes less useful to one, in consequence of the enjoyment by another, it is by accident, and because it is dependent on the exercise of the equal rights of others."[15]

These two cases marked a turning point in American legal development.[16] Anticipating a widespread movement away from property theories of natural use and priority, they introduced into American common law the entirely novel view that an explicit consideration of the relative efficiencies of conflicting property uses should be the paramount test of what constitutes legally justifiable injury. As a consequence, private economic loss and judicially determined legal injury, which for centuries had been more or less congruent, began to diverge.

Change in common-law doctrine, however, is rarely abrupt, especially when a major transformation in the meaning of property is involved. Common lawyers are more comfortable with a process of gradually giving new meanings to old formulas than with explicitly casting the old doctrines aside. Thus, it is not surprising that, in periods of great conceptual tension, there emerges a treatise writer who tries to smooth over existing stresses in the law. Some such writers try to nudge legal doctrine forward by extracting from the existing conflict principles that are implicit but have not yet been expressed. Joseph Story's work in equity or commercial law comes to mind as an example. Others seek to banish novelty and to return the law to an earlier and simpler past. Joseph Angell was of the latter variety.

In his treatise *Watercourses*, published in 1824, Angell reaffirmed the common-law view that all diversion and obstruction of the natural flow of water was actionable. His only concession to a rule of equal or proportionate use was to observe that since the common-law rules "are undoubtedly liable to a rational and liberal construction," they would not allow "a right of action for every trivial and insignificant deprivation."[17] Although in *Palmer* v. *Mulligan* the New York court had attempted to justify its break with the past by showing that the injury to the lower mill owner was slight, Angell attacked the decision as "certainly contrary to the authorities, and obviously unjust."[18] In short, Angell's treatise asserted the traditional common-law view that the only test for a reasonable use of water was the absence of all but the most trivial injury.

Though Angell sought to consolidate the past not a moment too early, his efforts hardly counted. The common law is especially cruel to those whom it casts aside. It either ignores them, soon forgetting that they ever existed, or, more usually, uses them as authority for propositions they did not accept. Angell's fate lay somewhere in between. In 1827, Justice Story wrote his influential opinion in *Tyler* v. *Wilkinson*,[19] citing all manner of contradictory authority, including, of course, Angell's treatise. Thereafter, Story was taken to have merely restated Angell's position and the clear inflexibility of the latter's analysis was forever replaced by the soothing, oracular quality of Story's formulation. Whenever Angell is cited afterwards, though the words be his, the meaning is supplied by Story.

Story's opinion is the classically transitional judicial opinion, filled with ambiguities sufficient to make any future legal developments possible.[20] It opens with a reaffirmation of traditional doctrine: the riparian owner "has a right to use of the water ... in its natural current, without diminution or obstruction ..."[21] But even as he stated this principle, Story seemed to perceive its harsh antidevelopmental tendencies and he attempted to qualify its rigor. "I do not mean to be understood," he wrote, "as holding the doctrine that there can be no diminution whatsoever, and no obstruction or impediment whatsoever ... for that would be to deny any valuable use .... The true test of the principle and extent of the use is, whether it is to the injury of the other proprietors or not." Some "diminution in quantity, or a retardation or acceleration of the natural current" is permissible if it is "not positively and sensibly injurious ...."[22]

By insisting, after all, that the true test of the riparian doctrine was reasonable use, but that reasonableness meant simply the absence of injury, Story managed to finesse the pressing problem of determining the extent to which conflicting and injurious uses of property could be regulated in the interest of economic development. Despite his invocation of the reasonable-use formula in *Tyler*, however, it is clear from later opinions[23] that he, like Angell, wished to perpetuate the principle of natural flow.[24]

Tyler v. *Wilkinson*, which spawned a line of decisions opposed to all diversion or obstruction of water regardless of any beneficial consequences,[25] marks the nineteenth-century high point in articulating the traditional conception of property that had already come under attack. Not only did it express a preproductive view of property as entailing the right to undisturbed ownership free from all outside interference, but proceeding from eighteenth-century conceptions of absolute property rights, it condemned all conflicting injurious uses of land without consideration of whether such exploitation would maximize total economic welfare.

Yet, by acknowledging that the utilitarian criterion of valuable use was the ultimate source of legal rules, Story's reasonable-use standard became almost immediately an open-ended formula through which common-law judges could implement their own conceptions of desirable social policy. As a result, *Tyler v. Wilkinson* is cited during the second quarter of the nineteenth century more often to support than to condemn the reasonableness of a mill's interference with the flow of water.

The effort to free property law from its antidevelopmental premises was still very much a struggle at mid-century. As late as 1852, Massachusetts Chief Justice Shaw still found it necessary to argue that the law did not bar all obstructions of a watercourse, "without diminution, acceleration, or retardation of the natural current," else "no proprietor could have any beneficial use of the stream, without an encroachment on another's right . . . ."[26] By the time of the Civil War, however, most courts had come to recognize a balancing test, making "reasonable use" of a stream "depend on the extent of detriment to the riparian proprietors below."[27]

"THE USAGES AND WANTS OF THE COMMUNITY"

It is important to appreciate the central role that the refashioning of American water law to the needs of industrial development played in the more general transformation of the law of property in the nineteenth century. Between 1820 and 1831 the productive capacity of American cotton mills increased six-fold.[28] Joseph Angell noted that more cases on the subject of water rights had been decided in the years between 1824 and 1833, when the first and second editions of his *Watercourses* appeared, than

during the entire previous history of the common law.[29] Under the powerful influence of this rapid development, judges began to understand that the traditional rights of property entailed the power to exclude would-be competitors and that some injurious use of property was an inevitable consequence of any scheme of competitive economic development. They sought to free the idea of property from its exclusionary bias by enlarging the range of noncompensable injuries. The increasing frequency with which courts appealed to the idea of *damnum absque injuria*[30] seems to have occurred in direct proportion to their recognition that conflicting and injurious uses of property were essential to economic improvement.

The most dramatic departure from common-law riparian principles took place in Massachusetts, where, ever since the colonial mill acts, it had been the practice to confer privileges on mill owners in order to promote the growth of industry. As mills proliferated, a new set of technological considerations began to upset conventional legal doctrine. Since the amount of water power that a mill could generate depended largely on the fall of water, an increase in the height of a lower dam often reduced the fall of water from an upper dam. At the same time, the construction of large integrated cotton mills after 1815 unleashed such an enormous demand for water power that, as one observer noted in 1829, "in very many cases, only one of many proprietors can, in fact, improve a (stream) because the occupation of one mill site may render the others useless. Which proprietor shall, in such case, be preferred?"[31]

Chief Justice Shaw pondered this question in *Cary v. Daniels*.[32] "One of the beneficial uses of a watercourse," he began, "and in this country one of the most important, is its application to the working of mills and machinery; a use profitable to the owner, and beneficial to the public." Proceeding from this new utilitarian orthodoxy, Shaw stated a legal doctrine strikingly different from Story's earlier formulation. Not only did the law require "a like reasonable use by the other proprietors of land, on the same stream, above and below," but it also took account of the "usages and wants of the community" and "the progress of improvement in hydraulic works." It required that "no one can wholly destroy or divert" a stream so as to prevent the water from flowing to the proprietor below, nor "wholly obstruct it" to the disadvantage of the proprietor above.[33] Thus, despite its invocation of "reasonable use," Shaw's formulation tended to erode a standard of proportionality: a mill owner who did not "wholly" obstruct a stream might claim that "the needs and wants of the community" justified his using more than a proportionate share of the water.

That Shaw intended this result is clear from *Cary* v. *Daniels* itself, in which the chief justice expressly rejected proportionality under the circumstances "growing out of the nature of the case."[34] Under manufacturing conditions then existing, he observed, beneficial uses of water were often, of necessity, mutually exclusive. Where the power needs of particular manufacturing establishments were such that maximum exploitation of limited water resources required a monopoly, "it seems to follow, as a necessary consequence from these principles, that ... the proprietor who first erects his dam for such a purpose has a right to maintain it, as against the proprietors above and below; and to this extent, prior occupancy gives a prior title to such use."[35]

Shaw's opinion is premised on the desirability of maximizing economic development even at the cost of equal distribution. There was, of course, no reason why he could not have held that the permissible limits of economic growth were reached at the point at which exploitation of water resources was equal, that large cotton mills had to pay their own way to the extent that their operation exceeded the limits of proportional appropriation. Indeed, judges could also have demanded, a half-century earlier, that equality of use be achieved through compensation of existing riparian owners. In the nineteenth century, however, there were few limits to the dominant mentality of maximization. When proportionate use was regarded as more efficient than priority, proportionality became the standard of reasonable use. When, in turn, proportionality stood in the way of the efficient use of water resources, the law returned to priority as the standard of reasonable use.

As *Cary* v. *Daniels* demonstrated, the doctrine of reasonable use could assimilate its historic antagonist—the rule of priority—and thereby make monopoly reasonable once again. Once the question of reasonableness of use became a question of efficiency, legal doctrine enabled common-law judges to choose the direction of American economic development. By the time of *Cary* v. *Daniels*, they were so captivated by the spirit of improvement that they were willing to manipulate the concept of property to conform to their own notions of the needs of industrialization. In the seventeen years after *Tyler* v. *Wilkinson*, the direction of the law had turned entirely around.

Conclusion

The American conception of property in the period between the Revolution and the Civil War was changed to permit the destruction of older forms of property by newer agents of economic development. In the process of change, land came to be viewed almost exclusively as a productive asset, and ownership of property was justified not for its own sake but for its contribution to increased national wealth. Legal doctrines, in turn, were transformed by this instrumental conception of property. At the beginning of the century, property law tended to encourage high-risk investment through a doctrine of priority which conferred exclusive property rights on the first developer. By the middle of the century,

Morton J. Horwitz

however, the law had shifted to a reasonable use or balancing test which allowed newer entrants to compete while destroying the claims that existing property owners had acquired under older legal doctrines. In the process of responding to the changing and often unstable utilitarian standard of efficiency, the American conception of property was harnessed to the paramount goal of economic development.

14

Leonard W. Levy

The Law of the Commonwealth and Chief Justice Shaw

A society reveals itself in its law. Its points of growth and the interests it values may be disclosed even in the decision of a seemingly technical and insignificant legal question. For example, one case confronted Chief Justice Lemuel Shaw with the question of a railroad employee's competency to testify as to the delivery of goods allegedly not delivered by his company. A common-law rule of evidence which had "existed for ages" would have excluded the testimony of an agent in behalf of his principal. But the Massachusetts chief justice made an exception to that rule, stating with more candor than is characteristic of judges that if the rule were followed, "business would be greatly impeded." The decision shows that the law reflected the needs of a new industry, the railroad. It shows, too, that the law was vitally concerned with the future of a recently emergent form of business, the corporation, for, as Shaw said, to follow the old rule "would nearly prevent the operations of corporate companies, who must act entirely through various classes of officers and agents."[1]

Reprinted from Leonard W. Levy, *The Law of the Commonwealth and Chief Justice Shaw*, 303-321, by permission. Copyright, 1957, The President and Fellows of Harvard College.

The ultimate question of legal history is, how does the law of a given time and place meaningfully connect with the society of which it is part? In the United States the question is all the more pressing because, as was noted by Burke, Tocqueville, and Dicey, Americans are the most legal-minded of people. Accordingly, American legal history should show in striking fashion how law is shaped by and in turn shapes the thought and experience of the American people. Tocqueville, a jurist in his own country, was astonished to discover that "scarcely any question arises in the United States which does not become, sooner or later, a subject of judicial debate."[2] In the guise of legal disputes between private parties, matters of high policy involving great stakes are referred ultimately to the courts for decision. Thus the opinions of judges are often political, economic, and social events, as well as legal events.

The relation of the individual to the state and of the states to the nation; the role of the government in the economy; the private and public interests deemed important enough to secure in permanent and authoritative form; the comparative valuation placed on different activities and goals, and on liberty and order; the

Leonard W. Levy

points of tension, growth, and power; and prevailing conceptions of rights, duties, and liabilities: all are exposed in the law.

For thirty years, Lemuel Shaw sat as chief justice, during an age which he said was remarkable for its "prodigious activity and energy in every department of life."[3] America was being transformed by the rise of railroads, steam power, the factory system, and the corporate form of business. A more complex society, urban and industrial, was superseding the older rural, agrarian one. Only a pace behind the astonishing rate of economic change came the democratization of politics and of life. The federal system lumbered toward its greatest crisis. During this time Shaw delivered what is probably a record number of opinions for a single judge: two thousand and two hundred, enough to fill about twenty volumes if separately collected.

At the time of his appointment to the bench, American law was in its formative period. Whole areas of law were largely uncultivated, many unknown, and few if any settled. Although Shaw was not writing on a completely clean slate, the strategy of time and place surely presented an unrivaled opportunity for a judge of strength and vision to mold the law.

In estimating the significance of Shaw's career it would be a mistake to search for the ways in which he altered the direction of social change, for that begins outside the law. Moreover, judges are in an unfavorable position to act as social engineers or innovators. They must wait until litigious battle casts up an issue for decision. Usage demands that they speak only to that issue in its legal character, that they do not unburden themselves on the subject at large, and that they stifle their personal preferences as to matters of wisdom or policy. In the course of deciding a given case, they can repair decayed parts of the legal structure or do some remodeling, but an architectural change takes a generation of decisions. Individual judges do well to keep the law in a state of good preservation so that it may be a place where social tensions are neutralized and the present may meet with and learn from the past.

But great judges like Shaw, who revitalize the law so that it may fulfill its function, can channel and legitimatize social change in as reasoned a way as is possible. This is surely a vital and civilizing task. Willard Hurst has remarked that the great judges have had an ability "to express the times or foretell the generation to come." They were the ones who "saw better where the times led and took their less imaginative, less flexible, or less courageous brethren in that direction with a minimum of waste or suffering."[4] Hurst might have been describing Shaw.

One of the major themes of his life work was the perpetuation of what Oscar and Mary Handlin have called "the commonwealth idea"[5] — essentially a quasi-mercantilist concept of the state within a democratic framework. In Europe where the state was not responsible to the people and was the product of remote historical forces, mercantilism served the ruling classes who controlled the state. In America men put the social-contract theory into practice and actually made their government. The people were the state; the state was their "Common Wealth." They identified themselves with it and felt that they should share, as of right, in the advantages that it could bring to them as a community. The state was their means of promoting the general interest.

A theory of the general interest was common. Shaw expressed it in his address to the Suffolk Bar in 1827 in language he was later to repeat from the bench. Speaking of the "theory of free government," he declared:

It regards men as by nature social, and endowed with powers adequate to enable them, by the establishment of government, to provide for defining and securing their social rights, and under a natural obligation to respect those of others, and it presupposes that all power resides originally in the whole people as a social community, that all political power is derived from them, is designed to be exercised solely for the general good, and limited to the accomplishment of that object; that no powers are, or ought to be, vested in the government, beyond those which are necessary and useful to promote the general security, happiness, and prosperity; and that all powers not delegated remain with the people.[6]

The commonwealth idea precluded the laissez faire state whose function was simply to keep peace and order, and then, like a little child, not be heard. The people of Massachusetts expected their commonwealth to participate actively in their economic affairs. As the Handlins point out, they found "manifestly erroneous" the notion that the economy should be left to its own devices, that the people individually, rather than their government, "are the judges of their interests." That principle was considered "subversive to the end and aim of all governments; and . . . utterly impracticable."[7]

Where risk capital feared to tread or needed franchises, powers of incorporation, or the boost of special powers like eminent domain, the duty of the state was to subsidize, grant, and supervise the whole process in the interests of the general welfare. But regulation was not restricted to those special interests which had been promoted by government aid. Banks, insurance companies, liquor dealers, food vendors, and others were all subjected to varying degrees of control, though the public trough had not been open to them. As the Handlins say, "Massachusetts observers conceived of the beneficent hand of the state as reaching out to touch every part of the economy."[8]

The commonwealth idea profoundly influenced the development of law in Massachusetts. It was largely responsible for the direction taken by the law of eminent domain, for the development of the police power, and for the general precedence given by the courts to public rights over merely private ones. As employed by

Shaw, the commonwealth idea gave rise to legal doctrines of the public interest by which the power of the state to govern the economy was judicially sustained.

The idea "that some privately owned corporations are more public in character than others," as Edwin Merrick Dodd noted, "had already begun to emerge in judicial decisions before 1830."[9] The grant of powers of eminent domain to early turnpike and canal companies had been upheld on grounds that they were public highways, although privately owned. The mill acts, which originated as a means of promoting water-powered gristmills, had also been sustained in early decisions on grounds that a public purpose was served. In this respect, the work of Theophilus Parsons and Isaac Parker, Shaw's predecessors, provided him with useful precedents in support of legislation that advanced both the commonwealth idea and industrial interests.

On the other hand, the earlier judges regretted the extension of the old gristmill acts to new manufacturing corporations. Shaw, by contrast, warmly accepted the mill acts because he believed that industrialization would bring prosperity and progress to the Commonwealth. Accordingly he declared that "a great mill-power for manufacturing purposes" was, like a railroad, a species of public works in which the public had a great interest. He even placed "steam manufactories" in the same class as water-powered mills, as devoted to a public use, although the former were never granted powers of eminent domain.[10] His opinions show reason for believing that he would have sustained far-reaching factory regulation if he had had the opportunity. In such a case, which never arose, the commonwealth idea would have explained his support of the legislature.

Certainly the commonwealth idea underlay those remarkably prophetic opinions of Shaw's that established the basis of the emerging law of public utilities. The old common law of common calling had considered only millers, carri-

Leonard W. Levy

ers, and innkeepers as "public employments"; it "knew no such persons as the common road-maker or the common water-supplier."[11] The "common road-maker," that is, the turnpike, bridge, and canal companies, were added to the list of public employments or public works while Shaw was still at the bar. But it was Shaw who settled the legal character of power companies, railroads, and water suppliers as public utilities, privately owned but subject to regulation for the public benefit. He would have included even manufacturers and banks. The commonwealth idea left no doubt as to whether the state would master, or be mastered by, its creatures, the corporations, or whether the welfare of the economy was a matter of public or private concern.

Indeed the police power may be regarded as the legal expression of the commonwealth idea, for it signifies the supremacy of public over private rights. To call the police power a Massachusetts doctrine would be an exaggeration, though not a great one. But it is certainly no coincidence that in Massachusetts, with its commonwealth tradition, the police power was first defined and carried to great extremes from the standpoint of vested interests. Shaw's foremost contribution in the field of public law was to the development of the police-power concept.

The power of the legislature "to trench somewhat largely on the profitable use of individual property," for the sake of the common good, as Shaw expressed the police power in *Commonwealth* v. *Alger*,[12] was consistently confirmed over thirty years of his opinions. Three decades later, when judges were acting on the supposition that the Fourteenth Amendment incorporated Herbert Spencer's *Social Statics*, the ideas expressed in Shaw's opinions seemed the very epitome of revolutionary socialism. Shaw's name was revered, but the implications of his police-power opinions were politely evaded. In the period between Shaw and the school of Holmes and Brandeis, American law became the graveyard of general-welfare or public-interest doctrines, and doctrines of vested rights dominated.

The trend toward legal Spencerianism was so pronounced by the end of the nineteenth century that legal historians concentrated on a search for the origins of doctrines of vested rights, almost as if contrary doctrines had never existed. When touching the pre–Civil War period, it is conventional to quote Tocqueville on the conservatism of the American bench and bar, to present American law almost exclusively in terms of Marshall, Story, and Kent, and to emphasize that the rights of property claimed the very warmest affections of the American judiciary. So familiar is this view of our legal history that we may summarize it with a paraphrase of Tennyson's "Northern Farmer, New Style":[13]

Proputty, proputty, proputty, proputty
That's what the judges and historians say.

If, however, the work of the state courts were better known, this view might be altered. But Gibson and Ruffin and Blackford are little more than distinguished names, their work forgotten. Shaw's superb exposition of the police power is respectfully remembered, but it is usually treated as exceptional, or mistreated as an attempt to confine the police power to the common-law maxim *sic utere tuo ut alienum non laedas*.

Shaw taught that "all property . . . is derived directly or indirectly from the government, and held subject to those general regulations, which are necessary to the common good and general welfare."[14] Roscoe Pound, in discussing the "extreme individualist view" of the common law concerning the rights of riparian property owners, says the common law asked simply, "was the defendant acting on his own land and committing no nuisance?"[15] But Shaw believed that the common law of nuisances, which was founded on the *sic utere* maxim, inadequately protected the public, because it was restricted to the abatement of existing nuisances. He believed that the general welfare required the anticipation and prevention of prospective wrongs from the use of private property. Accordingly he held that the legislature might interfere with the use of property before its owner became amenable to the common law. So a man could not even remove stones from his own beach if prohibited by the legislature, nor erect a wharf on his property beyond boundary lines fixed by it. Even if his use of his property would be "harmless" or "indifferent," the necessity of restraints was to be judged "by those to whom all legislative power is intrusted by the sovereign authority." Similarly the "reasonableness" of such restraints was a matter of "expediency" to be determined by the legislature, not the court. The simple expedient of having a precise statutory rule for the obedience of all was sufficient reason for a finding of constitutionality.[16]

Thus Shaw, using the commonwealth idea, established a broad base for the police power. He carried the law's conception of the public good and the power of government to protect it a long way from the straitjacketing ideas of Kent and Story. Their position may be summed up in Blackstone's language that "the public good is in nothing more essentially interested than the protection of every individual's private rights."[17]

A review of a few other decisions of the Shaw court on the police power will illustrate that the chief justice's *Alger* opinion was more than rhetoric. The authority of the legislature to shape private banking practices in the public interest was unequivocally sustained in two sweeping opinions. In one, Shaw said that a statute intended to prevent banks from "becoming dangerous to the public" was attacked as unconstitutional on the authority of Marshall, Story, and Kent. The statute allegedly operated retroactively against the bank in question; constituted a legislative assumption of judicial power because it required the Supreme Judicial Court to issue a preliminary injunction against banks on the

findings of a government commission; and violated the contract clause by providing for a perpetual injunction against the further doing of business, in effect a revocation of the charter. Rufus Choate probably never argued a stronger case. But Shaw sustained the statute and the injunction, peppering his opinion with references to the paramountcy of "the great interests of the community," the duty of the government to "provide security for its citizens," and the legitimacy of interferences with "the liberty of action, and even with the right of property, of such institutions."[18]

In a second bank case of the same year, 1839, the court refused "to raise banks above the control of the legislature." The holding was that a charter could be dissolved at the authority of the legislature, under the reserved police power, without a judicial proceeding.[19]

It has been said that from the standpoint of the doctrine of vested rights the most reprehensible legislation ever enacted was the prohibition of the sale of liquor. Such legislation wiped out the value of existing stocks and subjected violators to criminal sanctions, their property to public destruction. Similarly, buildings used for purposes of prostitution or gambling might, on the authority of the legislature, be torn down. The question presented by such statutes was whether the police power could justify uncompensated destruction of private property which had not been appropriated for a public use. The power of the Commonwealth over the health and morals of the public provided Shaw with the basis for sustaining legislation divesting vested rights.[20] On half a dozen occasions, the Wynehammer doctrine of substantive due process of law was repudiated in such cases.

Regulation of railroads was another subject for the exercise of the police power, according to the Shaw court. The same principles that justified grants of eminent domain to railroads, or to canals, bridges, turnpikes, power companies, and water suppliers, also provided the

Leonard W. Levy

basis for sustaining controls over their rates, profits, and services. Railroads, said Shaw, were a "public work, established by public authority, intended for the public use and benefit."[21] The power to charge rates was "in every respect a public grant, a franchise . . . subject to certain regulations, within the power of government, if it should become excessive."[22]

These dicta by Shaw became holdings at the first moment the railroads challenged the "reasonableness" of the rates and services fixed by government railroad commissions. "Reasonableness" was held to be a matter for determination by the legislature or the commission to which it delegated its powers. Those powers, in turn, were broadly construed. The court would not interfere with the regulatory process if the railroads had the benefit of notice, hearing, and other fair procedures.[23] Due process of law to the Shaw court meant according to legal forms, not according to legislation which the court approved or disapproved as a matter of policy.

A final illustration will show the scope of the police power as conceived by the Shaw court. It was held, in an opinion by the chief justice, that because the right to use land washed by tidewaters was a public rather than a private right, the government could validly authorize the uncompensated flooding of a tidemill-owner's property, destroying much of his business.[24] This decision rode roughshod over every doctrine of vested rights. The owner had the misfortune to be located where the "mere regulation of a public right, and not a taking," in Shaw's words, had caused his ruin. Here was a harsh application of the commonwealth idea based on the theory that the owner's loss had been inflicted by the government for the greater good of the community; moreover, that he was compensated by sharing with others in the advantages which derived from regulations of the public rights. As for compensation in the form of damages, it was a case of *damnum absque injuria*.

The latitudinarian attitude of the Shaw court toward the police power was unquestionably influenced by the strong tradition of judicial self-restraint among Massachusetts judges. Although they never questioned their power to hold a statute unconstitutional, they exercised that power only in rare and clear-cut cases. Theoretically, the explanation for such restraint was the doctrine of separation of powers. The courts would not invalidate an act whose wisdom they doubted on grounds of policy if it was passed within the compass of the legislature's delegated powers. Why Theophilus Parsons and Isaac Parker should have adhered so scrupulously to this rule when the federal judiciary and some other state courts did not is hard to understand, unless judicial self-restraint was an outgrowth of the commonwealth idea.

Shaw carried on the tradition of the Massachusetts judiciary in good faith. When he became chief justice, there were only two reported cases in which enactments had been held void by the Supreme Judicial Court. One related to an unimportant and expired act of Congress; the other to a special resolve of the Massachusetts legislature which suspended the statute of limitations in favor of a particular creditor.[25] During the thirty years that Shaw presided, there were only ten cases, one unreported, in which the Supreme Judicial Court voided legislative enactments.

Four of these cases in no way related to the police power. One involved a special legislative resolution confirming a private sale that had divested property rights of third persons without compensation.[26] The second concerned an act by which Charlestown was annexed to Boston without providing the citizens of Charlestown with representative districts and an opportunity to vote.[27] The third, an unreported case decided by Shaw sitting alone, involved the "personal liberty act," by which the state sought to evade Congress's Fugitive Slave Law.[28] Here Shaw felt bound by the national Constitution and by a decision of the Supreme Court of the United States. In the fourth case he invalidated a state act which dispensed with the ancient requirement of grand-jury proceedings in cases of high crimes.[29] In each of these four, the decisions are above any but trifling criticism.

Of the six cases bearing on the police power, three involved legislation egregiously violating procedural guarantees that are part of our civil liberties.[30] The statutes in question had validly prohibited the sale of liquor. But they invalidly stripped accused persons of virtually every safeguard of criminal justice, from the right to be free from unreasonable searches and seizures to the rights that cluster around the concept of fair trial. Shaw's decisions against these statutes, like his decisions ensuring the maintenance of grand-jury proceedings and the right to vote, were manifestations of judicial review in its best sense. There were also dicta by Shaw on the point that the legislature cannot restrain the use of property by ex post facto laws, by bills of attainder, or by discriminatory classifications.

Thus the limitations placed upon the police power by the Shaw court were indispensable to the protection of civil liberties.

The only exception to this generalization consists of the limitation derived from the contract clause of the United States Constitution. But there were only three cases during the long period of Shaw's chief justiceship in which this clause was the basis for the invalidation of statutes. In each of the three, the statutes were of limited operation and the decisions made no sacrifice of the public interest. The legislature in one case attempted to regulate in the absence of a reserved power to alter or amend public contracts; the court left a way open for the legislature's purpose to be achieved under common law.[31] In the other two cases, regulatory powers had been reserved but were exercised in particularly faithless and arbitrary ways: to increase substantially the obligations of a

corporation for a second time, in effect doubling a liability which had been paid off, and to repeal an explicit permission for another corporation to increase its capitalization in return for certain services rendered.[32] The legislature in all three cases had passed a high threshold of judicial tolerance for governmental interference with the sanctity of contracts. The decisions were hardly exceptional considering the facts of the cases and their dates—between 1854 and 1860, after scores of similar decisions by Federalist, Whig, and Jacksonian jurists alike in state and federal jurisdictions.

The striking fact is that there were so few such decisions by the Shaw court in thirty years. Handsome opportunities were provided again and again by litigants claiming impairment of their charters of incorporation by a meddlesome legislature. But the court's decisions were characterized by judicial self-restraint rather than an eagerness to erect a bulwark around chartered rights. In that sense the three cases wherein statutes were voided for conflict with the contract clause were exceptional.

Generally the attitude of the court was typified by Shaw's remark that "immunities and privileges [vested by charter] do not exempt corporations from the operations of those laws made for the general regulation . . ."[33] He habitually construed public grants in favor of the community and against private interests. When chartered powers were exercised in the public interest, he usually interpreted them broadly; but when they competed with the right of the community to protect itself or conserve its resources, he interpreted chartered powers narrowly. To be sure, he held that the police power could in certain respects be contracted away in return for some public benefit to be gained by the contract. But he did not permit the public control over matters of health, morals, or safety, nor the power of eminent domain, to be alienated by the contract clause.

In the face of such a record it is misleading to picture state courts assi-

Leonard W. Levy

duously searching for doctrines of vested rights to stymie the police power. Certainly no such doctrines appeared in the pre–Civil War decisions of the Supreme Judicial Court of Massachusetts, except for the one doctrine derived by John Marshall from the contract clause and so sparingly used by Shaw. The sources from which vested-rights doctrines were derived by others—the higher law, natural rights, the social compact, and other sources of implied, inherent limitations on majoritarian assemblies — were invoked by Shaw when he was checking impairments on personal liberties or traditional procedures of criminal justice.

If this picture does not fit the steoeotype of conservative Whig jurists, the stereotype may need revision. True enough, Shaw was capable of warning against the "encroachments of a wild and licentious democracy" or against the "irregular action of mere popular will."[34] He could applaud the restraints fixed by a well-balanced constitution, call for the "best members" of society to direct the government, and exalt the virtues of private property and the sanctity of chartered rights. Such rhetoric, however, was rare in his judicial utterances and was far outweighed by his affirmations of the power of government to "promote the general security, happiness, and prosperity" of the whole community.

On the great issue which has historically divided liberals from conservatives in politics—government controls over property and corporations—Shaw supported the government. Even when the commonwealth idea was being eroded away by those who welcomed the giveaway state but not the regulatory state, Shaw was still endorsing a concept of the police power that kept private interests under government surveillance and restraint. He would not permit the commonwealth idea to become just a rationale for legislative subventions and grants of chartered powers, with business as the only beneficiary. To Shaw, government aid implied government control, because the aid to business was merely incidental to the promotion of the public welfare. No general regulatory statute was invalidated while he was chief justice.

The idea of individualism was expressed in the law, cheek by jowl with the commonwealth idea, but it was an individualism that differed from that associated with the laissez faire state of the *fin de siécle*. It did not imply an absence of restraints upon private economic enterprise, though it did imply that individuals were economically self-sufficient. In constitutional law, individualism meant that a man's natural rights to life, liberty, and property could not be fettered by the state except by due process of law; nor could property be appropriated to any use but a public one and then only upon just compensation. The more aggressive individual rights, such as freedom of speech, press and religion, were also safeguarded. In criminal law individualism was apparent in the most fundamental of premises: a crime may be commited only by a free moral agent who acts voluntarily, is accountable for his conduct, and is the object of retributive justice.

The individualism of both criminal and constitutional law derived from the incorrigibly individualistic common law, which placed an unlimited valuation upon personal liberty and property. The common law knew society only as so many John Does and Richard Roes, which is to say that it had scant regard for society collectively. Social and economic problems were reflected in the common law merely as conflicts of personal interest between contending parties. They might possess an unequal status and power; their case might involve great and grave social interests. But to the common law, indifferently neutral and, in the hands of lesser judges, generally oblivious to public policy, the parties were theoretically interchangeable personalities to be dealt with on equal terms and with scant regard for others. The system made for impartial justice and protected the rights of persons and property; but its justice was sometimes harsh or indifferent to the general good.[35]

The hero of the common law was the property-owning, liberty-loving, self-reliant, reasonable man. He was also the hero of American society, celebrated by Jefferson as the freehold farmer, by Hamilton as the town merchant, by Jackson as the frontiersman. Between the American image of the common man and the common law's received ideal of Everyman there was a remarkable likeness.

In Shaw's time social conditions provided a congenial climate for the burgeoning of this individual in law and in society. America enjoyed an open class system in which power was fluid and plural, and everyone, including the industrial worker, lusted after capitalistic success. Where "the mentality of an independent entrepreneur" prevailed, as Louis Hartz observed, "two national impulses are bound to make themselves felt: the impulse towards democracy and the impulse towards capitalism."[36] Both made the "extreme individualism"[37] of the common law acceptable.

Individualism and the commonwealth idea were by no means incompatible, despite certain logical inconsistencies. The common law itself punished the injurious use of property by individuals, a fact which Shaw made a point of departure for expansion of the police power. The corporation, an individual in contemplation of law, although soulless, represented the collective enterprise of many individuals, as did the labor union. And both were smiled upon by the common law as construed by Shaw. Yet the corporation also represented a threat to strictly individualistic enterprisers, and on their behalf a grant of incorporation was accompanied by public governance of corporate organization and policy.

It was also on behalf of individuals, and the community too, that the common law frowned upon monopolies and sought to preserve a free competitive market. When, for example, the South Boston Iron Company bought out a shareholder at a price conditioned upon his bond that he would never thereafter engage in the iron business, the Shaw court found a violation of a common-law rule that "bonds in restraint of trade are void." This rule the court said was "suited to the genius of our government and nature of our institutions. It is founded on great principles of public policy and carries out our constitutional prohibition of monopolies and exclusive privileges."[38]

The court enumerated five specific considerations to prove the "unreasonableness" of contracts in restraint of trade.[39] The first, quite interestingly, protected individuals from themselves:

1. Such contracts injure the parties making them, because they diminish their means of procuring livelihoods and a competency for their families. They tempt improvident persons, for the sake of present gain, to deprive themselves of the power to make future acquisitions. And they expose such persons to imposition and oppression.

The other considerations, enumerated by the court, equally reflected the values and spirit of the time:

2. They tend to deprive the public of the services of men in the employments and capacities in which they may be most useful to the community as well as themselves.
3. They discourage industry and enterprise, and diminish the products of ingenuity and skill.
4. They prevent competition and enhance prices.
5. They expose the public to all the evils of monopoly.

The fifth consideration, declared the court, "especially is applicable to wealthy companies and large corporations, who have the means, unless restrained by law, to exclude rivalry, monopolize business and engross the market. Against evils like these, *wise laws protect individuals and the public,*

Leonard W. Levy

by declaring all such contracts void."[40] The "wise laws" of this case were judicial, not legislative, in character, but constituted state action nonetheless. The relationship between the commonwealth idea and individualism is clear enough.

The common law did not often protect individuals from themselves, from monopolies, or from anything. It tended more strongly to express its individualism not by tenderness but by harshly and uncompromisingly treating men as free-willed, self-reliant, risk-and-responsibility-taking individuals. The consequences of such an attitude were, as Roscoe Pound noted, a strict insistence upon full and exact performance of all duties legally undertaken, without allowance for accident or extenuating circumstances and without mercy for defaulters. If a man were tricked or coerced into a legal transaction, said Pound, the law might permit him to sue for the wrong, but declined to set aside the transaction. "If he could not guard his own interests, he must not ask the courts, which were only keeping the peace, to do so for him ... In other words, it held that every man of mature age must take care of himself. He need not expect to be saved from himself by legal paternalism ... When he acted, he was held to have acted at his own risk with his eyes open, and he must abide the appointed consequences."[41] One might add that the spirit of the common law was epitomized in the maxim, "Let the buyer beware" (caveat emptor).

The spirit manifested itself daily in the Shaw court in commercial law and in the law of private contracts. But its most important manifestation, from the standpoint of social consequences, was in cases of railroad and industrial accident, which fell within the compass of tort law. Here the fierce individualism of the common law, even though reflecting the self-reliance that America so highly valued, was devoid of humane considerations. No doubt the law could not have been expected to reward fools for their foolishness. Shaw would not allow damages to a man whose fingers were frozen

when he left the warmth of a stalled train to walk out in the cold in search of an inn, rather than wait with the other passengers for a rescue sleigh. The chief justice was right in ruling that because passengers can take care of themselves, the liability of a common carrier toward them is less than that toward goods entrusted to the carrier's care by a shipper. Yet when an accident occurred despite all precaution, Shaw held railroads liable for damage to freight, but not for injuries to passengers. They took the risk of accidents that might occur regardless of due care.

The rigorous individualism of the common law was especially noticeable in the emergent doctrine of contributory negligence, of which Shaw was a leading exponent.[42] That doctrine required a degree of care and skill which no one but the mythical "prudent" or "reasonable" man of the common law could match. A misstep, however slight, from the ideal standard of conduct, placed upon the injured party the whole burden of his loss, even though the railroad was also at fault and perhaps more so. Comparative rather than contributory negligence would have been a fairer test, or perhaps some rule by which damages could be apportioned.

Probably the furthermost limit of the common law's individualism in accident cases was expressed in the rule that a right to action is personal and dies with the injured party. This contributed to the related rule that the wrongful death of a human being was no ground for an action of damages. But for the intervention of the legislature, the common law would have left the relative of victims of fatal accident without a legal remedy to obtain compensation. It would also have made it more profitable for a railroad to kill a man outright than to scratch him, for if he lived he could sue.

The fellow-servant rule was the most far-reaching consequence of individualism in the law as Shaw expounded it. The rule was that a worker who was injured, through no fault of his own, by the negligence of a fellow employee, could not maintain a claim of damages against his employer. Shaw formulated this rule at a strategic moment for employers, because as industrialization expanded at an incredible pace, factory and railroad accidents multiplied frighteningly. Since the fellow-servant rule threw the whole loss from accidents upon innocent workers, capitalism was relieved of an enormous sum that would otherwise have been due as damages. The encouragement of "infant industries" had no greater social cost.

The fellow-servant rule was unmistakably an expression of legal thinking predicated upon the conception that a free man is one who is free to work out his own destiny, to pursue the calling of his choice, and to care for himself. If he undertakes a dangerous occupation, he voluntarily assumes the risks to which he has exposed himself. He should know that the others with whom he will have to work may cause him harm by their negligence. He must bear his loss because his voluntary conduct has implied his consent to assume it and to relieve his employer of it. On the other hand, there can be no implication that the employer has contracted to indemnify the worker for the negligence of anyone but himself. The employer, like his employees, is responsible for his own conduct, but cannot be liable without fault.

On such considerations Shaw exempted the employer from liability to his employees, although he was liable to the rest of the world for the tortious acts which they committed in the course of their employment. It is interesting to note that Shaw felt obliged to read the employee's assumption of risk into his contract of employment. This legal fiction also reflected the individualism of a time when it was felt that free men could not be bound except by a contract of their own making.

The public policy which Shaw confidently expounded in support of his reading of the law similarly expressed the independent man: safety would be promoted if each worker guarded himself against his own carelessness and just as prudently watched his neighbor; to remove this responsibility by setting up the liability of the employer would allegedly tend to create individual laxity rather than prudence. So Shaw reasoned. It seems not to have occurred to him that fear of being maimed prompted men to safety anyway, or that contributory negligence barred recovery of damages, or that freeing the employer from liability was no inducement to employ only the most careful persons and to utilize accident-saving devices. Nor, for all his reliance upon the voluntary choice of mature men, did it occur to Shaw that a worker undertook a dangerous occupation and "consented" to its risks because his poverty deprived him of real choice. For that matter, none of these considerations prompted the legislature to supersede the common law with employers' liability and workmen's compensation acts until many decades later. Shaw did no violence to the spirit of his age by the fellow-servant rule, or by the rules he applied in other personal injury cases, particularly those involving wrongful death. In all such cases his enlightened views, so evident in police-power cases, were absent, probably because government action was equally absent.

Part Five

Crime, Criminal Justice, and Violence

The history of criminal justice has been one of the most obscure and neglected corners of the history of American law, and of social history as well. But recently, a large body of interesting and stimulating work has appeared. One reason for this new interest has been public concern over the crime and violence that plague American urban life. People are afraid to walk the streets of New York and Chicago at night, a fear that hardly exists in London or Tokyo, and the statistics bear them out.

William Nelson studies criminal justice and its enforcement from 1760 to 1810, an age of revolution and of fundamental change in the functions of criminal justice. Colonial society equated crime with sin, and government spent much of its effort enforcing laws against what we would now call "victimless" crimes. But by the early nineteenth century, the emphasis had shifted dramatically; government had turned to the control of crimes against property, particularly to theft. To a certain extent, "economic distress" lay behind this shift, but Nelson's study invites us to search for a deeper meaning, and to find it in those social values that people sought to further through the use of criminal justice. Another theme

running through the pages of this book, the relationship of law and morality, is touched upon here as well.

Richard Maxwell Brown's work on violence and the vigilante movement deals more directly with violence in American society. Brown attempts to catalog episodes of violence and vigilantism, to put them in a broader context. He finds a relationship between class structure and vigilantism, and he traces how the movements respond to social disorder and failures in the legitimate legal order.

Brown's work appeared in a volume on the history of violence in America sponsored and issued in 1969 by the National Commission on the Causes and Prevention of Violence. Appointment of the commission itself was a response to public outcries over violence — urban rioting in particular. The article by Roger Lane was printed as part of the same collection, but it has a rather different message. Brown looked on vigilante movements as part of a series of important but sporadic eruptions of violence and disorder in our history. Lane argues that the long-term trend in the nineteenth century ran in the opposite direction from violence. The crime rate, Lane finds, was in the last century, slowly declining; over the long haul,

Crime, Criminal Justice, and Violence

urbanization had, he argues, a "settling, literally a civilizing, effect on the population involved," partly because an urban, industrial society cannot "afford" the disorders that can be tolerated in a rural society, where "fits of violence" did not "disrupt" any "vital patterns." The city and the factory need more tractable workers. The machinery of criminal justice — the police in particular — presumably helped "tame" the population, aided and abetted by the schools, churches, and other social institutions. If what Lane suggests in this provocative article is true, then the reader might well ask himself what, if anything, went wrong in our own more "violent" generation.

Further Reading

Lane, Roger. *Policing the City: Boston, 1822–1885.* Cambridge, Mass.: Harvard University Press, 1967.

Lewis, Walter David. *From Newgate to Dannemora: The Rise of the Penitentiary in New York, 1796–1848.* Ithaca, Cornell University Press, 1965.

Monkkonen, Eric H. *The Dangerous Class: Crime and Poverty in Columbus, Ohio, 1860–1885.* Cambridge, Mass.: Harvard University Press, 1975.

Rothman, David J. *The Discovery of the Asylum: Social Order and Disorder in the New Republic.* Boston: Little, Brown, and Co., 1971.

Williams, Jack K. *Vogues in Villainy: Crime and Retribution in Ante-Bellum South Carolina.* Columbia, S.C., University of South Carolina Press, 1959.

15

William E. Nelson

Emerging Notions of Modern Criminal Law in the Revolutionary Era: An Historical Perspective

Historians have devoted a great deal of attention to studying the law of the early American colonies, especially the criminal law,[1] and no jurisdiction has commanded as much attention as the Puritan colony of Massachusetts Bay.[2] One reason for this interest, perhaps, is that Puritan criminal law was vastly different from the criminal law of today. Religion "was a way of life"[3] for the early settlers of Massachusetts, and all of the Bay Colony's institutions reflected its religious values. Thus, the early settlers "adopt[ed] the Judicial Laws of Moses which were given to the Israelites of Old . . [and] punished Adultery . . [and] Blasphemy, with Death."[4] They equated crime with sin and thought of the state as the arm of God on earth. Modern law, on the other hand, rarely seeks to enforce morality and has thrown up a "wall of separation"[5] between religion and the state. Only incidentally is today's criminal considered a sinner; first and foremost he is regarded as a threat to the peace and order of society.

The purpose of this article is to study the forces which have altered criminal law since early colonial times — a subject

Reprinted, in abridged form, from New York University Law Review, 42 (1967), pp. 450-466, by permission.

much neglected in our legal history. Such a study requires close attention to trial-court records, and the large number of these records necessitates limitation to one locality. Middlesex County, Massachusetts,[6] was chosen largely for convenience, but also because it seems to have been more typical of Massachusetts and perhaps of the United States during the period under study than, for example, urban Boston or frontier Berkshire.

The court records indicate that most of the developments which transformed Puritan criminal law into the criminal law of today occurred during the three decades following the American Revolution. This article will concentrate upon that period. Of course changes, sometimes important ones, had occurred earlier, but nonetheless, the criminal law of prerevolutionary Massachusetts was remarkably similar to that of the Puritan era. The old Puritan ethic remained strong enough in the 1750s so that crime was still looked upon as sin, the criminal as sinner, and criminal law as the earthly arm of God. Criminal law surely was not the tool of the royal government in Boston, which was unconcerned with the outcome of most cases and, in any event, had little real power to influence that outcome. As a

William E. Nelson

result, the chief function of the courts, the primary law-enforcement agencies, remained, as in the early colonial era, the identification and punishment of sinners.

By 1810, some thirty years after the Revolution, a system of law enforcement similar to today's had emerged. This article will trace the development of the new system.

The Substance of the Law: From Preservation of Morality to Protection of Property

CRIMINAL LAW AT THE CLOSE OF THE COLONIAL PERIOD: 1760–1774

No scheme for the classification of crime was ever developed in colonial Massachusetts. Blackstone did develop a classification scheme in England, however, and, by the Revolution, lawyers in Massachusetts knew of it.[7] It included offense against God and religion, offenses against government, offenses against public justice, offenses against public trade and health, homicide, offenses against the person, and offenses against habitations and other private property.[8]

Most cases were within the category of offenses against God and religion. Between 1760 and 1774 there were 370 prosecutions in Middlesex in the Superior and General Sessions Courts. Of these, 210 were for fornication. Since only mothers of illegitimate children were brought into court, one might think that fornication was punished, not because it offended God but because it burdened towns with the support of the children.[9] Such a conclusion would be premature. Although the economic interests of the towns cannot be denied,[10] the fact is that prosecutions were brought even when no economic interests were at stake,[11] and the same penalties were imposed in those prosecutions as in cases where economic interests may have played a part. That the offense, when committed by a woman who did not marry, happened to burden her town was of little import; her offense against God was the essential evil for

which she, like the woman who did marry, was punished.

Also within Blackstone's category of offenses against God and religion were 27 prosecutions for violation of the Sabbath, 2 for cohabitation, and 1 for adultery. These 240 cases accounted for 65 percent of all prosecutions.

Statistically the next most significant category was that of offenses against habitations and other private property. Between 1760 and 1775, there were 32 larceny prosecutions and 15 prosecutions for burglary and breaking and entering — which, together with 6 miscellaneous cases within this category, amounted to 53 prosecutions, or 14 percent of the total.[12] The fact that Blackstone placed offenses against property in a separate category should not be taken to mean, however, that in prerevolutionary Massachusetts these crimes were prosecuted solely because their commission interfered with the enjoyment of property. Theft, like fornication and murder, was a sin against God, which government was obligated to suppress.[13]

Related to men's view of crime was their view of the criminal. The typical criminal was not, as today, an outcast from society, but only an ordinary member who had sinned. Like sin, crime could strike in any man's family or among any man's neighbors.

The court records of the 1760s and 1770s indicate that all elements of society committed crimes. Of forty-seven men accused between 1770 and 1774 of being fathers of illegitimate children, eighteen were laborers, fifteen were farmers, twelve were artisans, and two were gentlemen.[14] Moreover, unlike today, a convicted criminal was not placed in a prison and segregated from the rest of society; in the fifteen-year period before the Revolution, there was only one instance of a person being imprisoned for more than one year.[15] Colonial penalties usually did not sever a criminal's ties with society; fines and mild corporal punishments which left no permanent mark were the usual chastisements. Nor did the only punishment that was commonly of a long duration — the sale into servitude of a convicted thief unable to pay treble damages — result in the thief's segregation from society; rather, its probable effect was to integrate him more fully into society by reorienting him toward normal social contacts.

The years after the Revolution brought forth vast changes in attitudes toward crime and the criminal. Prosecutions for various sorts of immorality nearly ceased, while economically motivated crimes and prosecutions greatly increased. During this same period, old punishments were being discarded and new sanctions imposed.

THE DECLINE IN PROSECUTIONS FOR OFFENSES AGAINST GOD AND RELIGION

During the last fifteen years before the Revolution, there had been an average of fourteen prosecutions for fornication each year [in Middlesex]. The first ten years after the Revolution produced no change. However, in 1786, the General Court enacted a new statute for the punishment of fornication[16] that permitted a woman guilty of the crime to confess her guilt before a justice of the peace, pay an appropriate fine, and thereby avoid prosecution by way of indictment in the Court of General Sessions. Although the new law did not immediately produce any significant decline in prosecutions,[17] by 1789 only five convictions were recorded. The last indictment was returned in 1790, and, after 1791, women stopped confessing their guilt, apparently aware that even though they did not confess, they would not be indicted.

Prosecutions for Sabbath breaking also continued at the prewar rate of about two per year until the mid–1780s, after which, except for a brief interval in 1800–1802,[18] only three cases appear. As a publication issued in 1816 stated, "[F]or many years previous to 1814, the Laws of this State against profanations of the Sabbath, had fallen into general neglect . . . [T]housands of violations occurred every year,

with scarcely a single instance of punishment."[19]

The law's attitude toward adultery was also changing, although the number of prosecutions remained relatively constant. In 1793 three divorces were granted by the Supreme Judicial Court for the commission of adultery, but the guilty spouses were never criminally punished. After 1793 divorces for adultery were regular occurrences, yet only one prosecution was commenced. This increase in divorce indicates, not a rise in the incidence of adultery, but rather the development of an attitude of legal hypocrisy which made it possible, at least in divorce proceedings, for a court to acknowledge publicly the existence of sin without prosecuting it.

A parallel development occurred in paternity litigation. As prosecutions for fornication ceased, it appears that a question arose whether an unwed mother not convicted of the crime could bring a paternity action against the putative father. One woman instituted such a suit in 1790 and gave bond to appear at the next term of court to prosecute it. At that term, however, a new condition was added to her bond — namely, that she also appear to answer a criminal charge of fornication. Thus, the first attempt by a woman to sue without first suffering the consequences of her own misdeed failed. Yet within five years a new attempt had succeeded, and thereafter paternity suits by women not punished for their own sin succeeded regularly. Allowing such suits was a step even more radical than granting divorce for adultery without prosecuting the adulterer. In the divorce cases, the courts took merely a neutral attitude toward the sinner. In paternity cases, on the other hand, the courts not only ignored the plaintiff's "sinner" status, but also rendered the sinner affirmative help in obtaining relief from the consequences of her sin.

The deemphasis of prosecution for sin appears to have been related to what the Congregational ministry condemned as "a declension in morals."[20] President

William E. Nelson

Timothy Dwight of Yale traced the decline to the French and Indian War and, especially, to the Revolution, which, he said, added "to the depravation still remaining [from the French War] . . . a long train of immoral doctrines and practices, which spread into every corner of the country. The profanation of the Sabbath, before unusual, profaneness of language, drunkenness, gambling, and lewdness were exceedingly increased."[21] Others also alluded to habits of card playing and gambling, and to instances of social vice and illegitimacy.[22] Chief Justice William Cushing, for example, feared that "some men have been so liberal in thinking as to religion as to shake off all religion, & while they have labored to set up heathen above Christian morals, have shown themselves destitute of all morality."[23]

Notwithstanding these complaints, a modern author has concluded that there was no "deep-seated coarseness or general immorality"[24] during the closing years of the eighteenth century. What seems to have occurred after the Revolution was a relaxation, not of private, personal morality, but of what contemporaries referred to as public morality.[25] What occurred was "a general relaxing of social customs"[26] — an emergence, not of significantly more immorality, but of a new social and legal attitude toward the immorality that had always existed.

THE INCREASE IN PROSECUTIONS FOR OFFENSES AGAINST HABITATIONS AND PRIVATE PROPERTY

In the late eighteenth and early nineteenth centuries, prosecutions for offenses against habitations and private property greatly increased [in Middlesex], but the increase did not commence immediately after the Revolution. From 1776 to 1783, there was an average of three cases per year, the same as before the Revolution. But in 1784 the number of prosecutions quadrupled,[27] and then averaged eleven

per year for the remainder of the decade, a period of economic difficulty.[28] With the return of prosperity in the 1790s,[29] the average dropped to seven per year,[30] and, apart from an unexplained rise in 1800–1801,[31] remained constant until 1806. Then came the embargo of 1807, depression,[32] and an increase in the average of theft prosecutions during the remainder of the decade to twenty-one per year.[33]

Apart from the correspondence in time of the periods of economic distress and two of the periods of increasing prosecutions, there are other reasons for believing that the increases were results of the distress. As indicated by Josiah Quincy, Jr., in a speech on the relationship of "Poverty, Vice and Crime," larceny was a crime committed almost entirely by the urban poor.[34] Court records support this view. Of the thirty-eight theft prosecutions in the Supreme Judicial Court between 1807 and 1809, twenty-seven were against the urban poor,[35] and urban poor were defendants in fifty-three of seventy-one cases in all courts between 1784 and 1790.[36] It is also significant that many thought of crime as a product of idleness. Governor Strong, for example, told the legislature in 1802 that "a great proportion of crimes are the effects of idleness."[37] Such a view indicates that crime was often committed by the unemployed, such as poor laborers unable to find work during periods of economic dislocation.

Both the statistical and the impressionistic evidence suggests, then, that most theft was to some extent a consequence of poverty. Economic distress was apparently causing increasing numbers of the poor to turn to crimes against property during the postrevolutionary years.

THE USE OF HARD LABOR AS A PUNISHMENT

The third development occurring during the years between 1776 and 1810 was the gradual emergence of hard labor as a punishment in place of the wide variety of penalties used before the Revolution. Hard labor was first imposed with frequency in theft cases. Although there is no direct evidence of why the punishment was first used, the reason can be surmised by tracing the gradual evolution in the penalties imposed for theft during the revolutionary era.

The basic penalty for theft in prerevolutionary Massachusetts was twofold: first, a fine or some sort of mild corporal punishment was imposed on behalf of the government; second, the convicted thief was required to pay treble damages to the owner of the stolen goods. Enforcement of the second part of the penalty was apparently difficult, for many thieves simply could not pay. In such circumstances, the owner of the stolen goods was usually authorized to sell the defendant into service for a specified period varying according to the amount of the treble damages. The market for convict servants must have been depressed, however, for judgments as early as 1772 contain provisions that, if an owner could not sell a defendant within thirty days of his conviction, the defendant was to be released unless the owner compensated the government for the costs of keeping the defendant in jail. The government, it seems, did not want to be charged with the burden of supporting thieves. Its dilemma, though, was that setting convicted thieves free excused them from "that grievous . . . [penalty] of being sold in servitude" — the most severe of the penalties imposed upon them.

The dilemma was resolved in 1785, when the legislature provided for the imprisonment of thieves at hard labor,[38] for the state expected that the proceeds of such labor would pay the costs of imprisoning those so punished.[39] Originally hard labor was to be imposed only in cases where the old penalty of treble damages was not workable,[40] but the Supreme Judicial Court soon began to impose it even in cases where the old punishments could be used, apparently because the judges thought it a more efficacious penalty. At the same time, though, they continued to impose the old penalties in some cases. As a result, a defendant convicted of larceny could, by the early 1800s, look forward to almost any penalty.[41]

Meanwhile, a movement for general penology reform had begun. Having had its origin in Philadelphia in 1776,[42] this movement may have been partly responsible for the legislation of 1785. Any influence it may have had in 1785, however, was slight, for the legislature in that year explicitly decided to retain the old punishments for certain crimes.[43] This was directly contrary to the reform movement's aims, which are best stated in a message from Governor Hancock to the General Court in 1793:

> It may well be worthy of your attention to investigate the question whether the infamous punishments of cropping [ears] and branding, as well as that of the public whipping post, so frequently administered in this Government, are the best means to prevent the commission of crimes, or absolutely necessary to the good order of Government or to the security of the people. It is an indignity to human nature, and can have but little tendency to reclaim the sufferer. Crimes have generally idleness for their source, and where offences are not prevented by education, a sentence to hard labor will perhaps have a more salutary effect than mutilating or lacerating the human body . . . [44]

The movement reached fruition in 1805, when the state prison was reopened, [45] and corporal punishment and treble damages were imposed for the last time in a Middlesex county case.

THE NEW ATTITUDE TOWARD CRIME AND THE CRIMINAL

Each of the three developments discussed thus far was, of course, important in itself. Moreover, in combination with an ideological outgrowth of the Revolu-

William E. Nelson

tion, they transformed the legal and social attitudes toward crime and the criminal. Before the Revolution, two-thirds of all prosecutions were for immorality, and crime was pictured as sin. By 1810, on the other hand, crime was prosecuted to "insure the peace and safety of society"[46] and to relieve the public from the "depradations" of "notorious offenders"[47] and the "tax levied on the community by . . . privateering"[48] of thieves. More than 50 percent of all prosecutions were for theft, and only one-half of 1 percent for conduct offensive to morality. The criminal in 1810 was no longer envisioned as a sinner against God, but rather as one who preyed upon his fellow citizens.

The transition from the attitude of 1760 to that of 1810 seems to have occurred largely during the decade following the conclusion of peace with Britain in 1783. But the first step in the change began earlier, in the 1760s. During that decade and the first half of the following one, Massachusetts Tories carefully cultivated a fear that rebellion against British authority would lead ultimately to the destruction of all authority. The consequence of rebellion, they maintained, would be that "the bands of society would be dissolved, the harmony of the world confounded, and the order of nature subverted."[49] In a series of grand-jury charges given during the 1760s, Chief Justice Thomas Hutchinson suggested how law should be used to prevent the destruction of authority. Expressing his concern that "Disorders are seldom confined to one Point" and that "people who begin with one View, seldom end there,"[50] Hutchinson urged the jurors "to point out and bring forward all Crimes and Offenses against the Tranquillity and Order of the Society."[51]

Many Whigs had similar apprehensions. John Adams was as concerned as Hutchinson when, in 1765, a mob of rioters broke into a royal official's home. "To have his Garden torn in Pieces, his House broken open, his furniture destroyed and his whole family thrown into Confusion and Terror, is a very atrocious Violation of the Peace and of dangerous Tendency and Consequence."[52] By the outbreak of hostilities between the British and Americans in 1774–1775, apprehension of the danger of possible lawlessness and mob rule had grown into an obsession common to all. An example is the conduct of the people of Groton in sending supplies in 1774 for the relief of residents of Boston. With the supplies, the town clerk of Groton sent a letter: "The inhabitants of this Town have . . . this day sent forty bushels of grain . . . and we earnestly desire you will use your utmost endeavor to prevent and avoid all mobs, riots, and tumults, and the insulting of private persons and property."[53]

This emerging fear of the mob seems to have been primarily of a political nature. Adams and Hutchinson were not worried that *sinners* would break into their homes and take away their property: nor did they fear an individual thief motivated by a longing for personal material gain. Rather, they feared organized groups of malcontents bent upon the reconstruction of society. Yet they feared such political activity because they expected that it would be economically motivated. They were concerned that debtors would grow insolvent[54] and that mobs would "invade private rights."[55] In short, their fear was that the economically underprivileged would seek material gain by banding together to deprive more privileged persons of their wealth and standing.

Although quite real, the new concern had little support in the events of the time. During the 1760s and early 1770s, Middlesex County experienced relatively few violent attacks on property; indeed, during those two decades only four instances of such violence were prosecuted. Although there were undoubtedly additional cases, historians of the Revolution are nonetheless agreed that very little violence of the sort Adams and Hutchinson feared did take place during the course of struggle with Britain.[56]

In the 1780s, however, fears previously ungrounded were confirmed by a number of attacks upon authority and property. Between 1781 and 1786, there were four prosecutions for rioting and five for assaults on tax collectors, in one of which eighteen codefendents had participated. Then a most noteworthy attack occurred when, on September 12, 1786, the Court of General Sessions was scheduled by law to meet at Concord. "But a large armed Force, under the Command of one Job Shattuck of Groton (as it was said) being previously collected had taken Possession of the Court House to prevent their sitting, The Justices of the said Court did not attempt to open the Court." Thus did Shay's Rebellion, which sought to close the courts to prevent the collection of debts, extend eastward into Middlesex. It led to several prosecutions.

Culminating in open rebellion, these five years of violence undoubtedly strengthened the fear which society's well-to-do had of the designs of the lower classes upon their wealth and standing. The simultaneous increase in the incidence of theft appears to have contributed to both a strengthening and a modification of the fear. Adams and Hutchinson, it will be recalled, did not worry about individual thieves. A man living in 1786, however, must have viewed all attacks upon property, on the one hand, by poverty-stricken mobs and, on the other, by poverty-stricken individuals, as part of a single phenomenon. What was at stake, ultimately, was the security of his person and property, which members of the lower classes were seeking to disrupt. They used a variety of techniques: they rioted, they attacked courts and tax collectors; they refused to pay debts; they entered men's homes and carried away their possessions. Logically, though, their various techniques could be reduced to two. Some men — the thieves and recalcitrant debtors — broke the law and infringed property rights directly; others — the rioters and those who attacked the courts and tax collectors — worked indirectly by destroying the institutions of government upon which

enforcement of law, and thus security of property rights, rested. Thus, when Govenor Hancock, in an address to the legislature in 1793, suggested that the primary function of criminal law was to ensure "the good order of Government . . . [and] the security of the people,"[57] he was saying in effect that it must perform two functions: first, it must punish and deter direct attacks on property, and, second, it must preserve the power of government to perform that first function.

Hancock's address, which said nothing about the preservation of religion and morality, further shows that the old theocratic view of crime was rapidly dying. A "liberalizing of the older New England religious tradition" was occurring, especially among the upper classes of eastern Massachusetts.[58] As Chief Justice Cushing explained, when men rejected the old religious traditions, they also rejected many of the old moral ones, among them the theretofore unquestioned assumption that government should enforce morality. Such men, it would seem, were taking a step toward a modern view of criminal law — that its purpose is to protect men from unwanted invasions of their rights. At the same time, churchmen and others faithful to the old tradition were abandoning "the dream of theocracy," as it became "evident that the salvation of the nation . . . had to be won . . . with no assistance from any civil authority." The end result was that criminal law became secularized; its purpose came to be seen not as the preservation of morality, but rather as the protection of social order and property.

With the cessation in the 1790s of antigovernmental violence and prosecutions for immorality, criminal law in fact as well as in theory became concerned primarily with the punishment of theft. During the two decades after 1790, prosecutions for various sorts of theft amounted to 47 percent of all cases. This in turn produced a further modification of the theory of criminal law; by 1810 the obsession with mob violence was declining, and the law's purpose was coming to

William E. Nelson

be seen almost entirely as the relief of the public from the "depradations" of thieves.

Meanwhile, the criminal was becoming an outcast of society. Prior to the Revolution, all sorts of men became involved in crime. By 1810, though, the well-to-do rarely became involved with the criminal law, and it was greatly to be regretted "when the offender has some rank in society, with respectable connections who may suffer with him."[59] Such connections were rare, though, for the poverty of most criminals isolated them from the better elements of society on whom they preyed. Criminals in 1810, unlike the mere sinners of old, were different from other men. Nor were their differences and their consequent isolation from society ameliorated by the increasing use of hard labor as a punishment. As some began to observe soon after 1810, long terms of imprisonment did not reform men and enable them to take their place in society, but instead confirmed them in their criminal ways by giving them an opportunity "for corrupting one another."[60] Whereas God could forgive the sinner of old, the villain of 1810 kept returning to crime and was forever condemned to segregation from the society whose peace and prosperity he challenged.

16

Richard Maxwell Brown

Violence and Vigilantism in American History

American violence historically seems to fall into two major categories. The first is negative violence: violence that seems to be in no direct way connected with any socially or historically constructive development. Varieties of negative violence are feuds, lynching, riots and crimes arising from racial or religious prejudice.

Negative violence by no means exhausts the range of American violence. Positive violence is a broad term used to categorize the violence attached to popular and constructive movements. There has been a vast amount connected with some of the most important events of American history — events that are considered constructive, positive, and, indeed, among the noblest chapters in our national history. Thus the Revolutionary War —both in its origins and its progress — was shot through with domestic violence. The Civil War, by which the slave eventually gained his freedom and the union of the nation was assured, engendered vast waves of violence. The very land we occupy was gained over the centuries in a continuing war with the Indians. Vigilante violence was used to establish order and stability on the frontier. Agrarian uprisings occurred again and again to ease the plight of the farmer and yeoman. Labor violence was part and parcel of the industrial worker's struggle to gain recognition and a decent life. Police violence has always been invoked to protect society against the criminal and the disorderly. Again and again violence has been used as a means to ends that have been widely accepted and applauded.

Negative Violence

CRIMINAL VIOLENCE

The salient facts, chronologically arranged are: (1) Organized interstate gangs of criminals are an old story, going well back into the eighteenth-century. (2)

This is an edited and abridged version of two articles, "Historical Patterns of Violence in America," and "The American Vigilante Tradition," which appeared in Hugh D. Graham and Ted R. Gurr, *The History of Violence in America: A Report to the National Commission on the Causes and Prevention of Violence* (2 vols., Washington, D.C., U.S. Government Printing Office, 1969), vol. 1, pp. 35-64, 121-180. A recently revised and updated version of both articles appears in Richard Maxwell Brown, *Strain of Violence: Historical Studies of American Violence and Vigilantism* (New York, Oxford University Press, 1975), pp. 3-36, 95-133.

Richard Maxwell Brown

Before the Civil War, the most prevalent types of criminal activity — especially in frontier areas — were horse theft and the counterfeiting of the myriad private banknotes then in circulation. (3) After the Civil War a new era of crime began with the popularization of train robbery by the Reno brothers of Indiana and bank robbery by the James-Younger gang of Missouri. (4) The modern era of big-city organized crime with its police and political connections began to emerge in the early twentieth century.

THE FAMILY FEUD

One classic variety of negative American violence has been the family feud. This phenomenon has generally been associated with the "hillbilly" of the southern Appalachians, and, of the two great geographic locales of the family feud, one surely has been the southern mountains. Less generally recognized have been the family feuds that raged in Texas and the Southwest at the same time as murderous feuds were drenching the southern highlands with blood.

The family blood fued was virtually nonexistent in this country before the Civil War. It appeared on the scene quite dramatically in the decades following the war. The period between the Civil War and World War I is the great era of the southern mountain feud in Kentucky, West Virginia, and Virginia. This is the period that produced the Hatfield-McCoy feud (1873-1888) of the Kentucky-West Virginia border,[1] the Martin-Tolliver (1884-1887) and Hargis-Cockrell (1902-1903) feuds of eastern Kentucky, and the Allen family outburst at Hillsville in the Virginia Blue Ridge in 1912.[2]

The evidence is convincing that southern mountain feuding was triggered by the animosities generated by the Civil War. The mountain region was a divided country where Confederate and Union sympathizers fought in rival armies and slew each other in marauding guerrilla bands. After the war old hatreds did not die out, but, fueled anew by political partisanship and moonshine whisky in a region bedeviled by isolation, poverty, and ignorance, flamed up as never before. The formal law barely operated; its power was manipulated for selfish purposes by closely knit political and family factions. Because regular law and order were such frail reeds, families and individuals came increasingly to depend upon their own strong arms. Each feuding family for the sake of self-defense developed its own clan leader: a man who best combined in the highest quotients the qualities of physical strength, bravery, wealth, and leadership. Such men were "Devil Anse" Hatfield and Judge James Hargis. In the absence of an effective system of law and order, these men functioned as family "enforcers" around whom the feuding families rallied for protection.

In New Mexico Territory the family and factional feud was built into the political system.[3] New Mexico before World War I was probably the only North American state where assassination became a routine political tactic. The most deadly of all American feuds was fought in neighboring Arizona from 1886 to 1892. This was the Pleasant Valley War between the Graham and Tewksbury families, a conflict that was exacerbated by the Grahams' being cattlemen and the Tewksburys' being sheepmen. The bitter feud was fought, as described in the title of Zane Grey's novel about the vendetta, "to the last man." Only when a lone survivor remained from the two families did the feud come to an end.[4]

THE LYNCH MOB

Lynch law has been defined as "the practice or custom by which persons are punished for real or alleged crimes without due process of law."[5] The first organized movement of lynch law in the United States occurred in the South Carolina back country in 1767-1769. It appeared again in the Virginia Piedmont during the later years of the Revolutionary War near the present city of Lynchburg. The Virginia movement was initiated by Colonel

Charles Lynch (from whom the lynch law gained its name) and was employed against Tory miscreants.[6] Well into the nineteenth century, lynch law meant merely the infliction of corporal punishment — usually thirty-nine or more lashes well laid on with hickory withes, whips, or any other readily available frontier instrument. By the middle of the nineteenth century, lynch law had, however, come to be synonymous, mainly, with killing someone by illegal group action. By the term "lynch-mob" is meant an unorganized, spontaneous, mob which comes together briefly to do its fatal work and then breaks up. The more regular vigilante (or "regulator") movements engaged in a systematic usurpation of the functions of law and order.

Lynch-mob violence (in contrast to vigilante violence) was often resorted to in trans-Appalachian frontier areas before the Civil War, but it became even more common after the Civil War. In the postwar period (down to World War I) lynch-mob violence was frequently employed in all sections of the country and against whites as well as blacks, but it became preeminently the fate of southern Negroes. From 1882 to 1903 a staggering total of 1,985 Negroes were killed by southern lynch mobs. Supposedly the lynch-mob hanging (or, too often, the ghastly fate of being burned alive) was saved for the Negro murderer or rapist, but the statistics show that Negroes were frequently lynched for lesser crimes or in cases where there was no offense at all or the mere suspicion of one. Lynch-mob violence became an integral part of the post-Reconstruction system of white supremacy.[7]

Although predominant in the South, lynch-mob violence was far from being restricted to that section. In the West the ephemeral "necktie party" was often gathered for the summary disposal of thief, rapist, rustler, murderer, or all-around desperado. Frenzied mobs similarly worked their will in the North and East where (as in the West) villainous white men were the usual victims.[8]

VIOLENCE ARISING FROM RACIAL, ETHNIC, AND RELIGIOUS PREJUDICE

Lynch-mob activity by no means exhausts the violence involving whites against blacks. Racial conflict between Caucasians and Negroes is one of the most persistent themes in American violence, extending far back into the eighteenth century.

With the end of slavery and its slave patrols and black codes, the white men of the South developed a special organization for dealing with the Negro: The Ku Klux Klan. The Klan has been one of the most persistent institutions of the last hundred years of American violence. There have been three Ku Klux Klans: the first Klan of Reconstruction times, the second of the 1920s, and the third Klan of the 1950s and 1960s. The first Ku Klux Klan was organized to intimidate the Radical Republicans of the Reconstruction Era and, by violence and threats, to force the freedman to accept the renewed rule of southern whites.[9] The second Ku Klux Klan differed significantly from both its predecessor and its successor. Although it was founded in Atlanta in 1915, its greatest growth and strength actually took place beyond the borders of the old Confederacy. During the early 1920s it became a truly national organization. For a time it enjoyed great strength in the Southwest, West, North, and East. The strongest state Klan was in Indiana, and such wholly unsouthern states as Oregon and Colorado felt its vigor. The second Ku Klux Klan surely belongs to the violent history of America, but, unlike either the first or the third Klans, the Negro was only a secondary target. Although denunciation of Catholics and Jews ranked first and second in the rhetoric of the second Klan, recent students of the movement have shown that Klan violence — whippings, torture, and murder — were directed less against Catholics, Jews, and Negroes than against ne'er-do-wells and the allegedly immoral of the very same background as the Klansmen: white, Anglo-Saxon, and Protestant. The Klan thus attacked Americans of similar back-

Richard Maxwell Brown

ground and extraction who refused to conform to the Bible Belt morality that was the deepest passion of the Klan movement of the 1920s.[10] The Ku Klux Klan resurgence of the last ten years has been largely restricted to the South; it is only too well known for acts of violence against the civil rights movement and desegregation.

Paralleling the Ku Klux Klan have been a host of other movements of racial, ethnic, and religious malice. Before the Civil War the northeastern United States was frequently the scene of convent burnings and anti-Catholic riots.[11] This "Protestant Crusade" eventually bred the Know-Nothing movement. Anti-Chinese agitation that often burst into violence became a familiar feature of California and the West in the nineteenth century. In 1891, eleven Italian immigrants were the victims of a murderous mob in New Orleans.[12] The fear and loathing of Catholics (especially Irish and Italians) that often took a violent form was organized in the nonviolent but bigoted American Protective Association (APA) of 1887.[13] Labor clashes of the late nineteenth and early twentieth century were often in reality ethnic clashes with native old-stock Americans ranged on one side, as owners, foremen, and skilled workers, against growing numbers of unskilled immigrants — chiefly Jews, Slavs, Italians, and others from Southern and Eastern Europe.

URBAN VIOLENCE

Our cities have been in a state of more or less continuous turmoil since the colonial period. As early as the later part of the seventeenth century the beginnings of the organized North End and South End mobs that dominated Boston in the eighteenth century had already formed. Maritime riots occurred in Boston during the middle of the eighteenth century and were general in the colonies in the 1760s. Leading colonial cities of the revolutionary era — Charleston, New York, Boston, and Newport, Rhode Island — all had Liberty Boy troubles that resulted from an alliance of unskilled maritime workers, skilled artisans, and middle-class business and professional men in riotous dissent against toughening British colonial policy as exemplified by the Stamp Act and Townshend Acts.[14]

Economic and political conditions brought more urban turmoil in the post-revolutionary period of the 1780s and 1790s, and by the mid-nineteenth century, with rapid industrial and urban expansion, the cities of America found themselves in the grips of a new era of violence. The pattern of the urban immigrant slum as a matrix of poverty, vice, crime, and violence was set by Five Points in lower Manhattan before the Civil War. Ulcerating slums along the lines of Five Points and severe ethnic and religious strife stemming from the confrontation between burgeoning immigrant groups and the native American element made the 1830s, 1840s, and 1850s a period of sustained urban rioting, particularly in the great cities of the Northeast. It may have been the era of the greatest urban violence that American has ever experienced. During this period at least thirty-five major riots occurred in the four cities of Baltimore, Philadelphia, New York, and Boston. Baltimore had twelve, Philadelphia had eleven, New York had eight and Boston had four. The violence also extended into the growing cities of the Midwest and the lower Mississippi Valley — Cincinnati had four major riots during this period. Among the most important types were labor riots, election riots, antiabolitionist riots, anti-Negro riots, anti-Catholic riots, and riots of various sorts involving the turbulent volunteer firemen's units. Except for the Civil War draft riots, the urban violence subsided in the 1860s and 1870s until the year 1877 produced a tremendous nationwide railroad strike that began along the Baltimore and Ohio Railroad and spread to the Far West. Rioting left Baltimore and great stretches of Pittsburgh in smoking ruins.[15] (The similarity between what befell Baltimore and Pittsburgh in 1877 and the fate of Los Angeles, Chicago, Newark, Detroit,

Washington, and other cities in 1965-1968 is striking.) Many other cities suffered, but less seriously.

The forces of law and order responded strongly to the nineteenth-century urban violence. The modern urban police system was created in reaction to the riots of the 1830s, 1840s, and 1850s, and the National Guard system was developed in response to the uprisings of 1877. To deal with urban tumult, vigilantism was also used frequently in the nineteenth century. The greatest of all American vigilante movements occurred in the newly settled (by Americans) but thoroughly urban and up-to-date San Francisco of 1856; other nineteenth-century urban vigilante movements occurred in Los Angeles, New Orleans, San Antonio, St. Louis, Cincinnati, Rochester, and Natchez.

The era of the modern urban race riot was inaugurated around the turn of our present century. From 1900 to 1949 there were thirty-three major interracial disturbances in the United States. During this half century the peak period of violence was from 1915 to 1919 when twenty-two of the thirty-three disturbances occurred. (The 1915-1919 period of racial disorder was thus comparable to the period from 1964 to the present.) Major riots occurred in Atlanta (1906), Springfield, Illinois (1908), East St. Louis (1917), Chicago (1919), Harlem (1935 and 1943), and Detroit (1943). With the exception of the Harlem riots, whites emerged as the main aggressors in these riots, and most of the casualties were Negroes.[16] Not until the summer of 1964 with the Harlem and Rochester riots and Los Angeles's Watts riots of 1965 did the pattern decisively reverse itself to the present mode of Negro initiative. Since 1964 black rioting has concentrated on property destruction rather than on the taking of white lives; this is a new pattern, although it was foreshadowed in the Harlem riots of 1935 and 1943.

Positive Violence: The Police

The law-enforcement system in colonial America was quite simple, consisting

mainly of sheriffs for the counties and constables for the cities and towns. With the tremendous expansion of population and territory in the nineteenth century, the system took on much greater complexity. Added to the county sheriffs and local constables were municipal police systems, state police (including special and elite forces, such as the Rangers of Texas[17] and Arizona), and federal marshals and Treasury agents. The most important development of the century was the development of the modern urban police system in the midcentury years from 1844 to 1877. The new system was a direct response to the great urban riots of the 1830s, 1840s, and 1850s. The antiquated watch-and-ward system (daytime constables and nighttime watchmen) was simply inadequate to cope with the large-scale rioting and increasing urban disorder. The reform in the police system came first in New York, Philadelphia, Boston, and other cities which had acute problems of criminal violence and rioting.[18] Thus the riot era of the 1830s-1850s produced the present urban police system.

Scarcely less important than the development of the urban police system was the creation of the National Guard to replace the obsolete state-militia system that dated back to the eighteenth century. The rapid development of the National Guard system in the 1880s was largely a response to the great urban labor riots of 1877. The National Guard was established first and most rapidly in the leading industrial states of the North that were highly vulnerable to labor unrest: Massachusetts, Connecticut, New York, Pennsylvania, Ohio, and Illinois. By 1892, the system was complete throughout the nation.[19] Its officers were primarily business and professional men, and the Guard sometimes received large subsidies from wealthy industrialists. National Guard contingents were often called out to suppress labor violence from the late-nineteenth century down to the time of World War II.

In the later half of the nineteenth century there also grew up a sort of parapolice system with the founding of numerous private detective agencies (beginning with the famed Pinkerton National Detective Agency)[20] and the burgeoning of thousands of local anti-horse-thief associations or detecting societies which often were authorized by state laws and invested with limited law-enforcement powers.[21] After the Civil War, industrial corporations frequently set up their own police forces. The most notable of these were the private coal and iron police which the state of Pennsylvania authorized to deal with labor unrest in mines and mills.[22] It was during the nineteenth century as well that the science of crime detection was inaugurated.

Undue violence in the course of enforcing the law has long been a matter of concern. In an earlier generation the public worried about the employment of the "third degree" to obtain criminal confessions. In our own time the concern is with "police brutality," especially that directed against Negroes.

The American Vigilante Tradition

The vigilante tradition, in the classic sense, refers to organized, extralegal movements whose members take the law into their own hands. The first vigilante movement in American history occurred in 1767. From then until about 1900, vigilante activity was an almost constant factor in American life. Far from being a phenomenon only of the far-western frontier, there was much vigilantism in the eastern half of the United States. Although the first vigilante movement occurred in Piedmont, South Carolina in 1767-1769, most of the Atlantic Seaboard states were without significant vigilante activity. But beyond the Appalachians there were few states that did not have vigilante movements. There may have been as many as five hundred of them, but at the present only 326 have been documented.[23]

Vigilantism arose as a response to a typical American problem: the absence of effective law and order in a frontier region. It was a problem that occurred again and again beyond the Appalachian Mountains. It stimulated the formation of hundreds of frontier vigilante movements.[24] On the frontier the normal foundations of a stable, orderly society — churches, schools, cohesive community life — were either absent or present only in rough, immature forms. The regular legal system of law enforcement often proved to be woefully inadequate for the needs of the settlers.

Fundamentally, the pioneers took the law into their own hands for the purpose of establishing order and stability in newly settled areas. In the older settled areas person and property were secure, but the move to the frontier meant that it was necessary to start all over. Upright and ambitious frontiersmen wished to reestablish the values of a property-holder's society. The hurtful presence of outlaws and marginal elements in a context of weak and ineffectual law enforcement created the specter, and often the fact, of social chaos. The solution hit upon was vigilantism. A vigilante roundup of ne'er-do-wells and outlaws followed by their flogging, expulsion, or killing not only solved the problem of disorder but had crucial symbolic value as well. Vigilante action was a clear warning to disorderly inhabitants that the newness of settlement would provide no opportunity for eroding the established values of civilization. Vigilantism was a violent reaffirmation of the deeply cherished values of life and property.

Because the main thrust of vigilantism was to reestablish in each newly settled area the conservative values of life, property, law, and order, vigilante movements were usually led by the frontier elite. This was true of the greatest American vigilante movement — the San Francisco Vigilance Committee of 1856 — which was dominated by the leading merchants of the city. Again and again the most eminent local community leaders headed vigilante movements.

"Vigilance committee" or "committee of vigilance" were the common names of the organization, but originally — and far into the nineteenth century — vigilantes were known by the now obsolete term of "regulators." Variant names for vigilante groups were "slickers," "stranglers," "committees of safety," and, in central Texas, simply "mobs." Here "vigilante" will be used as a generic term to cover all phases of the general phenomenon of vigilantism. The duration of vigilante movements varied greatly, but movements which lasted as long as a year were considered to be long lived. More commonly they finished their business in a period of months or weeks. Vigilante movements (as distinguished from ephemeral lynch mobs) are thus identifiable by the two main characteristics of (1) regular (though illegal) organization and (2) existence for a definite (though possibly short) period of time.

EASTERN VIGILANTISM

Geographically, American vigilantism divides into eastern and western halves. Eastern and western vigilantism are distinct in regard to chronology. Eastern vigilantism mainly came to an end in the 1860s while western vigilantism began in the 1850s. Eastern vigilantism was largely a feature of the first half of the nineteenth century and western vigilantism of the second half. Eastern vigilantism fell between the Appalachian Mountains[25] and the 96th meridian, while western vigilantism stretched from the 96th meridian to the Pacific.[26] The Mississippi Valley, Great Lakes, and Gulf coast regions furnished the main scenes of eastern vigilantism; western vigilantism took in the arid and semiarid Great Plains and the Rocky Mountains and the Pacific coast. Eastern vigilantism was a response, chiefly, to frontier horse thieves, counterfeiters, and ne'er-do-well white people. West of the 96th meridian the vigilantes were concerned largely with disorder in mining camps, cattle towns, and on the open range.[27]

Counterfeiting and horse stealing were linked. Horse thieves commonly organized into gangs, stealing horses in one area and disposing of them hundreds of miles away — preferably across state lines. For obvious reasons, counterfeiting operations were best carried on in the same way, and it was simple to combine the two occupations. The link between counterfeiting and horse theft had an effect on the geographical distribution of regulator and vigilante movements. The latter tended to be found in wilderness areas, close to state lines, or near Indian borders — all were places favored by the horse thieves and counterfeiters.

From the 1790s well into the nineteenth century, vigilante activity was generally local in Kentucky, Tennessee, Indiana, and Illinois. Thereafter there were four major waves of vigilantism occurring in the early 1830s, the early 1840s, the late 1850s, and the late 1860s. The first wave was from 1830 to 1835, and it took place mainly in the lower southern states of Alabama and Mississippi where Captain Slick's bands operated against horse thieves and counterfeiters, and vigilantes attacked gamblers and the alleged Murrell conspiracy. The second wave took place in the early 1840s and included the Bellevue vigilante war in Iowa, the east Texas regulator-moderator conflict, the northern and southern Illinois regulators, and the Slicker War of the Missouri Ozarks. The vigilante wave of the early 1840s may have been a response to a shift in outlaw elements (caused by the 1830-1835 vigilante campaign) from the lower Mississippi River region of Alabama, Mississippi, Arkansas, and Louisiana to the upper Mississippi area (northern Illinois, eastern Iowa, and the Missouri Ozarks) and to the trans-Mississippi Southwest (east Texas.)

The third peak of vigilantism was from 1857 to 1859 and featured the Iron Hills and other vigilante movements of Iowa, the northern Indiana regulators, the San Antonio and New Orleans vigilantes, and the *comités de vigilance* of southwest Louisiana. The movements of the late 1850s may have been inspired by the San

Richard Maxwell Brown

Francisco Vigilance Committee of 1856,[28] which was well publicized throughout the nation. The fourth and final wave of vigilantism occurred in the immediate post–Civil War period (1866-1871) with major movements erupting in Missouri, Kentucky, Indiana, and Florida as a reaction to postwar lawlessness.

WESTERN VIGILANTISM

The natural resources of the West influenced the geography of frontier disorder. Repeated strikes of precious and valuable metals in the Sierras and Rockies set off mining rushes that brought miners and others into raw new camps and towns by the thousands. In such places the law was often absent or ineffectual, with vigilantism the result. The other great natural resource of the West was the grassy rangeland of the Great Plains and mountain plateaus. The open-range system afforded an irresistible attraction to cattle and horse thieves who, in turn, invited vigilante retaliation.

Beginning with the first significant outbreak of vigilantism in the gold-rush metropolis of San Francisco in 1849 and continuing for fifty-three years down to 1902 there were at least 210 vigilante movements in the West. No vigilante movements in American history were better organized or more powerful than the San Francisco Vigilance Committees of 1851 and 1856. The San Francisco movements had an immense impact on American vigilantism in general and upon California vigilantism in particular. During the 1850s, the San Francisco committees were copied all over the state in the new mining towns (Sacramento, Jackson) and in the old Spanish cities (Los Angeles, Monterey). Of California's forty-three movements, twenty-seven occurred in the 1850s.[29]

Montana was a most significant vigilante state. It had two of the most important movements in the history of the institution: the influential Bannack and Virginia City movement of 1863–1865 (which gave the term "vigilante" to

American English)[30] and the 1884 movement in northern and eastern Montana, which Granville Stuart led against horse and cattle thieves in a human roundup that claimed thirty-five victims and was the bloodiest of all American vigilante movements. In addition, Montana, from the 1860s to the 1880s, was in the grips of a territory-wide vigilante movement with headquarters apparently in the territorial capital, Helena.[31]

Texas had fifty-two vigilante movements — more than any other state. There were two important ante-bellum movements (Shelby County in east Texas, 1840–44 and San Antonio beginning in 1857), but the majority (at least twenty-seven, occurred in violence-torn central Texas in the post–Civil War period from 1865 to 1890. There were dozens and dozens of vigilante movements in most of the other western states; only Oregon and Utah did not have significant vigilante activity. Colorado's sixteen movements were headed by the Denver vigilantes of 1859–1861. New Mexico had three potent vigilante movements in Albuquerque (1871–1882), Las Vegas (1880–1882), and Socorro (1880–1884).[32] The Butler County vigilantes who enlisted almost eight hundred members and claimed eight victims formed the most notable of Kansas's nineteen movements.[33] Wyoming vigilantism began with two lethal movements in the wild railroad boom towns of Cheyenne and Laramie (1868–1869) and came to a climax with vigilantism's most famous failure, the cattlemen's regulator movement which precipitated the Johnson County War of 1862.[34]

For purposes of analysis, the 116 eastern vigilante movements and the 210 western vigilante movements have been divided into the categories of large — a large movement or one of particular significance; medium — a movement of medium size or significance; and small — a small movement or one for which there is insufficient information to otherwise categorize (see table No. 16.1).

Table 16.1. Eastern and Western Vigilante Movements

State	Movements				Total Number of Victims Killed
	Large	Medium	Small	Total	
Eastern					
Alabama	1	5	0	6	0
Arkansas	1	0	3	4	4
Florida	4	1	1	6	7
Georgia	2	1	1	4	6
Illinois	4	4	2	10	30
Indiana	3	2	6	11	15
Iowa	3	13	9	25	27
Kentucky	3	4	4	11	10
Louisiana	4	0	3	7	35
Minnesota	0	0	2	2	1
Mississippi	4	0	1	5	21
Missouri	4	1	7	12	21
Ohio	1	2	2	5	0
South Carolina	1	0	0	1	16
Tennessee	1	0	3	4	9
Virginia	0	2	0	2	0
Wisconsin	0	0	1	1	0
Subtotal	36	35	45	116	202
Western					
Arizona	0	3	3	6	11
California	10	23	10	43	101
Colorado	3	4	9	16	23
Idaho	4	1	0	5	35
Kansas	1	5	13	19	18
Montana	4	2	0	6	101
Nebraska	2	8	6	16	20
Nevada	1	2	10	13	7
New Mexico	3	3	5	11	17
North Dakota	0	1	0	1	0
Oklahoma	1	1	2	4	2
South Dakota	2	1	1	4	10
Texas	9	15	28	52	140
Utah	0	0	1	1	0
Washington	2	1	3	6	11
Wyoming	3	2	2	7	31
Subtotal	45	72	93	210	527
Total	81	107	138	326	729

There were 81 large movements; they extended, chronologically, from 1767 to 1897. Fifty-nine of the 81 large movements were clustered in the period from 1850 to 1889; 49 occurred in the midcentury decades from 1850 to 1879 when the nation was wracked by Civil War violence in the East and the tensions of rapid frontier settlement in the West. About three-fifths (190) of all vigilante movements took place after 1860, but here again it must be noted that the lack of specific information on many Kentucky, Tennessee, Indiana and Illinois movements leads to an understatement of pre-1860 vigilante movements; 180 of the 190 movements were concentrated in the three decades from 1861 to 1890 (see table 16.2). By the same token, about five-sevenths (511) of all the killed victims of vigilantism perished after 1860 (see table 16.3).

Behind the statistics lies the impact of vigilantism on the American consciousness. The original South Carolina regulator movement of 1767–1769 with its success in achieving order in the back country recommended itself to the pioneers who crossed the Appalachians and populated the Mississippi Valley. The regulator method was applauded as a tool for establishing frontier social stability until, in the 1840s, three anarchic movements in southern Illinois, the Missouri Ozarks, and east Texas gave the institution an increasingly bad name. Soon after, in 1851 and 1856, the restrained but deadly San Francisco Vigilance Committees restored to vigilantism

Table 16.2. Number of Movements Arranged by Periods

Period	Number of Movements
1767–1849	65
1850–1860	57
1861–1890	180
1891–110	10
Overlapped 2 periods	14
Total	326

Richard Maxwell Brown

Table 16.3. Number of Known Victims Killed

Period	Number of Victims Killed
1760–1769	16
1770–1779	0
1780–1789	0
1790–1799	0
1800–1809	0
1810–1819	0
1820–1829	3
1830–1839	5
1840–1849	64
1850–1859	119
1860–1869	179
1970–1879	125
1880–1889	107
1890–1899	25
1900–1909	1
Subtotal	644
Overlapped 2 or more periods	84[a]
Year or decade unknown	1
Total	729

	Killed
[a]1859–1860s	10
1860–1870s	10
1860–1890s	9
1870–1880s	30
1880–1890s	25
Total	84

the enormous prestige which it retained through the remainder of the century. Countless vigilante movements from coast to coast modeled themselves after the San Francisco committees. One of these was the vigilante movement of the gold camps of Bannack and Virginia City, Montana (1863–1865), which in turn had something of the same effect on American attitudes as the earlier South Carolina and San Francisco movements. Thomas Dimsdale's classic book, The Vigilantes of Montana (1866), not only spread the fame of the Montana movement but was a veritable textbook on the vigilante method.

Significant vigilante activity did not always take the shape of a formally organized movement with officers and trials. By the later half of the nineteenth century the ritual of organizing a vigilante movement had been carried out so many times on so many frontiers that to many settlers it often seemed an unnecessary delay to swift lynch-law justice. A local consensus in favor of immediate vigilante action without any of the traditional formalities produced instant vigilantism. Instant vigilantism was more prevalent in the West than in the East. Many of the "one-shot" vigilante actions in western states were the result of instant vigilantism, which existed side by side with the more formally organized variety. Instant vigilantism meant that the public mind had long since been made receptive to vigilante action when general conditions or a particular crime seemed to warrant it. The ritual process of organization had been gone through so many times, the rationale of vigilantism was so well understood, and the course of action so obvious on the basis of past precedents that the settlers readily proceeded to the lynching.

Instant vigilantism seems to have occurred in all western states but Oregon and Utah. It was particularly effective in California. In the Golden State, regular vigilante action took 101 lives, but the toll of instant vigilantism from 1851 to 1878 was almost as great, amounting to 79.[35] On a lesser scale the same thing occurred in other western states, where time and again precipitate lynchings were justified by the vigilante tradition.

Community Reconstruction and Vigilantism

New settlers ordinarily desire new opportunities but not social innovation. Their main desire is to re-create the life they left behind them by reconstructing the communities from which they came.

This is no great problem for communities that migrate together, of which there have been many examples. The Pilgrim settlers of Plymouth, Massachusetts, and the Mormon migrants to Great Salt Lake, Utah, are notable cases of "colonized" new communities.

More common have been the "cumulative" communities of inhabitants thrown together helter-skelter by the migration process.[36] The migrants to San Francisco, California, in 1849 and after furnish an example of the cumulative new community. The San Franciscans came from all over and were an immensely diverse lot. The only thing that united them initially was their common desire to profit form the California gold rush.

Basic to the reconstruction of the community is the reestablishment of the old community structure and its values. To the extent that both are achieved, an orderly and stable new community life will be achieved. Although American frontiersmen of the nineteenth century came to their new localities from all points of the compass and were usually unknown to one another, most came from essentially similar communities. The typical American community of the eighteenth and nineteenth centuries possessed a social structure of three levels.[37]

(1) The upper level consisted of the leading men and their families. Included were the well-to-do businessmen, the most eminent professional men, the affluent farmers and planters, and the prominent men of whatever occupation. This was the local elite, and in it were concentrated the community leaders.

(2) The middle level included the men of average means: farmers, craftsmen, tradesmen, and the less eminent lawyers, teachers, and other professionals. The industrious, honest middle level formed the core of the community. In this sector resided the American yeoman.

(3) The lower level included the honest poor and also those who were either marginal to or alientated from the remainder of the community. In but not really *of* the community (and spurned by it) were the ne'er-do-well, shiftless poor whites. They constituted a true *lower people*; they were viewed with contempt and loathing by the members of the upper and middle levels who could not abide their slovenly way of life, their spiritless lack of ambition, their often immoral conduct, and their disorganized family life.[38]

The lower people were not outlaws but often tended to lawlessness and were identified more with the outlaw element that with the law-abiding members of the community. The outlaw element lived on the fringes of the community. In some cases they sprang from the lower people, but then were often men of good background who chose the outlaw life or drifted into it. They were alienated from the values of the community, although some occasionally joined respectable community life as reformed men.

A community has behavioral boundaries just as it has geographic boundaries. Just as a new community establishes its geographic boundaries it must also establish its behavioral boundaries. The latter represent the positive, mutual values of the community.[39] The values which supported the three-level community and the basis upon which it rested were the linked ideals of respect for life and property. The American community of the eighteenth and nineteenth centuries was primarily a property-holder's community, and property was viewed as the very basis of life itself.

The vigilante leaders were drawn from the upper level of the community. The middle level supplied the rank-and-file. The lower people and outlaws represented the main threat to the reconstruction of the community and were the main targets of the vigilantes.

In the new cumulative communities of frontier America, the lower people and outlaws confronted the representatives of the middle and upper levels. The outlaws and lower people wished to burst their lower-level bounds and "take over" the new communities. In sociological terms the outlaws and lower people constituted a "contraculture."[40] They rejected the

Richard Maxwell Brown

respectable values of life and property and wished to upset the social structure in which the upper- and middle-level men were dominant. The lack of social boundaries in the new settlements was their opportunity. On the other hand, the men of upper-level background or aspirations were determined to reestablish the community structure in which they had been dominant. In this they had the support of the middle-level inhabitants, and with it they mounted vigilante campaigns to quell the insurgent outlaws and lower people.[41]

James Hall described the challenge which outlaws and lower people presented in the early years of midwestern settlement:

> We had whole settlements of counterfeiters, or horse thieves, with their sympathisers — where rogues could change names, or pass from house to house, so skillfully as to elude detection — and where if detected, the whole population were ready to rise to the rescue. There were other settlements of sturdy honest fellows, the regular backwoodsmen in which rogues were not tolerated. There was therefore a continual struggle between these parties — the honest people trying to expel the others by the terrors of the law, and when that mode failed, forming *regulating* companies, and driving them out by force.[42]

The loathing of upper-level men for the lower element — the contraculture — of the frontier was stated with feeling by Thomas Dimsdale, who cried that "for the low, brutal, cruel, lazy, ignorant, insolent, sensual and blasphemous miscreants that infest the frontier we entertain but one sentiment — aversion — deep, strong, and unchangeable,"[43] At times the deep aversion expressed itself in gruesome ways. Such an incident occurred in Rawlins, Wyoming, in 1881 where Dr. John E. Osborne (a future governor of Wyoming) attended the hanging of the brutal western outlaw, Big Nose George Parratt (or Paratti). The next day Dr. Osborne "skinned 'Big Nose' George

and cut away the top of the skull, in order to remove the brain. The skin was tanned and made into a medical instrument bag, razor strops, a pair of lady's shoes, and a tobacco pouch. The shoes were displayed in the Rawlins National Bank for years," and in effect, constituted an upper-level trophy in honor of the community values of life and property held by such men as Dr. Osborne.[44]

Vigilante Characteristics

Vigilante movements varied in size from the smallest of twelve to fifteen members (the Pierre, South Dakota, vigilance committee) to the six to eight thousand who belonged to the San Francisco Vigilance Committee of 1865.

The characteristic vigilante movement was organized in command or military fashion and usually had a constitution, articles, or a manifesto to which the members would subscribe. Outlaws or other alleged malefactors taken up by vigilantes were given formal (though illegal) trials in which the accused had counsel or at least an opportunity to defend himself. An example of a vigilante trial is found in the northern Illinois regulator movement of 1841. Two accused horse thieves and murderers were tried by 120 regulators in the presence of a crowd of 500 or more. A leading regulator served as judge. The defendants were given a chance to challenge objectionable men among the regulators, and, as a result, the number of regulators taking part in the trial was cut by nine men. Two lawyers were provided — one to represent the accused and one to represent the "people." Witnesses were sworn, an arraignment was made, and the trial proceeded. In summation, the prosecuting attorney urged immediate execution of the prisoners. The crowd voted unanimously for the fatal sentence, and, after an hour allotted to the two men for prayer, they were put to death. The accused were almost never acquitted, but the vigilantes' attention to the spirit of law and order caused them to provide, by their lights, a fair but speedy trial.

The punishments of whipping and expulsion were common in the early decades of vigilantism, but, as time passed, killing — usually by means of hanging — became the customary punishment. Through 1849 there are only 88 documented fatal victims of vigilance action (see table 16.3). In the next decade 105 persons were killed by vigilantes, and it was at about this time — the 1850s —that the transition in the meaning of the term "lynching" from whipping to killing was occurred. The killing character of vigilantism, made firm in the 1850s, was accentuated during the remainder of the century: from 1860 to 1909 vigilantes took at least 511 lives (see table 16.3).

The tendency among the 141 vigilante movements that were taking lives was to stop after claiming four or fewer victims. Thus 98 movements (or 70 percent of the 141 movements) inflicted from one to four deaths. Only 17 of the 141 movements (12 percent) took more than 10 lives. The most lethal movement was that in Montana in 1884 led by Granville Stuart against the horse and cattle thieves of the eastern and northern part of the territory; its toll was 35 persons.[45]

Vigilante leaders wished to reestablish the three-level community structure (in which they would be dominant) and the respect for life and property that supported it. Specifically, they wished to check disorder and crime, but in some situations the threat of the latter was mild. In such cases their desire to use vigilantism underscored their basic though implicit goals of implanting community structure and values.

All this they wished to achieve as cheaply as possible. They were the typical frontier entrepreneurs. Their enterprise in commerce or land was often speculative, and they frequently skated on financial thin ice. The delicate balance of their own personal finances could be easily upset; hence, they had a lively awareness of the cost of public ser-

vice and a desire to keep it down lest, as substantial taxpayers, their own circumstances suffer. No better resolution of the conflicting goals of public order and personal wealth could be found than vigilantism, which provided a maximum of the former at minimum cost to the ambitious and well-to-do.

The typical vigilante leaders were ambitious young men from the old settled areas of the East. They wished to establish themselves in the upper level of the new community, a status they had held or aspired to in the place of their origin. Two notable but representative examples of aggressive young vigilante leaders were William Tell Coleman and Wilbur Fisk Sanders.

Coleman was head of the San Francisco Vigilance Committee of 1856 when he was thirty-two years old. His father had been a Kentucky lawyer and legislator but died a bankrupt when the son was only nine years old. The future vigilante, deprived of educational opportunity, spent his early years moving restlessly about the Midwest (Illinois, Missouri, and Wisconsin) in a fruitless quest to regain the upper-level status of his father. Arriving overland in California in 1849 at the age of twenty-five, Coleman embarked on a career which, by 1856, found him one of San Francisco's most successful importers.[46] His participation as a vigilante leader was, in effect, an action to cement his position in the upper level of the new city and to consolidate the three-level system there.

Wilbur Fisk Sanders was the courageous and incisive prosecuting attorney of the vigilantes at Virginia City, Montana, in 1864. Like Coleman, Sanders came from an upper-level background but had not yet made firm his own position in that status. He was twenty-nine years old when he served as a vigilante and had not long before accompanied his uncle, Sidney Edgerton (who had been appointed territorial chief justice by Lincoln), from Ohio to Montana. Sanders's vigilante service did much to establish the three-level system in chaotic early

Richard Maxwell Brown

Montana, and it was the beginning of one of the most spectacular careers in the territory. Sanders went on to become one of the leading lawyers and top Republican politicians in Montana. He founded the Montana Bar Association and in 1889 was elected one of Montana's first two United States senators.

The Problem of Frontier Law Enforcement and Justice

In frontier areas, law and order were often tenuous. Outlaws — singly or in gangs — headed for the new areas and took every advantage they could of the social disorganization stemming from the newness of settlement and the weakness of the traditional institutions of state, society, and church.

Law enforcement was frequently inadequate. Throughout most of the nineteenth century (and not just on the frontier) it was pinned down to the immediate vicinity of county seat, town, or township.[47] Localities lacked the economic resources to support constables, policemen, and sheriffs in pursuit after lawbreakers. A really large expenditure of funds for the pursuit, capture, jailing, trial, and conviction of culprits could easily bankrupt the typical frontier county or town.

There was also the handicap of poor transportation. The mobility of sheriffs and others was only as rapid and flexible as their horses provided. A fugitive, having gained any sort of lead, was difficult to catch. The development of the railroad was a help but was not without its disadvantages. The officer was bound to the fixed route of the railroad. There were large gaps between the railroad lines — gaps into which the fugitives unerringly rode. In the hinterland stretches unserved by the railroads, the authorities were forced to make their way over poor roads and disappearing trails.

Linked with inadequate law enforcement was an uneven judicial system. Through fear, friendliness, or corruption, juries often failed to convict the criminal.

Lack of jails (in the early days) or their flimsy construction made it nearly impossible to prevent those in custody from escaping. The system presented numerous opportunities for manipulation by outlaws who could often command some measure of local support. Whenever possible, outlaws would obtain false witnesses in their behalf, pack juries, bribe officials, and, in extreme cases, intimidate the entire system: judges, juries and law-enforcement officials. Such deficiencies in the judicial system were the source of repeated complaints by frontiersmen. They made the familiar point that the American system of administering justice favored the accused rather than society. The guilty, they charged, utilized every loophole for the evasion of punishment. Compounding the problem was the genuinely heavy financial burden involved in maintaining an adequate "police establishment" and judicial system in a sparsely and economically underdeveloped frontier area.[48]

For many a frontiersman, vigilantism was the solution to these problems. W.N. Byers, an old Denver, Colorado, vigilante of 1860 reminisced: "We never hanged on circumstantial evidence. I have known a great many such executions, but I don't believe one of them was ever unjust. But when they were proved guilty, they were always hanged. There was no getting out it. No, *there were no appeals in those days; no writs of errors; no attorneys' fees; no pardon in six months. Punishment was swift, sure and certain.*"[49]

The Ideology of Vigilantism

Most vital to the philosophy of vigilantism was the democratic idea of popular sovereignty. Popular sovereignty was much more than a slogan used by the ambitious Stephen A. Douglas as a gimmick to solve the thorny problem of slavery in the territories; it represented a belief shared by Americans of whatever political persuasion. The regulators of the predominantly Republican countries of La Grange and Noble in northern Indiana saw no inconsistency (as they prepared for a lynch-law drive) in stating as the first of their resolutions on January 9, 1858: "Whereas, We are believers in the *doctrine of popular sovereignty;* that the people of this country are the real sovereigns, and that whenever the laws, made by those to whom they have delegated their authority, are found inadequate to their protection, it is the right of the people to take the protection of their property into their own hands, and deal with these villains according to their just deserts . . ."[50]

The same idea was put a bit more pithily in 1902 when the following jingle was found pinned to the body of a man hanged by the vigilantes of Casper, Wyoming:

> Process of law is a little slow
> So this is the road you'll have to go.
> Murderers and thieves, Beware!
> PEOPLE'S VERDICT.[51]

Although vigilantism rested on a bedrock democratic premise, the vigilante operation in practice was often not democratic. Ordinary men formed the rank and file of the vigilante organization, but, usually, its direction was firmly in the hands of the local elite. Vigilante leaders were often the local large taxpayers. They had the customary desire to whittle down the tax rate and keep local expenses in check. From this point of view there was a persuasive economic rationale, for vigilante justice was cheaper, as well as quicker and more certain, than regular justice. This was a theme that the vigilantes sounded time and again.

In 1858, northern Indiana regulators paraded under a banner that said simply "*No expense to the county.*"[52] A *Denver Tribune* reporter probed opinion in Golden, Colorado, in 1879 after a recent vigilante lynching and found that "on every side the popular verdict seemed to be that the hanging was not only well

merited, but a positive gain to the county, saving it at least five or six thousand dollars."[53]

The Two Models of Vigilantism

Two models of vigilante movements developed. One was the "good" or socially constructive model in which the vigilante movement dealt with a problem of disorder straightforwardly and then disbanded. The result was an increase in the social stability of the locality; the movement was, thus, socially constructive. The other model was the "bad" or socially destructive one in which a vigilante movement encountered such strong opposition that the result was an anarchic vigilante war. Some movements behaved according to the ideal theory of vigilantism while others did not. Some were socially successful; others were not.

THE SOCIALLY CONSTRUCTIVE MODEL

The socially constructive movement occurred where the vigilantes represented a genuine community consensus. Here a decided majority of the people either participated in the movement or approved of it. Vigilantism of this sort simply mobilized the community and overwhelmed the unruly outlaws and lower people. The community was left in a more orderly and stable condition, and the social functions of vigilantism were served: the problem of community order was solved by the consolidation of the three-level social structure and the solidification of the supporting community values.

Although the methods used were often harsh and arbitrary, most vigilante movements — large and small — conformed to the socially constructive model. One of the best examples was the northern Illinois regulator movement of 1841. The northern Illinois movement confronted a classic threat to community order: an agglomeration of outlaw gangs was nearing control of the area. With the regular government virtually powerless, the respectable leading men (the community

Richard Maxwell Brown

upper level) took the law into their own hands with the help of the middle-level farmers.

Since 1835 the situation in the Rock Valley of northern Illinois had gone from bad to worse. Several gangs of horse thieves and counterfeiters found the Rock River country a convenient corridor for illicit operations in Wisconsin, Illinois, Iowa, and Missouri. The Driscoll and Brodie gangs had made Ogle and De Kalb Counties virtual fiefs. The Oliver Gang dominated Winnebago County. The Bliss–Dewey–West ring waxed strong in Lee County, while the Birch gang of horse thieves ranged in all quarters. By 1840 the desperadoes were numerous enough to control elections in Ogle County and similarly threaten other counties. One summer the outlaws even went so far as to burn down the newly constructed courthouse at Oregon, Illinois.

Finally, in April 1841, fifteen "representative men" of Ogle County formed the first regulator company. In no time at all the counties were dotted with regulator squads, but the most vigorous were those of Ogle. The regulators embodied the social, economic, and political prestige of Ogle County: John Phelps was the county's oldest and wealthiest settler and the founder of the county seat, Oregon. Peter Smith combined a bank presidency with the ownership of 1,600 acres of land. The farmers who made up the bulk of the movement were substantial property holders; they had taken up government land claims ranging from 240 to 600 acres. These solid citizens brooked no opposition. They burned the Rockford *Star* to the ground soon after it published an anti-regulator editorial. But, on the whole, the local elite kept the movement under control. Having accomplished their purpose in a campaign of whipping, hanging, and firing squads, the regulator companies disbanded. Socially they left the Rock Valley in a better state than they found it.

The northern Illinois regulator movement exhibited the major characteristics of the successful frontier vigilante movement. It was organized in a rational way. Mass participation of respectable men was the rule, but the movement was clearly dominated by the social and economic elite of the area. The regulators were implacable in their war on the outlaws and unrelenting in the face of opposition. Although the Rockford *Star* opposed the regulators, no antiregulator coalition developed. The outlaw gangs were isolated and broken up. The vigilante leaders desired the assurance of their position at the upper level of their communities but were not power mad. With the outlaw threat put down, peace and order reigned.

THE SOCIALLY DESTRUCTIVE MODEL

In the socially destructive model, anarchy was the result of the vigilante movement. Because there was no community consensus behind the vigilante movement, strong opposition appeared, and civil conflict flared. In the socially constructive model, opposition to the vigilantes was narrowly restricted to outlaws and lower people who could gain no support from the remainder of the community. For the vigilantes to be stymied a broad antivigilante coalition was necessary. The formation of an antivigilante coalition almost inevitably condemned the community to a chaotic internecine struggle between the vigilantes and their opponents.

Examples of the socially destructive model are not as numerous as those for the constructive model, but they tend to be much more violent.

As the career of the socially destructive model proceeded, the moral standing of the vigilantes and the opposing coalition tended to be increasingly compromised. As the struggle became more violent, the respectable men of the antivigilante coalition put a higher premium on the violent tendencies of the outlaw element with which they otherwise had nothing in common. So too, did the original vigilantes themselves recruit criminals as mercenaries. With the community descending bloodily into chaos, wise and prudent men left if they could. The opposing movements tended to fall more and more into the control of the worst and most extreme of their adherents. About this time the desperate neutral residents would beseech state authorities for the intervention of the militia, and the "war" would subside fitfully in the presence of the state troops.

The regulator-moderator war of east Texas 1840–1844 was representative of the degenerate, socially destructive vigilante situation. The scene was the redland and piney-wood country of east Texas in the days of the Lone Star Republic. The center of the conflict was in Shelby County. Fronting on the Sabine River, where it formed the boundary between Louisiana and Texas, Shelby County lay in an old border area that had never been known for peace and calm. In 1840 the regulator movement arose as a quite honest and straightforward attack on a ring of corrupt county officials who specialized in fraudulent land transactions. The rise of the regulators was probably inevitable in any case, for the county had long suffered under a plague of counter-feiting, horse thievery, Negro stealing, and common murder and mayhem. However, the regulators overplayed their hand, especially after their original leader, Charles W. Jackson, was killed and replaced by the nefarious adventurer, Watt Moorman. Bad elements infiltrated both the regulators and their opponents, the moderators, but by comparison the latter seemed to become less obnoxious. Although some honorable and level-headed citizens like John W. Middleton stayed with the regulators to the end, an attitude of wild vengefulness came to be more characteristic of the band. The early ne'er-do-well group among the moderators dwindled. As more and more citizens were forced to take sides, many joined the moderators in reaction to the sadism and vindictiveness of the swashbuckling Watt Moorman, who affected a military uniform and blew great blasts on a hunting horn to summon his henchmen.

The original reasons for the founding of the regulator movement were all but forgotten. The war became a thing in itself, a complex of personal and family feuds that was consuming the area in blood lust. Several attempts to restore peace failed. Complete anarchy prevailed in 1844 when an all-out battle between two armies of several hundred men each was only forestalled by the dramatic intervention of Sam Houston and the militia. After four years, eighteen men had been killed and many more wounded. A stream in the vicinity was called "Widow's Creek." The killing of so many leaders and the exhaustion of the survivors probably explain why the war was not revived after Sam Houston and the militia withdrew. Ex-regulators and ex-moderators warily fought side by side in separate companies in the Mexican War, but for fifty years East Texans were reluctant to discuss the episode lest old enmities be rekindled.

Vigilantism as a Parallel Structure

Vigilantism characteristically appeared in two types of situations: (1) where the regular system of law and order was absent or ineffective, and (2) where the regular system was functioning satisfactorily. The first case found vigilantism filling a void. The second case revealed vigilantism functioning as an extralegal structure of justice that paralleled the regular system.

Why did vigilantes desire to erect a parallel structure when the regular one was adequate? There were a number of reasons. By usurping the functions of regular law enforcement and justice — or, at times, duplicating them — the cost of local government was greatly reduced. As taxpayers the vigilante leaders and the rank and file benefited from the reduction in public costs. Second, the process of community reconstruction through the re-creation of social structure and values could be carried on more dramatically by a vigilante movement than

Richard Maxwell Brown

was possible through the regular functioning of the law. A vigilante hanging was a graphic warning to all potentially disruptive elements that community values and structure were to be upheld.

The sort of impression that vigilantes wanted to make was that received by young Malcolm Campbell who arrived in Cheyenne, Wyoming, in 1868 at the age of twenty-eight. No sooner had he arrived than there were four vigilante hangings. "So in rapid succession," he recalled, "came before my eyes instances which demonstrated the strength of law [as carried out by vigilantes], and the impotence of the criminal. Undoubtedly, these incidents went far in shaping my future life and in guiding my feet properly in those trails of danger where I was later to apprehend some of the most dangerous outlaws of the plains"[54] (Campbell later became a leading Wyoming sheriff).

Finally, the vigilante movement sometimes existed for reasons that were essentially unrelated to the traditional problems of crime and disorder. The San Francisco Vigilance Committee of 1856 is one of the best examples of the vigilante movement as a parallel structure. The San Francisco vigilantes spoke of a crime problem, but examination of the evidence does not reveal a significant upsurge of crime in 1855-1856. The regular authorities had San Francisco crime well under control. Fundamentally, the San Francisco vigilantes were concerned with local political and fiscal reform. They wished to capture control of the government from the dominant faction of Irish Catholic Democrats. The vigilants actually left the routine enforcement of law to the regular police and intervened only in a few major cases. The parallel structure of the vigilante movement was utilized to organize a reform political party (the People's Party) and to shatter the Irish Catholic Democratic faction by exiling some of its leading operatives.

Sometimes the regular and parallel structures were intertwined. Law-enforcement officials often connived with vigilantes. Here a sheriff or police chief was not taken by surprise when a vigilante force bent on a lynching converged upon his jail, for he had helped plan the whole affair. Appearances were preserved, usually, by a token resistance on the part of the law officer, but it was well known in the community that he had shared in the vigilante plot.

Why would men violate their oaths and subvert their own functions as officers of the law? For some men the reason was that they were little more than hirelings of the local vigilante elite to whom were beholden for office. Other officers were of higher social status but, as large landholders or businessmen themselves, they shared the vigilante desire to keep down governmental costs. Little interested in legal niceties, the vigilante-minded law officers were happy to have a nefarious man disposed of quickly, cheaply, and permanently by a lynching.

17

Roger Lane

Urbanization and Criminal Violence in the Nineteenth Century: Massachusetts as a Test Case

America is now an urban nation, but Americans are still afraid of cities. There are many dimensions to this fear, but one of them is especially direct and starkly physical. The current concern with "safety in the streets" echoes a belief, as old as the Republic, that the city is dangerous, the breeding ground of vice and violence. Observers of varying sophistication have pointed out that dark streets hide dark deeds, and that the anonymity and freedom of urban society, its temptations and frenzied pace, all contribute to encourage criminal behavior. From this it is easy to conclude that with metropolitan growth and the multiplication of all these conditions, the rate of violent crime is inexorably multiplied also.

But constant repetition of a myth is no substitute for proof. Under some circumstances it does in fact seem clear that migration to the metropolis has been accompanied by disruption and violence. This does not mean that there is a necessary or inevitable connection between the growth of cities and the growth of crime. In fact the existing historical evidence

suggests the very reverse, that, over the long term, urbanization has had a settling, literally a civilizing, effect on the population involved.

The statistical evidence for such a long-term trend is necessarily fragmentary and local. But for this purpose local studies may well be more reliable than national. Figures for the United States as a whole, compiled by the Federal Bureau of Investigation, have been available only since 1930. Based on the records of police departments with widely varying standards of accuracy, these have provided a generation of criminologists with material for argument.[1] Analyses of crime rates in individual urban areas, on the other hand, are less complicated by discrepancies in definition and in police practice. While few of these reach back to any period before the FBI's Uniform Crime Reports, these few are significant. None points to any clear proportional increase in serious crime within particular cities, and the more recent suggest, on the contrary, a sometimes striking proportional decrease.[2]

Both the decrease and some of the explanation for it can be demonstrated — since it is necessary to choose a single area to represent the whole — by an exam-

Reprinted from the *Journal of Social History*, 2 (1968), 468-483, by permission. Copyright, 1968, by Peter N. Stearns, editor.

Roger Lane

ination of nineteenth-century Massachusetts. A stable eastern state, with one growing metropolis and a number of thriving smaller cities, the Commonwealth had a fairly typical experience with industrial urbanization. As a result of the legislature's enormous appetite for statistical information, its official records, including all those relating to criminal behavior, are probably better than any kept elsewhere.[3] And while criminal statistics are notoriously difficult to deal with, and by themselves offer no firm conclusions, the history of the Commonwealth has been abundantly studied, and may be used to help interpret the raw numerical data. Together, the statistics and the social record can illuminate several aspects of the history of criminal violence in America. These include: the changing incidence of disorder itself, the relation of this change to urban growth, the special conditions which may upset this relation, and, lastly, the problem of public attitudes or concern.

While all criminal statistics are subject to some doubt, the central conclusion about the figures from Massachusetts may be stated with confidence: serious crime in metropolitan Boston declined sharply between the middle of the nineteenth century and the middle of the twentieth. This often-ragged downward trend does not, of course, apply equally to all offenses, but it does to most of the more serious common-law crimes. Three independent studies, by a lawyer, a historian, and a sociologist, confirm this basic direction.[4] While the three cover different periods and employ somewhat different methods, they do fit together, and all are based essentially on police-arrest statistics, the index most widely used by contemporary criminologists.[5] The most comprehensive, covering the years from 1849 to 1951, shows a drop of nearly two-thirds in those crimes which the FBI classifies as "major."[6]

But only half the story, at best, can be told through the figures from the metropolis alone. Our concern is with the whole society. And it has been argued that the difference in crime rates between urban and nonurban areas may be great enough that a drop in the incidence of criminality in the cities is more than offset by the fact that a continually greater percentage of the population is living in them.[7] It is necessary, to meet this problem, to look at the statistics for Massachusetts as a whole.

For most of the nineteenth century the use of police records is neither possible nor desirable on a statewide basis.[8] But other indices of real criminal activity are available. And four of them may be used to establish the changing incidence of "serious" crime, defined as that which involves real injury to persons or loss of property.[9] These four are lower-court cases, jail commitments, grand-jury cases, and state-prison commitments, all involving the major common-law offenses against persons or property. The first date for which two of these indices were published in trustworthy form is 1834: the first year for which all four were compiled is 1860. The figures for these periods, expressed in three-year averages, may be compared with those for the end of the century in the table below.

The decline in the officially recorded crime rate is unmistakable here. And it is strongly probable that the real decline is greater than the statistics indicate. The key problem in the interpretation of criminal statistics is posed by "the dark figure" representing those illegal activities or incidents which never come to the light of official attention. But since in later years, as will be discussed below, there were both increasing intolerance of criminal activity and a great growth in the numbers of police and investigative agents, all evidence suggests that this "dark figure" was growing proportionately smaller as the century progressed. Thus Table 17.1 considerably understates the real decline.

For purposes of explanation it is almost equally important to note the pattern of this decline. The table lists offenses in the order of their severity: lower-court cases generally involve the least important crimes, jailings the next, indictments next, and imprisonments the most. And with one exception — the relative rise in

Table 17.1 Average yearly incidence of cases
per 100,000 population

	1834-36	1860-62	1899-1901
Lower court cases		777	707
Jail commitments		333	163
Grand-jury cases	89	117	63
Imprisonments	16.8	11.9	5.9

indictments between the 1830s and 1860s
which will be considered later — it is
especially notable that the recorded drop
in the crime rate is directly proportional
to the seriousness of the offense. This is
generally true also when the four indices
used are examined further and broken
into subcategories. Thus for example the
combined rate of commitments for homicide, rape, armed robbery, and arson in
1860–1862 was 6.8 per 100,000; by 1900 it
has dropped to 2.9 per 100,000. Most of
the other data point in the same direction
— not only a fall over time but a fall most
marked in the most serious categories.

Meanwhile, however, while the serious
crime rate was falling, the total crime rate
— or the officially recorded total — was
actually rising. This apparent paradox
results from the fact that the downward
curve described above may be wholly
reversed simply by adding a third official
category, "Crimes against Public Order,"
to the two above. When these offenses are
added in — drunkenness is by far the largest of them — the results for the lower
courts may be indicated as follows:

Table 17.2 Yearly incidence of cases per
100,000 population.

	1840	1860	1900
Total lower court cases	595	1,869	3,317

The pattern for these minor crimes is
the obverse of that for serious offenses, in
that the more trivial the degree of the
offense the larger its proportional increase
over time. While virtually no indictments
or imprisonments resulted from third-
class offenses, their addition makes less
difference in the case of jailings than of
lower- court cases:

Table 17.3 Yearly incidence of cases per
100,000 population

	1841	1860	1900
Total jail commitments	419	548	969

This upward curve in total offenses
does not have the same importance as the
other, downward curve in the incidence
of serious crime. The latter represents the
basic statistical conclusion, in that it
reflects a real situation, a real decline in
the rate of criminal activity. But the
former, while it is merely statistical, is
nontheless important. There is a comple-
mentary relationship between the two
trends, and the nature of this relationship
helps account for much that underlies the
numbers.

The entire increase in the criminal statistics of Massachusetts during the period
covered may in fact be attributed wholly
to the rise in cases of drunkenness. Indeed
this one offense, together with simple
assault, its constant companion, may
serve as a focus for much more. To understand the reasons for the rise in drunk
arrests is to understand much about the
social changes occurring in the nineteenth century, changes which affected all
its criminal patterns.

It is clear, first, that the mounting total
of cases fed into the official machinery of
justice does not reflect a real increase in
the consumption of alcohol. The misuse
of drink was throughout the nineteenth
century a problem of enormous dimensions. The continuing debate about the
nature of drunkenness, although some of
it anticipated the best of current thinking,
was on the whole punitive and tended to
blame the use of alcohol for virtually all
individual, and most social evils.[10] But
even the most ardent spirits in the temperance movement did not usually suggest
that there was any long-term rise in
drunken behavior. They and their opponents generally united in agreeing that
the situation, in ragged fashion, was
improving with time. Because much of
the alcohol was made and sold illegally,
especially in the countryside, it is diffi-

Roger Lane

cult to investigate this statistically. But certainly in the metropolis and probably elsewhere the evidence does suggest a decline. Early in the century even ministerial ordinations, to say nothing of less grave occasions, were frequently bibulous affairs.[11] By the 1830s a substantial portion of the middle class had renounced the use of hard liquor. The prohibition was extended later to all drinks, and its champions carried on a continuous political and educational campaign against it. In the 1830s, and again in the 1850s, law enforcement officers estimated that 1 in every 65 inhabitants of Boston — men, women, and children — were selling alcohol for a living, in the latter period in defiance of a state law which prohibited all private sales.[12] Certainly neither this proportion nor this widespread evasion of the law was matched later in the century; by about 1880 the ratio was down to 1 seller in 150 and rising fast.

On one level, the rising statistics of arrests for drunkenness simply reflect an increase in the numbers of professional police and in the penal apparatus. It was not until 1837 that Boston organized a squad of full-time professionals, and for many years these were the only ones in the Commonwealth. But by 1860 all of the larger cities had organized forces of varying sizes, and these had grown and spread to the smaller towns well before 1900.[13] The effect of this, and of a proportionate increase in the rest of the agents of justice, is easily demonstrated. In the absence of police, ordinary citizens were expected to make complaints on their own, and to call on constables only to execute warrants already sworn. But while private individuals may make the effort to initiate the processes of justice when directly injured, professionals are required to deal, in number, with those whose merely immoral or distasteful behavior hurts no one in particular. It takes real cops, in short, to arrest drunks.

Again on this level the relative shortage of official agents of law enforcement accounts for one of the most striking characteristics of Table 17.1 above. The farther back the figures go, as noted, the higher is the relative proportion of serious crimes. The authorities, with limited resources, obviously had to deal with felony first, indictable crime next, and misdemeanor only when resources permitted.

Conversely it is notable that as time advanced and it became easier for injured citizens to complain to a policeman, the tables indicate that proportionately fewer complaints were being made. In the city of Boston, at least, the result was a progressive decrease in the number of annual arrests made by each patrolman: in 1855, the average was seventy-one per man, while by 1885 this had dropped to thirty-seven.[14]

Drawn as a model, this development may explain the only apparent anomaly in table 17.1, already referred to. This is the fact that between the 1830s and the 1860s the figures show both a fall in prison commitments and a rise in grand-jury indictments. Perhaps — the subject will be investigated further — there is no great paradox at all. District attorneys in the 1830s, faced with a high incidence of truly violent criminal behavior, may have had to concentrate on the more important prisonable offenses to the neglect of others, even indictable ones. As their resources were increased and as the real crime rate fell, they would be able by the 1860s to catch up on lesser indictments.

But there remains a more fundamental level of explanation. To account for the rise in lesser offenses or the drop in more serious crimes simply in terms of the expansion of police, courts, and prosecutors is to misplace the emphasis. The expansion is not cause but symptom. The machinery of justice was increased because of a felt need, a growing intolerance of behavior which had earlier been tolerated, coupled with a belief that the state and not the individual citizen was required to do the necessary job.

This process is most evident in Boston itself. Leading citizens and governmental officials were always proud of their reputation for maintaining a tidy and well-governed "order" in the city. But the definition of what constituted "order" changed considerably with time.

Josiah Quincy, one of Boston's first mayors, was also the first to boast that in no other city "of equal population, are there fewer instances of those crimes, to which all populous places are subject."[15] He had in fact assumed charge, in 1823, of a newly incorporated city of about 45,000 inhabitants, which officially issued some 697 liquor licenses and ignored the existence of a large number of illegal sellers. Relatively little attention was paid to such common offenses as simple drunkenness and assault. The night watch, largely concerned with the danger of fire or arson, was afraid to enter some of the more notorious neighborhoods. No one patrolled anywhere in the daytime. Quincy's several terms of office were marked by frequent battles between rival gangs of firemen, whose hunger for looting threatened the whole institution of fire insurance. When, after one of the city's numerous "riots, routs, and tumultuous assemblies" had spluttered on for a full week during the long hot summer of 1825, Quincy was forced to take personal charge of a posse of citizens to put it down. This was clearly an unusual action, and the mayor refused later opportunities to risk his limbs and authority in physical combat, preferring to let mob violence burn out by itself. Nevertheless, neither he nor the voters were unduly alarmed by the prevailing level of disorder. Citizens were traditionally supposed to take care of themselves, with the help of family, friends, or servants when available. An organized professional police would certainly be expensive and might also be a threat to valued freedoms. Quincy was proud to point out, at the end of his official career, that he had not added a single constable or watchman to Boston's part-time corps of peace officers.

By the 1880s, when an aldermanic committee echoed Mayor Quincy's earlier claim that Boston was the most orderly of America's larger cities, the situation had changed considerably. In 1837, after three major riots in four years, the city had acquired a police force. Since then it had been growing steadily, at a rate faster than the population. By the Civil War, the citizens had abandoned their objections to uniforms, with their paramilitary connotations, and the patrolmen had begun to carry guns. By the 1880s the force had acquired most of its familiar modern characteristics and functions. And the demand for more men continued — despite the fact that the crime rate had been dropping for some time and, with it, the workload for each man on the force.

The demand for more men, then, reflected not a worsening situation but higher standards, a change in attitude. Really violent crime brought more severe retribution than formerly; the same offenses which had earned two-year sentences in the 1830s were now punished by three to four years or more in the state penitentiary, and the average was still going up. While the police stations were still being built for "defensibility," there had been — and would be — no large-scale riot for years.[16] It is impossible to imagine a late-century mayor wrestling with mobs as did Quincy in the twenties and Theodore Lyman in the thirties. All of the city had been brought under more or less effective patrol, and the voters were demanding that the streets be cleared not only of arsonists but of drunks, peddlers, and truants. Traffic problems were settled not by teamsters with their fists but by officers with whistles. The responsibility for individual safety had been decisively shifted to these agents of the law; uniformed men with revolvers were stationed not only in potentially dangerous areas but in the quiet confines of the public library.[17] And the end result, reflected in many arrests for minor breaches of conduct, was a degree of "order" which would have astonished and perhaps dismayed an earlier and rougher generation.

The progressive heightening of standards of propriety and with it the increasing reliance on official law enforcement were processes which,

Roger Lane

while most sharply visible in Boston, were common to the whole society. Traditionally, criminologists have interpreted the zigs and zags of recorded criminal statistics in terms of individual events or situations — war, for example, or depression. But the change in social behavior reflected in the two dominant curves of criminality in Massachusetts is so long term and so widespread as to suggest a connection with the most fundamental of contemporary social processes, that of industrial urbanization itself. The nature of that connection has never been studied in detail, but it may at least be outlined.

Massachusetts in 1835 had a population of some 660,940; 81 percent rural, overwhelmingly preindustrial, and native born.[18] Its citizens were used to considerable personal freedom. Whether teamsters, farmers, or artisans, they were all accustomed to settling their own schedules, and the nature of their work made them physically independent of each other. None of the more common occupations provided any built-in checks against various kinds of personal excess. Neither fits of violence nor bouts of drunkenness disrupted any vital patterns. Individual problems, sins, or even crimes were not generally cause for wider social concern.

Under these circumstances, while scarcely a frontier, the Commonwealth could afford a fairly high degree of lawlessness. No city in the state boasted a professional police, and the machinery of justice was not equipped to handle many cases. Many of the more common forms of violence or crime were simply not reported to the agents of law, as those affected either shrugged off their injuries or struck back directly.

But the impact of the twin movements to the city and to the factory, both just gathering force in 1835, had a progressive effect on personal behavior throughout the nineteenth century and into the twentieth. The factory demanded regularity of behavior, a life governed by obedience to the rhythms of clock and calender, the demands of foreman and supervisor. In the city or town the needs of living in closely packed neighborhoods inhibited many actions previously unobjectionable. Both blue- and white-collar employees in larger establishments were mutually dependent on their fellows; as one man's work fit into another's, so one man's business was no longer his own.

The results of the new organization of life and work were apparent by 1900, when some 76 percent of the 2,805,346 inhabitants of Massachusetts were classified as urbanites. Much violent or irregular behavior which had been tolerable in a casual, independent society was no longer acceptable in the more formalized, cooperative atmosphere of the later period. The private, direct response to criminal injury was no longer necessary or approved. All cities and most towns had acquired police forces, constantly expanding to meet greater expectations. Throughout the state, the victims of violence and theft were conditioned to seek official help. The move to the cities had, in short, produced a more tractable, more socialized, more "civilized" generation than its predecessors.[19]

The trend in the direction of higher standards and a lower level of violence may be measured from the early nineteenth century through much of the twentieth. But what is true in the long run is not necessarily evident in the short. While the process of urbanization has helped to raise standards of personal behavior, it may not do so by itself. And there is some indication in the history of nineteenth-century Massachusetts that under unfavorable conditions migration to the cities may at some times have increased the incidence of violently unsocial behavior. This may well be true, at least, of the long generation between 1835 and 1860.

The existing statistics alone are no sure guide to what was actually happening during these crucial early decades. The Boston arrest figures were not kept until 1849. For the state as a whole, much of the remaining evidence is ambiguous. As explained above, the two main indices, the rate of grand jury indictments and of imprisonments for felony, point stubbornly in opposite directions. But there is good reason to suspect that the period from the mid-1830s to the Civil War illustrates at least a partial, and important, exception to the general developments previously sketched.

From the war on to the end of the century and beyond, the industrial development of Massachusetts, however painful for those involved, was at least proceeding at a pace and along lines already laid out. The era just before was the one which witnessed the turbulence of transition. No similar timespan in fact encompassed a more rapid increase in the urban population. Between 1835 and 1860, while the total population was growing from 660,940 to 1,231,066, the proportion of city dwellers leaped from 19 to 44 percent of the total. At the same time, too, the major railroad lines were laid in patterns still existing. As steam began to replace water-power as the major source of industrial energy, the factories, earlier confined to rural sites near waterfalls, began to move into the cities.

Social dislocation, meanwhile, accompanied economic. All through the period, and especially during and after the "hungry forties," heavy Irish immigration exacerbated all of the problems of city living. By 1855, some 68,100 of the 168,031 residents of Boston were natives of Ireland.[20] Uprooted from a rural setting, wholly without skills, the newcomers experienced the kind of culture shock, prejudice, and alienation which would plague other waves of migrants later. Crowded into stinking hovels, some of them underground, their miserable conditions of living strained all of the city's institutions of charity and police. Smallpox, once virtually eliminated, became again a problem, cholera struck hard, and the death rate about the middle of the century climbed to the highest point in the city's recorded history.

In terms of its effect on behavior, all of these rapid and wrenching changes promoted the worst aspects of living in the city without benefit of its compensations.

It must be stressed that economic developments were not fully able to keep pace with migration. Between 1837 and 1845, it has been estimated, the amount of large-scale or factory employment did not increase at all, and in the fifteen years following, while the total of factory employees grew to something like 25,000 or 30,000, the number of outright paupers in the metropolitan area was increasing at an even faster rate, to reach a peak of nearly 13,000 in 1860. Without the discipline imposed by regular employment, this first large-scale flow of migrants into the city was a kind of mutual disaster. The raw arrivals from the countryside, Yankees as well as Irish, had not yet learned to weave warily through crowds with their arms held in close. Often radically insecure in neighborhoods still unstable, they sought release in drink. But to drink with strangers requires different rules and more restraints than drinking in more familiar situations. In this era of swinging elbows, bewilderment, and desperate unemployment, it is hard to find evidence that the level of violence was declining.

Indeed it is easy to find the opposite. During this whole period Massachusetts was wracked by political instability, aggravated by one unpopular war and the overhanging threat of another one. The 1850s in particular witnessed a resurgence of mob violence as Know-Nothings and Irishmen, opponents and defenders of slavery, all found occasions to take to the streets.[21] These clashes, superimposed on and partly resulting from the already unhealthy social condition of Boston, were deeply disturbing to the inhabitants. If the real incidence of criminal behavior was not actually rising at this time, then surely it was not falling at the rate apparent in the generations following the Civil War.

All evidence points to the long-term drop in criminal activity as normative and associated with urbanization. But the process was not complete without the accompaniment of rapid industrial development. It was this which provided the means of absorbing raw migrants, of fit-

Roger Lane

ting them into a "system" which socialized and accommodated them into more cooperative habits of life. Without this other process, migration to the city alone, simply by multiplying human contacts, may very well multiply the incidence of criminally violent interaction among inhabitants unsuited to its demands.

Because of its clear connection with ethnic prejudice and its dangerous political and social implications, the violent state of Boston during the 1850s was the source of considerable public concern. But the relation between concern about violence and violence itself is not always so uncomplicated. Both in the nineteenth and in the twentieth century, the attitudes of newspapers, scholars, and the public generally have been various and volatile, the product often of special interests or misinformation. This makes such attitudes difficult to measure. But they are nevertheless crucially important to the study of criminal disorder.

In the long run and in the short, popular concern has a direct effect on the shape of criminal statistics. As it was changing public standards which accounted for the rising total of arrests during the nineteenth century, so police departments still concentrate on those offenses of greatest current interest. Moreover, it is not simply the actual level of criminal activity, but the balance between this and social attitudes which determines how much violence is a "problem" at any given time.

While public "attitudes" are slippery concepts to compare, it does seem that, in the sense above, the state of Massachusetts, and the United States in general, had a criminal problem less worrisome in the nineteenth century than in the 1960s. The citizens of the Commonwealth, still close to their rural antecedents, were indeed afraid of cities, which one legislative committee called "the common sewers of the state." And one major source of this fear was the "poverty, vice, and crime" commonly associated with Boston in particular.[22] But hostile critics were more interested in the first two than

in the last, and reformers endlessly debated the causal relation between them. The charge that the city had lost control of its "dangerous classes" was used in several attempts to limit self-government in Boston, but mob action was the only form of violence which generally figured in these complaints, and "crime" was used typically as a synonym for "vice."[23] It is significant that the laws concerning drink especially were subject to constant revision, but except for a reduction in the number of cases involving the death penalty, the general criminal code was not. Legislative action or inaction mirrored public concern in this case. As the sons and daughters of Massachusetts migrated to the metropolis, the image conjured by the fearful was the rake or tempter, not the robber or rapist.

Nevertheless, however overshadowed by other issues, there were periodic outbursts of concern about violence or other crime. Often these occurred in response to some new development or threat for which the public or authorities were unprepared. In fact, the history of these threats and of the responses to them comprises much of the history of criminal-law enforcement.

Thus the multiplication of banks and bank notes, through the 1820s, provided golden opportunities for counterfeiters. The nature of the problem, in this case, required a network of private bankers' agents to cooperate across state and even national boundaries with the appropriate public authorities. Anti-Catholic rioting, in the 1830s, was a principal spur to the development of professional police. During the 1870s, the growing sophistication of professional criminals, dramatized by a spectacular series of bank robberies, led to an overhaul of existing detective methods in many American cities. During the same period, bands of healthy native vagrants, fugitives from the new industrial age, were a subject of great concern to the readers of sensational newspapers, who feared the violent potential in these "wild-eyed" strangers. The response in this case was harsher police action and a tightening of the rules governing charity and soup kitchens.

These concerns were at any rate, real and often had lasting effects, although they had little to do with the overall crime rate. Another and more frequent kind of scare resulted not from some genuinely new problem but from sudden attention focused on an old one. Lincoln Steffens, as a cub reporter in New York learned how easy it was to manufacture a "crime wave" with techniques still familiar.[24] Thus a particularly brutal murder or a series of muggings could touch off a wave of arrests "on suspicion."[25] Often it was simply an investigation or expose of some endemic form of crime which generated a sudden excitement, during which the public was assured that Boston was facing a threat of unprecedented proportions.

But it is impossible, from these brief scares, to get any clear sense of direction. While the definition of the tolerable was altering with time, it was altering slowly and imperceptibly. And there is no evidence that, as the century progressed, the gap between the level of order expected and the level actually obtaining was changing in any constant direction. It is true that the police often felt that they were faced with problems of unprecedented magnitude, and chiefs decades apart warned that the level of juvenile delinquency and the general breakdown of authority threatened the very basis of society. Other observers, too, perhaps beguiled by the image of a more peaceful golden age in the past, sometimes asserted that crime was growing faster than the population. But this tendency to fear was balanced throughout the century by pride in growth and progress. And the many apocalyptic statements may be countered with an equal number of others, more optimistic. Thus even in the troubled year of 1859, the state's attorney general could declare that "at no time in the history of Massachusetts have life, liberty, and property been more secure than at present."[26]

In short, while it is possible now to discover a long-term drop in the level of violence, contemporaries were simply not aware of this. The degree of public concern has never been, nor is it now, an accurate index of the degree of criminal activity. Indeed the reverse is often true. And it is doubly ironic that a drop in the actual incidence of disorder has been accompanied by — and contributed to — a heightened sensitivity to disorder. Such sensitivity, by leading to a more demanding standard of conduct, has been essential to the functioning of an interdependent urban society. But unless the process is recognized and understood, it may have unsettling effects. There are times when for various reasons the level of violence overbalances current expectations. In such situations the social pressure to maintain and extend high standards and to enforce them universally may result in frustration. The frustration may translate into fear. And this fear, in turn, may focus on the very urban process which helped to create those standards — on the growth of cities itself.

Part Six

Slavery and the Civil War

The legal and social realities that actually defined the "peculiar institution" — slavery — have long intrigued historians of the ante-bellum South. In the study that follows Kenneth Stampp examines the status of the slave in pre–Civil War state law. The premise that the slave was property rested at the foundation of ante-bellum southern law, and Stampp examines the rules and social controls that flowed from that premise. He also considers the fate of slaves given "virtual freedom" by their masters and other evidence of day-to-day practices that deviated from the system as we would describe it if we were drawing evidence only from statute books and court decisions.

How slavery worked in practice has recently been the subject of several major scholarly studies. Among them, Robert Fogel and Stanley Engerman's *Time on the Cross* (1974) argues that the system was far more benign than either the legal evidence or the work of most scholars, even those most familiar with plantation records and slave history, would suggest. This view, however, has not withstood critical scrutiny, including that of Stampp himself. Another intriguing alternative approach to slavery and the law was pro-vided by Eugene D. Genovese's *Roll, Jordan, Roll: The World the Slaves Made* (1976). But just as relevant to our knowledge of slavery as these more recent studies is the perceptive analysis of the law of slavery made in 1853 by William Goodell, a leading antislavery critic, when he sought "by an exhibition of the American Slave Code" to test the "moral character of American slaveholding." For "the practice," he wrote, "cannot be better than the code, or rule of conduct, that gives it licence and sanction." Without question, as Genovese and other scholars have pointed out, the slave community asserted in myriad ways the humanity of black people. No less certain was the fact that white Southerners carried a considerable burden of guilt, secret and open doubt, and even a willingness to soften certain features of the formal law so long as it did not threaten the institution of slavery itself. Yet, as Stampp demonstrates, what archaic, nineteenth-century rhetoric termed "the moral character" of the slave system meant, in the last analysis, that southern whites could guarantee the institution itself only by placing the values of property above those of humanity. Beneficent slavery is a contradiction in terms.

Slavery and the Civil War

The complex interrelations between southern fears of the blacks, southern concern that new constitutional doctrine might jeopardize the stability of the "peculiar institution," vigorous northern expansion into the western territories, and the classic constitutional issues of federalism and states' rights comprise the basis for Arthur E. Bestor's analysis of the Civil War as a constitutional crisis. As a corrective to an earlier interpretation that made economic issues and economic differences between North and South the essential explanation for the Civil War crisis, Bestor restores constitutional and legal questions to center stage. But he does so not in simplistic terms that depict the constitutional issues as abstractions commanding emotional support, nor even as a clash of doctrines that emerged reflexively as an expression of cultural differences between North and South. Instead, Bestor makes a telling argument for understanding southern intransigence and the ensuing constitutional debates of the 1850s as part of a dynamic process whose rich complexity he sets forth in bold terms.

Further Reading

Cover, Robert M. *Justice Accused: Antislavery and the Judicial Process.* New Haven: Yale University Press, 1975.

Davis, David Brion. *The Problem of Slavery in the Age of Revolution, 1770–1823.* Ithaca: Cornell University Press, 1975.

Hyman, Harold M. *A More Perfect Union: The Impact of the Civil War and Reconstruction on the Constitution.* New York: Alfred A. Knopf, 1973.

Nichols, Roy F. *American Leviathan: The Evolution and Process of Self-Government in the United States.* New York: Harper & Rowe, 1966. Also published as *Blueprints for Leviathan* (1963).

Paludan, Phillip S. *A Covenant with Death: The Constitution, Law, and Equality in the Civil War Era.* Urbana: University of Illinois Press, 1975.

Randall, J. G., and David Donald. *The Civil War and Reconstruction.* 2d ed. Boston: D. C. Heath, 1961.

Sydnor, Charles S. *Slavery in Mississippi.* 1933. Reprinted. Baton Rouge: Louisiana State University Press, 1966.

18

Kenneth M. Stampp

Chattels Personal

In Alabama's legal code of 1852 two clauses, standing in significant juxtaposition, recognized the dual character of the slave.[1]

The first clause confirmed his status as property — the right of the owner to his "time, labor and services" and to his obedient compliance with all lawful commands. Slavery thus being established by law, masters relied upon the state to use its power against white men who "tampered" with their bondsmen, and against bondsmen they could not subdue. Courts, police, and militia were indispensable parts of the machinery of control.

The second clause acknowledged the slave's status as a person. The law required that masters be humane to their slaves, furnish them adequate food and clothing, and provide care for them during sickness and in old age. In short, the state endowed masters with obligations as well as rights and assumed some responsibility for the welfare of the bondsmen.

But legislators and magistrates were caught in a dilemma whenever they found

that the slave's status as property was incompatible with his status as a person. Individual masters struggled with this dilemma in different ways, some conceding much to the dictates of humanity, others demanding the utmost return from their investment. Frederick Law Olmsted explained the problem succinctly: "It is difficult to handle simply as property, a creature possessing human passions and human feelings, . . . while, on the other hand, the absolute necessity of dealing with property as a thing, greatly embarrasses a man in any attempt to treat it as a person."

After adopting Draconian codes in the early eighteenth century, the various legislatures in some respects gradually humanized them, while the courts tempered their application; but there was no way to resolve the contradiction implicit in the very term "human property." Both legislators and judges frequently appeared erratic in dealing with bondsmen as both *things* and *persons*. Alabama's code defined the property status of the slave before acknowledging his human status, and throughout the ante-bellum South the cold language of statutes and judicial decisions made it evident that, legally, the slave was less a person than a thing . . .

Abridged from Kenneth M. Stampp, *The Peculiar Institution: Slavery in the Ante-Bellum South* 192-236. Copyright, 1956, Kenneth Stampp, by permission of Alfred A. Knopf, Inc.

Kenneth M. Stampp

In the customary phraseology of the ante-bellum codes, South Carolina's slaves were "deemed, held, taken, reputed and adjudged in law to be chattels personal, in the hands of their owners and possessors and their executors, administrators and assigns, to all intents, constructions and purposes whatsoever." Slaves had the attributes of personal property everywhere, except in Louisiana (and Kentucky before 1852) where they had the attributes of real estate. Neither the laws nor the courts, however, were altogether consistent. In states where slaves were generally considered as personalty, they were treated as realty for purposes of inheritance. In Louisiana, where they were supposedly like real property, they retained many of the characteristics of "chattels personal."

Though the slave was property "of a distinctive and peculiar character," though recognized as a person, he was legally at the disposal of his master, whose property right was very nearly absolute. "The master," proclaimed the Louisiana code, "may sell him, dispose of his person, his industry, and his labor: he can do nothing, possess nothing, nor acquire anything but what must belong to his master." Even in Kentucky, slaves had "no rights secured to them by the constitution, except of trial by jury in cases of felony."[2]

Legally a bondsman was unable to acquire title to property by purchase, gift, or devise; he could not be a party to a contract . . .

Nor could a chattel be a party to a suit, except indirectly when a free person represented him in a suit for freedom. In court he was not a competent witness, except in a case involving another slave. He had no civil rights, no political rights, no claim to his time, no freedom of movement.

Since slaves, as chattels, could not make contracts, marriages between them were not legally binding. "The relation between slaves is essentially different from that of man and wife joined in lawful wedlock," ruled the North Carolina Supreme Court, for "with slaves it may be dissolved at the pleasure of either party, or by the sale of one or both, depending upon the caprice or necessity of the owners." Their condition was compatible only with a form of concubinage, "voluntary on the part of the slaves, and permissive on that of the master." In law there was no such thing as fornication or adultery between slaves; nor was there bastardy, for, as a Kentucky judge noted, the father of a slave was "unknown" to the law.[3] No state legislature ever seriously entertained the thought of encroaching upon the master's rights by legalizing slave marriages.

On the contrary, the states guaranteed the rights of property in human chattels in every way feasible. Most southern constitutions prohibited the legislatures from emancipating slaves without both the consent of the owners and the payment of a full equivalent in money. Every state provided severe penalties for the theft of a slave — a common crime in the ante-bellum South. In Virginia the penalty was two to ten years in the penitentiary, in Tennessee it was five to fifteen years, and in many states it was death.

When a bondsman was executed for a capital crime the state usually compensated the owner, the normal compensation being something less than the full value assessed by a jury. In Arkansas, which gave no compensation, a slaveholder complained bitterly of the "injustice" done him when one of his slaves was hanged for rape. "I had, or ought to have, some claims upon the State for the destruction of my property," he thought. "That would be good policy and good law." Since the execution of a slave resembled the public seizure or condemnation of private property, most of the states recognized the justice of the owner's claim. Sometimes they levied a special tax on slaves and established a separate public fund for this purpose.

There were virtually no restrictions upon the owner's right to deed his bondsmen to others. Normally the courts nullified such transfers only if the seller fraudulently warranted a slave to be "free from defects" or "vices" such as the "habit of running away." In devising his chattels a testator had the power to divide them among his heirs in any way he saw fit — including the power to dissolve families for the purpose of making an equitable distribution. If a master died intestate, the division was made in accordance with the state's laws of inheritance.

Sometimes the division provided by a will, or the claims of heirs of a master who died intestate, could not be realized without a sale of slaves. In such cases the southern courts seldom tried to prevent the breaking up of slave families. The executor of an estate was expected to dispose of human chattels, like other property, in the way that was most profitable to the heirs. It may be "harsh" to separate members of families, said the North Carolina Supreme Court, yet "it must be done, if the executor discovers that the interest of the estate requires it; for he is not to indulge his charities at the expense of others" . . .

Since slaves were frequently sold on credit or used as security for loans, they were subject to seizure and sale for the benefit of creditors. A clause in the Virginia code added the proviso that human chattels were not to be seized "without the debtor's consent" when there were "other goods and chattels of such debtor for the purpose." Slaves who were seized were to be sold "at the court house of the county or corporation, between the hours of ten in the morning and four in the afternoon . . . on the first day of the court." In "execution sales," except for mothers and small children, family ties were ignored whenever it was beneficial to the debtor. As a witness testified before the Georgia Supreme Court, "It is not usual to put up negroes in families at Sheriff's sales"[4] . . .

Executors and administrators also sold slaves when it was necessary to satisfy the creditors of the deceased. Their notices of sales "for the purpose of paying debts" against estates appeared in the newspapers alongside the sheriff's notices. Sometimes their advertisements listed

bondsmen together with horses, mules, cows, farm implements, and other forms of personal property.

The unsentimental prose of legal codes and court records, of sheriff's notices and administrator's accounts, gave some indication of the dehumanizing effects of reducing people to "chattels personal." Masters who claimed their rights under the laws of property, and who developed the habit of thinking of their chattels in impersonal terms, provided further evidence. The laws, after all, were not abstractions; they were written by practical men who expected them to be applied to real situations. Accordingly, slaves *were* bartered, deeded, devised, pledged, seized, and auctioned. They were awarded as prizes in lotteries and raffles; they were wagered at gaming tables and horse races. They were, in short, property in fact as well as in law.

Men discussed the price of slaves with as much interest as the price of cotton or tobacco. Commenting upon the extraordinarily good prices in 1853, a South Carolina editor reported, "Boys weighing about fifty lbs. can be sold for about five hundred dollars." "It really seems that there is to be no stop to the rise," added a North Carolina editor. "This species of property is at least 30 percent higher now, (in the dull season of the year), than it was last January . . . What negroes will bring next January, it is impossible for mortal man to say"[5] . . .

In new regions — for example, in Alabama and Mississippi during the 1830s — the buying and selling of slaves and plantations was the favorite operation of speculators. Everywhere people invested cash in bondsmen as people in an industrial society would invest in stocks and bonds. Affluent parents liked to give slaves to their children as presents. "With us," said a Virginia judge, "nothing is so usual as to advance children by gifts of slaves. They stand with us instead of money." A Kentuckian, "in easy circumstances," was "in the habit of . . . presenting a slave to each of his grandchildren." "I buy . . . Negro boy Jessee," wrote a Ten-

Kenneth M. Stampp

nessee planter, "and send him as a gift to my daughter Eva and the heirs of her body."[6]

Slaveholders kept the courts busy with litigation involving titles and charges of fraudulent sales. "The plaintiff declares that the defendent . . . deceitfully represented the . . . slave to be sound except one hip, and a good house servant," ran a typical complaint. A lawyer, searching for legal precedents which might justify a claim of "unsoundness" in a slave recently sold, cited past judicial opinions "as regards horseflesh." Two South Carolinians presented to the state court of appeals the question of whether the seller or buyer must suffer the loss of a slave who had committed suicide during the course of the transaction.[7] Families were sometimes rent asunder as relatives fought for years, in court and out, over claims to bondsmen.

Litigation between slaveholders and their creditors also brought much business to the southern courts. Many masters who would have refused to sell bondsmen to traders nevertheless mortgaged them and thus often made sales inevitable when their estates were settled, if not before. A Tennesseean with "heavy debts over him" escaped the sheriff by fleeing to Texas with his slaves. This was a familiar story in the Old South, so familiar that the phrase "gone to Texas" was applied to any debtor who fled from his creditors. A slaveholder would abandon his lands and escape in the night with his movable chattels. The courts heard case after case like that of a Georgian who "clandestinely removed his property, consisting of negroes, to . . . Alabama, . . . to avoid the payment of his debts," and of a Mississippian, who "ran off . . . into Texas, certain negro slaves, with a view of defrauding his creditors."[8]

The reduction of bondsmen to mere pawns in disputes over titles and in actions by creditors was a sordid business. But the suits for trespass masters brought against those who had injured their chattels were no less depressing. For example, when a Kentucky bondsman "died in consequence of injuries inflicted on him by Thos. Kennedy and others," the owner sued and recovered a judgment for one hundred and ninety-five dollars and costs. A Tennessee slave was hired to a man who permitted him to die of neglect. An indignant judge affirmed that "the hirer of a slave should be taught . . . that more is required of him than to exact from the slave the greatest amount of service, with the least degree of attention to his comfort, health, or even life" — and gave a judgment of five hundred dollars for the master, the sole penalty. An Alabama slave was scarred by severe whippings inflicted by his hirer. The owner brought suit on the ground that the slave's "market value . . . was permanently injured."[9]

In all these ways the slave as property clearly had priority over the slave as a person. Contrary to tradition, this was equally the case when masters executed their last wills and testaments. To be sure, some exhibited tender solicitude for their "people" and made special provisions for them, but they were decidedly exceptional. In addition to those who died intestate and thus left the fate of their slaves to be settled by the courts, most testators — Virginians as well as Mississippians, large as well as small — merely explained how they wished their chattels to be divided among the heirs . . .

Testators often specifically authorized or ordered the sale of slaves. In 1849 Martha DuBose, of Fairfield District, South Carolina, provided for a division of slaves among her devisees "either by sale or otherwise." Stephen Taylor, of Edgecombe County, North Carolina, in 1848 bequeathed to his wife five slaves during her life, after which they were "to be sold and the money arising therefrom to be equally divided" among several heirs. In 1842 James Atkinson, also of Edgecombe County, instructed his executor to sell nine slaves immediately after his death; upon his wife's death his two remaining slaves were to be "sold at public sale to the highest bidder and the monies arising from said sale equally divided among my lawful heirs."

The offspring of slave women were frequently devised before they were born — occasionally before they were conceived. In Fairfield District, South Carolina, in 1830 Mary Kincaid gave a slave woman named Sillar to a grandchild, and Sillar's two children to other grandchildren. If Sillar should have a third child, it was to go to still another grandchild. If not, "I will that her two children now living be sold at twelve years of age and the proceeds equally divided among my said grand children." In Mecklenburg County, North Carolina, George Houston in 1839 willed to one daughter a slave named Charity and to another daughter "the first child that . . . Charity shal have . . ."

Every slave state had a slave code. Besides establishing the property rights of those who owned human chattels, these codes supported masters in maintaining discipline and provided safeguards for the white community against slave rebellions. In addition, they held slaves, as thinking beings, morally responsible and punishable for misdemeanors and felonies.

Fundamentally the slave codes were much alike. Those of the Deep South were somewhat more severe than those of the upper South, but most of the variations were in minor details. The similarities were due, in part, to the fact that new states patterned their codes after those of the old. South Carolina's code of 1712 was almost a copy of the Barbadian code; Georgia's code of 1770 duplicated South Carolina's code of 1740; and later the Gulf states borrowed heavily from both. In the upper South, Tennessee virtually adopted North Carolina's code, while Kentucky and Missouri lifted many passages from Virginia's. But the similarities were also due to the fact that slavery, wherever it existed, made necessary certain kinds of regulatory laws. The South Carolina code would probably have been essentially the same if the Barbadian code had never been written.

After a generation of liberalization following the American Revolution, the codes underwent a reverse trend toward increasing restrictions. This trend was clearly evident by the 1820s, when rising slave prices and expansion into the Southwest caused more and more Southerners to accept slavery as a permanent institution. The Nat Turner rebellion and northern abolitionist attacks merely accelerated a trend which had already begun.

In practice the slave codes went through alternating periods of rigid and lax enforcement. Sometimes slaveholders demanded even more rigorous codes, and sometimes they were remiss in enforcing parts of existing ones. When the danger of attack from without or of rebellion from within seemed most acute, they looked anxiously to the state governments for additional protection. After the Turner uprising, Governor John Floyd advised the Virginia legislature: "As the means of guarding against the possible repetition of these sanguinary scenes, I cannot fail to recommend to your early attention, the revision of all the laws, intended to preserve in due subordination the slave population of our State."[10] The legislature responded with several harsh additions to the code, but enforcement during the next three decades continued to be spasmodic.

At the heart of every code was the requirement that slaves submit to their masters and respect all white men. The Louisiana code of 1806 proclaimed this most lucidly: "The condition of the slave being merely a passive one, his subordination to his master and to all who represent him is not susceptible of modification or restriction . . . He owes to his master, and to all his family, a respect without bounds, and an absolute obedience, and he is consequently to execute all the orders which he receives from him, his said master, or from them." A slave was neither to raise his hand against a white man nor to use insulting or abusive language. Any number of acts, said a North Carolina judge, may constitute "insolence" — it may be merely "a look, the pointing of a finger, a refusal or neglect to step out of the way when a white person is seen to approach. But each of such acts violates the rules of propriety, and if tolerated, would destroy that subordination, upon which our social system rests."[11]

The codes rigidly controlled the slave's movements and his communication with others. A slave was not to be "at large" without a pass which he must show to any white man who asked to see it; if he forged a pass or free papers he was guilty of a felony. Except in a few localities, he was prohibited from hiring his own time, finding his own employment, or living by himself. A slave was not to preach, except to his master's own slaves on his master's premises in the presence of whites. A gathering of more than a few slaves (usually five) away from home, unattended by a white, was an "unlawful assembly" regardless of its purpose or orderly decorum.

No person, not even the master, was to teach a slave to read or write, employ him in setting type in a printing office, or give him books or pamphlets. A religious publication asked rhetorically: "Is there any great moral reason why we should incur the tremendous risk of having our wives slaughtered in consequence of our slaves being taught to read incendiary publications?" They did not need to read the Bible to find salvation: "Millions of those now in heaven never owned a bible."[12]

Farms and plantations employing slaves were to be under the supervision of resident white men, and not left to the sole direction of slave foremen. Slaves were not to beat drums, blow horns, or possess guns; periodically their cabins were to be searched for weapons. They were not to administer drugs to whites or practice medicine. "A slave under pretence of practicing medicine," warned a Tennessee judge, "might convey intelligence from one plantation to another, of a contemplated insurrectionary movement; and thus enable the slaves to act in concert."[13]

A slave was not to possess liquor, or purchase it without a written order from his owner. He was not to trade without a permit, or gamble with whites or with other slaves. He was not to raise cotton, swine, horses, mules, or cattle. Allowing a slave to own animals, explained the North Carolina Supreme Court, tended "to make other slaves dissatisfied . . . and thereby excite . . . a spirit of insubordination."[14]

Southern cities and towns supplemented the state codes with additional regulations. Most of them prohibited slaves from being on the streets after curfew or living in dwellings separate from their masters'. Richmond required Negroes and mulattoes to step aside when whites passed by, and barred them from riding in carriages except in the capacity of menials. Charleston slaves could not swear, smoke, walk with a cane, assemble at military parades, or make joyful demonstrations. In Washington, North Carolina, the town commissioners prohibited "all disorderly shouting and dancing, and all disorderly . . . assemblies . . . of slaves and free Negroes in the streets, market and other public places." In Natchez, all "strange slaves" had to leave the city by four o'clock on Sunday afternoon.[15]

Violations of the state and local codes were misdemeanors or felonies subject to punishment by justices, sheriffs, police, and constabulary. Whipping was the most common form of public punishment for less than capital offenses. Except in Louisiana, imprisonment was rare. By the mid–nineteenth century branding and mutilation had declined, though they had not been abolished everywhere. South Carolina did not prohibit branding until 1833, and occasionally thereafter slave felons still had their ears cropped. Mississippi and Alabama continued to enforce the penalty of "burning in the hand" for felonies not capitally punished.[16]

But most slave offenders were simply tied up in the jail or at a whipping post and flogged. Some states in the upper South limited to thirty-nine the number of stripes that could be administered at any one time, though more could be given in a series of whippings over a period of days or weeks. In the Deep South floggings could legally be more severe. Alabama permitted up to one hundred stripes on the bare back of a slave who forged a pass or engaged in "riots, routs, unlawful assemblies, trespasses, and seditious speeches."

State criminal codes dealt more severely with slaves and free Negroes than with whites. In the first place, they made certain acts felonies when committed by Negroes but not when committed by whites; and in the second place, they assigned heavier penalties to Negroes than whites convicted of the same offense. Every southern state defined a substantial number of felonies carrying capital punishment for slaves and lesser punishments for whites. In addition to murder of any degree, slaves received the death penalty for attempted murder, manslaughter, rape and attempted rape upon a white woman, rebellion and attempted rebellion, poisoning, robbery, and arson. A battery upon a white person might also carry a sentence of death under certain circumstances . . .

The codes were quite unmerciful toward whites who interfered with slave discipline. Heavy fines were levied upon persons who unlawfully traded with slaves, sold them liquor without the master's permission, gave them passes, gambled with them, or taught them to read or write . . .

Every slave state made it a felony to say or write anything that might lead, directly or indirectly, to discontent or rebellion. In 1837 the Missouri legislature passed an act "to prohibit the publication, circulation, and promulgation of the abolition doctrines." The Virginia code of 1849 provided a fine and imprisonment for any person who maintained "that owners have not right of property in their slaves." Louisiana made it a capital offense to use "language in any public discourse, from the bar, the bench, the stage, the pulpit, or in any place whatsoever" that might produce "insubordination among the slaves." Most southern

states used their police power to prohibit the circulation of "incendiary" material through the United States mail; on numerous occasions local postmasters, public officials, or mobs seized and destroyed antislavery publications.

Southerners justified these seizures on the ground that some slaves were literate in spite of the laws against teaching them to read. A petition to the South Carolina legislature claimed that "the ability to read exists on probably every plantation in the state; and it is utterly impossible for even the masters to prevent this — as is apparent from the cases in which servants learn to write by stealth." But whether or not slaves could read, the "corrupting influence" of antislavery propaganda was bound to reach them unless it was suppressed. There seemed to be no choice but to construct an "intellectual blockade" against ideas hostile to slavery if property were to be protected and the peace of society secured. Hence the laws controlled the voices and pens of white men as well as black[17] . . .

Southern slave codes protected the owners of bondsmen who attempted to abscond by requiring officers to assist in their recapture and by giving all white men power to arrest them. Every state required the owner of a fugitive to compensate the captor for his trouble. Because of the magnitude of the problem, Kentucky obligated masters to pay a reward of one hundred dollars for runaways taken "in a State where slavery is not tolerated by law." In an effort to induce the return of fugitives escaping to Mexico, Texas promised a reward of one-third the value of a slave who fled "beyond the limits of the slave territories of the United States."[18]

A slave was legally a runaway if found without a pass beyond a certain prescribed distance from home — eight miles in Mississippi, twenty in Missouri. If his master could not be located or lived far away, the fugitive was delivered to a justice of the peace who committed him to jail. The slave of an unknown master was advertised for a period ranging from

Kenneth M. Stampp

three months to one year, and if he was not claimed by the end of this time he was sold to the highest bidder. The proceeds, of the sale, minus the reward, jail fees, and other costs, were recoverable by the master should he appear at some future date.

North Carolina authorized the outlawing of a "vicious" runaway. For example, two justices of New Hanover County gave notice that the slave London was "lurking about" and "committing acts of felony and other misdeeds." London was therefore outlawed; unless he surrendered immediately, "any person may KILL and DESTROY the said slave by such means as he or they may think fit, without accusation or impeachment of any crime or offense for so doing." At the same time, London's master offered a reward of fifty dollars for his confinement in jail, or one hundred dollars for his head. Louisiana permitted a person to shoot a runaway who would not stop when ordered to do so. The state Supreme Court cautioned pursuers that they ought to try to avoid giving a fugitive a "mortal wound," but if he were killed "the homicide is a consequence of the permission to fire upon him."[19]

Occasionally a band of runaways was too formidable to be dispersed by volunteers, and the governor called upon the militia to capture or destroy it. Ordinarily, however, this and other organized police activity was delegated to the slave patrols. A system of patrols, often more or less loosely connected with the militia, existed in every slave state. Virginia empowered each county or corporation court to "appoint, for a term not exceeding three months, one or more patrols" to visit "all negro quarters and other places suspected of having therein unlawful assemblies," and to arrest "such slaves as may stroll from one plantation to another without permission." Alabama compelled every slaveowner under sixty and every nonslaveholder under forty-five to perform patrol duty. The justices of each precinct divided the eligible males into detachments which had to patrol at least one night a week during their terms of service. Everywhere the patrols played a major role in the system of control.

The patrols were naturally more active and efficient in regions with many slaves than in regions with few. In some places patrol activity was sporadic, at least between insurrection panics. "We should always act as if we had an enemy in the very bosom of the State," warned a group of Charlestonians after the Vesey conspiracy.[20] But when their fears subsided, many Southerners looked upon patrol service as an irksome duty and escaped it when possible. Even the slaveholders often preferred to pay the fines levied for nonperformance of this duty, or to hire substitutes as they were sometimes permitted to do. The complaint of an editor in Austin, Texas, that the state patrol law was not effective, "in consequence of the indisposition of parties to perform their duties," was frequently heard — until the whites were again alarmed by rumors of rebellion.[21]

But complaints about patrols abusing their powers were as common as complaints about their failing to function. The nonslaveholding whites, to whom most patrol service was relegated, frequently disliked the masters almost as intensely as the Negroes, and as patrollers they were in a position to vent their feelings toward both. Slaveholders repeatedly went to the courts with charges that patrollers had invaded their premises and whipped their slaves excessively or illegally. The slaves in turn both hated and feared the "paterollers" and retaliated against them when they could. Yet masters looked upon the patrol as an essential police system, and none ever seriously suggested abolishing it.

The final clauses in the southern legal codes relating directly to the control of slaves were those governing free Negroes. The laws reflected the general opinion that these people were an anomaly, a living denial "that nature's God intended the African for the *status* of slavery." They "embitter by their presence the happiness of those who remain slaves. They entice them and furnish them with facilities to elope." They were potential allies of the slaves in the event of a rebellion. In 1830, David Walker, a free Negro who moved from North Carolina to Boston, wrote and attempted to circulate in the South a pamphlet which urged the slaves to fight for their freedom. He thus aroused southern legislatures to the menace of the free Negro.[22]

The trend of ante-bellum legislation was toward ever more stringent controls. Free Negroes could not move from one state to another, and those who left their own state for any purpose could not return. In South Carolina and the Gulf states Negro seamen were arrested and kept in custody while their vessels were in port. Though free Negroes could make contracts and own property, in most other respects their civil rights were as circumscribed as those of slaves. They were the victims of the white man's fears, of racial prejudice, and of the desire to convince slaves that winning freedom was scarcely worth the effort.

Many Southerners desired the complete expulsion of the free Negroes, or the re-enslavement of those who would not leave. Petitions poured into the state legislatures demanding laws that would implement one or the other of these policies. In 1849 a petition from Augusta County, Virginia, asked the legislature to make an appropriation for a program of gradual removal; all free Negroes who refused to go to Liberia should be expelled from the state within five years.[23] In 1859 the Arkansas legislature required sheriffs to order the state's handful of free Negroes to leave. Those who remained were to be hired out as slaves for a year, after which those who still remained were to be sold into permanent bondage.

A Texas editor caught the spirit of the extreme proslavery element during the 1850s when he proclaimed that the time was "near at hand for determined action." Southern free Negroes were "destined to be remitted back into slavery," which was their "true condition."[24]

In this last ante-bellum decade most states adopted laws authorizing the " voluntary enslavement" of these people and enabling them to select their own masters. Virginia went a step further and permitted the sale into "absolute slavery" of free Negroes convicted of offenses "punishable by confinement in the penitentiary"; Florida applied the same penalty to those who were "idle" or "dissolute." This problem, some apparently felt, would remain unsolved until all Negroes and "mulattoes" were not only *presumed* to be slaves but were in *fact* slaves.

"A slave," said a Tennessee judge, "is not in the condition of a horse . . . He has mental capacities, and an immortal principle in his nature." The laws did not "extinguish his high-born nature nor deprive him of many rights which are inherent in man."[25] All the southern codes recognized the slave as a person for purposes other than holding him accountable for crimes. Many state constitutions required the legislature "to pass such laws as may be necessary to oblige the owners of slaves to treat them with humanity; to provide for them necessary clothing and provisions; [and] to abstain from all injuries to them, extending to life or limb."

The legislatures responded with laws extending some protection to the persons of slaves. Masters who refused to feed and clothe slaves properly might be fined; in several states the court might order them to be sold, the proceeds going to the dispossessed owners. Those who abandoned or neglected insane, aged, or infirm slaves were also liable to fines. In Virginia the overseers of the poor were required to care for such slaves and to charge their masters.

Now and then a master was tried and convicted for the violation of one of these laws. In 1849 the South Carolina Supreme Court upheld the conviction of a slaveholder who "did not give his negroes enough even of [corn] meal, the only provision he did give." In such a case, said the court, the law had to be

Kenneth M. Stampp

enforced for the sake of "public sentiment, . . . and to protect property from
the depredation of famishing slaves." [26]
But prosecutions were infrequent. Since
a slave could neither file a complaint nor
give evidence against his master, action
depended upon the willingness of whites
to testify in the slave's behalf. This happened only under unusual circumstances.

Some of the codes regulated the hours
of labor. As early as 1740 South Carolina
limited the working day to fifteen hours
from March to September and fourteen
hours from September to March. All the
codes forbade field labor on Sunday. In
Virginia a master who worked his slaves
on Sunday, "except in household or
other work of necessity or charity," was
to be fined two dollars for each offense. It
was permissible, however, to let slaves
labor on the Sabbath for wages; and the
North Carolina Supreme Court ruled that
it was not an indictable offense to give
them Sunday tasks as a punishment.[27]
With rare exceptions, masters who were
so inclined violated these laws with
impunity.

The early colonial codes had assessed
only light penalties, or none at all, for
killing a slave. South Carolina, "to
restrain and prevent barbarity being exercised toward slaves," provided, in 1740,
that a white who willfully murdered a
slave was to be punished by a fine of
seven hundred pounds or imprisonment
at hard labor for seven years. Killing a
slave in "sudden heat or passion" or by
"undue correction" carried a fine of three
hundred and fifty pounds. In Georgia
prior to 1770, and in North Carolina prior
to 1775, taking a slave's life was not a
felony.

After the American Revolution there
was a drastic change of policy. Virginia,
in 1788, and North Carolina, in 1791,
defined the malicious killing of a slave as
murder subject to the same penalty
imposed upon the murderer of a freeman.
In 1817 North Carolina applied this principle to persons convicted of manslaughter. Georgia's Constitution of 1798
contained a clause that was copied, in

substance, into the constitutions of several states in the Southwest: "Any person
who shall maliciously dismember or
deprive a slave of life shall suffer such
punishment as would be inflicted in case
the like offence had been committed on a
free white person."

Eventually all the southern states
adopted laws of this kind. In 1821 South
Carolina belatedly provided that a person
who killed a slave "willfully, maliciously, and deliberately" was to suffer
death, and a person who killed a slave in
"sudden heat or passion" was to be fined
up to five hundred dollars and imprisoned up to six months. In Alabama a person who, "with malice aforethought,"
caused the death of a slave "by cruel
whipping or beating, or by any inhuman
treatment, or by the use of any weapon in
its nature calculated to produce death,"
was guilty of murder in the first degree.
A master or overseer causing death by
cruel whipping or by other cruel punishment, "though without any intention to
kill," was guilty of murder in the second
degree.

By the 1850s, most of the codes had
made cruelty a public offense even when
not resulting in death. Alabama masters
and overseers who inflicted brutal punishments were subject to fines of from
twenty-five to one thousand dollars. A
person who committed an assault and
battery upon a slave not his own, "without just cause or excuse," was guilty of a
misdemeanor. Louisiana prohibited the
owner from punishing a slave with
"unusual rigor" or "so as to maim or
mutilate him." Georgia more explicitly
prohibited "cutting, or wounding, or . . .
cruelly and unnecessarily biting or tearing with dogs." In Kentucky a slave who
was treated cruelly might be taken from
his master and sold.

But these laws invariably had significant qualifications. For example, the
accidental death of a slave while receiving "moderate correction" was not homicide. Killing a slave in the act of
rebellion or when resisting legal arrest
was always "justifiable homicide." South

Carolina permitted a white person to "apprehend and moderately correct" a slave who was at large without a pass and refused to submit to examination; "and if any such slave shall assault and strike such white person, such slave may be lawfully killed." The South Carolina law against cruelty concluded with a nullifying clause: "nothing herein contained shall be so construed as to prevent the owner or person having charge of any slave from inflicting on such slave such punishment as may be necessary for the good government of the same." Southern courts, by their interpretations of the laws, in effect added further qualifications. Thus the North Carolina Supreme Court ruled that a homicide upon a slave did not require as much provocation as a homicide upon a white to make it justifiable.

Under most circumstances a slave was powerless to defend himself from an assault by a white man. According to the Tennessee Supreme Court, severe chastisement by the master did not justify resistance. If a master exercised his right to punish, "with or without cause, [and] the slave resist and slay him, it is murder . . . because the law cannot recognize the violence of the master as a legitimate cause of provocation." According to the Georgia Supreme Court, even if the owner should "exceed the bounds of reason . . . in his chastisement, the slave must submit . . . unless the attack . . . be calculated to produce death."[28]

On rare occasions a court refused to convict a bondsman for killing a brutal overseer (never a brutal master) while resisting an assault that might have caused his death. In 1834, the North Carolina Supreme Court reversed the decision of a lower court which had sentenced a slave to be hanged for the homicide of an overseer under these circumstances. Though the slave's "general duty" was unconditional submission, he nevertheless had the right to defend himself against "an unlawful attempt . . . to deprive him of life." But Chief Justice Thomas Ruffin, in a similar

case, expressed the apprehension many Southerners felt when a slave was exonerated for an assault on a white man. To hold that slaves could decide when they were entitled to resist white men was a dangerous doctrine, said Ruffin. It might encourage them to denounce "the injustice of slavery itself, and, upon that pretext, band together to throw off their common bondage entirely."[29]

In a few notable cases the courts enforced the laws against the killing of slaves . . . Decisions such as these were exceptional. Only a handful of whites suffered capital punishment for murdering slaves, and they were usually persons who had committed the offense upon slaves not their own. When a master was convicted, it was generally for a lesser crime, such as killing in "sudden heat or passion" or by "undue correction." And a convicted killer, whether or not the master, rarely received as heavy a penalty as he would have for a homicide upon a white.

Actually, the great majority of whites who, by a reasonable interpretation of the law, were guilty of feloniously killing slaves escaped without any punishment at all. Of those who were indicted, most were either acquitted or never brought to trial. For several reasons this was almost inevitable.

One major reason was that neither slaves nor free Negroes could testify against whites. There were, as one Southerner observed, "a thousand incidents of plantation life concealed from public view," witnessed only by slaves, which the law could not reach. One of slavery's "most vulnerable points," a defender of the institution agreed, was the "helpless position of the slave" when his master was "placed in opposition to him." His "mouth being closed as a witness," he had to depend upon whites to testify in his behalf.[30] But here was the second major obstacle in the way of convictions: white witnesses were reluctant to testify against white offenders . . . And there was still a third obstacle. Even when whites agreed to testify, there remained

Kenneth M. *Stampp*

the problem of getting a white jury to convict . . .

In Maryland, Frederick Douglass remembered hearing white men say that it was "worth but half a cent to kill a nigger, and half a cent to bury him."[31] This surely was not the attitude of the average Southerner, but it did indicate how lightly all too many of them regarded the laws against the killing of slaves. It would be too much to say that the codes gave slaves no protection at all. But it would also be too much to say that they extended equal justice and protection to slaves and freemen. If they had, there would unquestionably have been fewer felonious assaults upon slaves.

"There are many persons," complained a Mississippi editor, "who think they have the same right to shoot a negro . . . that they have to shoot down a dog, but there are laws for the protection of slaves as well as the master, and the sooner the error alluded to is removed, the better it will be for both parties."[32] Slavery and the racial attitudes it encouraged caused this "error" to persist throughout the ante-bellum period.

The fate of a slave who was the principal, rather than the victim, of an alleged misdemeanor or felony was highly uncertain. The state codes established regular judicial procedures for the trial of slaves accused of public offenses, but probably most minor offenses, such as petit larceny, were disposed of without resort to the courts. For instance, when an Alabama slave was caught stealing from a neighboring plantation, the proprietor agreed not to prosecute if the overseer punished the slave himself. The state supreme court sanctioned the informal settlement of such cases. Even though an offense was "criminally punishable," said the court, so far as the public was concerned it was better to have the punishment "admeasured by a domestic tribunal."[33]

Nevertheless, many bondsmen who violated the law were given public trials. In colonial days they were always arraigned before special "Negro courts,"

which were usually less concerned about formalities of traditional English justice than about speedy verdicts and certain punishments. A slave accused of a capital offense, according to the South Carolina Code of 1740, was to be tried "in the most summary and expeditious manner"; on conviction he was to suffer death by such means as would be "most effectual to deter others from offending in the like manner." Justice in the "Negro courts" was at best capricious.

For misdemeanors, and in some states for crimes not punished capitally, the summary processes of "Negro courts" survived until the abolition of slavery. Louisiana tried slaves for noncapital felonies before one justice and four slaveholders, Mississippi before two justices and five slaveholders, and Georgia before three justices. Alabama tried slaves for minor offenses before a justice (who could assign a maximum penalty of thirty-nine lashes), and for noncapital felonies before the judge of the probate court and two justices of the peace. The states of the upper South generally subjected slaves accused of misdemeanors to similar informal and summary trials.

In the nineteenth century most states gave slaves jury trials in the regular courts when accused of capital crimes; some went further and gave them this privilege when accused of any felony. The Missouri Constitution of 1820 and the Texas Constitution of 1845 provided that in criminal cases slaves were to have an impartial trial by jury. On conviction, a Missouri slave was to suffer "the same degree of punishment, and no other, that would be inflicted on a free white person for a like offense." North Carolina slaves accused of capital offenses were tried in the superior courts, and the law required the trials to be conducted as the trials of freemen. In Alabama, they were tried before the circuit court of the county, "in the mode provided by law for the trial of white persons," except that two-thirds of the jurors had to be slaveholders. In Georgia, capital crimes continued to be tried before three justices until 1850, when the superior courts were given jurisdiction.

A few states never granted jury trial or abandoned the informal courts and summary procedures even in capital cases. The Virginia code declared that the county and corporation courts, consisting of at least five justices, "shall be courts of *oyer* and *terminer* for the trial of negroes charged with felony . . . Such trials shall be . . . without a jury." Louisiana tried slaves for capital offenses before two justices and ten slaveholders, and South Carolina tried them for all offenses before a justice and five freeholders without a jury.

Many Southerners trained in the law recognized the possibilities for miscarriages of justice in the "Negro courts." A South Carolina judge called these courts "the worst system that could be devised."In his message to the legislature in 1833, Governor Robert Y. Hayne acknowledged that reform was "imperiously called for." "Capital offenses committed by slaves, involving the nicest questions of the law, are often tried by courts composed of persons ignorant of the law." An editor affirmed that the life of the slave and the property of the master were in jeopardy "from the ignorance and malice of unworthy magistrates."[34] However, criticism such as this produced few reforms.

In practice, the quality of justice slaves received from juries and regular courts was not consistently better than the justice they received from "Negro courts." When tension was great and the passions of white men were running high, a slave found it as difficult to get a fair trial before a jury in one of the superior courts of North Carolina or Alabama as he did before the justices in one of the informal courts of South Carolina or Virginia. Nowhere, regardless of constitutional or statutory requirements, was the trial of a bondsman apt to be like the trial of a freeman. Though counsel was guaranteed, though jurors might be challenged, though Negroes could testify in cases involving members of their own race, the

trial of a slave was never the trial of a man by his peers. Rather, it was the trial of a man with inferior rights by his superiors — of a man who was property as well as a person. Inevitably, most justices, judges, and jurors permitted questions of discipline and control to obscure considerations of even justice.

A slave accused of committing violence upon another slave, rather than upon a white, had a better chance for a fair trial. Here the deeper issues of discipline and racial subordination were not involved, and the court could hear the case calmly and decide it on its merits. Moreover, the penalty on conviction was usually relatively light. Slaves were capitally punished for the murder of other slaves almost as rarely as whites were capitally punished for the murder of slaves. A bondsman in Rapides Parish, Louisiana, accused of beating another bondsman to death, was found guilty of "misbehavior" and sentenced to receive one hundred lashes on four successive days and to wear a ball and chain for three months. A slave in Clay County, Missouri, convicted of murdering another slave, received thirty-nine lashes and was sold out of the state.[35]

The southern codes did not prescribe lighter penalties for slaves who murdered other slaves than for slaves who murdered whites. The theory of the law was that one offense was as serious as the other. But the white men who applied the law usually thought otherwise.

When a Louisiana slave accused of murdering a white man (not his master) had the benefit of two mistrials, an overseer wrote in disgust: "there are some slave owners who think that a white man's life is worth nothing in comparison with that of a slave." For some, such as this overseer, the wheels of justice even in the "Negro courts" turned all too slowly; and critics often held the masters responsible for it.

Fortunately for the slave, his lack of civil rights and helplessness in the courts was mitigated somewhat by either the master's self-interest or paternalism, or both. Sometimes bondsmen had the help of their masters in escaping conviction for legal offenses or were sheltered from the harshest features of the slave codes.

Though slaves were not legally permitted to live independently, a few masters nevertheless gave them virtual freedom. The North Carolina Supreme Court noted a custom that had developed, "particularly among that class of citizens who were opposed to slavery, of permitting persons of color, who, by law, are their slaves, to go at large as free, — thereby introducing a species of *quasi* emancipation, contrary to the law, and against the policy of the State." Quakers frequently owned slaves "having nothing but the name, and working for their own benefit." Free Negroes with titles to slaves usually made their bondage nominal. Maryland doubtless contained more Negroes living in an "intermediate status between slavery and freedom" than any other southern state.[36]

Masters softened the state codes not only by evading them but also by going beyond the mere letter of the law in recognizing their slaves as human beings. No slaveholder needed to respect the marital ties of his slaves; yet a Tennesseean purchased several slaves at a public sale, not because he needed them, but because of "their intermarriage with my servants and their appeals to me to do so." A Kentucky mistress tried to buy the wife of her slave before moving to Missouri. Another Kentuckian, when obliged to sell his slaves, gave each an opportunity to find a satisfactory purchaser and refused to sell any to persons residing outside the neighborhood.

Finally, a few slaveholders tempered the codes by refusing to bequeath their human chattels as they did ordinary property. True, wills showing solicitude for slaves were unusual; they often singled out just one or two from the rest for special consideration; and the favored ones were nearly always being rewarded for loyalty and obedience. Even so, these expressions of gratitude were touching reminders that some masters could never completely forget the human qualities in their "people" . . .

Masters who ignored the demands of discipline by flagrantly violating the slave codes, who elevated their slaves to virtual freedom, who treated them with utter disregard for their status as property, and who strictly regulated their use when bequeathing them to heirs are justly celebrated in the folklore of slavery. But they are celebrated because their conduct was so abnormal. Had other masters imitated them, the slave system would have disintegrated — and a nation might have been spared a civil war.

"A free African population is a curse to any country," the Chancellor of the South Carolina Court of Appeals once flatly affirmed. "This race, . . . in a state of freedom, and in the midst of a civilized community, are a dead weight to the progress of improvement." Free Negroes became "pilferers and maurauders," "consumers, without being producers . . . governed mainly by the instincts of animal nature."[37] Racial attitudes such as these, the fear of free Negroes as a social menace, and respect for the rights of property caused the southern states to adopt constitutional prohibitions against the legislative emancipation of slaves without the consent of their owners.

But the state constitutions put few obstacles in the way of masters who wished to manumit their own slaves. In the border states of Delaware, Maryland (until 1860), Kentucky, and Missouri, the sole legislative restrictions were that creditors' claims must be respected and that a manumitted slave must not become a burden to the public because of age or infirmity. Virginia added the further condition that a manumitted slave was not to remain in the state for more than a year "without lawful permission." A county or corporation court might grant this permission if it had evidence that the freedman was "of good character, sober, peaceable, orderly and industrious." In North Carolina an emancipated slave had to leave the state within ninety days, unless a superior court made an exception because of "meritorious service." In Tennessee a slave freed after 1831 had to be sent beyond her borders immediately; after 1854 he had to be sent to the west coast of Africa.

In the Deep South the trend was toward increasingly severe legislative restrictions. In Louisiana (for many years the most liberal of these states) an act of 1807 limited the privilege of manumission to slaves who were at least thirty years old and who had not been guilty of bad conduct during the previous four years. In 1830 Louisiana required emancipated slaves to leave the state within thirty days; after 1852 they had to leave the United States within twelve months. Five years later, Louisiana entirely prohibited private emancipations within the state.

The remaining states of the lower South had outlawed private emancipations early in the nineteenth century, except when granted by a special act of the legislature as a reward for "meritorious service" . . .

The laws prohibiting private emancipations did not in themselves prevent a testator from directing in his will that his slaves be removed from the state and freed elsewhere. But the court might scrupulously examine the wording of such a bequest. The Georgia Supreme Court invalidated wills specifying that slaves be "manumitted and sent to a free state," because "emancipation . . . was to take effect in Georgia." However, if the verbs were transposed, if the slaves were to be "sent to a free state and manumitted," the will was valid, because it was not unlawful to direct emancipation outside the state. Judge Joseph H. Lumpkin urged the Georgia legislature to remedy this "defect" in the law. "I have no partiality for foreign any more than domestic manumission," he confessed. "Especially do I object to the colonization of our negroes upon our northwestern frontier. They facilitate the escape of our fugitive slaves. In case of civil war, they would become an element of strength to the enemy."[38]

Several states in the Deep South took the step Judge Lumpkin suggested and prohibited emancipation by last will and testament. South Carolina acted as early as 1841, when it voided all deeds and wills designed to free slaves before or after removal from the state. Mississippi, Georgia, Arkansas, and Alabama adopted similar laws during the next two decades.

Occasionally a testator attempted to circumvent the statutes against emancipation, but almost invariably the court invalidated his will. "This is another of those cases," the South Carolina Court Appeals once complained, "in which the superstitious weakness of dying men, proceeding from an astonishing ignorance of the solid moral and scriptural foundations upon which the institution of slavery rests, . . . induces them, in their last moments, to emancipate their slaves, in fraud of the . . . declared policy of the State." A Charleston editor thought it was sheer hypocrisy for an "old sinner" who had "enjoyed the profits of the labor of his slaves, during his life time" to emancipate them on his deathbed.[39]

The truth was, of course, that *living* masters in all the southern states — even in those which prohibited manumission by last will and testament — always had the right to remove their slaves to a free state and there release them from bondage. Though no slave state could deprive them of this right, few made use of it.

Moreover, only a handful of slaveholders wrote wills providing for manumissions in states where this continued to be legal. An even smaller number would have done so in the Deep South had the privilege remained open to them. In no slave state, early or late in the antebellum period, were the total yearly emancipations more than a small fraction of the natural increase of the slave population. For example, in 1859, only three thousand slaves were emancipated throughout the entire South. At that time both Virginia and Kentucky permitted manumissions by deed or will. Yet Virginia, with a slave population of a half million, freed only two hundred and seventy-seven; Kentucky, with a slave population of nearly a quarter million, freed only one hundred and seventy-six.

Clearly, if the decline of slavery were to await the voluntary acts of individuals, the time of its demise was still in the distant future. The failure of voluntary emancipation was evident long before the 1830s when, according to Judge Lumpkin, "the blind zealots of the North" began their "unwarrantable interference."[40] James H. Hammond got at the crux of the matter when he asked whether any people in history had ever voluntarily surrendered two billion dollars worth of property.

One of the minority, a North Carolin-ian, who willed the unconditional emancipation of his slaves gave four reasons for his action: "Reason the first. Agreeably to the rights of man, every human being, be his or her colour what it may, is entitled to freedom . . . Reason the second. My conscience, the great criterion, condemns me for keeping them in slavery. Reason the third. The golden rule directs us to do unto every human creature, as we would wish to be done unto; and sure I am, that there is not one of us would agree to be kept in slavery during a long life. Reason the fourth and last. I wish to die with a clear conscience, that I may not be ashamed to appear before my master in a future World . . . I wish every human creature seriously to deliberate on my reasons."[41]

19

Arthur Bestor

The American Civil War as a Constitutional Crisis

Within the span of a single generation — during the thirty-odd years that began with the annexation of Texas in 1845 and ended with the withdrawal of the last Union troops from the South in 1877 — the United States underwent a succession of constitutional crises more severe and menacing than any before or since. From 1845 on, for some fifteen years, a constitutional dispute over the expansion of slavery into the western territories grew increasingly tense until a paralysis of normal constitutional functioning set in. Abruptly, in 1860–1861, this particular constitutional crisis was transformed into another: namely, that of secession. Though the new crisis was intimately linked with the old, its constitutional character was fundamentally different. The question of how the Constitution ought to operate as a piece of working machinery was superseded by the question of whether it might and should be dismantled. A showdown had come, and the four-year convulsion of Civil War ensued. Then, when hostilities ended in 1865, there came not the hoped for dawn of peace, but instead a third great consti-

tutional struggle over Reconstruction, which lasted a dozen years and proved as harsh and divisive as any cold war in history. When the nation finally emerged from three decades of corrosive strife, no observer could miss the profound alterations that its institutions had undergone. Into the prodigious vortex of crisis and war every current of American life had ultimately been drawn.

So all-devouring was the conflict and so momentous its effects, that to characterize it (as I have done) as a series of constitutional crises will seem to many readers an almost irresponsible use of language, a grotesque belittling of the issues. Powerful economic forces, it will be pointed out, were pitted against one another in the struggle. Profound moral perplexities were generated by the existence of slavery, and the attacks upon it had social and psychological repercussions of incredible complexity. The various questions at issue penetrated into the arena of politics, shattering established parties and making or breaking the public careers of national and local leaders. Ought so massive a conflict to be discussed in terms of so rarefied an abstraction as constitutional theory?

To ask such a question, however, is to mistake the character of constitutional

Reprinted from *American Historical Review*, 69 (1964), 327-352, by permission crises in general. When or why or how should they arise if not in a context of social, economic, and ideological upheaval? A constitution, after all, is nothing other than the aggregate of laws, traditions, and understandings — in other words, the complex of institutions and procedures — by which a nation brings to political and legal decision the substantive conflicts engendered by changes in all the varied aspects of its societal life. In normal times, to be sure, routine and recurrent questions of public policy are not thought of as constitutional questions. Alternative policies are discussed in terms of their wisdom or desirability. Conflicts are resolved by the ordinary operation of familiar constitutional machinery. A decision is reached that is essentially a political decision, measuring, in some rough way, the political strength of the forces that are backing or opposing some particular program of action, a program that both sides concede to be constitutionally possible, though not necessarily prudent or desirable.

When controversies begin to cut deep, however, the constitutional legitimacy of a given course of action is likely to be challenged. Questions of policy give place to questions of power; questions of wisdom to questions of legality. Attention shifts to the Constitution itself, for the fate of each particular policy has come to hinge upon the interpretation given to the fundamental law. In debating these constitutional questions, men are not evading the substantive issues. They are facing them in precisely the manner that the situation now requires. A constitutional dispute has been superadded to the controversies already present.

Should the conflict become so intense as to test the adequacy of existing mechanisms to handle it at all, then it mounts to the level of a constitutional crisis. Indeed the capability of producing a constitutional crisis is an ultimate measure of the intensity of the substantive conflicts themselves. If, in the end, the situation explodes into violence, then the catastrophe is necessarily a constitutional one, for its very essence is the failure and the threatened destruction of the constitutional framework itself.

The secession crisis of 1860–1861 was obviously an event of this kind. It was a constitutional catastrophe in the most direct sense, for it resulted in a civil war that destroyed, albeit temporarily, the fabric of the Union.

There is, however, another sense — subtler, but perhaps more significant — in which the American Civil War may be characterized as a constitutional crisis. To put the matter succinctly, the very form that the conflict finally took was determined by the preexisting form of the constitutional system. The way the opposing forces were arrayed against each other in war was a consequence of the way the Constitution had operated to array them in peace. Because the Union could be, and frequently had been, viewed as not more than a compact among sovereign states, the dissolution of the compact was a conceivable thing. It was constitutional theorizing, carried on from the very birth of the Republic, which made secession the ultimate recourse of any group that considered its vital interests threatened.

Since the American system was a federal one, secession, when it finally occurred, put the secessionists into immediate possession of fully organized governments, capable of acting as no ad hoc insurrectionary regime could possibly have acted. Though sometimes described as a "rebellion" and sometimes as a "civil war," the American conflict was, in a strict sense, neither. It was a war between preexisting political entities. But it was not (to use a third description) a "war between the states," for in war the states did not act severally. Instead, the war was waged between two federations of these states: one the historic Union, the other a Confederacy that, though newly created, was shaped by the same constitutional tradition as its opponent. In short, only the preexisting structure of the American Constitution can explain the actual configuration even of the war itself.

The *configurative* role that constitutional issues played is the point of crucial importance. When discussed in their own terms and for their own sakes, constitutional questions are admittedly theoretical questions. One may indeed say (borrowing a phrase that even academicians perfidiously employ) that they are academic questions. Only by becoming involved with other (and in a sense more "substantive") issues, do they become highly charged. But when they do become so involved, constitutional questions turn out to be momentous ones, for every theoretical premise draws after it a train of practical consequences. Abstract though constitutional issues may be, they exert a powerful shaping effect upon the course that events will in actuality take. They give a particular direction to forces already at work. They impose upon the conflict as a whole a unique, and an otherwise inexplicable, pattern or configuration.

To speak of a configuration of forces in history is to rule out, as essentially meaningless, many kinds of questions that are popularly supposed to be both answerable and important. In particular, it rules out as futile any effort to decide which one of the various forces at work in a given historical situation was "*the* most important cause" of the events that followed, or "*the* decisive factor" in bringing them about, or "*the* crucial issue" involved. The reason is simple. The steady operation of a single force, unopposed and uninterrupted, would result in a development so continuous as to be, in the most literal sense, eventless. To produce an event, one force must impinge upon at least one other. The event is the consequence of their interaction. Historical explanation is, of necessity, an explanation of such interactions.

If interaction is the crucial matter, then it is absurd to think of assigning to any factor in history an intrinsic or absolute weight, independent of its context. In the study of history, the context is all-important. Each individual factor derives its significance from the position it occupies in a complex structure of interrelationships. The fundamental historical problem, in short, is not to measure the relative weight of various causal· elements, but

instead to discover the pattern of their interaction with one another.[1]

A cogent illustration of this particular point is afforded by the controversy over slavery, which played so significant a role in the crisis with which this paper deals. Powerful emotions, pro and con, were aroused by the very existence of slavery. Powerful economic interests were involved with the fate of the institution. Nevertheless, differences of opinion, violent though they were, cannot by themselves account for the peculiar configuration of events that historically occurred. The forces unleashed by the slavery controversy were essentially indeterminate; that is to say, they could lead to any number of different outcomes, ranging from simple legislative emancipation to bloody servile insurrection. In the British West Indies the former occurred; in Haiti, the latter. In the United States, by contrast with both, events took an exceedingly complicated course. The crisis can be said to have commenced with a fifteen-year dispute not over slavery itself, but over its expansion into the territories. It eventuated in a four-year war that was avowedly fought not over the issue of slavery, but over the question of the legal perpetuity of the Union. The slavery controversy, isolated from all other issues, cannot begin to explain why events followed so complex and devious a course. On the other hand, though other factors must be taken into account in explaining the configuration of events, these other factors, isolated from those connected with slavery, cannot explain why tensions mounted so high as to reach the breaking point of war.

No single factor, whatever its nature, can account for the distinctive form that the mid-nineteenth-century American crisis assumed. Several forces converged, producing a unique configuration. Men were debating a variety of issues simultaneously, and their various arguments intertwined. Each conflict tended to intensify the others, and not only to intensify them but also to alter and deflect them in complicated ways. The crisis was born of interaction.

Arthur Bestor

The nature of these various converging conflicts is abundantly clear. They are spread at length upon the historical record. Documents, to be sure, are not always to be taken at face value; there are occasions when it is legitimate to read between the lines. Nevertheless, the documentary record is the foundation upon which historical knowledge rests. It can be explained, but it cannot be explained away, as many writers on the causes of the Civil War attempt to do. Most current myths, indeed, depend on such wholesale dismissals of evidence. Southern apologetics took form as early as 1868 when Alexander H. Stephens unblinkingly asserted that "this whole subject of Slavery, so-called, . . . was, to the Seceding States, but a drop in the ocean compared with . . . other considerations,"[2] by which he meant considerations of constitutional principle. The dogma of economic determinism can be sustained only by dismissing, as did Charles and Mary Beard in 1927, not merely that part of the record which Stephens rejected but also the part he accepted. Having decided, like Stephens, that "the institution of slavery was not the fundamental issue," the Beards went on to assert that constitutional issues likewise "were minor factors in the grand dispute."[3]

When the historical record is as vast as the one produced by the mid-nineteenth-century American crisis — when arguments were so wearisomely repeated by such multitudes of men — it is sheer fantasy to assume that the issues discussed were not the real issues. The arguments of the period were public ones, addressed to contemporaries and designed to influence their actions. If these had not touched upon genuine issues, they would hardly have been so often reiterated. Had other lines of argument possessed a more compelling force, they would certainly have been employed.

The only tenable assumption, one that would require an overwhelming mass of contrary evidence to rebut, is that men and women knew perfectly well what they were quarreling about. And what do

we find? They argued about economic measures — the tariff, the banking system, and the Homestead Act — for the obvious reason that economic interests of their own were at stake. They argued about slavery because they considered the issues it raised to be vital ones — vital to those who adhered to the ideal of a free society and vital to those who feared to disturb the status quo. They argued about the territories because they felt a deep concern for the kind of social order that would grow up there. They argued about the Constitution because they accepted its obligations (whatever they considered them to be) as binding.

These are the data with which the historian must reckon. Four issues were mentioned in the preceding paragraph: the issue of economic policy, the issue of slavery, the issue of the territories, and the issue of constitutional interpretation. At the very least, the historian must take all these into account. Other factors there indubitably were. To trace the interaction of these four, however, will perhaps suffice to reveal the underlying pattern of the crisis and to make clear how one of these factors, the constitutional issue, exerted a configurative effect that cannot possibly be ignored.

Conflicts over economic policy are endemic in modern societies. They formed a recurrent element in nineteenth-century American political conflict. To disregard them would be an even greater folly than to assume that they determined, by themselves, the entire course of events. Between a plantation economy dependent upon the sale of staples to a world market and an economy in which commerce, finance, and manufacturing were rapidly advancing, the points of conflict were numerous, real, and important. At issue were such matters as banks and corporations, tariffs, internal improvements, land grants to railroads, and free homesteads to settlers. In a general way, the line of division on matters of economic policy tended, at mid-century, to coincide with the line of division on the question of slavery. To the extent that it did so (and it did so far less clearly than many economic determinists assume), the economic conflict added its weight to the divisive forces at work in 1860–1861.

More significant, perhaps, was another and different sort of relationship between the persistent economic conflict and the rapidly mounting crisis before the Civil War. To put the matter briefly, the constitutional theories that came to be applied with such disruptive effects to the slavery dispute had been developed, in the first instance, largely in connection with strictly economic issues. Thus the doctrine of strict construction was pitted against the doctrine of loose construction as early as 1791, when Alexander Hamilton originated the proposal for a central bank. And the doctrine of nullification was worked out with ingenious thoroughness in 1832 as a weapon against the protective tariff. Whatever crises these doctrines precipitated proved to be relatively minor ones so long as the doctrines were applied to purely economic issues. Within this realm, compromise always turned out to be possible. The explosive force of irreconcilable constitutional theories became apparent only when the latter were brought to bear upon the dispute over slavery.

Inherent in the slavery controversy itself (the second factor with which we must reckon) were certain elements that made compromise and accommodation vastly more difficult than in the realm of economic policy. To be sure, slavery itself had its economic aspect. It was, among other things, a labor system. The economic life of many regions rested upon it. The economic interests that would be affected by any tampering with the institution were powerful interests, and they made their influence felt.

Nevertheless, it was the noneconomic aspect of slavery that made the issues it engendered so inflammatory. As Ulrich B. Phillips puts it, "Slavery was instituted not merely to provide control of labor but also as a system of racial adjustment and social order." The word "adjustment" is an obvious euphemism; elsewhere Phillips speaks frankly of "race control." The effort to maintain that control, he maintains, has been "the central theme of Southern history." The factor that has made the South "a land with a unity despite its diversity," Phillips concludes, is "a common resolve indomitably maintained — that it shall be and remain a white man's country."[4]

It was this indomitable resolve — say rather, this imperious demand — that lay at the heart of the slavery controversy, as it lies at the heart of the struggle over civil rights today. To put the matter bluntly, the demand was that of a master race for a completely free hand to deal as it might choose with its own subject population. The word "sovereignty" was constantly on the lips of southern politicians. The concept they were invoking was one that Blackstone had defined as "supreme, irresistible, absolute, uncontrolled authority."[5] This was the kind of authority that slaveholders exercised over their chattels. What they were insisting on, in the political realm, was that the same species of power should be recognized as belonging to the slaveholding states when dealing with their racial minorities. "State Sovereignty" was, in essence, the slaveowner's authority writ large.

If slavery had been a static system, confined geographically to the areas where the institution was an inheritance from earlier days, then the demand of the slaveholding states for unrestricted, "sovereign" power to deal with it was a demand to which the majority of Americans would probably have reconciled themselves for a long time. In 1861, at any rate, even Lincoln and the Republicans were prepared to support an ironclad guarantee that the Constitution would never be amended in such a way as to interfere with the institution within the slaveholding states. An irrepealable amendment to that effect passed both houses of Congress by the necessary two-thirds vote during the week before Lincoln's inauguration.[6] The incoming President announced that he had "no objection" to the pending amendment,[7] and three states (two of them free) actually gave their ratifications in 1861 and 1862.[8] If the problems created by slavery had actually been, as slaveowners so vehemently maintained, of a sort that the slaveholding states were perfectly capable of handling by themselves, then the security offered by this measure might well have been deemed absolute.

As the historical record shows, however, the proposed amendment never came close to meeting the demands of the proslavery forces. These demands, and the crisis they produced, stemmed directly from the fact that slavery was not a static and local institution; it was a prodigiously expanding one. By 1860 the census revealed that more than half the slaves in the nation were held in bondage *outside* the boundaries of the thirteen states that had composed the original Union.[9] The expansion of slavery meant that hundreds of thousands of slaves were being carried beyond the territorial jurisdictions of the states under whose laws they had originally been held in servitude. Even to reach another slaveholding state, they presumably entered that stream of "Commerce . . . among the several States," which the Constitution gave Congress a power "to regulate."[10] If they were carried to United States territories that had not yet been made states, their presence there raised questions about the source and validity of the law that kept them in bondage.

Territorial expansion, the third factor in our catalogue, was thus a crucial element in the pattern of interaction that produced the crisis. The timing of the latter, indeed, indicates clearly the role that expansion played. Slavery had existed in English-speaking America for two centuries without producing any paralyzing convulsion. The institution had been brought to an end in the original states of the East and North by unspectacular exercises of legislative or judicial authority. Federal ordinances barring slavery from the Old Northwest had operated effectually yet inconspicuously since 1787. At many other points federal authority had dealt

with slavery, outlawing the foreign slave trade on the one hand and providing for the return of fugitive slaves on the other. Prior to the 1840s constitutional challenges to its authority in these matters had been few and unimportant. Indeed, the one true crisis of the period, that of 1819–1821 over Missouri, was rooted in expansionism, precisely as the later one was to be. The nation was awakening to the fact that slavery had pushed its way northward and westward into the virgin lands of the Louisiana Purchase. Only when limits were drawn for it across the whole national domain did the crisis subside.

Suddenly, in the election of 1844, the question of territorial expansion came to the fore again. Events moved rapidly. Within the space of precisely a decade, between the beginning of 1845 and the end of 1854, four successive annexations added a million and a quarter square miles to the area under undisputed American soveignty.[11] Expansion itself was explosive; its interaction with the smoldering controversy over slavery made the latter issue explosive also.

The annexation of Texas in 1845, the war with Mexico that followed, and the conquests in the Southwest which that war brought about gave to the campaign against slavery a new and unprecedented urgency. Within living memory the plains along the Gulf of Mexico had been inundated by the westward-moving tide of slavery. Alabama and Mississippi, to say nothing of Arkansas and Missouri, furnished startling proof of how quickly and ineradicably the institution could establish itself throughout great new regions. Paricularly telling was the example of Texas. There slavery had been carried by American settlers to nominally free soil beyond the boundaries of the United States; yet in the end the area itself was being incorporated in the Union. To guard against any possible repetition of these developments, antislavery forces reacted to the outbreak of the Mexican War by introducing and supporting the Wilmot Proviso. Originally designed to apply simply to territory that might be acquired from Mexico, it was quickly changed into an all-encompassing prohibition: "That there shall be neither slavery nor involuntary servitude in any territory on the continent of America which shall hereafter be acquired by or annexed to the United States . . . in any . . . manner whatever."[12] The steadfast refusal of the Senate to accept the proviso did not kill it, for the prospect of continuing expansion kept the doctrine alive and made it the rallying point of antislavery sentiment until the Civil War.

This prospect of continuing expansion is sometimes forgotten by historians who regard the issue of slavery in the territories as somehow bafflingly unreal. Since 1854, it is true, no contiguous territory has actually been added to the "continental" United States. No one in the later 1850s, however, could know that this was to be the historic fact. There were ample reasons to expect otherwise. A strong faction had worked for the annexation of the whole of Mexico in 1848. Filibustering expeditions in the Caribbean and Central America were sporadic from 1849 to 1860. As if to spell out the implications of these moves, the notorious Ostend Manifesto of 1854 had announced (over the signatures of three American envoys, including a future president) that the United States could not "permit Cuba to be Africanized" (in plainer language, could not allow the slaves in Cuba to become free of white domination and control), and had defiantly proclaimed that if Spain should refuse to sell the island, "then, by every law, human and divine, we shall be justified in wresting it from Spain if we possess the power."[13] This was "higher law" doctrine with a vengeance.

Behind the intransigent refusal of the Republicans in 1860–1861 to accept any sort of compromise on the territorial question lay these all too recent developments. Lincoln's letters during the interval between his election and his inauguration contained pointed allusions to filibustering and to Cuba.[14] And his most explicit instructions on policy, written on February 1, 1861, to William H. Seward, soon to

take office as his secretary of state, were adamant against any further extension of slavery in any manner:

> I say now, . . . as I have all the while said, that on the territorial question — that is, the question of extending slavery under the national auspices, — I am inflexible. I am for no compromise which *assists* or *permits* the extension of the institution on soil owned by the nation. And any trick by which the nation is to acquire territory, and then allow some local authority to spread slavery over it, is as obnoxious as any other.

The obnoxious "trick" that Lincoln feared was, of course, the acceptance of Stephen A. Douglas's doctrine of popular sovereignty. The supreme importance that Lincoln attached to the territorial issue was underlined by the final paragraph of his letter, wherein he discussed four other issues on which antislavery feeling ran high: the Fugitive Slave Act, the existence of slavery in the national capital, the domestic slave trade, and the slave code that the territorial legislature of New Mexico had enacted in 1859. Concerning these matters, Lincoln wrote Seward: "As to fugitive slaves, District of Columbia, slave trade among the slave states, and whatever springs of necessity from the fact that the institution is amongst us, I care but little, so that what is done be comely, and not altogether outrageous. Nor do I care much about New-Mexico, if further extension were hedged against."[15]

The issues raised by territorial expansion were, however, not merely prospective ones. Expansion was a present fact, and from 1845 onward its problems were immediate ones. Population was moving so rapidly into various parts of the newly acquired West, most spectacularly into California, that the establishment of civil governments within the region could hardly be postponed. Accordingly, within the single decade already delimited (that is, from the beginning of 1845 until the end of 1854), state or terrorial forms of government were actually provided for every remaining part of the national domain, except the relatively small enclave known as the Indian Territory (now Oklahoma). The result was an actual doubling of the area of the United States within which organized civil governments existed.[16] This process of political creation occurred not only in the new acquisitions, but it also covered vast areas, previously acquired, that had been left unorganized, notably the northern part of the old Louisiana Purchase. There, in 1854, the new territories of Kansas and Nebraska suddenly appeared on the map. With equal suddenness these new names appeared in the newspapers connected with ominous events.

The process of territorial organization brought into the very center of the crisis a fourth factor, the last in our original catalogue, namely, the constitutional one. The organization of new territories and the admission of new states were, after all, elements in a constitution-making process. Territorial expansion drastically changed the character of the dispute over slavery by entangling it with the constitutional problem of devising forms of government for the rapidly settling West. Slavery at last became, in the most direct and immediate sense, a constitutional question, and thus a question capable of disrupting the Union. It did so by assuming the form of a question about the power of Congress to legislate for the territories.

This brings us face to face with the central paradox in the pre-Civil War crisis. Slavery was being attacked in places where it did not, in present actuality, exist. The slaves, close to four million of them, were in the states, yet responsible leaders of the antislavery party pledged themselves not to interfere with them there.[17] In the territories, where the prohibition of slavery was being so intransigently demanded and so belligerently resisted, there had never been more than a handful of slaves during the long period of crisis. Consider the bare statistics. The census of 1860, taken just before the final descent into Civil War, showed far fewer than a hundred slaves in all the territories,[18] despite the abrogation of restrictions by the Kansas-Nebraska Act and the Dred Scott decision. Especially revealing was the situation in Kansas. Though blood had been spilled over the introduction of slavery into that territory, there were actually only 627 colored persons, slave or free, within its boundaries on the eve of its admission to statehood (January 29, 1861). The same situation obtained throughout the West. In 1846, at the time the Wilmot Proviso was introduced, the Union had comprised twenty-eight states. By the outbreak of the Civil War, more than two and a third million persons were to be found in the western areas beyond the boundaries of these older twenty-eight states, yet among them were only 7,687 Negroes, free or slave.[19] There was much truth in the wry observation of a contemporary: "The whole controversy over the Territories ... related to an imaginary negro in an impossible place."[20]

The paradox was undeniable, and many historians treat it as evidence of a growing retreat from reality. Thus James G. Randall writes that the "larger phases of the slavery question ... seemed to recede as the controversies of the fifties developed." In other words, "while the struggle sharpened it also narrowed." The attention of the country was "diverted from the fundamentals of slavery in its moral, economic, and social aspects," and instead "became concentrated upon the collateral problem as to what Congress should do with respect to slavery in the territories." Hence "it was this narrow phase of the slavery question which became, or seemed, central in the succession of political events which actually produced the Civil War." As Randall sees it, the struggle "centered upon a political issue which lent itself to slogan making rather than to political analysis."[21]

Slogan making, to be sure, is an important adjunct of political propaganda, and slogans can easily blind men to the relatively minor character of the tangible interests actually at stake. Nevertheless, a much more profound force was at work, shaping the crisis in this peculiar way.

This configurative force was at work, shaping the crisis in this peculiar way. The indirectness of the attack upon slavery, that is to say, the attack upon it in the territories, where it was merely a future possibility, instead of in the states, where the institution existed in force, was the unmistakable consequence of certain structural features of the American Constitution itself.

A centralized national state could have employed a number of different methods of dealing with the question of slavery. Against most of these the American Constitution interposed a barrier that was both insuperable and respected.[22] By blocking every form of frontal attack, it compelled the adoption of a strategy so indirect as to appear on the surface almost timid and equivocal.[23] In effect, the strategy adopted was a strategy of "containment." Lincoln traced it to the founding fathers themselves. They had, he asserted, put into effect a twofold policy with respect to slavery: "restricting it from the new Territories where it had not gone, and legislating to cut off its source by the abrogation of the slave trade." Taken together these amounted to "putting the seal of legislation against its spread." The second part of their policy was still in effect, but the first, said Lincoln, had been irresponsibly set aside. To restore it was his avowed object: "I believe if we could arrest the spread [of slavery] and place it where Washington, and Jefferson, and Madison placed it, it would be in the course of ultimate extinction, and the public mind would, as for eighty years past, believe that it was in the course of ultimate extinction. The crisis would be past."[24]

Whether or not slavery could have been brought to an end in this manner is a totally unanswerable question, but it requires no answer. The historical fact is that the defenders of slavery regarded the policy of containment as so dangerous to their interests that they interpreted it as signifying "that a war must be waged against slavery until it shall cease throughout the United States."[25] On the other hand, the opponents of slavery took an uncompromising stand in favor of this particular policy because it was the only one that the Constitution appeared to leave open. To retreat from it would be to accept as inevitable what Lincoln called "the perpetuity and nationalization of slavery."[26]

To understand the shaping effect of the Constitution upon the crisis, one must take seriously not only the ambiguities that contemporaries discovered in it, but also the features that all alike considered settled. The latter point is often neglected. Where constitutional understandings were clear and unambiguous, responsible leaders on both sides accepted without serious question the limitations imposed by the federal system. The most striking illustration has already been given. Antislavery leaders were willing to have written into the Constitution an absolute and perpetual ban upon congressional interference with slavery inside the slaveholding states. They were willing to do so because, as Lincoln said, they considered "such a provision to now be implied constitutional law," which might without objection be "made express, and irrevocable."[27]

Equally firm was the constitutional understanding that Congress had full power to suppress the foreign slave trade. On the eve of secession, to be sure, a few fire-eaters proposed a resumption of the importation of slaves. The true index of southern opinion, however, is the fact that the Constitution of the Confederate States outlawed the foreign slave trade in terms far more explicit than any found in the Constitution of the United States.[28]

Far more surprising to a modern student is a third constitutional understanding that somehow held firm throughout the crisis. The Constitution grants Congress an unquestioned power "to regulate Commerce with foreign Nations, and among the several States, and with the Indian Tribes."[29] Employing this power, Congress had outlawed the foreign slave trade in 1808, with the general acquiescence that we have just noted. To anyone familiar with twentieth-century American constitutional law, the commerce clause would seem to furnish an obvious weapon for use against the domestic slave trade as well. Since the 1890s the power of Congress to regulate interstate commerce has been directed successively against lotteries, prostitution, child labor, and innumerable other social evils that are observed to propagate themselves through the channels of interstate commerce.

The suppression of the domestic slave trade, moreover, would have struck a far more telling blow at slavery than any that could possibly have been delivered in the territories. Only the unhampered transportation and sale of slaves from the older seaboard regions can account for the creation of the black belt that stretched westward through the new Gulf states. By 1840 there were already as many slaves in Alabama and Mississippi together as in Virginia. During the twenty years that followed, the number of slaves in the two Gulf states almost doubled, while the number of slaves in Virginia remained almost stationary.[30]

The migration of slaveholding families with the slaves they already possessed can account for only part of this change. The domestic slave trader was a key figure in the process. His operations, moreover, had the indirect effect of pouring money back into older slaveholding states like Virginia, where slavery as an economic system had seemed, in the days of the Revolution, on the verge of bankruptcy. Futhermore, a direct attack upon the domestic slave trade might well have aroused less emotional resentment than the attack actually made upon the migration of slaveholders to the territories, for the slave trader was a universally reprobated figure, the object not only of antislavery invective but even of southern distrust and aversion.

No serious and sustained effort, however, was ever made to employ against the domestic slave trade the power of Congress to regulate interstate commerce. The idea was suggested, to be sure, but it never received significant support from responsible political leaders or from public opinion. No party platform of the entire period, not even the comprehensive, detailed, and defiant one offered by the Liberty party of 1844, contained a clear-cut proposal for using the commerce power to suppress the interstate traffic in slaves. Public opinion seems to have accepted as virtually axiomatic the constitutional principle that Henry Clay (who was, after all, no strict constructionist) phrased as follows in the set of resolutions from which the Compromise of 1850 ultimately grew: "*Resolved*, That Congress has no power to prohibit or obstruct the trade in slaves between the slaveholding States; but that the admission or exclusion of slaves brought from one into another of them, depends exclusively upon their own particular laws."[31]

Careful students of constitutional history have long been at pains to point out that the broad interpretation that John Marshall gave to the commerce clause in 1824 in the notable case of *Gibbons v. Ogden*[32] represented a strengthening of federal power in only one of its two possible dimensions. The decision upheld the power of Congress to sweep aside every obstruction to the free flow of interstate commerce. Not until the end of the nineteenth century, however, did the commerce power begin to be used extensively for the purpose of regulation in the modern sense, that is to say, restrictive regulation. The concept of a "federal police power," derived from the commerce clause, received its first clear-cut endorsement from the Supreme Court in the Lottery Case,[33] decided in 1903. These facts are well known. Few scholars, however, have called attention to the dramatic illustration of the difference between nineteenth- and twentieth-century views of the Constitution that is afforded by the fact that the commerce clause was never seriously invoked in connection with the slavery dispute. This same fact illustrates another point as well: how averse to innovation in constitutional matters the antislavery forces actually were, despite allegations to the contrary by their opponents.

Various other constitutional understandings weathered the crisis without particular difficulty, but to catalogue them is needless. The essential point has been made. The clearly stated provisions of the Constitution were accepted as binding. So also were at least two constitutional principles that rested upon no specific written text, but were firmly ingrained in public opinion: the plenary authority of the slaveholding states over the institution within their boundaries and the immunity of the domestic slave trade to federal interference.

In the Constitution as it stood, however, there were certain ambiguities and certain gaps. These pricked out, as on a geological map, the fault line along which earthquakes were likely to occur, should internal stresses build up to the danger point.

Several such points clustered about the fugitive-slave clause of the Constitution.[34] Clear enough was the principle that slaves might not secure their freedom by absconding into the free states. Three vital questions, however, were left without a clear answer. In the first place, did responsibility for returning the slaves to their masters rest with the states or the federal government? As early as 1842, the Supreme Court, in a divided opinion, placed responsibility upon the latter.[35] This decision brought to the fore a second question. How far might the free states go in refusing cooperation and even impeding the process of rendition? The so-called personal liberty laws of various northern states probed this particular constitutional question. Even South Carolina, originator of the doctrine of nullification, saw no inconsistency in its wrathful denunciation of these enactments, "which either nullify the Acts of Congress or render useless any attempt to execute them."[36] A third question arose in connection with the measures adopted by Congress to carry out the constitutional provision, notably the revised Fugitive Slave Act of 1850. Were the methods of enforcement prescribed by federal statute consistent with the procedural guarantees and underlying spirit of the Bill of Rights? From the twentieth-century viewpoint, this was perhaps the most profound of all the constitutional issues raised by the slavery dispute. It amounted to a direct confrontation between the philosophy of freedom and the incompatible philosophy of slavery. Important and disturbing though the issues were, the mandate of the fugitive-slave clause was sufficiently clear and direct to restrain all but the most extreme leaders from outright repudiation of it.[37]

Of all the ambiguities in the written Constitution, therefore, the most portentous proved in fact to be the ones that lurked in the clause dealing with territory: "The Congress shall have Power to dispose of and make all needful Rules and Regulations respecting the Territory or other Property belonging to the United States."[38] At first glance the provision seems clear enough, but questions were possible about its meaning. Eventually they were raised, and when raised they turned out to have so direct a bearing upon the problem of slavery that they would not down. What did the Constitution mean by mingling both "Territory" and "other Property," and speaking first of the power "to dispose of" such property? Was Congress in reality given a power to govern, or merely a proprietor's right to make regulations for the orderly management of the real estate he expected eventually to sell? If it were a power to govern, did it extend to all the subjects on which a full-fledged state was authorized to legislate? Did it therefore endow Congress with powers that were not federal powers at all but municipal ones, normally reserved to the states? In particular, did it bestow upon Congress, where the territories were concerned, a police power competent to deal with domestic relations and institutions like slavery?

This chain of seemingly trivial questions, it will be observed, led inexorably to the gravest question of the day: the future of slavery in an impetuously expanding nation. On many matters the decisions made by territorial governments might be regarded as unimportant, for the territorial stage was temporary and transitional. With respect to slavery, however, the initial decision was obviously a crucial one. A single article of the Ordinance of 1787 had eventuated in the admission of one free state after another in the old Northwest. The omission of a comparable article from other territorial enactments had cleared the way for the growth of a black belt of slavery from Alabama through Arkansas. An identical conclusion was drawn by both sides. The power to decide the question of slavery for the territories was the power to determine the future of slavery itself.

In whose hands, then, had the Constitution placed the power of decision with respect to slavery in the territories? This was, in the last analysis, the constitutional question that split the Union. To it, three mutually irreconcilable answers were offered.

The first answer was certainly the most straightforward. The territories were part of the "Property belonging to the United States." The Constitution gave Congress power to "make all needful Rules and Regulations" respecting them. Only a definite provision of the Constitution, either limiting this power or specifying exceptions to it, could destroy the comprehensiveness of the grant. No such limitations or exceptions were stated. Therefore, Congress was fully authorized by the Constitution to prohibit slavery in any or all of the territories, or to permit its spread thereto, as that body, in exercise of normal legislative discretion, might decide.

This was the straightforward answer; it was also the traditional answer. The Continental Congress had given that answer in the Ordinance of 1787, and the first Congress under the Constitution had ratified it. For half a century thereafter the precedents accumulated, including the precedent of the Missouri Compromise of 1820. Only in the 1840s were these precedents challenged.

Because this was the traditional answer, it was (by definition, if you like) the conservative answer. When the breaking point was finally reached in 1860–1861 and four identifiable conflicting groups offered four constitutional doctrines, two of them accepted this general answer, but each gave it a peculiar twist.

Among the four political factions of 1860, the least well organized was the group that can properly be described as the genuine conservatives. Their vehicle in the election of 1860 was the Constitutional Union party, and a rattletrap vehicle it certainly was. In a very real sense, however, they were the heirs of the old Whig party and particularly of the ideas of Henry Clay. Deeply ingrained was the instinct for compromise. They accepted the view just stated, that the power of decision with respect to slavery in a particular territory belonged to Congress. But they insisted that one additional understanding, hallowed by tradition, should likewise be considered constitutionally binding. In actually organizing the earlier territories, Congress had customarily balanced the prohibition of slavery in one area by the erection elsewhere of a territory wherein slaveholding would be permitted. To conservatives, this was more than a precedent; it was a constitutional principle. When, on December 18, 1860, the venerable John J. Crittenden offered to the Senate the resolutions summing up the conservative answer to the crisis, he was not in reality offering a new plan of compromise. He was, in effect, proposing to write into the Constitution itself the understandings that had governed politics in earlier, less crisis-ridden times. The heart of his plan was the reestablishment of the old Missouri Compromise line, dividing free territories from slave.[39] An irrepealable amendment was to change this from a principle of policy into a mandate of constitutional law.

That Congress was empowered to decide the question of slavery for the territories was the view not only of the conservatives, but also of the Republicans. The arguments of the two parties were identical, up to a point; indeed, up to the point just discussed. Though territories in the past had been apportioned between freedom and slavery, the Republicans refused to consider this policy as anything more than a policy, capable of being altered at any time. The Wilmot Proviso of 1846 announced, in effect, that the time had come to abandon the policy. Radical though the proviso may have been in a political sense, it was hardly so in a constitutional sense. The existence of a congressional power is the basic constitutional question. In arguing for the existence of such a power over slavery in the territories, the Republicans took the same ground as the conservatives. In refusing to permit mere precedent to hamper the discretion of Congress in the use of that power, they broke with the conservatives. But the distinction they made between power and discretion, that is, between constitutional law and political policy, was neither radical nor unsound.

One innovation did find a place in antislavery, and hence in Republican, constitutional doctrine. Though precedent alone ought not to hamper the discretion of Congress, specific provisions of the Constitution could, and in Republican eyes did, limit and control that discretion. With respect to congressional action on slavery in the territories, so the antislavery forces maintained, the due process clause of the Fifth Amendment constituted such an express limitation. "Our Republican fathers," said the first national platform of the new party in 1856, "ordained that no person shall be deprived of life, liberty, or property, without due process of law." To establish slavery in the territories "by positive legislation" would violate this guarantee. Accordingly the Constitution itself operated to "deny the authority of Congress, of a Territorial Legislation [sic], of any individual, or association of individuals, to give legal existence to Slavery in

any Territory of the United States."[40] The Free Soil platform of 1848 had summed the argument up in an aphorism: "Congress has no more power to make a SLAVE than to make a KING; no more power to institute or establish SLAVERY, than to institute or establish a MONARCHY."[41] As a doctrine of constitutional law, the result was this: the federal government had full authority over the territories, but so far as slavery was concerned, Congress might exercise this authority in only one way, by prohibiting the institution there.

The conservatives and the Republicans took the constitutional system as it stood, a combination of written text and historical precedent, and evolved their variant doctrines therefrom. By contrast, the two other factions of 1860 — the northern Democrats under Stephen A. Douglas, and the southern Democrats whose senatorial leader was Jefferson Davis and whose presidential candidate was John C. Breckinridge — appealed primarily to constitutional theories above and beyond the written document and the precedents. If slogans are meaningfully applied, these two factions (each in its own way) were the ones who, in 1860, appealed to a "higher law."

For Douglas, this higher law was the indefeasible right of every community to decide for itself the social institutions it would accept and establish, "Territorial Sovereignty" (a more precise label than "popular sovereignty") meant that this right of decision on slavery belonged to the settlers in a new territory fully as much as to the people of a full-fledged state. At bottom the argument was one from analogy. The Constitution assigned responsibility for national affairs and interstate relations to the federal government; authority over matters of purely local and domestic concern were reserved to the states. So far as this division of power was concerned, Douglas argued, a territory stood on the same footing as a state. It might not yet have sufficient population to entitle it to a vote in Congress, but its people were entitled to self-government from the moment they were "organized into political communities." Douglas took his stand on what he regarded as a fundamental principle of American political philosophy: "that the people of every separate political community (dependent colonies, Provinces, and Territories as well as sovereign States) have an inalienable right to govern themselves in respect to their internal polity."[42]

Having thus virtually erased the constitutional distinction between a territory and a state — a distinction that was vital (as we shall see) to the state-sovereignty interpretation — Douglas proceeded to deal with the argument that since a territorial government was a creation of Congress, the powers it exercised were delegated ones, which Congress itself was free to limit, to overrule, or even to exercise through direct legislation of its own. He met the argument with an ingenious distinction. "Congress," he wrote, "may institute governments for the Territories," and, having done so, may "invest them with powers which Congress does not possess and can not exercise under the Constitution." He continued: "The powers which Congress may thus *confer* but can not *exercise*, are such as relate to the domestic affairs and internal polity of the Territory."[43] Their source is not to be sought in any provision of the written Constitution, certainly not in the so-called territorial clause,[44] but in the underlying principle of self-government.

Though Douglas insisted that the doctrine of popular sovereignty embodied "the ideas and principles of the fathers of the Revolution," his appeal to history was vitiated by special pleading. In his most elaborate review of the precedents (the article in *Harper's Magazine* from which quotations have already been taken), he passed over in silence the Northwest Ordinance of 1787, with its clear-cut congressional ban on slavery.[45] Douglas chose instead to dwell at length upon the "Jeffersonian Plan of government for the Territories," embodied in the Ordinance of 1784.[46] This plan, it is true, treated the territories as virtually equal with the member states of the Union, and thus supported (as against subsequent enactments) Douglas's plea for the largest measure of local self-government. When, however, Douglas went on to imply that the "Jeffersonian Plan" precluded, in principle, any congressional interference with slavery in the territories, he was guilty of outright misrepresentation. Jefferson's original draft (still extant in his own hand) included a forthright prohibition of slavery in all the territories.[47] The Continental Congress, it is true, refused at the time to adopt this particular provision, a fact that Douglas mentioned,[48] but there is no evidence whatever to show that they believed they lacked the power to do so. Three years later, the same body exercised this very power by unanimous vote of the eight states present.[49]

Disingenuousness reached its peak in Douglas's assertion that the Ordinance of 1784 "stood on the statute book unrepealed and irrepealable . . . when, on the 14th day of May, 1787, the Federal Convention assembled at Philadelphia and proceeded to form the Constitution under which we now live."[50] Unrepealed the ordinance still was, and likewise unimplemented, but irrepealable it was not. Sixty days later, on July 13, 1787, Congress repealed it outright and substituted in its place the Northwest Ordinance,[51] which Douglas chose not to discuss.

Despite these lapses, Douglas was, in truth, basing his doctrine upon one undeniably important element in the historic tradition of American political philosophy. In 1860 he was the only thoroughgoing advocate of local self-determination and local autonomy. He could justly maintain that he was upholding this particular aspect of the constitutional tradition not only against the conservatives and the Republicans, but also (and most emphatically) against the southern wing of his own party, which bitterly repudiated the whole notion of local self-government, when it meant that the people of a territory might exclude slavery from their midst.

This brings us to the fourth of the parties that contested the election of 1860, and to the third and last of the answers that were given to the question of where the Constitution placed the power to deal with slavery in the territories.

At first glance there would appear to be only two possible answers. Either the power of decision lay with the federal government, to which the territories had been ceded or by which they had been acquired; or else the decision rested with the people of the territories, by virtue of some inherent right of self-government. Neither answer, however, was acceptable to the proslavery forces. By the later 1850s they were committed to a third doctrine, state sovereignty.

The theory of state sovereignty takes on a deceptive appearance of simplicity in most historical accounts. This is because it is usually examined only in the context of the secession crisis. In that situation the corollaries drawn from the theory of state sovereignty were, in fact, exceedingly simple. If the Union was simply a compact among states that retained their ultimate sovereignty, then one or more of them could legally and peacefully withdraw from it, for reasons which they, as sovereigns, might judge sufficient. Often overlooked is the fact that secession itself was responsible for reducing the argument over state sovereignty to such simple terms. The right to secede was only one among many corollaries of the complex and intricate doctrine of the sovereignty of the states. In the winter and spring of 1860–61, this particular corollary, naked and alone, became the issue on which events turned. Earlier applications of the doctrine became irrelevant. As they dropped from view, they were more or less forgotten. The theory of state sovereignty came to be regarded simply as a theory that had to do with the perpetuity of the Union.

The simplicity of the theory is, however, an illusion. The illusion is a conse-

quence of reading history backward. The proslavery constitutional argument with respect to slavery in the territories cannot possibly be understood if the fifteen years of debate prior to 1860 are regarded simply as a dress rehearsal for secession. When applied to the question of slavery, state sovereignty was a positive doctrine, a doctrine of power, specifically, a doctrine designed to place in the hands of the slaveholding states a power sufficient to uphold slavery and promote its expansion *within* the Union. Secession might be an ultimate recourse, but secession offered no answer whatever to the problems of power that were of vital concern to the slaveholding states so long as they remained in the Union and used the Constitution as a piece of working machinery.

As a theory of how the Constitution should operate, as distinguished from a theory of how it might be dismantled, state sovereignty gave its own distinctive answer to the question of where the authority lay to deal with matters involving slavery in the territories. All such authority, the theory insisted, resided in the sovereign states. But how, one may well ask, was such authority to be exercised? The answer was ingenious. The laws that maintained slavery — which were, of course, the laws of the slaveholding states — must be given extraterritorial or extrajurisdictional effect.[52] In other words, the laws that established a property in slaves were to be respected, and if necessary enforced, by the federal government, acting as agent for its principals, the sovereign states of the Union.

At the very beginning of the controversy, on January 15, 1847, five months after the introduction of the Wilmot Proviso, Robert Barnwell Rhett of South Carolina showed how that measure could be countered, and proslavery demands supported, by an appeal to the *mystique* of the sovereignty of the several states:

Their sovereignty, unalienated and unimpaired ... exists in all its plenitude over our territories; as much so, as within the limits of the States themselves ... The only

Arthur Bestor

effect, and probably the only object of their reserved sovereignty, is, that it secures to each State the right to enter the territories with her citizens, and settle and occupy them with their property — with whatever is recognised as property by each State. The ingress of the citizen, is the ingress of his sovereign, who is bound to protect him in his settlement.[53]

Nine years later the doctrine had become the dominant one in proslavery thinking, and on January 24, 1856, Robert Toombs of Georgia summed it up succinctly: "Congress has no power to limit, restrain, or in any manner to impair slavery: but, on the contrary, it is bound to protect and maintain it in the States where it exists, and wherever its flag floats, and its jurisdiction is paramount."[54] In effect, the laws of slavery were to become an integral part of the laws of the Union, so far as the territories were concerned.

Four irreconcilable constitutional doctrines were presented to the American people in 1860. There was no consensus, and the stage was set for civil war. The issues in which the long controversy culminated were abstruse. They concerned a seemingly minor detail of the constitutional system. The arguments that supported the various positions were intricate and theoretical. But the abstractness of constitutional issues has nothing to do, one way or the other, with the role they may happen to play at a moment of crisis. The sole question is the load that events have laid upon them. Thanks to the structure of the American constitutional system itself, the abstruse issue of slavery in the territories was required to carry the burden of well-nigh all the emotional drives, well-nigh all the political and economic tensions, and well-nigh all the moral perplexities that resulted from the existence in the United States of an archaic system of labor and an intolerable policy of racial subjection. To change the metaphor, the constitutional question of legislative authority over the territories became, so to speak, the narrow channel through which surged the torrent of ideas and interests and anxieties that flooded down from every drenched hillside upon which the storm cloud of slavery discharged its poisoned rain.

Part Seven

The New Legal Order: Reconstruction and the Gilded Age

Each of the articles in this section explodes what had been a long-accepted interpretive view of post–Civil War constitutional history. In his study of the reconstruction of federal judicial power, William Wiecek subjects to close reappraisal the conventional wisdom — also challenged tellingly in a recent book by Stanley I. Kutler — that depicted the immediate postwar years as a period of "congressional ascendency," when the Supreme Court and the federal judiciary generally were intimidated by the Radicals in Congress. Wiecek carefully examines the legal and constitutional history of the removal power, for example, and demonstrates that the triumph of centralized federalism as the result of the Civil War in fact brought an attendant expansion of federal judicial power. The augmented jurisdiction and power of the national courts, Wiecek maintains, "proved to be one of the most important and most lasting legacies of Reconstruction." Both institutional and statutory innovation established the framework for vigorous federal judicial intervention in the affairs of the nation during the years that followed.

Precisely why such innovations were of such crucial importance is clarified by Charles W. McCurdy's study of Justice Stephen Field and "the jurisprudence of government-business relations." It has long been a staple concern of constitutional historians to appraise the role of the Supreme Court in ordering the relations between business and government in the late nineteenth century. That the Gilded Age produced a classic, full-blown "judicial conservatism" — the most notable product of which was the transformation of the Fourteenth Amendment into a charter of "entrepreneurial liberty" — is indeed a view difficult to fault. What McCurdy decisively corrects, however, is the simplistic understanding of Gilded Age constitutional law that long underlay this view. Lawyers and historians built their analysis of judicial conservatism mainly upon study of the fate of regulatory legislation in the hands of the Supreme Court. McCurdy argues that they accepted too easily the thesis that Justice Field was the architect of a constitutional version of laissez faire that tried to reduce state power to ordinary police functions. But an alternative view of the leading economic issues of late-nineteenth-century constitutional litigation is possible; McCurdy, by stressing elements in Field's jurisprudence that left the state with a vigorous set of powers clearly differentiated from private-sector concerns, casts a sharply focused new light on judicial conservatism.

Further Reading

Belz, Herman J. *Reconstructing the Union: Conflicts of Theory and Policy during the Civil War*. Ithaca: Cornell University Press, 1969.

Beth, Loren P. *The Development of the American Constitution, 1877–1917*. New York: Harper & Row, 1971.

Fairman, Charles. *Mr. Justice Miller and the Supreme Court, 1862–1890*. Cambridge: Harvard University Press, 1939.

———. *Reconstruction and Reunion, 1864–88. Oliver Wendell Holmes Devise History of the U.S. Supreme Court*. New York: Macmillan, 1971. Vol. 6, pt.1.

Fine, Sidney B. *Laissez Faire and the General Welfare State*. Ann Arbor: University of Michigan Press, 1956.

Graham, Howard J. *Everyman's Constitution*. Madison: State Historical Society of Wisconsin, 1968.

Kutler, Stanley. *Judicial Power and Reconstruction Politics*. Chicago: University of Chicago Press, 1968.

Twiss, Benjamin. *Lawyers and the Constitution*. Princeton: Princeton University Press, 1942.

See also works by Hyman, Paludan, and Randall and Donald, in "Further Reading," Part 6.

20

William M. Wiecek

The Reconstruction of Federal Judicial Power, 1863–1876

In no comparable period of our nation's history have the federal courts, lower and Supreme, enjoyed so great an expansion of their jurisdiction as they did in the years of Reconstruction, 1863 to 1876. To a court, jurisdiction is power: power to decide certain types of cases, power to hear the pleas and defenses of different groups of litigants, power to settle policy questions which affect the lives, liberty, or purses of men, corporations, and governments. An increase in a court's jurisdiction allows that court to take on new powers, open its doors to new parties, and command the obedience of men formerly strangers to its writ. Thus it is that in crabbed and obscure jurisdictional statutes a hundred years old we may trace out great shifts of power, shifts that left the nation supreme over the states in 1876 and that gave the federal courts a greater control over the policies of Congress than they had before the Civil War.

The courts' jurisdiction was enlarged in five ways. First, Congress permitted many cases that had been begun in state courts to be taken out of them and tried in federal courts. This procedure, known as "remo-

val," first gave the federal courts new responsibilities for protecting the rights of Negroes and federal officials in the South. It was later used by corporations seeking to evade the hostility of Granger juries in state courts by resorting to the more sympathetic purlieus of the federal courts. Second, Congress extended the habeas corpus powers of the federal courts and transformed the nature of the Great Writ itself. Third, Congress organized a new federal court, the United States Court of Claims, to handle claims against the federal government, and allowed appeals to go from it to the United States Supreme Court. Fourth, Congress enacted a bankruptcy law which transferred much of the individual and corporate insolvency business from the state courts to the federal courts. By creating a claims court and making federal district judges bankruptcy arbiters, Congress gave the federal courts wide powers to regulate the national economy. Not all of these jurisdictional innovations stuck. Congress repealed the bankruptcy statute only eleven years after its passage. Yet in the long run, all the jurisdictional statutes of the Reconstruction era laid the groundwork for the judicial self-assertiveness of the late nineteenth and early twentieth centuries.

Abridged from *American Journal of Legal History*, 13 (1969), 333-359, by permission.

William M. Wiecek

In the twentieth century, removal became a means of protecting the civil liberties of all Americans, not just of southern Negroes. Habeas jurisdiction enabled federal courts to supervise the administration of justice in state courts. Removal and habeas corpus became two of the chief procedural supports for expanding concepts of Fourteenth Amendment liberties. Congress enacted a permanent bankruptcy statute, shorn of the faults of its predecessor, in 1898. In the 1960s, the Court of Claims annually processed millions of dollars of claims.

The responsibility for this accretion of power to the courts lies primarily with Congress. Federal judges cannot confer jurisdiction on themselves, *ab initio*, because the Constitution gives to Congress alone the ability to make "exceptions and regulations" controlling the jurisdiction of any federal court.[1] The President's role in expanding or narrowing the jurisdiction of the courts is usually minimal.[2] It is Congress in the first instance that gives new powers to the courts or takes them away. When Congress expanded the jurisdiction of the federal courts during Reconstruction, it did so sometimes deliberately, sometimes absentmindedly; its intention was clear in one statute, ambiguous and vague in another. But the result by 1876 was clear: Congress had determined to expand the power of the federal courts, sometimes at its own expense, more often at the states', to make them partners in implementing national policy.

Until recently historians have scouted the part played by the federal courts, especially the Supreme Court, in Reconstruction. Because they emphasized Congress's forceful assertion of its powers after the death of Lincoln, historians tended to see the Supreme Court as intimidated by Congress. The justices, according to this view, were so abjectly cowed by Radical threats to strip the courts of their jurisdiction that they offered no resistance to unconstitutional laws. When judges did dare to flap their robes in protest against the usurpation of power by the legislative branch,

congressional Radicals maliciously lopped off this or that segment of their jurisdiction. The courts, we once read, were bullied into submission to Congress and were left impotent to deflect the subjugation of the white South.[3]

This prevalent misapprehension about the federal courts' powers is derived from two errors commonly made by historians hostile to Republican accomplishments: first, they exaggerated the importance of selected contemporary sources; and second, they failed to investigate carefully the statutes and courts' opinions of the period. The extraordinary and unrepresentative act of Congress in 1868 that withdrew recently granted jurisdictional authorization so as to prevent William McCardle from taking his habeas corpus appeal to the Supreme Court brought down the wrath of Democrats and conservative Republicans on the heads of the Radicals and the Supreme Court justices. It is from these biased observers that historians have taken their views of the courts' power just after the Civil War.[4] Contemporaries and historians alike conveniently ignored numerous statutes increasing the federal courts' jurisdiction, as well as Supreme Court opinions vigorously implementing this statutory grant. This paper reviews some of those statutes and opinions in an attempt to restore some realistic perspective to congressional-judicial relations in the Reconstruction era.

The most important source of new federal judicial power was the removal legislation of the postwar years.[5] The removal jurisdiction of the federal courts had been narrowly restricted before the Civil War. Because the constitution nowhere expressly authorized federal courts to hear suits removed from state courts,[6] it was not clear that removal was constitutionally permissible until Justice Joseph Story's opinion in *Martin v. Hunter's Lessee*.[7] Story there held that the Constitution implicitly sanctioned removal, and that even cases which had gone to judgment in the state courts could be removed to federal courts. He also insisted that

Congress was obliged to enact statutes vesting in the federal courts all constitutionally authorized jurisdiction. Congress eventually did this in the Reconstruction years.

The original grant of removal jurisdiction, section 12 of the 1789 Judiciary Act, was quite limited.[8] Congress might have provided that any party could remove a suit presenting a federal question or a suit in which a party on one side lived in a state different from the residence of a party on the other.[9] Instead, it refused to permit removal of federal question cases as such. Only diversity suits could be removed, and then only by the defendant who was an alien or who did not reside in the forum state.[10] In addition, no suit could be removed unless the "matter" involved had a financial value of at least five hundred dollars.[11]

The shortcomings of section 12 became apparent within twenty-five years after its enactment. When New England shipowners harassed federal customs officers by vexatious lawsuits during the War of 1812, Congress responded by passing the removal provisions of the Revenue Act of February 4, 1815.[12] Section 8 of this statute made removal available in actions begun "for any thing done, or omitted to be done, as an officer of the customs, or for any thing done by virtue of this act." Congress again turned to the courts for help in implementing its policies in 1833 when it passed the Force Act to suppress South Carolina's resistance to the enforcement of federal revenue laws.[13] Section 3 of the act permitted the removal of suits involving "any right, authority, or title" under any federal revenue statute.

On the eve of the Civil War, Congress had thus hesitantly groped toward a comprehensive system of removal legislation in the 1789, 1815, and 1833 statutes, but it had not come near to giving the federal courts plenary removal jurisdiction.[14] Only the recurring crises of the war and Reconstruction years could provide impetus for that. Congress conferred this plenary jurisdiction incrementally and in two ways. First, it authorized removal as an auxiliary procedural device for protecting the enforcement of substantive policies unrelated to removal; second, it enacted other removal statutes with the explicit and primary objective of expanding federal judicial power.

Many Reconstruction statutes which provided for the enforcement of federal laws or for the protection of an individual's rights under the federal Constitution also included removal provisions. Such removal sections were always ancillary to some other policy objective, such as collecting revenue or protecting freedmen. They also reflected a growing Republican disenchantment with state courts. As congressmen's respect for the independence of the state benches diminished when they came to believe that local judges were trying to thwart national policy, they did not hesitate to by-pass the state judicial machinery altogether in order to protect federal officers and freedmen. This can be most clearly seen by looking at four statutes in chronological order: the Habeas Corpus Act of 1863, the 1866 amendment to the 1863 Habeas Corpus Act, the Internal Revenue Act of 1866, and the 1871 Voting Rights Act.

The removal provisions of the 1863 Habeas Corpus Act[15] were modeled on earlier removal legislation and were designed to protect federal officials who arrested persons from suits for false imprisonment. The act also contained a new increment to the expansion of federal removal power: its umbrella of protection was not limited to acts done under any one federal statute. It gave blanket protection to federal officers from all civil and criminal actions arising out of any official acts.

When Congress amended the 1863 Act in 1866, it included provisions that showed its increasing annoyance with state judges and prosecuting attorneys who, it believed, flouted federal removal laws. The 1866 amendment voided all proceedings in state courts after removal and made any person involved in such void proceedings liable to the removing party for damages and double costs.[16]

William M. Wiecek

The 1871 Voting Rights Enforcement Act made it still easier to by-pass the state courts.[17] The removing party no longer needed the assent of the state judge to remove the action; he had merely to file his petition for removal in the federal court. The court would then issue its writ of certiorari to the state court, a writ which emphasized the inferior status of the state court. Any persons taking part in state proceedings after such removal, including the judge, were made guilty of a misdemeanor and triable for contempt in the court to which the action had been removed.

Congress enacted the Separable Controversies Act of 1866[18] to get around an old decision of Chief Justice John Marshall, *Strawbridge* v. *Curtis*,[19] which required that all parties on one side of a suit have citizenship different from all parties on the opposite side in order for federal courts to take the suit on removal under their diversity jurisdiction. Canny resident plaintiffs in southern-state courts supposedly abused the Strawbridge rule and stymied federal removal jurisdiction by joining a nominal resident party to the real and nonresident defendant. To stop this, the Separable Controversies Act permitted the nonresident defendant to remove the action against him to the federal court, leaving the remainder of the suit in the state court, if that portion of the controversy that pertained to him could be finally decided in the federal court. This statute was the first which permitted parties to split a cause of action, leaving part in the state court and bringing another part to the federal court. In the long run, this splitting greatly increased the business of the federal courts.[20]

Southern hostility to nonresident litigants was also the occasion for the Local Prejudice Act of 1867.[21] The original version of the bill, in fact, was limited in its application to "states lately in insurrection."[22] This limitation was dropped, and the act as passed permitted either party to a suit in a state court anywhere in the nation to remove by filing an affidavit "stating that he has reason to, and does believe that, from prejudice or local influence, he will not be able to obtain justice in such state court." As with the Separable Controversies Act, Congress enlarged federal jurisdiction to protect the administration of justice by providing an impartial forum to litigants when the state courts proved inadequate or obstructive.[23]

By 1875 congressional Republicans' humanitarian concern for the freedmen was nearly spent. The flourishing economic development of the postwar years led most Republicans to substitute sympathies for entrepreneurial interests in place of their earlier care for the freedmen. It was no accident that the most important later use of removal jurisdiction redounded to the benefit of businessmen and corporations rather than Negroes. Congress abandoned its suspicions of southern courts and concentrated its attention on the midwestern courts and legislatures infected with Granger resentment toward eastern capitalists.[24]

The impetus for enactment of a comprehensive removal statute in 1875 was provided in a negative way by the United States Supreme Court. On March 3, 1874, the court handed down its decision in the Sewing Machine Company Cases,[25] holding that under the Local Prejudice Act and the Separate Controversies Act a party could not remove an entire suit to the federal courts if one of the parties on the opposite side lacked diversity. The Jurisdiction and Removal Act of 1875[26] permitted any party to remove; reversed the Sewing Machine Company Cases and authorized removal of the whole suit if the real controversy was between diverse parties; allowed removal of all diversity actions, whether or not one of the parties lived in the forum state; and, most important of all, permitted removal of all federal question suits. Section 1 of the act made analogous changes in the original jurisdiction of the lower federal courts. The lower federal courts were at last given original and removal jurisdiction as broad as the Constitution authorized.

Senator Matt Carpenter (R., Wis.) explained at length the motives of the

Senate Judiciary Committee in reporting out such an expansive bill. In 1789, he stated, extensive federal jurisdiction was not needed because the nation's commerce was small and waterborne; but in 1875, it "crosses the continent; our people have become vitally changed in their methods of doing business." To accommodate this changed commerce, the former railroad attorney noted, required an expansion of the jurisdiction of the federal courts.[27] Congress, it would appear, was determined not to let the particularist animosities of state court judges and juries impede the national market.

The second major accretion to federal judicial power came with section 1 of the 1867 Habeas Corpus Act. Not only did this statute expand the power of the courts; it changed the nature of the Great Writ itself. Before 1867, habeas corpus was principally a means of testing the legality of confinements by *executive* authority. After the 1867 act, the writ became a means of reviewing *judicial* confinement; appellate courts took on power to determine whether lower courts acted properly when they deprived a man of his liberty.

More controversial, then and now, was the shift of power embodied in the 1867 act. Before 1867, the courts of the nation and the states were insulated from each other in habeas corpus matters by the old maxim that habeas corpus cannot be used as a writ of error. Habeas corpus could not call into question the judgment of a jurisdictionally competent court. Under the 1867 act, however, federal courts got the power to review the judgments of state courts, even after these had been affirmed by the state supreme courts. The salvos of the controversy this brought on thundered for nearly a century; their echoes resound today.

The Constitution did not set the bounds of the federal courts' habeas powers; it dealt only with the reasons for suspending the writ.[28] The courts therefore depended entirely on Congress for their habeas powers; without statutory authorization no court could issue the Great Writ

except the Supreme Court, and then only in aid of its rarely invoked original jurisdiction.[29] The federal courts did not have power to supervise the rulings of the state courts by habeas corpus. A person on trial in a state court depended completely on the states for the protection of his rights guaranteed by the federal Constitution; he had no recourse to the national courts by habeas corpus.

The First Congress did not delay in giving the federal courts habeas jurisdiction, but its jurisdiction grant, section 14 of the 1789 Judiciary Act, was niggardly.[30] The most crippling part of section 14 was contained in its proviso "that writs of habeas corpus shall in no case extend to prisoners in gaol, unless where they are in custody, under or by colour of the authority of the United States, or are necessary to be brought into court to testify."

This proviso meant that the federal writ could not reach the man held under the order of a state court. No matter how outrageous the violation of his rights under the Constitution, no matter how emphatically he was protected by federal laws, a man in the grasp of the state courts could not be pried out by federal habeas corpus.

By 1860, federal habeas power was thus narrowly circumscribed. The Great Writ could not be used in any court to review an order of a jurisdictionally competent tribunal; it was exclusively a pretrial remedy used to test confinement by executive order. Within the American federal system, the national courts could not use the writ as a means of liberating prisoners held under the authority of the state. Both these restrictions were swept away by the Habeas Corpus Act of 1867. After a century of judicial development of the 1867 act, the Great Writ has become a procedural device for reviewing convictions after trial in courts which had jurisdiction of the person and the subject matter, and it has been used by federal courts to supervise the administration of justice in state courts.

The origins of the 1867 Habeas Corpus Act may be traced to Republican concern for the condition of southern freedmen.

William M. Wiecek

As a means of enforcing the Thirteenth Amendment, Representative James F. Wilson (R., Iowa) introduced a bill "to secure the writ of habeas corpus to persons held in slavery."[31] In the House Judiciary Committee, Wilson's bill was replaced by a new two-part bill and reported out. Section 1[32] of this substitute bill provided that federal courts and judges could grant a writ of habeas corpus "in all cases where any person may be restrained of his or her liberty in violation of the Constitution, or of any treaty or law of the United States."

The newborn statute nearly suffered infanticide a year later, when the United States Supreme Court announced that it would take jurisdiction in a habeas appeal of one William McCardle.[33] McCardle was a Mississippi editor awaiting trial by a military commission; a federal circuit court had refused his petition for a writ of habeas corpus, and he appealed this refusal to the Supreme Court. Democrats in Congress assumed that the Court was about to hold the military reconstruction acts of 1867 unconstitutional. This possibility, unreal though it appears in retrospect,[34] thoroughly frightened congressional Republicans, and they responded by repealing as much of the 1867 act as would authorize the United States Supreme Court to review a lower federal court's disposition of a habeas petition.[35] Supporters of the "McCardle repealer," as it has been called, were at pains to point out that the repealer did not affect previous grants of habeas jurisdiction; but they did not have quite enough candor to admit that the bill was designed merely to keep McCardle out of the Supreme Court.[36]

The court accepted the repealer and dismissed McCardle's petition, but it passed a useful hint on to counsel, reminding them that the federal habeas jurisdiction, except for the 1867 act, remained unaffected by the repealer.[37] The hint was taken up by attorneys for Edward M. Yerger, a Mississippian who had been arrested by the army for killing an army officer. The court accepted Yerger's habeas petition as coming up under the 1789 Judiciary Act provisions rather than the 1867 act, and granted the writ.[38] The effect of the Yerger decision was to nullify the impact of the McCardle repealer as far as federal (not state) prisoners were concerned. In 1885, after the passions of Reconstruction had subsided, Congress restored the McCardle-type jurisdiction it had excised in 1868.[39] Thus the 1867 act, less than two decades after its passage, was restored to its full force.

The McCardle episode proved to be only a temporary diversion from the mainstream of habeas development in the nineteenth century. The Great Writ emerged as a post-conviction form of relief. State resentment of federal review, smoldering since *Cohens v. Virginia* and *Martin v. Hunter's Lessee* earlier in the century, flared up again as persons convicted in state courts sought relief in the federal courts. Partisans of the state judiciary came to realize that the 1867 act contained no limitations on collateral review by federal courts of state court convictions, and they denounced this "abuse" vociferously in law journals and petitions to Congress.[40]

The Court lent a sympathetic ear to those who complained that the dignity of state courts was abased by having convictions, some of them affirmed by state supreme courts, overturned by lower federal courts by habeas petitions. It began narrowing the sweep of the 1867 act by formulating the "exhaustion" doctrine of *Ex parte Royall*,[41] by which federal courts may require that a would-be habeas petitioner first be tried by the state courts or exhaust his appeals through the state court system before federal courts grant collateral habeas review. This was done to give the state courts an opportunity to pass on the merits of the case before the federal courts step in.

The Supreme Court's new restrictive mood was further evinced in *In re Wood*, where the court instructed lower federal courts not to retry the merits of federal constitutional questions raised in a habeas petition under the 1867 act unless the state court lacked jurisdiction of person or cause.[42] This holding, in apparent conflict with congressional intent in passing the 1867 act, nevertheless suited the new mood of hostility toward federal review. By emphasizing the one desideratum of finality in litigation, the court sacrificed another, that of full judicial protection for individual constitutional rights.

It appeared by 1900 that the expansive possibilities of the 1867 act had been severely curtailed by judicial surgery. Aside from its use after conviction, habeas corpus had not wrought any drastic changes in the federal system. Yet the act remained in the Revised Statutes, its potential dormant but surviving the winter of judicial "conservatism" in the late nineteenth century. It was revived dramatically in the 1920s by a bare majority on the court that insisted that federal courts should retry factual issues which, if proved, deprived the petitioner of federal constitutional rights.[43] This began a trend, culminating in several post-World War II cases, toward realizing the full promise of the 1867 act by permitting federal courts to review the merits of all federal constitutional questions arising in a state court trial.[44]

Reconstruction Congresses enhanced the role of the federal courts in the area of economic regulation in two principal ways: by creating a Court of Claims having jurisdiction over claims suits against the sovereign and by enacting a bankruptcy statute to be administered by the federal courts. In both cases, the federal court system took on broad new powers to implement national policy respecting the country's transportation network and other aspects of the national economy.

The problem of providing justice, both procedural and substantive, to persons who had a claim against the United States had plagued Congress ever since 1789. Because the national government was a sovereign, it could not be sued unless it waived its sovereign immunity; yet congressmen always had felt that it would be inequitable to use sovereign immunity as a cloak for evading just obligations. Hence they had experimented with various devices for processing claims against the federal government.

Between 1789 and about 1820, Congress made claims determination primarily the responsibility of the executive branch of the government by funneling claims through the Treasury Department and, after the War of 1812, through an ad hoc administrative commission which processed claims growing out of the war.[45] Beginning sometime in the 1820s and extending to 1855, Congress took on itself the power of adjudicating claims through its committees.[46] The workload of the committees was so time-consuming, however, that Congress was forced, in the mid-fifties, to turn to a quasi-judicial body to handle claims adjudication.

Congress was impeded in its efforts to work out a claims procedure before and during the Civil War by two principal considerations, one practical and one constitutional. The latter stemmed from the seventh clause of Article I, section 9: "No Money shall be drawn from the Treasury, but in Consequence of Appropriations made by Law." The practical difficulty was simply that Congress did not want to relinquish its control of the national purse strings to some extralegislative body it could not control. Both difficulties hampered the establishment of a court of claims during the war and Reconstruction.

By 1855, the time wasted in claims committees had become intolerable to congressmen, and they tried to rid themselves of the unwelcome burden of claims processing by creating a "court" to decide claims.[47] But their reluctance to part with the power they exercised over claims, together perhaps with scruples about the constitutionality of a wholly independent judicial body whose judgments would have to be honored by the Treasury, led them in the next year to refuse finality to the judgments of the court.[48] Successful plaintiffs in the claims court still had to have Congress authorize appropriations for their judgments, unsuccessful ones still had their resort to Congress despite an adverse judgment. It was this unsatisfactory structure that still operated when the Civil War broke out. It became obvious that Congress would soon be inundated with war claims.

President Lincoln, in his first annual message,[49] called on Congress to set up a claims court whose judgments would be final, but Congress did not get around to doing so until 1863. Then it reorganized the court of claims and tried to give finality to its judgments by authorizing them to be paid out of general appropriations made for that purpose, rather than by specific appropriations. At the end of debates, an opponent of finality, Senator John P. Hale (R., N.H.) inserted an amendment to the bill which provided that no claim could be paid until it had been "estimated for" by the secretary of the treasury. With this amendment, the bill passed and the modern Court of Claims made its debut.[50]

The new court, naturally, did a booming business, and it seemed that all doubts about its constitutional status as an Article III court and the finality of its judgments had been laid to rest. Hence the 1865 holding of the Supreme Court in *Gordon v. United States* came as a shock everywhere. In a brief and opaque opinion the new chief justice, Salmon P. Chase, stated that the authority given to the secretary of the treasury to "revise" the decisions of the Court of Claims denied the court Article III judicial status. As a result, appeals could not be taken from it to the United States Supreme Court. Chase's holding left the Court of Claims in existence, but its decisions were by implication not necessarily binding on Congress or the Treasury.[51]

Congress immediately repealed the section of the 1863 act that Chase had found objectionable, emphasizing its original intention that the Court of Claims be an authentic Article III court.[52] By preserving the right of appeal from Court of Claims decisions to the United States Supreme Court, Congress necessarily gave up its

power to revise the judgments of the court, a considerable shift of power from the supposedly hostile Congress to the supposedly intimidated federal courts.

Regulation of the railroad system was an unexpected bonus of the Bankruptcy Act of 1867. That relatively short-lived statute (it was repealed in 1878) marks another major increment of power passed on to the federal courts by Congress in the Reconstruction era.

Earlier attempts at providing the federal courts with power to supervise insolvencies had failed. The Bankruptcy Law of 1800,[53] a creditor-oriented statute which failed to satisfy its intended beneficiaries, was repealed in 1803.[54] The 1841 Bankruptcy Act, a Whig measure, made available the procedure of voluntary bankruptcy, and broadened the powers of federal courts in supervising the administration of bankrupts' estates. Democrats, southerners, and even creditors were dissatisfied with the actual workings of the act, and it too was repealed within two years.[55] The failure of both statutes indicated that any national bankruptcy legislation would have to appeal to all sections of the country and to both creditor and debtor interests. During the Civil War practical pressures for a new bankruptcy act came as a result of business failures caused by the cancellation of southern indebtedness and the depreciation of currency, North and South, as well as from widespread financial failures in the South because of the war. These pressures brought about the enactment of a third federal bankruptcy statute in 1867.[56]

The 1867 Bankruptcy Act permitted voluntary as well as involuntary bankruptcies. Federal district courts were made "courts of bankruptcy" and were again given the quasi-equitable jurisdiction of bankruptcy in all cases involving a bankrupt's financial affairs, the interest of his creditors in his property, or the property itself. Appeals from the district courts were provided to the circuit and Supreme courts. This new bankruptcy statute added considerably to the volume of cases in the federal courts.[57]

To the routine bankruptcy business of the federal courts there was soon added a novel function: the supervision of railroad reorganization. Analogous in most respects to certain bankruptcy proceedings, railroad reorganization came to occupy a major part of the time of certain district courts. Railroad-receivership suits soon became quasi-permanent proceedings, and federal judges took on the unwonted duty of railroad management. Receivership almost became an end in itself, not an ancillary incident to an equity suit. Receivership was not confined to small intrastate feeder lines. A contemporary estimated that "the larger portion of all the railroads in the country are in a condition which would justify [federal courts] in placing them in the hands of receivers."[58] Receivership and railroad reorganization were becoming staples in the business of the lower federal courts by the end of Reconstruction.

The 1867 act was repealed because of sectional and interest-group opposition. Nineteenth-century bankruptcy laws had a way of alienating those whom they were intended to benefit. Some northern creditors felt the act was too lenient on southern debtors. Southerners and westerners voiced their instinctive fears of federal courts and national laws providing for the collection of debts. The voluntary bankruptcy provisions seem to have been most unpopular in the South and West, while northeastern creditors disliked the involuntary provisions, a reaction the opposite of what one might have expected. Creditors demanded bigger dividends and more protection; they complained of frauds and high fees.[59] President Grant recommended repeal of the act in 1878, and Congress soon complied.[60] But the need for national bankruptcy legislation was obvious; it was apparent that if the defects of the 1867 act could be ironed out, a national bankruptcy law became every day more necessary with the expansion of American commercial activity. The 1898 Chandler Act omitted most of the flaws of the 1867 act and remains

today the basis of our national bankruptcy legislation.

The traditional picture of a vindictive and ruthless Congress intimidating a supine judiciary during Reconstruction is derived from a few exceptional scraps of historical evidence exaggerated by partisan historians. The seeds of fact in this husk of fiction are occasional proposals to abolish the Supreme Court's appellate jurisdiction or to strip the Court of its power of judicial review, together with one successful attempt at trimming federal appellate review, the McCardle repealer. Of these, two things should be noted. First, the amputation in McCardle was not done with a cleaver but with a surgical knife. Congress did not withdraw all habeas review, but only a small portion of it recently conferred. This was far from being an "emasculation" of the Supreme Court, as a recent writer has termed it.[61] Second, the proposals to abolish judicial review are significant, not for what was done, but for what was not done. No such proposal received the approval of either house [of Congress] in the Reconstruction era.

The scope of federal judicial authority was broadened for the most part at the expense of the states. State court determinations affecting a person's federal constitutional or statutory rights were made reviewable by the federal bench. Whole categories of cases could be, and were, taken out of the state judicial systems entirely. This was a consequence of the nationalizing process of Reconstruction: a strong federal bench assured the dominance of the federal government over the states.

The federal judiciary emerged from the turmoil of reconstructing the Union triumphant, vigorous, conscious of its power, and willing to exercise it exuberantly in the decades to come. This reconstruction of federal judicial power proved to be one of the most important and most lasting legacies of Reconstruction.

21

Charles W. McCurdy

Justice Field and the Jurisprudence of Government-Business Relations: Some Parameters of Laissez Faire Constitutionalism, 1863–1897

The institutional and economic growth of American society through the mid-nineteenth century entailed close cooperation between the public and private sectors. Antebellum state and local politicians viewed government's resources as a means to attain the developmental goals of a society dedicated to material growth; public officials were more than willing "to seek the public good through private negotiations."[1] State legislatures chartered hundreds of corporations and lavished them with land grants, lottery franchises, eminent-domain privileges, and tax exemptions.[2] Local governments, too, engaged in the scramble for regional development and readily opened their treasures to railroad corporations and other businesses.[3] By the 1870s, however, various socioeconomic groups began to perceive that their interests were no longer congruent with those of the corporations that government had created and subsidized. In that decade, shippers waged successful struggles to impose stiff regulatory laws on grain warehousemen and railroad companies; local govern-

ments became "convinced that they had not gotten their money's worth" and repudiated their indebtedness; finally, state legislatures resolutely moved to divest corporations of the valuable special grants that preceding policy makers had bargained away.[4] The simultaneous emergence of regulation, repudiation, and revulsion against corporate privileges threatened a multitude of vested interests on an unprecedented scale. Thus, as Justice Stephen J. Field put it in 1890, post-Civil War constitutional controversies "exceed[ed], in the magnitude of the property interests involved, and in the importance of the public questions presented, all cases brought within the same [short] period before any court of Christendom."[5]

The Supreme Court, armed with an enlarged jurisdiction and three new constitutional amendments as a result of the Civil War, had both the power and the opportunity to forge new doctrine and fix new boundaries between the public and private sectors.[6] In the ensuing thirty-year intra-court debate on how to use those powers, and for what purposes, Field was a pivotal figure. He sought to persuade his colleagues to use all the Court's powers, "broadly and liberally interpreted," to

Reprinted from *Journal of American History*, 61 (1975), 970-1005, by permission. Copyright, 1975, Organization of American Historians.

"close the door . . . on the introduction of improper elements to control" the legislative process and to "draw the line between regulation and confiscation."[7] He was remarkably successful. The post-Civil War Court reconsidered the scope of the states' police and eminent-domain powers, restricted the range of policy tools government might employ to subsidize private businesses, and imposed new limitations on government's power to regulate prices. The outcome was a constitutional revolution that set the legal basis of government-business relations upon an entirely new footing.

Field's historical reputation largely stems from his role as "pioneer and prophet" of a substantive interpretation of the Fourteenth Amendment.[8] Since the court often invoked the due-process clause to "stave off adverse regulation," historians have relentlessly marched to the conclusion that Field was a mere handmaiden for "business needs" who believed that "protection of economic privilege was government's one excuse for being."[9] By focusing on regulatory issues alone, however, scholars get a distorted view of Field's government-business jurisprudence. Regulatory agitation emerged at the very time that state and local governments were also repudiating internal-improvement bonds and divesting corporations of tax exemptions, lottery rights, and other special grants. All the ensuing controversies involved judicial consideration of the legitimacy of governmental interventions in economic life, and all resulted in significant doctrinal innovations — not only under the newly adopted Fourteenth Amendment but also under the contract clause and the inchoate "public purpose" maxim. Moreover, the convergence of litigation on these several questions was especially important in that at common law regulatory and promotional legislation were part of a single doctrinal continuum. Private businesses that had been granted special privileges by state and local governments did not hold their property by "common right" and were therefore subject to regulation.[10] As a result, litigation resulting from regulatory statutes involved a reconsideration of governmental interventions on the promotional side, and vice versa. Thus, "if one regarded each case as though it came up spontaneously and in isolation, one would fail to grasp the great underlying problems" that the justices perceived.[11]

What follows in this essay is a reconsideration of the parameters and underlying rationale of Field's jurisprudence on both sides of the promotional-regulatory continuum. The first part focuses on his signal contributions to American property law and reappraises the court's crucial Fourteenth Amendment opinions on government's police and eminent-domain powers. New light is cast upon Field's concerns in the Slaughterhouse Cases — concerns that subsequently spilled over into corporation law generally, and controlled his position in cash subsidy and regulatory controversies. The second part offers a new view of Field's convictions vis-à-vis "economic privilege." Here, postbellum developments in contract clause law are mapped out to delineate Field's role in the formulation of the important but neglected "public trust" doctrine, which ultimately relegated *Fletcher* v. *Peck* to the "status of a judicial relic."[12] In the third part, a line of doctrinal continuity is traced linking Field's landmark dissents in the Granger Cases to earlier court rulings on eminent-domain, municipal-bond, and exclusive-privilege questions. Along this route, one discovers that Field's jurisprudence was neither "cut from the same bolt of cloth" as William G. Sumner's Social Darwinism, nor a product "of the Gilded Age with its Great Barbecue for the Robber Barons and for the rest — 'let the public be damned' "[13] Instead, one finds that Field shaped his government-business jurisprudence to provide "final" solutions to the many-faceted, "great underlying problem" of the 1870s: government's legitimate role in American economic life. The final product was an extraordinarily consistent body of immutable rules designed to sepa-

Charles W. McCurdy

rate the public and private sectors into fixed and inviolable spheres.

The fundamental theorem of Field's government-business jurisprudence was derived from the Jacksonian, radical antislavery precept that under "the declaration of 1776" each individual had a natural right "to pursue the ordinary avocations of life without other restraint than such as effects all others and to enjoy with them the fruits of his labor."[14] The Fourteenth Amendment, he periodically asserted, was "undoubtedly intended" to protect both the title to a person's property and his liberty to dictate its use and "enjoy" its income.[15] This was a novel proposition in American constitutional law, if not in social theory, and it exerted a profound impact on government's role in economic life through the third decade of the twentieth century.[16]

Field conceded that state governments had certain inherent powers that necessarily subjected property rights to a degree of public interference. The states could regulate the use of property in order to protect the safety, health, and morals of the community — in short, to exercise the police power. Government might also take a portion of a person's property by way of taxation for the support of governmental operations or local improvements. Finally, the states could provide public improvements — gas and water works, highways, railroads, and the like — and might employ the power of eminent domain on behalf of those ends. Thus property might be taken for public use upon payment of just compensation. All these powers, however, might be abused by government, and therfore Field subjected each of them to important and essentially coextensive constitutional limitations.

Nineteenth-century eminent-domain law was primarily a state matter, and the Supreme Court of the United States played "only an occasional, and mainly validating, role in support of the state judiciaries' initiatives."[17] The Court did, however, often reiterate that private property could only be expropriated "in execution of works in which the public is interested."[18] Railroads and other public-utility concerns might take property at administered prices because "the public at large" could use the facilities by right, "not as a favor," and government might protect the public's interest in those businesses by enacting appropriate legislation, including "public regulations as to tolls."[19] Purely private firms had to make land purchases in the marketplace, for "the right of eminent domain nowhere justifies taking private property for a private use."[20] Thus Field indicated that takings under the eminent-domain power were "proper matter[s] for judicial cognizance."[21]

The court's dicta pertaining to the "public use" limitations on the eminent-domain power were merely reassertions of doctrine that was well-established in the states.[22] In *Pumpelly* v. *Green Bay and Mississippi Canal Co.*, however, the court reappraised and modified a long line of state court decisions on the just compensation provision.[23] Before the Civil War, "the nagging scarcity of fluid capital" that had initially led to governmental promotion of private corporations also encouraged the state courts to develop legal doctrine that reduced the costs of doing business.[24] Indirect legal subsidies were an especially prominent feature of eminent-domain law. The several state courts so narrowed the definition of a "taking" that railroad and canal companies had to pay compensation only to persons who had been forced to give up title to their property. As a result, landowners whose crops and buildings were flooded or otherwise damaged in the course of transport construction had no legal remedy.[25] The word "take", Pennsylvania's Chief Justice John Bannister Gibson explained in a widely followed opinion, "means taking the property altogether; not a *consequential* injury which is not a taking at all."[26]

In *Pumpelly* the court dealt a decisive blow to the ante-bellum state judiciaries' "general disposition not to cramp these [growth-inducing] enterprises by a too sweeping or extreme compensation."[27] In that case, a canal company had raised the height of its dam on a Wisconsin lake, which had the unintended effect of flooding the farm of an adjoining landowner. Speaking for a unanimous court, Justice Samuel F. Miller held that:

It would be a very curious and unsatisfactory result, if in construing a provision of constitutional law, always understood to have been adopted for protection and security to the rights of the individual as against the government [just compensation clauses] . . .it shall be held that if the government refrains from the absolute conversion of real property to the use of the public it can destroy its value entirely, can inflict irreparable and permanent injury to any extent, can, in effect, subject it to total destruction without making any compensation, because, in the narrowest sense of the word, it is not *taken* for the public use. Such a construction would . . . make it authority for invasion of private right under the pretext of the public good, which had no warrant in the laws or practices of our ancestors.[28]

Indeed, in Field's view, the property right entailed the right to use and enjoyment as well as formal title, and therefore the plaintiff's right to compensation was unquestionable. But Field was prepared to go further and, in slightly modified form, extend the narrow "public use" and broad "taking" docrines of eminent-domain law to the police power as well.

The celebrated Slaughterhouse Cases came up from Louisiana at a time when northern "adventurers" and old-line southern Whigs had "become convinced that the same industry and commerce which had transformed the North would revolutionize the South."[29] During the late 1860s virtually all the southern states embarked on massive programs of public aid to railroads, and, simultaneously, major marketing centers made desperate attempts to recapture commercial hegemony in "natural" hinterland zones.[30] The New Orleans slaughterhouse monopoly was part of that city's "organic plan" to secure control of the Texas cattle trade.[31] In order to take full advantage of its locational superiority, city boosters advocated both railroad expansion and the construction of efficient slaughtering facilities that could withstand the competitive pressures imposed by packers in St. Louis and Chicago. New Orleans commercial interests ultimately succeeded in procuring the exclusive grant, as the Louisiana Supreme Court later observed, by "corrupting and improperly influencing members of the state legislature."[32] But the statute conferring the monopoly also threw hundreds of meatcutters out of work. The unemployed butchers claimed that the state legislature had divested them of valuable constitutional rights, while counsel for Louisiana defended the measure as a police regulation designed to protect the public health. In 1873 the ensuing litigation evoked the court's first construction of the Fourteenth Amendment.

Field's associates probably concurred with his assertion that the alleged public-health rationale of the enactment was a "shallow . . . pretence" for an "odious monopoly."[33] Nevertheless, a narrow majority upheld the statute on the ground that the Fourteenth Amendment had not been designed to make the court "a perpetual censor upon all the legislation of the states."[34] Field dissented. He conceded that slaughterhouses had long been considered prima facie nuisances, and he insisted that state legislatures might altogether prohibit butchers from plying their noxious trade in densely populated cities.[35] But in his view, the state's duty to protect the people from unhealthful businesses could not "possibly justify" legislation framed "for the benefit of a single corporation."[36] Field was particularly concerned with the implications of Thomas Durant's brief for the state of Louisiana, in which it was argued that a state legislature might make any business "the exclusive privilege of a few . . . if the sovereign judges that the interests of society will be better promoted."[37] Field flatly stated that Durant's position had no support in the common law. The only business firms which might be granted exclusive privileges, he asserted, were those that held "franchise of a public character appertaining to government."[38] The classic examples were hackmen, wharfingers, bridge proprietors, and ferry operators. Those businessmen could not engage in their calling by common right because they required special easements in the public streets or public rivers and, as quid pro quo for the government's grant of privilege, public officials might prescribe "the conditions under which it [the franchise] is enjoyed."[39] Railroad and other public-utility corporations had assumed similar liabilities to the public by dint of exercising eminent-domain powers.[40] The meat-cutting business, however, was a purely private, "ordinary trade." As a result, Field contended, it had to be open to all persons "without other restraint than such as effects all others."[41] Thus, in his view, the Louisiana statute "present[ed] the naked case, unaccompanied by any public consideration, where a right to pursue a lawful and necessary calling, previously enjoyed by every citizen . . . is taken away" in contraventon of the Fourteenth Amendment.[42]

Field's vigorous defense of the butcher's right to pursue his calling unfettered by state-sanctioned monopolies, if not by "legitimate" police regulations, cannot be considered idiosyncratic. Field's colleagues, although not prepared to "proclaim the faith that was in him both in season and out . . . shared [it] none the less."[43] Indeed, the North had just finished fighting a war that, in Abraham Lincoln's words, was a "people's contest . . . for maintaining in the world that *form and substance* of government whose leading object is to elevate the condition of man; to lift artificial weights from all shoulders; to clear the paths of laudable pursuit for all; to afford all men an unfettered start and a fair chance in the race of life."[44] Thus Field was not being presumptuous when he claimed that the individual's right to pursue one of the "ordinary trades" was "in many respects . . . a distinguishing feature of our republican institutions."[45] In his view, the Fourteenth Amendment would become a "vain and idle enactment, which accomplished nothing" if the court continued to permit the state legislatures to "farm out the ordinary avocations of life."[46] And while Field stubbornly maintained his position, he kept his colleagues aware that, on the whole, they shared the same values and convictions. The strategy of dissent and persistence, aided by changes in the court's composition, ultimately succeeded. In 1886 the major components of Field's Slaughterhouse Cases dissent received the approbation of the court.[47]

Even as Field persuaded his associates to adopt a substantive interpretation of the Fourteenth Amendment, he became alarmed at the bar's "apparent misconception" of his views.[48] In the zeal of dissent Field had indeed maintained several implausible positions, had cited such dubious authorities as Adam Smith's *Wealth of Nations*, and had given the impression that he was an advocate of unrestrained individualism. But after 1874, Field tried to make it clear that he recognized the states' police power "in its fullest extent," and he was in fact prepared to accord state governments considerable policy discretion.[49] He upheld statutes that prohibited certain businesses altogether as detrimental to the public welfare, recognized government's right to prescribe standards of fitness for lawyers and doctors, and sustained legislation that required railroad corporations to erect cattle guards and eliminate grade crossings at their own expense.[50] Moreover, Field acknowledged the several states' authority to improve the condition of "the poor and dependent" classes of society, including " the laborers in our factories and workshops"; hence he readily affirmed laws that prescribed maximum working hours or compelled employers in hazardous businesses to compensate workers who were injured on the job.[51] The court would invalidate police regulations, he asserted in *Soon Hing v. Crowley*, only "when persons engaged in the same business are subjected to different restrictions."[52] So-called special legislation was not unconstitutional merely "because like restrictions are not imposed upon other businesses of a different kind."[53] Field, then, provided government with ample room to give "the under fellow a show in this life."[54] Eight years after he retired, however, the court invalidated a maximum-hour law for New York bakery workers.[55] But in the process the majority had to disregard the rule Field had handed down in *Soon Hing*, which "was precedent, in order to draw support from his [Slaughterhouse Cases] dicta . . . which was not precedent."[56] Indeed, if Field's landmark dissents ultimately became the "fountainhead" of the dubious "liberty of contract" doctrine, it was because "another generation" of jurists, with entirely different concerns, wrenched Field's principles out of their original context.[57]

Field also held that although health and safety measures invariably "lessen[ed] the value of the property affected," government was not required to compensate property owners who had sustained pecuniary losses.[58] Takings under the eminent-domain power were compensable, even if government "refrain[ed] from the absolute conversion of real property to the use of the public," because the individual's property was necessary either for the public work itself or, as in *Pumpelly*, as an easement for "water, earth, sand or other materials."[59] But the police power stood on a different footing. Police regulations impaired property rights because, as Justice Joseph P. Bradley put it, "the property itself is the cause of the public detriment."[60] In Field's view, this was a vital distinction. Effective takings under the police power were justifiable, he declared in *Barbier v. Connolly*, because "special burdens are often necessary for general benefits."[61] So long as the public did not make positive use of private property, the courts would "presume he [who thereby suffered] is compensated by sharing in the advantages arising from such beneficial regulation."[62]

Field did make it clear, however, that government's police regulations had to provide "general benefits." Under "the pretense of prescribing a police regulation," government could not create monopolies in the "ordinary trades;" solve unemployment problems by forbidding Chinese laborers to work for railroad companies; or provide dairy interests with a protective umbrella by proscribing the manufacture and sale of oleomargarine.[63] Field contended that those laws, "as disclosed on the face of the act, or inferable from their operation," manifestly "discriminated against some [persons] and favored others."[64] Since men had property rights in their occupations, statutes of that variety effectively took the property of one class of persons and vested it in another, private group.[65] In other words, Field imposed limitations on the police power, not to protect individuals from enactments designed to "promote . . . the general good," but rather to prevent powerful socioeconomic interests, through the use of corruption or the force of sheer numbers, from utilizing the legislative process as a weapon to improve their own position at the expense of other individuals' "just rights."[66] In his view, this was a proper judicial function. As in eminent-domain law, only the courts could determine whether public policy actually "car[ied] out a public purpose."[67]

Field's crusade to fix a precise boundary between private rights and legitimate governmental interventions also entailed a reconsideration of "public purpose" doctrine in taxation law. By the 1870s, this was a particularly muddled area of American jurisprudence. The legal controversy stemmed from the public's clamor for internal improvements, especially rail connections, which after 1840 had resulted in state laws authorizing local governments to commit themselves to stock purchases and outright gifts to privately owned businesses. In the East and Midwest, ante-bellum local politicians had been mesmerized by booster-ism. Between 1840 and 1880 the nation's aggregate local indebtedness leaped from $25 million to $840 million, much of which flowed into the coffers of private corporations.[68] During the 1860s and 1870s, however, local officials from New York to Iowa recognized that they had overestimated both their power to influ-ence rate structures and their ability to service enormous public debts. Thus a wave of repudiation, and bondholder suits to enforce the contractual obliga-tions of local governments, coincided with the emergence of regulatory agitation.[69]

The cycle of promotion, repudiation, and regulation frightened investors and profoundly disturbed the conservative community.[70] What must have been most unsettling to Field was the fact that in much of the South and trans-Mississippi West the same process was still in its formative stages. Moreover, as one scholar has observed, "the Western prov-inces" were even more "creative in devising techniques to abet their own self-exploitation" than their eastern brethren had been.[71] In Kansas, for exam-ple, local governments not only granted subsidies to railroad companies but also by 1874 had appropriated over two mil-lion dollars to aid such "ordinary trades" as hotel and manufacturing establish-ments.[72] The politics of economic policy were particularly chaotic in Wisconsin. During the 1870s, communities in the southeastern portion of the state had both repudiated their indebtedness and forced a regulatory law through the state legisla-ture. At the same time, representatives from the undeveloped northern counties not only opposed regulation but also suc-ceeded in enacting a statute authorizing local aid to railroads, dry-dock compa-nies, manufacturing firms, and steamship companies.[73] For Field, these were omi-nous developments. He was well aware that private firms that had feasted upon government's largess were, by the same token, subject to regulation. Thus judicial validation of public-sector cash grants to

the "ordinary trades" would bring manu-facturing, hotel, and dry-dock companies into the same vortex of hostile govern-mental regulation that was simultan-eously threatening railroad corporations. Field, however, believed that persons engaged in the "ordinary trades" had a natural right, consistent only with the health and safety of others, to dictate the use and "enjoy" the income of their property unfettered by governmental interference. As a result, he concluded that it was up to the judiciary to establish an inviolable boundary — equally applic-able for eminent-domain, exclusive privi-lege, subsidy, and regulatory purposes — that would distinguish purely private businesses from those that executed works in which the public had an inter-est.

The state courts, however, only con-tributed additional uncertainty to the existing, unstable state of affairs. In over twenty jurisdictions, the state judiciaries required defaulting communities to adhere to contractual obligations incurred on behalf of railroad develop-ment.[74] Jurists in Michigan and Wiscon-sin, however, refused to provide remedies for bondholders. Judge Thomas M. Cooley, the influential author of *Con-stitutional Limitations* (1868), was the leading advocate of the latter position. Speaking for the Michigan court in an 1870 bondholder suit, Cooley held that a railroad was "exclusively private prop-erty, owned, controlled, and operated by a private corporation for the benefit of its own members"; as such, it was "not dis-tinguishable from any other" variety of private enterprise and therefore was not a legitimate recipient of public subsidies.[75] The Wisconsin court reached the same conclusion only months afterward.[76] At the very time that midwestern legisla-tures were enacting statutes to protect the public's interest in rate matters, then, influential jurists were ruling that railroads were "exclusively private" for tax purposes. The state courts' response to the convergence of regulatory and pro-motional issues, Charles Francis Adams,

Jr., lamented in 1870, "furnishes a very curious illustration of the extreme difficulty which . . . now attends any attempt to definitely fix legal principles."[77] Field concurred.

Since diversity of citizenship could usually be established, some three-hundred municipal-bond cases came up during Field's tenure on the court. Two of the more important cases were *Olcott v. Supervisors of Fond Du Lac County* (1873) and *Pine Grove Township v. Talcott* (1874), which came up from Wisconsin and Michigan, respectively, in the years immediately following state court rulings that public aid to railroads was unconstitutional. In each case, the court refused to affirm the state's "public-purpose" doctrine. The court would follow state decisions on "local questions peculiar to themselves," Justice Samuel Nelson asserted in *Pine Grove Township*, but "here, commercial securities are involved" and therefore the issues "belong to the domain of general jurisprudence."[78] The court held that the public's interest in railroad expansion was undeniable: "Where they go they animate the sources of prosperity, and minister to the growth of the cities and towns within the sphere of their influence."[79] Moreover, Justice William Strong contended in *Olcott*, railroads were "public highways" even when constructed and owned by private persons. Their "uses are so far public that the right of eminent domain . . . may be exerted to facilitate . . . construction" and that had "been the doctrine of all the courts ever since such conveniences for passage and transportation had any existence."[80] The conclusion was inexorable, Strong declared, that public funds might be given as subsidies and "tolls and rates for transportation might [also] be limited" by public officials.[81]

The court's municipal-bond decisions exerted a salutary effect on American money markets by restoring confidence in an important class of commercial paper.[82] But the bench divided on the legitimacy of the court's heavy-handed use of "general jurisprudence" principles to protect bondholders. Three factions within the court can be identified. Chief Justice Salmon P. Chase and Justices Miller and David Davis generally dissented on the ground that the court lacked authority to overrule state court decisions when bona fide federal questions had not been raised.[83] Justices Nelson, Nathan Clifford, Noah H. Swayne, Bradley, and Strong (later joined by Morrison R. Waite, Ward Hunt, and Harlan) stubbornly resisted every form of railroad-subsidy repudiation. Those men were, Miller commented, "if not monomaniacs, as much bigots and fanatics on that subject as is the most unhesitating Mahemodan in regard to his religion. In four cases out of five the case is decided when it is seen by the pleadings that it is a suit to enforce a contract against a city, or town, or a county. If there is a written instrument its validity is a foregone conclusion".[84] In the majority's view, continued economic growth necessitated vigorous judicial protection of bondholders. "Within the last few years," Nelson wrote in *White v. Vermont & Massachusetts R. R. Co.*, "large masses of . . . [municipal bonds] have gone into general circulation and in which capitalists have invested their money." If the court then denied their negotiability, the instrumental value of such securities "as a means of furnishing the funds for the accomplishment of many of the greatest and most useful enterprises of the day would be impaired."[85]

Field's views were unique. Before the convergence of promotional and regulatory issues during the early 1870s, he was not certain that local promotion of railroad expansion was legitimately "within the objects to be accomplished" by municipalities.[86] Moreover, he was deeply troubled by the corruption and opportunism that pervaded the local-aid process; when entrepreneurs and local politicians conspired to thrust massive tax burdens on unsuspecting citizens, he consistently voted against the rights of bond holders. Thus he often joined the dissenters.[87] *Olcott* and *Pine Grove Township* came up, however, at a decisive moment in the development of Field's jurisprudence of government-business relations and dictated a reevaluation of his position vis-à-vis municipal repudiation of internal improvement bonds. By then the Slaughterhouse Cases had been argued, and he was well into the process of formulating his notion of "public use" or "public purpose" with respect to the extent of the states, police and eminent-domain powers. Railroad corporations had been granted eminent-domain privileges; hence they were clearly not "ordinary trades." As a result, Field joined the majority in both *Olcott* and *Pine Grove Township*. In his view, the need to formulate universal rules determining the legitimate range of public interventions in economic life took precedence over the immediate consequences his position involved, even if it entailed the exploitation of local governments by railroad corporations or irreparable damages to bondholders. For Field, once the character of the use had been fixed, it was immutable and applied to all governmental interventions. At stake in the subsidy controversies, then, was not only government's promotional discretion but also the legitimate scope of the public sector's regulatory powers.

Under Field's "public use" doctrine, it was axiomatic that local governments had no authority to grant cash subsidies to businessmen engaged in the "ordinary trades." The Court considered one such instance in the leading 1874 case of *Loan Association* v. *Topeka*.[88] Through a vigorous promotional campaign involving a hundred-thousand-dollar subsidy, the citizens of Topeka had lured the nation's largest manufacturer of wrought-iron bridges to their city. Subsequently the city repudiated its indebtedness, and with only Clifford dissenting, the Court ruled that the bondholders' contract with Topeka was not enforceable. Speaking for the majority, Miller held that the general public had not received a consideration — the right to use the facilities on terms

set by government — for the city's grant, and the people's tax monies could not "be used for purposes of private interest instead of public use."[89] "To lay with one hand the power of government on the property of the citizen, and with the other to bestow it upon favored individuals to . . . build up private fortunes," he asserted, "is none the less robbery because it is done under the forms of law and is called taxation."[90]

Field was undoubtedly pleased that Miller had invoked concepts and employed language that closely conformed to his Slaughterhouse Cases dissent. Nevertheless, he recognized that a gap remained between their respective positions. For Miller, who had written the majority opinion in the Slaughterhouse Cases and had filed virulent dissents in the leading railroad subsidy cases, the decisive aspect of *Loan Association* was that it had come up from a federal court on a subject for which pertinent state law had not been formulated. Thus he spurned the due-process clause altogether and held that the Topeka "robbery" violated "principles of general constitutional law."[91] More importantly, Miller declared that "it may not be easy to draw the line in all cases so as to decide what is a public use in this sense and what is not."[92] By declining to hand down a firm rule specifying the exact boundaries of the "public use" doctrine, the court retained discretion to include or exclude particular fact situations as new controversies arose. But that was precisely what Field feared. And four years later he stood in lone dissent when the court upheld payment of subsidies to mill owners. The majority, speaking through Hunt, believed that "it would require great nicety of reasoning" to define a public use such that it included "a gristmill run by water, and exclude [d] one operated by steam; or . . . [showed] that the means of transportation were more valuable to the people of Kansas than the means of obtaining bread."[93] Field did not write a dissenting opinion, but he was almost certainly prepared to make the "nice" distinction the majority had dismissed. Owners of gristmills driven by waterwheels held "franchises of a public character" in that they had flooded adjoining land under the several states' mill acts. Steam-powered mills were "ordinary trades" and, in Field's view, could neither be subjected to governmental control nor be recipients of public subsidies. He believed that doctrine separating the public and private sectors had to be immutable if it was to be effective. As a result, Field refused to condone any deviation from his syllogistic version of the "public use" concept, even when he was required to stand alone in order to maintain a consistent position.

Field's exposition of the constitutional limitations on the exercise of the states' inherent powers — police, taxation, and eminent domain — was uncommonly systematic. Indeed, Field would have reduced the legitimate bounds within which the police and taxation powers might be exercised to embody the eminent-domain constraint of "public use." By applying the body of rules that logically flowed from the "public use" doctrine, Field assumed he could mechanically maintain a viable separation of public-sector and private-sector activities. This is the stuff of laissez faire. But Field's principles carried him still further. If individuals had natural rights which required constitutional protection from the vagaries of government, so too did the states have certain social duties which, according to Field, correct constitutional doctrine recognized as inalienable, inherent powers.

Before the Civil War, judicial concern with the reconciliation of private rights and governmental powers largely focused on the protection of rights vested in private corporations by state legislatures. Therefore, Article I, section 10 of the Constitution, which provides that "no state shall pass any law impairing the obligation of contracts," was by far the signal constitutional limitation on

legislative abuse of private rights. Beginning with the leading case of *Fletcher* v. *Peck*, the Marshall Court held that once government had granted land, perpetual tax exemptions, or corporate charters to private groups, the state could not thereafter take away those privileges.[94] Most importantly, John Marshall indicated that it was not "within the province of the judiciary" to take notice of corruption or examine the mischievous effects of legislative grants in determining their validity.[95] "We have no knowledge of any authority or principle," Justice Joseph Story announced in *Terrett* v. *Taylor*, "which would support the doctrine that a legislative grant is revocable in its own nature."[96]

The Marshall Court's construction of the contract clause became a crucial "link between capitalism and constitutionalism" during the formative years of nineteenth-century economic development.[97] Nevertheless, Marshall's views were subjected to significant modifications in the ante-bellum era. First, in *Dartmouth College*, Story suggested in a concurring opinion that the states might insert special clauses in corporate charters reserving to themselves the powers of amendment and repeal. Most states quickly availed themselves of this practice, and by mid-century it was an accepted feature of American corporation law.[98] Then two decades later in *Charles River Bridge* v. *Warren Bridge*, Chief Justice Roger B. Taney held that the court would thereafter strictly construe corporate charters.[99] In practical application, this doctrine meant that corporate privileges and immunities not expressly granted by the legislature were retained by the state.

Taney's approach to the contract clause reflected his concern for the course of American economic development. He feared that if the court chose to presume that legislative grants embodied exclusive privileges, it might discourage investment in new and competing forms of enterprise.[100] But there were other judicial concerns that made strict con-

Charles W. McCurdy

struction of corporate charters particularly appropriate at a time when legislatures served as "annexes to the marketplace."[101] Speaking for the court in *Ohio Life Insurance & Trust Co. v. Debolt*, Taney declared:

> For it is a matter of public history, which this Court cannot refuse to notice, that almost every bill for the incorporation . . . is drawn originally by the parties who are personally interested in obtaining the charter; and that they are often passed by the legislature in the last days of its session, when, from the nature of our political institutions, the business is unavoidably transacted in a hurried manner, and it is impossible that every member can deliberately examine every provision in every bill upon which he is called on to act.
>
> On the other hand, those who accept the charter have abundant time to examine and consider its provisions, before they invest their money.[102]

Field agreed. He occasionally referred to the economic rationale of the strict-construction rule, but he believed that the doctrine primarily served "to defeat any purpose concealed by the skillful use of terms, to accomplish something not apparent on the face of the act, and thus [it] sanctions only open dealing with legislative bodies."[103] Field, however, was prepared to extend Taney's position further and restrict the application of *Fletcher* v. *Peck*. He believed that "open dealing" alone had failed to arrest the baneful effects of the private quest for special privileges. Adept lobbyists still might persuade policymakers to waive future powers of amendment and, as Justice John A. Campbell put it, the Court's construction of the contract clause made the judiciary "the patron of such legislation, by furnishing motives of incalculable power to the corporation to stimulate it, and security to the successful effort."[104] Field contended that, since the Court had, in fact, taken notice of the turbulent resource-allocation process, there was no reason why it should not also scrutinize the substance of special legislative grants. In his view, corporations were not created to extort special privileges from the states, nor were governments instituted to dispense their several attributes of sovereignty to the highest bidder. Thus he concluded that the Court's proper function was to "close the door . . . on the introduction of improper elements to control" the legislative process and ensure that unwarranted grants, made against implicit public policy, were not enforced.[105]

Field had some support in precedent for his antagonism to sweeping grants of special immunities. In the leading case of *West River Bridge* v. *Dix*, the Court held that the property of a corporation, including its very franchise, might be taken for public use under the power of eminent domain, even if that corporation had earlier exercised that power. The sovereign power of eminent domain was inalienable. Into all contracts, Justice Peter V. Daniel asserted for the majority, "there enter conditions which arise not out of the literal terms of the contract itself; they are superinduced by the preëxisting and higher authority of the law of nature, of nations, or of the community to which the parties belong."[106] Field was prepared to apply this principle to all the states' essential powers. If the states could not divest themselves forever of their power of eminent domain, he contended, their powers of taxation and police and their ownership and control of the navigable waters within their respective political jurisdictions were to no less a degree inalienable.[107]

Tax immunity controversies swelled the Court's docket during the 1870s. Throughout the antebellum period, state legislatures had granted growth-inducing private interests special tax concessions as a stimulus to development. Policy measures of that variety were particularly popular among politicians because no direct allocation of public funds was necessary.[108] Nevertheless, the suspicion persisted, doubtless with some justification, that the source of tax-immunity grants lay in "careless or corrupt legislature[s]" rather than enlightened public policy.[109] As a result, when developmental goals had been fulfilled and middle-class groups began to complain about high taxes, public officials invariably waged concerted campaigns against corruption and corporate privilege and attempted to reassert the power earlier legislatures had bargained away.[110] The summary repeal of special tax immunities was particularly threatening to the fifty-five railroad companies that by 1870 had secured tax exemptions worth some thirteen million dollars from at least nineteen states.[111] The result was a flood of litigation in which corporations confidently argued that their position was impregnable: in *New Jersey* v. *Wilson*, the Marshall Court had already brought tax immunities within the protective umbrella of the contract clause.[112]

Few of Field's colleagues shared his belief that Wilson was not good law. In their view, any ruling by the Court that tended to undermine a leading case or impair the sanctity of contracts would give an unnecessary shock to the economic system.[113] Thus in *Home of the Friendless* v. *Rousse*, with only Field, Miller, and Chase dissenting, the court vigorously affirmed Marshall's tax-exemption decision. The dissenters, speaking through Miller, filed an uncompromising critique of doctrine that sustained government's right to bargain away its essential powers. The power to tax, Miller declared,

> is a power which, in modern political societies, is absolutely necessary to the continued existence of every such society . . . To hold, then, that any one of the annual legislatures can, by contract, deprive the State forever of the power of taxation, is to hold that they can destroy the government which they are appointed to serve . . .

The result of such a principle, under the growing tendency to special and partial legislation, would be, to exempt the rich from taxation, and cast all the burdens of the support of government, and the payment of its debts, on those who are too poor or too honest to purchase such immunity.[114]

Indeed, Field believed, as he later indicated in the Income Tax Case, that partial and unequal tax laws effectively transferred property from one socioeconomic group to another in contravention of the fundamental precept that property could not be taken for private use.[115]

Despite the setback in *Rousse*, Field ultimately succeeded in modifying the relative position of corporations and the public sector in tax-immunity controversies. Speaking for the court in two leading cases handed down in the 1870s, Field held that once business corporations changed hands on sale of execution or were consolidated such that the original concerns had forfeited their status as distinct corporations, all franchises and privileges not "essential to the operation of the corporation," including tax immunities, might be revoked by state legislatures.[116] Moreover, the *Rousse* dissenters' unrestrained advocacy of government's inherent power to tax mobilized substantial support both in the legal profession and on the state benches. In virtually every state, jurists refused to uphold the validity of tax immunities.[117] Thus private interests were required either to expend large sums of money on appeal or bargain with state authorities who were often prepared to offer alternative, though less valuable, concessions as *quid pro quo* for giving up perpetual exemptions.[118] State pressures, combined with the Court's propensity to invoke all doctrinal weapons short of reversing *Wilson*, effectively destroyed vested rights in special tax concessions. By 1890 the question was of little importance as a practical matter or a legal issue.

Field met less resistance in establishing the inalienability of the police power. The tyranny of established constitutional doctrine was not a factor, as in the tax exemption cases, and "vested rights in liquor, lottery tickets, gambling, and sex never appealed much to nineteenth century judges."[119] The leading cases came up from the South during Reconstruction, when policymakers had employed the age-old technique of stimulating capital formation by grants of lottery privileges.[120] The giant southern lottery corporations, particularly the infamous Louisiana State Lottery Company, were notoriously corrupt and often "exercised a power greater than that of the State government itself."[121] As "redeemer" governments acquired power, they generally revoked the charters of those concerns, thereby precipitating litigation.

In *Boyd* v. *Alabama*, an agent for a state-chartered mutual-aid association had been convicted of selling lottery tickets in violation of the state's antilottery law. The 1868 charter of the company, however, not only explicitly granted it the right to carry on a lottery, but the state had also failed to include any provision for amending the twenty-year grant of privilege. Thus Boyd claimed that the statute was void insofar as it applied to his activities, because it impaired the state's obligation of contract. The court actually resolved the issue by referring to the antilogrolling provision in the Alabama constitution. The act of incorporation and the grant of lottery privileges were embraced in the same statute, violating the prohibition of laws involving more than one subject. Nevertheless, in his opinion for the court, Field explained that he was "not prepared to admit that it is competent for one legislature, by any contract with an individual to restrain the power of a subsequent legislature to legislate for the public welfare, and to that end to suppress [by the exercise of the police power] any and all practices tending to corrupt the public morals."[122]

In *Stone* v. *Mississippi*, the court refused to provide contract-clause protection for a lottery corporation on the inalienability doctrine alone.[123] The inalienability of the police power, Field reiterated in 1884, "is a principle of vital importance," because "its habitual observance" by the state "is essential to wise and valid execution of the trust committed to the legislature."[124]

Field's development of the "public trust" doctrine and the simultaneous erosion of *Fletcher* v. *Peck* reached their apogee in the leading 1892 case of *Illinois Central R. R. Co.* v. *Illinois*.[125] In 1869 the state of Illinois conveyed to the railroad corporation, as part of a larger grant, title to the submerged lands along the entire Chicago waterfront. When the state sought to repossess the property, Illinois Central balked, and its attorneys attempted to restrain state action by invoking the contract clause. Field, speaking for a narrow majority, held that the contract authorizing the original grant could not be enforced. The state had no right, he declared, to grant away in perpetuity lands covered by the navigable waters of the sovereign. Navigable lakes and rivers were "public highways" which the state held in trust for the use of all shippers and carriers.[126] Thus the state could make grants of them only for purposes of constructing wharves, docks, and other aids to commerce, and then only to the extent that they did "not substantially impair the public interest in the water remaining."[127] The principle permitting limited grants for public benefit, Field concluded,

is a very different doctrine from the one which would sanction the abdication of the general control of the state over the navigable waters of an entire harbor or bay, or of a sea or lake. Such abdication is not consistent with the exercise of that trust which requires the government of the state to preserve such waters for the use of the public. The trust devolving upon the state for the public, and which can only be discharged by the management and control of property in which the public has an interest, cannot be relinquished by a transfer of property.[128]

It was preposterous, Field contended, that "a corporation created for . . . [railroad] purpose[s]" could be "converted into a corporation to manage and practically control the harbor of the City of Chicago, not simply for its own purpose as a railroad corporation, but for its own profit generally."[129] To allow such a grant was to concede that the public and private sectors had common interests. But, as his several references to "management," "purpose," and "profit" indicated, Field believed that public and private institutions had diametrically opposed reasons for existence; legislation that vested public property in private corporations would invariably lead to situations in which the people would be subject to private greed, Thus, in his view, the court had to "meet the very suggestion of evil, and strike down the contract from its inception."[130]

The fact that Field was willing summarily to divest a major American corporation of exceedingly valuable property should be viewed as more than a legal curiosity. In his version of the American system, there was room for neither corruption and special privilege nor a self-denying spirit of largess on the part of government, and his "radical" opinions on the "public trust" doctrine were an integral part of his larger vision of government-business relations under the Constitution.[131] On the one hand, he enjoined the several state legislatures to refrain from exercising their "trinity of powers" — police, taxation, and eminent domain — so as arbitrarily to transfer property rights from one socioeconomic group to another. On the other hand, Field reprimanded legislatures that would contract away the right to exercise those very powers and, except in the case of tax-immunity grants, succeeded in persuading his associates that the states' inherent powers were "held in trust" for the public and therefore inalienable. What he attempted to take from government with one hand he sought to restore with the other; the doctrine Field handed down in *Illinois Central R. R. Co. v. Illinois* demonstrates in disarming proportions the degree to which he was committed to upholding powers which, in his view, fell on the public side of the line. By enlarging judicial cognizance of the consequences of ill-considered public policy and exercising all its powers,

"broadly and liberally interpreted," Field believed the court could proscribe virtually every form of special privilege. The result would be a harmonious system in which the public and private sectors pursued appropriate goals within proper spheres of action. But an all-encompassing separation of the public and private sectors was impossible. Certain businesses, though private in ownership, were public in "use." Thus much of Field's judicial energy was expended in formulating rules fixing the areas in which the public might lawfully intervene in the affairs of private businesses and the extent to which any such interference would be a violation of property rights.

The concept of businesses "affected with a public interest," a major constitutional doctrine for over half a century, was born in the 1877 case of *Munn v. Illinois*.[132] Deriving its doctrinal reasoning from the seventeenth-century treatises of Lord Hale, the court held, as Justice Bradley explained a year later in the Sinking Fund Cases, that "when an employment or business becomes a matter of such public interest and importance as to create a common charge or burden upon the citizens; in other words, when it becomes a practical monopoly, to which the citizen is compelled to resort, and by means of which a tribute can be exacted from the community, it is subject to regulation by the legislative power."[133] Grain warehousemen, Chief Justice Waite wrote for the majority, "stand . . . in the very 'gateway of commerce' and take toll from all who pass": and therefore "exercise a sort of public office" comparable to that enjoyed by wharfingers, ferry operators, hackney coachmen, and railroad corporations.[134]

Field dissented. In his view, the affectation doctrine, as employed by the majority, was a contorted misapplication of Hale's precepts. According to Field, when Hale had suggested that property might cease to be *juris privati*, that is when it ceased to be held by private right, he referred to "property the use of which was granted by the government, or in connection with which special privileges were conferred."[135] But the firm of Munn and Scott was a partnership. It held no corporate charter, and it had been granted no special privileges. The firm's property, then, had never ceased to be *juris privati*, and there was no legitimate rationale for regulation.

Field's position in *Munn* did not stem, however, from a careful reading of Lord Hale. Instead, his construction of "practical monopoly" and "affected with a public interest" had been carefully worked out four years earlier in the Slaughterhouse Cases. "It is also sought to justify the act in question," Field had asserted in that case,

on the same principle that exclusive grants for ferries, bridges and turnpikes are sanctioned. But it can find no support there. Those grants are of franchises of a public character appertaining to the government. Their use usually requires the exercise of the sovereign right of eminent domain. It is for the government to determine when one of them shall be granted, and the conditions under which it shall be enjoyed ... The grant, with exclusive privileges, of a right thus appertaining to the government, is a very different thing from a grant ... of a right to pursue one of the ordinary trades or callings of life, which is a right appertaining solely to the individual.[136]

In order to fulfill a public purpose, then, special privileges, including exclusive monopolies or cash subsidies, might be conferred on corporations that necessarily employed powers "appertaining to government." Moreover, the governmental character of those businesses subjected them to legislative control of "the conditions upon which" the franchises might "be enjoyed." "The recipient of the privilege," Field explained in *Munn*, "stipulates to comply with the conditions" set by government, and "it is the public privilege conferred with the use of

the property which creates the public interest in it."[137] But the public had no interest whatsoever in slaughterhouses and grain elevators. There could be no legal monopoly because such firms could not lawfully exercise governmental powers or privileges, and there could be no "practical monopoly," and hence no rationale for regulation, because no special privileges were held and therefore anyone might take up the calling. Munn and Scott had been engaged in the "ordinary trades" only. In that instance, reasonable prices might be determined only by normal market mechanisms.

"The great difficulty in the future," Chief Justice Waite commented shortly after *Munn* was handed down, "will be to establish the boundary between what is private, and that in which the public has an interest. The elevators furnished an extreme case and there was little difficulty in determining on which side of the line they properly belonged."[138] Indeed, the Chicago warehousemen not only stood "in the very gateway of commerce," but also had collusive lease agreements for the use of railroad rights of way; hence they were, in fact, "practical monopol[ists].[139] But in *Munn*, as in *Illinois Central R.R. Co. v. Illinois*, Field was concerned with high policy rather then with the outcome of one particular controversy, and the "great difficulty" to which Waite referred molded his dissenting opinion. In his view, there was simply no way for the court to uphold the grain-elevator statute without opening the door for any combination of interest groups, through the "magic ... [of] language," to change an unpopular "private business into a public one" and leave its owner "at the mercy of a majority of the legislature."[140] "There is hardly an enterprise or business engaging the attention and labor of any considerable portion of the community," he remarked, "in which the public has not an interest in the sense in which that term is used by the court."[141] Yet Field believed that the exigencies of the turbulent 1870s required the judiciary resolutely to perform its "main purpose, namely, that of setting metes and bounds to legislative power."[142] The Granger Laws and public vacillation — first subsidizing private enterprises, then repudiating the bonded indebtedness incurred — had thoroughly disrupted the nation's economy.[143] Moreover, regulatory agitation and the ensuing clash of regional and functional interest groups had increased at the very time that governments in the trans-Mississippi West and in the South had increased their promotion — through cash subsidies and exclusive grants — of otherwise "ordinary trades." In the Slaughterhouse Cases, *Loan Association v. Topeka*, and *Munn*, however, the court had failed to make a firm distinction between private businesses and those in which the public had an interest. The court's decisions, Field indicated, would encourage further ill-advised interventions in economic life, perpetuate the inordinate instability that had characterized the early 1870s, and necessitate continuous debate as to which businessmen engaged in purely private concerns and which "exercise[d] a sort of public office." The mechanical public-use doctrine, however, had been designed to restore stability by resolving for all time the era's pressing policy questions on both sides of the promotional-regulatory continuum. Through the end of his long career, Field continued to believe that the majority had committed a grave error and, as Justice Harlan noted, he periodically turned "his face towards the setting sun, wondering . . . whether the *Munn* case or the eternal principles of right and justice, [would] ultimately prevail."[144]

The court's decisions in the Granger Railroad Cases flowed logically from the principles articulated in *Munn*.[145] Railroad corporations were "affected with a public interest" and therefore might be regulated at the discretion of the legislature. "The controlling fact," Waite wrote for the majority, "is the power to regulate at all. If that exists, the right to establish the maximum of charge . . . is implied." And he added,

"We know that it is a power which may be abused; but that is no argument against its existence. For protection against abuses by legislatures the people must resort to the polls, not to the courts."[146] Justice Bradley had anticipated and described the rationale behind this dictum two years earlier in *Baltimore & Ohio R.R. Co. v. Maryland*. The states' power to fix rates charged by transport firms, he asserted, "in its very nature is unrestricted and uncontrolled" because of "the simple fact that they are its own works, or are constructed under its authority."[147] State legislatures, Bradley explained a decade later, had a "duty" to provide transport facilities for the convenience of the public. When a railroad corporation was chartered, government only empowered it to act "as an agent of the State for furnishing public accommodation." Therefore, it was the legislature's "prerogative to fix the fares and freights which they may charge for their services. When merely a road or a canal is to be constructed, it is for the legislature to fix the tolls to be paid by those who use it; when a company is chartered not only to build a road, but to carry on public transportation upon it, it is for the legislature to fix the charges for such transportation."[148] According to Bradley, and probably the entire Granger Railroad Cases majority, then, a railroad corporation was no different from a state-owned canal or publicly operated toll road; hence the legislature might fix rates of carriage at its discretion.

Once again Field dissented. He conceded that transport firms were devoted to "public use," and he recognized that state legislatures had generally reserved the power to alter rates fixed in corporate charters.[149] As a result, he admitted that the states' power to regulate transport tariffs was incontrovertible. What he could not accept, however, was the court's contention that railroad corporations were mere "agents of the State." In his view, the majority had converted private concerns with public duties into wholly public corporations. That position, Field contended, was neither good policy nor good law. The public's interest in railroads necessitated the mobilization of private investment capital, and the state of railroad credit wholly depended upon certainty of return. But investors could not be attracted, and economic growth perpetuated, if their property was entirely at the mercy of hostile legislatures.[150] Thus Field contended that the court's clear duty was to "define the limits of the power of the State over its corporations . . . so that, on the one hand, the property interest of the stockholder would be protected from practical confiscation, and, on the other hand, the people would be protected from arbitrary and extortionate charges."[151] Field must have been most upset because only one year earlier, in *Lake Superior & Mississippi R.R. Co. v. United States*, Bradley had drawn just such a line in holding that railroad corporations had certain rights in their property which the public could not take without just compensation.[152]

In 1864 Congress granted land on the public domain to the state of Minnesota to be conveyed, in turn, to the Lake Superior and Mississippi Railroad Company as a bounty for the construction of a "first class" line. The statute contained the following provision: "The railroad shall be, and remain a *public highway* free from all toll or other charge [upon] the transportation of any property or troops of the United States." Federal attorneys liberally construed the act to mean that government shipments were to be transported toll-free by the company. The corporation demurred, filed suit in the United States Court of Claims and, after losing there, appealed to the Supreme Court of the United States. Speaking through Bradley, a narrow majority sustained the railroad's contention that the government had to pay the company for the cost of its services. The word "public highway," Bradley declared, "cannot, without doing violence to language . . . be extended to embrace the rolling-stock or other personal property of the railroad company."[153]

How Bradley and Waite, who had joined the majority in the land-grant case, reconciled government's "unrestricted and uncontrolled" discretion to fix rates with the right of railroad corporations to refuse carriage without compensation is unclear. But for Field, the difference was only one of degree. As a result of the pervasive, rancorous conflict among merchants, farmers, and railroad companies during the preceding decade. Field had imbibed a profound distrust of the legislative process. Thus he was readily convinced that greedy shippers had fixed rates "without reference to the expenses of the carriage, or the obligations incurred in the construction of the roads."[154] In the Wisconsin rate cases, however, the state court had held that even if tariffs fixed by the legislature diminished income below costs, the judiciary could not provide a remedy, and the court, by remanding the companies to the polls, had implicitly sustained the Wisconsin court's assertion that a compensable "taking" necessitated "appropriation by the state itself, for its own use . . . of the whole thing confiscated."[155] That doctrine, however, ignored the crucial transformation of the property right which the court had, in Field's view, brought to fruition in *Pumpelly v. Green Bay & Mississippi Canal Co.*[156] If, indeed, rates had been fixed such that carriage was required without remuneration, then the stockholders' track and rolling stock, like the property of landowners in "consequential" eminent-domain takings, had been effectively taken for the public's use without compensation. Moreover, Field contended, rate regulation was not analogous to health and safety measures for which compensation need not be paid even if the value of property had been diminished.[157] By regulating railway tariffs, government did not destroy property because it was detrimental. Instead, the public made positive use of the regulated property. In that instance, Field asserted, "if the constitutional guaranty extends no further than to prevent a deprivation of title and possession, and allows a deprivation of use, and the fruits of that use, it does not merit the encomiums it has received."[158]

Field did not reject the Court's position in the Granger Railroad Cases on eminent-domain analogies alone. He believed that his approach to regulatory questions was also deeply rooted in American corporation law and constituted a logical application of contract-clause doctrine the Court had handed down during the early 1870s. Speaking for a unanimous Court in *Tomlinson* v. *Jessup*, Field had conceded that a state legislature might amend corporate charters if a specific reservation retaining that power had been inserted in either the act of incorporation or the constitution of the state. He had added, however, that "rights and interests acquired by the company, not constituting a part of the contract of incorporation, stand upon a different footing."[159]

For Field, then, franchise privileges might be altered or revoked altogether; but the state retained control only over what it granted. Contractual agreements and corporate property made or acquired in the exercise of the charter privileges were collateral to the grant of incorporation and could not be impaired or taken without compensation. Insofar as the property of the corporators — whether in the form of stock, bonds, or commonly held capital goods — had been vested, then, the state might exert no other power than that which it exercised over the property of individuals. "And such must be the case," Field reiterated in the Sinking Fund Cases, "or there would be no safety in dealing with the government where such a [reservation] clause is inserted in its legislation." Otherwise, government "could undo at pleasure every thing done under its authority, and despoil of their property those [investors] who had trusted to its faith."[160]

Field's construction of the contract clause was not unique. In both the state courts and in the Supreme Court, jurists had long agreed that reservation clauses did not authorize legislative interference with property rights held outside of, and

collateral to, the corporate franchise.[161] The Court divided, however, on the application of that doctrine to cases in which government asserted the right to alter maximum rates fixed in the dated charters of railroad and other public-service corporations. The Granger Railroad Cases majority ruled that the contract clause was inapplicable and held that the only "controlling fact is the right to regulate at all." Field, however, contended that, although the states might regulate the rates charged by businesses that "held franchises of a public character," the policy makers' discretion was limited by the established principle that "no amendment or alteration of the charter can take away the property rights which have become vested under a legitimate exercise of the powers given."[162] In his view, if a public-service corporation were required "to take as compensation" rates which were "less than the expenses" which the company had incurred in building and operating the road, the stock and bondholders would be deprived of property "as effectually as if the legislature had ordered its forcible dispossession."[163] But Field dissented, not because the several railroad corporations had conclusively shown that property rights of stockholders had been impaired, but rather to expose fully the disparity between his position and the doctrine handed down by the majority.[164] Subsequently in *Ruggles* v. *Illinois*, he concurred when the Court sustained a maximum-rate law "on the ground that no proof was made that the rate prescribed by the legislature was unreasonable."[165] The burden of proof lay with the corporation.[166] The legislature only had to take care that maximum-rate laws provided each company with income commensurate with its costs and, since the property right subsumed the right to the fruits of its use, furnished stockholders with a fair return on their investment.

Field never altered this position. He merely waited for the rest of the Court to assume his posture. After 1886, however, neither Field nor the Court invoked the contract clause as a restraint on rate maxima.[167] But this did not indicate inconsistency or opportunism on his part. Instead, in the Railroad Commission Cases, Chief Justice Waite asserted that the states' regulatory power was subject to the "taking" provision of the due-process clause.[168] This landmark concession made it no longer necessary to look through the corporate entity to its stockholders and creditors. Thus Field's persistent demolition work on the discretion doctrine of *Munn* bore fruit even as its contract-clause rationale became obscured; by 1888 he was able to summarize his position while speaking for a unanimous court. Railroad corporations, he asserted in *Georgia Banking and Railroad Co.* v. *Smith*, were subject to regulation in order to "prevent extortion by unreasonable charges, and favoritism by unjust discrimination" because there had been a "grant to it of special privileges to carry out the object of its incorporation, particularly the authority to exercise the State's right of eminent domain."[169] But regulation was "subject to the limitation that the carriage is not required without reward, or upon conditions amounting to the taking of property for public use without just compensation."[170] This restriction was directly applied in the leading case of *Chicago, Milwaukee & St. Paul Ry. Co.* v. *Minnesota*, and in 1898 the Court began reviewing state regulatory legislation to ascertain its probable effect on the distribution of corporate assets and liabilities.[171] Judicial review of fact in so complex an area as corporate finance added burdensome judicial duties to an already overcrowded docket. But that was of no consequence to Field. Public and private rights not only had to be defined, but the rights of each had to be protected from "arbitrary" encroachment by the other. That, above all else, was what Field conceived to be the role of law.

In the immediate post–Civil War period, the socioeconomic dislocation that accompanied three decades of rapid growth eroded the unifying, ante-bellum

conception of "the commonwealth" and Americans became "obsessed ... with the necessity for making the distinction between public and private spheres of action."[172] But the issues arising from the collapse of cooperation between the public and private sectors affected different groups in different ways, and men drew the line as their particularistic interests dictated. Thus railroad leaders saw no reason why government should not grant them tax exemptions, cash subsidies, or even an entire harbor. They claimed the rate-making power, however, as a sovereign right of management "that cannot be disturbed by *any* legislative action."[173] Merchants and farmers were equally opportunistic. In their view internal-improvement bonds might be repudiated because railroad and manufacturing companies were "exclusively private," but the same firms that were ineligible for subsidies or perpetual immunities might be regulated at the legislature's discretion because they were "affected with a public interest."[174]

Field's approach to the ensuing constitutional controversies was more than a narrow philosophy of the bank account. He, too, was obsessed with formulating rules that separated the public and private sectors as far as practicable. But he refused to provide "a harbor where refuge can be found" for the inconsistent claims of any particular interest group.[175] Instead, Field believed that the proper solution to the nation's policy conflicts lay in uncompromising judicial application, on both sides of the promotional regulatory continuum, of the long-established eminent-domain concepts of "public purpose," inalienability, and just compensation for public use of private property. In his view, the body of doctrine that logically flowed from those precepts was so consistent and so conducive to "the peace of society and to its progress and improvement" that he was certain his entire system would ultimately prevail.[176] *Munn* and all other "grave departure[s] from the purposes of the Constitution," he told a New York crowd at the court's centennial celebration, were "bound to die." Any decision that did "not fit harmoniously with other rulings," Field declared, "will collide with them, and thus compel explanations and qualifications until the error is eliminated . . . Truth alone is immortal, and in the end [it] will assert its rightful supremacy."[177]

But Field's "immortal truths," if viable at all, provided solutions only for the policy issues of the 1870s. The "public use" and inalienability doctrines offered no guidance whatsoever on questions involving labor-management strife or governmental control of such "ordinary trades" as sugar and oil refining. For the judicial conservatives that succeeded him, then, the system of immutable rules that Field had formulated to separate the public and private sectors was irrelevant for the issues that loomed largest in their minds.[178] And by 1920, the Court had not

only transformed Field's police-power dicta into an iron law of "liberty to contract" but also had permitted the states to devolve eminent-domain powers to mining companies and had sustained payment of subsidies to housing-construction firms.[179] As a result, when the affectation doctrine of *Munn* was finally overthrown in *Nebbia v. New York*, it did indeed no longer "fit harmoniously with other rulings." The concerns of Field's generation had expired, and the Court flatly stated that "there is no closed class or category of businesses affected with a public interest."[180] Field's government-business jurisprudence perished, however, not because it had been internally incosistent or had failed to reflect the ideological commitments of post–Civil War Americans, but rather because his doctrinal system proved to be incongruent with the rapidly changing needs of an ever-expanding capitalist society.

Part Eight

Progressivism and the Law

The most significant developments in the period following the Civil War were not the short-term changes and events, but the long-term social trends: the migration of people from farm to city and from agricultural to industrial pursuits; the massive inflow of immigrants, and the rise of modern business. These huge social changes brought new social problems and were the incentive for new social movements as well.

Historians have wrangled among themselves over the definition and nature of one of these movements, loosely called progressivism. For our purposes it can be defined as a nineteenth-century and early twentieth-century reform movement that attempted to end corruption, oligarchical power, and social privilege in politics, and to curb the power of big business, but within the framework of a constitutional government and a capitalist economy.

Reform of political and social structure meant, necessarily, reform through law: constitutional change, new legislation, court decisions. As a result, the courts and the legislatures became major battlegrounds of progressivism.

American society had never been shy about the use of law. Characteristically, post-Civil War society also turned to organization and the formation of interest groups to achieve its ends; Americans were, and are, in Arthur Schlesinger's phrase, "a nation of joiners." Labor unionized; farmers organized; business formed trade associations and agglomerated enterprises into pools, combinations, and trusts. The trades and professions sought consolidation and monopoly status through occupational licensing. The clashes among these interest groups often took the form of legal battles that eventually resulted in such major legislation as the Sherman Antitrust Act and the Interstate Commerce Act and in legal doctrines and legal processes (for example, the rise of the labor injunction).

The two articles in this section chronicle some of these legal battles. Lawrence Friedman and Jack Ladinsky chart the rise and fall of the "fellow-servant rule" — the development of industrial-accident law from a clear-cut, but harsh, set of rules favoring enterprise to the more complicated, but more balanced, system of workmen's compensation. In the battles of progressivism, however, there were few, if any, absolute winners and losers. The legal system developed through a series of ragged compromises; each side gave a little, got a little. The reformers were not

Progressivism and the Law

doctrinaire idealists, but even if they had been, they would have had to reckon with the power of business, just as business ultimately had to reckon, however reluctantly, with the power of labor.

Friedman and Ladinsky also attack the notion of cultural lag, at least as it is applied to law. They argue that the law responds to social forces and hence, almost by definition, cannot be "behind the times." What at first sight may appear archaic or recalcitrant in a legal system, on closer view reflects the equilibrium point of a tug of war among interest groups, each defending itself and at the same time seeking to encroach on the others' territory.

Arnold M. Paul's article looks closely at the attitudes of the legal profession in the 1890s. A vigorous, activist — and conservative — Supreme Court handed down a number of opinions which aroused great outrage, not only outside the profession but inside it as well. This trend was paralleled by decisions in the state courts. Although the leaders of the bar generally applauded the conservative trend of the nineties, an important minority did not.

In any event, by the end of the decade the controversy died down somewhat, in part at least because court decisions temporarily became more liberal. The conflict over the court's work in reviewing legislation on economic and social questions was not over, however; it would prove to be a recurrent one.

Further Reading

Jacobs, Clyde. *Law Writers and the Court.* Berkeley: University of California Press, 1954.

Kolko, Gabriel. *Railroads and Regulation, 1877–1916.* Princeton: Princeton University Press, 1965.

Letwin, William. *Law and Economic Policy in America: The Evolution of the Sherman Antitrust Act.* New York: Random House, 1965.

Miller, George H. *Railroads and the Granger Laws.* Madison: University of Wisconsin Press, 1971.

Paul, Arnold M. *Conservative Crisis and the Rule of Law, Attitudes of Bar and Bench, 1887–1895.* New York: Harper & Row, 1969.

22

Lawrence M. Friedman and Jack Ladinsky

Social Change and the Law of Industrial Accidents

Sociologists recognize, in a general way, the essential role of legal institutions in the social order. They concede, as well, the responsiveness of law to social change and have made important explorations of the interrelations involved. Nevertheless, the role law plays in initiating — or reflecting — social change has never been fully explicated, either in theory or through research. The evolution of American industrial-accident law from tort principles to compensation systems is an appropriate subject for a case study on this subject. It is a topic that has been carefully treated by legal scholars, and it is also recognized by sociologists to be a significant instance of social change. This essay, using concepts drawn from both legal and sociological disciplines, aims at clarifying the concept of social change and illustrating its relationship to change in the law.

Background of the Fellow-Servant Rule

At the dawn of the industrial revolution, the common law of torts afforded a remedy, as it still does, for those who had suffered injuries at the hands of others. If

Reprinted, with changes, from *Columbia Law Review*, 67 (1967), 50-82, by permission.

a man injured another by direct action — by striking him, or slandering him, or by trespassing on his property — the victim could sue for his damages. Similarly, the victim of certain kinds of negligent behavior had a remedy at law. But tort law was not highly developed. Negligence in particular did not loom large in the reports, and it was not prominently discussed in books of theory or practice.[1] Indeed, no treatise on tort law appeared in America until Francis Hilliard's in 1859; the first English treatise came out in 1860.

In theory, at least, recovery for industrial accidents might have been assimilated into the existing system of tort law. The fundamental principles were broad and simple. If a factory worker was injured through the negligence of another person — including his employer — an action for damages would lie. Although as a practical matter servants did not usually sue their master nor workers their employers, in principle they had the right to do so. In principle, too, a worker might have had an action against his employer for any injury caused by the negligence of any other employee. The doctrine of *respondeat superior* was familiar and fundamental law. A principal was liable for the negligent acts of his agent. As Black-

Lawrence M. Friedman and Jack Ladinsky

stone put it: "He who does a thing by the agency of another, does it himself . . . If an innkeeper's servants rob his guests, the master is bound to restitution . . . So likewise if the drawer at a tavern sells a man bad wine, whereby his health is injured, he may bring an action against the master."[2]

Conceivably, then one member of an industrial work force might sue his employer for injuries caused by the negligence of a fellow worker. A definitive body of doctrine was slow to develop, however. When it did, it rejected the broad principle of *respondeat superior* and took instead the form of the so-called fellow-servant rule. Under this rule, a servant (employee) could not sue his master (employer) for injuries caused by the negligence of another employee. The consequences of this doctrine were far reaching. An employee retained the right to sue the employer for injuries, provided they were caused by the employer's personal misconduct. But the factory system and corporate ownership of industry made this right virtually meaningless. The factory owner was likely to be a "soulless" legal entity; even if the owner was an individual entrepreneur, he was unlikely to concern himself physically with factory operations. In work accidents, then, legal fault would be ascribed to fellow employees, if to anyone. But fellow employees were men without wealth or insurance. The fellow-servant rule was an instrument capable of relieving employers from almost all the legal consequences of industrial injuries. Moreover the doctrine left an injured worker without any effective recourse but an empty action against his co-worker.

Origin and Acceptance of the Rule

The origin of the fellow-servant rule is usually ascribed to Lord Abinger's opinion in *Priestley* v. *Fowler*,[3] decided in 1837. Yet the case on its facts did not pose the question of the industrial accident as later generations would understand it; rather, it concerned the employment relationships of tradesmen. The defendant, a butcher, instructed the plaintiff, his servant, to deliver goods which had been loaded on a van by another employee. The van, which had been overloaded, broke down, and plaintiff fractured his thigh in the accident. Lord Abinger, in his rather diffuse and unperceptive opinion, reached his holding that the servant had no cause of action by arguing from analogies drawn neither from industry nor from trade:

> If the master be liable to the servant in this action, the principle of that liability will . . . carry us to an alarming extent . . . The footman . . . may have an action against his master for a defect in the carriage owing to the negligence of the coachmaker . . . The master . . . would be liable to the servant for the negligence of the chambermaid, for putting him into a damp bed; . . . for the negligence of the cook in not properly cleaning the copper vessels used in the kitchen . . .

These and similar passages in the opinion suggest that Abinger was worried about the disruptive effects of a master's liability upon his household staff. These considerations were perhaps irrelevant to the case at hand, the facts of which did not deal with the household of a nobleman, great landowner, or rich merchant; *a fortiori* the decision itself did not concern relationships within an industrial establishment. Certainly the opinion made extension of the rule to the factory setting somewhat easier to enunciate and formulate technically. But it did not justify the existence of an industrial fellow-servant rule. The case might have been totally forgotten — or overruled — had not the onrush of the industrial revolution put the question again and again to courts, each time more forcefully. *Priestley* v. *Fowler* and the doctrine of *respondeat superior* each stood for a broad principle. Whether the one or the other (or neither) would find a place in the law relative to industrial accidents depended upon needs felt and expressed by legal institutions in response to societal demands. Had there been no *Priestley* v. *Fowler*, it would have been necessary — and hardly difficult — to invent one.

In the United States, the leading case on the fellow-servant situation was *Farwell v. Boston & Worcester Railroad Corp.*[4] decided by Massachusetts's highest court in 1842. The case arose out of a true industrial accident in a rapidly developing industrial state. Farwell was an engineer who lost a hand when his train ran off the track due to a switchman's negligence. As Chief Justice Shaw, writing for the court, saw it, the problem of *Farwell* was how best to apportion the risks of railroad accidents. In his view, it was superficial to analyze the problem according to the tort concepts of fault and negligence. His opinion spoke the language of contract, and employed the stern logic of nineteenth-century economic thought. Some occupations are more dangerous than others. Other things being equal, a worker will choose the least dangerous occupation available. Hence, to get workers an employer will have to pay an additional wage for dangerous work. The market, therefore, has already made an adjustment in the wage rate to compensate for the possibility of accident, and a cost somewhat similar to an insurance cost has been allocated to the company. As Shaw put it, "He who engages in the employment of another for the performance of specified duties and services, for compensation, takes upon himself the natural and ordinary risks and perils incident to the performance of such services, and *in legal presumption, the compensation is adjusted accordingly.*"[5] The worker therefore has assumed the risk of injury — for a price. The "implied contract of employment" between the worker and employer did not require the employer to bear any additional costs of injury (except for those caused by the employer's personal negligence).

Shaw's opinion has a certain heartlessness of tone. A disabled worker without resources was likely to be pauperized if he had no realistic right to damages. Unless his family could help him, he would have to fall back upon poor relief, the costs of which were borne by the public through taxation. The railroads and other industrial employers paid a share as taxpayers and, in addition, a kind of insurance cost as part of their wage rate — but no more. Additional damages had to be borne by the worker; if he could not bear them, society generally would pay the welfare costs. Thus the opinion expresses a preference for charging the welfare cost of industrial accidents to the public rather than to the particular enterprise involved.

It is not surprising that such a preference was expressed. Shaw's generation placed an extremely high value on economic growth. As Willard Hurst has noted, that generation was thoroughly convinced it was "socially desirable that there be broad opportunity for the release of creative human energy," particularly in the "realm of the economy."[6] The establishment of a functioning railroad net was an essential element in economic growth.

In addition, while social welfare is looked upon today as a task of government, and government can lay claim to far greater resources to accomplish welfare goals, in Shaw's day, private charity was assigned a higher place in the relief of misery. Probably most people would have agreed that the disabled and wretched poor ought not to starve; where private philanthropy failed, local poor relief stepped in. But it was the most miserable sort of minimum, though its deficiencies were not apparent to the average middle- or upper-class citizen. Furthermore, in Shaw's day certain kinds of crisis and risks had to be accepted as inevitable — far more of them than would be acceptable today. High mortality rates from disease threatened all classes of society. Business entrepreneurs ran heavy risks; business failure was common and could be avoided only by great skill and good fortune. The instability of the monetary system threatened an entrepreneur with sudden, unpredictable, and uninsurable ruin. The present national bankruptcy system also did not yet exist, and local insolvency laws were chaotic and unpredictable.[7] Men like Shaw, the bearers of

Lawrence M. Friedman and Jack Ladinsky

power and influence, might have conceded that the misfortunes of factory workers were real, but they would have said that insecurity of economic position cursed the lot of all but the very rich. The problem was one of *general* insecurity.

Shaw and his generation placed their hopes of salvation on rapid economic growth. Perhaps they were anxious to see that the tort system of accident compensation did not add to the problems of new industry. Few people imagined that accidents would become so numerous as to create severe economic and social dislocations. On the contrary, rash extension of certain principles of tort law to industrial accidents might upset social progress by imposing extreme costs on business in its economic infancy. The 1840s and 1850s were decades of massive economic development in New England and the Midwest. Textiles, and then iron, spearheaded the industrial revolution; westward expansion and the railroads created new markets. Communities and states made a social contribution to the construction of railroads through cash subsidies, stock subscriptions, and tax exemptions. The courts, using the fellow-servant doctrine and the concepts of assumption of risk and contributory negligence,[8] socialized the accident costs of building the roads. That these solutions represented the consensus, however uneasy, of those with authority and responsibility is supported by the fact that every court of the country, with but one transient exception,[9] reached the same conclusion in the years immediately following *Farwell*. Moreover, the fellow-servant rule was not abolished by any legislature in those early years. Although legislative inaction is not necessarily a sign of acquiescence, it at least indicates lack of strong feelings of revulsion.

Weakening the Rule

A general pattern may be discerned which is common to the judicial history of many rules of law. The courts enunciate a rule by which they intend to "solve" a social problem — that is, they seek to lay down a stable and clear-cut principle by which men can govern their conduct or, alternatively, by which the legal system can govern men. If the rule comports with some kind of consensus, it will in fact work a solution — that is, it will go unchallenged, or, if challenged, will prevail. Challenges will not usually continue, since the small chance of overturning the rule is not worth the cost of litigation. If, however, the rule is weakened — if courts engraft exceptions to it, for example — then fresh challenges probing new weaknesses will be encouraged. Even if the rule retains some support, it will no longer be efficient and clear-cut. Ultimately, the rule may no longer serve *anybody's* purposes. At this point, a fresh (perhaps wholly new) "solution" will be attempted.

The history of the fellow-servant rule rather neatly fits this scheme. Shaw wrote his *Farwell* opinion in 1842. During the later part of the century, judges began to reject his reasoning. The "tendency in nearly all jurisdictions," said a Connecticut court in 1885, was to "limit rather than enlarge" the range of the fellow-servant rule.[10] A Missouri judge in 1891 candidly expressed the change in attitude:

In the progress of society, and the general substitution of ideal and invisible masters and employers for the actual and visible ones of former times, in the forms of corporations engaged in varied, detached and widespread operations . . . it has been seen and felt that the universal application of the [fellow-servant] rule often resulted in hardship and injustice. Accordingly, the tendency of the more modern authorities appears to be in the direction of such a modification and limitation of the rule as shall eventually devolve upon the employer under these circumstances a due and just share of the responsibility for the lives and limbs of the persons in its employ.[11]

The rule was strong medicine, and it depended for its efficacy upon continued, relatively certain, and unswerving legal loyalty. Ideally, if the rule were strong and commanded nearly total respect from the various agencies of law, it would eliminate much of the mass of litigation that might otherwise arise. Undoubtedly it did prevent countless thousands of law suits; but it did not succeed in choking off industrial-accident litigation. For example, industrial-accident litigation dominated the docket of the Wisconsin Supreme Court at the beginning of the age of workmen's compensation; far more cases arose under that heading than under any other single field of law.[12] Undoubtedly, this appellate caseload was merely the visible portion of a vast iceberg of litigation. Thus the rule did not command the respect required for efficient operation and hence, in the long run, survival.

One reason for the continued litigation may have been simply the great number of accidents that occurred. At the beginning of the industrial revolution, when Shaw wrote, the human consequences of that technological change were unforeseeable. In particular, the toll it would take of human life was unknown. But by the last quarter of the nineteenth century the number of industrial accidents had grown enormously. After 1900, it is estimated, 35,000 deaths and 2,000,000 injuries occurred every year in the United States. One quarter of the injuries produced disabilities lasting more than one week. The railway injury rate doubled in the seventeen years between 1889 and 1906.[13]

In addition to the sheer number of accidents, other reasons for the increasing number of challenges to the rule in the later nineteenth century are apparent. If the injury resulted in death or permanent disability, it broke off the employment relationship; the plaintiff or his family thereafter had nothing to lose except the costs of suit. The development of the contingent-fee system provided the poor man with the means to hire a lawyer.

The contingent-fee system was no more than a mechanism, however. A losing plaintiff's lawyer receives no fee; that is the essence of the system. The fact is that

plaintiffs won many of their lawsuits; in so doing they not only weakened the fellow-servant rule, but they encouraged still more plaintiffs to try their hand, still more attorneys to make a living from personal-injury suits. In trial courts the pressure of particular cases — the "hard" cases in which the plight of the plaintiff was pitiful or dramatic — tempted judges and juries to find in favor of the little man and against the corporate defendant. In Shaw's generation, many leading appellate judges shared his view of the role of the judge; they took it as their duty to lay down grand legal principles to govern whole segments of the economic order. Thus individual hardship cases had to be ignored for the sake of higher duty. But this was not the exclusive judicial style, even in the appellate courts. In personal injury cases, lower-court judges and juries were especially prone to tailor justice to the case at hand. For example, in Wisconsin, of 307 personal injury cases involving workers that appeared before the state supreme court up to 1907, nearly two-thirds had been decided in favor of the worker in the lower courts. In the state supreme court, however, only two-fifths were decided for the worker.[14] Other states undoubtedly had similar experiences. Whether for reasons of sympathy with individual plaintiffs, or with the working class in general, courts and juries often circumvented the formal dictates of the doctrines of the common law.

Some weakening of the doctrine took place by means of the control exercised by the trial-court judge and jury over findings of fact. But sympathy for injured workers manifested itself also in changes in doctrines. On the appellate-court level, a number of mitigations of the fellow-servant rule developed near the end of the nineteenth century. For example, it had always been conceded that the employer was liable if he was personally responsible (through his own negligence) for his worker's injury. Thus, in a Massachusetts case, a stable owner gave directions to his employee, who was driving a wagon, that caused an accident and injury to the driver (or so the jury found). The employer was held liable.[15] Out of this simple proposition grew the so-called vice-principal rule, which allowed an employee to sue his employer where the negligent employee occupied a supervisory position such that he could more properly be regarded as an alter ego of the principal than a mere fellow servant. This was a substantial weakening of the fellow-servant doctrine. Yet some states never accepted the vice-principal rule; in those that did, it, too, spawned a bewildering multiplicity of decisions, sub-rules, and sub-sub-rules. "The decisions on the subject, indeed, are conflicting to a degree which, it may safely be affirmed, is without a parallel in any department of jurisprudence."[16] This statement appeared in a treatise, written on the eve of workmen's compensation, which devoted no fewer than 524 pages to a discussion of the ramifications of the vice-principal rule.

There were scores of other "exceptions" to the fellow-servant rule enunciated in one or more states. Some of them were of great importance. In general, an employer was said to have certain duties that were not "delegable;" these he must do or have done, and a failure to perform them laid him open to liability for personal injuries. Among these was the duty to furnish a safe place to work, safe tools, and safe appliances. Litigation on these points was enormous, and here, too, the cases cannot readily be summed up or even explained. In *Wedgwood* v. *Chicago & Northwestern Railway Co.*[17] the plaintiff, a brakeman, was injured by a "large and long bolt, out of place, and which unnecessarily, carelessly and unskillfully projected beyond the frame, beam or brakehead, in the way of the brakeman going to couple the cars." The trial court threw the case out, but the Wisconsin Supreme Court reversed: "It is true, the defendant . . . is a railroad corporation, and can only act through officers or agents. But this does not relieve it from responsibility for the negligence of its officers and agents whose duty it is to provide safe and suitable machinery for

its road which its employees are to operate."

So phrased, of course, the exception comes close to swallowing the rule. Had the courts been so inclined, they might have eliminated the fellow-servant rule, without admitting it, simply by expanding the safe-place and safe-tool rules. They were never quite willing to go that far, and the safe-tool doctrine was itself subject to numerous exceptions. In some jurisdictions, for example, the so-called simple-tool rule applied: "Tools of ordinary and everyday use, which are simple in structure and requiring no skill in handling — such as hammers and axes — not obviously defective, do not impose a liability upon employer[s] for injuries resulting from such defects."[18]

Doctrinal complexity and vacillation in the upper courts coupled with jury freedom in the lower courts meant that by the end of the century the fellow-servant rule had lost much of its reason for existence: it was no longer an efficient cost-allocating doctrine. Even though the exceptions did not go the length of obliterating the rule, and even though many (perhaps most) injured workers who had a possible cause of action did not or could not recover, the instability and unpredictability of operation of the common-law rule was a significant fact.

The numerous judge-made exceptions reflected a good deal of uncertainty about underlying social policy. The same uncertainty was reflected in another sphere of legal activity — the legislature. Though the rule was not formally abrogated, it was weakened by statute in a number of jurisdictions. Liability statutes, as will be seen, were rudimentary and in many ways ineffective. This was partly because of genuine uncertainty about the proper attitude to take toward industrial-accident costs — an uncertainty reflected in the cases as well. The early nineteenth century cannot be uncritically described as a period that accepted without question business values and practices. Rather it accepted the ideal of economic growth, which certain kinds of enterprise seemed to hinder. Thus in the age of Jackson, as is well known, popular feeling ran high against financial institutions, chiefly the chartered banks. Banks were believed to have far too much economic power; they corrupted both the currency and the government. They were a "clog upon the industry of this country."[19] But many a good judge, who decried the soulless corporation (meaning chiefly the moneyed kind) in the best Jacksonian tradition, may at the same time have upheld the fellow-servant rule. One did not, in other words, necessarily identify the interests of the common man with industrial liability for personal injuries.

Later on, the railroads replaced the banks as popular bogeymen. By the 1850s some of the fear of excessive economic power was transferred to them. Disregard for safety was one more black mark against the railroads; farmers, small businessmen, and the emerging railroad unions might use the safety argument to enlist widespread support for general regulation of railroads, but the essential thrust of the movement was economic. The railroads were feared and hated because of their power over access to the market. They became "monopolistic" as the small local lines were gradually amalgamated into large groupings controlled by "robber barons." Interstate railroad nets were no longer subject to local political control — if anything, they controlled local politics, or so it plausibly appeared to much of the public. Farmers organized and fought back against what they identified as their economic enemy. It is not coincidental that the earliest derogations from the strictness of the fellow-servant rule applied *only* to railroads. For example, the first statutory modification, passed in Georgia in 1856, allowed railroad employees to recover for injuries caused by the acts of fellow servants, provided they themselves were free from negligence.[20] A similar act was passed in Iowa in 1862.[21] Other statutes were passed in Wyoming (1869)[22] and Kansas (1874).[23] The chro-

nology suggests — though direct evidence is lacking — that some of these statutes were connected with the general revolt of farmers against the power of the railroad companies, a revolt associated with the Granger movement, which achieved its maximum power in the 1870s.[24] Wisconsin in 1875 abolished the fellow-servant rule for railroads ; in 1880, however, when more conservative forces regained control of the legislature, the act was repealed.[25]

Despite the fall of Granger legislatures, the legal and economic position of the railroads was permanently altered. By 1911 twenty-five states had laws modifying or abrogating the fellow-servant doctrine for railroads.[26] Railroad accident law reached a state of maturity earlier than the law of industrial accidents generally; safety controls were imposed on the roads, and the common-law tort system was greatly modified by removal of the employer's most effective defense. The Interstate Commerce Commission called a conference of state regulatory authorities in 1889; the safety problem was discussed, and the commission was urged to investigate the problem and recommend legislation.[27] In 1893 Congress required interstate railroads to equip themselves with safety appliances, and provided that any employee injured "by any locomotive, car, or train in use" without such appliances would not "be deemed . . . to have assumed the risk thereby occasioned."[28]

The Federal Employers' Liability Act (FELA) of 1908[29] went much further; it abolished the fellow-servant rule for railroads and greatly reduced the strength of contributory negligence and assumption of risk as defenses. Once the employers had been stripped of these potent weapons, the relative probability of recovery by injured railroad employees was high enough that workmen's compensation never seemed as essential for the railroads as for industry generally. The highly modified FELA tort system survives (in amended form) to this day for the railroads.[30] It is an anachronism,

Lawrence M. Friedman and Jack Ladinsky

but one which apparently grants some modest satisfaction to both sides. Labor and management both express discontent with FELA, but neither side has been so firmly in favor of a change to workmen's compensation as to make it a major issue.[31]

FELA shows one of many possible outcomes of the decline in efficacy of the fellow-servant rule. Under it, the rule was eliminated, and the law turned to a "pure" tort system — pure in the sense that the proclivities of juries were not interfered with by doctrines designed to limit the chances of a worker's recovery. But the railroads were a special case. Aside from the special history of regulation, the interstate character of the major railroads made them subject to national safety standards and control by a single national authority. For other industrial employers, the FELA route was not taken; instead, workmen's compensation acts were passed. In either case, however, the fellow-servant rule was abolished, or virtually so. Either course reflects, we can assume, some kind of general agreement that the costs of the rule outweighed its benefits.

Rising Pressures for Change

The common-law doctrines were designed to preserve a certain economic balance in the community. When the courts and legislatures created numerous exceptions, the rules lost much of their efficiency as a limitation on the liability of businessmen. The rules prevented many plaintiffs from recovering, but not all; a few plaintiffs recovered large verdicts. There were costs of settlements, costs of liability insurance, costs of administration, legal fees and the salaries of staff lawyers. These costs rose steadily at the very time when American business, especially big business, was striving to rationalize and bureaucratize its operations. It was desirable to be able to predict costs and insure against fluctuating, unpredictable risks. The costs of industrial-accident liability were not eas-

ily predictable, partly because the legal consequences of accidents were not predictable. Insurance, though available, was expensive.

In addition, industry faced a serious problem of labor unrest. Workers and their unions were dissatisfied with many aspects of factory life. The lack of compensation for industrial accidents was one obvious weakness. Relatively few injured workers received compensation. Under the primitive state employers' liability statutes, the issue of liability and the amount awarded still depended upon court rulings and jury verdicts. Furthermore the employer and the insurance carrier might contest a claim or otherwise delay settlement in hopes of bringing the employee to terms. The New York Employers' Liability Commission in 1910 reported that delay ran from six months to six years.

> The injured workman is driven to accept whatever his employer or an insurance company chooses to give him or take his chance in a lawsuit. Half of the time his lawsuit is doomed to failure because he has been hurt by some trade risk or lacks proof for his case. At best he has a right to retain a lawyer, spend two months on the pleadings, watch his case from six months to two years on a calender and then undergo the lottery of a jury trial, with a technical system of law and rules of evidence, and beyond that appeals and perhaps reversals on questions that do not go to the merits . . . If he wins, he wins months after his most urgent need is over.

When an employee did recover, the amount was usually small. The New York Commission found that of forty-eight fatal cases studied in Manhattan, eighteen families received no compensation; only four received over $2,000; most received less than $500. The deceased workers had averaged $15.22 a week in wages; only eight families recovered as much as three times their average yearly earnings. The same inadequacies turned up in Wisconsin in 1907. Of fifty-one fatal injuries studied, thirty-four received settlements under $500; only eight received over $1,000.

Litigation costs consumed much of whatever was recovered. It was estimated that in 1907 "of every $100 paid out by [employers in New York] on account of work accidents but $56 reached the injured workmen and their dependents." Even this figure was unrepresentative because it included voluntary payments by employers. "A fairer test of employers' liability is afforded by the $192,538 paid by these same employers as a result of law suits or to avoid law suits, whereof only $80,888, or forty-two percent, reached the beneficiaries." A large fraction of the disbursed payments, about one-third, went to attorneys who accepted the cases on a contingent basis.

These figures on the inadequacy of recoveries are usually cited to show how little the workers received for their pains. But what did these figures mean to employers? Assuming that employers, as rational men, were anxious to pay as little compensation as was necessary to preserve industrial peace and maintain a healthy work force, the better course might be to pay a higher *net* amount directly to employees. Employers had little or nothing to gain from their big payments to insurance companies, lawyers, and court officials. Perhaps at some unmeasurable point the existing tort system crossed an invisible line and thereafter, purely in economic terms, represented on balance a net loss to the industrial establishment. From that point on, the success of a movement for change in the system was certain, provided that businessmen could be convinced that indeed their self-interest lay in the direction of reform and that a change in compensation systems did not drag with it other unknowable and harmful consequences.

When considerations of politics were added to those of business economics and industrial peace, it was not surprising to find that businessmen gradually withdrew their veto against workmen's compensation statutes. They began to say that a reformed system was inevitable — and even desirable. A guaranteed, insurable cost — one which could be computed in advance on the basis of accident experience — would, in the long run, cost business less than the existing system.[32] In 1910 the president of the National Association of Manufacturers (NAM) appointed a committee to study the possibility of compensating injured workmen without time-consuming and expensive litigation, and the convention that year heard a speaker tell them that no one was satisfied with the present state of the law — that the employers' liability system was "antagonistic to harmonious relations between employers and wage workers."[33] By 1911 the NAM appeared convinced that a compensation system was inevitable and that prudence dictated that business play a positive role in shaping the design of the law — otherwise the law would be "settled for us by the demagogue, and agitator and the socialist with a vengeance."[34] Business would benefit economically and politically from a compensation system, but only if certain conditions were present. Business, therefore, had an interest in pressing for a specific kind of program, and turned its attention to the details of the new system. For example, it was imperative that the new system be in fact as actuarially predictable as business demanded; it was important that the costs of the program be fair and equal in their impact upon particular industries, so that no competitive advantage or disadvantage flowed from the scheme. Consequently the old tort actions had to be eliminated, along with the old defenses of the company. In exchange for certainty of recovery by the worker, the companies were prepared to demand certainty and predictability of loss — that is, limitation of recovery. The jury's caprice had to be dispensed with. In short, when workmen's compensation became law as a

Lawrence M. Friedman and Jack Ladinsky

solution to the industrial-accident problem, it did so on terms acceptable to industry. Other pressures were there to be sure, but when workmen's compensation was enacted, businessmen had come to look on it as a positive benefit rather than as a threat to their interests and profits.

The Emergence of Workmen's Compensation Statutes

The change of the businessman's, the judge's, and the general public's attitudes toward industrial injuries was accelerated by the availability of fresh information on the extent of accidents and their cost to both management and workers. By 1900 industrial accidents and the shortcomings of the fellow-servant rule were widely perceived as problems that had to be solved. After 1900 state legislatures began to look for a "solution" by setting up commissions to gather statistics, to investigate possible new systems, and to recommend legislation.[35] The commissions held public hearings and called upon employers, labor, insurance companies, and lawyers to express their opinions and propose changes. A number of commissions collected statistics on industrial accidents, costs of insurance, and amounts disbursed to injured workmen. By 1916 many states and the federal government had received more or less extensive public reports from these investigating bodies.[36] The reports included studies of industrial-accident cases in the major industries, traced the legal history of the cases, and looked into the plight of the injured workmen and their families.

From the information collected the commissions were able to calculate the costs of workmen's compensation systems and compare them with costs under employers' liability. Most of the commissions concluded that a compensation system would be no more expensive than the existing method,[37] and most of them recommended adoption, in one form or another, of workmen's compensation. In

spite of wide variations in the systems proposed, there was agreement on one point: workmen's compensation must fix liability upon the employer regardless of fault.

Between 1910 and 1920 the method of compensating employees injured on the job was fundamentally altered in the United States. In brief, workmen's-compensation statutes eliminated (or tried to eliminate) the process of fixing civil liability for industrial accidents through litigation in common-law courts. Under the statutes, compensation was based on statutory schedules, and the responsibility for initial determination of employee claims was taken from the courts and given to an administrative agency. Finally, the statutes abolished the fellow-servant rule and the defenses of assumption of risk and contributory negligence. Wisconsin's law, passed in 1911, was the first general compensation act to survive a court test.[38] Mississippi, the last state in the Union to adopt a compensation law, did so in 1948.[39]

Compensation systems varied from state to state, but they had many features in common. The original Wisconsin law was representative of the earlier group of statutes. It set up a voluntary system — a response to the fact that New York's courts had held a compulsory scheme unconstitutional on due-process grounds.[40] Wisconsin abolished the fellow-servant rule and the defense of assumption of risk for employers of four or more employees. In turn, the compensation scheme, for employers who elected to come under it, was made the "exclusive remedy" for an employee injured accidentally on the job. The element of "fault" or "negligence" was eliminated, and the mere fact of injury at work "proximately caused by accident" and not the result of "wilful misconduct" made the employer liable to pay compensation but exempt from ordinary tort liability.[41] The state aimed to make it expensive for employers to stay out of the system. Any employer who did so was liable to suit by injured employees, and the employer was denied the common-law defenses.

The compensation plans strictly limited the employee's amount of recovery. In Wisconsin, for example, if an accident caused "partial disability," the worker was to receive 65 percent of his weekly loss in wages during the period of disability, not to exceed four times his average annual earnings.[42] The statutes, therefore, were compensatory, not punitive, and the measure of compensation was, subject to strict limitations, the loss of earning power of the worker. In the original Wisconsin act, death benefits were also payable to dependents of the worker. If the worker who died left "no person dependent upon him for support," the death benefit was limited to "the reasonable expense of his burial, not exceeding $100."[43] Neither death nor injury as such gave rise to a right to compensation — only the fact of economic loss to someone, either the worker himself or his family. The Wisconsin act authorized employers to buy annuities from private insurance companies to cover projected losses. Most states later made insurance or self-insurance compulsory. Some states have socialized compensation insurance, but most allow the purchase of private policies.[44]

In essence, then, workmen's compensation was designed to replace a highly unsatisfactory system with a rational, actuarial one. It should not be viewed as the replacement of a fault-oriented compensation system with one unconcerned with fault. It should not be viewed as a victory of employees over employers. In its initial stages, the fellow-servant rule was not concerned with fault, either, but with establishing a clear-cut, workable, and predictable rule, one which substantively placed much (if not all) of the risk on the worker. Industrial accidents were not seen as a social problem, but at most as an economic problem. As value perceptions changed, the rule weakened; it developed exceptions and lost its efficiency. The exceptions and counterexceptions can be looked at as a series of brief, ad hoc, and unstable compromises between the clashing interests of labor and management. When both sides became convinced that the game was mutually unprofitable, a compensation system became possible. But this system was itself a compromise: an attempt at a new, workable, and predictable mode of handling accident liability which neatly balanced the interests of labor and management.

The Concept of Cultural Lag

The problem of "fair and efficient incidence of industrial accident costs," in the words of Willard Hurst, "followed a fumbling course in courts and legislature for fifty years before the first broad-scale direction [leading to workmen's compensation] was applied."[45] In a famous book written in 1922, the sociologist William Fielding Ogburn used the example of workmen's compensation and the fifty-year period of fumbling to verify his "hypothesis of cultural lag."[46] "Where one part of culture changes first," said Ogburn, "through some discovery or invention, and occasions changes in some part of culture dependent upon it, there frequently is a delay . . . The extent of this lag will vary . . . but may exist for . . . years, during which time there may be said to be a maladjustment." In the case of workmen's compensation, the lag period was from the time when industrial accidents became numerous until the time when workmen's compensation laws were passed, "about a half-century, from 1850-70 to 1915." During this period, "the old adaptive culture, the common law of employers' liability, hung over after the material conditions had changed."

The concept of cultural lag is still widely used, in social science and out, particularly since its popularization by Stuart Chase in *The Proper Study of Mankind*.[47] The notion that law fails to adjust promptly to the call for change is also commonly voiced. In popular parlance, this or that aspect of the law is

Lawrence M. Friedman and Jack Ladinsky

often said to "lag behind the times." This idea is so pervasive that it deserves comment quite apart from its present status in sociological thought.

The lesson of industrial-accident law as here described may be quite the opposite of the lesson that Ogburn drew. In a purely objective (nonteleological) sense, social processes — and the legal system — cannot aptly be explained by the notion of lag. When, in the face of changed technology and new problems, a social arrangement stubbornly persists, there are *social* reasons why this is so; there are explanations why no change or slow change occurs. The legal system is a part of the total culture; it is not a self-operating machine. The rate of response to a call for change is slow or fast in the law depending upon who issues the call and who (if anybody) resists it. "Progress" or "catching up" is not inevitable or predictable. Legal change, like social change, is a change in behavior of individuals and groups in interaction. The rate of change depends upon the kind of interaction. To say that institutions "lag" is usually to say no more than they are slow to make changes of a particular type.

But why are they slow? Often the answer rests on the fact that these institutions are controlled by, or respond to, groups or individuals who are opposed to the specific change. This is lag only if we feel we can confidently state that these groups or individuals are wrong as to their own self-interest as well as that of society. Of course, people *are* often wrong about their own self-interest; they can be and are short-sighted, ignorant, maladroit. But ignorance of this kind exists among progressives as well as among conservatives — among those who want change as well as among those who oppose it. Resistance to change is "lag" only if there is only one "true" definition of a problem — and one "true" solution.

There were important reasons why fifty years elapsed before workmen's compensation became part of the law. Roscoe Pound once remarked that the twentieth

century accepts the idea of insuring those unable to bear economic loss at the expense of the nearest person at hand who is able to bear it.[48] This conception was relatively unknown and unacceptable to judges of the nineteenth century. The fellow-servant rule could not be replaced until economic affluence, business conditions, and the state of safety technology made feasible a more social solution. Labor unions of the mid–nineteenth century did not call for a compensation plan; they were concerned with more basic (and practical) issues such as wages and hours. Social insurance, as much as private insurance, requires standardization and rationalization of business, predictability of risk, and reliability and financial responsibility of economic institutions. These were present in 1909, but not in 1850.

Prior to workmen's compensation, the legal system reflected existing conflicts of value quite clearly; the manifold exceptions to the fellow-servant rule and the primitive liability statutes bear witness to this fact. These were not symptoms of "lag"; rather they were a measure of the constant adjustments that inevitably take place within a legal system that is not insulated from the larger society but is an integral part of it. To be sure, the courts frequently reflected values of the business community and so did the legislatures, but populist expressions can easily be found in the work of judges, legislatures, and juries. In the absence of a sophisticated measuring rod of past public opinion — and sophisticated concepts of the role of public opinion in nineteenth-century society — who is to say that the legal system "lagged" behind some hypothetical general will of the public or some hypothetically correct solution?

The concept of lag may also be employed in the criticism of the courts' use of judicial review to retard the efficacy of social-welfare legislation. In 1911 the New York Court of Appeals declared the state's compulsory Workmen's Compensation Act unconstitutional. As a result of this holding, the state constitution had to be amended — two years later — before workmen's compensation was legally possible in New York.[49] Because of the New York experience, six states also amended their constitutions and others enacted voluntary plans. The issue was not finally settled until 1917, when the United States Supreme Court held both compulsory and elective plans to be constitutional.[50] But it adds little to an understanding of social process to describe this delay in terms of the concept of cultural lag. Courts do not act on their own initiative. Each case of judicial review was instigated by a litigant who represented a group in society which was fighting for its interests as it perceived them; these were current, real interests, not interests of sentiment or inertia. This is completely apart from consideration of what social interests the courts thought they were serving in deciding these cases — interests which hindsight condemns as futile or wrong, but which were living issues and interests of the day.

Conflicts of value also arose in the legislatures when they began to consider compensation laws. The Massachusetts investigating commission of 1903 reported a workmen's-compensation bill to the legislature, but the bill was killed in committee on the ground that Massachusetts could not afford to increase the production costs of commodities manufactured in the state.[51] Once more, the emergence of compensation depended upon a perception of inevitability — which could cancel the business detriment to particular states that enacted compensation laws — and of general economic gain from the new system. It is not enough to sense that a social problem exists. Rational collective action demands relatively precise and detailed information about the problem, and clear placement of responsibility for proposing and implementing a solution. For many years legislatures simply did not consider it their responsibility to do anything about industrial injuries. Since they did not view accidents as a major

social problem, and since state legislatures were weak political structures, they were content at first to leave accidents to tort law and the courts.[52] Moreover, state agencies were not delegated the task of collecting information on the nature and extent of industrial accidents until relatively late. The Wisconsin legislature created a Bureau of Labor and Industrial Statistics in 1883, but it did not provide for the collection of data on industrial accidents until 1905.[53] When a need for accident legislation was perceived, individual legislators under pressure from constituencies began to introduce work-accident indemnity bills. Some were inadequately drafted; most were poorly understood. In order to appraise potential legislation, investigating commissions were created to collect information, weigh the costs, and report back alternative solutions.

What appears to some as an era of "lag" was actually a period in which issues were collectively defined and alternative solutions posed, and during which interest groups bargained for favorable formulations of law. It was a period of "false starts" — unstable compromise formulations by decision makers armed with few facts, lacking organizational machinery, and facing great, often contradictory, demands from many publics. There was no easy and suitable solution, in the light of the problem and the alignment of powers. Indeed, workmen's compensation — which today appears to be a stable solution — was only a compromise, an answer acceptable to enough people and interest groups to endure over a reasonably long period of time.

Part of what was later called "lag," then, is this period of false starts — the inadequate compromises by decision makers faced with contradictory interest groups pressing inconsistent solutions. There may not be a "solution" in light of the alignment of interests and powers with respect to the problem at any given time. Perhaps only a compromise "solution" is possible. What later appears to be the final answer is in fact itself a compro-

Lawrence M. Friedman and Jack Ladinsky

mise — one which is stable over some significant period of time. Sociologically that is what a "solution" to a problem is: nothing more than a stable compromise acceptable to enough people and interest groups to maintain itself over a significant period of time. Theoretically, of course, the total victory of one competing interest and the total defeat of another is possible. But in a functioning democratic society, total victories and total defeats are uncommon. Total defeat would mean that a losing group was so utterly powerless that it could exert no bargaining pressure whatsoever; total victory similarly would imply unlimited power. In the struggle over industrial-accident legislation, none of the interests could be described that way. Different preceptions of the problem, based at least in part on different economic and social stakes, led to different views of existing and potential law. When these views collided, compromises were hammered out. Workmen's compensation took form not because it was (or is) perfect, but because it represented a solution sufficiently acceptable to enough interests to outweigh the costs of additional struggle and bargaining. If there was "lag" in the process, it consisted of acquiescence in apparently acceptable solutions which turned out to be inadequate or unstable in the long run. "Lag", therefore, at most means present-minded pragmatism rather than long-term rational planning.[54]

23

Arnold M. Paul

Legal Progressivism, the Courts, and the Crisis of the 1890s

The significance of the courts as instruments of conservative defense in the half-century 1887–1937 has long been established. The decisive years in the development of this judicial conservatism were the 1890s, when rising social tension and popular unrest seemed to demand new and vigorous exercises of judicial power. The transformation of the due-process clause into a substantive check upon legislative regulation, the elaboration of the labor injunction as an antistrike weapon, the emasculation of the Sherman Act in the E. C. Knight case, and the overthrow of the federal income tax in the Pollock case were related aspects of a massive judicial entry into the socioeconomic scene. American constitutionalism underwent a revolution in the 1890s, a conservative-oriented revolution which vastly expanded the scope of judicial supremacy, with great consequence for American economic and political history.[1]

The advance of judicial conservatism in the 1890s was not, however, uncontested. The legal profession itself, contrary to most assumptions, was sharply divided

on many phases of the new judicial interventionism, and an important minority of legal progressives[2] protested vigorously against judicial guardianship of the status quo.[3] Suspicious of the growing power of corporate capital with its techniques of consolidation and control, sensitive to the exploitation of labor in factories and mines, the legal progressives of the 1890s represented the traditions of a more equalitarian, more socially aware America. Though ideas for reform varied and were often ill-defined, several main themes predominated in progressive legal thought: destruction or close control of the "trusts," strict regulation of the railroads and other public-service corporations, protection of workingmen from unconscionable employers, income and inheritance taxes on great wealth.[4] How these progressives reacted to the changing social atmosphere of the 1890s, and more particularly to the new role of the judiciary, is a revealing addendum to the story of American social protest.[5]

In the late 1880s legal progressives had cause for encouragement. The tensions aroused by the Haymarket Riot of 1886 had gradually receded, while the movement for social regulation was gaining strength. The federal government had

Reprinted, from Business History Review, 83 (1959), 497-509, by permission.

enacted the Interstate Commerce Act, many states were passing antitrust acts with great pressure mounting for a sweeping federal antitrust law, and state protection against abuses of the labor contract appeared to be a growing trend.[6] Most significant to lawyers, the United States Supreme Court was apparently standing firm by its broad underwriting of the state police power in the great case of *Munn v. Illinois*.[7] In that case, one of the famous Granger cases of 1877, the Court had upheld the power of the states to regulate the rates of businesses affected with a public interest, and had declared that the reasonableness of the rates established was a legislative, not a judicial, question. Though in 1886 the Court had permitted corporations to be included under the term "persons" as used in the due–process clause of the Fourteenth Amendment,[8] successive cases had reaffirmed, and even extended, the power of the state to regulate private property.[9] The high point in this series of cases had been reached in April 1888, when the Supreme Court had sustained a Pennsylvania law prohibiting the manufacture of oleomargarine, Justice Harlan holding that to challenge the good faith of the legislature was to raise "questions of fact and of public policy which belong to the legislative department to determine."[10]

In response to these trends legal progressives were highly optimistic on the eve of the 1890s. Charles C. Bonney, former president of the Illinois Bar Association, issued a confident call to the American bar in midsummer 1888 to take the lead in behalf of popular right "in the great conflict now impending between the people and the giant forces that are striving for the practical control of the republic."[11] Urging greatly expanded state control over labor relations, Bonney declared it a paramount duty of government "to protect the weak against the strong, and to prevent, by stringent laws and their vigorous enforcement, the oppression of the poor and friendless by the rich and powerful." A.H. Wintersteen, the successful counsel for the state in the

Pennsylvania oleomargarine case, predicted in the March 1889 issue of the *American Law Register* that the recent string of Supreme Court decisions would sustain the widest range of legislative discretion.[12] "In a complex social system," he wrote, "the tendency necessarily must be towards affirmative exercise of governmental powers."

Three months later, in March 1890, the legal, if not the political, compass veered sharply, as the United States Supreme Court handed down its decision in the case of *Chicago, Milwaukee & St. Paul Railway Co. v. Minnesota*,[13] the first of a series of judicial retreats from the *Munn* case. Striking down a Minnesota act establishing a railway commission with power to set schedules of rates to be considered final and conclusive, the Court declared that a commission's schedules must be subject to judicial review by the regular courts of law. The reasonableness of rate regulations, said the Court majority, was "eminently a question for judicial investigation, requiring due process of law for its determination."[14] Three justices dissented, maintaining that *Munn v. Illinois* had been practically overruled, and warning that courts all over the land would now be called upon to review decisions of state railroad commissions.[15]

Legal progressives were indignant. Seymour D. Thompson, a well-known writer of legal texts, senior editor of the widely read *American Law Review*, and for ten years judge of the St. Louis Court of Appeals,[16] asserted in an editorial that the effect of the Supreme Court's opinion was "to subject the legislation of the States to judicial superintendence upon the mere question of its *reasonableness*."[17] The Court's decision, Thompson continued, was thus "an overturning of the fundamental principles upon which all our American governments are founded . . . that the three coordinate departments . . . are independent of each other."

An even fiercer attack on the Supreme Court was made by Allan B. Brown of the Chicago bar. As Brown saw it, the overriding evils of the age — the condition of labor, "the enormous concentration of wealth in a few hands," and the abuse of corporate privileges - had been perpetuated and aggravated by the Supreme Court. From the decisions of John Marshall's day, applying the federal contract clause to state-granted corporation charters, to recent declarations that a corporation was a "person" and a "citizen" and entitled to judicial protection from "unreasonable" regulation, the Supreme Court had thwarted the popular will and elevated the corporation above the state. As a preventive of more such decisions, Brown gave this fervent advice: "Put men on the bench who will not hesitate to defy precedent, and pull down the moldy monstrosities Marshall and his compeers set up. Make your judges elective so you can keep them in touch with the people and you will find them correspondingly jealous of the people's rights."[18]

At the same time that legal progressives were responding sharply to the Supreme Court's new shift to economic conservatism, they were equally concerned over developments in the state courts, particularly the rise of the doctrine of freedom of contract. The origins and growth of this remarkable doctrine, which would attain an unenviable reputation for judicial opacity before its atrophy in the late 1930s, have been well chronicled by constitutional historians.[19] By "freedom of contract" or "liberty of contract" was meant the alleged right of employer and employee under the due-process clause to contract at will on the terms of employment, unhampered by legislative prohibitions or requirements. Though first used by state courts in the mid-1880s,[20] the doctrine had languished until 1889 when a sudden rash of decisions aroused professional attention. Among the laws annulled in the next few years were "store order" acts of West Virginia, Illinois, and Missouri prohibiting payment of wages in company "scrip";[21] a city of Los Angeles ordinance prescribing the eight-hour day for employees of municipal contractors;[22] the Massachusetts weavers' fines bill, prohibiting fines or deductions of wages

because of alleged inferior work;[23] an Illinois coal "screening" law regulating computation of wages to miners;[24] a Texas statute requiring railroads to pay all back wages within eight days after termination of employment;[25] and a weekly payment law of Illinois.[26] What made many of these cases especially striking were the frank laissez faire statements appearing in the opinions. Judge Snyder of the West Virginia Court of Appeals, for example, denied the right of the state to regulate the labor contract on the view that government was not authorized "to do for its people what they can do for themselves. The natural law of supply and demand is the best law of trade."[27]

The attack on freedom of contract was led by Seymour D. Thompson, the St. Louis judge and law editor and easily the most articulate of the legal progressives. "What mockery to talk about the freedom of contract," exclaimed Thompson addressing the Kansas Bar Association in January 1892, "where only *one* of the contracting parties is free! What mockery to talk about the freedom of contract as between the corporation which has everything and a day laborer who has nothing!"[28]

Thompson's midwestern denunciation of freedom of contract was soon followed by two New England criticisms considerably less oratorical but almost equally severe. Herbert H. Darling of Boston, just graduated from the Harvard Law School, argued in the May 1892 issue of the *Harvard Law Review* that the basic question in all the freedom-of-contract cases was the degree of legislative discretion under the police power. As Darling put it, "An ostensible exercise of the power which in reality cannot be sustained *from any point of view* . . . is undoubtedly invalid; but if there is any doubt, however slight, that doubt must be resolved in favor of the legislature."[29] Several months later, Conrad Reno, a well-known Boston lawyer,[30] writing in the *American Law Review* in support of a system of state arbitration boards which would be empowered, in cases submitted to it by either side, to set minimum wages and maximum hours enforceable at law, had this to say about the freedom-of-contract cases:

> If there be any benefit in maintaining the independence of the three departments of government, the time seems to have arrived to call a halt upon the encroachments of the judiciary. Progress along economic lines must cease, if the courts have the power to seize upon vague clauses in the constitution to perpetuate the economic views of the past, and to fasten them upon the present as matters of constitutional law, of which the courts are the final judge.[31]

Perhaps the most significant indictment of the freedom-of-contract decisions came from the Far West in an article by C. B. Labatt, a San Francisco attorney and frequent contributor to legal periodicals. Condemning several of the court opinions as, variously, "breathing the very spirit of Mr. Herbert Spencer," distorted by "class prejudices," and filled with "economic prepossessions," Labatt cautioned the judges against building constitutional law on the precepts of political economy. The demands of the laboring classes for legislative protection were bound to increase, he predicted, and the continued intercession of the courts on such doubtful grounds could "scarcely fail to strengthen the impression which is already widely prevalent among workingmen, that the courts are a mere stronghold of capital."[32]

While legal progressives were assessing the impact of new judicial doctrines affecting rate regulation and labor legislation, another new technique of judicial power, the labor injunction, was becoming significant. The labor injunction, first used sporadically in strike situations of the 1880s, attained national prominence in the depression years 1893 and 1894 as widespread industrial conflict and class antagonism brought forth vigorous judicial intervention in behalf of property and order. The climax of the labor strife of the 1890s — and the occasion for the most celebrated uses of the injunction — was, of course, the great Chicago railway strike of June 1894, when the 150,000-man American Railway Union of Eugene V. Debs undertook a nationwide sympathy strike on behalf of the 3,000 strikers of the Pullman Corporation. The intervention of the federal courts, and of federal troops to enforce the process of the courts, quickly ended the strike, though not before an atmosphere of class conflict, marked by considerable bloodshed and destruction of property, had sharply intensified the crisis psychology of the times.[33]

The labor militancy of 1893–1894 and the new uses of the injunction created a conflict of attitudes for legal progressivism. Though legal progressives had long championed the workingman against the corporation and denounced judicial interference with labor laws, they were ambivalent toward unionism: on the one hand, progressives acknowledged the inevitability of unions as counterbalances to capital; on the other hand, many progressives feared that powerful labor organization could crush individualism as easily as could powerful capital organization. Partly on this basis, and partly because lawyers of all persuasions generally favored protection of property from actual or potential depredation, legal progressives such as Seymour D. Thompson had welcomed the early labor injunctions.[34] Extreme applications of the injunction, such as the Northern Pacific orders of United States Circuit Judge Jenkins prohibiting the mere quitting of work,[35] had been strongly disapproved by Thompson and others.[36] The Debs railway strike, however, with its accompanying violence and social excitements, seemed to confirm for these progressives the dangers of militant labor unionism and the need for judicial protection. Thompson, writing in July 1894, when crisis psychology was endemic, castigated Debs as an "irresponsible vagabond" and a "fiend," and described the strike as "in the nature of a servile insurrection"; the interventions of the courts and the troops, he held, were utter necessities to forestall "anarchy" and "revolution."[37] Ardemus Stewart of the *American Law Register*, progressive on most issues, denounced every strike as a menace to legal right and advocated "repressive legislation, the more stringent the better."[38]

Progressive rationalism had not vanished, however. Judge B. D. Tarlton, Chief Justice of the Court of Civil Appeals at Forth Worth, while expressing disapproval of strikes and boycotts as remedies for labor's grievances, insisted that the root of industrial conflict lay in the "economic servitude" of the masses of workers. Recommending that labor leaders concentrate their efforts on courts and legislatures, Tarlton advocated destruction of the trust with its "unreasonable depression of wages" and a general expansion in the scope of protective legislation.[39] Lee Thornton of Memphis, reading a paper to the Tennessee Bar Association, explained that labor organizations were legal so long as they were not unlawfully coercive, and urged that the law "reach by summary remedy the calm, cool, calculating combination of capital, as it reaches the turbulent, impulsive one of labor."[40] And Seymour D. Thompson, replying perhaps apologetically to a correspondent's criticism in the *American Law Review*, maintained that "government by injunction was better than no government at all."[41]

If the legal progressives were in disarray in 1894, buffeted by class militancy and national hysteria, in 1895 they were on solid ground again, with issues clearly defined. For in the early months of 1895 the judicial conservatism of the 1890s reached its apogee, as the United States Supreme Court effected the wreckage — for the time at least — of two of progressivism's most cherished programs, prosecution of the trusts and taxation of large incomes.

The first of the great cases of 1895 was *United States v. E. C. Knight Co.,*[42] decided January 21. By this opinion, declaring the Sherman Antitrust Act of 1890 inapplicable to the American Sugar Refining Company, despite its more than 90 percent monopoly, because the company was a combination in manufacturing only "indirectly" affecting commerce, the Supreme Court at one swoop negated the major intent of the Sherman Act and fractured the national commerce power. Justice John Marshall Harlan, then emerging as the Court's leading sympathizer with the progressive point of view, filed a strong dissent, attacking the opinion as placing the Constitution in "a condition of helplessness . . . while capital combines . . . to destroy competition."[43]

The legal progressives were thrown into an uproar. Ardemus Stewart, the associate editor of the *American Law Register*, concluded a bitter attack on the Court's decision with these words: "It is enough to say that if this decision stands, and it is true that the national government is powerless to protect the people against such combinations as this . . . then this government is a failure, and the sooner the social and political revolution which many far-sighted men can see already darkening the horizon overtakes us, the better."[44]

Seymour D. Thompson was equally infuriated: "Such, we are told is the Constitution which our fathers made for us. They conquered political liberty for us through seven years of blood and privation, and then gave us a constitution under which we are handed over, helpless, bound hand-and-foot, to industrial and commercial slavery." Although amendment of the Constitution might be frustrated, the Supreme Court itself, Thompson gave prophetic warning, could be amended — "even by as drastic a measure as the amendment of the House of Lords by the creation of new peers."[45]

The sensation of the *E. C. Knight case* and the bitterness of progressive reactions were soon overshadowed by the even more arresting *Pollock* case.[46] The *Pollock* case declared unconstitutional the income tax of 1894, a 2 percent tax on incomes over four thousand dollars and the first federal income tax in more than twenty years. The many extraordinary features of the *Pollock* case, which have given it a special notoriety in American constitutional history, need no recounting here. It is enough to recall, among other items, that the two hearings required to decide the case were both accompanied by unusual press and public interest, that distinguished counsel on both sides engaged in highly emotional appeals to class and sectional partisanship, that the final vote demolishing the tax was five to four, that this narrow margin for the negative appeared attributable to one justice having changed his mind between the first and second opinion, that the constitutional interpretation on which the Court hinged its decision overthrew a hundred years of firmly settled precedent, and that the four minority justices each delivered forceful dissents, Justice Harlan's being particularly impassioned.[47]

The wrath of the legal progressives seemed to know few bounds. Seymour D. Thompson, writing in the *American Law Review*, accused the Supreme Court of continually encroaching upon the legislative power and "doing it in almost every case in the interest of the rich and powerful and against the rights and interests of the masses of the people." In a stinging critique of "Government by Lawyers" at the Texas Bar Association, he warned that unless the profession became more responsive to the people, some mighty "popular tempest" could well bring down the entire fabric of law and government.[48] At the Tennessee Bar Association, Henry H. Ingersoll, a former judge of the Tennessee Supreme Court,[49] made this ominous parallel:

> Forty years ago the owners of peculiar property in the South appealed to the Federal courts for protection against the aggressive agitation of the dominant sentiment of the Christian world ... and the Dred Scott decision became famous on two continents. But the contention involved in that case could not abide such judicial decision; agita-

tion increased and it was settled on appeal to arms and by wager of battles ... In 1895 the owners of vast property in the North appealed to the Federal courts for protection against the popular demand that they who get the benefits of government shall bear their just share of its expenses; and they get it in this decision of the Supreme Court in the income tax cases; Dives wins, Plebs loses. Is the contention settled?[50]

The attack upon the tax case was only one facet of a mounting progressive revolt against judicial interventionism in 1895–1896. The anger of the legal progressives was turned upon the increasing stream of freedom-of-contract cases, and in particular the *Ritchie* case of March 1895, that nullified the Illinois eight-hour law for women in garment manufacturing.[51] In the words of one writer, the courts had "disregarded elementary principles of constitutional construction"; another accused the courts of enforcing the "dungeon" of the sweatshop and overturning laws which were "the very bulwark of liberty."[52] The Supreme Court decision unanimously upholding the Debs injunctions,[53] though seldom criticized in its own right (as noted above, most legal progressives had opposed the Pullman boycott), was unfavorably regarded for its striking contrast to the *E. C. Knight* and *Pollock* cases: a clear demonstration, it was asserted, of judicial one-sidedness on behalf of the wealthy classes.[54]

Accompanying these attacks upon specific aspects of the new judicial supremacy was the emergence of a wave of constitutional radicalism. In a series of articles in the *American Law Review*, Sylvester Pennoyer, former Democratic-Populist governor of Oregon, characterized the system of judicial review as "usurpation" by "judicial oligarchy," first instigated by the " plausible sophistries" of John Marshall. Congress should impeach the majority justices in the tax case, he declared, teach the Court a well-deserved lesson, and thus restore the Constitution to its original purity.[55] Pennoyer was soon joined by Justice Walter Clark of the North Carolina Supreme Court, advocating constitutional amendments which would make elective, and for a term only, all federal judges.[56]

The expanding professional protest against judicial conservatism merged with the political crisis of 1896. As Populists and left-wing Democrats gained strength, the Supreme Court was soon lumped with Wall Street and President Grover Cleveland as objects of radical scorn. Illinois Governor John P. Altgeld, who had bitterly denounced Cleveland's intervention in the Pullman strike as "Government by Injunction" and the Supreme Court as "lackeys of capitalism," became perhaps the most powerful behind-the-scenes figure in the Democratic intraparty conflict.[57]

The Democratic insurgents who captured the Chicago convention and nominated William Jennings Bryan on a free-silver anti-Wall Street platform also took due notice of the judiciary. Three separate anticourt planks were included in the platform: one criticizing the income-tax decision and hinting that the Supreme Court might well be packed to secure a reversal, another characterizing government by injunction as a form of judicial "oppression," and a third opposing life tenure in the public service except as provided in the Constitution.[58] The effect of these planks on the following campaign was considerable; for with traditional symbols under challenge in both the constitutional and the monetary fields, the conservative defense became especially fierce and proved effective. In the legal profession, men of both parties worked actively against Bryan, isolating the advanced progressives.[59]

The campaign of 1896 turned out to be the last peak in the crisis of the 1890s. Shortly after the defeat of Bryan, the business cycle moved upward again, social tension lessened, and the public was soon absorbed in the Cuban situation. The trend of court decisions became, temporarily, more liberal,[60] and the forces of social protest were channeled into less sensitive areas. The conflict over the courts in the mid-1890s, however, had clearly foreshadowed the more decisive struggle of the 1930s, when a politically conservative Supreme Court in a time of crisis would again arouse a formidable progressive revolt against judicial supremacy.

Part Nine

Crime and Social Control in the Twentieth Century

The next two articles continue the exploration of history of American crime and punishment. David Rothman looks at national attitudes toward punishment, especially toward imprisonment, and how imprisonment has become the customary method of dealing with convicted criminals. The penitentiary is an American invention of the early nineteenth century; these vast, austere prisons with their strict regimes assumed a larger and larger role in the "science" of penology as the century progressed and as "correction" was increasingly looked upon as a branch of applied knowledge to be run by professionals. A further striking development of the same period was the rapid expansion of professionalization linked with an increase in discretionary power among those dealings with criminals. Discretion has always been a feature of criminal justice (consider, for example, the jury). But the influence of psychiatry, the notion of parole, and the use of the indeterminate sentence considerably increased the discretionary powers placed in the hands of professionals. In the last generation, "a new and persuasive critique" of our penal and related institutions has emerged; and Rothman touches on this movement as well.

Rothman's attention is directed to those in prison — the losers caught in the web of the legal system, convicted, and sentenced. Mark H. Haller discusses quite another side of modern criminal justice. Great areas of behavior are defined as criminal under the penal codes, but they survive and flourish nonetheless, either because enforcement lacks public support or because the "criminal" protects himself through corrupt manipulation of the criminal-justice system and political alliances. Many people grow rich off gambling and other "crimes," which thus provide an avenue of escape for young people otherwise doomed to a life in the slums. The members of the "criminal underworld . . . were not outsiders." They had a "secure place in this new social structure."

In a sense, organized crime was a business like any other; it filled a need. It offered commodities and services for sale that people wanted, but could not legally obtain — gambling, easy sex, and pornography. Because the commodities were illegal, the business was attended by certain risks and costs, and this was one reason for the complicated relationships between crime and legitimate law-enforcement organizations.

Crime and Social Control in the Twentieth Century

Organized crime was intimately connected with entertainment — sports, gambling, nightlife. Hence, it was a kind of bastard child of that feverish rebirth of moralism of the late nineteenth and early twentieth centuries, a movement that ended up labeling as "criminal" many of the leisure-time activities of ordinary Americans. It was a morality, in consequence, that was purchased at heavy cost. Part of that price was a weakened and corrupted system of criminal justice — a system that reformers had failed to understand and hence could not cope with. These problems are clearly still with us. The contemporary "crisis" in criminal justice is related both to the correctional failures described by Rothman and to the enforcement failures and reform misconceptions that Haller analyzes.

Further Reading

Eisenstein, James, and Herbert Jacob. *Felony Justice: An Organizational Analysis of Criminal Courts*. Boston: Little, Brown and Co. 1977.

Ianni, Francis A. J. *A Family Business: Kinship and Social Control in Organized Crime*. New York: Russell Sage Foundation, 1972.

Moley, Raymond. *Our Criminal Courts*. New York: Minton, Balch and Co., 1930.

Morse, Wayne L. and Ronald H. Beattie. *Survey of the Administration of Criminal Justice in Oregon*. Eugene: University of Oregon Press, 1932.

Richardson, James F. *Urban Police in the United States*. Port Washington, New York: Kennikat Press, 1974.

24

David J. Rothman

Behavior Modification in Total Institutions: An Historical Overview

Although the term "behavior modification" is of recent origin, first popularized by psychologists in the post-World War II period, the ideal of altering the conduct of persons labeled deviant has a long and important history. In early-nineteenth-century America, "regeneration" and "reform" were the key words; later, "rehabilitation" became the fashionable expression. But in every period, intervention in the name of behavior modification was regarded as a benevolent and proper exercise of authority. Nowhere has this judgment had greater impact or significance than in the field of incarceration. The genesis and perpetuation of total institutions for the deviant, be they state prisons or mental hospitals, cannot be understood apart from the allure of reform. This goal of character reformation not only shaped the internal routine and programs of institutions; more importantly, it played the crucial role in legitimating them. What we might be reluctant or unwilling to do in the name of retribution, deterrence, or incapacitation, we do eagerly and enthu-

siastically in the name of rehabilitation. This is no less true in our own day than it was one hundred and fifty years ago.

Promise to Cure

The concept of rehabilitation and the practice of incarceration are relatively modern developments, which first emerged in this country during the Jacksonian period, the 1820s, '30s, and '40s. In the eighteenth century, the criminal justice system had been one with far more circumscribed purposes: to deter and incapacitate the offender and to punish the sinner. The highly insular and static colonial communities sentenced the petty offender to the stocks, to shame him into conformity; or whipped or fined him, to make crime painful and costly; or banished him to force some other town to deal with his behavior. For the particularly heinous offender, the murderer or the recidivist who simply would not leave the community in peace, towns had regular recourse to the gallows. Mental illness, to the limited degree that it evoked official attention, was defined not as a treatable disease, but as a special problem in relief or public order. The impoverished insane who posed no threat to others were boarded with a local family at the taxpayer's expense; violent cases were con-

Reprinted from *Hastings Center Report*, vol. 5 no. 1 (February 1975), 17-24, by permission. Copyright, 1975, Institute of Society, Ethics and the Life Sciences, 360 Broadway, Hastings on Hudson, New York 10706.

David J. Rothman

fined to the basement of a jail or some other building. All these were essentially stopgap measures. They were intended to protect the citizenry and to minimize inconvenience, not to cure the deviant.

Beginning in the post-Revolutionary War period, American attitudes and programs changed dramatically. For the first time the goal of intervention became behavior modification — that is, reform of the criminal and the mentally ill. A heady patriotic enthusiasm encouraged citizens of the new republic to believe that no task, however grandiose, was beyond their ability to accomplish. This nation unlike corrupt, monarchial European ones, could abolish crime and insanity, thereby demonstrating the superiority of its political and social arrangements. Moreover, the Enlightment view of man as a plastic creature, shaped by his environment, replaced traditional Calvinist notions of innate depravity. Thus would-be reformers had all the more reason to believe that if only the right influences could be brought to bear, the deviant would be cured.

But these right influences, Americans in the Jacksonian period believed, were not to be found within the community. Their open and mobile society, where men could move westward to new lands or into the growing number of eastern cities, into new occupations or up and down the social ladder, was too chaotic and too corrupting to reclaim the deviant. Rather, for the purposes of reform, they had to create a specially designed environment, a quasi-utopian setting. In these microcosms of the perfect society, the criminal and the insane would acquire what they lacked, the vital habits of obedience, discipline, and good order. These ambitions eventually led to the establishment of the state penitentiary and the insane asylum, and coincidentally, the almshouse, orphan asylum, and reformatory. The "total" character of these institutions, their ability to completely structure the environment and to order the daily routine of the deviant, was to be the very guarantor of their success.

Under the influence of this ideology, the institutions took their shape. They were, first and foremost, places of order and discipline. Bell-ringing punctuality and set periods for working, eating, and sleeping characterized the schedules of both prisons and mental hospitals. The corruptions at loose in the community were not allowed to intrude into the institutions. All such establishments were located at a distance from population centers. All of them had massive walls, as much to keep people out as inmates in. All of them kept correspondence between insiders and outsiders to a minimum. In a similar spirit, the courts handed down lengthy sentences to offenders; the criminal needed long exposure to the regenerative influences of his new environment. So, too, legislatures established a minimum of procedural requirements for committing the insane. Why allow them to languish on a courtroom bench if they could be receiving effective treatment?

The prospect of reform shone so brightly that these institutions proliferated and became the pride of the republic. One cannot find any challenge during these decades to the wisdom of a policy of incarceration. The promise to cure made state intervention not merely acceptable but altogether noble.

Legitimation despite Failure

It is not difficult to sympathize with this initial enthusiasm for incarceration. Indeed, under the management of the first generation of medical superintendents and wardens, prisons and hospitals were places of good order. Every observer insisted that reform was actually taking place. And when one Ohio medical superintendent announced one-hundred-percent cures in his institution, his statement generated applause, not skepticism. But then beginning in the 1850s, more clearly in the 1870s, still more clearly in the 1890s, it became obvious that the institutions were not fulfilling the promises of their founders. Incarceration was not reforming the offender or curing the insane — rates of crime and insanity were not diminished by it. Worse yet, as numerous state and private investigators discovered, the institutions were typically overcrowded, filthy, corrupt, and brutal. Now one learned about wardens who exploited for their own profit the labor of convicts and of the prevalence of horrible punishments behind the walls. One reads these revelations today with a certain tension: after absorbing one hundred detailed pages of gruesome discipline, of inmates hanging by their thumbs for hours on end or stretched out on racks of medieval design, one wonders how state legislators will conclude their report. Will they pronounce incarceration an experiment gone bad and search for alternatives? Will they ring the bell on this venture and call for a new departure?

Invariably they did not. One state committee after another, one benevolent society after another, one professional organization after another recounted the abuses and denounced the barbarisms. Then they urged the construction of bigger and better institutions. More cells, more wards, more humane administrators, more skilled guards and attendants — these were their recommendations. The faults lay, they argued, not in the policy of incarceration but in its implementation. The concept was marvelous; it was practice that had to be improved. How did they arrive at this judgment, justify it, and explain it? Why did these men so doggedly defend the institutions? How was the legitimacy of incarceration preserved once the grim reality had become so apparent?

For some observers and commentators, the goal of reform was so noble that a program linked with such a goal, however tenuously, could not be abandoned. The rhetoric of rehabilitation was enough to justify the continued investment in incarceration. If they incessantly reminded the managers to strive to this end, perhaps then the institutions would measure up. For others the convenience of incarceration, its very functional qualities, legitimated the institutions' existence. After

all, by the late nineteenth century immigrants had begun to flood not only our shores, but our prison cells and hospital wards as well. These aliens were dangerous enough in their ghettos; when they flouted the law or went insane, incarceration seemed an appropriate solution. No matter how miserable institutional conditions were, they were decent enough for the Irish — and then, later, decent enough for the blacks.

Still other reformers believed it right and just to defend the idea of incarceration because of their own very special reading of history. Their view of the past trapped them into defending existing realities instead of inviting them to devise alternatives. As they saw it, in half-truth fashion, incarceration in the 1820s and 1830s had replaced a fundamentally cruel and barbaric system, one in which all criminals went to the gallows and all the insane were chained in jails. Hence these reformers feared that if incarceration were eliminated as a public policy, the nation would automatically and immediately revert to those loathsome practices. It was the dungeon and the gallows, or it was the institutions. Faced with such a choice, reformers believed it the better part of wisdom to work for the reform, not the abolition, of institutions. Finally, they suffered a failure of nerve and imagination; frightened of the future, they accommodated themselves to the present.

The legitimacy of incarceration in this period was further rationalized by the skillful way in which prison and asylum managers juggled incapacitation and rehabilitation. When challenged for not fulfilling the goals of reform, they justified procedures on the grounds of incapacitation. The institutions confined dangerous people, protecting society from the havoc they would cause. But when questioned on the propriety of confining those who were not especially dangerous, they shifted to rehabilitation. The institutions treated the deviant and released him when cured. It was a masterful tactic which kept critics off balance and prevented them from attacking the system itself. The weakness of a defense that joined together two such divergent goals, that claimed that institutions could simultaneously incapacitate and rehabilitate, went unnoticed.

Those in the best position to mount an attack upon incarceration — state officials and medical professionals — played a more supportive than antagonistic role. By the 1890s, most states had established boards of charities and correction to investigate institutional conditions; invariably the members of these boards were unwilling to question the legitimacy of the system. When particular abuses came to light, they preferred to sit down with the directors and managers and talk things over man to man, gentleman to gentleman. In training, outlook, and class the state board members and the asylum directors were alike; with good will assumed on both sides, particular difficulties could surely be overcome. There seemed to be no cause for launching a fundamental attack on the way a peer conducted his business, especially when the other option was to ally oneself with the dangerous immigrant classes.

A devastating critique of the failures of the mental hospitals might have come from the growing number of neurologists in the late nineteenth century. To be sure, neurologists did attack the medical superintendents for ignoring research, for not running better pathology laboratories, for not examining more carefully the somatic basis for mental disorders, but they had no quarrel with the idea of incarceration itself. Their advice on how to administer an institution differed little from the practices of the medical superintendents. All that the neurologists wanted was more laboratory space in the asylums, not a basic change in the daily routine.

Finally, the legitimacy of incarceration received additional support from the existence of "model" institutions. If nine hundred ninety-nine institutions failed to live up to standards but one did, then the nine hundred ninety-nine failures reflected faulty administration, not a flaw

in the system itself. The problem rested with a poorly trained staff or inadequate resources, not with the policy of incarceration. There was a Sodom-and-Gomorrah quality to this rationale — if ten good men could save a city from God's wrath then one good institution could salvage the entire network of institutions. In this period, New York's Elmira Reformatory served as the model. Its graded system of classification and its work and early release procedures seemed to high-minded observers to set the standards which other institutions should meet. Whatever message the nine hundred ninety-nine failures had to transmit about the inherent limitations of the system was drowned out in the chorus of admiration for the one good prison — a mode of thought from which we are no more immune than our predecessors. The result was to confirm the idea of building bigger and better institutions, not to raise doubts about the wisdom of a policy of confinement.

The Impact of Psychiatric Thought

About 1900 a third stage emerged in the complex relationship between the ideal of behavior modification and the history of total institutions, a stage that has persisted almost to the present. The most distinguishing characteristic of this period was the crucial influence of psychiatric thought in both mental health and criminal justice. These years witnessed the general triumph of the "medical model."

These new doctrines evoked an optimism reminiscent of the Jacksonian era. Psychiatrists and their social-worker allies promised to reduce substantially, if not to eliminate altogether, the problem of deviancy. They would uncover the psychodynamics of the deviant personality and explore the psychological processes that made persons mentally ill or criminal. Then, in therapeutic encounters, the doctor would review and explain these dynamics to the patient, assisting him to adjust successfully to his environment.

The encounter itself, not an institutional routine, would be the instrument of rehabilitation. Accordingly, the new theories looked to the community and away from incarceration as the treatment center of first resort.

But at the same time the psychological doctrines encouraged a massive expansion of the mental health and criminal justice systems and, in doing so, extended the power and reach of doctors, wardens, superintendents, and judges. Even more troubling than this expansion was the creation of a new category of deviancy. Implicit in the pledge to cure some of the deviants was the definition of another class of persons who were beyond assistance, persons who, because of their inherited physical deficiencies or the gross character of their malady, were unable to respond to a therapeutic encounter. For them extended confinement, perhaps even life-long confinement, was the only alternative. Thus, as psychiatrists encouraged opening the door of the asylum partway for some, they simultaneously helped to close it more firmly behind others. The promise to rehabilitate did move society away from a total reliance upon incarceration, but by the same definition, it legitimated its prolonged use.

The prospect of a cure through a therapeutic encounter helped to create the first alternatives to confinement. Probation was one by-product. Some criminals did not need to enter a prison; rather, the probation officer-social worker would be able to rehabilitate the deviant within the community. Parole was another. Convicted offenders could be released from prison to the supervision of a parole officer-social worker; in weekly meetings they would explore and eliminate the psychological roots of disturbed behavior. Concomitantly, the first outpatient mental-health clinics sprang up. Instead of committing the mentally ill to an asylum, psychiatrists would treat them within the community. Psychopathic hospitals, dedicated to short-term and intensive programs, were created during these years. A brief period of confinement would be followed by a longer period of treatment after the patient returned home.

Expansion of Discretion

Yet rationales and practices that initially promised to be less intrusive and less onerous nevertheless served to encourage an extension of state authority. The impact of the new ideology was to expand intervention, not to restrict it.

The medical model stimulated and legitimated a vast increase in discretionary decision making. "Treat the criminal, not the crime," became the slogan; the system was to concern itself not with the "act" of the offender but with his "state of mind." Hence, the interventions that were appropriate for one type of offender were not necessarily appropriate for another — and officials had to have the leeway to decide among them. Under the impact of this doctrine, the indeterminate sentence flourished, expanding the prerogatives of judges and parole boards. Instead of legislatures continuing to set fixed terms for an offender — three or four years for a burglar, for example — they now established widely divergent minimum and maximum terms — two years to eight — and left it to the judge to make his choice. The judge exercised his discretion: in one case, he could settle on a sentence of two to four years; in another identical one, he could choose a term of three to eight. Then, in turn, he passed on to a parole board the discretion to select the moment for final release. It could discharge the inmate at the minimum term set, or midway through his sentence, or at the expiration of the maximum. Thus in the name of treating the criminal not the crime the justice system became unpredictable and ultimately arbitrary. And whatever inequities occurred were interpreted as a necessary and proper by-product of individualized treatment.

An enlarged definition of the type of information considered necessary for

David J. Rothman

decision making also took hold during this period. If the system was to treat the criminal, to decide who should go on probation and who should make parole, then officials had to know the most intimate details of the offender's life. To this end, psychiatrists and social workers compiled pre-sentence reports and parole dossiers, including data on the offender's family life, his relationship to his parents, how he got on with his wife and friends, the level of his occupational and educational training, his work history, his social attitudes, his feelings, and his IQ score. His fate now hinged, not on what he had done, but upon his motivation, his attitudes, and his psychological state. There was nothing private left to the individual; the system had a right and a need to know everything. This probing without limits was not seen as an intrusion into privacy or violation of personal rights. Since the goal was rehabilitation, the means were legitimate. Just as the doctor was entitled to compile a social history in order to diagnose and cure the sick, so the psychiatrist was entitled to compile a social history in order to diagnose and cure the deviant.

Moreover, it was the psychiatrists' definition of time that ruled in criminal justice and mental health: not the particular and exact measurement of time — seconds as well as minutes and hours — which now marked both work and play in industrializing America; not even "medical time." For surgeons, after all, think of intervention in terms of minutes. The good surgeon is the quick surgeon, one who will boast of being in and out in twenty minutes. But psychiatrists work to a different clock. Psychiatrists will matter-of-factly admit that it took a year and a half to overcome a patient's resistance to therapy. A four-year therapeutic encounter is considered average; weeks of bad sessions must be expected; even years of bad sessions must be tolerated. After all, psychiatrists accept a theoretical construction that is very fluid about time. The patient is ill precisely because he is still

reacting to events buried deep in his past; that trauma at age three is still with him at age forty — it is as if time had not passed. Thus, they are often reluctant to predict how long therapy will take, indeed to say how long therapy should take. And this concept of time, imported into determinations of sentence length and commitment terms, helped to expand the period for which intervention was permissible. If indeterminate sentences proved to be longer than fixed ones, if commitments in state hospitals were for five or ten years, the rehabilitative process demanded it. Once again, psychiatric doctrines worked to break down, not to build up, clear and defined limits.

The rehabilitative ethic also expanded the reach of the criminal justice and mental-health systems, bringing new sectors of the population under supervision and treatment. Programs designed in the first instance as alternatives to incarceration quickly developed into supplements to incarceration. It appears, for example, that probation did not reduce the number of offenders confined to state prisons. Rather, it gave judges the opportunity to place under supervision a class of persons who otherwise would have received suspended sentences or release under their own recognizance. So, too, the first outpatient mental-health clinics seem not to have reduced hospital populations. Instead, they serviced members of the community who heretofore had not received treatment. It may well be that these persons profited from the intervention, that probation and community clinics provided useful supporting services. But the point remains that these innovations probably did more to enlarge the network of clients than to provide practical alternatives to total institutions.

Incarceration further Legitimated

In a curious way, the new programs actually enhanced the legitimacy of state prisons and mental hospitals. The process worked in two ways. First the existence of new programs encouraged the public to believe that those behind the walls undoubtedly belonged there. If the offender was tractable, he would be freed on probation; if he had learned his lessons, he would be released on parole. If the mentally ill were manageable, they would be in outpatient clinics, or, at worst, in psychopathic hospitals. Therefore, anyone still found inside a prison or state mental hospital was simply too dangerous or too bizarre to stay in the community. Second, the institutions could now present themselves as testing grounds for social adjustment. Once the prisoner behaved well inside, he could be trusted to behave well outside; once the patient functioned adequately within the hospital, he would function adequately outside it. Both perspectives gave powerful support to a policy of incarceration. The institutions had accepted the challenge that the community refused. They held the hard-core deviant until he was cured.

It was not a long step from this conclusion to a compelling justification for life-long commitment. And this step was taken in the first decades of the twentieth century. Between 1900 and 1920, institutions for the permanent confinement of the mentally retarded proliferated. In 1890 there were fourteen institutions for the retarded in this country; by 1910 there were twenty-six, and by 1923, forty. In the 1920s and 1930s, numerous states passed their first habitual-offender laws, providing life sentences for third-time felons. Simultaneously they created the first institutions to confine indefinitely the defective delinquent, that class of persons with low IQs and high recidivism, and sexual psychopaths, that catch-all term for the dangerous and the disturbed.

In part, these developments reflected the new popularity of eugenic theories. Americans were panicked at the prospect of defectives multiplying themselves and passing on their incapacities until their numbers eventually overran the community. The Jukeses and Kallikaks were nightmare families whose threat to the social order had to be eliminated at all cost. In part, these developments reflected an acute concern about crime waves. Crime seemed to be increasing so rapidly that life in the nation's cities would soon become intolerable unless some drastic measures were adopted. But probably more basic to an understanding of these changes was the fear that the new release procedures would allow the hard-core deviant, the retarded, the professional criminal, and the sexual psychopath to return easily and quickly to the community. Just when probation, parole, and out-patient clinics were being established, the state also created institutions for long-term commitment, in effect providing for preventive detention.

Psychiatric theories and the psychiatrists themselves played a crucial role in making this procedure appear legitimate, indeed constitutionally acceptable. Practically every institution for the retarded and for the defective delinquent was headed by a psychiatrist. The simple logic of the situation made this an odd choice. By definition, the retarded and the defective delinquent were beyond psychiatric assistance. Typically the institutions that held them were farms on which they carried out menial agricultural chores. A skilled administrator, a competent businessman, or a farmer would have been a more sensible choice than a psychiatrist to superintend such places. Why, then, this choice of a psychiatrist?

To a degree, the decision may reflect our society's predilection for giving over the care of the "dying" to a doctor. The medical profession does assume responsibility for those suffering from chronic illness; hence, by extension, they should have responsibility for the chronic deviant. Furthermore, the rationale for preventive detention rested on the deviant's state of mind, not on any particular acts he might have committed. Therefore, it seemed appropriate to let

David J. Rothman

the expert in states of mind head up the institutions. Moreover, the vast discretion allowed by the law in selecting persons for this type of incarceration might have been challenged as arbitrary and capricious unless it was exercised by someone with impeccable and impressive credentials. Finally, the choice of a psychiatrist helped to dress preventive detention in the garb of rehabilitation. If the retarded or defective delinquent could possibly be reformed, then the psychiatrist would do it; and if he could not treat them, then confinement was an appropriate policy. In other words, the link between incarceration and rehabilitation was unbreakable. When forced to justify extended commitments, officials could raise the prospect of cure. When confronted with the fact that the institutions were not treatment centers, that the staff of professionals was pitifully small, and that rehabilitation programs were practically nonexistent, then they could vividly describe just how dangerous their inmate population was. As we shall soon see, this equivocation is no less prevalent today — and frequently the public role of the psychiatrist is not altogether different either.

A New Critique

Since the mid-1960s, a new and persuasive critique of total institutions has emerged. Rationales that once buttressed the practice of incarceration now seem flimsy. As faith in the ability of total institutions to rehabilitate the deviant had declined, so has support for incarceration. For the first time, reformers are not focusing their attack on the inadequacies of one particular institution or the failing of one group of administrators but on the very idea of confinement. Unlike their predecessors, who invariably responded to scandals by calling for bigger and better prisons and asylums, and greater state intervention, critics today are blaming the system, not its wardens or superintendents. Since the arrangements that are ostensibly susceptible to

improvement within incarceration are well-nigh endless, from the administrative hierarchy to the quality of the staff, to the nature of the daily programs, the ability to transcend this particular angle of vision and achieve a more generalized analysis is genuinely impressive.

Part of the credit for this breakthrough belongs to such theorists as Erving Goffman. His study, *Asylums*, argues compellingly that the inherent characteristics of total institutions make impossible the achievement of rehabilitative goals. A series of sociological studies has also been important in demonstrating the failure of existing penal programs. These findings have influenced a wide and diverse group of observers. The contemporary dissatisfaction with incarceration does not follow political lines. It includes conservative as well as liberal members of government commissions, left-wing writers and former wardens, psychiatric superintendents and federal judges.

And yet for all the novelty and popularity of this perspective, for all the unanimity in calling for a moratorium on the construction of new institutions and for a reduction in the number of inmates and patients, there is little cause to believe that our long and grim history of incarceration is nearing the end, that state intervention will decline. The anti-institutional program is vulnerable in several important respects.

First, it is a faint trumpet that now calls us to reform. The attack upon incarceration is generally a negative one, a dissatisfication with current arrangements, without any promise that alternatives will promote massive cure. Unlike the first promoters of asylums, the new breed of reformers does not claim to be able to rid the streets of crime or the community of mental illness. Their aims are more modest: to reduce the harm done by intervention, to lower the costs of care, to make treatment less cruel and inhumane. Their goals are sensible and decent, but not dramatic or glamorous.

Further, the first attempts to bring the incarcerated back into the community have not been without drawbacks of their own. Although the experiment is only a few years old, there is mounting evidence of a backlash. To date reformers have been more concerned with emptying the institutions than with thinking through the modes of community care and treatment. Activist lawyers won the major legal battles which helped reduce institutional populations — it was not, however, within their skill or province to design alternatives. In addition, many observers are so shocked at the inadequacy of institutional conditions that they feel compelled to press for immediate reduction in the numbers of the incarcerated and to leave for later the problem of alternatives. (In the words of one crusading psychiatrist, when you have Buchenwald, you don't worry first about alternatives to Buchenwald.) But the effect of these approaches, particularly in the field of mental health, has been to force ex-patients into settings almost as bad as, and in some cases perhaps worse than, the institutions they have left. And tolerance for the deviant, no matter how harmless he may be, is very limited; communities simply will not, in their own terms, gamble with safety. Hence, before nonincarcerative programs are able to learn from their own mistakes, they may be put out of business.

A still more significant development, whose thrust is much more pro-institutional and conducive to maximizing state intervention, is the burgeoning faith in the power of behavior-modification techniques to rehabilitate the deviant. Not everyone, it seems, is so pessimistic about the prospects for cure. Indeed, at a time when so many others are abandoning the goal of rehabilitation as an unrealistic and ultimately a mischievous one upon which to base public policy, those who claim to have answers, those who present themselves as problem solvers, receive a very attentive and enthusiastic audience.

The optimism comes from several quarters, and the term "behavior modification" does not fit easily over all of them. Some psychiatrists insist that the environment of a total institution or the compulsory character of treatment within it need not weaken efforts at rehabilitation. They insist that group-therapy sessions with inmates, whether conducted by more orthodox psychiatrists or encounter-group leaders, can work well; they argue that if psychiatrists hold the key to release from confinement, if the inmate must reckon with the fact that either he cooperates with his doctor or remains inside, then progress is all the more likely. (Many of the staff at Patuxent, Maryland's institution for defective delinquents, subscribe to this position.) Still other psychiatrists find this to be an appropriate time for wide-open experimentation with all kinds of therapeutic techniques, proven or unproven, traditional or novel. Perhaps effective treatment will emerge from the work of drama therapists, or Synanon-type models, or human-resources-development-type models, or in heart-to-heart discussions between cons and ex-cons. (The plans for the new federal treatment center at Butner, North Carolina, illustrate this approach.) And finally, there are the behavior modifiers in the strict sense of the term, the most aggressive and optimistic of the lot, those persuaded that operant conditioning holds the key to effective cure. Convinced that they can curb the eating habits of the overweight and eliminate the cigarette habit of the chain smoker, they stand ready to apply their skills to the deviant.

To date most of their efforts have been applied to the hard-core deviant, the institutional dregs, the toughest cases. In Connecticut's prison at Somers, behavior modifiers have used their techniques on pedophiles, the child molesters who so shock the community conscience that they typically remain incarcerated for decades. In *Clockwork Orange* fashion, the behavior modifiers attach electrodes to the inmate's skin, flash on the screen pictures of nubile and naked boys and girls, and then simultaneously apply electric shock. They have also intervened with the most troublesome inmates in the federal-prison system. At the Springfield, Missouri, treatment center, the behavior modifiers took inmates with long records as troublemakers in other federal prisons, those who had spent months in solitary and disciplinary cells, and placed them in the START program. Through a careful meting out of rewards and punishments, they promised to turn them into obedient inmates and, ostensibly, obedient citizens.

Because they have worked with the hard core, the behavior modifiers can argue more or less in good conscience that, however unpleasant their techniques, the inmates otherwise confront an even worse fate. You may not like shock conditioning, but remember that the alternative is to keep pedophiles locked up forever; the START program may be rough, but surely it is no worse than months in solitary. They further argue that nothing else works with this segment of the deviant population. Just as doctors will use experimental drugs on terminally ill patients, so, too, behavior modifiers should be allowed to use their techniques on the chronic deviant. We have nothing to lose, they tell us, and much to gain through their efforts.

Another Turn for Rehabilitation?

One ought not for a moment to minimize the power of this appeal. Since the alternatives to this type of intervention are so unsatisfactory, many officials, administrators, and judges are prepared to let them have their turn. To be sure, the START program was canceled by the Federal Bureau of Prisons just as it was about to lose a court challenge on the constitutionality of its procedures, and at least for the time being, the bureau has prohibited further behavior-modification programs. But there is little cause for complacency. Any program that can link itself to the ethic of rehabilitation still stands a good chance of implementation.

One need look no further than recent, and enlightened, federal court decisions

in the area of incarceration to confirm this view. Federal courts have intervened in the conduct of state mental hospitals, and helped to empty their wards, precisely because judges found that treatment was not being conducted. But the "right to treatment" doctrine is a two-edged sword. If the ratio of staff to patients is high, if the rhetoric is one of rehabilitation, if there are "treatment plans" for the patient, then the institution will receive the courts' blessings, even if patients are not actually being cured. The institution at Patuxent, for example, has won numerous legal contests because the judges were impressed with the good intentions of its administrators and the number of professionals on its payroll.

Moreover, while the federal courts have struck down as unconstitutional many prison practices, from prohibitions on letter writing to barbaric solitary cells, they have often done so because they could find no rehabilitative purposes to the measures. But these decisions leave the door wide open to procedures that can enter under the guise of rehabilitation. "A prison regulation," declared one recent court decision, "restricting freedom of expression would be justifiable if its purpose was to rehabilitate prisoners." Announced another: courts will keep their "hands off" prison administration as soon as officials attempt to rehabilitate inmates. When Texas prison officials defended their solitary cells as places of treatment, a federal court allowed them to continue: "Our role as judges," it stated, "is not to determine which of these treatments is more rehabilitative than another." In short, the ideal of rehabilitation remains so attractive and appealing, that one cannot be too cautious about any procedure that attempts to come under its umbrella.

We are not the first generation to confront the mischief that can be perpetuated in the name of rehabilitation. The historical record of behavior modification and total institutions does alert us to many potential danger points. First, as behavior modifiers attempt to win acceptance for their programs, and attempt they surely will, we should be especially sensitive to the perils implicit in the assumption that, since the existing system is so rotten, any alternative should be given a try. Such a perspective places the burden of proof, not on the innovator, where it properly belongs, but on the critic. An attitude of "if not me, the gallows" can end up creating worse nightmares than those we now live with. So, too, a willingness to accept the promise to do good as the equivalent of the ability to do good is certain to legitimate a network of intervention schemes which would otherwise be suspect.

Second, we must insist on distinguishing between such diverse and mutually antagonistic goals as custody and rehabilitation. We cannot permit administrators to slip so conveniently from one rationale to another. If we choose to hold some persons in custody, let us call it that and decide whether we as a society are willing to pay such a price in civil liberties for the sake of our safety. But we cannot debate preventive detention if it calls itself rehabilitation, and if we are incarcerating people for treatment purposes, then let us measure the effectiveness of treatment, not hide behind the claim that these people are dangerous.

Third, we must not let the credentials of an administrator substitute for performance. The presence of a doctor as head of an institution is no guarantee that treatment will occur and no guarantee that ethical standards will be adhered to. Fourth, we must be especially wary of "model" programs. There is not sufficient cause to assume that all such programs will be effective and decent simply because one charismatic personality manages to effect some good, or because

one institution is able to bring more benefit than harm to its inmates, or that a system constructed on its principles will function well. We must ask whether the model is exportable, whether other institutions will live up to the standard. We must concern ourselves with the unintended consequences of legitimating this mode of intervention.

Finally, we must be acutely aware of the issue of trade-offs. If behavior modifiers promise to release one class of inmates at the expense of keeping others in for extended periods of time, we must recognize the dilemma and make our choice in full cognizance of the implications. If Patuxent officials tell us that some persons, who at another institution would have been incarcerated for thirty years, leave their institution in only five, we must remember to ask about the others, those who might have been confined elsewhere for only five, and end up spending thirty at Patuxent. So, too, those committed to operant-conditioning techniques may come up with their own trade-offs. They may ally themselves with the anti-institutional position, promising to release in one year those we normally confine for five, and to release them cured. Here we must remember not only to query the promise of results, to insist upon scrutinizing research findings ourselves, but to calculate whether in all probability such techniques will spread the net of state intervention still wider without actually reducing institutional populations. The dismal experience of the first probation, parole, and outpatient procedures ought not to be repeated. A historical overview, unfortunately, does not provide any firm answers to the problems we face. But at least it can help us to ask the right questions.

25

Mark H. Haller

Urban Crime and Criminal Justice: The Chicago Case

The history of crime and criminal justice in American cities is a topic that has remained relatively unexplored by professional historians. Yet its importance is clear. Crime has had enduring ties with urban political factions, played a crucial part in the social life of ethnic groups struggling upward in the urban slums, been linked to labor and business activities, and made urban life dangerous. The police, the courts, and other criminal justice institutions have performed various functions. They have provided favors for political factions, been under pressure from some groups to eliminate pleasures enjoyed by other groups, and always had such meager resources that criminal justice has often involved regulation rather than abatement of criminal activity. Finally, campaigns of civic leaders for law and order are far from modern, and these campaigns have often revealed much about the values of reformers and the structure of urban society. An examination of the complex interrelations of

Reprinted from the *Journal of American History*, 57 (1970), 619-635, by permission. Copyright, 1970, Organization of American Historians.

crime, criminal justice, and reform in Chicago from 1900 to 1930 raises many of the important questions and problems that require historical exploration.

During the period, a variety of reformers conducted intensive and often dramatic campaigns to reform the criminal-justice system. To the extent that historians have examined such reform movements, they have tended to accept the reformers' views of the system's deficiencies. The reformers, however, lived largely outside the world of criminal justice, and often held values and expectations that were incompatible with the expectations of persons who were a part of the system. As a result, reformers often misunderstood both the system and the impact of their reforms.

Criminal justice involved a working relationship among three groups: officials, such as the police, prosecutors, judges, bailiffs, and probation officers; mediators between the legal system and criminals, such as bail bondsmen, criminal lawyers, fixers, and politicians; and finally, criminals, whose behavior was influenced by contact with enforcement officials. These groups, by frequent contact, developed diverse informal relationships and mutual obligations. In order to understand how the criminal-justice system actually functioned, it is as important to understand the criminal-justice subculture as to understand the characteristics of the formal system.

In Chicago, criminal activity and the criminal-justice system were rooted in the city's ethnic neighborhoods and were means of social mobility for persons of marginal social and economic position in society. (The ethnic political machines served the same purpose.) As a result, criminals, politicians, and enforcement officials often shared common experiences and values.

According to a 1930 study of 108 directors of the Chicago underworld, 30 percent were of Italian background, 29 percent were of Irish background, 20 percent were of Jewish background, and 12 percent were blacks; but "not a single leader was recorded as native white American of native born stock." A few groups virtually monopolized the upper levels of crime in Chicago.[1] Official positions within the criminal-justice system were also distributed largely among the same groups. As might be expected, 76 percent of the police captains were Irish. Judgeships were a reward for party service, and each party slated judges so that the various ethnic groups in the city would be represented. Judgeships often provided social mobility for lawyers whose training at unprestigious law schools or whose ethnic or religious background denied them admission to leading firms. Indeed, most of the positions within the system, elected or appointed, were rewards for party service. Politicians within the urban political machines looked upon the criminal-justice system as one of many means of maintaining the political organization.[2]

Most of the people processed by the criminal-justice system were the unorganized offenders: juvenile delinquents, drunkards, wife beaters, and amateur thieves. Other lawbreakers were part of the more organized underworld. The organized underworld, for purposes of analysis, can be seen to consist of three types: professional thieves, business or labor racketeers, and participants in organized crime.

Professional thieves included pickpockets, shoplifters, burglars, jewel thieves, confidence men, and other specialists. They had a loose subculture of their own. They met in hangouts, exchanged gossip and information, developed their own argot, and generally accepted a common system of values in terms of which they awarded prestige and governed behavior among themselves. The probable extent of professional crime in Chicago is illustrated by the fact that a city-council committee on crime in 1915 was able to locate one hundred criminal hangouts and three hundred "fences" in the city.[3]

Professional thieves often developed relatively stable relations within the criminal subculture and with other segments of society. Most such criminals worked with a mob. The mob often maintained continuing relations with a fence, in order to dispose of stolen goods, and also with a lawyer, fixer, or bail bondsman, for assistance in case of arrest. Professional thieves might also develop special relationships with policemen or politicians. The 1915 city-council committee, for example, had three of its investigators pose as pickpockets newly arrived in the city. The alleged pickpockets soon made contact with a city detective who explained the best place to practice their trade, put them in touch with a reliable fixer and fence, and then provided them with on-the-job police protection in return for 50 percent of the take. For nearly thirty years one of Chicago's best-known thieves, Eddie Jackson, was called the "Immune Pickpocket." In part, he earned his immunity through services to a political faction; on election day he was in charge of a band of voters who voted early and often.[4]

There are a number of accounts of the underworld of professional thieves, based mostly upon the reminiscences of individual thieves, but almost nothing is known about changes in the underworld of thieves. For example, what explains the fact that in 1929 most pickpockets in Chicago were of Jewish background, while most confidence men were Anglo-Saxon Protestants? And what changes have taken place in recruitment and operations of professional criminals since then? How, indeed, have changes in technology and consumer tastes affected the operation of thieves?[5]

Racketeering in business and in labor unions took several forms. One was control over a labor union for personal profit, either by misuse of the union treasury or by agreeing to negotiate "sweetheart" contracts. An even more fully developed cooperation between union racketeers and employers occurred when the union, by strikes or by violence, helped to maintain prices among firms or drive out competitors. Another form of racketeering consisted of using violence in order to persuade small businesses to purchase a particular product. In the late 1920s, for example, many taverns and similar establishments in the Chicago area were forced to accept slot machines.[6]

Little is known about racketeering in American labor unions and small business enterprises. But in Chicago, racketeering was endemic. George "Red" Barker, who by violence and threats took over thirty-three unions during the late 1920s, enjoyed local fame. By the early 1930s members of the Capone organization appeared to be involved in a systematic attempt to dominate vulnerable unions. Racketeering elements had also come into control of a variety of trade associations: barber shops, miniature-golf courses, kosher butchers, junk peddlers, and many others. The types of businesses that came under racketeering control often shared two characteristics. They were small, relatively marginal, and powerless; and they were highly competitive, so that racketeers performed an economic service by regulating prices and competition.[7]

Organized crime, the distribution and sale of illegal goods and services, such as gambling, prostitution, narcotics, and, in the 1920s, booze, was generally the most systematic aspect of underworld activity, with an on-going and pervasive impact upon criminal justice. The man engaged in organized crime was set apart from the professional thief because he had customers, not victims. The need to develop congenial, long-term relations with customers was itself a factor leading to systematic organization of the enterprise. The customers, in fact, were often co-conspirators in the violation of law. Indeed, the distribution and sale of alcoholic beverages in Chicago during prohibition resulted in widespread public recognition of the wealth and customer support that characterized the city's underworld.[8]

In many ways organized crime resembled a legitimate business. It often included a substantial capital investment, a regular payroll, and problems of manufacture, distribution, and retailing. For example, in various phases of gambling there were internal factors that led to coordination. Bookmaking required a wire service. From early in the twentieth century, Mont Tennes monopolized wire services. Using this as a basis — but also employing political connections and occasional violence — he gained control of most bookmaking in Chicago and extended his influence through much of the United States. Most forms of gambling also had economic aspects that contributed to consolidation. Since a small-time gambler lacked the capital to cover his losses on a bad day, the local bookmaker or policy man was part of a larger organization that handled financing and protection. According to one estimate made in the late 1920s, three hundred policy writers worked for a single wheel in Chicago's black ghetto, and there were more than six thousand policy writers in the ghetto.[9]

The need for protection also led to coordination of organized criminal activities. In the early years of the twentieth century, Chicago's red-light district achieved well-deserved fame, based on the high quality of its better houses and the wide variety of services available. Those classic aldermen from the First Ward, Michael "Hinky Dink" Kenna and "Bathhouse John" Coughlin, presided over political protection of vice in the ward. Saloons, gambling houses, and bordellos provided the funds that nurtured the aldermen's political organization and paid enthusiastic workers who supported the party's efforts on election day. In addition to arrangements with Hinky Dink and Bathhouse John, operators also made business arrangements with the local police. Protection not only exempted some enterprises from police interference but also became part of a process for eliminating competition. Those who were not part of the protection arrangement would be raided and harassed. The protection arrangement, in addition, involved agreements for regulating fraud and violence, both in order to give customers confidence in the product and to avoid open scandal that would embarrass law-enforcement agencies. Thus the stable and systematic relationships with politicians and police protected criminal activity and served the economic functions of regulating competition and fraud.

Throughout the period, underworld figures held important positions as civic leaders and political brokers. In addition to the relationships based on mutual interest and favors that linked the underworld to enforcement officials and politicians, there were friendships and ethnic loyalties that linked gangsters to segments of legitimate society. The members of ethnic groups who achieved success in business, politics, or the professions often had ties with gangsters stemming from youthful friendship and from mutual participation in ethnic social life. The successful criminal or racketeer was almost automatically at that time an important figure in urban ethnic communities.[10]

The many ties of the underworld and the upperworld were seldom displayed publicly. Occasionally a ceremonial event, such as a political banquet or a funeral, would bring together leaders from many walks of life. Indeed, the splendid funerals of gangsters at which judges and aldermen mingled with underworld figures shocked the decent citizens of Chicago. Gangsters also associated with other segments of society in the night life of the city, for the leaders of the underworld were both participants in and sponsors of the restaurants and clubs around which the night life revolved.[11]

The relations of the criminal underworld to other segments of the city's social structure were highly complex. Reformers, in attempting to alter the criminal-justice system, faced opposition partly because the public desired the services provided by the underworld, partly because of the ethnic and class loyalties that racketeers and criminals could sometimes summon to their defense, and partly because of the entrenched relationships of criminals with politicians and with the criminal-justice system. In contrast to those who staffed the institutions of criminal justice, reform leaders tended to be Protestant and native American in origin. Moreover, the reformers lived in upper-income areas dominated by native Americans: the Hyde Park and Woodlawn areas surrounding the University of Chicago, the Gold Coast along Lake Michigan, and the elite northern suburbs. Even the attorneys and law professors who were reformers had little in common with the lawyers who practiced criminal law; indeed, they often did not bother to conceal their contempt for the training and ethics of the lawyers who practiced regularly in the criminal courts.[12]

Reformers, then, approached criminal justice with values and life experiences that differed from those of city politicians and the men who staffed the system. The reformers most valued "efficiency" — the idea that the criminal-justice system should be uniform and impartial in the enforcement of law and the punishment of criminals. Reformers demanded increased vigor in law enforcement and the elimination of political favoritism and corruption from the criminal-justice system. They sought higher standards of competence for officials — from policemen to prison guards — and wanted criminal justice insulated from partisan politics.[13]

There were, however, differences within the ranks of reformers. One group — especially leading lawyers, businessmen, and newspaper editors — believed that the major function of criminal justice was to deter crime through punishment of criminals; and they worked to eliminate delays in justice, leniency, and "coddling." In general, they also believed that the police should concentrate chiefly upon crimes against property and persons: assault, rape, burglary, robbery, and larceny.[14] The other group — social settlement workers, professors, and some clergymen — wished in part to use the criminal-justice system for social-reform purposes. They hoped to rehabilitate the criminals brought within the system and eliminate vice and temptations from the urban environment. To provide a decent environment for children, they worked to close brothels, dance halls, taverns, and other traps for the unwary. To protect the income of a husband for his family, they struggled to drive out gambling and to curtail or eliminate the temptation to drink. The city, in short, was a cesspool of iniquity; but the criminal-justice system might reduce the sinful stench.[15]

The goals of criminal-justice reformers — efficiency, elimination of political corruption and favoritism, higher competence for political officials, creation of a more moral urban environment — were central to the values of the progressive movement of the early twentieth century and of "good government" movements generally. During the period before World War I, the group that sought to use the criminal-justice system in order to improve the urban neighborhood and rehabilitate youthful delinquents generally predominated; after the war, the dominant group wanted to make criminal justice more punitive and deterrent. In criminal-justice reform, then, as in so many reform movements, a generally humanitarian impulse in the period before the war took on a less humanitarian impulse in the period following the war.

In attempting to influence criminal justice, reformers were at a disadvantage, partly because they were only marginally related to the political factions that controlled the city and partly because they were seldom directly involved in the criminal-justice system. Yet reformers had a number of advantages that stemmed from their social prestige, relative wealth, and organizational skills. They controlled the press; their values were almost universally acknowledged as normative, and they had the resources to conduct investigations and work for specific reform goals.

An examination of three reform activities provides an opportunity to explore some of the patterns by which reformers influenced criminal behavior and criminal justice. The first was the establishment in Cook County of the earliest juvenile court in the United States. The court was the creation of reformers with a variety of backgrounds, including social settlement work, leadership in the prestigious Chicago Women's Club, and membership in the Chicago Bar Association. The founders of the juvenile court believed that criminal justice could serve the goals of reform and rehabilitation, and the reformers shaped the juvenile court to their own values and goals.[16]

The new court, established by the state legislature in 1899, was not intended to be a criminal court. There were no "prosecutors" or "defendants", and no one was formally found guilty of a crime. Instead, a boy under the age of seventeen or a girl under the age of eighteen could be brought into court if there was evidence of delinquency or neglect. If the court found the youth to be dependent or delinquent, it could then make him a ward of the state and put him on probation with his parents, place him with a guardian, or assign him to an appropriate institution. The important point about the court was the discretionary power that the judge was expected to exercise in the interests of the child.

After its establishment, the court's discretion was exercised under the guidance of the reformers. For a while, the juvenile court, with a detention center, was located across the street from Hull House.

When the legislature, in establishing the court, failed to appropriate funds for probation officers, the reformers established the Juvenile Court Committee which, through contributions from wealthy patrons, selected and paid the salaries of the early probation officers. When public authorities assumed financial responsibility for the court personnel in 1907, reformers continued their efforts to bar political influence from the selection of probation officers and insisted that the officers be persons with a demonstrated competence in social welfare. The reformers also helped to select the judge who was named each year to administer the juvenile court. In the early years two women from the Juvenile Court Committee often sat with the judge and helped shape decisions.[17]

Discretion in the interest of rehabilitation was the formal basis for the court's decisions. Many reformers believed, however, that such decisions could be made "scientifically." The probation officers were expected to have social-work training and to provide background information on each youth to guide the judge's decision. In 1909, in order to further scientific understanding of delinquency, reformers took the initiative in founding a Juvenile Psychopathic Institute. Under Dr. William Healy, the institute became a leading center for research into the causes of delinquency and made recommendations to the court concerning specific delinquents referred to the institute.[18]

The juvenile court was intended not only to rehabilitate delinquents but also to intervene to aid those youths being led astray by the temptations of city life. Under Illinois law, a juvenile might be declared delinquent if he "is growing up in idleness or crime; or knowingly frequents a house of ill-repute; . . . or frequents any saloon or dram shop where intoxicating liquors are sold; or patronizes or visits any public pool room or bucket shop; or wanders about the street in the nighttime without being on any lawful business . . . or uses vile, obscene,

vulgar, profane, or indecent language in any public place or about any schoolhouse". While the court generally dealt with more serious behavior by youths, the language of the law reflected the hopes and views of some reformers.[19]

Reformers, then, replaced the adversary model of the criminal court with a rehabilitative model, and the juvenile court lacked the procedural safeguards of the criminal courts. As a result, some scholars have argued that the founders of the juvenile court were insensitive to the civil liberties of the young. In fact, many of the founders were acutely aware that the adversary system often victimized the youths brought before the criminal courts. Prior to the establishment of the juvenile court, young offenders seldom had defense attorneys and thus went to trial undefended. When a delinquent did have a defense attorney, the attorney was often more interested in his fee than in the defense, so that the cost of the defense attorney was sometimes another way that the adversary system victimized the defendant. If civic reformers acted from an exaggerated faith in the possibilities of rehabilitation, they also acted from a genuinely realistic recognition of the failures of adversary justice for the young and poor.[20]

Like so many urban criminal-justice institutions, the juvenile court was soon overburdened. Probation officers handled far more cases than they could reasonably investigate or supervise, This made it difficult to maintain the rehabilitative standards that were supposed to govern the court. The number of youths found delinquent often depended more upon the availability of resources for processing them than upon the behavior of the youths themselves. Between 1913 and 1914 the number of delinquents referred to the court rose from 1,956 to 2,916, an increase of nearly 50 percent in the delinquency rate for Cook County. The reason for the increase was that twenty-three additional probation officers were hired in 1914, and the court could handle more cases.[21] Given the intentions of the court's founders and the realities of its operation, there are a number of questions that need exploration, including the impact of the juvenile court upon the definition of delinquency, upon the behavior of young persons, and upon the opportunities for a variety of professionals to study and influence youthful behavior in the streets of the city.

Reformers proved less successful in their efforts to influence the adult criminal-justice system. Their activities encountered resistance that stemmed from vested interests, different values, and the influence of the criminal underworld within urban politics. During the Progressive era, for example, Chicago's reformers began a systematic campaign to rid the city of its world-famous vice districts. In 1907 a group of businessmen representing the city's prestigious clubs formed a Joint Club Committee to combat the white-slave trade. Religious leaders, too, were active. In October 1909, evangelist Gipsy Smith led a protest parade of twelve-thousand law-abiding citizens through the red-light district. The next year, the Church Federation of Chicago asked the mayor to appoint a vice commission to investigate the problem. The vice commission, whose members included both leading reformers and politicians, made a careful report in 1911. It described in detail the vice conditions in Chicago and recommended an end to segregated districts. In that same year, a number of business and civic leaders formed the Committee of Fifteen to undertake a permanent campaign to eliminate commercialized vice. With a full-time executive secretary and investigative staff, the committee was the chief reform organization to fight vice and the white-slave trade in Chicago. [22]

The reformers' demands to end commercialized vice conflicted with the vested relationships of both the police and politicians. The demands also conflicted with the police conception about the proper methods of enforcing vice laws in the city. Chicago police, like all American police, were faced with more

violations of law than could be prosecuted. Discretion was built into daily police work.[23] Police in Chicago were often primarily concerned with maintaining order or, perhaps more accurately, the appearance of order. The police sought to eliminate the open violations of law that would bring complaints from local citizens or the scrutiny of reformers intent upon finding scandal. Law enforcement was more vigorous in relatively wealthy neighborhoods than in poorer neighborhoods. Such a policy represented the expectations of the local residents about the amount of violence or vice that was tolerable. This meant that in marginal neighborhoods, where organized criminals were powerful and other citizens exercised little effective opposition, vice could flourish without creating local scandal.[24]

Furthermore, the police appear to have been generally quite tolerant of vice, gambling, and liquor violations — to have adopted the view that such activities were part of human nature and could not be effectively suppressed by law enforcement. In 1912, when the city council held hearings to decide whether to continue the segregated districts, police chiefs from twenty cities testified that segregated districts were preferable to the scattering of vice that would inevitably result from a policy of suppression. Even more significant, perhaps, police officials issued orders in April 1910 in order to head off the campaign against the red-light districts. Although operating or frequenting a house of prostitution was illegal, Chicago police regulations prescribed that "no house of ill-fame shall be permitted outside of certain restricted districts, or to be established within two blocks of any school, church, hospital, or public institution, or upon any street car line". Children between the ages of three and eighteen — including messenger boys, — were not to be allowed in the district; no persons were to be held in a house of prostitution by force; and open soliciting was not to be permitted. Furthermore, "short skirts, transparent gowns or other improper attire shall not be permitted in the parlors, or public rooms," and "obscene exhibitions or pictures shall not be permitted."[25] In short, the police response to demands that laws against prostitution be enforced was to tighten informal regulation rather than enforcement.

During the antivice crusade, the mayor and the state's attorney, faced with reform pressure and periodic scandals, took action to obtain the semblance of effective police enforcement. Eventually the mayor created a special vice squad and removed the police chief and a police captain from their commands. Many officers, as a result of civil-service investigations, were dismissed from the force. Although the campaign suffered many setbacks, one by one the famous houses closed their doors, and vice either went underground in Chicago or moved to working-class suburbs. By the end of 1914 the Committee of Fifteen declared with some satisfaction, "it is admitted by all who are in a position to know the facts that the old vice district of the south side is practically closed."[26]

Reformers could disperse the segregated vice district because organized criminal activity was vulnerable to certain types of pressure. The continued threat of raids or liquor-license revocations discouraged customers and generally made the business unprofitable. The Committee of Fifteen was able to harass the vice operations because, in 1916, the state passed an injunction and abatement law. Under the law, private individuals could go to court and, if they proved that a building was being used for immoral purposes, obtain a court order closing the building completely for a year. The committee's investigators no longer needed to rely upon the police to make arrests under the criminal law. They could circumvent the criminal process altogether and effectively strike at the profitability of organized prostitution.[27]

While reformers successfully rearranged the patterns of vice in the city, they did not substantially alter relationships among police, politicians, and criminals. In 1915, William "Big Bill" Thompson became mayor of Chicago. He gradually removed the honest police from positions of responsibility. Investigators for the Committee of Fifteen soon found the police uncooperative. Thompson inaugurated an era of almost unprecedented cooperation between politicians and criminals — a cooperation that grew rapidly with the coming of prohibition. Nor did the reformers succeed in jailing the vice lords. A few went out of business. But many moved their operations to the suburbs or, in the 1920s, became successful bootleggers.[28] Reformers were too peripheral to change the vested relations of criminals with police and politicians.

A final illustration of reform activity is provided by the Chicago Crime Commission. The commission, established by the Chicago Association of Commerce in 1919 after a particularly flagrant payroll robbery, acted as a watchdog for the business community. The commission's operating director, Henry B. Chamberlin, a former newspaperman, attorney, and civic reformer, took steps to develop personal contacts with key officials such as the police chief, state's attorney, and various judges in the municipal and criminal courts. He also placed observers in the courts to keep notes on all felony trials in the county. The orientation of the commission was punitive, and its major goal was to make "justice" more certain, swift, and severe.[29]

The Chicago Crime Commission undertook numerous campaigns to reform criminal justice. By the later 1920s it had decided that the major area of corruption and laxity in the criminal courts was the system of plea bargaining by which criminals received reduced sentences or were found guilty of a lesser offense than the original charge. The bargaining system was rooted in the impossible trial load placed upon the criminal courts. In Cook County it was necessary not only that most felony cases be dismissed before indictment but also that most indicted cases be settled by means other than trial.

Mark H. Haller

In 1926 there were 13,117 felony arrests. Fully 70 percent of the cases were dismissed at preliminary or grand-jury hearings. Only .94 percent of the defendants were found guilty of the original charge after trial; another 2.6 percent pleaded guilty to the original charge; and 11 percent were found guilty of a lesser charge, generally by a plea of guilty.[30] Criminal trials played only a minor part in the disposition of criminal cases. Criminal-court dispositions resulted from a system of bargaining in which the defendant (or his lawyer) attempted to secure a lesser charge or an agreement to a moderate sentence in return for a plea of guilty. Because the court and state's attorney lacked resources to try cases and the defendant generally believed he received a better break by bargaining than he might by trial, the system of plea bargaining was strongly entrenched within the criminal-justice system.

The commission's strategy was based upon a misperception. Although plea bargaining was rooted in institutional necessities, the commission assumed that the system stemmed from the corruption or inefficiency of individual judges. During the first three months of 1928, therefore, the commission's observers in the criminal courts kept a record of felony waivers granted by each of the seven judges. Three judges were found to have waived the felony count in 364 cases, and the other four judges waived the felony count in 205 cases. The three judges not only granted felony waivers with the greatest liberality but also seemed to represent the alliance between the courts and politics that civic leaders deplored. Judge Emmanuel Eller, a Republican and a leader of what was believed to be one of the most corrupt political rings in the city, allegedly held court on the sidewalk outside a polling place in order to release election officials arrested by the police for violations of election laws.[31]

In late April 1928, Frank J. Loesch, president of the Chicago Crime Commission, demanded that the three judges be removed from the criminal courts. The judges requested a judicial investigation of the charges. As a result, a panel of six judges was established to hear evidence. Neither the impugned judges nor the commission defended the system of felony waivers and plea bargaining, although it was then, and remains today, a basic feature of criminal justice. Instead, the commission attempted to place the blame upon the judges, and the judges attempted to place the blame upon the state's attorney. After hearing evidence, the panel of judges brought in a report that placed responsibility for felony waivers upon the state's attorney. To no one's surprise, the judges were exonerated.[32]

During the next few years, as Loesch surveyed the courts, he periodically issued bitter charges, fatherly admonitions, and grudging praise. In the long run, however, his campaign exercised little influence upon the essentially discretionary and bargaining nature of the criminal-court process. The reformers continued to believe that the discretionary administration of justice resulted from corruption or laziness, and the judges never offered a reasoned justification for the system which departed so greatly from the way the courts were supposed to operate.[33]

There were a number of factors, then, that undermined the universalistic standards of the legal system and that explained the informal relations of criminals, politicians, and criminal-justice officials. One was the heterogeneity of the neighborhoods and life styles of the city. Gambling was widely accepted among some groups and within certain neighborhoods; violation of liquor laws before prohibition and violation of prohibition laws in the 1920s had wide support among some ethnic groups for whom drinking was part of a way of life; even prostitution in certain red-light districts became part of the standard entertainment and business activity of the area. Where such activities were accepted, the police were under little day-to-day pressure to enforce unpopular laws and, in fact, were under considerable pressure to develop informal relations that would maintain order rather than enforce the law. The criminal-justice system, as part of the larger political system, often operated to provide jobs, favors, and income for politicians and officials. Futhermore, the criminal-justice system was overburdened. Policemen, faced with more petty and serious crimes than could be handled by arrest, had to develop informal standards to guide their behavior. The court system, presented with more cases than could be tried, had to dispose of cases by rapid processing, dismissals, and bargaining. An informal system largely replaced the formal system. The combination of political and personal favoritism with informal discretion meant that criminal justice departed widely from the impartial, due-process model that was written into law and supported by civic reformers.

The weakness of civic reformers stemmed partly from the fact that their moral values were not shared by a number of their fellow citizens and their legal values were not shared by politicians and officials. But this should not be overemphasized. There was in Chicago a widespread concern with the impact of commercialized vice, saloons, crime, and official corruption. The major weakness of civic reformers was that they lived outside the intellectual and geographical communities they wished to reform, and they were not participants in the criminal-justice system they wished to change. While they often achieved satisfactory law enforcement in their own communities, they were generally unable to have their standards of enforcement accepted throughout the city. And, while they achieved success in the juvenile court system, they remained peripheral to the adult system and to the political factions that controlled it. Despite their wealth and prestige, they were outsiders to the subculture of politics, crime, and criminal justice.

The strength of the criminal underworld lay in the fact that its members were not outsiders. They could frequently maintain mutually satisfactory, if sometimes ambiguous, relations with enforcement officials. They were tied to politics by a shared belief that the system should operate on the basis of friendship and favors. They played a part in organized labor and in many aspects of business activity. Within the red-light district and in other parts of the city, they participated in a social life of saloons, hangouts, and gambling parlors. They had a secure place within the social structure of Chicago and other American cities at the turn of the century.

Part Ten

Race Relations and the Law

What character the federal Union would assume was the central political and constitutional question of the Republic's first half-century, but by the 1850s the problem of slavery was casting that question in new form. From that time on the problem of racial equality under the law was to be a dominant theme in the legal and constitutional evolution of the nation; for while the Civil War finally established the supremacy of the central government, it did not come close to ending racial disharmony. What remained to be determined was whether or not the nation would extend true equality before the law to its non-white citizens. Over time the courts, the legislatures, and the people had to face increasingly bitter and strident demands for extension of equal rights to minorities.

Using three distinct modes of analysis, the essays that follow explore important features of the legal history of race relations. The historian William Cohen, in his article on involuntary servitude of blacks in the South after 1865, examines southern state-court decisions and statutes to reveal the manifold forms that "servitude" took in the efforts by white society to keep blacks bound to forced labor. Although the subject has not been studied

previously with such precision, Cohen's technique is the classic methodology and his sources are the type of evidence that legal historians have traditionally used to define the boundaries and content of the legal system.

If the fate of thousands of dispossessed people in the courts, prisons, cities, and farms of the South is the stuff of black history, nonetheless the major thrust for legal change came from the distant and rarefied forum of the federal Supreme Court. William B. Hixson studies how one prominent lawyer played a central role in the dramas staged there in the nation's "struggle for equality." Through biography, Hixson probes the motivations, style, and accomplishments of Moorfield Storey, a man who exemplified how a creative lawyer can seek social change through law. A subsidiary, but important, theme in this essay is the work of the NAACP in the courts — a significant example of organized legal action financed and promoted by a voluntary association contending for the rights of a disadvantaged group.

The climax of the long struggle in the courts, exemplified by Storey's career, came in the case of *Brown v. Board of Education* in 1954. This great case was, of

Race Relations and the Law

course, a beginning as well as a culmination of an historic legal confrontation. The Warren Court followed it with decisions that reshaped constitutional law in race relations, giving new meaning to the phrase "equal protection of the laws" in the Fourteenth Amendment. These decisions also paved the way for the modern phase of the civil rights movement — and the "Black Power" movement as well. The political scientist S. Sidney Ulmer, in a case study of Earl Warren and the *Brown* decision, provides an illustration of how contemporary social science has contributed to the analysis of judicial behavior and judicial politics.

Further Reading

Abraham, Henry J. *Freedom and the Court: Civil Rights and Liberties in the United States.* 2d ed. New York: Oxford University Press, 1972.

———. *The Judicial Process.* 3d ed. New York: Oxford University Press, 1976. Includes fullest available bibliography on the Supreme Court and civil rights.

Daniel, Pete. *The Shadow of Slavery: Peonage in the South, 1901–1969.* New York: Oxford University Press, 1972.

Harris, Robert J. *The Quest for Equality.* Baton Rouge: Louisiana State University Press, 1960.

Kurland, Philip B. *Politics, the Constitution, and the Warren Court.* Chicago: University of Chicago Press, 1973.

Lyons, Thomas, with Harry N. Scheiber. *The Supreme Court and Individual Rights in Contemporary Society.* Menlo Park; Calif.: Addison Wesley, 1975.

Murphy, Paul L. *The Constitution in Crisis Times, 1918–1969.* New York: Harper & Row, 1972.

Meier, August, and Elliott Rudwick. *CORE: A Study in the Civil Rights Movement, 1942–1968.* New York: Oxford University Press, 1973.

Peltason, J. W. *Fifty-Eight Lonely Men: Southern Federal Judges and School Desegregation.* New York: Harcourt, Brace, 1961.

26

William Cohen

Negro Involuntary Servitude in the South, 1865-1940: A Preliminary Analysis

The Thirteenth Amendment formally ended slavery, but the legacy of bondage proved stubbornly persistent. Seventy-five years after emancipation black forced labor remained common in many areas of the South. While historians of the South have devoted much attention to the oppressive effects of sharecropping, tenantry, the crop-lien system, and peonage, few have addressed themselves to the larger system of involuntary servitude within which these factors operated. From a legal standpoint this system comprised a variety of state laws aimed at making it possible for both individuals and local governments to acquire and hold black labor virtually at will. Beyond this, involuntary servitude was a creature of custom dependent upon community attitudes which sanctioned the use of forced labor. Occasionally such attitudes even allowed whites to compel labor from Negroes without the pretense of a legal justification.[1]

Contained in embryo in the Black Codes and gaining increasing strength in the years immediately after Reconstruction, the system of involuntary servitude remained largely hidden until 1907, when the Department of Justice published Assistant Attorney General Charles W. Russell's "Report . . . Relative to Peonage Matters." The title is misleading. The central argument of this work was that peonage constituted only one dimension of a more comprehensive system of involuntary servitude having its roots in laws "considered to have been passed to force negro laborers to work." Peonage had a precise and narrow meaning. For this condition to exist an individual had to be held to labor against his will in order to satisfy a debt. According to Russell many southern statutes were being used to compel laborers to work against their will even without a claim of debt. In such cases the federal government was virtually powerless, for the Peonage Act of 1867 seemed to be the only tool that could be used to stop forced labor, and this law applied only in situations where a debt was alleged. Seeking to change this situation, Russell suggested: "It might even be well to abandon the use of the word 'peonage' and pass a law forbidding involuntary servitude." His plea went unheeded.[2]

Reprinted in slightly abridged form, from *The Journal of Southern History*, vol. 42, No. 1 (February 1976), 31-60. Copyright, 1976, by the Southern Historical Association, by permission of the Managing Editor and the author.

William Cohen

Whether focusing upon peonage or involuntary servitude, earlier studies assert or imply that latter-day bondage was widespread; however, large-scale Negro migration from one southern state to another and later from the South to the North indicates that the southern labor system did not immobilize the Negro labor force. This essay will seek to describe the system of involuntary servitude within a conceptual framework that accounts for this paradox. At the same time it will attempt to describe the nineteenth-century origins of the system.[3]

Far less rigid than slavery, the system of involuntary servitude that emerged after the Civil War was a fluid, flexible affair which alternated between free and forced labor in time to the rhythm of the southern labor market. Employers had the legal and social tools to compel labor from blacks, but the use of such measures was not obligatory. When labor was plentiful, Draconian powers were unneeded. When it was scarce, they were readily at hand. Thus whites had no reason to impede black mobility except when faced with a real or anticipated shortage of hands, and the system had something of a "now you see it, now you don't" quality about it. Still, compulsion was frequent enough. Even when unused, force posed an omnipresent threat which had a pervasive effect upon the tone of the southern labor system.

The laws of involuntary servitude facilitated both the recruitment and the retention of black labor. Enticement statutes established the proprietary claims of employers to "their" Negroes by making it a crime to hire away a laborer under contract to another man. Emigrant-agent laws assessed prohibitive license fees against those who made their living by moving labor from one state to another, and a variety of contract-enforcement statutes virtually legalized peonage. In some cases contract legislation went still further and made it a criminal offense to break a labor contract even when no debt was involved. Broadly drawn vagrancy statutes enabled police to round up idle blacks in times of labor scarcity and also gave employers a coercive tool that might be used to keep workers on the job. Those jailed on charges of vagrancy or any other petty crime were then vulnerable to the operations of the criminal-surety system, which gave the offender an "opportunity" to sign a voluntary labor contract with his former employer or some other white who agreed to post bond. Convict-labor laws began where the surety system ended, and those who had no surety often wound up on chain gangs, which in effect were a state-sponsored part of the system of involuntary servitude.[4]

These statutes need not have created the system of involuntary servitude. Vagrancy and convict-leasing acts existed in the North, and, taken at face value, many contract-enforcement laws simply aimed at penalizing fraud. What gave life to the system was the intent of the men who wrote its laws and the spirit in which these measures were enforced. Most of the laws discussed here made no mention of race, but Southerners knew that the laws were intended to maintain white control of the labor system, and local enforcement authorities implemented them with this in mind. Custom transcended statute; and, with the full assent of the white community, these acts served as a skeleton which was fleshed out with a host of extralegal and illegal practices designed to keep blacks hewing wood and drawing water.

Writing in September 1865, Henry William Ravenel voiced sentiments that would remain a common southern theme for generations when he said: "There must . . . be stringent laws to control the negroes, & require them to fulfill their contracts of labour on the farms."[5] Responding to such pleas, from 1865 to 1867 one southern legislature after another enacted Black Codes designed to preserve white hegemony. The story of these codes is well known, and this essay will consider only those portions which laid the groundwork for the system of involuntary servitude. The code provisions dealing with contract enforcement and vagrancy have often been described, but less attention has been paid to related statutes. Also enacted at this time were laws dealing with enticement and measures foreshadowing later legislation pertaining to emigrant agents, convict labor, and the criminal-surety system.[6]

Reconstruction voided most Black Code legislation, including many statutes dealing with enticement, contract enforcement, and vagrancy. Once the Redeemers took power, however, the former Confederate states began to resurrect the labor controls established from 1865 to 1867. In the years after Reconstruction there was a spate of new laws aimed at keeping blacks on the farm. Significantly, when court action invalidated some of these measures, the states often replaced them with others of similar ilk. A survey of the laws of involuntary servitude and of the ways in which they were applied will reveal both the nature of the system of involuntary servitude and its persistence into the twentieth century.

Enticement Laws

More than any other form of legislation, the enticement acts embodied the essence of the system of involuntary servitude. They re-created in modified form the proprietary relationship that had existed between master and slave. With precedents going back to fourteenth-century England, these laws had an extensive history in both criminal and civil law. Seventeenth-century Americans often viewed the enticement of a servant as a crime against society (that is, a violation of criminal law), but later generations took the matter less seriously and treated it as a civil wrong involving only private rights. By the mid-nineteenth century criminal prosecutions for enticing a servant had become virtually nonexistent, and civil cases were rare. Thus, it is highly significant that when the South resurrected the enticement laws after the Civil War almost every former Confederate state chose to make them criminal statutes.

Ten southern states enacted enticement laws from 1865 to 1867. They were the most common measures aimed at controlling the Negro labor force adopted in these years. Only Tennessee failed to pass such an act then, and it did so in 1875. Of the remaining states, Virginia alone failed to make enticement a *criminal* offense. Georgia made it a crime to entice a worker "by offering higher wages or in any other way whatever." Some states made it illegal to hire a contract breaker, and a few penalized those who harbored, detained, or fed such a person. Louisiana's law punished "any one who shall persuade or entice away, feed, harbor or secrete any person who leaves his or her employer."[7]

Frequently amended, the enticement statutes remained active law until World War II. Most of the changes occurred before 1910, but some came later. South Carolina and Mississippi brought the enticement of minors within the purview of their laws in 1913 and 1924, respectively. Alabama made attempted enticement a crime in 1920. Three years later Arkansas increased the maximum penalties for those convicted under her law, and in 1928 Mississippi weakened her statute by making it applicable only to willful violators. As was often the case, this change was the result of a restrictive court decision. North Carolina had four enticement laws. One of these was enacted in 1905 and applied only to tenants and croppers living in certain specified counties. Between 1920 and 1951 ten separate acts added fourteen more counties to the fourteen originally listed in this act.

Mississippi made extensive use of her enticement law, and in 1917 when the constitutionality of that act came before the state supreme court, Assistant Attorney General Frank Roberson noted that the statute had been before the high court on at least twenty previous occasions. He went on to argue that such a law was an absolute necessity "in an agricultural state where long time contracts are made and monies necessarily advanced in anticipation of the fulfillment of a contract." Then he added: "This is without reference to the fact that incidentally the larger part of the labor may be negroes." Whether Roberson meant to say that race was irrelevant to the issue, or subtly to imply the opposite, is not known. Whatever his intent, enticement cases in Mississippi and elsewhere almost always involved situations ᐧin which a white planter was seeking to entice a black laborer.[8]

Even in North Carolina, where whites generally outnumbered Negroes by a ratio of two to one, blacks figured in the great majority of enticement cases. When two black "orphans" ran away from a Sampson County planter in 1872 he published a notice saying: "I hereby forbid anyone employing them . . . or giving aid or comfort in any way to them upon penalties of law." In 1911 John Bridges, a Negro who lived in the vicinity of Wake Forest, entered into a contract with A. M. Harris, a white man. Bridges later quit as a result of a dispute over wages, and Harris proceeded to harass him from job to job by threatening to bring each new employer into court under charges of enticement. Finally, one employer, Jonathan C. Fort, refused to fire Bridges, and Harris brought suit against Fort. At the same time he arranged to have Bridges thrown in jail on unknown charges. Such practices still obtained on the eve of World War II, and in 1939 the *Caswell Messenger* of Yanceyville, North Carolina, carried the following advertisement: "NOTICE — I forbid any one to hire or harbor Herman Miles, colored, during the year 1939. A. P. Dabbs, Route I, Yanceyville."[9]

The laws of enticement can be distinguished from contract-enforcement legislation by their emphasis upon regulating the behavior of employers rather than laborers. Nevertheless, the line between these types of law was often hazy, and the two could sometimes be combined in a single act. The law invoked by Dabbs against Miles was probably a 1905 statute making it a crime for tenants and croppers in certain specified counties to abandon their crops without first repaying any advances made by their landlords. A further clause penalized anyone who knowingly employed a laborer who had violated this provision. In 1909 the North Carolina Supreme Court declared the law unconstitutional except where the indictment alleged that the tenant had entered into his contract with the intention of defrauding his landlord. Taken on its face the statute was completely unconstitutional, for, until it was amended in 1945, it contained no reference to fraud.

By bringing in the unmentioned matter of fraud, the court left just enough room for the statute to remain on the books, and this gave local magistrates an opportunity to use it without regard to its constitutionality. Responding to an inquiry from the editor of the Chapel Hill *Weekly*, a Yanceyville man familiar with the courts and county offices in the area asserted that notices like those placed by Dabbs were still being used to "put the fear of God into Negroes and ignorant white folks." He termed the law permitting this "archaic," but said that "many of our magistrates still hold it is good law and zealously support its use in upholding the contentions of landlords who resent any dissatisfaction on the part of tenants to whom they have advanced as much as 50 cents for rations on which to make a crop . . . As long as folks don't know the statute is unconstitutional it can be made to serve its intended purpose. The Caswell legislator who would try to take that law off the books would lose many votes."[10]

Emigrant-Agent Laws

White planters concerned about maintaining a stable work force saw enticement as a threat to their labor system, and they took the same view of the "emigrant agents" who made a living as interstate labor brokers. Here, too, their main concern was to regulate the behavior of whites. In ante-bellum days slave traders played a necessary role in the southern economy by arranging for the reallocation of labor from areas where it was superabundant to places where it was scarce. After emancipation emigrant agents served the same function. In so doing they fell heir to the social stigma that attached to their predecessors.

A useful though despised breed, the emigrant agents represented a menace to those who feared the loss of their workers. Thus, emigrant-agent laws came first in those states which felt themselves most threatened by Negro out-migration. Hard hit by black movement to the West, Georgia took the lead in 1876, when she levied an annual tax of one hundred dollars for each county in which a recruiter sought labor. A year later she raised the amount to five hundred dollars. All the southern states which acted to outlaw emigrant agents followed this pattern and attempted to levy prohibitively high license or occupation taxes. Roughly similar measures were soon adopted in Alabama (1879), North Carolina (1891), South Carolina (1891), Florida (1903), and Mississippi (1912).

The massive wave of black migration that began in 1916 and continued sporadically through the 1920s provoked more legislation. Tennessee (1917), Virginia (1924), and Texas (1929) joined the list of states having emigrant-agent laws, and Florida, Georgia, and Alabama drastically increased the severity of their statutes. License fees and penalties rose sharply. In addition, Georgia broadened the definition of an agent to include virtually anyone who sought to take labor out of the state. Agents were required to make daily reports and to post bond to cover any debts which might be owed by those being transported to out-of-state jobs. These provisions were mild compared with those of Alabama, which defined the term "emigrant agent" so broadly that it included assistants, messengers, and even the printer who ran off recruiting handbills. Each such person had to pay a five-thousand-dollars-per-county annual license fee, and each had to supply a recommendation signed by twenty "householders and freeholders" testifying to his good moral character and to the fact that he had been a state resident for at least six months.

The Great Depression rendered laws like this unnecessary, but prior to this time they were a powerful deterrent to the open solicitation of black labor. An occasional agent found it possible to pay the occupation tax and make a profit. For the most part, however, law and public opinion combined to drive them underground. Even before Mississippi legislated against the agents, her citizens made their disdain for recruiters abundantly clear. In 1908 the steamer *America* landed at a Natchez wharf and waited while agents sought to add more laborers to the number already on board. Mobilizing to fight this threat, local businessmen "organized the 'Bankers' and Merchants' Labor' Agency for the purpose of keeping the negroes at home." Meeting with a large group of blacks assembled at the pier, a committee of white citizens used methods which a southern reporter described as "so emphatic that the negroes concluded to abandon their idea of leaving." That same day fifteen local labor agents (two of whom were Negroes)were told to leave town.[11]

Official efforts to curb the recruiters often complemented informal actions like this. Sometimes the target might be a professional like R. A. "Pegleg" Williams of Atlanta, but more often than not the whites who ran afoul of the emigrant-agent laws were private employers like C. W. Lane, a West Virginia construction company official. Operating openly, Williams paid the Georgia license fee and transported thousands of blacks to the Southwest in the 1890s. Still, local authorities harassed him, and he invited prosecution by refusing to pay the license tax. Georgia officials gladly obliged, and he then fought the case all the way to the United States Supreme Court. In 1900 this body upheld the right of the states to license emigrant agents as they saw fit and denied Williams's argument that such licensing interfered with interstate commerce. Unlike Williams, Lane sought workers for his own use and not for a third party, but this did not stop the sheriff of Rowan County, North Carolina, from arresting him in 1905 for attempting to hire men to build a railroad in West Virginia. Lane won his release by paying the license tax and subsequently sued for the return of his money. The North Carolina

William Cohen

Supreme Court sustained his contention that he was not an agent within the meaning of the law. Typical of many, this case illustrates the frequent failure of local police to distinguish between the professionals and others who might also be recruiting black workers.[12] Even in states that regulated only the professionals, custom rendered suspect any solicitation of Negro laborers.

Inhibited by such laws and customs, whites needing labor often turned to Negro agents, subagents, and informal recruiters. These blacks knew where to find workers and could enter and leave Negro areas less conspicuously than whites. With some frequency, law-enforcement authorities arrested Negroes for recruiting without a license. Whether this reflected the degree to which whites actually used Negro surrogates as recruiters, or whether it mirrored differential treatment at the hands of sheriffs and police is not known.[13]

Implicit in the sanctions against emigrant agents as well as in the enticement acts was a widely held proprietary attitude toward blacks which had its roots in the property relations of slavery. If whites sometimes thought of themselves as the guardians of child-like Negroes, they more often responded to the presence of "enticers" or labor agents as though they thought their goods were about to be stolen.

Contract-Enforcement Laws

Unlike the emigrant-agent and enticement acts, which focused on white behavior, contract-enforcement statutes aimed directly at regulating blacks. As in other areas, the Black Codes set the tone for later legislation. In 1865 Mississippi required Negroes to enter into labor contracts by a specified day each January. South Carolina, Louisiana, Texas, and Arkansas required employers to grant discharge certificates to laborers who had legitimately left their service. A subsequent employer who hired a worker without a certificate would render himself liable to prosecution for enticement. Most Draconian of all,

Florida's contract law made "willful disobedience of orders," "wanton impudence," or the failure to perform assigned work crimes punishable in the same manner as vagrancy. At the discretion of the employer this penalty might be waived and the laborer remanded back to his custody.

This law continued into the 1890s, but the other statutes mentioned above disappeared during Reconstruction. Then, in the 1880s, they began to reemerge in more subdued forms. The most common successor was the "false pretenses" act, which made it a crime to take advances and then break a contract if one had entered the agreement with the intention of subsequently violating it. Enacted in Alabama (1885), North Carolina (1889, 1891), and Florida (1891), these early statutes spread a veneer of legitimacy over legal proceedings that were nothing less than criminal prosecutions for breach of contract. Refusing to go along with the ruse, the Alabama Supreme Court insisted that valid convictions could only be had when it was proved that an intent to defraud existed when the contract was made.

In 1903 Alabama plugged this loophole by adding a proviso making the unjustified refusal or failure to do the work called for in the contract or to refund any advances that had been made "prima facie evidence of the intent to injure or defraud his employer." North Carolina (1905) and Florida (1907) soon followed suit. In the wake of Alabama's early lead, four states which had no false-pretenses acts at all saw fit to adopt such laws, and each included a prima facie clause in its new legislation. These states were Georgia (1903), Mississippi (1906), Arkansas (1907), and South Carolina (1908). If there had been any doubt as to the intent of the first false-pretenses acts, the new measures made it clear that what concerned the legislatures was not fraud but breach of contract. Law-enforcement officers acted accordingly, and only rarely did the evidence suggest that those accused under these laws had intended to commit fraud.

In *Bailey* v. *Alabama* (1911) the United

States Supreme Court overturned the Alabama statute on the ground that it contravened the Federal Peonage Act of 1867 and the Thirteenth Amendment. The Court reasoned that, despite the law's apparent aim of penalizing fraud, the presumption of guilt contained in the prima facie clause created a condition of peonage. This alone would have justified the rejection of the law, but, in addition, the Court expressed concern that Alabama did not permit the defendent to give rebuttal testimony about his uncommunicated motives or intentions. As a result of the *Bailey* decision Arkansas and Mississippi belatedly removed the false-pretenses laws from their legal codes.[14]

Elsewhere the states sought to preserve such statutes. In 1911 Alabama passed a new measure which did not contain a prima facie clause. South Carolina followed suit a year later. North Carolina's high court held the clause invalid but sanctioned the rest óf the law. With appropriate caveats the unconstitutional clause repeatedly appeared in the state code until 1943. Ignoring the essence of the *Bailey* decision, Georgia's supreme court held that this case did not apply to its law since the state had no rule forbidding rebuttal testimony against prima facie evidence. In 1913 Florida enacted a new statute designed to meet some of the objections of the federal court, but in 1919, after this measure proved defective, she adopted yet another act complete with prima facie clause. Both the Georgia and Florida laws continued in use until the high court struck them down during World War II.[15]

As Table 26.1 shows, Georgia's law was the subject of a good deal of higher-court litigation prior to 1932.[16] The mere fact that so many contract cases came to these courts for adjudication suggests their wide use at the local level. Appeals were expensive and required support, and many cases must never have moved beyond the county courts. Contract cases came before Georgia's high courts more often than did vagrancy cases, and this too suggests the popularity of the false-pretenses act. It should be remembered, however, that

Table 26.1 Reported Cases from the Higher Courts of Georgia Involving Litigation Under The State Vagrancy and Labor-Contract Statutes

Period	Supreme Court Cases		Appellate Court Cases	
	Contract Cases	Vagrancy Cases	Contract Cases	Vagrancy Cases
1903-1911	23	10	39	7
1912-1921	1	—	41	4
1922-1931	—	—	17	7
1932-1942	2	—	4	1

there was far less dispute about the legal issues involved in vagrancy cases than in cases arising under the contract law. During the 1930s Georgia's higher courts heard fewer cases in both categories, and this partially reflects the impact of the Great Depression.

Paralleling the false-pretenses acts, still other statutes virtually made the breach of a labor contract per se a criminal offense rather than a civil offense. In the early twentieth century Alabama, Mississippi, and Louisiana had active measures to this effect, but they were soon nullified by action of the state supreme courts. Perhaps because their legislators knew that custom and other statutes rendered such acts superfluous these states took no action to replace their fallen laws.[17]

In 1869, with Radical Reconstruction at full tide, South Carolina adopted a contract law holding that a worker who failed to give the labor reasonably required of him or refused to abide by the conditions of his contract would "be liable to fine or imprisonment, according to the gravity of the offense." Quite unspecific regarding the punishment of laborers, this same act provided that landowners who defrauded their workers might be fined from fifty dollars to five hundred dollars. In 1889 these differential punishments provided the grounds for a court challenge. Even before the state supreme court rendered its decision the legislature hastened to correct the defect by providing equal penalties for both landlords and laborers. Eight years later a supplementary act promised imprisonment for from twenty to thirty days or a fine of from twenty-five to a hundred dollars for "any laborer working on shares of crop or for wages . . . who shall receive advances . . . and thereafter willfully and without just cause fail to perform the reasonable service required of him." Two 1904 amendments stiffened the penalties and provided that a conviction would not release the laborer from the duty of discharging his previous contractual obligation after he had been released from prison.[18]

In 1907 two courts declared this amended law (Section 357, South Carolina, *Criminal Code*, 1902) unconstitutional on the ground that it placed laborers in a condition of peonage. In overturning the measure, both the state supreme court and the federal district court said explicitly that it had been created to control Negro labor. Federal judge William Huggins Brawley summarized one of the arguments favoring the retention of the statute, saying that "the legislation complained of is a part of a system of local administration in matters of great concern to the industrial life of the state; . . . under our system of local self-government the power of the state in that sphere is supreme; and . . . the white people of the state, now charged with the responsibility of its government, being better acquainted with the negro, his capacities and limitations, can determine better than those outside of it what policy will best subserve his interest and their own."[19]

Himself a Confederate veteran and a proud scion of the slaveholding class, Brawley nonetheless contended, "The one sufficient answer to the argument is that the question of human liberty is not one of merely local concern. It rests upon the Constitution of the United States." Moreover, the courts had no higher duty than to construe liberally the provisions for personal security and liberty which were the foundations of free government. In a different vein, he also observed that South Carolina's efforts to promote foreign immigration would be to no avail "so long as our statute books hold legislation tending to create a system of forced labor, which in its

essentials is as degrading as that of slavery."[20]

Such sentiments notwithstanding, South Carolina was in no mood to abandon her system of involuntary servitude, and the complex and tortuous path of her contract legislation was the direct result of her attempt to maintain this system against court assaults. Four laws adopted between 1907 and 1918 testify to the state's determination. Together with a 1912 act and portions of the 1869 law this legislation remained on the books until at least 1962.

Vagrancy Laws

The contract system could work only if there was some way of forcing blacks to sign labor agreements in the first place. Vagrancy statutes provided just such a means, and all the former Confederate states except Tennessee and Arkansas passed new vagrancy laws in 1865 or 1866. Defining vagrancy in sweeping terms, these nine states gave local authorities a virtual mandate to arrest any poor man who did not have a labor contract. Significantly, all the new vagrancy laws except that of North Carolina provided for the hiring out of convicted offenders. Florida, Louisiana, Georgia, and South Carolina set maximum terms of up to one year. Alabama and Mississippi established penalties that combined fines and jail in such a manner as to mean at least a year's labor for anyone who could not pay his fine. Virginia and Texas provided milder punishments, and North Carolina set no limit to either the term in the workhouse or the size of the fine.

Between 1890 and 1910 there was a rash of racially motivated legislation, including the infamous Jim Crow laws as well as a host of acts relating to the southern labor system. Taken as a whole, these measures indicated southern determination to make the existing system of caste and involuntary servitude even more rigid than it had already become. As part of this pattern all the former Confederate states except Tennessee adopted new vagrancy laws between 1893 and 1909. These laws defined the crime of vagrancy in painstaking detail, and yet, paradoxically, they were even broader and vaguer than before. Alabama's 1866 statute began by stating that "any person who, having no visible means of support, or being dependent on his labor, lives without employment, or habitually neglects his employment . . ." The 1903 replacement read that "any person wandering or strolling about in idleness, who is able to work, and has no property to support him; or any person leading an idle, immoral, profligate life, having no property to support him . . ." This wording was identical with that of Georgia's 1866 law and was also adopted by Mississippi (1904) and North Carolina (1905). Georgia let her definition of vagrancy stand, but she did increase the range of penalties. From now on vagrancy would be punished "as for a misdemeanor," and this meant that judges might impose one or more of the following maximum penalties: a thousand-dollar fine, six months on the state chain gang, or twelve months on the county chain gang. No other state went so far, but, on the whole, the new laws were harsher than those that preceded them. With little change these acts remained in effect into the 1960s.

Actual enforcement of the vagrancy laws varied. Immediately after the Civil War southerners were convinced that the Negro would not work without coercion, and they also knew that the northern conquerers were not averse to using vagrancy measures when they saw fit. At the same time they became increasingly aware of a sharp northern reaction against the Black Codes. As a result of these crosscurrents some areas experienced a vigorous enforcement of the vagrancy statutes, while others did not. Whether enforced or not, these laws served as a threat to those who might hestitate to enter into labor contracts, and this was their central purpose.

However limited their enforcement may have been before 1880, by the early twentieth century the vagrancy acts had become a mainstay of the system of involuntary servitude. More than for any other category of legislation, the use of these laws reflected the continuing belief of whites that they had the right to appropriate Negro labor whenever "the good of society" demanded it. In addition, the times at which the vagrancy statutes were invoked show clearly the way the free-labor market came and went according to the supply of black labor and how Negro migration could exist side by side with a system that could and did limit Negro mobility.

At harvest time cotton farms experienced an acute need for a large work force, and it was precisely at such times that the police became most active in discovering vagrants. So common was the practice that the Atlanta *Constitution* could quip to the police: "Cotton is ripening, See that the 'vags' get busy." Local officials at all levels endorsed such tactics, and in 1910 a Memphis police-court judge announced a new policy whereby blacks brought before him on vagrancy charges would be allowed "to go free provided they would accept jobs offered by farmers who have set up a cry over scarcity of 'hands.'" Warmly endorsed by the mayor and police commissioner, this plan was accompanied by the announcement that the police would "renew their efforts to clear the city of all vagrants and loiterers."[21]

For cities, too, vagrancy statutes served as a means of recruiting black labor to serve the needs of white society. In 1910, as this country's romance with the car was beginning, the Automobile Club of America selected Savannah as the site of its International Grand Prize Race. When news of the decision reached the city, overjoyed local officials announced that in anticipation of this action they had already taken two hundred convicts off their normal jobs to put them to work on the racecourse. The superintendent of county public works said this would mean that all other public works requiring convict labor would have to be neglected. The next day "Negro loafers and vagrants were rounded up by the scores in all parts of Savannah." This dragnet brought in more than a hundred blacks, and it was announced that

William Cohen

those who could not "prove their innocence" would be sent to work on the racecourse.[22]

Down through the years Southerners continued to use vagrancy laws to compel community service from blacks. In 1937, when depression-ridden Miami, Florida, could not find the funds to maintain its trash collection schedule, it began to use Negro prisoners as garbage men. The Miami *Daily News* sarcastically reported the ensuing events: "Unfortunately there weren't enough prisoners of the proper persuasion [that is, Negroes] available, but that didn't stop the astute officials. They simply sent an SOS to police, who promptly went out and rounded up a hatful of negro vagrants. As soon as the current crop of prisoners concludes its time, another batch will be forthcoming, promise the police." Investigating this report Justice Department lawyers learned that fifty-five blacks had been rounded up and that seventeen had been convicted of vagrancy. Although there was no evidence of similar white arrests, federal officials concluded that the vagrancy law was being impartially enforced.

World War II accelerated the socioeconomic changes that were gradually eroding the system of involuntary servitude, but remnants of the old ways persisted. In September 1943, acting in conformity with Alabama's "Work or Fight" program, the sheriff of Mobile County charged fifty-five Negroes with vagrancy. Included in this number were two men picked up at the specific request of their employer, the Ruberoid Company, because they had been absent from work for at least one day a week over the past one hundred weeks.

All these instances were linked by the theme of service to the white community. Whether the setting was Savannah, Georgia or Miami, Florida, Negroes provided a ready pool of involuntary labor that could be tapped whenever whites faced any sort of labor emergency. Southern use of the vagrancy statutes had often been treated simply as a dimension of peonage, but to stop there is to miss the larger picture. Certainly debt servitude existed, and certainly

vagrancy arrests could lead to peonage, but the cases given above have been selected to show that white southerners also made wide use of the vagrancy laws in situations where the element of debt was nonexistent or, at most, incidental.

Criminal-Surety Laws

Still, peonage remained a major element within the system of involuntary servitude. Contract-enforcement laws served as one means by which blacks might be held in peonage; the criminal-surety system provided another route toward the same end. Under this system employers paid the fines and costs of individuals convicted of minor offenses like vagrancy, petty larceny, or public drunkenness. Such persons were, in turn, contractually obligated to repay the money advanced on their behalf. In a variant of this system, a planter sometimes bailed out a worker before a trial. The authorities then dropped the matter, leaving the black beholden to his new employer for the money advanced on his behalf and fearful that misbehavior would bring a return to jail.[23]

With roots that probably went back to the antebellum mistreatment of poor whites and free Negroes, the criminal-surety system apparently came into wide use shortly after the Civil War. It remained in use well into the twentieth century, but only Georgia and Alabama gave it the sanction of state law. Elsewhere in the South, however, it at least had the endorsement of custom, and further research may show that it was written into law at the local level. In 1874 Georgia made it lawful for misdemeanor convicts working off their fines to hire themselves "to any citizen of this state who pays the amount of said sentence, for said prescribed term." Twenty years later the state supreme court held that this provision had been repealed by an 1878 convict law. As will be seen, the practice continued at the local level. Adopted in 1883, Alabama's complex surety law penalized those who signed a labor contract to get out of jail and then failed to perform the work called for in the agreement.

This measure stipulated that the surety contract had to be signed in open court, but a 1907 enactment provided that such agreements would also be valid if signed in the presence of a mayor or city recorder. The 1907 law symbolized Alabama's determination to maintain the system of involuntary servitude at all costs, for it came in the wake of a series of major federal peonage prosecutions, and it aimed to facilitate further the process by which blacks might be bound to labor for the most trivial offenses.[24]

Upheld by the Alabama Supreme Court in 1883, the Alabama surety law came before this court on at least fifteen other occasions prior to 1914. Again, the volume of higher-court litigation suggests a heavy use at the local level. In 1914, however, the United States Supreme Court declared the law to be in violation of the Thirteenth Amendment (*United States* v. *Reynolds*). In this case Ed Rivers, a Negro convicted of petty larceny, had been sentenced to pay a $15 fine plus court costs of $43.75. Working these charges off in jail would have taken Rivers sixty-eight days, but instead he chose to sign a surety contract obligating him to work nine months and twenty-four days to pay off his fine and fees at the rate of $6 a month. Before fulfilling his agreement Rivers deserted his new employer and was rearrested. This time the judge sentenced him to pay a fine of one cent plus costs of $87.75, and Rivers signed a new surety contract with G. W. Broughton in which he promised to work for over fourteen months to pay his newly acquired debt. Concurring with the majority opinion, Justice Oliver Wendell Holmes observed: "The successive contracts, each for a longer term than the last, are the inevitable, and must be taken to have been the contemplated outcome of the Alabama laws [of 1883 and 1907.]"[25]

As events on the infamous Jasper County, Georgia, peonage farm of John S. Williams would show, the Reynolds decision invalidated the Alabama surety laws, but it did not end the practice of recruiting labor from southern jails. In 1921, fearing discovery by government agents, Williams

arranged the murder of ten of his peons and personally killed an eleventh Negro. Subsequent investigation revealed that these workers had been acquired from the jails of Atlanta, Macon, and other nearby towns. Testifying in his own behalf, Williams said: "I am like most farmers that I know, that at times I have bonded out and paid fines for niggers with actual agreement that they would stay there till their fines were paid, or till he was relieved from his bonds." Although self-serving, this statement rings true when measured against evidence that local jailers were so casual in releasing prisoners to farmers like Williams that they did not even bother to record the names of sureties. Clearly, there was nothing unusual in the way Williams acquired his labor. Almost three weeks after Williams and his foreman were found guilty of murder, the head of the Atlanta office of the Federal Bureau of Investigation said he was receiving new reports of peonage daily.[26]

Convict Labor

When Ed Rivers chose to accept a ten-month surety contract in lieu of a sixty-eight-day jail sentence he made a rational choice, for the southern penal system stood as the ultimate sanction behind the surety system and every other aspect of involuntary servitude. Those who could not, or would not, be bound to a surety would work for the direct benefit of government instead. The methods of handling convicts that evolved in the post-Civil War era aimed to provide a maximum of deterrence and punishment at minimal cost to the taxpayers. Thus, between 1865 and 1867, Alabama, Georgia, South Carolina, Texas, and Virginia gave local authorities the right to use county prisoners on such public projects as roads and bridges. These five states together with Florida and Mississippi also made explicit provision for the hiring out of county prisoners or those who had committed minor crimes and could not pay their fines.[27] This procedure did not require the convict's consent, and

William Cohen

he did not have to sign a surety agreement.

The southern states were somewhat slower to lease the inmates of their penitentiaries than they were to permit hiring out at the county level, but this changed as it became clear that the states could make a profit from convict leasing. By 1880 every former Confederate state except Virginia had a full-blown state leasing program. The lessees paid the states for the right to extract a maximum of labor from the prisoners, and they took the responsibility for guarding and maintaining them. Using shackles, dogs, whips, and guns, they created a living hell for the prisoners, which often bore a striking similarity to the most lurid abolitionist stereotypes of slavery.[28]

Mortality rates were shocking. Of 285 convicts sent to build South Carolina's Greenwood and Augusta Railroad between 1877 and 1880, 128, or 44.9 percent died. Tennessee boasted a model leasing program, but during the biennium 1884 -1885, when she had an average of 600 prisoners, there were 163 deaths. Convicts generally fared worse than this in other southern states. By way of contrast, the annual death rate in the prisons of New Hampshire, Ohio, Iowa, and Illinois during the period 1881–1885 was slightly more than one percent. South Carolina's warden remarked in 1879 that "the casualties would have been less if the convicts were property having a value to preserve."[29] His remark implies that most of the convicts were black, and this was indeed the case. Taking population differences into accounts, in the period around 1880 the ratios of Negro to white prisoners in North Carolina, Georgia, and South Carolina were roughly 13:1, 11:1, and 7:1, respectively.[30]

Figures like these were not accidental, for the southern prison system was being shaped specifically to deal with blacks. Guided by a white determination to return the Negro to "his place," the problems of crime, tax relief, internal development, and control of the labor force all intersected in the convict-lease system. Advocating this system in 1877, South Carolina Redeemer George D. Tillman asserted, "The negro has a constitutional propensity to steal, and in short to violate most of the ten commandments. The State should farm out such convicts even for only their subsistence, rather than compel taxpayers to support them in idleness." The returns from convict labor far exceeded subsistence. State prisoners played major roles in phosphate mining and turpentining (Florida), in coal mining (Alabama, Tennessee, and Georgia), and in road building (North Carolina and other states). Most important of all was the involuntary contribution of convicts to the South's railroads. In the capital-starved post-Civil War era they helped construct or reconstruct the railroads of every southern state save Louisiana. There, the levees took precedence.[31] Not surprisingly, as the advantages of convict labor became more apparent, the zeal of law-enforcement authorities showed a corresponding rise.

By 1910, when Ed Rivers signed his first surety agreement, the southern prison system was improving, but not so fast as to induce him to opt for a short jail term. The leasing system was on the road to extinction, and the states were taking responsibility for guarding and maintaining prisoners even when they were let out to private contractors. During the next three decades conditions continued to improve, at least when compare to the barbarous 1880s. In 1928 Alabama became the last state formally to abandon the leasing system, and by 1932 the annual mortality rate of its Negro convicts was 2.5 percent. The comparable figure for white prisoners, however, was 0.7 percent. Less is known about conditions at the county level, where misdemeanants often served their terms, but there is reason to believe that improvement proceeded more slowly here. In some states, for example, county leasing remained legal after the practice had been abolished at the state level. Such improvements as there were may well have escaped the attention of convicts on the chain gangs. Brutality remained omnipresent, and the convicts who built the

South's roads were often housed in movable cages that provided less space per man than would a six-by-four-by-four-foot box.[32]

During the 1930s blacks still constituted the great majority of those serving on the chain gangs of Alabama, Georgia, Virginia, and Florida, and the situation was certainly similar elsewhere in the South. In September 1932, Alabama's 1,089-man road force was composed entirely of Negroes. In Georgia, where blacks accounted for only 37 percent of the total population in 1930, they constituted 83 percent of the total prison population in 1932.[33] Even within the prison population, there was a further differential. As Table 26.2 shows, the percentage of white felons serving on Georgia's chain gangs was only somewhat less than the comparable figure for Negroes (79 percent versus 90 percent).[34] Considered outcasts, Georgia's white felons were treated none too gently. Misdemeanants posed a different problem, and only a handful of whites received jail sentences for minor offenses. Overwhelmingly those jailed for misdemeanors in Georgia were blacks, and beyond this disparity the percentage assigned to county labor far exceeded the percentage of whites given similar sentences. With but few exceptions, those assigned to county labor worked on the chain gang, either fixing or building roads (2,348 misdemeanants served in this capacity) or doing other arduous labor.[35]

The situation in Georgia is indicative of that in other southern states. In 1932 only 23 percent of the South's state prisoners (largely felons) served on chain gangs, while 49 percent of its county prisoners (largely misdemeanants) were engaged in road work. That the overwhelming majority of these county prisoners were black is beyond doubt.[36] Even in the 1930s the southern prison system continued to supply cost-free labor for internal development. At the same time the continuing harshness of the prison system served as a potential weapon for any white seeking to intimidate his Negro employees.

In September 1937, Warren County, Georgia, cotton growers sought to prevent farmers of adjoining Glascock County from enticing away their black laborers. Desperate for hands, the men from Glascock County had offered almost double the rate being paid for cotton pickers in Warren County. Unwilling to abide by the law of supply and demand, Warren County planters mobilized to stop the depletion of their labor force. Sheriff G. P. Hogan described the ensuing events: "There was no trouble, although a number of them [the Warren County men] carried guns and fired them into the air. They told the pickers there was plenty of cotton to pick in Warren County and asked them to stay home and pick it. They decided to stay."[37]

Conclusion

The planters of Warren County might have brought charges of enticement against their competitors, but they did not. Yet this incident is at least as representa-

Table 26.2 Distribution of Georgia Prisoners
December 31, 1932

Race	Felons			Misdemeanants		
	Total	State Farm	Chain Gang	Total	State Farm	County Labor
Negro	3,229	331	2,898	3,925	212	3,713
	100%	10%	90%	100%	5%	95%
White	1,196	247	949	273	141	132
	100%	21%	79%	100%	52%	48%
Total	4,425	578	3,847	4,198	353	3,845
% Negro	73.0	57.3	75.3	93.5	60.1	96.6

William Cohen

tive of the workings of the system of involuntary servitude as the many cases where legal and quasi-legal processes came into play. Law gave the system structure and the appearance of legitimacy, but at base it was rooted in a state of mind that arrogated to whites the right to use Negro labor when and as they chose. Transcending peonage as it transcended the legal structure which partially defined it, the system of involuntary servitude was a unique blend of slavery and freedom which gave whites the option of limiting black movement while leaving Negroes otherwise free to come and go as they pleased.

It was this feature of the system which created the paradoxical situation whereby involuntary servitude coexisted with a good deal of black mobility. Prior to 1916 many Negroes moved from the Southeast to the Southwest, and after that date large numbers began moving north. Such movement was possible within the framework of involuntary servitude because it often occurred at times and places where labor was superabundant. When this was not the case, white southerners frequently took steps to prevent blacks from departing. This had been the purpose of the emigrant-agent laws, and it was also the aim of those who sought to use all means, including violence, to prevent blacks from leaving the South in 1916 and 1917.[38] The system of involuntary servitude did not always function perfectly; resourceful blacks could and did get around its restrictions. Just as the laws of slavery defined the ideals and fears of the slaveholders rather than the realities of the system, so too with the laws of involuntary servitude.

Writing in 1938 Jonathan Daniels quoted a southern editor as telling him; "Slavery is still in force . . . but not generally profitable.[39] The statement was an exaggeration, but hardly so far from the truth as one would like to believe.

27

William B. Hixson, Jr.

Moorfield Storey and the Struggle for Equality

The organization of the National Association for the Advancement of Colored People in 1909 and 1910 was the joint achievement of Negro militants and of white reformers. That some Negroes decided to assert their human dignity and demand their constitutional rights is not surprising. What is surprising, since anti-Negro prejudice was far more bitter and more widespread then than now, is that some white men and women joined them in their struggle for equality.

Two of the white founders of the Association—Oswald Garrison Villard and Mary White Ovington—have, in their autobiographies, indicated some of the factors that impelled them toward championing the Negro's cause.[1] Both—Villard, particularly, because of his Garrison ancestry—have some claim to be considered inheritors of the civil rights tradition of the previous century. But Ovington, as a social worker trying to alleviate the condition of the poor, and Villard, as a crusading journalist and an ardent civil-libertarian, tended to sympathize automatically with the victims and outcasts of society, a reaction more

characteristic of twentieth-century liberalism than of nineteenth-century reform. It is unclear, therefore, whether their dedication to the Negro's cause came primarily from the abolitionist memories of their childhoods or from the liberal environment in which they spent their careers.

In contrast, the first president of the Association and its counsel in its first three important cases before the Supreme Court cannot be considered a twentieth-century liberal. Until he died in 1929 at the age of eighty-four, Moorfield Storey adhered to the values he had acquired as a pillar of the legal profession and as a Mugwump reformer in the late nineteenth century. Although willing to accept social legislation on the state level, he consistently opposed federal intervention and remained suspicious of the more ambitious programs of the progressive movement. Storey's outlook on racial matters was little different from that of Villard and Ovington, but because the reinforcing effect of a general liberalism is absent, the sources of his dedication to the Negro's cause is easier to follow. Specifically, his legal arguments on behalf of the National Association for the Advancement of Colored People reveal the influence of Charles Sumner, who made the most not-

Reprinted from the *Journal of American History*, vol. 60, no. 3 (1968), 533-554 by permission. Copyright, 1968, Organization of American Historians.

able nineteenth-century argument that the law must make no racial distinctions.

As they found that the general statements of equality in the state constitutions failed to reach the massive discrimination against the free Negroes of the North, abolitionists tended to demand specific prohibitions on racial discrimination.[2] In 1849 Sumner introduced into American jurisprudence this new meaning of the phrase "equality before the law." In that year, he served as counsel for a Negro couple whose daughter was prohibited by the rules of the Boston School Committee from attending the neighborhood public school because it was restricted to whites. Since only Negro children were prevented from attending the schools nearest them and were instead sent to all-Negro schools often at a considerable distance, they were made, Sumner argued, to feel inferior, and white children were made to regard them as such. The Negro schools did not have facilities equal to those attended by whites, but even if they had been equal, Sumner explained, "this compulsory segregation from the mass of the citizens is of itself an *inequality* we condemn". In view of the general principles of "equality before the law" embodied in the Massachusetts constitution, the Boston School Committee could not, in justice, make such a distinction.[3]

Sumner took this commitment to civil equality with him into the Senate two years later and, once emancipation became a certainty, devoted the remaining years of his career to securing civil equality for all the citizens of the United States. Though directly responsible for minor gains for Negroes during the Civil War,[4] his greater significance lies in his articulation of the emerging postwar northern sentiment that the Negro be granted the rights of citizenship.[5] Ultimately, his persistent demands for universal manhood suffrage were realized in the Fifteenth Amendment; but his other great goal, a bill prohibiting segregation in all public facilities for education, recreation, and transportation, remained unfulfilled at the time of his death.[6]

This was the man with whom Moorfield Storey had spent two of the most impressionable years of his life. Through his father he had received an invitation in the fall of 1867 to become Sumner's personal secretary, and in late November of that year the twenty-two-year-old Storey, fresh from a year at Harvard Law School, left for Washington.[7] Upon moving into Sumner's house the following January, Storey soon became aware of some of the senator's idiosyncracies: "Mr. Sumner is not great at conversation, properly so called, I think. He can make himself very agreeable if he likes, and frequently does, but he either does all the talking himself and goes off into long disquisitions, or he simply draws out the other person and lets him do the talking, so it is a monologue on one side or the other."[8]

As the months passed, Storey became the daily companion of a man desperately in search of friendship beyond the calculated associations of official Washington. That Sumner himself bore much of the responsibility for his social isolation has been one of the main arguments of his recent biographer,[9] but Sumner seems to have had a genuine affection for Storey, one which the younger man returned in full.

In the spring of 1869, Storey completed his clerkship with Sumner and returned to Boston. Apparently he had cut himself off from the influence of Sumner's ideas as well. During the last three decades of the nineteenth century, he enjoyed a prosperous legal career and devoted his remaining time to the various civic interests of his fellow Mugwumps: civil-service reform, low tariffs, independent politics, and anti-imperialism. The Mugwumps began as opponents of both the corruption of the Grant administration and the radicalism of the Greenbackers. Regarding themselves as the guardians of social and moral order, they began to question the unlimited application of the principle of self-government; the first victim of their growing skepticism about democracy was the recently enfranchised freedman.

Seeing only the corruption of the Radical regimes in the South, as early as 1872 many Mugwumps urged the end of Reconstruction; and they soon became among the most articulate supporters of the idea of sectional reconciliation. President Rutherford B. Hayes's withdrawal of federal troops from the South in the spring of 1877 was more symbolic than substantial; of far greater importance in the "road to reunion" were the Supreme Court decisions, between 1875 and 1883, which seriously weakened the Reconstruction legislation protecting the freedmen's civil rights. Like the other Mugwumps, Storey does not appear to have protested the Court's decisions. Indeed, when Senator George F. Hoar and Representative Henry Cabot Lodge made a final effort to restore federal protection to Negro voters in 1890, Storey condemned their bill as attacking "the root of constitutional government and . . . parent of the grossest abuses and gravest disturbances."[10]

Though it is doubtful that many Mugwumps preserved the concern for the freedmen that they had shown in the aftermath of the Civil War, it is quite possible that a minority of them (Storey, for example) acquiesced in the dismantling of federal protection of civil rights in the 1870s and 1880s on the assumption that, since Southerners themselves appeared to accept Negro rights, there was no need for federal interference. Certainly, both the pledges of southern leaders such as Wade Hampton, Lucius Q. C. Lamar, and Alexander Stephens, and the investigations of the former abolitionist Thomas Wentworth Higginson confirmed this view.[11] It is easy to say that Higginson, a staunch supporter of Hayes's policy, and the Southerners, still fearful of the reassertion of federal power, had vested interests in the Compromise of 1877 and that this bias may have colored their views. But, if the argument advanced by numerous modern

scholars is to be accepted, integrated facilities and Negro participation in politics continued in many parts of the South until the turn of the century.

In the 1890s, to heal the wounds from the bitter fights between industry-oriented Redeemers and angry farmers, the doctrine of "white supremacy" was invoked in full force. The proscriptive devices which followed—the "legal" disfranchisement and statutory segregation of the Negro—received constitutional endorsement from the Supreme Court and widespread approval by the American public. No Mugwump had tried harder to assimilate "home rule" for the South with equal rights for the Negro than Carl Schurz. But this new proscription, beginning in the 1890s, led Schurz to write Storey that "unless the reaction now going on be stopped, we shall have to fight the old anti-slavery battle again";[12] and before his death Schurz publicly warned the South against finding itself "once more in a position provokingly offensive to the moral sense and the enlightened spirit of the world outside.[13]

The trend, beginning in the 1890s, seems to have evoked within Storey the dedication to civil equality that he had received from his close association with Sumner. By the early years of the twentieth century, his concept of civil equality (like Sumner's) embraced not only the Negro but also all minorities. "The absurd prejudices of race and color" would become, for Storey, equally obnoxious and equally worthy of attack "whether they bar the Negro from his rights as a man, the foreigner from his welcome to our shores, the Filipino from his birthright of independence, or the Hebrew from social recognition."[14] He sharply qualified the anti-immigrant aspersions he had made in his Mugwump days and began to defend immigrant citizenship;[15] after 1899 he fought continuously on behalf of Philippine independence. But his main concern was, as Sumner's had been, with the protection of the Negro American's civil and political rights and with the expansion of his opportunity for advancement in all areas of American society.

Storey's defense of the Negro first emerged as a theme in the debate over Philippine annexation in 1899–1900. Unlike some of his associates in the anti-imperialist movement whose prejudices led them to oppose the incorporation of another colored people,[16] he was shifting his own attitudes in a different direction. The denial of self-government to the Filipinos was wrong in itself, he argued, but doubly wrong because it would be used to rationalize the denial of civil and political rights to Negroes at home. By the time of his anti-imperialist campaign for Congress in 1900, Storey had firmly linked in his own mind the suppression of Negroes in the South and the suppression of the natives in the Pacific possessions:

> No man of anti-slavery antecedents can fail to regard with horror the treatment of the colored race in the South and the attempt to disfranchise them. The whole reaction against this unhappy race, both in the northern and southern states, is deplorable. While, however, the President and the Republican Party are denying the doctrine of human equality which the party was formed to maintain, and are justifying conquest and despotic methods in the Philippines and Porto Rico by the argument that the inhabitants of these islands are unfit for freedom because of their race or color, it is only to be expected that the same doctrines will be applied at home.[17]

Four years later, as the Roosevelt administration took no action to stem the mounting tide of disfranchisement and segregation, the reasons seemed apparent. "The Philippine war has paralyzed the conscience of the Republican Party," Storey said; "it cannot denounce the suppression of the Negro vote in the South by any argument that does not return to condemn the suppression of the Philippine vote in Luzon and Samar."[18]

Significantly, it was a remark attributed to the administrator of Roosevelt's Philip-pine policy, Secretary of War Elihu Root, that Negro suffrage had been a failure, which elicited Storey's first major public defense of Negro citizenship. Just as no country had the right to deny national independence to another, no race within a country had the right to deny citizenship to another. The purpose of congressional Reconstruction, he told an audience, had not been to establish good government, but to grant self-government to the emancipated slaves:

> The object was not primarily to secure well-tilled fields, well-ordered towns, an industrious laboring class, nor even a legislature, a bench, and an executive taken from the ablest men in the state. All these results had been secured by slavery. Had these been the object of our policy, slavery need never have been destroyed. It was because these advantages, the material prosperity of a few, had been gained by the degradation of a whole race,—because millions of human beings had been denied the rights and hopes of humanity, that slavery was abolished, and unless we carried the work through we had better never have begun it. The same reason that led us to abolish slavery forbade us to establish any legal inequality between man and man. Anything less than equality of rights was sure to be the seed of future trouble.[19]

There had been corruption under the Reconstruction regimes, "an orgy of corruption after Negro suffrage was granted" – this Storey freely admitted. "But," he asked, pointing to the current outcry against the "bosses," "can we insist that the color is the cause? While Pennsylvania bows to Quay; while Montana elects Clark; while Addicks owns Delaware; while the trials at St. Louis reveal the nature of her rulers, and Minneapolis is punishing Ames, are we sure that white suffrage is a success?" And the South, which was still fighting corruption, could hardly blame its present condition on the black man, for, in the broadest sense, "since 1876 Negro suffrage *has not been tried* and therefore has not failed."[20]

In his defense of civil rights, Storey may have begun as one of those who, as his friend Charles Francis Adams, Jr., put it, "plant themselves firmly on what Rufus Choate once referred to as the 'glittering generalities of the Declaration of Independence.'"[21] But, in an age when moral judgments were increasingly argued on the basis of empirical evidence, Storey found that his commitments led to factual disagreements. His first debate was with the historians. Although Storey was consulted by his friend James Ford Rhodes when Rhodes wrote his multivolume history, Storey, nevertheless, remained one of the more persistent critics of the completed work.[22] Rhodes, Storey felt, had drawn a one-sided picture of actual conditions during Reconstruction; discussions with prominent white Southerners had given Storey the impression – at least he wrote to Rhodes – "that we in the North have a very exaggerated notion of the trouble in the South" occasioned by the carpetbag regimes.[23]

Simultaneously Storey carried on a somewhat more extended debate with Adams. Increasingly drawn to the South through his researches on Robert E. Lee, Adams thought that "the reconstruction policy of 1866 we forced on the helpless states of the Confederacy was worse than a crime; it was a political blunder, as ungenerous as it was gross."[24] But it was not true, Storey wrote to Adams, "that the reconstruction policy was 'conceived in passion' and devoid of statesmanship. It is the fashion to forget that white reconstruction was tried faithfully and that Johnson's white legislatures at once passed laws which in effect re-established slavery."[25] Nor was it true, Storey argued, that Reconstruction had been engineered by a small group of "vindictive" Radicals:

> The reconstruction policy was largely framed and was supported by the most conservative men in the Senate like Trumbull, Grimes, Sherman and the group that voted against impeachment ... the policy was adopted in view of the exigencies of the time by the sober judgment of the men who were

then in control of the Republican Party, and Thad Stevens was only one force.[26]

Against the natural and social scientists, Storey was less sure in his arguments than he had been against the historians. By the time he died, he had acquired a notable collection of books on Negro history and society, but studies in psychology and anthropology were absent. He had been isolated too long from scientific thought to be more than vaguely aware that a new wave of anthropologists was attacking long-established notions of biological and cultural "superiority."[27] Instead, he used whatever arguments he could and combined the general knowledge acquired in a liberal education, the personal experience of sixty years, and the discipline of a sharp legal mind. In 1913, for example, he exchanged views on "race purity" with Harvard's president, Charles W. Eliot. For Eliot, who is currently enjoying a reputation as an exponent of racial tolerance,[28] "the experience of the world demonstrates upon an immense scale that peoples far advanced in the scale of civilization cannot profitably mix with backward peoples. The purer a race is kept, the more likely it is to maintain itself and prosper."[29] Storey disagreed and argued:

> *A priori*, it is hard to see why the admixture of different breeds which has produced such wonderful results in the vegetable and animal worlds should be so disastrous to the human race. Nature demands variety, and intermarriage between members of the same family or class long persisted in tends to produce degenerates. Even the fact that the results are jeered at and called hard names is not conclusive. The term "cur" has long been a term of reproach, but no one who knows dogs can fail to admit that the most admirable qualities of canine nature are very commonly found in dogs of very mixed ancestry.[30]

Whatever the merits of the abstract issue, Storey never doubted the absurdity

William B. Hixson, Jr.

of "race purity" in American society, where there had been widespread sexual contact:

> You wish to keep the white blood pure [he wrote a southern correspondent] and free from contamination with an inferior strain. Let me ask you, do you? If the public opinion of the South disgraced a man who established relations with colored women, and became the parent of colored children, I should acquiesce in your contention, but it does not, and it is not the presence of a marriage ceremony which makes the contamination but the mingling of blood as a fact. From the time when the colored people were first brought into this country until now there has been no instinct which prevents the mingling of blood, and until there is I feel that it is not race pride which controls the action of the white people of the South.[31]

Whatever the causes of the trend toward racial discrimination, a sudden awareness of the need to preserve "racial purity" was not one of them. Storey had traveled in the South before the days of institutionalized Jim Crow, and he particularly remembered one incident of interracial harmony on a New Orleans streetcar:

> There was no trace of objection to this association of white and colored during the whole trip, but had we crossed the street and taken the railroad train these same people would have been given separate cars. Such discrimination is fashion, not instinct, and other illustrations in abundance could be given. It is a bad fashion, not an uncontrollable instinct, against which we contend.[32]

To all those—whether historians or biologists, his friends or occasional correspondents — who justified their demands for the subjugation of the Negro by his supposed "inferiority," Storey answered that their case against the Negro remained unproven:

> When the colored men have had an equal chance with the white man, and as for many

years, we can then form a sound opinion as to their respective abilities, but in my own time I have seen men belonging to races which were deemed inferior establish their right to be regarded as the equal of all their fellow men. A notable instance is the case of the Jews, who are treated in Russia very much as the colored men are treated in the South, are denied social equality, herded together in quarters, and generally regarded as hopelessly inferior. We know in the United States that this opinion is unfounded.[33]

Those who wanted to subjugate the Negro were really unsure of the racial "inferiority" they tried to establish. He asked the irrefutable questions, "If the Negro is so hopelessly inferior, why do the whites fear the effect of education? Why do they struggle against his progress upward?" He could only conclude: "The attempt to prevent him from rising, by violence or by adverse legislation, is a confession that the assumption of white superiority is unsafe".[34]

Storey's contention that Negroes could not be fairly judged unless granted equal opportunities is best revealed in his continual fight against discrimination in private institutions. His correspondence is full of incidents of minor indignities suffered by Negroes: a doctor barred from the staff of a public hospital, a girl refused dormitory accommodations at Smith College, a worker barred from employment by a "lily-white" union.[35] In two notable campaigns he successfully fought against the exclusion of Negroes from the American Bar Association[36] and against the segregation of Negro students in separate dormitories at Harvard College.[37] But, in the presence of mounting racial oppression, Storey had long recognized that individual gestures on behalf of equal opportunity would do little to turn the tide: "The whites in the South are one party in the contest, and the interests of the other party are not safe in their hands. They had the full charge of the Negro problem for a great many years, and they made a great mess of it, so that I desire to reserve the right to bring to bear all the public opinion that we can muster in favor of the Negro in the South and elsewhere."[38] To implement his argument that the United States "is the country of all its citizens, and black men have under our Constitution all the rights of white men,"[39] in 1910 he accepted the presidency of the National Association for the Advancement of Colored People.

Unlike W. E. B. Du Bois, Villard, Ovington, and Joel and Arthur Spingarn, Storey had little to do with the day-to-day problems of the NAACP. Any organization devoted to securing complete equality before the law, however, would be largely dependent upon litigation for the realization of its goals, and here someone with Storey's legal skill and professional prestige was invaluable. Relying on the careful investigations conducted by Association branches and the preliminary preparation of cases by local lawyers, Storey appears to have determined the constitutional basis for the Association's arguments. In several notable cases before the Supreme Court, he was thus able to halt the judicial trend of three decades toward racial proscription.

When the Association was formed, the effective expression of civil equality in public policy had been severely limited by two judicial doctrines: "state action," which appeared to exempt private discrimination and intimidation from the prohibitions of the Fourteenth Amendment,[40] and the "separate but equal" doctrine, which required proof of actual inequality of facilities to show a denial of "the equal protection of the laws."[41] Though opposed to segregation on principle, the NAACP was forced to work within that framework – fully aware that only those acts of government whose denial of "equal protection" were blatant would be declared unconstitutional by the Supreme Court.[42] In the years since Reconstruction, there were two main decisions to which the association could appeal as precedents: a West Virginia case affirming the constitutional right of

Negroes to sit on juries,[43] and a California case striking down those building requirements for laundries framed in such a way as effectively to prohibit Chinese establishments alone.[44]

The first Supreme Court case in which Storey appeared for the Association involved the constitutionality of the Oklahoma "grandfather clause." The grandfather clause was one aspect of the "legal" disfranchisement of the Negro in the southern states. States imposed restrictive suffrage requirements while at the same time passing exemptive clauses under which illiterate whites might vote.[45] In a case arising from the first of the disfranchising states, Mississippi, the Court had held that the requirements themselves, by-passing as they did "race, color, or previous condition of servitude," did not violate the prohibitions of the Fifteenth Amendment; only the discriminatory enforcement of those requirements would be unconstitutional.[46] In several other cases decided during this period, the Court dismissed voting suits on a variety of grounds: the election in question had already been held; registration could not be enforced under the provisions which the plaintiff charged were invalid; and plaintiffs could not sue for damages in equity.[47]

In 1907 Oklahoma was admitted to the Union. Its constitution provided for universal manhood suffrage, with only residence requirements. In 1910, however, an amendment was added which required a literacy test for all voters except those who were "on January 1, 1866, or at any time prior thereto, entitled to vote under any form of government" or anyone who was a "lineal descendant of such person." Obviously, few Negroes were entitled to vote in the United States of 1865. Acting under a Reconstruction statute, still viable as far as intimidation in congressional elections was concerned, the federal government brought indictments against certain registrars, in part for their administration of the act. They were convicted and sentenced to one year in a federal penitentiary. They appealed to the Eighth Circuit Court; the sentence was affirmed; they appealed to the Supreme Court. Action on the part of the government had been continued during the transition from the Taft to the Wilson administrations; when the case was finally argued, the government was represented by John W. Davis, a decade away from his presidential nomination. The role of the NAACP was limited to an amicus curiae brief, which had been filed by Storey.

In his own attitudes toward suffrage, Storey differentiated between personal principle and legal precedent. As a matter of principle, "I rather agree with Clay that no people is fit for any government except self-government, though I do not feel certain that any of us are any too competent."[48] But as a matter of law, "the denial or abridgement of the right to vote need not be illegal or unconstitutional. An educational qualification for example, is neither ... The same would be true of a property qualification."[49] But, even though such restrictions might be "constitutional," if they were used, the second section of the Fourteenth Amendment would automatically come into force "when any state denies to any male person who is an inhabitant of that state and at the same time a citizen of the United States the right to vote, or in any way abridges it, except for participation in rebellion or other crime, the basis of representation shall be reduced" [Storey's paraphrase].

But if the Court accepted his argument on this point and "reactivated" the second section, two consequences might occur. On the one hand, "if the South finds that it loses power because the basis of representation is reduced, it would be a constant motive to modify their laws and admit colored men to the polls ..." On the other hand, Storey felt, the South just might accept such conditions as the price of white supremacy. If it did, the Negroes would remain disfranchised while the North would be apt to say "that they would not disturb the situation as long as

they profited by it in the increased representation [for themselves]."[50] With this unfortunate possibility in mind, he dropped any idea of relying on the Fourteenth Amendment in his argument and decided to litigate under the Fifteenth Amendment instead.

Because he favored the latter approach, Storey was personally committed to his brief in the "grandfather-clause" case. "If it is possible for an ingenious scrivener to accomplish that purpose of disfranchisement by careful phrasing, the provisions of the Constitution which establish and protect the rights of some ten million colored citizens of the United States are not worth the paper on which they are written, and all constitutional safeguards are weakened."[51] Like Davis, he argued that the *effect* of the Oklahoma amendment was discriminatory and, therefore (citing the *Yick Wo* v. *Hopkins* precedent), unconstitutional. In its decision, the Court paid homage to state control over elections: "The [Fifteenth] Amendment does not change, modify or deprive the States of their full power as to suffrage except of course as to the subject with which the Amendment deals and to the extent that obedience to its command is necessary." This case, however, was manifestly one involving the denial of suffrage for reasons of "race, color or previous condition of servitude." The Court concluded:

> We are unable to discover how, unless the prohibitions of the Fifteenth Amendment were considered, the slightest reason was afforded for basing the classification upon a period of time prior to the Fifteenth Amendment. Certainly it cannot be said that there was any peculiar necromancy in the time named which engendered attributes affecting the qualification to vote which would not exist at another and different period unless the Fifteenth Amendment was in view.[52]

Though the Supreme Court struck down the grandfather clauses, other barriers—among them, the all-white primaries of a one-party South—remained for those Negroes who were courageous enough to attempt to vote. In Texas the Democratic state committee passed a resolution in 1922 excluding Negroes from the party primaries. One Negro sued, and again the Supreme Court on appeal ruled that no issue was presented since the election had already occurred.[53] Various factions within Texas politics pushed for a more thorough exclusion, and in 1923 the legislature passed a bill which prohibited Negro participation in party primaries. Dr. L. A. Nixon, head of the El Paso NAACP chapter, brought suit for damages; the suit was dismissed by the district court, but finally taken on appeal by the Supreme Court. Storey had regarded the statute as "absurd" and hoped "the Supreme Court [would] sustain the case".[54] Though the NAACP's case was finally argued by Fred Knollenberg and Arthur Spingarn, Storey helped to prepare the brief. Its main point was that the 1923 act violated the Fifteenth as well as the Fourteenth Amendment because Texas statutes considered the primary a public election; thus Negro exclusion violated the prohibition of denial of the suffrage because of "race, color, or previous condition of servitude" of the one amendment, and the guarantee of "the equal protection of the laws" of the other.[55] Speaking for the Court, Oliver Wendell Holmes succinctly declared the Texas statute unconstitutional: "We find it unnecessary to consider the Fifteenth Amendment, because it seems to us hard to imagine a more direct and obvious infringement of the Fourteenth."[56]

In addition to the more blatant disfranchising procedures, another area that seemed to the Association to involve discriminatory "state action" was enforced residential segregation. The first targets were residential-segregation ordinances. The original of such ordinances involved the Chinese in San Francisco and was declared unconstitutional by a United States District Court as violating both the treaty with China and the Fourteenth

Amendment.[57] In the early years of the twentieth century, however, the device more often represented the conclusion of the trend toward racial proscription in the South. Beginning with Baltimore, southern cities passed ordinances freezing areas with a majority of one race into permanent "white" or "black" sections.[58] The Baltimore ordinance was declared unconstitutional by the Maryland Supreme Court on the grounds that it did not adequately protect the rights of the present owners of property and that a municipality did not have the authority to enact such an ordinance.[59] Where the rights of owners were clearly protected, however, state courts tended to uphold similar statutes.[60]

The city of Louisville passed an ordinance classifying certain blocks as "white" and "colored", and no owner or resident of the other race on such a block would be compelled to sell his property, but, should he do so, the property would revert to the predominant race in the classified area. Drawn as it was to protect rights of ownership, the ordinance passed a test in the Kentucky State Supreme Court.[61] For the NAACP, already active in the fight against enforced segregation, the Kentucky decision presented a major challenge. The Association decided to test the ordinance. In the fall of 1914, therefore, William Warley, head of the Louisville chapter, arranged to buy a lot for two hundred fifty dollars from a sympathetic white, Charles H. Buchanan. To provide a cause for legal action, Warley said he would pay the final one hundred dollars after he made sure the transaction did not violate the ordinance. When he found that it did, he then refused to pay; Buchanan brought suit, but the chancery court ruled for Warley. Buchanan then appealed to the state supreme court, which also ruled against him. By 1916 the case was on the docket of the United States Supreme Court, and Storey, assisted by the Louisville attorney Clayton L. Blakey, was prepared to present the NAACP's argument. Perhaps because only seven justices were sitting at the time, Chief Justice Edward J. White ordered a rehearing the following term, and the case was finally argued early in 1917.

The spectacle of the NAACP defending a white property owner trying to collect payment from an unwilling Negro (even if it was prearranged) was not without its ironies. The defendant, as Storey explained, "is not complaining of discrimination against the colored race. He is not trying to enforce their rights, but to enforce his own."[62] By restricting the freedom of Louisville citizens, black and white, to buy and sell property, the ordinance had deprived them of income from the sale of property without the due process of law and thus had violated the Fourteenth Amendment. That may have been Storey's most persuasive argument as far as the Court was concerned, but for him there were more important reasons for arguing the case. Nowhere else in a court of law was Storey's passionate dedication to civil equality so apparent.

The law ostensibly was passed to curtail "ill-feeling between the races," but Storey ridiculed the idea that an alley could serve as an effective barrier between racially different blocks; and he then went on to challenge the whole presumption of "race purity." The defendant's counsel talked of "racial barriers which Providence and not human law has erected." Storey argued, "Had Providence in fact erected such a barrier it would have been impassable and no human law would have been needed. It is because no such divine barrier exists that they seek to establish one by human legislation."[63] The ordinance discriminated against "the better class of Negroes" who wished to move out of the ghetto, and this discrimination, he claimed, was the purpose of the ordinance. "No one outside a courtroom would imagine for an instant that the predominant purpose of this ordinance was not to prevent the Negro citizens of Louisville—however industrious, thrifty, and well-educated they might be—from approaching that condition vaguely described as 'social equality.' "[64] It was specious to say that the law also affected whites, for it was the Negro's advancement that was being hindered. Storey quoted Anatole France's aphorism that the law forbids the rich, as well as the poor, from sleeping under the bridges of Paris and added, "A law which forbids a Negro to rise is not made just because it forbids a white man to fall."[65]

With the intention of hindering the mobility of its Negro population, Louisville was not only denying it property rights secured by the "privileges and immunities" clause of the Fourteenth Amendment but was also denying it "equal protection of the laws." Whatever the trend of decisions from *Plessy* v. *Ferguson* onward, Storey concluded, the separate-but-equal doctrine had no relevance in a case of such obvious statutory discrimination. Nor, as the city's representatives claimed, could the ordinance be regarded as a legitimate exercise of the police power. Such power could operate only against the "injurious consequences of individuals," not against classes. The Negro was the victim, not the instigator, of social disorder; just because white men "do not like him as a neighbor, they pass an ordinance depriving him of his right to live where he pleases, and they justify it on the ground that it is necessary to protect them from being tempted to assault him if he exercises that right."[66]

In his argument Storey compared Negroes with employers, who were also victims, as he saw it, of an organized assault upon their rights as property owners. Such analogies reflected his own view, but no doubt also pleased a conservative Court. Indeed, some commentators have argued that it was solicitude for property rights, and not for the victims of discrimination, that motivated the Court to rule for Storey's client.[67] It is true that the decision made no mention of the aspirations of Negroes. Significantly, however, the Court did impose limitations upon the "separate-but-equal" doctrine and the sociological assumptions behind it: "That there exists a serious and difficult problem arising from a feeling of race hostility which the law is powerless to control, and to which it must give a measure of consideration, may be freely admitted. But its solution cannot be promoted by depriving citizens of their constitutional rights privileges."[68] There were situations in which, under the *Plessy* precedent, it would uphold segregation legislation, the Court continued, and it would not permit such legislation to restrict the right to buy and sell property, secured under the "privileges-and-immunities" clause. By limiting real-estate transactions to persons of the same race, the Louisville ordinance—and all other such ordinances—restricted that right and thus were unconstitutional.

Storey, who had been worried before he argued the case ("You know how ingenious the Court sometimes is in finding a method of avoiding a disagreeable question"[69]), was overjoyed with the decision. "I cannot help thinking," he wrote Villard, "it is the most important decision that has been made since the *Dred Scott* Case, and happily this time it is the right way."[70]

As Negroes began moving in large numbers to the North during and after World War I, new devices were found to keep them segregated. The most prominent was the restrictive convenant, a contractual agreement among property owners not to sell to Negroes for a specified number of years; the courts would enforce the agreements. California and Michigan courts declared the future restriction void, but concurred with other state courts on the validity of restrictions against current purchase or occupancy.[71] Storey denied the validity of the restrictions and cited the Buchanan ruling that the "attempt to prevent the alienation of the property in question to a person of color was not a legitimate exercise of the police power of the State."[72] He argued that "if public policy does not justify the state in making this restriction, neither does it justify the restriction when imposed by a private citizen."[73] The case

the NAACP entered came from the Supreme Court of the District of Columbia. One party to a covenant, John J. Buckley, had successfully sought an injunction against another, Irene H. Corrigan, to prevent the sale of property to a Negro, Helen Curtis. Louis Marshall argued the case on appeal before the United States Supreme Court, but Storey played a major role in preparing the brief.

To a greater extent than the previous briefs the NAACP had prepared for the Supreme Court, that of Marshall and Storey in this case attempted to counter in advance any questions the Court might raise. Their first point was that enforcement of the covenant by the lower court deprived Corrigan of the right to dispose of her property without the "due process of law" guaranteed by the Fifth Amendment. Partly because both men hoped that a favorable ruling from the Court would void all such covenants throughout the United States, and partly because Storey at least believed that the Fourteenth Amendment extended to all territory under American jurisdiction,[74] their brief also contended that judicial enforcement of those covenants violated the Fourteenth Amendment as well. Yet, as far as the Court was concerned, the Fourteenth Amendment, even more than the Fifth, applied only to cases of "state action." What if the Court dismissed the case on the ground that the covenant constituted private discrimination?

To counter this contingency, Marshall and Storey decided to argue that the covenant went against "public policy."[75] "Public policy," as Marshall had written to Storey, "is largely based upon constitutional and statutory definitions as to what the policy of a State is"[76]—in this case, the common law prohibitions on contracts in restraint of the alienation of property, statutory prohibitions on contracts in restraint of trade, and, most of all, the implications of the Court's decision in *Buchanan v. Warley*. There the Court had prohibited municipal governments from segregating residential areas. Since "there can be no permissible distinction between citizens based on race, creed, or color if we are to remain a harmonious nation,"[77] the Court could not now permit such segregation to be furthered through judicially enforced private agreements.

As Marshall and Storey had foreseen, the Court could find no case of "state action" presented. But it also refused to consider their "public policy" argument and, in a somewhat opaque decision, dismissed the case for want of jurisdiction.[78] Storey was "not surprised at the decision," and wrote; "I deplore it bitterly for the same rules will be tried not only against colored people but against everybody who by social position, nationality, religion, or perhaps politics is objected to by their neighbors."[79] This, the only major case lost by the NAACP in Storey's lifetime, was only a temporary defeat. Twenty years later, the Supreme Court decided that the judicial enforcement of restrictive covenants was indeed "state action" and therefore unconstitutional.[80] In a companion case, the Court extended its ruling to the District of Columbia.[81]

"Those who would hold the Negroes down, who would deprive them of their rights, now understand that any attempt of that sort is going to be met by proceedings in the courts backed by an adequate organization," Storey wrote prophetically in 1926, "and in the courts our rights are safer than anywhere else in this great country."[82] The NAACP's success in achieving the total destruction of the legal embodiment of "white supremacy" was launched with the victories won by Storey. It has been said that the founding of the National Association for the Advancement of Colored People represented a "new abolitionism," a second commitment of some white Americans to fight for the freedom of their black countrymen. In the case of Storey's advocacy on behalf of the NAACP, it would be more accurate to say that it represented the culmination of the original abolitionist commitment—that of Charles Sumner and his idea of "equality before the law."

28

S. Sidney Ulmer

Earl Warren and the Brown Decision

If asked to name the most important decision made by the Supreme Court during the chief justiceship of Earl Warren, the layman could be excused if he answered quickly: the decision about segregation in the *Brown* case. For it is that decision that marked the new chief justice in 1954 as a major force in the American constitutional system. It is that decision that gave the Court's work a tenor and a tone that was to characterize it throughout Warren's tenure. When Warren himself was asked the same question in 1968, he selected *Brown* v. *Board of Education*[1] as one of the two most important cases decided by his Court, placing it only behind *Baker* v. *Carr*[2] in significance. It seems unquestionable, however, that the personal influence of the chief justice was more readily felt in the *Brown* case, in which he wrote the "opinion of the Court," than in the reapportionment case, in which the opinion was written by Justice Brennan. For Warren's opinion in *Brown* received unanimous support, a feat that most students of the Court would have thought unlikely, if not impossible, at the time.

Reprinted from *Journal of Politics*, 33 (1971), 690-702, by permission.

The phenomenon of unanimity in *Brown* has elicited considerable speculation. One observer has written:

Conceivably, we will some day know how unanimity was reached. What was the role of the Chief Justice's predecessor? Was it necessary to woo and win those members of the Court with Southern backgrounds? How were the lines drawn in December of 1953, when the cases were argued for a second time? Are the speculations correct which credit the newly arrived Chief Justice with the unanimous statement? Was the opinion in the cases shaped by adamant refusals to concur unless this or that approach was utilized?[3]

Answers to such questions would, of course, go far in helping one to assess correctly the contribution of Earl Warren to the decision in the Segregation Cases. Until now, however, a lack of appropriate data had inhibited the investigation. The recent opening of the Harold H. Burton Papers presents an opportunity to attempt a fuller and more complete evaluation of Warren's role than has heretofore been possible.[4] That is the purpose of this short paper.[5]

S. Sidney Ulmer

The background for the decision in Brown was laid by the Vinson Court, probable jurisdiction being noted on June 9, 1952.[6] On October 8th, it was decided to continue the cases so that they could be heard with the developing District of Columbia case.[7] This could have been a play for time, for the distinction between the applicable Fourteenth and Fifth Amendments was such as to complicate the finding of common ground for the federal and state cases. Or strategical considerations may have been involved. Some justices may have reasoned that a decision to ban segregation in the "federal city" would increase the pressure to bar it in the states. In any event, by so structuring the situation, the Court underscored its concern with public school segregation as a social rather than a legal problem. After initial arguments, the Court, on June 8, 1953, redocketed the cases and scheduled reargument for October 12.

All the above decisions were made by the Vinson Court, and they suggest that, in this period, the justices were finding a solution difficult. Just how difficult is reflected in the report of the conference held on December 13, 1952,[8] i.e., in the interim between oral argument and the redocketing of the cases. Speaking first in the conference, Vinson observed that public schools in the District of Columbia were segregated in 1868 when the Fourteenth Amendment was adopted. Moreover, the Congress sitting at that time declined to pass a statute barring racial segregation in District schools. Though he voiced no disagreement with Harlan's dissent in Plessy v. Ferguson,[9] he argued that Harlan was careful to avoid a reference to public schools. This, he thought, was highly significant since the opinion otherwise bore down so heavily on racial segregation. With regard to the role of the Court, Vinson expressed the view that if Congress failed to act, the Court would have to confront the problem and would need wisdom to deal with it. He is recorded by Burton as probably upholding the validity of segregation at that time.

The views of the other justices at that point appear to have been as follows: favoring or leaning toward reversal— Black, Douglas, Burton, and Minton; favoring or leaning toward affirmance— Vinson, Reed, Frankfurter, Jackson, and Clark. Had this situation been inherited by Warren in October 1953,[10] it seems quite unlikely that the Court could have reached a decision to reverse, much less a decision unanimously taken.

Although reargument was scheduled initially for October, it did not occur until two months later. A conference was held on December 12 with Warren presiding and, as chief justice, required to speak first. Knowing, as he undoubtedly did, the disparate views prevailing on his Court, knowing the views of his predecessor, and lacking prior experience on the bench, Warren might have been expected to proceed with caution. His statement, however, did not reflect such constraints. Remarking on the high quality of the arguments presented several days earlier, he quickly stated that the Court could not evade the issue but must decide whether segregation was allowable in the public schools. While he was concerned about the possible necessity of overruling earlier cases and lines of reasoning, he concluded that such segregation must now be prohibited. For in his view the only basis for segregation and separate but equal rights was the inherent inferiority of the colored race. This, he thought, was the theory of Plessy and would have to be the theory of the present Court if segregation was to be approved.

Warren could not understand how, in that day and age, one group could be set apart on the basis of race and denied rights given to others. To do so, he argued, violated the Thirteenth, Fourteenth, and Fifteenth Amendments — amendments clearly designed to make slaves equal with all others. On a personal level, he could not fathom how — "today" — segregation could be justified solely on the basis of race. In discussing a possible remedy, he thought it important to avoid precipitous acts that would inflame the situation more than necessary. Conditions in the different states would have to be recognized. Kansas and Delaware with their Negro populations he considered little different from California with its Mexican and Japanese populations. In the Deep South, however, he believed it would require all the wisdom at the command of the Court to abolish segregation with minimal upheaval and strife. He particularly stressed that *how* segregation was abolished was important. In summing up he is recorded by Burton as stating that his "instincts and feelings would lead [him] to say that in these cases [we] should abolish in a tolerant way the practices of segregation in public schools."

Upon reflection Warren's opening statement was a masterly one. It condemned no one; it was unemotional; it recognized differences among the states and in conditions relevant to the problem; it suggested tolerance in disposing of the matter; it referred humbly to the need for wisdom. Thus it projected a reasonable and concerned man with malice toward none — a judge faced with a case to decide whatever the impediments. At the same time one must be struck by the firmness with which Warren asserted at the outset that he was prepared and that the Court was obliged to bar consciously segregated public schools. Given the uncertainties with which some of the other justices were plagued at this time, strong leadership on the question was undoubtedly a key factor in the ultimate solution.

By taking the unambiguous position that segregation by race could only be justified by a belief in the inherent inferiority of the Negro, Warren forced those in opposition to subscribe to a questionable theory or show that such a theory was not a fundamental support for the practice.

Finally, it may be noted that Warren made no reference to the inconclusive history of, or the intentions behind, the Fourteenth or other amendments. Indeed, he asserted that all three of the Civil War amendments were violated. But beyond

that legal reference, his opening comment was not laden with "law language" or frequent reference to "constitutional requirements." Instead he sought to deny the inferiority of Negroes, to suggest that such anachronistic practices as segregation had no place in the modern day, and to follow his instincts and feelings in banning it. Clearly, we see here a man who had enlarged his horizons from the day when, as governor of California, he had been a leading proponent of Japanese exclusion from the West Coast [during World War II].

The reactions of the other justices to Warren's views were mixed. Three of them were of southern background although only one, Black, came from a Deep South state. Reed, of Kentucky, indicated that he understood Warren's attitude and that he (Reed) recognized the dynamic character of the Constitution. He conceded that the Constitution of *Plessy* might not be the Constitution of today and that equal protection, as defined by *Plessy*, had resulted in neither equal facilities nor equal justice for Negroes. Responding directly to Warren, however, Reed observed that the argument was not made before the Court that the Negro was an inferior race, adding that, of course, there was no inferior race. Though Warren expressed no concern about the meaning of the Civil War amendments, Reed reminded his colleague that segregated schools had not been barred by the Congress that framed the amendments. With regard to the legality of segregation, Reed argued that it was not a denial of liberty to say that people must go to separate schools. It was merely the exercise of a police power.

A second Southerner was absent from this conference. Hugo Black, Burton recorded, had departed for Alabama and Florida on December 10. Black's sister-in-law was near death in Birmingham.[11] Thus Black could not have been influenced one way or the other by Warren's opening efforts to eliminate public school segregation from the national scene.

The member from Texas, Tom Clark, was present and ready to grapple with the question. Pointing out that he was closer to the problem, having lived with it, than any other justice except Black, Clark stressed the seriousness of the issues involved. He acknowledged that in some Mississippi and Alabama counties, the Negro population was as much as 60 percent of the total. He noted South Carolina Governor Jimmy Byrnes's threat to abolish public schools. But while opposed to relief by fiat, Clark was willing to pursue a flexible approach. He was surprised at the legislative history of the Fourteenth Amendment. He had always thought the amendment banned segregation by race, but he saw now that Congress had not ignored the question—that it had recognized segregated schools—and that the legislative history could not be used. Nevertheless, he was willing to support Warren if relief were carefully worked out with variations to fit different situations. Thus, the two "southern" justices present at this conference appear to have had opposite preferences at this stage of the proceedings.

The remaining justices on the Court also expressed divergent views. Minton and Douglas were clearly in agreement with Warren, thus maintaining the positions they had taken in the earlier conference in the Vinson Court. Minton could simply imagine no valid distinction based on race or color. He was in favor of outlawing public school segregation on both equal-protection and due-process grounds and was inclined to let the district courts have their heads in the matter. Douglas shared Warren's views concerning the states, though he believed that the legislative history shed a mixed light on the intention of the "framers." His position was essentially that discrimination by race or color could no longer be sanctioned. With regard to the District of Columbia case, he favored sending it back to the Court of Appeals to determine whether segregation in the District was mandatory or permissive.

The last two justices recorded by Burton, Frankfurter and Jackson, provided some contrast in their responses to the new chief justice. Quoting Cardozo to the effect that the Court's work is partly statutory interpretation and partly politics, Jackson asserted that the Segregation Cases required a political decision. This, he said, was no problem for him, but he did not know how to justify the abolition of segregation on judicial grounds. The problem for him was how to create a judicial basis for a political conclusion. He indicated that he could support a political decision, but he may have threatened to label the decision as such. Suggesting that he had no particular loyalty to southern schools, Jackson predicted that trouble would occur when white children were sent to colored schools and colored teachers.

Frankfurter's position at this point was typically philosophical. He began by deploring the fact that the Court was the guardian of the due-process clause. Other nations (India, Australia, Ireland), he observed, had not burdened their high courts with this function. Like Reed and others, Frankfurter doubted that the legislative history of the amendments suggested the unconstitutional status of school segregation. To eliminate it would, he thought, require some psychological adjustments. In any event, he advised against a self-righteous attitude on the part of the Court.

Regarding Burton's position, some initial ambiguity exists. Burton did not record his own remarks in the conference dealing with segregation. His diary likewise reveals nothing of what he may have said in the conferences. Yet, we know that he was heavily involved in the intra-Court interactions that preceded and followed the Segregation Cases and the decisions in them. Burton records that conversations on these cases with one or more justices occurred on a number of occasions between December 1952 and June 1955. The most frequently mentioned justices were Frankfurter and Warren. On April 20, 1954, for example, Burton wrote, "After lunch the Chief Justice and [I] took a walk around the Capitol, then went to his chambers where he [one word illegible] his preliminary thoughts as to [one word illegible] Segregation Cases."[12] Conversations with Warren were also recorded throughout May. In these conversations Burton indicated a high level of agreement with the way in which Warren was handling the cases. It may be inferred that Burton's position was never far from that of Warren. Certainly Burton was not among those justices to whom Warren had to "sell a bill of goods."

When Warren opened the conference reported above, he suggested that discussion be informal and that no vote be taken. Thus no formal vote was cast. Yet, if one had to speculate about the outcome of a vote at that time, it seems likely that Warren would have had a majority with him. Added to his vote would have been those of Minton, Douglas, and Black (consistent with their earlier positions). He could also have counted on Burton and Clark. On the other hand, Jackson and Reed appear to have been two "no" votes while Frankfurter was negative at least regarding the state cases.[13] Thus it appears that Warren began his tenure on the Court with a 6–3 majority in favor of barring public school segregation in the states.

In his diary Harold Burton records the view that, in May 1953, six members of the Court were in favor of and three were opposed to outlawing segregation – with Chief Justice Vinson in dissent. According to Burton a major reason for postponing a decision was the hope of getting a better result later.[14] In any event, Burton's comment suggest that either Frankfurter, Reed, or Jackson was a member of the majority in May 1953 and implies that a 7–2 lineup existed in December 1953.[15]

It does not appear from the evidence available that Warren made any converts to his position between coming to the Court in October and the conclusion of the December 12 conference. This inference is buttressed further by a diary entry

made by Burton on December 17, 1953: "After lunch the Chief Justice told me of his plan to try [and] direct discussion of segregation cases toward the decree – as probably was the best chance of unanimity in that phase."[16] This information serves two purposes. It tells us definitely that the conference held on December 12 had failed to produce the unanimity that Warren clearly sought. Beyond that it reveals poor judgment on Warren's part since the subsequent processes by which a decree was produced proved to be much more complicated and difficult than the processes leading to the initial decision. That this mistake was soon recognized is reflected in the May 1954 decision, which was not a decree but a highly general opinion and decision which did, indeed, have unanimous support.[17]

Was Warren responsible for the unanimity that eventually prevailed in the Segregation Cases? Reaching complete agreement in the Court on so volatile a social issue, as opposed to a divided Court with the Chief Justice in dissent, seems to have been important to Warren. He not only worked to achieve unanimity on the vote but also wanted his opinion in the cases to have the support of all the justices. To obtain the latter, he offered an appealing format in a memorandum sent to his brethren on May 7, 1954. The opinion, he wrote, should be short, nonrhetorical, unemotional and, above all, nonaccusatory.[18]

That the Court finally stood as one in the Segregation Cases is attributed by Burton to the chief justice. In his diary for May 8, 1954, Burton records: "In AM the Chief Justice brought his draft of his segregation cases memoranda. They were in accord with our conversations. In PM I read them and wrote him my enthusiastic approval – with a few minor suggestions. He had done, I believe, a magnificent job that may win a unanimous court."[19] And on May 12, he writes: "The Chief Justice also read to me his latest revision (slight) of his drafts in the Segregation cases. It looks like a unanimous opinion. A major accomplishment for his leadership."[20]

Producing a unanimous opinion was indeed a major accomplishment. For only five days before the opinion was to be handed down, Burton was still uncertain whether there would be unanimous backing for it. The holdouts or doubtful members appear to have been Frankfurter and Jackson, or one of them. It seems not to have been Justice Reed, who lunched with Warren and Burton on that very day. Reed is also recorded as having lunch with Burton and Warren at least twenty times between the initial conference and May 8, including several days in April and early May. While this group was frequently joined by Clark and Minton, and less frequently by Black and Douglas, it was never joined by Frankfurter and Jackson. The inference is that Burton was probably more familiar with Reed's thinking on the question at that time than with that of Frankfurter or Jackson. Comments made by these justices in conference are also consistent with such an interpretation. Subsequent to the *Brown* decision, Frankfurter is on record as saying that "it is not fair to say that the South has always denied the Negroes this Constitutional right. It was not a constitutional right till May 17/54."[21] Taking together all the evidence on Frankfurter, it seems likely that he was in doubt on the state cases until the last possible moment.

After maximizing support for his opinion, Warren considered it necessary to engage in a kind of administrative management that is undoubtedly rare in the Court. It appears that he and other justices were concerned lest there be "leaks" about the upcoming decision. Thus steps were taken to assure that the matter would remain private until decision day. Warren *personally* circulated his final draft opinion among the justices.[22] Burton tells us that on May 15, in conference, the opinions were "finally approved."[23] But, then, "no previous notice was given to [the] office staff, etc. so as to avoid leaks."[24] To avoid suspicion of leaks by the justices themselves, Burton writes that "most of us – including me – handed back the circulated prints to the C.J. to avoid possible leaks."[25]

Managing the timing of news releases is nothing new in government, but the measures taken here were unusual. It seems that the Court placed great importance on being the first to announce its own judgment. These maneuvers also hint that leaks from the Court prior to a formal announcement of case results are more common that one might suspect. Since Burton's recording of these arrangements suggests that they were rare, we have evidence that the Court was particularly sensitive to the subject matter of the cases and the social implications of the decisions in them.[26]

What answers can now be given to the questions quoted at the beginning of this article? Clearly, when Warren came to the Court, a majority of the justices were already in favor of holding public school segregation unconstitutional. Though we can credit him with refraining from action that might have lost him that majority, we cannot conclude that Warren was responsible for it. At the same time, there were strong views in the Court as to how the decision should be formulated and carried out. Warren's low-key approach emphasizing fairness, understanding, and tolerance, combined with a strong plea for justice, clearly contributed to keeping the question on a mature level of discussion and to muting the differences (minor and major) among the justices.

Wooing the southern justices does not appear to have been necessary, at least as regards Black and Clark. It probably did occur in Reed's case. The southern backgrounds of first Vinson and, later, Reed, Black, and Clark were not, however, immaterial for the decision in the Segregation Cases and were of particular importance in the formulation of the 1955 decrees. Each southern justice was not only aware of his southern background, but referred to it in conference. Indeed, having a southern background provided a justice with the aura of an "expert" who had lived with the problem, knew its magnitude, and understood the attitudes and ingrained habits of southern whites – an expert who could foresee the consequences of proceeding in alternative ways.

Deference to the "southern justice" familiar with the "Negro problem" is reflected in Frankfurter's apologetic comment that he had never lived closely with Negroes but had gained some insight into the matter while serving as assistant counsel to the NAACP. He also thought it pertinent to remark that he was a member of the Jewish community.[27] Presumably this gave him some understanding of the treatment of minorities in the United States. In any event, it is clear that the background of a justice was not thought to be beyond the pale of judicial notice.

Robert H. Jackson admitted with embarrassment that he had never really been conscious of the racial issue until he came to Washington. There he discovered that white lawyers, Catholic and Jewish, discriminated against Negroes.[28] Even Reed, from Kentucky, was moved to state that he did not know the Deep South – thereby suggesting that a knowledge of the Deep South was relevant to a decision in the case and that Black and Clark (particularly Black) were better informed and qualified to speak than those without such a background.[29] Neither Black nor Clark hesitated to draw upon his background and familiarity with racial matters in Alabama and Texas. Thus, on balance, it seems likely that the treatment of segregated public schools would have been harsher, in the sense of more immediate and demanding remedies, had the Court been deprived of southern representation at this stage. Southern critics who have been upset with the southern justices for their roles

in the Segregation Cases and the decrees that followed have not adequately appreciated the more subtle influences exerted by those justices on the actions taken.

The unanimous opinion in the case must, of course, be attributed to Warren. Though he was reported as saying in 1968, "Well, gee, the Chief Justice doesn't write all of the important decisions,"[30] he did assign the Segregation Cases to himself and worked for unanimity from the start. Since we know he did not inherit a unanimous Court, it is probably correct to credit him with achieving the full agreement that ultimately prevailed. There is no hard and fast rule by which we can evaluate the significance of unanimity in these cases, though one supposes that the unanimity of the Court enhanced the acceptability of the decision. Had there been dissents, it is possible that dissidents in the concerned public might have rallied around the dissenters. But that is mere speculation, for no appropriate historical evidence is available from earlier cases, and certainly none is available from this decision, for there were no dissents.

The influence of the other justices on the segregation decisions was substantial. Undoubtedly the views of the Court accounted for the gradualism of the social change required and served to temper any tendencies toward precipitous action that might have been present in the Court. All of the justices were aware of the limitations on their ability to effect major social change quickly, and they reflected that belief in their words and actions. It is in circumstances like these that the possible value of having former political leaders on the Court can be appreciated. For political experience tempers the impulse to choose extreme options.

Part Eleven

The Bar and the New Jurisprudence

In the United States the practice of law requires formal training and admission to the bar. At present there are more than 400,000 practitioners, – far more in proportion to population than in any other country. Lawyers in America are influential and ubiquitous: active in business, prominent in politics, and, despite their reputation for conservatism, in the forefront of reform (consider, for example, Ralph Nader and the "public interest" lawyers). American legal and constitutional history cannot be fully understood without some consideration of the role of the lawyer. Jerold Auerbach's essay examines the career of two very prominent lawyers, one a Democrat and one a Republican, and concludes that, despite differences in their political and personal leanings, they both served essentially the same master – big business. There *was* a liberal branch of the profession before the New Deal as afterwards but the dominant voice of the bar defended the prevailing economic order.

Before the twentieth century, despite the work of a few "giants" such as Kent and Story, there was hardly anything in American legal thought worthy of the name, and, compared to continental Europe, academic lawyers still show little interest in legal theory and legal philosophy. But one intellectual movement – legal realism – did flourish in the 1920s and the 1930s, evoking considerable interest both here and abroad, and it still influences scholarship. (It may also affect the behavior of lawyers and judges, but this is much harder to measure.) Edward Purcell's study of legal realism emphasizes its background in ethical relativism and in the exaltation of natural science. The realists were skeptical about legal logic. The clear, precise surfaces of law and the gapless network of rules, they felt, concealed the reality that judges were in fact making law on a case-by-case basis. The realists wanted to be candid and open about the judge's power, hoping in this way to harness it on behalf of the public interest.

Ironically, though the realists were almost invariably liberals, they were vulnerable to the charge that their philosophy ignored justice and the rights of man, delivering the citizen to the tender mercies of the all-powerful state. This was a potent criticism, especially in the growing shadow of Hitler in the 1930s. Under pressure from a powerful and varied group of critics, the realists backed off somewhat, trying to reconcile their view

The Bar and the New Jurisprudence

of the judges' role in fact with their view of a good and just society.

Further Reading

Auerbach, Jerold S. *Unequal Justice, Lawyers and Social change in Modern America.* New York: Oxford University Press, 1976.

Grossman, Joel B. *Lawyers and Judges: The ABA and the Politics of Judicial Selection.* New York: John Wiley & Sons, 1965.

Harbaugh, William H. *Lawyer's Lawyer: The Life of John W. Davis.* New York: Oxford University Press, 1973.

Johnstone, Quintin, and Dan Hopson, Jr. *Lawyers and Their Work: An Analysis of the Legal Profession in the United States and England.* Indianapolis: Bobbs-Merrill & Co., 1967.

Rumble, Wilfred E. *American Legal Realism: Skepticism, Reform, and the Judicial Process.* Ithaca: Cornell University Press, 1968.

Todd, A. L. *Justice on Trial: The Case of Louis D. Brandeis.* Chicago: University of Chicago Press, 1964.

29

Jerold S. Auerbach

Lawyers and Clients in the Twentieth Century

Toward the end of the nineteenth century when Charles Evans Hughes and John W. Davis decided to practice law, the American legal profession had begun to experience the growing pains of modernization. Especially at the metropolitan bar, traditional folkways were unsuited to the changing demographic patterns, accelerating pace, and shifting values of an urban industrial society. Bar associations expressed an impulse toward professional cohesion. Bar admission standards were tightened, and ethical norms were promulgated to define and deter deviance. University legal education, especially the case method, elevated academic excellence above practical experience and encouraged the professionalization of law teaching. Systematized recruitment patterns channeled the talent flow to new corporate firms, which provided comprehensive services to a restricted clientele. Within a generation a sprawling, stratified profession pulled away from the old moorings, its transformation in structure and values complete: from individualism to organization; from apprenticeship to

formal training; from advocacy to counseling; from the disruptive fluidity of the late nineteenth century to the uncertain stability of the early twentieth century.[1]

Hughes and Davis ascended to eminence within the new professional culture. No professional honor and barely a high public office escaped their grasp. Hughes was governor of New York, associate justice of the Supreme Court, secretary of state, and chief justice of the United States. Davis was a congressman from West Virginia, solicitor general, and ambassador to England. They were presidents of the American Bar Association a year apart and, had a Republican been elected in 1916 and a Democrat in 1924, Davis might have followed Hughes to the White House. No chief justice after Marshall did more than Hughes to preserve the Supreme Court from attack upon its institutional power. No advocate after Webster argued more cases than Davis before the Court or won more glowing plaudits from its members. Hughes and Davis were the consummate statesmen of the legal profession in the first half of this century. Not only did the appellation "lawyer's lawyer" describe them; their personal and professional attributes virtually defined the accolade.

Reprinted with changes, from the *Harvard Law Review*, 87 (1974), 1100-11, by permission. Copyright, 1974, by the Harvard Law Review Association.

Hughes, the son of an upstate New York minister, was a precocious child and a voracious student who was driven relentlessly by his parents to excel. Equipped with a formidable intelligence, a law degree from Columbia, and letters of recommendation from his father's well-placed friends, he entered the law office of Walter S. Carter, the architect of the modern law firm who institutionalized its symbiotic relationship with university law schools and business corporations.[2] "These highly privileged firms," Hughes recalled, "seemed to hold in an enduring grasp the best professional opportunities and to leave little room for young aspirants outside the favored groups." Hughes was an insider who capitalized on his opportunities: within five years he and Paul D. Cravath (whom Hughes had met at Columbia) were Carter's partners, and Hughes became Carter's son-in-law. Two decades in practice, interrupted by a brief hiatus on the Cornell law faculty, preceded his meteoric rise in public life after he served as counsel to the New York gas and insurance investigations. To Hughes, the lessons of his career were self-evident: "If the young lawyer sees to it that his work is of the best and if by intelligence and industry he stands well in his own generation, he can afford to await his share of the privileges and responsibilities which to that generation are bound to come."

Davis followed a more circuitous path to Wall Street. He lacked Hughes's intellect; Mrs. Davis observed knowingly that her son was not brilliant, but he would work as hard as anyone. Washington and Lee, where Davis attended college and law school, was a parochial institution that reinforced his orthodoxies. From his father, a prominent Clarksburg attorney, Davis had learned to misread Jefferson in support of natural law, constitutional fundamentalism, and states' rights. College refined his ability to reason from fixed principles and to deport himself as a gentleman. His legal education was no less conventional. His teachers, he reminisced without criticism, wanted their students to learn what law was, not speculate about what it ought to be. Davis was a good student. Orthodoxy did not impede success in Clarksburg, especially for the son of an established lawyer. Davis & Davis was not Carter, Hughes & Cravath but, as the elder Davis reminded his neophyte partner, no young attorney in West Virginia enjoyed more opportunities at the outset of practice. The father's clientele provided initial security; the surging prosperity of local railroads and mining companies offered subsequent opportunity. Young Davis was blunt about his ends. He conceded that he was "after every dollar in sight" that he would "do any amount of work on the *chance* of gaining prestige by it." The strain of working and earning showed. Once he hit an attorney in court; another time he threw an inkwell.

By 1910, when Hughes was appointed to the Supreme Court, Davis had reached the pinnacle of the West Virginia bar. A reluctant candidate for the House of Representatives, he quickly won distinction in Washington as the ablest lawyer in Congress and as an outstanding solicitor general. When he relinquished his ambassadorship in 1921 he was certified by his government experience for the professional elite. As Hughes left Wall Street for Washington, Davis arrived on Wall Street from Washington. Their careers, converging at the apex of professional life, demonstrated that success was possible for educated white Anglo-Saxon Protestant sons of professional fathers whose positions provided a boost on the mobility ladder.[3]

But Hughes and Davis paid for their success in ways that neither their society nor their profession prepared them to comprehend. Hughes, from the age of six when he composed a "Plan of Study," was so driven by the compulsion to work, and to ascribe his work to the dictates of duty, that his professional and public life were constant sources of psychic distress. Law school exhausted him; practice left him "nervously depressed because of the steady grind." He accepted the professorship at Cornell with expectations of surcease. But Cornell also was a "hive of industry," where Hughes remained ensnared in "constant toil". Regaining his "nervous poise," he returned to practice and to periodic "fits of depression." Much of his professional life, he conceded, was "unrequited drudgery." Public service was also private torment. During the life insurance investigation he felt "worn out and utterly depressed"; as governor he was "nervously worn"; when he joined the Court he felt "tired out." Back in practice, he "almost suffered a breakdown." Only duty (he claimed) enabled him to accept the gubernatorial nomination and the Supreme Court appointment. He told President Taft that he could "withstand any personal inclination" to serve on the bench "if it were opposed to the obligations of public duty." It "reassured" Hughes, upon reflection, to discover that his duty to serve impelled him to accept what mere desire (to say nothing of ambition) never could.

What Hughes did from the spur of duty, Davis did for the love of money. He, too, was frustrated by work that consumed his energies and required stringent control over his emotions, yet left him feeling "peevish & fretful." (His absorption with work elicited the poignant lament from his daughter: "What I wanted from him was his time, and he had little to spare.") The harder he worked the more he earned; the more he earned the more he craved. He spurned a teaching offer for the "millions" he wanted from practice. Asked to run for Congress, he pleaded financial insecurity with an annual income (in 1910) of $10,000 and $83,000 in investments. In search of "congenial partners and a remunerative situation," he joined the Stetson firm (whose major client was J. P. Morgan and Co.), although only recently he had described some results of Stetson's craft as "abnormal" and "immoral." He declined a feeler for the Supreme Court because he wanted "some economic independence," provoking Chief

Justice Taft to complain: "If you people in New York were not so eager for money . . . you might have some representatives on our bench." Davis suffered severe reversals after the 1929 crash: his average annual income declined from $400,000 to $275,000 and rising taxes made it a struggle to maintain his Long Island estate and his Fifth Avenue apartment (each with its staff of six). Too much was never enough, as Davis probably sensed when he conceded: "I feel even poorer perhaps than I am."

At critical junctures in their careers public accountability was demanded of Davis and Hughes for their personal and professional choices. As Davis edged closer to the presidential nomination in 1924, the Morgan retainer, his major economic asset, became a political liability. Davis found refuge in the duty "to serve those who call on him" without regard for the implications of service for personal popularity or political reward. "Any lawyer who surrenders this independence or shades this duty . . . disparages and degrades the great profession to which he should be proud to belong." Six years later, when Hughes was nominated for Chief Justice, he was "most bitterly and unjustly attacked," he claimed in his *Notes*, for his corporate counseling. Hughes, like Davis, was distressed by "prejudice arising from a misconception of the character and effect of the activities of a lawyer in active practice."

Their indignation was misplaced. Critics did not question their right to choose corporate practice for the ample financial and professional rewards it assured; they asked only that Davis and Hughes be accountable for their choices. Both lawyers evaded accountability by seeking refuge in professional duty, which was sufficiently resilient to accommodate any demand upon it. But a lawyer who was obligated to serve well those who called was hardly compelled to engage in practice which virtually eliminated noncorporate callers. It was sophistry for Davis to claim that he was asked to betray his professional independence when, in fact,

Jerold S. Auerbach

he was being urged to demonstrate it. Hughes, who casually dismissed any inference that a lawyer might be judged by the clients he kept, cited Professor Zechariah Chafee, Jr., approvingly for declaring that Hughes had merely fulfilled his "duty to represent loyally the client for whom he happened to be working." But the question was not whether loyal representation was provided. It was whether the recipients of loyal representation constituted a restricted, identifiable clientele whose interests shaped a lawyer's practice, values, and politics, and thus his qualification for public office.

Hughes and Davis were momentarily embarrassed by their professional identity, but they were not impeded by it. Hughes was confirmed; Davis remained the acknowledged leader of the corporate bar. But the accumulation of prestige and dollars exposed the nagging predicament of Davis' career: he was a Jeffersonian individualist whose corporate retainers, William H. Harbaugh suggests, "imposed subtle restraints on his freedom of action." Unable to reconcile constitutional fundamentalism with social change, he violated in practice every precept of his Jeffersonian and professional faith. He displayed a "consuming concern for the preservation of individual liberties," but corporate counseling, Harbaugh concludes, "slowly forced him to inure himself to the injustices wrought against individuals." He defended states' rights, but, Harbaugh notes, "it was the national corporations on whose boards Davis sat ... that set in motion the subversion of states' rights." He defended strict constructionism and limited federal power, but he demanded the broadest construction of treason and the war powers during World War I. He claimed that he would take any case that came into his office, but when Gus Hall, a Communist convicted under the Smith Act, approached him, Davis responded that he was too busy.

It is an article of professional faith that when constitutional freedoms are in jeopardy bar leaders like Hughes and Davis will rise to the responsibility of defending unpopular and beleaguered persons. Indeed, Hughes protested against the expulsion of duly elected Socialist members of the New York legislature during the red scare, and Davis carried an appeal to the Supreme Court on behalf of a theologian who claimed that selective conscientious objection should not disqualify him from citizenship. Yet there lurks the suspicion that incidents like these are celebrated less because they are typical than because they are exceptional, despite Davis's insistence that it was the "supreme function" of lawyers to serve as "sleepless sentinels on the ramparts of human liberty and there to sound the alarm whenever an enemy appears."

In fact Davis slumbered on the ramparts of liberty, secure in the knowledge that federal power was the enemy, and Liberty Leagues were necessary only when New Dealers regulated corporations. Not that Davis was exceptional. Twenty-three other lawyers also refused to provide Communist Party leader Gus Hall with counsel, but no one ever accused them of devotion to professional ideals.

Learned Hand was so enamored of the quality of Hughes's character that "to question the sincerity and purity of his motives betrayed either that you had not understood what he was after, or that your own standards needed scrutiny." Hand also was so captivated by Davis's "eloquence and charm" that he feared he might disregard the merits of any case that Davis argued. Davis (who belonged to an intimate dinner club with Learned and Augustus Hand) was mindful of the advantages bestowed. He once said of the Second Circuit, on which both Hands sat: "Nobody can hurt me in this Court!" Harbaugh concludes that "tough-minded jurists had to fight off his seductive charm." Elegance, grace, style, charm — some elusive components of character — are the recurrent adjectives that lawyers used to describe Davis, in part, no doubt, because he possessed these qualities and in part, one suspects, from the desire to cover substance with manner. But Felix Frankfurter, among others, knew the underside of "character": it was one of those "high-falutin' expressions for personal likes and dislikes, or class, or color, or religious partialities or antipathies."[4]

The Davis Polk firm, like other prestigious Wall Street firms, institutionalized these qualities of character. Not coincidentally, it also gained a reputation as "the most socially exclusive office on Wall Street." This achievement culminated a process within corporate firms that began back when Hughes and Cravath joined Carter. Mass immigration and urbanization threatened the dominant Anglo-Saxon culture. The fortunate few created sanctuaries for the preservation of their group power and status in eastern schools, careers in business and financial bureaucracies, and corporate law-firm partnerships.[5] Reserved for those who possessed proper Anglo-Saxon social credentials (character and ethnicity did not mix, as elite opposition to the Brandeis nomination in 1916 demonstrated), the Wall Street firm was a crucial link between corporate capitalism and social elitism. White Anglo-Saxon Protestants dominated the partnership roster, transforming it into an appendix to the *Social Register*. Davis must have done more then "acquiesce" in this pattern; his presence (including, doubtlessly, his genteel racism and anti-Semitism), as Harbaugh notes, "was felt everywhere within the firm." An occasional Roman Catholic was tolerable, but blacks of course were not, nor were new immigrants. Years earlier Davis had described himself as one of those "who resent all immigration in general and that of the Russian Jew in particular." Davis Polk and its counterparts on Wall Street, State Street, and LaSalle Street were oases for club members whose social origins and character eased their journey to elite status.

Character was necessary for club membership but insufficient for professional distinction. Craft was the *sine qua non* of elite professionalism. Only lawyers with Davis's "compulsion for technical perfec-tion" and "dedication to the case at hand" were elevated to the highest state of professional grace. Craft required skills: mastery of facts and knowledge of law; reasoning acuity; and, as an advocate, "the ability to simplify complex matters with a few pithy Anglo-Saxon phrases devoid of adjectives and drained of all emotion." But craft also required a particular definition of the lawyer's role, which disguised volition and values under the cloak of technical proficiency. Davis was "just a law lawyer" (according to his friend, Charles C. Burlingham, a prominent New York attorney) who, Harbaugh writes, "adhered absolutely to the principle that the lawyer's duty was to represent his client's interest to the limit of the law, not to moralize on the social and economic implications of the client's lawful actions." As Davis reminisced: "It was my duty to find out what the law was, and to tell my client what rule of life to follow. That was my job. If the rules changed, well and good." For Davis, the lawyer was merely a technician ("He does not create. All he does is lubricate the wheels of society") wearing a surgeon's mask ("The lawyer must steel himself . . . to think only of the subject before him & not of the pain his knife may cause"). Such professional tunnel vision was designed to obliterate those disturbing substantive issues that Davis preferred to ignore: once the laws regulating corporate activity changed in the 1930s, he found it neither well nor good; his lubricant was selectively sold and applied; the clients whose retainers he avidly procured were immune to the pain he inflicted.

Exaltation of craft eliminated the political and social implications of a lawyer's work from consideration and sustained the illusion that law was science, not politics. Proficiency certainly matters: how well something is done is never inconsequential, but the "morality of process," to quote a recent phrase of Alexander Bickel,[6] is the highest morality only for those trained from their first day in law school to separate method from substance. It is important to know, for example, that Solicitor General Davis presented an argument in support of broad federal power over commerce and civil rights that was as technically impeccable as the argument that private attorney Davis made in opposition to both policies. But preoccupation with craft ignores the substantive differences between these policies, the social consequence of those differences, and the fact that Davis argued the government's cases for six years and corporations' cases for half a century. The point is not that Davis was a hired gun, but that he consistently sold his craft to the highest bidder while claiming that the practice of law was "an avenue for service and not a means for private gain."

Fifty years ago when Davis ran for President, Professor Felix Frankfurter, dismayed by the "crass materialism" of his students, wrote that "it is good nei-ther for these lads that I see passing through this School from year to year, nor for this country, . . . that we should reward with the Presidency one to whom big money was the big thing."[7] Although the White House eluded Davis and Hughes, virtually nothing that their profession could offer exceeded the reach of these supremely successful practicing attorneys. Nevertheless, the professional culture exacted its toll. Its elevation of craft as the ultimate criterion of value detached process from purpose and divided the psyches of its ablest practitioners. Although it sanctified these debilitating divisions and rewarded as lawyer's lawyers those who submerged their personal lives in their professional careers, both Davis and Hughes displayed persistent symptoms of discomfort, avoidance, and repression.

30

Edward A. Purcell, Jr.

American Jurisprudence between the Wars: Legal Realism and the Crisis of Democratic Theory

During the 1930s the American legal profession became the forum for one of the most bitter and sustained intellectual debates in the nation's history. A new generation of legal scholars, inspired by Justice Oliver Wendell Holmes, Jr., and attempting a scientific study of law, was developing a sweeping critique of American jurisprudence that went far beyond the criticisms of such sociological jurists as Roscoe Pound and Benjamin N. Cardozo. By 1930 their stinging attacks on established legal conceptions had alarmed traditionally-minded jurists and within a few years had raised distressing questions from the standpoint of democratic theory about the nature and basis of law. The frightening challenge of totalitarianism in the late thirties moved the debate out of the realm of mere juristic speculation and gave it a tone of urgency and crisis.

The new legal criticism developed out of the same intellectual environment that generated new attitudes throughout American intellectual life. The increasing prominence of the physical sciences, at least since the time of Charles Darwin,

had been convincing more and more individuals that knowledge of the physical world and of human beings themselves could only be attained through the use of the scientific method. By the beginning of the twentieth century the pragmatism of William James and especially of John Dewey had provided a broad philosophy that attempted to explain the human and social meaning of science and that suggested how the scientific method could be employed to understand and resolve human problems on all levels. Large numbers of American thinkers in many diverse fields began to adopt a more empirical, experimental, and relativistic attitude toward the problems and guiding assumptions of their disciplines. The impact of science and pragmatism, together with the desire for the improvement of man's social and political life that many intellectuals shared, brought new vitality, ideas, and methods to the expanding social sciences.

Through such approaches as functionalism and behaviorism, American psychologists were striving to make their discipline experimental; the new science began to play an increasingly prominent role in the social thought of the twentieth century. By offering to explain the sources

Reprinted from *American Historical Review,* 75 (1969), 424-446 by permission.

Edward A. Purcell, Jr.

and nature of human behavior, psychology promised to bring the elusive human factor under control and to enable social scientists to make their work wholly empirical. "The importance of the rapid rise of psychology in recent years," explained Edward S. Robinson, a psychologist working with Yale University Law School, "is that it supplies a background for a natural science of society which has hitherto been lacking."[1] Because psychology seemed to answer an intellectual need that had grown acute by the twenties, many social scientists turned toward its discoveries and theories with renewed hope and enthusiasm.

Rejecting the prescriptive theories of classical economics, such scholars as Thorstein Veblen and Wesley Mitchell studied production and distribution as problems in the institutional behavior of individuals and groups. "Economics," Mitchell declared, "is a science of human behavior."[2] Charles Merriam urged his fellow political scientists to apply the discoveries of psychology and the other social sciences to the study of politics, and along with many of his colleagues produced closely detailed studies of the actual operations of governments, politicians, and pressure groups. Bronislaw Malinowski refined techniques of careful observation and description in anthropological field work and developed a theory of society based on the functional interrelationships of all parts of a culture.[3] Throughout those disciplines the new empirical, experimental approach emphasized the importance of analyzing social phenomena in terms of functions and behavior.

Along with the primary reliance upon scientific methods came a pervasive epistemological and ethical relativism. Because valid knowledge had to be based on empirical evidence, all a priori absolutes were unproved and unprovable. All knowledge was necessarily tentative and subject to change. Since science supposedly dealt only with objective facts and was morally neutral, the one practically reliable method of reaching truths was inoperative where questions of an ethical nature were concerned. Although a few men such as Dewey maintained that the scientific method could develop and substantiate moral values, most scholars in the interwar decades were not convinced. The empirical documentation of widespread cultural relativism by anthropologists like Ruth Benedict confirmed the relativistic trend, as did the analyses of the nature of historical knowledge by such scholars as Carl Becker and Charles Beard. By the early thirties both Beard and Becker were arguing that historical judgments could never be truly objective because they were based on partial evidence, were not subject to experimental testing, and were warped by the desires and beliefs of the historian. Value judgments, Beard concluded along with most of his contemporaries, "cannot be 'proved' by reference to historical occurrences or anything else."[4]

While the basic attitudes of an empirical and relativistic social science spread throughout most of American intellectual life, they penetrated legal thinking slowly and haltingly. As late as the 1920s the predominant legal theory still claimed that judicial decisions were made on the basis of rules and precedents defined historically and applied mechanically. The eighteenth-century concept of natural law served vaguely as the moral foundation for legislative and judicial actions, while Sir William Blackstone's statement of the common law provided many of the supposed first principles on which judicial decisions were based. The old legal theory claimed that reasoning proceeded syllogistically from those rules and precedents through the particular facts of a case to a clear decision. The sole function of the judge was to discover the proper rules and precedents involved and to apply them to the case as first premises. Once he had done that, the judge could decide the case logically with certainty and uniformity.[5]

In spite of its established predominance, however, the old legal theory had already come under forceful attack by the beginning of the twenties. As early as 1881 Justice Holmes, then a young lawyer in Boston, had published his famous study of the common law, which he placed in an evolutionary Darwinistic framework. Holmes argued that practical expedients, necessitated by the needs and conflicts of human society, were much more central to the development of law than were any logical propositions. *The Common Law* was, to use a congenial Holmesian metaphor, the first cannon shot in his fifty-year battle against the armies of legalistic formalism.

By 1897 the basic outline of his scientific, relativist attack was clear. Law was not an abstract problem of logic, but a practical question of social management. Judges did not in fact settle cases by deductive reasoning; rather they necessarily decided what was socially desirable according to their personal and class beliefs. Those beliefs, like all moral values, were wholly relative and determined by one's particular environment. The power of deductive logic and the ethical and social absolutes that the method claimed to establish were simply illusions that masked the actual working of the legal process. By the law, Holmes declared, he meant no metaphysical truths or grand moral principles such as a rationally knowable "natural law," but only "the incidence of the public force through the instrumentality of the courts." The lawyer's sole duty was to predict how the courts would use that force, and hence to advise his clients most effectively. Thus defining the law in empirical, behavioral terms, Holmes urged his colleagues to study "the operations of the law" rather than its phraseology or moral connotations.[6]

By the first decade of the twentieth century other scholars were beginning to follow Holmes's lead and to apply the insights of the new scientific, pragmatic outlook. John Chipman Gray, a professor of law at Harvard University, stressed the preeminent role of the individual judge as opposed to the logic of the law itself in deciding particular cases. Louis D. Brandeis and, later, Felix Frankfurter argued that judges must consciously consider the probable social results of their decisions. Scientific studies of social needs and problems, rather than syllogistic reasoning, should be the determining factor. To guide the judges in their assessment of those social results, both men employed briefs loaded with a maximum of sociological evidence and a minimum of logical argumentation.[7]

Much of the theoretical justification for the "Brandeis brief" came from the work of a young law professor at the University of Nebraska, Roscoe Pound, who wrote a series of articles showing the need for and relevance of a new sociological jurisprudence. "The sociological movement in jurisprudence," he explained in 1908, "is a movement for pragmatism as a philosophy of law."[8] Agreeing with Holmes that legal scholars must study the way laws operate in practice, Pound insisted that the overemphasis on logical uniformity and theoretical certainty that characterized much of the older approach often frustrated the just practical settlement of particular cases. Only by studying the social impact of legal principles and rules could men know whether the law in fact brought about the administration of real justice. While Pound and Holmes agreed on many points, especially on the mechanical and abstract nature of the older legal theory, Pound's greater emphasis on the ideal of justice conflicted with Holmes's more cynical view of moral values in the law. Ultimately that difference would be one of the central reasons for Pound's rejection of Holmes's disciples, who were to some extent also his own, in the 1930s.

It was thus in a rigid and formalistic profession that nevertheless had produced a Holmes and a Pound, and in a broader intellectual environment that recognized science as the method of reaching truth, that the so-called legal realists came of age. Of a sample of twenty-two of the most important new critics only five had been born before 1880, while eight were born during the

Edward A. Purcell, Jr.

1880s, and nine after 1890. By 1930 when their collective efforts were first termed "legal realism" their average age was still only forty-two.[9] Thus the realists formed a younger generation of scholars, less committed to what they regarded as the rigid ways of the past and more willing to follow new methods and ideas. Having grown up with the spread of the scientific outlook and the successful growth of the social sciences, they readily accepted a critical, empirical attitude and hoped to apply it to the study of the legal process. Facing the need to discuss the observed facts of judicial behavior, many of the realists turned toward psychological theory for a scientific framework within which to work.

While their pragmatic attitude made them hostile toward the older legal theory and their age put them in the position of a new generation ready to criticize established methods, the state of American law invited and even necessitated their devastating attacks. The inconsistencies between the practices of a rapidly changing industrial nation and the claims of a mechanical juristic system had grown so acute by the 1920s that in the minds of an increasing number of individuals the old jurisprudence could no longer justify and explain contemporary practice. It had become clear, Judge Cardozo declared in 1932, that "the agitations and the promptings of a changing civilization" demanded more flexible legal forms and demanded equally "a jurisprudence and philosophy adequate to justify the change."[10]

At the same time even many of the strict proponents of the old jurisprudence had to admit that widespread confusion and uncertainty threatened the American legal system. Such a stalwart of orthodoxy as Elihu Root acknowledged that "the confusion, the uncertainty, was growing worse from year to year" and that as a result "the law was becoming guesswork."[11] Root, like many other lawyers, found the cause of confusion primarily in the massive growth of case law during the previous decades. The whole case law system had, in fact, become unwieldy since the 1870s when the National Reporter system was inaugurated. At that time the West Publishing Company had begun printing all federal court opinions throughout the United States, in addition to all higher and some lower state court decisions. By the beginning of the twentieth century the National Reporter system had turned the inevitably increasing number of cases into an avalanche of reported precedents that made it impossible for judges to stay properly informed.[12] To their great chagrin and bewilderment, members of the legal profession began uncovering contradictory and conflicting decisions with ever-increasing frequency.

That plight was so widely recognized that in 1923 Root and a number of his orthodox colleagues helped establish the American Law Institute to abolish confusion by a clear and updated "restatement" of the law. The organization's first report emphasized, in addition to the flood of precedents, a number of other contributing causes of legal uncertainty, including a lack of precision in the use of legal terms and a lack of agreement on basic common-law principles.[13] For many of the young critics the widely acknowledged confusion was clear evidence that the syllogistic certainty of the law was a hollow claim and that the actual role of the individual judge was much wider and more crucial than the older jurisprudence allowed.

The very fact that the new American Law Institute was attempting a "restatement" of the law was an additional factor provoking the new critique. Such a restatement assumed that law preexisted in some whole form that could be discovered by logical analysis and that the job of the American Law Institute was merely to write it down. Most of the members of the institute still believed in the validity of the older juristic method and thought that a more rigorous application would resolve all difficulties. Convinced that law was a human product related to changing social and cultural conditions, the new critics rejected the idea of an official restatement as an impossible goal.[14]

The practical experience of many of the realists served to strengthen their awareness of the changing and subjective elements in the legal system. The great majority of them had practiced law for at least a year before starting to teach, and they were aware of the many individual, human factors that lay behind the actions of lawyers and judges. They knew firsthand the conflicting and confused nature of many precedents and rules. Such practical experience, as well as their pragmatic outlook, helped lead many of them to hostility toward the older jurisprudence. Recognizing the need both to understand the actual relationship between law and a changing society and to explain the reasons behind contemporary practice, they began their concerted though diverse probing for a new and scientific jurisprudence.

By the end of the twenties Yale, Columbia, and Johns Hopkins had become the centers of the new legal criticism. Charles E. Clark, who succeeded Robert M. Hutchins as dean of the Yale University Law School in 1929, brought such aggressive scholars as Jerome Frank, Walter Nelles, William O. Douglas, Thurman Arnold, and Robinson to New Haven. In cooperation with Johns Hopkins University three of the most scientific minded critics, Walter Wheeler Cook, Herman Oliphant, and Hessel E. Yntema, founded the research-oriented Institute of Law in 1929. At Columbia University Karl N. Llewellyn, often regarded as the most important of the new critics, joined with Edwin W. Patterson, Underhill Moore, and others in publishing sharp essays probing the weaknesses of traditional jurisprudence. Dean Leon Green of Northwestern University, Felix S. Cohen of the New School for Social Research, Max Radin of the University of California, Thomas Reed Powell of Harvard University, and Judge Joseph C. Hutcheson of the United States District Court in Texas were among those whose work placed them in the forefront of the new movement.

The intense debate over legal realism as a collective movement began in 1930 when Llewellyn and Frank, then an attorney practicing in New York, published separate essays that struck the legal profession in rapid succession. Llewellyn used the phrase "Realistic Jurisprudence" to describe his suggested approach, and soon the term "legal realism" came to stand for the general attitude of all the new critics. While most of the so-called realists disliked the label, their enemies seized upon it as an epithet to brand what they considered an unsound and often dangerous attitude.

Llewellyn's article on "Realistic Jurisprudence" centered on the distinction between abstract legal verbalisms and concrete empirical facts. "The traditional approach is in terms of words; it centers on words," he explained, adding pointedly, "it has the utmost difficulty in getting beyond words".[15] Legal phrases and concepts were simple devices to make the world more manageable, but the history of American law showed that those necessary abstractions "tend to take on an appearance of solidarity, reality and inherent value which has no foundation in experience".[16] Hence they led to a rigidity that forced new facts and situations to conform to outmoded concepts or else ignored the new altogether. Much of the law was an exercise in painful definition and strained syllogism that bore little resemblance to the real world it was supposed to govern.

Such an important concept as that of the legal rule was a perfect example of the danger and ambiguity inherent in rigid abstractions, Llewellyn declared. While such authoritative rules were supposed to lead judges to proper decisions, they were in fact so vague and confused as often to be no help at all. When lawyers talked of legal rules, no one knew whether they were the lawyer's rule or the court's; whether they represented what the courts should do, or what they had done in fact; whether courts actually followed them, or merely used them to justify a decision reached on other grounds. Such fuzzy conceptions of legal rules led to large-scale uncertainty and

Edward A. Purcell, Jr.

contradiction in actual decisions and caused massive and often absurd twisting of terms in legal argumentation. Fundamental conceptual imprecision, Llewellyn concluded, could only mean "confusion, profuse and inevitable."[17]

He insisted that there was almost always a gap between the so-called rules of a case and its practical settlement. Admitting that legal rules had some uncertain influence on judges, he resolutely maintained that a realistic study of the law demanded an examination of the extent to which the rules actually controlled or influenced the case. "You cannot generalize on this, *without investigation*", Llewellyn insisted. If men were ever to understand the legal system, they would have to study individual cases empirically. "The significance of the particular rule", he stressed, "will appear only *after* the investigation of the vital, focal phenomenon: the behavior".[18] Llewellyn's empirical approach concentrated on behavior as the proper subject of study for the legal scholar. Behavior was real, whereas most legal argumentation was simply verbal game playing. Following Holmes's lead, Llewellyn defined law in terms of the coercive actions taken by government officials. Regardless of syllogisms and definitions, the actual law was what the public force would support. "What these officials do about disputes," Llewellyn wrote in a sentence that returned to haunt him, "is, to my mind, the law itself".[19] Using such a definition, the whole legal process was clearly susceptible to empirical study. Again following Holmes, Llewellyn declared that concepts of justice and ethical right had to be ignored when the actual operations of the law were analyzed. Such concepts merely confused the investigator by mixing considerations of "ought" where only the realities of "is" were relevant. "The most fruitful thinking about law," he remarked, "has run steadily toward regarding law as an engine (a heterogeneous multitude of engines) having purposes, not values in itself".[20]

Accepting most of Llewellyn's ideas, Frank went far beyond them in earning his reputation as one of the most extreme realists. Whereas Llewellyn believed that rules and precedents were relevant and of some importance, Frank did not even consider them a meaningful part of the law. To him law meant a particular judicial determination upon a particular and singular set of facts. Reducing law to what he considered an unequivocal empirical minimum, Frank equated it solely with the specific individual judicial decisions. "Until a court has passed on these facts," he insisted, "no law on that subject is yet in existence."[21]

Rules and precedents were not part of the law because they had little if any effect on actual judicial decisions. No one could reason out a decision by syllogism, Frank declared. Instead judges had "hunches" about how cases should be decided and then looked up the proper rules that would support their "hunch." "Judicial judgments, like other judgments," Frank maintained, "doubtless in most cases, are worked out backward from conclusions tentatively formulated."[22] A judicial opinion was actually only the judge's rationalization, not the real explanation for his decision. Judges manipulated precedents in the same way: after they made their decision, they sought favorable precedents or reinterpreted unfavorable ones to support it. "What the courts in fact do," Frank charged, "is to manipulate the language of former decisions."[23]

As a result of realistic, empirical analysis of actual decisions, it became clear that the law was not a rational whole, nor even largely logical. In addition to personal prejudices, judicial objectivity was further deflected by the necessity of relying on secondhand evidence concerning the facts, relayed by lawyers, parties to the case, and witnesses who distorted the facts through prejudice, misunderstanding, ignorance, or simple falsification. The facts of any case were thus necessarily elusive and essentially subjective. The law was vague, uncertain, and necessarily partial and prejudiced. "To predict the decisions of the courts on many a point," Frank argued, "is impossible."[24]

In spite of the practical uncertainty and subjectivity, Frank continued, most lawyers and judges still insisted that law was essentially rational and certain. The explanation for that contradiction, he suggested, lay in what he called the "legal absolutist" mind. The father-child pattern, bred deeply during every individual's childhood, drove most men continually to seek some powerful authority figure which would act as a substitute for the "Father-as-Infallible-Judge."[25] Because the law served as a natural authority figure, Frank concluded, it subconsciously stimulated the latent childish emotions of those who studied it. "We would seem to be justified in surmising that the subject-matter of the law is one which evokes, almost irresistibly, regressive emotions."[26] Most lawyers and judges, therefore, unconsciously developed an "absolutist" viewpoint that made them see the law as a father-like authority figure, necessarily certain and just in operation. That subconscious drive prevented them from recognizing the true nature of the legal system.

The manipulation of abstract concepts provided the method with which lawyers and judges could construct a façade of certainty and absolute rationality over the confused legal process. Referring to such manipulation as "Platonism" and "Scholasticism," he charged that the "absolutists" used "magical phrases" to convince themselves that all was well and to rationalize awkward facts. Frank considered concrete facts as the only important reality. Such abstract rationalizations were merely escapes and delusions. "Virtually empty concepts," Frank remarked, "seem to give to the metaphysician the stable world he requires."[27] Because the concepts were empirically empty — they did not bear a definite and constant relation to any concrete reality — they were liable to all kinds of twisting and reinterpreting. In such a way lawyers were able to reconcile completely contradictory judicial decisions as "logical" under the same principle or precedent.

Although he declared that the great majority of men believed in the certainty of law, Frank was primarily interested in, and hostile toward, traditional legal theories and their contemporary advocates who controlled the bench and the bar. Using a technique reminiscent of that of Veblen, Frank on several occasions remarked in footnotes or appendixes that his psychoanalytic approach provided only a partial explanation for the legal quest for certainty. But after making that qualification in obscure places, usually he continued in the text to write as if that approach were the only explanation. Indeed, while consistently proclaiming lawyers and judges highly intelligent and learned men, he described them throughout as immature, childish, and irrational.

The two works by Frank and Llewellyn had an immediate impact. Pound, then dean of the Harvard Law School and the most renowned legal scholar in America, responded early in 1931, ironically in an issue of the *Harvard Law Review* dedicated to Justice Holmes on his ninetieth birthday. Although Pound had earlier espoused many of the attitudes associated with realism, by 1931 he had become wary of some of the more radical implications of pragmatism and positivism in the law. He was perhaps, in addition, moved to reply by the fact that both Llewellyn and Frank had specifically attacked his work on juristic theory. Undoubtedly having Frank most clearly in mind, Pound accused an unnamed group of "realists" of allowing their naïve faith in empiricism to lead them into a philosophical nominalism that denied the existence of legal rules, doctrines, principles, and concepts. They overemphasized irregularities and contradictions and ignored the uniformity and reasonableness of the law. By focusing on subjective motives and behavior of judges, Pound asserted, the realists were leading legal science into a dead end.[28]

Considering his attack unfair, Llewellyn and Frank replied jointly and claimed Pound's criticisms were almost wholly unwarranted. The importance of the reply was that Llewellyn and Frank gathered together and defended twenty of the better-known critics who, they explained, could be taken as a fair sample of the new approach to the law. While emphasizing that the twenty represented no "school" and were by no means in complete agreement in their own attitudes, Frank and Llewellyn admitted that their criticisms of existing legal theory gave them a unified approach. By the end of 1931 the new critics had been attacked and defended, and, most importantly, they had been personally identified and categorized.[29]

While Frank alone had attempted a sweeping psychoanalytic interpretation, he and Llewellyn had agreed on several key points. They assumed that human knowledge could never be certain and uniformly logical and that law was a constantly changing phenomenon. They denounced abstract verbal formulas and absolutes as the bane of clear thinking, legal or otherwise. They agreed that the "is" and the "ought" should be temporarily separated for the purpose of precise study. Finally Llewellyn and Frank were united in calling for careful empirical studies of the way the law actually operated in society, with an emphasis on the dubious practical impact of legal rules and the likelihood that judicial opinions were at least partly rationalizations. Because of that focus on judicial motivation, both of them, like most realists, looked to their colleagues in psychology for clues to help explain the legal process. Behaviorism, Freudianism, and abnormal psychology all played a role in the new movement.[30] Around those basic attitudes the realists centered their attacks on traditional jurisprudence.

Although the young critics were firm believers in democracy, most of them embraced an empirical relativism that raised both practical and theoretical questions about the nature of democratic government. The most important practical point of their argument was to question and in many cases to reject the idea of a government of laws rather than of men. While most democratic legal theories — and the United States Constitution — held that established and known laws alone should be binding on free citizens, the realists maintained that such laws were nonexistent and impossible to attain. Frank had argued that law was uncertain in administration and depended largely on the subjective motivations of the particular judge who heard the case. "It is fantastic, then," he had declared, "to say that usually men can warrantably act in reliance upon 'established law.'"[31]

Frank based much of his analysis of the judicial process on the work of Judge Hutcheson, who claimed that all judges reached their decisions by "hunches" based on an "intuitive flash of understanding" that revealed the proper decision in a case. He was referring, Hutcheson pointed out, not to the rationalization or the "logomachy" that the judge used to explain his opinion, but to the actual way in which he decided a case. "The vital, motivating impulse for the decision," he remarked, "is an intuitive sense of what is right or wrong for that case".[32] If that were the process of decision, then the social, economic, and moral values of the judge were far more important than the rest of the legal structure, and the law was clearly a subjective, changeable phenomenon.

Most of the new critics accepted an analysis similar to Hutcheson's and tried to base their legal theory on a subjective conception of judicial decisions. Radin emphasized the number of conflicting rules that pertained to any case. In such a situation the judge was forced to decide cases on an expectation of their probable social results. Since that meant a reliance on the judge's subjective value standards, the process was actually a matter of personal motivation. "Judges, we know, are people," Radin commented, and they thus make their decisions like all other people.[33] Yntema make the point even more explicitly: "The ideal of a government of laws and not of men," he maintained, "is a dream."[34] The subjective motives of the judge, not the existence of rules, or even constitutions, provided the key to understanding the law.

Morris R. Cohen, a philosopher at the City College of New York and a leading critic of realism, pointed to the antidemocratic implication of such a judicial theory. "To be ruled by a judge," Cohen declared, "is, to the extent that he is not bound by law, tyranny or despotism."[35] When the realists claimed that the judge's subjective decision was the only law, he implied, they were justifying judicial despotism.

At that point, the theoretical force of the realist critique became clear, for it rejected any concept of a higher law that could provide judges with objective, rational guidance to assure a just operative law. A pervasive scientific relativism that seemed to undermine any objective or absolute moral standard underlay the realist approach. Llewellyn and Frank had both assailed abstract logic and deductive rationalism and scorned the absolutes that those approaches generated. Their determination to make concrete empirical facts the touchstone for all analytical concepts seemed necessarily to exclude ideas of "ought" in favor of facts about "is." If what men ought to do was not identical with what they did in fact, then there was no basis in their approach for discussing moral concepts except as mere psychological data. It would, in any case, be impossible to establish the objective validity of any such ethical values.

Some of the realists made their relativism explicit and direct. Cook, another of the founders of the Institute of Law at Johns Hopkins University who had been trained first as a physicist, looked enthusiastically to the physical sciences for his legal inspiration. Scorning the futility of deduction, he emphasized that human knowledge had "reached the era of relativity." By relativity, he explained, he

meant "a point of view, which, whatever may happen to specific doctrines, seems destined to remain as a permanent achievement in human thought."[36] Neither legal nor moral theory could escape that era.

Applying the scientific, relativist approach to the question of legal and moral standards, Moore, who taught first at Columbia University and later at Yale, similarly rejected the idea of absolutes: "Ultimates are phantoms drifting upon the stream of day dreams." Arguing for a pragmatic standard of judgment, he insisted that "human experience discloses no ultimates."[37] Nelles, a professor at Yale University, carried the approach to its extreme. "I deny ethical *right* and *ought* without qualification," he declared in 1933. He scorned the possibility of both scientific and deductive ethics. "In the twentieth century," he remarked, "popular feeling of the wickedness of denying ethical *right* and *ought* can no longer command the unconscious deference of an important mind."[38] In the minds of most of the realists there could be no such thing as a demonstrable moral standard.

The pragmatism and apparent ethical relativism of men like Cook, Moore, and Nelles shocked much of the legal profession. Although the counterattack did not reach its bitterest phase until after 1935, it had clearly begun by the early thirties. John Dickinson, one of Pound's leading disciples, and Hermann Kantorowicz, a professor at the New School for Social Research, criticized the realists for dismissing the importance of rules and pointed to the philosophical difficulties in their approach.[39] Hutchins, then president of the University of Chicago, and Mortimer Adler, a prominent philosopher, joined the assault on realism, basing their attacks on an Aristotelian-Thomistic philosophy. Rationally knowable moral principles, not inchoate empirical facts, were the proper foundation of jurisprudence.[40] By excluding ethical considerations and reverting to a philosophical nominalism, many scholars believed, the realists were necessarily making force the only meaningful arbiter of human affairs and destroying the ethical basis of democracy.

To harm the cause of democratic government was the last thing the realists hoped to do. In attacking traditional abstractions and nonempirical concepts of justice, they were usually assailing what they considered the practical injustices of American society. Abstraction in economics and politics, as in the law, they believed, had been one of the biggest obstacles to the attainment of a truly democratic society. Frank, Oliphant, Clark, Arnold, Douglas, and Felix Cohen were all ardent New Dealers who shared a strong hostility to the method of juristic reasoning that struck down social-welfare laws and wrought what they considered great human injustices. Most of the other realists expressed equally strong disapproval of the social and economic situation of the thirties. The new criticism was thus not intentionally hostile toward the idea of democratic government. Indeed, after 1932 it lent itself readily to the support of concrete political reform. As early as 1931 Frank defended the realists against charges that they excluded ethical considerations from the law. "*The point is,*" he retorted, "*that the rational and ethical factors are thwarted in their operations by the conventional tendency to ignore the non-rational and non-ethical factors.*"[41] The problem was not whether there was something abstract called justice, but rather how human relations could be made more just in practice. Though the theoretical problems the realists raised left them open to bitter attack, the obtuse formalism of American constitutional interpretation throughout the first third of the twentieth century helped drive them to their extreme positions. The manifest human needs created by the depression further convinced them of the need for a more realistic and flexible legal theory to attain what they considered a truly democratic society.

While the early critiques of legal realism tended to be mild and often discriminating, by 1936 they were becoming wholly denunciatory. The tone of the attack grew in bitterness in proportion to the spread of fear and uncertainty created by the success of the totalitarian governments of Europe. As Americans became more acutely aware of the despotic and repressive practices in Russia, in Italy, and most especially in Germany, the great majority condemned them in clear and forceful terms. As the possibility of another war drew nearer, they clung more tightly to the ideal of democracy as the best and morally ideal form of government. The realists had raised, unintentionally, fundamental questions about the possibility and validity of democratic government at a time when the country needed reassurance and conviction.

Inside the ominous framework constructed by the existence of the totalitarian governments, a new extremism in the realist movement itself was working to invite the bitter attack. In 1935 Robinson and Arnold, who jointly conducted siminars at the Yale University Law School on psychology and the law, published studies that assumed a sweeping ethical relativism. Robinson, who revealed a marked antipathy toward traditional deductive juristic thought, argued that the whole legal system should be reformed in line with the discoveries of modern scientific psychology. Committed to a thoroughgoing empiricism, he charged that "there is not now and never has been a deductive science of ethics."[42] Moral values developed, instead, out of concrete situations and were intelligible only in that context. No absolute, abstract, or universal moral values existed.

Arnold went beyond Robinson's position and argued that abstract theories and moral values were not only unfounded, but were wholly mythical. Moral ideals served only as satisfying symbols for emotional needs and had no further connection with anything real. The proper way to study theories and ideals, Arnold explained, was to ignore them as "principles of truth" and regard them simply "as symbolic thinking and conduct which condition the behavior of men in groups."[43] In fact, he concluded, if theories were to be effective as emotional symbols, they would have to be empirically false. In his sweeping rejection of the validity of such ideals Arnold left no basis for distinguishing between morally good or bad symbols or for establishing the legitimacy of any ethical position whatever. In his approach ethical values faded through relativism and out of existence.

Shortly after their two books were published, at a time when men could see the rampant brutality of Nazism, the vigorous counterattack began its harshest phase. Rufus C. Harris, dean of the Tulane University Law School, Philip Mecham, a professor at the University of Iowa Law School, and Morris R. Cohen all charged that realism paved the way for totalitarianism by denying objective ethical standards and making law an amoral coercive force.[44] Edgar Bodenheimer, an attorney in the Solicitor's Office in the Department of Labor, argued the same line in his important work on jurisprudence. "There is a certain danger that the skepticism of realistic jurisprudence may, perhaps very much against the intents and wishes of its representatives, prepare the intellectual ground for a tendency toward totalitarianism."[45]

The growing condemnation of realism reached a climax in 1940 when two of the most prominent legal scholars in the country, Pound and Lon L. Fuller of Duke University, published lectures assailing the new movement. Pound had long been critical of realism, and by 1940 he was ready to name it a "give-it-up philosophy." Refusing to discuss the work of any particular individual, he issued a blanket charge against them all: "The political and juristic preaching of today leads logically to [political] absolutism."[46] Fuller, like Pound, had earlier shared some of the attitudes associated with realism, but by 1934 he had turned into a stalwart critic. Realism attempted the impossible, he argued, for man could never ignore the ethical problems in the law, not even for the alleged purpose of scientific scholarship. In the end realism "remains formal and sterile". Such a negative attitude spreading through society was a major cause, he explained, "in bringing Germany and Spain to the disasters which engulfed those countries."[47]

Though Pound and Fuller attacked realism vigorously, the most severe and extreme attacks came from a number of Catholic legal scholars who during the thirties helped to generate a resurgent Neo-Scholastic legal movement in the United States. Much of the impetus came from the work of the American Catholic Philosophical Association, which established a round table on philosophy and law at its meeting in 1933. In addition to sponsoring scholarly papers and monographs, the round table attempted to organize a unified jurisprudence among professors at all Christian church-related law schools in the country. Although relatively few non-Catholics expressed interest, the suggestion drew support from many Catholics who saw the situation as desperate.

As other critics had done, the Catholics pictured realism as ethical relativism undermining the foundations of democracy. Those who adhered to such doctrines as pragmatism and empiricism, as the realists did, declared Dean Clarence Manion of the Notre Dame University Law School, were betraying the American citizen and "preparing to sell him into slavery."[48] Such dire predictions exceeded those of most other critics, for many of the Catholics refused to qualify them in any way. They saw such a definite and direct causal connection between ethical relativism and totalitarianism that they seemed to believe in what has been called the autonomy of ideas. Disregarding such factors as economic structures and political institu-

Edward A. Purcell, Jr.

tions, they argued that the ideas associated with legal realism and ethical relativism, by themselves, would lead naturally and inevitably away from traditional democracy to a ruthless totalitarianism. "Godless Behaviorism and Pragmatism are the headhunters, with Democracy and popular sovereignty the victims," declared Father Francis E. Lucey, a regent of the Georgetown University School of Law. "Democracy *versus* the Absolute State means Natural Law *versus* Realism."[49]

While the reaction against pragmatism and relativism was bitterest in the legal profession, the attack spread through all areas of American intellectual life. In the fields of history, philosophy, literature, and the social sciences many scholars began pointing to the dangerous implications of scientific relativism and condemning their colleagues who had embraced some form of it. By 1937 Walter Lippmann had completely rejected his earlier pragmatism and condemned the "aimless and turbulent moral relativity" of twentieth-century social thought.[50] Hans Kohn, Lewis Mumford, Reinhold Niebuhr, Thomas Mann, Alvin Johnson, and Van Wyck Brooks were among those who joined in blaming pragmatists and relativists for the desperate state of world affairs. "This recognition of guilt must pave the way, not to maudlin regrets," they declared in a united manifesto, "but to immediate atonement."[51]

Although the critics of legal realism undoubtedly believed that the new attitude directly threatened the existence of democracy, many of them were animated also by other social motives. Some critics, for example, were representatives of the wealthy groups that had violently opposed the New Deal since 1934 and correctly understood the devastating relevance of realism to their strained method of constitutional interpretation. One of the most extreme attacks, for example, came from a New York lawyer, Raoul E. Desvernine, who had been in charge of the Legal Division of the American Lib-

erty League. When he charged in 1941 that realism was "radically subversive of the American way of life," few could have doubted that he had specifically in mind the realist argument for a more permissive constitutional attitude toward New Deal legislation.[52] For those who already regarded the New Deal as prototototalitarian there was no real distinction between attacking the Roosevelt administration and condemning legal realism as antidemocratic. Rather, the accepted fact of New Deal regimentation gave evidence to the charge against the legal attitude that defended and justified such regimentation.

There was a different ulterior motive behind the attacks of most of the Catholics, who politically were generally sympathetic to the New Deal. The intellectual attitudes they associated with legal realism denied their deepest articles of religious faith and emotional conviction. The Catholic faith in its fundamentals was indissolubly linked with a hierarchical institution that claimed ability to interpret an absolutely true moral law, based on the truths of revelation and reason. Realism and modern empiricism rejected those foundations, and the Catholics began their assault in defense, not just of their conception of democracy, but of their Church. Because of their religious and philosophical conviction that such attitudes were false and evil, they quickly identified them with the practice of totalitarianism, which was also false and evil. A number went so far as to identify American democratic ideas with their own Catholic philosophy. The "definite American philosophy of life," explained one typical writer, was "drawn directly from the Catholic philosophy of life."[53] Having long been considered not completely American, the Catholics were at last able to assert their legitimacy by defining themselves as the true descendants of the American Revolution, and at the same time discrediting their dangerous intellectual adversaries.[54]

Whatever their motivations, the attacks had an effect. Much of the work of the realists had slighted the importance of ethical theory. Their philosophical assumptions had undermined the concept of a rational moral standard. Their ethical relativism seemed to many to mean that no Nazi barbarity could be justly branded as evil, while their identification of law with the actions of government officials gave even the most offensive Nazi edict the sanction of true law. Juxtaposing that logic to the actions of the totalitarian states, the critics had painted realism in the most ominous and shocking colors.

The damning charges forced the realists to assert their innocence. "I hope," declared Radin, "I have never said that ideas like wrong and right, or any ideas, are worthless or meaningless terms."[55] An empiricism that tried to predict actual decisions was "an *incomplete* way to see law," Llewellyn admitted in 1940, for "the heart and core of Jurisprudence" was the problem of ethical purpose in the law. "I for one," Llewellyn exclaimed, "am ready to do open penance for any part I may have played in giving occasion for the feeling that modern jurisprudes or any of them had ever lost sight of this."[56] Frank, Yntema, Patterson, and Felix Cohen all explicitly defended the realists against their critics, arguing that they had never denied an ethical goal in the law.[57] That defense was only partially relevant, however, since the fundamental question was actually whether the basic philosophical and methodological assumptions that characterized realism left any rational basis for affirming the legitimacy of an ethical goal.

Facing a barrage of criticism for his extreme views, Frank ultimately drew closer to the natural-law school than any of the other realists. During the early forties he looked increasingly for the moral justification of democracy and seemed to find it in the Thomistic concept of natural law. By 1945 he was maintaining that most Americans refused to accept the concept of natural law only because of a confusion in terminology that gave them the wrong idea of its true meaning.

"Most intelligent Americans, if the 'basic principles' of Scholastic natural law are described to them," he argued, "will find them completely acceptable."[58] Three years later he made his position clear and unequivocal: "I do not understand how any decent men today can refuse to adopt, as the basis of modern civilization, the fundamental principles of Natural Law, relative to human conduct, as stated by Thomas Aquinas."[59] Although Frank still called for empirical analysis of the legal system and insisted on the uncertainty and confusion in the application of principles, he had come a long way from the philosophical implications of *Law and the Modern Mind*.

Llewellyn, too, moved in the direction of natural law, though he stopped short of Frank's enthusiastic acceptance. Although he acknowledged a recent "debt" to Aquinas for the Schoolman's work on the philosophy of law, Llewellyn embraced neither Thomism nor the whole doctrine of natural law.[60] He accepted instead the general idea of a natural law, but translated it into a less precise and more intuitive concept. Natural law, he believed, was the name given for a universal human "urge" or "drive" for "right, or decency, or justice". Rather than being the opposite of legal empiricism as many had charged, Llewellyn declared, natural law was "an interesting and highly useful complement".[61]

While Llewellyn added a general concept of natural law to his legal theory and emphasized the importance of proper ethical ends in law, he remained true to his empiricism and retained a sharp skepticism concerning the powers of deductive logic. "When it comes to ultimate substance of the Good," he wrote early in 1942, "I repeat that I can find no clarity, or any conviction of reason, or of deduction as to specific matters, from the broad ultimates others have found clear" If pressed for an ultimate justification for democratic government, or for any values, he admitted, "I have no answer".[62]

In spite of their early leadership, neither Llewellyn nor Frank was typical of the other realists in the move toward natural law. Radin perhaps best represented the others. Acknowledging that realism must place an added weight on ethical considerations, he declared that "the lawyer's task is ultimately concerned with justice" and emphasized that "any legal teaching that ignored justice had missed most of its point."[63] But even with the modification in his outlook, Radin remained a convinced empiricist with no use for abstract formulations. Justice or any other idea, he declared in 1940, "has no objective existence". Hence it existed only in the minds of men and was, therefore, only meaningful to the extent that actual men subscribed to it. In that case the concept of justice held by juridical officials was the source of a community's operative concept of justice. "In the last analysis," Radin argued, "justice must be a common denominator of what a specific group— the judges themselves—think is just."[64] "Objectified" justice was real, fundamental, and essential, but it was necessarily a changing justice, wholly relative to the moral beliefs of the community in general and of the judges in particular.

Thus, while the realists modified their tone and protested their innocence, they did not, with the exception of Frank, give in to their critics on any fundamental point. They agreed that deduction was sterile in the field of values and claimed that their critics were as unable as they were to demonstrate conclusively the ultimate validity of any ethical ideals. Most would have agreed with Cook, who compared the advocates of deductive ethical systems to the infants in John Watson's experiments who exhibited "fear reaction" when they lost their sense of physical support. "They fear the loss of support of fixed principles which can be used automatically in cases of doubt," Cook charged, and hence they struck out wildly at those who pointed to the limits of human reason and suggested the true relativity to be found in reality.[65]

As most of the realists lost little of their confidence in science, so, too, they lost little of their ability to retaliate. Pound's condemnation of realism in light of his own earlier work, Yntema charged, "bears a tragic aspect of schizologic aberration."[66] Fuller's legal theory, Patterson pointed out, was marred throughout by a pervasive ambiguity. "Surely the clarification of basic confusions does not hamper the exercise of the creative reason," he commented dryly.[67] Myres S. McDougal, a young professor at Yale University, accused Fuller of "preaching pseudo-inspirational sermons." The day would come, McDougal hoped, when lawyers could be trained as scientific scholars "and not as priests in outworn and meaningless faiths whether of 'law' or of 'ethics'."[68] Fred Rodell, another of the younger realists, charged that all those legal thinkers who spoke in sacred terms of some abstract "Law" had been "taught in mental goose-step."[69] It was only appropriate to the spirit of much of the debate that Walter B. Kennedy, a leading Catholic scholar at Fordham University, returned the same charge in 1941 by calling realism a "goose-step philosophy."[70]

By 1941 when America entered the Second World War, the bitter debate within the legal profession had reached its most intense phase, and it revealed a number of important facts about American thought in general and legal theory in particular. Most important, the debate demonstrated the depth of a basic split that divided two groups of American intellectuals who, for want of better terms, might be called scientific relativists and rational absolutists. On the one hand, the realists owed their inspiration and intellectual attitudes to a cluster of ideas associated with modern science. Truth was wholly dependent on empirically established facts and hypotheses, they agreed, and it was necessarily tentative and relative. On the other hand, the absolutists, such as Hutchins, Adler, and the Catholics, believed that human reason could discover certain universal principles of justice by analyzing philosophically the nature of reality. Deductive logic could demonstrate the truth of propositions and lead man to correct applications in settling particular, practical questions. The universal principles formed for the absolutists the basis for all ethical knowledge, which was demonstrably certain.

These two fundamentally irreconcilable attitudes were in large part responsible for the intensity and extremism in the debate. Since both sides started from widely divergent assumptions, they were often unable to understand, let alone sympathize with, their enemy's position. The realists saw rational absolutism as pointless and often subjected it to ridicule and scorn. Felix Cohen referred to it as "Transcendental Nonsense," while Arnold and Frank compared it to superstitious incantations chanted by witch doctors and faith healers. The rational absolutists returned the scorn in full, charging the realists with everything from atheism to Communism to nihilism. As the realists were often unable to understand how anyone could accept some of the canons of rational absolutism in light of the discoveries of modern science and philosophy, their critics were equally unable to see how any man could fail to accept that which was self-evident and necessary to give support to a universally valid ethical system. Such a system was necessary, they continually insisted, if men were to condemn totalitarianism rationally. With each side committed to its own obvious truths and faced with an implacable opponent, vilification and the questioning of motives became an almost automatic recourse. Those who would not see must have some hidden and unworthy purpose.

That deep division was also evident in the awkward positions taken by Pound, Fuller, Morris Cohen, and a number of other critics of realism. Such scholars knew the severe limitations of deductive logic and were committed to some form of legal empiricism. At the same time, however, they saw many of the theoretical problems realism created, and they agreed, when faced with the challenge of totalitarian ideology and practice, that some supralegal moral standard was necessary as the basis for ethical judgments. Torn between two conflicting attitudes, they tried desperately to reconcile them or to develop a coherent ethical position that would withstand the criticisms from both sides. Fuller's concept of natural law, for example, placed him distinctly outside the realist movement, but failed to bring him into any real philosophical agreement with the Thomists. It was too abstract for the one side and too positivistic for the other.

The long debate also clearly revealed the plight of ethical theory in the middle of the twentieth century. The incisive criticisms of modern philosophy and the dramatic impact of experimental science had made rational absolutism untenable in the minds of most educated Americans. Many were ready to conclude that moral justification in any ultimate sense was an impossible and meaningless concept. "Having surrendered the quest for certainty," Cook insisted, quoting Dewey, "we can offer no guarantees."[71] Though difficult to deny intellectually, that conclusion was dissatisfying to most Americans at the time when Nazism was perpetrating its outrages on both Germany and the rest of Europe.

The apparent success and spread of the totalitarian ideologies, backed by military might, exacerbated the internal division in American thought and placed the fundamental problem of the ethical basis of democracy into clear relief. The barbarity and repression evident in the various totalitarian countries enraged most American intellectuals. Feeling the deep need to condemn them in the clearest and strongest terms, they were forced to deal in some way with rationally based ethical judgments. That necessity created immense stress in the minds of many who either doubted the possibility of such judgments or found themselves unable to produce them. Some, like Becker and Malinowski, turned on much of their earlier work and argued that there were broad moral values that in fact did support the ideal of democracy and that showed equally that totalitarianism was evil. Others, such as Percy W. Bridgman and Stuart A. Rice, admitted that there was no ultimate ethical sanction for democracy and suggested only that human experience indicated that the great majority of men preferred it to Nazism. Most intellectuals finally had to ignore their doubts and the intellectual difficulties that plagued ethical theory and in the end simply assert the evil of totalitarianism and the relative goodness and desirability of democracy.

Although the Catholics in contrast expressed great certainty in the power of reason to discover ultimate principles, the debate revealed a defensive attitude on their part that at times reached extreme proportions. In spite of their fervent religious and intellectual convictions, they realized that they were fighting a battle against the ever-strengthening intellectual trends of the past three hundred years. Abstract rationalism simply could not stand against the combined forces of pragmatism, scientific empiricism, and modern critical philosophy. The vitriolic tone and extreme, unfounded accusations made against such movements as legal realism showed clearly the sense of intellectual frustration and institutional anxiety that underlay Catholic legal thought in the 1930s. The identification of realism and relativism with totalitarianism was the ground on which the Catholics hoped to make their belated victorious stand against the intellectual forces of the twentieth century. Though they had some limited success during the time of most severe intellectual crisis in the late thirties and early forties, their counterattack failed, and the Catholics themselves eventually modified some of their more strident positions.

Finally, the debate suggested the course that American legal thinking would take in the years after the Second World War. While the idea of natural law grew somewhat in importance — and certainly proved useful for such purposes as trying war criminals — through the late forties and early fifties, it died down again and became mainly an isolated and parochial concept that enjoyed little support outside of a few Catholic law schools. Where it did have vitality it was made part of a broader empirical synthesis as in the work of F.S.C. Northrop. While ignoring some of its more extreme theoretical tendencies, the profession generally accepted many of the ideas associated with legal realism. That movement helped establish the importance of factual research in law, the necessity of empirical studies of the legal process, the legitimacy of a more flexible constitutional interpretation, and the acceptance of a pragmatic, operational concept of law. In spite of the problems the realists presented, both philosophically and legally, they were pointing toward the future by suggesting fruitful courses of study and more useful methods of analysis. The alliance the realists helped forge between legal theory and empirical analysis fortified the trend toward sociological jurisprudence that had begun forty years before and that was to become a commonly accepted part of American law in the years after the Second World War.

Part Twelve

The Regulatory and Welfare State

The following study by the legal scholar Charles Reich is, in a sense, an obituary for liberal reform and a sweeping critique of its consequences. It concerns the effects of the profound transformation that occurred in the American legal and governmental systems after 1933. Some of the foundations for this transformation were laid much earlier, with the establishment of the "independent regulatory agencies," of which the Interstate Commerce Commission (1887) was the first; nevertheless to a remarkable extent the modern administrative state was the product of the Great Depression of the 1930s and of the New Deal. The New Deal instituted fundamental revisions of governmental structure, constitutional doctrine, socio-economic policy, and consequently of the power relationships in American society.

Since 1933 the dramatic shift in real power within the federal system has allowed the central government decisively to displace the states as the locus for most major policy decisions. The sum of governmental power over the private sector has increased massively as well. Among the functions assumed by public authorities and centralized in the national government are extensive regulation of

business and responsibility for social welfare. Agriculture was made a federally managed sector in the 1930s; regional planning and development emerged, under federal auspices; and many key industries became subject to governmental control of entry, markets, and prices or rates. The central government has also effectively preempted the most flexible and productive of revenue sources, the income tax. Other federal payroll taxes, financing the social-security system, also became a major component of overall tax collections. In the Nixon presidency this trend accelerated so rapidly as to become a quiet (and regressive) revolution in government finance. As federal programs expanded, both taxes and government spending as a component of national income rose dramatically. Since the mid-thirties the national government has been committed to a counter cyclical fiscal policy that uses federal revenues and spending as the key instruments for dealing with recession and depression.

These developments were accompanied by a shift in the content of constitutional doctrine, beginning with a wholesale reversal by the late 1930s of the Supreme Court's position on such critical issues as the commerce power, federal

The Regulatory and Welfare State

regulatory power, labor law, and the legitimate distribution of authority between the states and the central government. The Court has largely validated the whole range of welfare-state and regulatory-state initiatives.

Charles Reich here assesses these developments in the context of concomitant changes in the private sector. He considers how changes in the constitutional order and the American political economy have transformed the fundamental meaning and functions of private property. Revisited in this article are some major themes from earlier studies in this volume — for example, the interplay of privatism, community values, and governmental power and the ideals of the legal progressives who sought a more egalitarian legal system. It is probably fair to say that the popular, nineteenth-century American view of the positive social functions that private property could perform as portrayed by Hurst is not very different from Reich's view. But Reich contends that, whereas in the earlier era property institutions *did* provide "zones of privacy" and protect individuality whatever their other failures, today they have been overwhelmed by the governmental structures of the regulatory and welfare state. He argues that because of this, and also because of the continuing concentration of power in private hands, new legal concepts and structures are required to assure the protection of individuality and personal dignity in modern life.

Further Reading

Berle, Adolph A. *The American Economic Republic*. New York: Harcourt, Brace, 1965.

Boulding, Kenneth E. *The Organizational Revolution*. New York: Harper & Row, 1953.

McCloskey, Robert G., ed. *Essays in Constitutional Law*. New York: Alfred A. Knopf, 1957.

―――. *The Modern Supreme Court*. Cambridge: Harvard University Press, 1972.

McConnell, Grant. *Private Power and American Democracy*. New York: Alfred A. Knopf, 1966.

Mason, Alpheus T. *Security through Freedom: American Political Thought and Practice*. Ithaca: Cornell University Press, 1955.

Miller, Arthur Selwyn. *The Modern Corporate State: Private Governments and the American Constitution*. Westport, Conn.: Greenwood Press, 1976.

―――. *The Supreme Court and American Capitalism*. New York: Free Press, 1968.

Pritchett, C. Herman. *The Roosevelt Court: A Study in Judicial Politics and Values, 1937–1947*. New York: Macmillan, 1948.

Scheiber, Harry N. *The Condition of American Federalism: An Historian's View*. 89th Cong., 2d sess., Senate Committee on Government Operations print. Washington, D.C., 1966.

Shapiro, Martin. *The Supreme Court and Administrative Agencies*. New York: Free Press, 1968.

31

Charles A. Reich

The New Property

One of the most important developments in the United States during the past decade had been the emergence of government as a major source of wealth. Government is a gigantic siphon. It draws in revenue and power and pours forth wealth: money, benefits, services, contracts, franchises, and licenses. Government has always had this function. But while in early times it was minor, today's distribution of largess is on a vast, imperial scale.

The valuables dispensed by government take many forms, but they all share one characteristic. They are steadily taking the place of traditional forms of wealth — forms which are held as private property. Social insurance substitutes for savings; a government contract replaces a businessman's customers and good will. The wealth of more and more Americans depends on a relationship to government. Increasingly, Americans live on government largess — allocated by government on its own terms, and held by recipients subject to conditions which express "the public interest."

Reprinted, with changes, from *Yale Law Journal*, 73 (1964), 733-787, by permission of the Yale Law Journal Company and Fred B. Rothman & Company.

The growth of government largess accompanied by a distinctive system of law is having profound consequences. It affects the underpinnings of individualism and independence. It influences the workings of the Bill of Rights. It has an impact on the power of private interests in their relation to each other and to government. It is helping to create a new society.

The Largess of Government

THE FORMS OF GOVERNMENT-CREATED WEALTH

The valuables which derive from relationships to government are of many kinds. Some primarily concern individuals, others flow to businesses and organizations. Some are obvious forms of wealth, such as direct payments of money, while others, like licenses and franchises, are indirectly valuable.

Income and Benefits For a large number of people, government is a direct source of income although they hold no public job. Their eligibility arises from legal status. Examples are Social Security benefits, unemployment compensation, aid to dependent children, veterans' bene-

Charles A. Reich

fits, and the whole scheme of state and local welfare. These represent a principal source of income to a substantial segment of the community. Total federal, state, and local social-welfare expenditures in 1961 were almost fifty-eight billion dollars.

Jobs. More than nine million persons receive income from public funds because they are directly employed by federal, state, or local government. The size of the publicly employed work force has increased steadily since the founding of the United States, and it seems likely to keep on increasing. If the three to four million persons employed in defense industries (which exist mainly on government funds) are added to the nine million directly employed [by government] it can be estimated that 15 to 20 percent of the labor force receives its primary income from government.

Occupational licenses Licenses are required before one may engage in many kinds of work, from practicing medicine to guiding hunters through the woods. Even occupations which require little education or training, like that of longshoremen, often are subject to strict licensing. Such licenses, which are dispensed by government, make it possible for their holders to receive what is ordinarily their chief source of income.

Franchises A franchise, which may be held by an individual or by a company, is a partial monopoly created and handed out by government, Its value depends largely upon governmental power; by limiting the number of franchises, government can make them extremely remunerative. A New York City taxi medallion, which costs very little when originally obtained from the city, can be sold for over twenty thousand dollars. The reason for this high price is that the city has not issued new transferable medallions despite the rise in population and traffic. A television channel, handed out free, can often be sold for many millions. Government distributes wealth when it dispenses route permits to truckers, charters to bus lines, routes to air carriers, certificates to oil and gas pipelines, licenses to liquor stores, allotments to growers of cotton or wheat, and concessions in national parks.

Contracts Many individuals and many more businesses enjoy public generosity in the form of government contracts. Fifty billion dollars annually flow from the federal government in the form of defense spending. These contracts often resemble subsidies; it is virtually impossible to lose money on them. Businesses sometimes make the government their principal source of income, and many "free enterprises" are set up primarily to do business with the government.

Subsidies Analogous to welfare payments for individuals who cannot manage independently in the economy are subsidies to business. Agriculture is subsidized to help it survive against better organized (and less competitive) sectors of the economy, and the shipping industry is given a dole because of its inability to compete with foreign lines. Local airlines are also on the dole. So are the other major industries, notably housing. Still others, such as the railroads, are eagerly seeking help. Government also supports many nonbusiness activities in such areas as scientific research, health, and education.

Use of public resources A very large part of the American economy is publicly owned. Government owns or controls hundreds of millions of acres of public lands valuable for mining, grazing, lumbering, and recreation; sources of energy such as the hydroelectric power of all major rivers, the tidelands reservoirs of oil, and the infant giant of nuclear power; routes of travel and commerce such as the airways, highways, and rivers; the radio-television spectrum which is the avenue for all broadcasting; hoards of surplus crops and materials; public buildings and facilities, and much more. These resources are available for utilization by private businesses and individuals; such use is often equivalent to a subsidy. The radio-television industry uses the scarce channels of the air free of charge; electric companies use publicly owned water power; stockmen graze sheep and cattle on public lands at nominal cost; ships and airplanes arrive and depart from publicly owned docks and airports; the atomic-energy industry uses government materials, facilities, and know-how, and all are entitled to make a profit.

Services Like resources, government services are a source of wealth. Some of these are plainly of commercial value; postal service for periodicals, newspapers, advertisers, and mail-order houses; insurance for home builders and savings banks; technical information for agriculture. Other services dispensed by government include sewage, sanitation, police and fire protection, and public transportation. The communications satellite represents an unusual type of subsidy through service — the turning over of government research and know-how to a quasi-private organization. The most important public service of all, education, is one of the greatest sources of value to the individual.

THE IMPORTANCE OF GOVERNMENT LARGESS

How important is governmentally dispensed wealth in relation to the total economic life of the nation? In 1961, when personal income totaled $416,432,-000,000, government expenditures on all levels amounted to $164,875,000,000. The government payroll alone approached $45 billion. And these figures do not take account of the vast intangible wealth represented by licenses, franchises, services, and resources. Moreover, the *proportion* of governmental wealth is increasing. Hardly any citizen leads his life without at least partial dependence on wealth flowing through the giant government syphon.

In many cases, this dependence is not voluntary. Valuables that flow from government are often substitutes for, rather than supplements to, other forms of wealth. Social security and other forms of public insurance and compensation are supported by taxes. This tax money is no longer available for individual savings or insurance. The taxpayer is a participant in public insurance by compulsion, and his ability to care for his own needs independently is correspondingly reduced. Similarly, there is no choice about using public transportation, public lands for recreation, public airport terminals, or public insurance on savings deposits. In these and countless other areas, government is the sole supplier. Moreover, the increasing dominance of scientific technology, so largely a product of government research and development, generates an even greater dependence on government.

Dependence creates a vicious circle of dependence. It is as hard for a business to give up government help as it is for an individual to live on a reduced income. And when one sector of the economy is subsidized, others are forced to seek comparable participation. This is true of geographical areas; government contracts can fundamentally influence the economy of a region. It is also true of different components of the economy. If one form of transportation is subsidized, other types of transportation may be compelled to seek subsidies. When some occupations are subsidized, others, which help to pay the bill, find themselves disadvantaged as a class.

LARGESS AND THE CHANGING FORMS OF WEALTH

The significance of government largess is increased by certain underlying changes in the forms of private wealth in the United States. Changes in the forms of wealth are not remarkable in themselves; the forms are constantly changing and differ in every culture. But today more and more of our wealth takes the form of rights or status rather than of tangible goods. An individual's profession or occupation is a prime example. To many others, a job with a particular employer is the principal form of wealth. A profession or a job is frequently far more valuable than a house or bank account, for a new house can be bought,

Charles A. Reich

and a new bank account created, once a profession or job is secure. For the jobless, their status as governmentally assisted or insured persons may be the main source of subsistence.

The automobile dealer's chief wealth is his franchise from the manufacturer which gives him exclusive sales rights within a certain territory, for it is his guarantee of income. His building, his stock of cars, his organization, and his good will may all be less valuable than his franchise. Franchises represent the principal asset of many businesses: the gasoline station, chain restaurant, motel or drug store, and many other retail suppliers. To the large manufacturer, contracts, business arrangements, and organization may be the most valuable assets. The steel company's relationships with coal and iron producers and automobile manufacturers, and construction companies may be worth more than all its plant and equipment.

The kinds of wealth dispensed by government consist almost entirely of those forms which are in the ascendancy today. To the individual, these new forms, such as a profession, job, or right to receive income, are the basis of his various statuses in society, and may therefore be the most meaningful and distinctive wealth he possesses.

The Emerging System of Law

Wealth or value is created by culture and by society; it is culture that makes a diamond valuable and a pebble worthless. Property, on the other hand, is the creation of law. A man who has property has certain legal rights with respect to an item of wealth; property represents a relationship between wealth and its "owner." Government largess is plainly "wealth," but it is not necessarily "property."

Government largess has given rise to a distinctive system of law. This system can be viewed from at least three perspectives: the rights of holders of largess, the powers of government over largess, and the procedure by which holders' rights and governmental power are adjusted. At this point, analysis will not be aided by attempting to apply or to reject the label "property." What is important is to survey − without the use of labels − the unique legal system that is emerging.

INDIVIDUAL RIGHTS IN LARGESS

As government largess has grown in importance, quite naturally there has been pressure for the protection of individual interests in it. The holder of a broadcast license or a motor-carrier permit or a grazing permit for public lands tends to consider this wealth his "own" and to seek legal protection against interference with his enjoyment of it. The development of individual interests has been substantial, but it has not come easily.

From the beginning, individual rights in largess have been greatly affected by several traditional legal concepts, each of which has had lasting significance.

Right versus privilege The early law is marked by courts' attempts to distinguish which forms of largess were "rights" and which were "privileges." Legal protection of the former was by far the greater. If the holder of a license had a "right," he might be entitled to a hearing before the license could be revoked; a "mere privilege" might be revoked without notice or hearing.

The gratuity principle Government largess has often been considered a "gratuity" furnished by the state. Hence it is said that the state can withhold, grant, or revoke the largess at its pleasure. Under this theory, government is considered to be in somewhat the same position as a private giver.

The whole and the parts Related to the gratuity theory is the idea that, since government may completely withhold a benefit, it may grant it subject to any terms or conditions whatever. This theory is essentially an exercise in logic: the whole power must include all its parts.

Internal management Particularly in relation to its own contracts, government has been permitted extensive power on the theory that it should have control over its own housekeeping or internal management functions. Under this theory, government is treated like a private business. In its dealings with outsiders it is permitted much of the freedom to grant contracts and licenses that a private business would have.

Quite often these four theories are blurred in a single statement of judicial attitude. For example: "A taxicab is a common carrier and use by it of the public streets is not a right but a privilege or license which can be granted on such conditions as the legislature may impose."[1]

But individual interests have grown up nonetheless. The most common forms of protection are procedural, coupled with an insistence that government action be based on standards that are not "arbitrary" or unauthorized. Development has varied mainly according to the particular type of wealth involved. The courts have most readily granted protection to those types which are intimately bound up with the individual's freedom to earn a living. They have been reluctant to grant individual rights in those types of largess which seem to be exercises of the managerial functions of government, such as subsidies and government contracts.

Occupational licenses   After some initial hesitation, courts have generally held that an occupational or professional license may not be denied or revoked without affording the applicant notice and a hearing. Doctors, lawyers, real estate brokers, and taxi drivers may not be denied their livelihood without some minimum procedure of this sort.

Drivers' licenses   Licenses not specifically tied to a particular occupation, such as drivers' licenses, have to some extent been assimilated under the umbrella of occupational licenses. New York's highest court declared that a driver's license is "of tremendous value to the individual and may not be taken away except by due process.[2]

Franchises   A franchise is less of a "natural right" than an occupational license because it confers an exclusive or monopoly position established by government. But the courts early took the position that certain types of franchises were "property" protected by the Constitution.[3]

Benefits   With somewhat greater reluctance, the courts have moved toward a measure of legal protection for benefits. The District of Columbia Court of Appeals questioned whether Congress could authorize an administrator to revoke a veteran's disability pension without some standards to guide him.[4] The Supreme Court held that a state cannot deny unemployment benefits on grounds which interfere with freedom of religion.[5]

Contracts   Government contracts might seem the best possible example of a type of valuable that no one has any right to receive and that represents only the government's managerial function. But even here, at least one court has said that a would-be contractor may not be wholly debarred from eligibility as a consequence of arbitrary government action: "While they do not have a right to contract with the United States on their own terms, appellants do have a right not to be invalidly denied equal opportunity under applicable law to seek contracts on government projects."[6]

In all the cases concerning individual rights in largess the exact nature of the government action which precipitates the controversy makes a great difference. A controversy over government largess may arise from such diverse situations as denial of the right to apply, denial of an application, attaching of conditions to a grant, modification of a grant already made, suspension or revocation of a grant, or some other sanction. In general, courts tend to afford the greatest measure of protection in revocation or suspension cases. The theory seems to be that here some sort of rights have "vested" which may not be taken away without proper procedure. On the other hand, an applicant for largess is thought to have less at stake and is therefore entitled to less protection. The mere

Charles A. Reich

fact that a particular form of largess is protected in one context does not mean that it will be protected in all others.

When the public interest demands that the government take over "property," the Constitution requires that just compensation be paid to the owner. But when largess is revoked in the public interest, the holder ordinarily receives no compensation. For example, if a television station's license were revoked, not for bad behavior on the part of the operator, but in order to provide a channel in another locality, or to provide an outlet for educational television, the holder would not be compensated for its loss. This principle applies to government largess of all types.

In addition to being revocable without compensation, most forms of largess are subject to considerable limitations on their use. Social Security cannot be sold or transferred. A television license can be transferred only with FCC permission. The possessor of a grazing permit has no right to change, improve, or destroy the landscape. Use of most largess is limited to specified purposes. Some welfare grants, for example, must be applied to support dependent children.

The most significant limitation on use is more subtle. To some extent at least, the holder of government largess is expected to act as the agent of "the public interest" rather than solely in the service of his own self-interest. The theory of broadcast licensing is that the channels belong to the public and should be used for the public's benefit, but that a variety of private operators are likely to perform this function more successfully than government; the holder of a radio or television license is therefore expected to broadcast in "the public interest." The opportunity for private profit is intended to serve as a lure to make private operators serve the public.

The "mix" of public and private, and the degree to which the possessor acts as the government's agent, varies from situation to situation. The government contractor is explicitly the agent of the government in what he does; in theory he could equally well be the manager of a government-owned factory. Only his right to profits and his control over how the job is done distinguish his private status. The taxi driver performs the public service of transportation (which the government might otherwise perform) subject to regulation but with more freedom than the contractor. The doctor serves the public with still greater freedom. The mother of a child entitled to public aid acts as the state's agent in supporting the child with the funds thus provided, but her freedom is even greater, and the responsibility of her agency still less defined.

The result of all of this is a breaking down of distinctions between public and private and a resultant blurring or fusing of public and private. Many of the functions of government are performed by private persons; much private activity is carried on in a way that is no longer private.

LARGESS AND THE POWER OF GOVERNMENT

Affirmative powers When government — national, state, or local — hands out something of value, whether a relief check or a television license, government's power grows forthwith; it automatically gains such power as is necessary and proper to supervise its largess. It obtains new rights to investigate, to regulate, and to punish. This increase in power is furthered by an easy and wide-ranging concept of relevance. A government contractor finds that he must comply with wage-hour and child-labor requirements. Television and radio licenses learn that their possible violation of the antitrust laws or allegedly misleading statements to the FCC are relevant to their right to a license. Doctors find they can lose their licenses for inflating bills that are used as a basis for claims against insurance companies in accident cases, and theaters are threatened with loss of licenses for engaging in illegal ticket-sale practices. The New York State Board of Regents includes in its definition of "unprofessional conduct" by doctors, dentists, and other licensed professions any discrimination against patients or clients on the basis of race, color, or creed. Real estate brokers can be suspended for taking advantage of racial tensions by the practice called "blockbusting." California has used its power over the privilege of selling alcoholic beverages in order to compel licensed establishments to cease discriminating.

One of the most significant regulatory by-products of government largess is power over the recipients' "moral character." Some random illustrations will suggest the meaning and application of this phrase. The District of Columbia denied a married man in his forties a permit to operate a taxi partly because when he was a young man in his twenties, he and a woman had been discovered about to have sexual intercourse in his car.[7] Men with criminal records have been denied licenses to work as longshoremen and chenangoes and prevented from holding union office for the same reason. A license to operate a rooming house may be refused for lack of good character.[8]

Political activities are also regulated by use of largess power. The Hatch Act forbids federal employees to engage in political activities on pain of losing their jobs; the act was also made applicable to state employees engaged in activities aided by the federal government. But political activities thought to be subversive or communistic have been the chief area of concern. One of the earliest illustrations is the Emergency Relief Appropriation Act, which sought to prevent any member of the Communist Party or Nazi Bund from getting work under the act. Another example is the effort — ultimately frustrated by the courts — to bar communists or subversives from occupying public housing. Membership in the Communist Party or subversive organizations has been considered relevant to the right to pursue a number of important occupations and professions, including that of lawyer, radio-telegraph operator, and port worker. Nor does the list stop at occupations. Ohio required a loyalty oath to receive unemployment compensation. For a time a loyalty oath was required under the National Defense Education Act. New York has provided for the mandatory revocation of the driver's license of any motorist convicted under the Smith Act of advocating the overthrow of the government.

The restrictions which derive from these expanded notions of relevance are enforceable not merely by withholding largess, but also by imposing sanctions. Along with largess goes the power to punish new crimes. Misuse of the gift becomes criminal, and hence new standards of lawful behavior are set: government can make it a crime to fail to spend welfare funds in such a manner as accords with the best interests of the children.

Government largess not only increases the legal basis for government power; it increases the political basis as well. When an individual or a business uses public money or enjoys a government privilege or occupies part of the public domain, it is easier to argue for a degree of regulation which might not be accepted if applied to businesses or individuals generally. Objections to regulation fade, whether in the minds of the general public or legal scholars, before the argument that government should make sure that its bounty is used in the public interest. Benefits, subsidies, and privileges are seen as "gifts" to be given on conditions, and thus the political and legal sources of government power merge into one.

The magnification of governmental power by administrative discretion Broad as is the power derived from largess, it is magnified by many administrative factors when it is brought to bear on a recipient. First, the agency granting government largess generally has a wide measure of discretion to interpret its own power. Second, the nature of administrative agencies, the functions they combine, and the sanctions they possess give them additional power. Third, the circumstances in which the recipients find themselves sometimes make them abettors, rather than resisters, of the further growth of power.

The legislature generally delegates to an administrative agency its authority with respect to a given form of largess. In this

Charles A. Reich

very process of delegation there can be an enlargement of power. The courts allow the agencies a wide measure of discretion to make policy and to interpret legislative policy. Sometimes a legislature gives the agency several different, possibly conflicting, policies, allowing it (perhaps unintentionally) to enforce now one and now another. There is little if any requirement of consistency or adherence to precedent, and the agency may, instead of promulgating rules of general application, make and change its policies in the process of case-to-case adjudication. For example, New Jersey's Waterfront Commission has power "in its discretion" to deny the right to work to any longshoreman if he is a person "whose presence at the piers or other waterfront terminals in the Port of New York is found by the commission on the basis of the facts and evidence before it, to constitute a danger to the public peace or safety." The discretion of an agency is even broader and even less reviewable when the subject matter is highly technical. In such fields, which are increasing in number, "experts" or professionals come to power, and their actions are even harder to confine within legislatively fixed limits. Discretion as to enforcement or punishment is one of the greatest of agency powers. A licensing agency often has power to choose between forgiveness, suspension, and permanent revocation of a license after a violation.

Most dispensing agencies possess the power of delay. They also possess the power of investigation and harassment; they can initiate inquiries which will prove expensive and embarrassing to an applicant. Surveillance alone can make a recipient of largess uncomfortable. Agencies have so many criteria to use, so many available grounds of decision, and so much discretion that they, like the FCC, can usually find other grounds to accomplish what they cannot do directly. This is a temptation to the honest but zealous administrator, and an invitation to the official who is less than scrupulous. In addition, the broader the regulation, the greater the chance that everyone violates the law

in some way and the greater the discretion to forgive or to punish. But even if a dispensing agency is self-restrained and scrupulous beyond the requirements of statutes, the function of dispensing will make its power grow. The dispensing of largess is a continuing process. The threat of an unfavorable attitude in the future should be sufficient persuasion for today.

The recipients of largess themselves add to the powers of government by their uncertainty over their rights, and their efforts to please. Unsure of their ground, they are often unwilling to contest a decision. The penalties for being wrong, in terms of possible loss of largess in the future, are very severe.[9] Seeking to stay on the safe side of an uncertain and often unknowable line, people dependent on largess are likely to eschew any activities that might incur official displeasure. Beneficiaries of government bounty fear to offend, lest ways and means be found in the obscure corners of discretion to deny these favors in the future.

LARGESS AND PROCEDURAL SAFEGUARDS

The procedural law of government largess is as distinctive as the substantive. In addition to the general law governing the grant and revocation of largess, there are special aspects of unusual interest: the power to conduct trials of persons for alleged violations of law, and the authority to apply sanctions and punishments.

Procedures in general The granting, regulation, and revocation of government largess are carried on by procedures which, in varying degrees, represent short-cuts that tend to augment the power of the grantor at the expense of the recipient. In the first place, the tribunal is likely to be an arm of the granting agency rather than independent and impartial. For example, when disputes arise over government contracts, the tribunal may turn out to be the government contracting officer, himself a party to the dispute, followed by a series of contract appeals boards likewise composed of government contracting officials. More commonly the initial tribunal is a hearing officer, but the final decision is by the dispensing agency itself. Thus a charge that a television licensee is violating the terms of its license is ultimately passed upon by the FCC itself. A pilot can be suspended by the CAB, which previously investigated the accident out of which the suspension resulted, and earlier found in a "probable cause" investigation and hearing that the accident was due to pilot error.

Sometimes there is no hearing at all. For example, the SEC has been upheld in suspending, without a hearing, a broker-dealer license for alleged violations. Driver's licenses are also sometimes suspended without a hearing.

Decisions concerning government largess are not always subject to effective review in the courts. An application for a savings-and-loan charter can be granted or denied without judicial review. The matter rests in the "vast discretion" of a federal board. A local agricultural committee, exercising authority under the federal soil-bank subsidy program, has virtually unreviewable authority to find a farmer in violation of the rules of the program, making him subject to statutory forfeitures. At present there is a trend toward more judicial review, but the important question is what kind of review; review limited to constitutional or jurisdictional questions may prove inadequate to curb possible agency abuses.

Trial Violations of law are normally determined by courts. But in dispensing largess government has not always been willing to rely on courts to determine whether laws have been violated. In an increasing number of cases it has undertaken to make such determinations independently ... The CAB can take away a pilot's license on the basis of an agency "trial" proving that he violated regulations. The FCC had "found" that an applicant for a broadcast license was guilty of an attempt to deceive the commission. A New York City taxicab driver was brought before a police captain and charged with having withheld change from a passenger.

The officer found him guilty, and his license was revoked. The New York Court of Appeals subsequently held that the procedures used by the police violated due process, but the court seemed to agree that the police could "try" taxi drivers if they observed better procedures.[10]

Administrative "trials" are not even limited to conduct that might violate some law. Agencies can deny government largess for "bad" conduct which is lawful. This often happens when a license is denied because of "bad character." Many largess-dispensing agencies are concerned with character – from the SEC to state boxing commissions. The entire federal loyalty-security program for public employees involves trials of character. Here the "gift" of a public job has been the justification for a process by which countless individuals have been "tried" for "offenses" which vary from conduct approaching treason to the most trivial departure from orthodoxy. These security trials and the character investigations which are made for innumerable licenses and permits attempt to search out every crevice and recess of an individual's life. The agencies try, not an offense, but the whole of a man, his strengths and weaknesses, his moments of honor and of temptation.[11]

New and unusual punishments Administering largess carries with it not only the power to conduct trials, but also the power to inflict many sorts of sanctions not classified as criminal punishments. The most obvious penalty is simply denial or deprivation of some form of wealth or privilege that the agency dispenses. How badly this punishment hurts depends upon how essential the benefit is to the individual or business affected. The loss of some privileges or subsidies may be quite trivial. But for the government contractor placed on a blacklist the consequences may be financial ruin if the government is one of its major customers. The television station that loses its license is out of business; so is the doctor who loses his medical license.

Charles A. Reich

Although the denial of benefits is consistently held not to be penal in nature, it is perfectly clear that on occasion the government uses this power as a sanction. The FCC has denied a radio or television license as a sanction for the applicant's misrepresentations to the commission. Government contractors who are guilty of undesirable conduct may be officially "debarred" from contracting for a specified term of years. Persons guilty of prior crimes may be disqualified from office in waterfront unions. But denial of benefits by no means exhausts the list of sanctions available to government. Severe harm can be inflicted by adverse publicity resulting from investigations, findings of violation, blacklisting, or forfeitures for cause. A striking instance is the SEC practice, upheld by the courts, of placing alleged violators of certain of its regulations on a public blacklist. Forfeitures are imposed under agricultural stabilization programs. The mere pendency of proceedings may be harmful, especially if accompanied by costly and harassing investigation and interminable delay.

The Public-Interest State

What are the consequences of the rise of government largess and its attendant legal system? What is the impact on the recipient, on constitutional guarantees of liberty, on the structure of power in the nation? It is important to try to picture the society that is emerging, and to seek its underlying philosophy. The dominant theme, as we have seen, is "the public interest," and out of it there grows the "public-interest state."

THE EROSION OF INDEPENDENCE

The recipient of largess, whether an organization or an individual, feels the government's power. The company that is heavily subsidized or dependent on government contracts is subjected to an added amount of regulation and inspection, sometimes to the point of having resident government officials in its plant. And it is subject to added government pressures.

The well-known episode when the large steel companies were forced to rescind a price rise, partly by the threat of loss of government contracts, illustrates this. Perhaps the most elaborate and onerous regulation of businesses with government contracts is the industrial security system which places all employees in defense industries under government scrutiny and subjects them, even high executives, to dismissal if they fail to win government approval.

Universities also feel the power of government largess. Research and development grants to universities tend to influence the direction of university activities, and in addition inhibit the university from pursuing activities it might otherwise undertake. In order to qualify for government contracts, Harvard University was required, despite extreme reluctance, to report the number of Negroes employed in each department. The university kept no such information and contended that gathering it would emphasize the very racial distinctions that the government was trying to minimize. Nevertheless, the university was forced to yield to the government's demand.

Individuals are also subject to great pressures. Dr. Edward K. Barsky, a New York physician and surgeon since 1919, was for a time chairman of the Joint Anti-Fascist Refugee Committee. In 1946 he was summoned before the House Committee on Un-American Activities. In the course of his examination he refused, on constitutional grounds, to produce records of the organization's contributions and expenditures. For this refusal he served six months in jail for contempt of Congress. Thereafter the New York State Education Department filed a complaint against him under a provision of law making any doctor convicted of a crime subject to discipline. Although there was no evidence in any way touching Dr. Barsky's activities as a physician, the department's Medical Grievance Committee suspended his medical license for six months. The New York courts upheld the suspension.

If the businessman, the teacher, and the professional man find themselves subject to the power of government largess, the man on public assistance is even more dependent. Welfare officials, often with the best of motivations, impose conditions intended to better a client, which sometimes are a deep invasion of his freedom of action. In a memorable case in New York, an old man was denied welfare because he insisted on living under unsanitary conditions, sleeping in a barn in a pile of rags. The court's opinion expresses a characteristic philosophy:

> Appellant also argues that he has a right to live as he pleases while being supported by public charity. One would admire his independence if he were not so dependent, but he has no right to defy the standards and conventions of civilized society while being supported at public expense . . .
>
> It is true, as appellant argues, that the hardy pioneers of our country slept in beds no better than the one he has chosen. But, unlike the appellant, they did it from necessity, and unlike the appellant, they did not call upon the public to support them, while doing it.

To envision how sweeping the powers derived from government largess can become, one may turn to New York City, where the Commissioner of Licenses holds sway over a long list of gainful employments. With broad discretion, he dispenses and revokes licenses for exhibitions and performances, billiard and pool tables, bowling alleys, miniature golf, sidewalk cafes and stands, sightseeing guides, street musicians, public carts, expressmen, porters, junk dealers, second-hand dealers, pawnbrokers, auctioneers, laundries, wardrobe concessionaires, locksmiths, masseurs, bargain sales, bathhouse keepers, rooming houses, barbers, garages, refuse removal, cabarets, coffee houses, and cannon firing. The license commissioner has used his broad powers to deny licenses to many persons on the basis of "bad character." A parking-lot license was denied to an applicant for failure to disclose arrests for book-making which had occurred some twelve years previously. Whatever the merits of individual denials, the commissioner seems to

have no standards to guide him. Nor has the commissioner limited himself to denials for bad character. He has used his power of revocation to regulate his licensees in many ways. He threatened to revoke the licenses of theaters if he found them accepting kickbacks on tickets. He revoked the licenses of three of New York's eight dance halls that provide hostesses and initiated proceedings against others, charging that they were "lewd" and "offensive to public decency."

Vast discretion tends to corrupt. The New York State Liquor Authority, having the power to grant valuable liquor licenses to a favored few, having inadequately objective standards by which to make the choice, and operating in secret, fell into a pattern of corruption in which it would dispense its favors only in return for bribes and pay-offs, refusing to grant privileges to those who were too honest, too ignorant, or too poor to play its game. Thus a dispensing agency of government became little better than a shakedown racket.

PRESSURES AGAINST THE BILL OF RIGHTS

The chief legal bulwark of the individual against oppressive government power is the Bill of Rights. But government largess may impair the individual's enjoyment of those rights. A radio-operator's license was denied by the FCC because the applicant pleaded the privilege against self-incrimination. Pressures are also applied against the protection of the Fourth Amendment.

In the case of many public-assistance programs, a power to make unannounced searches of recipients' premises is asserted by administrators.

> In the sample of active cases studied some instances were reported in which the special-investigation teams in a surprise visit in the middle of the night pushed past the one who answered the door and looked in the closets and under the bed for evidence of male occupancy. One family interviewed in this study complained of repeated harassment of this kind. The family consisted of a mother, her teenage son and younger daughter. The mother and daughter slept in the combina-

tion living room, dining room and bedroom, and the son slept in a small converted closet off the bedroom. One night they were awakened at three o'clock in the morning by loud knocking at their door. The son went to the door, which opened into the bedroom occupied by the mother and daughter. Two men pushed past him without identifying themselves as investigators from the Department of Public Aid, and said they were looking for the father who was reported to have returned home. Without apology they left, but returned several weeks later at one o'clock in the morning, repeating the same performance, again without finding their man. This experience has had an unnerving effect on the entire family.

Largess also brings pressure against First Amendment rights. The Pacifica Foundation was for a long period in danger of losing its three radio licenses because of "controversial" broadcasts, including "extreme" political views. For an extended period the FCC delayed action on the foundation's application for renewals. Then the FCC demanded that the foundation's directors, officers, and mangers give answers disclosing whether they were, or had been, members of the Communist Party or of any group advocating or teaching the overthrow of government by force. The foundation refused to answer. Eventually the FCC renewed the licenses.

FROM GOVERNMENT POWER TO PRIVATE POWER

Inequalities lie deep in the administrative structure of government largess. The whole process of acquiring it and keeping it favors some applicants and recipients over others. The administrative process is characterized by uncertainty, delay, and inordinate expense; to operate within it requires considerable know-how. All of these factors strongly favor larger, richer, more experienced companies or individuals over smaller ones. Only the most secure can weather delay or seemingly endless uncertainty. A company accused of misusing a license can engage counsel to fight the action without being ruined by the

expenses of the defense; an individual may find revocation proceedings are enough to send him to the poorhouse regardless of the outcome. And the large and the small are not always treated alike. For example, small firms which deal with the government are sometimes placed on a blacklist because of delinquencies in performance, thus losing out on all government contracts, but giant contractors who are guilty of similar delinquencies are apparently not subject to this drastic punishment. Similarly, regulation of taxicabs tends to be harder on the individual owner or driver, who may lose his driver's license,— while little harm comes to the company controlling a fleet, which may lose drivers but not its precious franchise.

All these inequalities modify somewhat the simple picture of a government-private dichotomy. But a second modification is required: government and the private sector (or a favored part of it) are often partners rather than opposing interests. The concept of partnership covers many quite different situations. Sometimes government largess serves to aid the private objectives of an industry, as when government supplies grazing land to stockmen, timber to the lumber industry, and scientific know-how to the private investors in Telstar. A second type of partnership exists where governmental action protects the recipient of largess from adverse forces with which he would otherwise have to contend; this is illustrated by the defense contract, with its virtual guarantee against losses due to most economic or management factors. The Atomic Energy Commission provides insurance against public liability due to negligence. Just as frequently, government largess offers protection against the disadvantages of competition. ICC motor-carrier regulation provides partial monopolies for each trucker. CAB routes give partial monopolies to airlines. Professional or occupational licensing limits competition and adds a tone of respectability and reliability as well. Often the leaders in seeking regulation have been the persons affected, and not government or the general community; the professional and occupational groups want government protection just as the property owner wants zoning. Sometimes licensing is a particularly obvious cover for monopoly. An ordinance in Seattle limited to a handful the number of persons or firms who could be licensed to operate juke boxes, but allowed each licensee to have a large number of juke boxes in different establishments; this effectively restricted the business to a small but highly privileged group. The partnership of government and private enterprise may give further protection — not merely from the consequences of competition, but also from the legal consequences of eliminating competition. Some privilege-dispensing agencies can exempt their clients from the antitrust laws, and, like the Maritime Board, use this power in connection with the grant of franchises to make lawful all sort of anticompetitive practices that otherwise would violate the Sherman Act. The federal government's role in defense research and development has created new forms of partnership. Substantial sectors of the economy become committed to a system of government contracting in which both the contractors and the politicians have a tremendous stake in the continuance of the system.

In any society with powerful or dominant private groups, it is not unexpected that governmental systems of power will be utilized by private groups. Hence the frequency with which regulatory agencies are taken over by those they are supposed to regulate. Significantly, most of these agencies are also the chief federal dispensers of largess. They quarrel with the industries they regulate, but seen in a larger perspective these quarrels are all in the family. In sum, the great system of power created by government largess is a ready means to further the interests of certain private groups and not merely an advance in the position of government over what is "private" in society as a whole.

THE NEW FEUDALISM

The characteristics of the public-interest state are varied, but there is an underlying philosophy that unites them. This is the doctrine that the wealth that flows from government is held by its recipients conditionally, subject to confiscation in the interest of the paramount state. Just as the feudal system linked lord and vassal through a system of mutual dependence, obligation, and loyalty, so government largess binds man to the state — and, it may be added, loyalty or fealty to the state is often one of the essential conditions of modern tenure. In the many decisions taking away government largess for refusal to sign loyalty oaths, belonging to "subversive" organizations, or other similar grounds, there is more than a suggestion of the condition of fealty demanded in older times.

The comparison to the general outlines of the feudal system may best be seen by recapitulating some of the chief features of government largess. (1) Increasingly we turn over wealth and rights to government, which reallocates and redistributes them in the many forms of largess; (2) there is a merging of public and private, in which lines of private ownership are blurred; (3) the administration of the system has given rise to special laws and special tribunals outside the ordinary structure of government; (4) the right to possess and use government largess is bound up with the recipient's legal status; status is both the basis for receiving largess and a consequence of receiving it; hence the new wealth is not readily transferable; (5) individuals hold the wealth conditionally rather than absolutely; the conditions are usually obligations owed to the government or to the public and may include the obligation of loyalty to the government; the obligations may be changed or increased at the will of the state; (6) for breach of condition the wealth may be forfeited or escheated back to the government; (7) the sovereign power is shared with large private interests; (8) the object of the whole system is to enforce "the public interest" — the interest of the state or society or the lord paramount — by means of the distribution and use of wealth in such a way as to create and maintain dependence.

Charles A. Reich

If the day comes when most private ownership is supplanted by government largess, how then will governmental power over individuals be contained? What will dependence do to the American character? What will happen to the Constitution, and particularly the Bill of Rights, if their limits may be by-passed by purchase, and if people lack an independent base from which to assert their individuality and claim their rights? Without the security of the person that individual wealth provides — and that largess fails to provide — what, indeed, will we become?

Property and the Public Interest: An Old Debate Revisited

The public-interest state, as visualized above, represents in one sense the triumph of society over private property. This triumph is the end point of a great and necessary movement for reform. But somehow the result is different from what the reformers wanted. Somehow the idealistic concept of the public interest has summoned up a doctrine monstrous and oppressive. It is time to take another look at private property and at the "public interest" philosophy that dominates its modern substitute, the largess of government.

PROPERTY AND LIBERTY

Property is a legal institution the essence of which is the creation and protection of certain private rights in wealth of any kind. The institution performs many different functions. One of these functions is to draw a boundary between public and private power. Property draws a circle around the activities of each private individual or organization. Within that circle, the owner has a greater degree of freedom than without. Outside, he must justify or explain his actions, and show his authority. Within, he is master, and the state must explain and justify any interference. It is as if property shifted the burden of proof; outside, the individual has the burden; inside, the burden is on government to demonstrate that something the owner wishes to do should not be done.

Thus, property performs the function of maintaining independence, dignity, and pluralism in society by creating zones within which the majority has to yield to the owner. Whim, caprice, irrationality, and "antisocial" activities are given the protection of law; the owner may do what all or most of his neighbors decry. The Bill of Rights also serves this function, but while the Bill of Rights comes into play only at extraordinary moments of conflict or crisis, property affords day-to-day protection in the ordinary affairs of life. Indeed, in the final analysis, the Bill of Rights depends upon the existence of private property. Political rights presuppose that individuals and private groups have the will and the means to act independently. But so long as individuals are motivated largely by self-interest, their well-being must first be independent. Civil liberties must have a basis in property or bills of rights will not preserve them.

Property is not a natural right but a deliberate construction by society. If such an institution did not exist, it would be necessary to create it in order to have the kind of society we wish to have. The majority cannot be expected, on specific issues, to yield its power to a minority. Only if the minority's will is established as a general principle can it keep the majority at bay in a given instance. Like the Bill of Rights, property represents a general, long-range protection of individual and private interests, created by the majority for the ultimate good of all.

Today, however, it is widely thought that property and liberty are separable things; that there may, in fact, be conflicts between "property rights" and "personal rights." Why has this view been accepted? The explanation is found at least partly in the transformations which have taken place in property.

During the industrial revolution, when property was liberated from feudal restraints, philosophers hailed property as the basis of liberty and argued that it must be free from the demands of government society. But as private property grew, so did abuses resulting from its use. In a crowded world a man's use of his property increasingly affected his neighbor, and one man's exercise of a right might seriously impair the rights of others. Property became power over others; the farm landowner, the city landlord, and the working man's boss were able to oppress their tenants or employees. Great aggregations of property resulted in private control of entire industries and basic services capable of affecting a whole area or even a nation. At the same time, much private property lost its individuality and in effect became socialized. Multiple ownership of corporations helped to separate personality from property, and property from power. When the corporations began to stop competing, to merge, agree, and make mutual plans, they became private governments. Finally, they sought the aid and partnership of the state, and thus by their own volition became part of public government. These changes led to a movement for reform which sought to limit arbitrary private power and protect the common man. Property rights were considered more the enemy than the friend of liberty. The reformers argued that property must be separated from personality.

During the first half of the twentieth century, the reformers enacted into law their conviction that private power was a chief enemy of society and of individual liberty. Property was subjected to "reasonable" limitations in the interests of society. The regulatory agencies, federal and state, were born of the reform. In sustaining these major inroads on private property, the Supreme Court rejected the older idea that property and liberty were one, and wrote a series of classic opinions upholding the power of the people to regulate and limit private rights.

The struggle between abuse and reform made it easy to forget the basic importance of individual private property. The defense of private property was almost entirely a defense of its abuses – an attempt to defend, not individual property, but arbitrary private power over other human beings. Since this defense was cloaked in a defense of private property, it was natural for the reformers to attack too broadly.

The reform took away some of the power of the corporations and transferred it to government. In this transfer there was much good, for power was made responsive to the majority rather than to the arbitrary and selfish few. But the reform did not restore the individual to his domain. What the corporation had taken from him, the reform simply handed on to government, and government carried further the powers formerly exercised by the corporation. Government as an employer, or as a dispenser of wealth, has used the theory that it was handing out gratuities to claim a managerial power as great as that which the capitalists claimed. Moreover the corporations allied themselves with, or actually took over, part of government's system of power. Today it is the combined power of government and the corporations that presses against the individual.

From the individual's point of view, it is not any particular kind of power, but all kinds of power, that are to be feared. This is the lesson of the public-interest state. The mere fact that power is derived from the majority does not necessarily make it less oppressive. Liberty is more than the right to do what the majority wants, or to do what is "reasonable." Liberty is the right to defy the majority and to do what is unreasonable. The great error of the public-interest state is that it assumes an identity between the public interest and the interest of the majority.

The reform, then, has not done away with the importance of private property. More than ever the individual needs to possess, in whatever form, a small but sovereign island of his own. If individualism and pluralism are to be preserved, this must be done, not by marching backwards, but by building these values into today's society. If public and private are now blurred, it will be necessary to draw a new zone of privacy. If private property can no longer perform its protective functions, it will be necessary to establish institutions to carry on the work that private property once did but can no longer do.

Charles A. Reich

In these efforts government largess must play a major role. As we move toward a welfare state, largess will be an ever more important form of wealth. And largess is a vital link in the relationship between the government and private sides of society. It is necessary, then, that largess begin to do the work of property.

The chief obstacle to the creation of private rights in largess has been the fact that it is orginally public property, comes from the state, and may be withheld completely. But this need not be an obstacle. Traditional property also comes from the state, and in much the same way. Land, for example, traces back to grants from the sovereign. In a less obvious sense, personal property also stems from government. Personal property is created by law; it owes its origin and continuance to laws supported by the people as a whole. These laws "give" the property to one who performs certain actions.

Like largess, real and personal property were also originally dispensed on conditions and were subject to forfeiture if the conditions failed. The conditions in the sovereign grants, such as colonization, were generally made explicit, and so was the forfeiture resulting from failure to fulfill them. In the case of the Preemption and Homestead Acts, there were also specific conditions. Even now land is subject to forfeiture for neglect; if it is unused it may be deemed abandoned to the state or forfeited to an adverse possessor. In a very similar way, personal property may be forfeited by abandonment or loss. Hence, all property might be described as government largess, given on condition and subject to loss.

If all property is government largess, why is it not regulated to the same degree as present-day largess? Regulation of property has been limited, not because society had no interest in property, but because it was in the interest of society that property be free. Once property is seen not as a natural right but as a construction designed to serve certain functions, then its origin ceases to be decisive in determining how much regulation should be imposed. The conditions that can be attached to receipt, ownership, and use depend not on where property came from, but on what job it should be expected to perform. Thus in the case of government largess, nothing turns on the fact that it orginated in government. The real issue is how it functions and how it should function.

CONSTITUTIONAL LIMITS

The most clearly defined problem posed by government largess is the way it can be used to apply pressures against the exercise of constitutional rights. A first principle should be that government must have no power to "buy up" rights guaranteed by the Constitution. It should not be able to impose any condition on largess that would be invalid if imposed on something other than a "gratuity." Thus, for example, government should not be able to deny largess because of invocation of the privilege against self-incrimination.

The problem becomes more complicated when a court attempts, as current doctrine seems to require, to "balance" the deterrence of a constitutional right against some opposing interest. In any balancing process, no weight should be given to the contention that what is at stake is a mere gratuity. It should be recognized that pressure against constitutional rights from denial of a "gratuity" may be as great or greater than pressure from criminal punishment. And the concept of the public interest should be given a meaning broad enough to include general injury to independence and constitutional rights. It is not possible to consider detailed problems here. It is enough to say that government should gain no power, as against constitutional limitations, by reason of its role as a dispenser of wealth.

SUBSTANTIVE LIMITS

Beyond the limits deriving from the Constitution, what limits should be imposed on governmental power over largess? Such limits, whatever they may be, must be largely self-imposed and self-policed by legislatures; the Constitution sets only a bare minimum of limitations on legislative policy. The first type of limit should be on relevance. It has proved possible to argue that practically anything in the way of regulation is relevant to some legitimate legislative purpose. But this does not mean that it is desirable for legislatures to make such use of their powers.

Courts sometimes manage, by statutory construction, to place limits on relevance. One example is the judicial reaction to attempts to ban "disloyal tenants" from government-aided housing projects. The Wisconsin Court said: "Counsel for the defendant Authority have failed to point out to this court how the occupation of any units of a federally aided housing project by tenants who may be members of a subversive organization threatens the successful operation of such housing projects."[12] It is impossible to confine the concept of relevance. But legislatures should strive for a meaningful, judicious concept of relevance if regulation of largess is not to become a handle for regulating everything else.

Besides relevance, a second important limit on substantive power might be concerned with discretion. To the extent possible, delegated power to make rules ought to be confined within ascertainable limits, and regulating agencies should not be assigned the task of enforcing conflicting policies. Also, agencies should be enjoined to use their powers only for the purposes for which they were designed. In a perhaps naïve attempt to accomplish this, Senator Lausche introduced a bill to prohibit United States government contracting officers from using their contracting authority for purposes of duress. This bill, in its own words, would prohibit officials from denying contracts, or the right to bid on contracts, with the intent of forcing the would-be contractor to perform or refrain from performing any act which such person had no legal obligation to perform or not perform. Although this bill might not be a very effective piece of legislation, it does suggest a desirable objective.

A final limit on substantive power, one that should be of growing importance, might be a principle that policy-making authority ought not to be delegated to essentially private organizations. The increasing practice of giving professional associations and occupational organizations authority in areas of government largess tends to make an individual subject to a guild of his fellows. A guild system, when attached to government largess, adds to the feudal characteristics of the system.

PROCEDURAL SAFEGUARDS

Because it is so hard to confine relevance and discretion, procedure offers a valuable means for restraining arbitrary action. This was recognized in the strong procedural emphasis of the Bill of Rights, and it is being recognized in the increasingly procedural emphasis of administrative law. The law of government largess has developed with little regard for procedure. Reversal of this trend is long overdue.

The grant, denial, revocation, and administration of all types of government largess should be subject to scrupulous observance of fair procedures. Action should be open to hearing and contest and based upon a record subject to judicial review. The denial of any form of privilege or benefit on the basis of undisclosed reasons should no longer be tolerated. Nor should the same person sit as legislator, prosecutor, judge, and jury, combining all the functions of government in such a way as to make fairness virtually impossible. There is no justification for the survival of arbitrary methods where valuable rights are at stake.

FROM LARGESS TO RIGHT

The proposals discussed above, however salutary, are by themselves far from adequate to assure the status of individual man with respect to largess. The problems go deeper. First, the growth of government power based on the dispensing of wealth must be kept within bounds. Second, there must be a zone of privacy for each individ-

Charles A. Reich

ual beyond which neither government nor private power can push – a hiding place from the all-pervasive system of regulation and control. Finally, it must be recognized that we are becoming a society based upon relationship and status – status deriving primarily from source of livelihood. Status is so closely linked to personality that destruction of one may well destroy the other. Status must therefore be surrounded with the kind of safeguards once reserved for personality.

Eventually those forms of largess which are closely linked to status must be deemed to be held as of right. Like property, such largess could be governed by a system of regulation plus civil or criminal sanctions, rather than by a system based upon denial, suspension, and revocation. As things now stand, violations lead to forfeitures – outright confiscation of wealth and status, but there is surely no need for these drastic results. Confiscation, if used at all, should be the ultimate, not the most common and convenient, penalty. The presumption should be that the professional man will keep his license and the welfare recipient his pension. These interests should be "vested." If revocation is necessary, not by reason of the fault of the individual holder but by reason of overriding demands of public policy, perhaps payment of just compensation would be appropriate. The individual should not bear the entire loss for a remedy primarily intended to benefit the community.

The concept of right is most urgently needed with respect to benefits such as unemployment compensation, public assistance, and old-age insurance. These benefits are based upon a recognition that misfortune and deprivation are often caused by forces far beyond the control of the individual, such as technological change, variations in demand for goods, depressions, or wars. The aim of these benefits is to preserve the self-sufficiency of

the individual, to rehabilitate him where necessary, and to allow him to be a valuable member of a family and a community; in theory they represent part of the individual's rightful share in the commonwealth. Only by making such benefits into rights can the welfare state achieve its goal of providing a secure minimum basis for individual well-being and dignity in a society where each man cannot be wholly the master of his own destiny.

Conclusion

The time has come for us to remember what the framers of the Constitution knew so well — that "a power over a man's subsistence amounts to a power over his will." We cannot safely entrust our livelihoods and our rights to the discretion of authorities, examiners, boards of control, character committees, regents, or license commissioners. We cannot permit any official or agency to pretend to sole knowledge of the public good. We cannot put the independence of any man wholly in the power of other men.

If the individual is to survive in a collective society, he must have protection against its ruthless pressures. There must be sanctuaries or enclaves where no majority can reach. To shelter the solitary human spirit does not merely make possible the fulfillment of individuals; it also gives society the power to change, to grow, and to regenerate, and hence to endure. These were the objects which property sought to achieve, and can no longer achieve. The challenge of the future will be to construct, for the society that is coming, institutions and laws to carry on this work. Just as the Homestead Act was a deliberate effort to foster individual values at an earlier time, so we must try to build an economic basis for liberty today — a Homestead Act for rootless twentieth-century man. We must create a new property.

Part Thirteen

The Contemporary Legal Order

Both John P. Frank and Herbert Wechsler, writing in the 1950s about the work of the United States Supreme Court, expressed criticism. It is interesting to see how attitudes can shift within the span of a few short years. Frank assesses the work of the Supreme Court and its effect on civil liberties, and he finds the Court wanting: the court never, he concludes, stood firm on the side of civil liberties during a crisis. Judicial review "has not been of any great significance to the civil liberties of the American people." Frank wrote before the landmark egalitarian and civil-liberties decisions of the Warren Court had been decided. No doubt, after the passage of twenty years, he would now want to revise his opinion. But this does not alter the basic finding that the Court has, in fact, not been zealous in defense of civil liberites to the extent that a convinced civil libertarian would have wanted it to be. We still cannot tell whether the Warren Court and its work reflect a lasting trend, or are only an interlude.

Herbert Wechsler's much discussed article was originally delivered as a lecture at the Harvard Law School in 1959. The Warren Court decisions on criminal rights still lay in the future, and its most revolutionary work had been in civil

rights. But this work together with a few of the bolder opinions of its predecessors were enough to alarm Wechsler. The court, he said, was deciding cases which it could not justify on the basis of general principle, solely because it approved of their results in the light of some assumed goal of social policy. Wechsler's critique implies that some kind of long-range harm is likely to ensue from the assumption of an activist role by the court. This is certainly a possibility, though one difficult to verify, and one wonders if the advantages of judicial restraint, whatever they might be, are worth the price of giving up those important new doctrines which came out of the Warren Court. Wechsler's criticisms of the Court remind one of the attacks on the legal realists. Indeed, the failures of judicial craftsmanship that he deplores are, in a sense, a translation of realist principles into decisional law. But, in the light of the massive social change in this century, one wonders whether assigning a more modest role to the courts would be worth the social cost.

The final essay, by David M. Potter, asks a fundamental and lasting question, but one unlikely to have been posed before the turbulent decade of the 1960s. Law in

395

The Contemporary Legal Order

this country was always connected, as it is in most countries, with order, and order invariably was tied to some sort of community consensus. No society is strong enough to sustain itself by force alone, though there are totalitarian societies that have come very close. For societies that are in any way "open," stability depends on adherence to some number of common beliefs. In the 1960s, against a background of war in Vietnam, urban rioting, and social unrest, it was only fair to ask, as Potter does, "What happens to law based on the norms of the community if there is no prevailing community, but only a multiplicity of conflicting communities? What happens to the principle of consent if the social structure has no center which can even speak the voice of consent?"

As this book is being put together, a new, more tranquil (perhaps complacent) mood has at least partly replaced the turbulence of the 1960s. This reminds us that the fundamental questions of law in society are always raising themselves, in somewhat different forms. What seems to be an answer in one period is not even worthy of a question in the next. Nonetheless the basic problem which David Potter discussed remains at the core of this enterprise: if there is one theme which the

majority of these essays share, it is the intimate connection between the legal system and its social context. Less obvious, but implicit at least, is the assumption that the legal order, once shaped by society, in turn helps mold the particular forms of social life, or at least sustains and maintains their structure. As society becomes ever more complex, ever more subject to the subtle interplay of forces, ever less able to call upon shared beliefs, it becomes ever more dependent upon law, and yet law itself is dependent upon community.

Further Reading

Bickel, Alexander M. *The Least Dangerous Branch: The Supreme Court at the Bar of Politics.* Indianapolis: Bobbs-Merrill & Co., 1962.

Johnson, Earl, Jr. *Justice and Reform: The Formative Years of the OEO Legal Services Program.* New York: Russell Sage Foundation, 1974.

Horowitz, Donald L. *The Courts and Social Policy.* Washington, D.C.: The Brookings Institution, 1977.

Swindler, William F. *Court and Constitution in the 20th Century: The New Legality, 1932–1968.* Indianapolis: Bobbs-Merrill & Co., 1970.

32

John P. Frank

Judicial Review and Basic Liberties

Introduction

. . . One hundred and fifty years ago, John Marshall for the Supreme Court declared the American doctrine of judicial review of the validity of acts of Congress . . .

. . . We have lived under the system for a century and a half, and we may fairly examine whether we like it, and whether it needs any improvements, basic or slight.

In this discussion, I will cling closely to certain partially self imposed jurisdictional limitations in my own subject matter in the belief that one precise problem needs close attention. That precise problem is the relation of judicial review to civil liberty, to the rights of free speech, pess, religion, assembly and to the great procedural rights of the Constitution. For this purpose, the term judicial review is to be given the narrowest of several available constructions. To emphasize this narrow construction, the term "pure judicial review" will occasionally be used. It will

Abridged from *Supreme Court and Supreme Law*, ed. Edmond Cahn, 109-136, by permission of the author and Indiana University Press. Copyright, 1954, by the Law Center Foundation, New York University.

mean here no more and no less than what was involved in the *Marbury* case, that is, review by the Supreme Court of the validity of acts of Congress. This excludes several matters commonly included within the meaning of the term. Specifically excluded are (a) review of acts of Congress by tribunals other than the Supreme Court, which is put aside as quantitatively insignificant; (b) review by the Supreme Court of state legislation, which is based on the Constitution's supremacy clause quite apart from *Marbury* v. *Madison*; and (c) review by the Supreme Court of executive action. The excluded matters will be discussed only where they bear on review of the validity of federal legislation.

Uses of the Power

INVALIDATIONS

The most obvious measure of judicial review is in the instances where it has been used. Here, so far as civil liberties are concerned, the balance is if anything against judicial review.

Using Mr. Warren's list[1] brought up to date, there have been 78 instances of invalidations. Of these, the overwhelming bulk had no direct bearing on basic liber-

John P. Frank

ties. They dealt, as *Marbury* v. *Madison* did, with distribution of the powers of government or, as in *Adkins* v. *Children's Hospital*,[2] with economic matters. A numerical breakdown will make the point:

Distribution of All Invalidations

Cases unrelated to basic liberties		59
Total cases bearing on basic liberties		19
Holdings aiding liberty	3	
Holdings limiting liberty	8	
Holdings peripheral to civil liberties	8	
Total invalidations		78

The eight peripheral cases are those which involve civil liberties either of a minor sort or in a minor way, and are decisions which could fairly well have gone either way without greatly affecting the course of the republic. Three involve minor points of criminal administration in the District of Columbia,[3] and a fourth relates to the type of jury required in Alaska.[4]

The other four of these peripheral cases are somewhat more substantial. *Tot* v. *United States*[5] involved a point as to permissible presumptions in criminal statutes, and the *Cohen Grocery*[6] case made a contribution to the requirement of definiteness in statutes. *Boyd* v. *United States*[7] and *Counselman* v. *Hitchcock*,[8] the remaining two of this group, have helped shape the law of searches and seizuires and of self-incrimination.

. . . [T]hree cases [were] listed above as holdings aiding liberty. . .

. . . *Ex parte Garland*,[9] a distinctly benign holding, invalidated the test oath for lawyers after the Civil War. One of its largest practical results was to retain for the country the services of Mr. Garland, an outstanding lawyer and, later, Attorney General. A second case was that of *Wong Wing*[10] a holding giving some procedural rights to aliens; specifically the holding prohibits imprisonment of aliens at hard labor without judicial process. (It should be noted in passing that a subsequent decision permits their imprisonment, without bail, for protracted periods

pending hearing, largely on the say-so of the Department of Justice.[11]) A third case, the most recent, is that of Messrs. Watson, Dodd, and Lovett,[12] whom Congress attempted to strike from all present and future government employment by name. The Court, going back to the *Garland* case as a precedent, held the congressional effort a bill of attainder. The holding was undoubtedly of substantial importance, for Congress regarded the naming of the three as a test case and would undoubtedly have followed with further proscriptions had the door been left open by the Court.

Against these blows in behalf of basic liberties, specialized as they are, must be balanced prodigious counterblows. In eight cases the Court's holdings, putting aside any issue of how good their constitutional law may have been, had the effect of limiting liberty. Concededly this is a matter of interpretation. What one reader thinks limits liberty, another may think extends it. Let me put it this way: most students north of the Mason-Dixon line and many students south of it will think that the decisions now under discussion limited, rather than extended, basic liberties.

This group begins with Dred Scott's case[13] declaring that Congress could not preclude slavery in the territories. The other seven cases are all invalidations of legislation passed primarily for the protection of Negroes under the Civil War Amendments. The leading three of these cases include, first, *United States* v. *Reese*,[14] holding invalid under the Fifteenth Amendment a statute forbidding state election officials from keeping "any citizen" from voting. The second was *United States* v. *Harris*,[15] holding the punishment of a lynch mob beyond the federal power. The third is the Civil Rights Cases,[16] which held that Congress could not use Fourteenth Amendment powers to prevent private acts of racial discrimination.

On the basis of this brief enumeration this much seems inescapable: if the test of the value of judicial review to the preservation of basic liberties were to be rested solely on consideration of actual invalidations, the balance is against judicial review. On the benefit side lie abolition of the test oaths after the Civil War, the benefit to aliens from Wong Wing's case, and the repudiation of congressional proscription lists. On the loss side, still using benefit to liberty as the sole test, is the destruction of what was intended to be comprehensive legislation to give some measure of equality to the vast number of Negroes in our midst.

This conclusion by no means requires the further conclusion that judicial review is valueless to basic liberties. What it does mean is that the case for judicial review must be made, if any can be made, on some basis other than consideration of the Court's direct use of its power.

THE COURT IN THE FLOW OF HISTORY

The same result is reached if the Court is studied in terms of the general trends of American history. Neither the spirit of liberty nor the spirit of repression is ever totally absent from the American scene. From time to time, one or the other achieves sufficient dominance to provide the basis for a cyclical interpretation of the history of liberty in America. If I may repeat here a theory often advanced before, the cycle of liberty and repression is, in some superficial respects at least, similar to the more familiar economic cycle of prosperity and depression. To accentuate the similarity of form, we may use as a parallel to the economic term "depression" the term "repression" to symbolize the downsweeps in this cycle. It may be noted in passing that repressions usually occur at the opposite end of an economic cycle from a depression — our repressions are frequently concomitants of prosperity.

The term "repression" may be defined thus: it is an intense spasm of social fury in which a commonly latent impulse to destroy opposition without regard to the norms of democratic behavior becomes a dominantly conspicuous element in the American scene. It normally results in some destruction of opposition and, to date, has always been followed by a period of renewed affection for democratic values.

The most striking fact in the relation of the history of repressions to the history of judicial review in particular or to the Supreme Court in general is that no direct action by the Court has ever had any significant bearing in either *stopping* or *slowing* a repression. I am not speaking here of the effects of the Court's decisions in moments of calm upon our conduct in moments of frenzy, nor of the effects of individual expressions by particular justices, but solely of the effect of the Court at the storm center during the storm. This may be illustrated tabularly, including for this purpose every kind of judicial review no matter how broadly considered:

Supreme Court Response to Repressions

EPISODE	JUDICIAL RESPONSE
Alien and sedition scare, 1795–1801	None called for
Anti-Masonry, ca. 1830	None called for
Climax of nativism, ca. 1850	None called for
Anti-anarchism 1880s–1890s	No restraint
Espionage and Bolshevik flurries, 1917–1927	No restraint
Contemporary repression, at pinnacle 1946–	No restraint[17]

If the foregoing is true as to the action of the Court in all fields, including review of state laws, review of the executive, and interpretation of statutes, it is *a fortiori* true of the more narrow judicial review. The bald fact is that, except for the very narrow points involved in the *Garland* and *Lovett* cases, Congress has never yet passed a statute in a fit of repression which the Supreme Court has invalidated. On the contrary, except for the very special and unusual reaction after the Civil War (excluded from this table because of its unique circumstances), the Court has stamped the repressionist acts as "Approved." The dominant lesson of our history in the relation of the judiciary to repressions is that courts love liberty most when it is under pressure least.

One is compelled to conclude again that if judicial review has had any whole-

John P. Frank

some effect on the basic liberties of Americans, that effect must be found elsewhere than on the occasions of the direct exercise of the power.

The Interaction of Judicial Review and Noncongressional Interferences with Liberty

In a familiar passage, Mr. Justice Holmes said, "I do not think the United States would come to an end if we lost our power to declare an Act of Congress void. I do think the Union would be imperiled if we could not make that declaration as to the laws of the several states."[18]

This statement, it seems to me, is sound in both its halves. It does, however, suggest a completeness of disjunction between these two types of judicial review which could be misleading. I have already excluded from consideration the Supreme Court's review of executive action and of state legislation, except insofar as they must be commingled with discussion of "pure" judicial review; but there is an area in which they cannot be separated.

There is in fact a dual interaction between pure judicial review, or review of acts of Congress, and review of state action. This dual quality can be discussed separately, in terms of (a) the effect of judicial review on the states (or on the executive), and (b) the effect of review of state action on pure judicial review.

EFFECT OF JUDICIAL REVIEW ON STATE (OR EXECUTIVE) REVIEW

The principal consequences of pure judicial review on review of state action are wholly psychological, rather than tangible, but they are immensely important. The very existence of the power of judicial review is the greatest single source of the Supreme Court's prestige. That prestige in turn gives the Court's decisions on state laws far more effect than they otherwise would have, and also greatly increases the self-confidence of the Court.

The great, the almost mystical admiration for this feature of our governmental system is unending; it is old and new. In the nineteenth century, Bryce described judicial review as one of the most admirable features of our system. More recently a Supreme Court justice quoted *Marbury* v. *Madison*, and said, "Upon this rock the nation has been built."[19]

Whether these enthusiasms are warranted or not is outside the scope of this essay, which deals with only one fragment of the whole of judicial review. What is important is that these attitudes exist and are generally shared, whether warranted or not, and their very existence has the broadest of consequences on basic liberties. The Court may be timid, it may be (as I think) unduly timid in standing up to Congress; but it has not been nearly as timid in standing up to the states or to the president. In these battles, the aura of prestige stemming from the power of judicial review undoubtedly aids its effectiveness.

It is not accident that the episodes of state or of executive defiance of the judiciary antedate the establishment of judicial review as a common practice. Today the president and the states largely accept the Court's mandates. The current acquiescence in judicial decisions is very different from the response of the sovereign state of Virginia to the cases of *Hunter's Lessee* or of *Cohens*[20] 125 years ago; or the response of Ohio to the decisions on its attempted abolition of certain bank-tax exemptions;[21] or President Jackson's famous "John Marshall had made his decision"; or Abraham Lincoln's defiance of Chief Justice Taney over the matter of Merryman. In those days, judicial review was not a workaday practice.

This is to say that the mere possession of the power of judicial review gives the opinions of the Supreme Court an extra prestige in wholly unrelated matters. The Court is a little like the multimillionaire whose opinion is asked on Paris art or the affairs of the world when he returns from Europe — perhaps his possessions should not give these extraneous opinions any added weight, but nonetheless they do. There is no way of knowing how much of the Court's prestige comes from its possession of the power of judicial review, but undoubtedly some of it does.

That prestige is directly useful to basic liberties. The libertarian decisions of the Hughes Court in the 1930s in such cases as *Near* v. *Minnesota, Herndon* v. *Lowry, Lovell* v. *Griffin,*[22] and a dozen other decisions were accepted by the states which received them in remarkably good grace. The invalidation of many forms of racial discrimination in the last several years, such as white primaries, restrictive covenants, segregated transportation and law schools, and restrictions on alien land use have none of them directly involved judicial reveiw. Nonetheless each of them flew in the teeth of strong local sentiment, and the consequences of the decisions for good have ranged from at least a little to a great deal in the various areas mentioned. The acceptance of each of the decisions mentioned is, to some unknown but real extent, aided by the fact that the Court which made them had in addition the power of judicial review. One may suspect, though one cannot know, that the self-confidence with which the Court sailed into those tough problems was also increased by its possession of the larger power.

To a lesser extent this is also true of the relations of the judiciary and the executive. Whether the steel-seizure case[23] involved a "basic liberty" as that term is being used here is arguable; but at least the instant acquiescence of the president may have been conditioned by his acceptance of the Court's power over acts of Congress. From *Ex parte Milligan*[24] to *Ex parte Quirin,*[25] in which the Court overrode without discussion executive interference with habeas corpus, to the Hawaiian martial-law cases,[26] the Court has approached the problem of occasionally rampaging executives with a sense of power nurtured in part by its possession of the power of judicial review. In this indirect, but important, sense the existence of the power of judicial review has contributed to the maintenance of basic liberty in the United States.

EFFECT OF STATE REVIEW ON JUDICIAL REVIEW

The effect of state review on judicial review is doctrinal. Since some parts of the Bill of Rights are equated to the "liberty" of the Fourteenth Amendment (or to the "privileges and immunities" of that amendment), and since equal-protection concepts can be read back into the Fifth Amendment's due-process clause, there is no necessary doctrinal difference between review of some state conduct and of some federal conduct. The clear-and-present-danger concept, for example, originated in interpretation of the First Amendment, languished for a time in interpretation of the Fourteenth, was developed to some glory in the thirties and early forties as an interpretation of both, and then collapsed to its present toothless state in the fifties as a matter of interpretation of both.

Because of the interacting quality of the substantive doctrines used in judicial review and in state review, judicial review has these two additional indirect consequences to basic liberty. (1) Historically it has somewhat raised the standard to which state laws relating to liberty, particularly to free speech, are held. Before the *Gitlow* case[27] there was no federal review of state free-speech infractions, and, but for the judicial review cases clustered around World War I, it is extremely doubtful that jurisdiction would ever have been asserted in *Gitlow*. That some good to liberty has come from the assumption of jurisdiction in that case is too obvious to warrant elaboration. (2) The existence of a reservoir of cases on state law enlarges the body of civil-liberties law. To the extent that Fourteenth Amendment law and First Amendment law are the same, the mere existence of these state cases operates to give the Congress a few more hazards to circumvent when it would restrict basic liberties.

Let me enlarge briefly on this last thought by way of preface to the following section. It has been seen that so far as direct consequences to basic liberties are concerned, judicial review has in fact operated as more of a drag than a protection to freedom. But the indirect consequences may alter the total picture. As one indirect consequence, the sheer existence of judicial review makes the Court more effective in protecting basic liberties outside the scope of judicial review. As another, judicial review has had the effect of fostering review of state intrusions upon liberty and of giving a doctrinal base for the inspection of intrusions.

But the greatest indirect consequence of judicial review, at least theoretically, might be its restraining effect upon the Congress. Whether Congress in fact is more moderate in its laws than it would otherwise be because of respect for judicial review is the subject next to be considered. But certainly the interacting quality of the two types of review materially increases the education of Congress. Before the *Lovett* case, if Congress was to pass a bill in the nature of a bill of attainder, it had to consider *Cummings* v. *Missouri*[28] (state review) as much as *Ex parte Garland* (pure judicial review). When it was passing the Smith and McCarran Acts, *Herndon* v. *Lowry* (state review) was as relevant as *Abrams* v. *United States*[29] (pure judicial review). One important indirect effect of judicial review, therefore, is that it contributes to the development of a related body of doctrine which may have the effect of restraining Congress in passing laws restrictive of liberty.

Consequences in Congress

Judicial review, even though it resulted in negligible invalidations or indeed in no invalidations at all, might have a very substantial effect on the legislative process, whether for good or for evil. Some of these consequences could be:

1. Congress might abstain from passing repressive legislation because of a fear that it would be invalidated — or, at a minimum, might eliminate some of the more repressive features of legislation for that reason.

2. On the other hand, the fact that judicial review is in the offing might cause Congress to abandon any serious constitutional consideration, passing the responsibility to the Court.

3. Judicial review might at least have the effect of slowing and sobering congressional action while constitutional issues are considered.

4. Judicial review might furnish the rhetoric of legislative discussion, providing useful symbols for debate as well as furnishing concrete information to legislators.

REVIEW AND RHETORIC

The latter two of these possibilities, while important, are subordinate to the first two and will be discussed briefly. In this connection I have considered the legislative history of a series of bills which might be considered test cases: the Smith Act of 1940; the legislation of 1940 aimed at deporting Harry Bridges; the oath provisions of the Taft-Hartley Act of 1947; and the McCarran Internal Security Act of 1950.[30]

As to rhetoric, there is no doubt that judicial review has furnished much of the verbalization for our discussion of constitutional issues. For this result, however, judicial review was unnecessary. While judicial review was contemplated from the beginning, the power went almost unexercised until the Civil War[31] and yet, for the first seventy years of national experience, almost all issues of moment were debated in constitutional terms. A listing would only enumerate the obvious; indeed the level of constitutional argument in Madison's Remonstrance on the Alien and Sedition Acts, or Lincoln's address at Cooper Union, or Binney's pamphlets on habeas corpus is, qualitatively, far superior to any recent debate by public figures on constitutional questions. There is a very serious possibility that by enmeshing great principles in the minute details of the case system, judicial review has rendered serious public discussion of constitutional questions less, instead of more, valuable; there is in any case no evidence that the quality of discussion has been improved greatly by judicial review. The great dissents are rhetorically helpful, but *quaere* whether on balance they are worth the cost

Insofar as judicial review has increased the stock of constitutional rhetoric, it may be a misfortune. There are two angles to be considered: (a) the consequence of excessive attention to constitutionalism and lack of attention to the merits; (b) the related equating of constitutionality with merit.

As to the first, Chafee has pointed out the vice of discussion which concentrates excessively on constitutional factors. "What you are really saying then is that [a legislature] ought not to pass the measure even though they are not persuaded that it is undesirable. Whatever they think about it, the Supreme Court will annul it and so it will be useless. But this argument will fail unless you can convince your hearers that the Court will in fact be against the measure. In order to do this, you have to turn aside from the reasons about desirability which are part of everybody's thinking and *stick to the kind of language which lawyers use* [emphasis added]. You have to be absolutely sure of your ground, for if other lawyers (on the legislative committee or elsewhere) can raise plausible doubts about the validity of your constitutional position, you will get nowhere."[32]

For the reasons already stated, judicial review cannot be blamed for the American habit of debating issues in constitutional terms, with too little regard for the merits. That habit was ingrained long before judicial review became routine. But Chafee does raise serious doubt as to whether the lawyer's talk into which judicial review has pushed these debates has been an improvement.

The second branch of the subject is more serious; the practice of judicial review has tended to equate constitutionality with merit. No matter how loudly the Supreme Court proclaims that it is not passing upon the wisdom of legislation, validation is treated as an imprimatur. An extreme instance is the outbreak of anti-Jehovah's Witness riots which followed the Court's approval of the enforced flag salute.[33] The act of upholding a statute has a way, not always but very frequently, of ending debate on the merits; the syndicalism acts, once upheld, not only stay on the books permanently but become models for future statutes.

Without judicial review, we would experience the constitutional discussion but there never would be a final resolution of the issue by a single dramatic act. Hence the debate on the merits would not so brusquely end. There are of course exceptions to what is being said here, but it is at least a reasonable hypothesis that frequently, as judicial review has worked in fact in relation to basic liberties, it has depressed the status of those liberties toward the lowest common level of constitutional acceptance.

As to whether the case law flowing from judicial review has slowed and sobered congressional discussion, a fuller discussion follows immediately below. Suffice it to say here that there have been few instances of a substantial sobering effect. In most, but not all, cases of serious constitutional doubt, the constitutional element of the discussion is ritualistic. Proponents of the bill under discussion arm themselves with legal opinions upholding its constitutionality. These memoranda, written by leading members of the American Bar Association, may be introduced as a first point of business in committee hearings.[34] For most Congressmen, the stately opinions end all need for further intellectual ferment. When opponents of the bill arrive with legal memoranda on the other side, their statements will ordinarily be received into the record with politeness but without even a modicum of discussion.[35] Some witnesses may be questioned at length on nonconstitutional matters; if they persist on a constitutional line, they may be assured that the committee has a memorandum that clears everything up.[36] When debate reaches the floor, the prepared opinions may again be cited,[37] and only a minute fragment of debate time is usually consumed in a spontaneous discussion of constitutional principles. The serious consequences of judicial review, if any, lie elsewhere.

JUDICIAL REVIEW: LEGISLATIVE RESTRAINT OR EXCUSE?

The precise problem here is whether judicial review operates, on the one hand, to restrain the Congress or on the other to give it a sense of irresponsibility.

This discussion is exclusively in the context of legislation restrictive of civil liberties. Everyone knows that judicial review may have a major role in some fields. For example, *Willing v. Chicago Auditorium Ass'n*,[38] by casting doubt on the validity of the declaratory judgment, slowed that procedural reform for years; and the Brandeis opinion[39] invalidating one Frazier-Lemke Act became a model for design of the next.[40] But there is no strong impulse to repress basic liberties except when emotion is hot, hotter than it becomes over procedural reform, or over bankruptcy or production control. In this respect basic liberties might be in a special class.

The discussion must begin with the concession that there can be no assured conclusions. It must proceed into legislative history as its only available source, there to discover a pattern of words and acts. But no matter how much talk on constitutional points is found, not even the fiercest proponent of content analysis will claim that social science techniques can determine the motives underlying an utterance or the precise effect these symbols have upon the attitudes of others.[41] Systematic content analysis rejected, the analyst is cast back upon judgments via impression. His impressions may be based in part on (1) quantity and quality of constitutional discussion; and (2) ostensible response to constitutional discussion.

(1) Quantity and quality of constitutional discussion: The legislative history of the Taft-Hartley Act reveals only a single occasion upon which the constitutionality of the non-Communist–affidavit requirement for union officers was even perfunctorily drawn into question,[42] and this though Justices Murphy and Rutledge still sat on the Court. Nor was this paucity of consideration attributable to unawareness of the affidavit clause; the measure was fully considered, with a lengthy discussion of alternative proposals to reach past as well as present Communist Party members.[43] Yet constitutional power to enact the provision was either assumed or regarded as an improper matter for legislative concern.

The famous advocacy-of-overthrow section of the Smith Act,[44] as another example, received only slightly more constitutional consideration in Congress. Direct references to constitutionality were made twice in the House[45] and once in the Senate,[46] and in all instances the debate was casual. One discussion ended with a disclaimer of opinion as to the constitutionlity of his own bill by Representative Smith. ("I cannot tell . . . anymore when anything is constitutional or unconstitutional."[47]) In the hearings, discussion was equally negligible; one witness received a polite request for the citation of the *Gitlow* case from which he had earlier quoted.

On the other hand, the McCarran Act was accompanied by considerable legal discussion, although the arguments were not brought squarely into relation one to another, the two sides simply passing each other by. The only legislative debate studied in which constitutional discussion took foremost consideration was in the abortive congressional attempt in 1940 to deport Harry Bridges by name. Here Congress was squarely confronted with *Ex parte Garland* and the related state-review decision of *Cummings v. Missouri*, and there was abundant discussion of the relation of these cases to the bill.

When constitutional discussion does appear, its quality is extremely variable. Many Congressmen are not lawyers, and, of those who are, many have only a remote acquaintance with the Constitution. Hence discussion may be ornamented with a good deal that is irrelevant, and some that is absurd. For example, the Senate managers of Taft-Hartley felt compelled to read to their colleagues a lengthy and citation-laden memorandum supporting the proposition that the union-shop provisions of the bill were valid under the commerce clause — a matter not open to much dispute.[48] Helen Gahagan Douglas, a nonlawyer, solemnly predicted to the House that the whole act would be invalidated because in two labor board cases, the Court had said that collective bargaining was a good thing.[49]

This much may be concluded as to quantity and quality: The quantity of constitutional consideration of legislation is irrationally unpredictable, and even where discussion occurs it may pass by the hard points to center on the obvious. Much of it is ritualistic, taking the form of statements put in the record simply as part of the routine, like the first and second readings of a bill. On the other hand, some of it is squarely to the point. Quality is uneven, varying from the silly to the acute. Insofar as the words reflect what is actually felt, one must conclude that for many a congressman, the practical effect of judicial review is to create a mass of cases too large and complex to be digested.

(2) *Responses to constitutional discussion:* Responses of individual legislators to constitutional arguments are of three types, typified in the discussion of the Bridges bill:

1. The legislative buckpasser,e.g., Representative Case: "This bill may be unconstitutional; the lawyers here seem divided on that question; the balance of us can only register the heart and mind of America on the broad question involved."[50]

2. The stickler for constitutional regularity as he sees it, e.g., Representative O'Connor: "We have got something at stake here today much bigger than Harry Bridges. Of course, I will agree with my friend; I think he ought to rot. The gentleman is right. But . . . do you want your

Constitution to become punctured with holes like this, by reason of which it will gradually be broken down? . . . The precedent we are establishing this afternoon will rise up to plague us in the future."[51]

3. The conscientious compromiser, e.g., Senator Danaher, on a different phase of the Bridges bill, after a proposal of his own had been included: "I believe most, if not all, of my objection has been met, chiefly for the reason that if there be any question as to the constitutionality of someone undertaking to organize a society to overthrow the Government of the United States by force or violence, I would much rather err in favor of the public policy of sustaining the Government's right to protect itself than I would to protect the rights of an individual" of criminal intent.[52]

While the separate types may be identified, the insoluble problem remains as to how many of each type may be expected to be found in a Congress. The Bridges bill is a good test: how many men could be found who would vote *against* their convictions on the merits because of constitutional persuasion? The excellence of the bill for purposes of this text is that a large number of legislators might reasonably have been expected to entertain constitutional doubts here if ever they would.

There were a few. Representative Dickstein rested on the constitutional point alone.[53] Representative Leavy, who had ten years of experience as a trial judge, pledged himself to vote for the bill if it could be revised into constitutional form, but not otherwise.[54] Representative Hobbs, remembered equally for his legal integrity and his passionate attacks on Communism, applauded the deportation of Bridges as a goal, but said, "I deplore, strongly, the proposed means."[55] And so with a few others, each relying on *Garland* and *Cummings.*

The bill passed the House 330 to 42, but its attainder characteristics were removed in Senate committee, and it was eventually enacted without them. The Senate committee's report makes clear

John P. Frank

that its action was heavily, though not exclusively, influenced by the cases.[56]

Here is an instance, then, in which well-defined Supreme Court decisions prevented a congressional relapse into the precise activity previously proscribed. But even here, 330 members of the House of Representatives withstood the clearest of Court holdings and the most lucid floor discussion.

As has been noted, in the Smith and Taft-Hartley Acts, the Constitution had not even rhetorical significance. Not so for the McCarran Act, which was appreciably affected by constitutional discussion. The effect, however, was of a sort quite different from that of the Bridges bill. In the McCarran Act the constitutional discussion went to perfecting details, so that the decisions became one vast map showing how the legislation could be brought safely to its designed end.

Some basic decisions may have been influenced by fears of invalidation. The House Committee report on the McCarran Act shows that serious consideration was given to proposals to outlaw the Communist Party outright, which were rejected because of "risk of [its] being held unconstitutional."[57] Provisions in the Smith Act concerning the outlawing of civilian military organizations were stricken because of "questionable constitutionality."[58] Apart from these examples, possibly important, there was little serious constitutional impact. For example, a provision that the attorney general should determine an organization's Communist tinge read, "having regard to some or all of the following considerations," followed by a series of criteria. This was attacked as unconstitutionally vague, and was therefore redrafted to read: "The Board shall take into consideration the extent to which" the same criteria are present.[59]

The big constitutional debate in connection with the McCarran Act went to the so-called concentration-camp provisions. As the bill was approaching final action in the Senate, it contained provisions for registration of Communists and for dealing with alien Communists. The following legislative history is exceedingly confusing, but appears to be this: The liberal bloc in the Senate, foreseeing the passage of the act, offered the Kilgore substitute, a provision which would have permitted the ruthless incarceration of "subversives" in time of actual war, but would have eliminated most of the other provisions of the act. Their move seems to have been intended as a tactic to defeat the peacetime provisions of the measure.

Foreseeing this result, Senators McCarran and Ferguson immediately opposed the "concentration camp" provision on a number of constitutional grounds. Senator McCarran pointed out that the substitute would amount to a total elimination of the provisions of his own bill, and that it would replace his bill with a thoroughly unconstitutional measure because detention (a) would be without warrant, (b) would prevent a speedy public trial, (c) would deny trial by jury, (d) would not provide for confrontation of witnesses and cross-examination, (e) would deny the right to process for obtaining witnesses in the detainee's behalf, and (f) might result in involuntary servitude.

The Senate thus observed the unusual phenomenon of Senators Kilgore and Douglas defending a bill against the charge that it invaded personal liberty and Senators McCarran, Ferguson, and Mundt attacking the same measure on the ground that it violated the Bill of Rights. But once the Kilgore measure was defeated, Senator McCarran added a detention-camp provision to his own bill.[60] On September 12, 1950, one day after he attacked the Kilgore measure as unconstitutional, he defended his own version as curing the defects of the Kilgore proposal.

The intriguing fact about the McCarran measure is that, while it cures some of the Kilgore defects, it denies several of the identical rights which Senator

McCarran had found wanting in the Kilgore measure. He complained of want of trial by jury;[61] his own bill has an administrative procedure and no jury.[62] He complained of want of a speedy public trial;[63] again, his own measure is administrative and some of the evidence may be kept secret.[64] He complained of want of confrontation;[65] his own measure permits the attorney general to withhold from the detainee the "identity or evidence" of witnesses and to put in "confidential evidence" when security requires.[66]

There is scarcely a blunter exposure of the Constitution as rhetoric rather than as substance than this McCarran Act history. For reasons of strategy, the liberals pushed a bill of most doubtful constitutionality; the conservatives opposed the bill on constitutional grounds and then within twenty-four hours were sponsoring legislation with many of the very vices they had just decried. In such a situation surely the prospect of judicial review is having no effective bearing on the affairs of the Capitol.

CONCLUSION

Measures restrictive of basic liberties usually spring from a strong legislative demand. With a preponderant number of legislators, the existence of judicial review has negligible effect on the demand except where outstanding cases are so directly in point that they are inescapable; even then, doubtful legislation can pass, as the Bridges bill swept through the House. Individual legislators will stick to constitutional principle, just as Representative Bingham, a leading House radical, voted against the Civil Rights Act of 1866 because he thought it would be unconstitutional without the Fourteenth Amendment. But for a variety of reasons including simple want of understanding of legal refinements, the Binghams and the Hobbses are the colorful exceptions.

If we had not become a "judicial democracy," we might have become, in a sense, a "parliamentary democracy," with exclusive authority in Congress to interpret the Constitution. Whether, from the standpoint of liberty, this would have been for the best is arguable; there is no way of knowing whether greater responsibility might have gone with greater power. Before the Civil War, when judicial review was largely theoretical, constitutional debate in Congress was of a higher order than we now know,[67] but whether it was more objective and responsible is not demonstrated. In the great debate of the 1830s and 1840s over the right of abolitionists to petition Congress, the discussion was constitutional, but the final vote was sectional.[68] Perhaps most Americans from the beginning have subordinated their constitutional judgments to their substantive wishes — the point is not proved either way.

It is distinctly possible that judicial review has encouraged a tendency to congressional irresponsibility (a) by proliferating the law through so many decisions that Congress cannot be expected to cope with it; and (b) by giving an appearance of a judicial veto in the field of liberty when in fact there is almost none. The average congressman would be surprised to know how little actual restraint the Court puts upon him. The repeated episodes of buck passing exemplify Congress's refusal to trouble itself about legal issues in a comfortable, if mistaken, assurance that the judiciary will correct the worst errors.

33

Herbert Wechsler

Toward Neutral Principles of Constitutional Law

The Standards of Review

If courts cannot escape the duty of deciding whether actions of the other branches of the government are consistent with the Constitution, when a case is properly before them you will not doubt the relevancy and importance of demanding what, if any, are the standards to be followed in interpretation. Are there, indeed, any criteria that both the Supreme Court and those who undertake to praise or to condemn its judgments are morally and intellectually obligated to support? By this I mean criteria that can be framed and tested as an exercise of reason and not merely as an act of willfulness or will. Even to put the problem is, of course, to raise an issue no less old than our culture. Those who perceive in law only the element of fiat, in whose conception of the legal cosmos reason has no meaning or no place, will not join gladly in the search for standards of the kind I have in mind. So, too, must I anticipate dissent from those more numerous among us who, vouching no philosophy to warranty, frankly or covertly make the test of virtue in inter-

pretation whether its result in the immediate decision seems to hinder or advance the interests or the values they support.

The man who simply lets his judgment turn on the immediate result may not, however, realize that his position implies that the courts are free to function as a naked power organ, that it is an empty affirmation to regard them, as ambivalently he so often does, as courts of law. If he may know he disapproves of a decision when all he knows is that it has sustained a claim put forward by a labor union or a taxpayer, a Negro or a segregationist, a corporation or a Communist — he acquiesces in the proposition that a man of different sympathy but equal information may no less properly conclude that he approves.

You will not charge me with exaggeration if I say that this type of ad hoc evaluation is, as it has always been, the deepest problem of our constitutionalism, not only with respect to judgments of the courts but also in the wider realm in which conflicting constitutional positions have played a part in our politics.

Did not New England challenge the embargo that the South supported on the very ground on which the South was to resist New England's demand for a protec-

Reprinted, in slightly abridged form, from *Harvard Law Review*, 73 (1959), pp. 10-35, by permission.

tive tariff?[1] Was not Jefferson in the Louisiana Purchase forced to rest on an expansive reading of the clauses granting national authority of the very kind that he had steadfastly opposed in his attacks upon the Bank?[2] Can you square his disappointment about Burr's acquittal on the treason charge and his subsequent request for legislation[3] with the attitude toward freedom and repression most enduringly associated with his name? Were the abolitionists who rescued fugitives and were acquitted in defiance of the evidence able to distinguish their view of the compulsion of a law of the United States from that advanced by South Carolina in the ordinance that they despised?

To bring the matter even more directly home, what shall we think of the Harvard records of the Class of 1829, the class of Mr. Justice Curtis, which, we are told, praised at length the justice's dissent in the Dred Scott case but then added, "Again, *and seemingly adverse to the above*, in October, 1862, he prepared a legal opinion and argument, which was published in Boston in pamphlet form, to the effect that President Lincoln's Proclamation of prospective emancipation of the slaves in the rebellious States is *unconstitutional*."

Of course, a man who thought and, as a justice, voted and maintained that a free Negro could be a citizen of the United States and therefore of a state, within the meaning of the constitutional and statutory clauses defining the diversity jurisdiction; that Congress had authority to forbid slavery within a territory, even one acquired after the formation of the Union; and that such a prohibition worked emancipation of a slave whose owner brought him to reside in such a territory — a man who thought all these things detracted obviously from the force of his positions if he also thought the president was without authority to abrogate a form of property established and protected by state law within the states where it was located, states which the president and his critic alike maintained had not effectively

seceded from the Union and were not a foreign enemy at war. How simple the class historian could make it all by treating as the only thing that mattered whether Mr. Justice Curtis had, on the occasions noted, helped or hindered the attainment of the freedom of the slaves.

I have cited these examples from the early years of our history since time has bred aloofness that may give them added force. What a wealth of illustration is at hand today! How many of the constitutional attacks upon congressional investigations of suspected Communists have their authors felt obliged to launch against the inquiries respecting the activities of Goldfine or of Hoffa or of others I might name? How often have those who think the Smith Act, as construed, inconsistent with the First Amendment made clear that they also stand for constitutional immunity for racial agitators fanning flames of prejudice and discontent? Turning the case around, are those who in relation to the Smith Act see no virtue in distinguishing between advocacy of merely abstract doctrine and advocacy which is planned to instigate unlawful action,[4] equally unable to see virtue in the same distinction in relation, let us say, to advocacy of resistance to the judgments of the courts, especially perhaps to judgments vindicating claims that equal protection of the laws has been denied? I may live a uniquely sheltered life, but am I wrong in thinking I discerned in some extremely warm enthusiasts for jury trial a certain diminution of enthusiasm as the issue was presented in the course of the debate in 1957 on the bill to extend federal protection of our civil rights?

All I have said, you may reply, is something no one will deny, that principles are largely instrumental as they are employed in politics, instrumental in relation to results that a controlling sentiment demands at any given time. Politicians recognize this fact of life and are obliged to trim and shape their speech and votes accordingly, unless perchance they are prepared to step aside. The example that

Herbert Wechsler

John Quincy Adams set somehow is rarely followed.

That is, indeed, all I have said, but I now add that whether you are tolerant, perhaps more tolerant than I, of the ad hoc in politics, with principle reduced to a manipulative tool, are you not also ready to agree that something else is called for from the courts? I put it to you that the main constituent of the judicial process is precisely that it must be genuinely principled, resting with respect to every step that is involved in reaching judgment on analysis and reasons quite transcending the immediate result that is achieved. To be sure, the courts decide, or should decide, only the case they have before them. But must they not decide on grounds of adequate neutrality and generality, tested not only by the instant application but by others that the principles imply? Is it not the very essence of judicial method to insist upon attending to such other cases, preferably those involving an opposing interest, in evaluating any principle avowed?

Here, too, I do not think that I am stating any novel or momentous insight. But now, as Holmes said long ago in speaking of "the unrest which seems to wonder vaguely whether law and order pay," we "need education in the obvious."[5] We need it more particularly now respecting constitutional interpretation, since it has become a commonplace to grant what many for so long denied: that courts in constitutional determinations face issues that are inescapably "political" — political in the third sense that I have used that word — in that they involve a choice among competing values or desires, a choice reflected in the legislative or executive action in question, which the court must either condemn or condone.

What is crucial, I submit, is not the nature of the question but the nature of the answer that may validly be given by the courts. No legislature or executive is obligated by the nature of its function to support its choice of values by the type of reasoned explanation that I have suggested is intrinsic to judicial action —

however much we may admire such a reasoned exposition when we find it in those other realms.

Does not the special duty of the courts to judge by neutral principles addressed to all the issues make it inapposite to contend, as Judge Hand does, that no court can review the legislative choice — by any standard other than a fixed "historical meaning" of constitutional provisions[6] — without becoming a "third legislative chamber?"[7] Is there not, in short, a vital difference between legislative freedom to appraise the gains and losses in projected measures and the kind of principled appraisal, in respect of values that can reasonably be asserted to have constitutional dimension, that alone is in the province of the courts? Does not the difference yield a middle ground between a judicial House of Lords and the abandonment of any limitation on the other branches — a middle ground consisting of judicial action that embodies what are surely the main qualities of law, its generality and its neutrality? This must, it seems to me, have been in Mr. Justice Jackson's mind when in his chapter on the Supreme Court "as a political institution" he wrote[8] in words that I find stirring: "Liberty is not the mere absence of restraint, it is not a spontaneous product of majority rule, it is not achieved merely by lifting underprivileged classes to power, nor is it the inevitable by-product of technological expansion. It is achieved only by a rule of law." Is it not also what Mr. Justice Frankfurter must mean in calling upon judges for "allegiance to nothing except the effort, amid tangled words and limited insights, to find the path through precedent, through policy, through history, to the best judgment that fallible creatures can reach in that most difficult of all tasks: the achievement of justice between man and man, between man and state, through reason called law?"[9]

You will not understand my emphasis upon the role of reason and of principle in the judicial, as distinguished from the legislative or executive, appraisal of conflicting values to imply that I depreciate the duty of fidelity to the text of the Constitution, when its words may be decisive — though I would certainly remind you of the caution stated by Chief Justice Hughes: "Behind the words of the constitutional provisions are postulates which limit and control."[10] Nor will you take me to deny that history has weight in the elucidation of the text, though it is surely subtle business to appraise it as a guide. Nor will you even think that I deem precedent without importance, for we surely must agree with Holmes that "imitation of the past, until we have a clear reason for change, no more needs justification than appetite."[11] But after all, it was Chief Justice Taney who declared his willingness "that it be regarded hereafter as the law of this court, that its opinion upon the construction of the Constitution is always open to discussion when it is supposed to have been founded in error, and that its judicial authority should hereafter depend altogether on the force of the reasoning by which it is supported."[12] Would any of us have it otherwise, given the nature of the problems that confront the courts?

At all events, is not the relative compulsion of the language of the Constitution, of history and precedent — where they do not combine to make an answer clear — itself a matter to be judged, so far as possible, by neutral principles — by standards that transcend the case at hand? I know, of course, that it is common to distinguish, as Judge Hand did, clauses like "due process," cast "in such sweeping terms that their history does not elucidate their contents,"[13] from other provisions of the Bill of Rights addressed to more specific problems. But the contrast, as it seems to me, often implies an overstatement of the specificity or the immutability these other clauses really have — at least when problems under them arise.

No one would argue, for example, that there need not be indictment and a jury trial in prosecutions for a felony in district courts. What made a question of some difficulty was the issue whether service wives charged with the murders of their husbands overseas could be tried there before a military court.[14] Does the language of the double-jeopardy clause or its preconstitutional history actually help to decide whether a defendant tried for murder in the first degree and convicted of murder in the second, who wins a reversal of the judgment on appeal, may be tried again for murder in the first or only murder in the second?[15] Is there significance in the fact that it is "jeopardy of life or limb" that is forbidden, now that no one is in jeopardy of limb but only of imprisonment or fine? The right to "have the assistance of counsel" was considered, I am sure, when the Sixth Amendment was proposed, a right to defend by counsel if you have one, contrary to what was then the English law.[16] That does not seem to me sufficient to avert extension of its meaning to imply a right to court-appointed counsel when the defendant is too poor to find such aid[17] — though I admit that I once urged the point sincerely as a lawyer for the government.[18] It is difficult for me to think the Fourth Amendment freezes for all time the common law of search and of arrest as it prevailed when the amendment was adopted, whatever the exigencies of police problems may now be or may become. Nor should we, in my view, lament the fact that "the" freedom of speech or press that Congress is forbidden by the First Amendment to impair is not determined only by the scope such freedom had in the late eighteenth century, though the word "the" might have been taken to impose a limitation to the concept of that time — a time when, Benjamin Wright has recently reminded us, there was remarkable consensus about matters of this kind.[19]

Even "due process," on the other hand, might have been confined, as Mr. Justice Brandeis urged originally,[20] to a guarantee of fair procedure, coupled perhaps with prohibition of executive displacement of established law — the analogue for us of what the barons meant in Magna Carta. Equal protection could be taken as no more than an assurance that no one may be placed beyond the safeguards of the law, outlawing, as it were, the possibility of outlawry, but nothing else. Here, too, I cannot find it in my heart to regret that interpretation did not ground itself in ancient history, but rather has perceived in these provisions a compendious affirmation of the basic values of a free society, values that must be given weight in legislation and administration at the risk of courting trouble in the courts.

So far as possible, to finish with my point, I argue that we should prefer to see the other clauses of the Bill of Rights read as an affirmation of the special values they embody rather than as statements of a finite rule of law, its limits fixed by the consensus of a century long past, with problems very different from our own. To read them in the former way is to leave room for adaptation and adjustment if and when competing values, also having constitutional dimension, enter on the scene.

Let me repeat what I have thus far tried to say. The courts have both the title and the duty when a case is properly before them to review the actions of the other branches in the light of constitutional provisions, even though the action involves value choices, as invariably action does. In doing so, however, they are bound to function otherwise than as a naked power organ; they participate as courts of law. This calls for facing how determinations of this kind can be asserted to have any legal quality. The answer, I suggest, inheres primarily in that they are — or are obliged to be — entirely principled. A principled decision, in the sense I have in mind, is one that rests on reasons with respect to all the issues in the case, reasons that in their generality and their neutrality transcend any immediate result that is involved. When no sufficient reasons of this kind can be assigned for overturning value choices of the other branches of the government or of a state, those choices must, of course, survive. Otherwise, as Holmes said in his first opinion for the Court, "a constitution, instead of embodying only relatively fundamental rules of right, as generally understood by all English-speaking communities, would become the partisan of a particular set of ethical or economical opinions."[21]

The virtue or demerit of a judgment turns, therefore, entirely on the reasons that support it and their adequacy to maintain any choice of values it decrees, or, it is vital that we add, to maintain the rejection of a claim that any given choice should be decreed. The critic's role, as T. R. Powell showed throughout so many fruitful years, is the sustained, disinterested, merciless examination of the reasons that the courts advance, measured by standards of the kind I have attempted to describe. I wish that more of us today could imitate his dedication to that task.

Some Appraisals of Review

One who has ventured to advance such generalities about the courts and constitutional interpretation is surely challenged to apply them to some concrete problems — if only to make clear that he believes in what he says.

1. I start by noting two important fields of present interest in which the Court has been decreeing value choices in a way that makes it quite impossible to speak of principled determinations or the statement and evaluation of judicial reasons, since the Court has not disclosed the grounds on which its judgments rest.

The first of these involves the sequel to the *Burstyn* case,[22] in which, as you recall, the Court decided that the motion picture is a medium of expression included in the "speech" and "press" to which the safeguards of the First Amendment, made applicable to the states by the Fourteenth, apply. But *Burstyn* left open, as it was of course obliged to do, the extent of the protection that the movies are accorded, and even the question whether any censorship is valid, involving as it does prior restraint. The judgment rested, and quite properly, upon the vice inherent in suppression based upon a finding that the film involved was "sacrilegious" — with the breadth and vagueness that that term had been accorded in

New York. "Whether a state may censor motion pictures under a clearly drawn statute designed and applied to prevent the showing of obscene films" was said to be "a very different question" not decided by the Court.[23] In five succeeding cases, decisions sustaining censorship of different films under standards variously framed have been reversed, but only by per curiam decisions. In one of these,[24] in which I should avow I was of counsel, the standard was undoubtedly too vague for any argument upon the merits. I find it hard to think that this was clearly so in all the others. Given the subtlety and difficulty of the problem, the need and opportunity for clarifying explanation, are such unexplained decisions in a new domain of constitutional interpretation consonant with standards of judicial action that the Court or we can possibly defend? I realize that nine men often find it easier to reach agreement on result than upon reasons and that such a difficulty may be posed within this field. Is it not preferable, however, indeed essential, that if this is so the variations of position be disclosed?[25]

The second group of cases to which I shall call attention involves what may be called the progeny of the school-segregation ruling of 1954. Here again the Court has written on the merits of the constitutional issue posed by state segregation only once;[26] its subsequent opinions on the form of the decree[27] and the defiance in Arkansas[28] deal, of course, with other matters. The original opinion, you recall, was firmly focused on state segregation in the public schools, its reasoning accorded import to the nature of the educational process, and its conclusion was that separate educational facilities are "inherently unequal."

What shall we think, then, of the Court's extension of the ruling to other public facilities, such as public transportation, parks, golf courses, bathhouses, and beaches, which no one is obliged to use — all by per curiam decisions?[29] That these situations present a weaker case against state segregation is not, of course, what I am saying. I am saying

that the question whether it is stronger, weaker, or of equal weight appears to me to call for principled decision. I do not know, and I submit you cannot know, whether the per curiam affirmance in the *Dawson* case, involving public bathhouses and beaches, embraced the broad opinion of the circuit court that all state-enforced racial segregation is invalid or approved only its immediate result and, if the latter, on what ground. Is this "process of law," to borrow the words Ernest S. Brown has used so pointedly in writing of such unexplained decisions upon matters far more technical[30] — the process that alone affords the Court its title and its duty to adjudicate a claim that state action is repugnant to the Constitution?

Were I a prudent man I would, no doubt, confine myself to problems of this order, involving, not the substance, but the method of decision — for other illustrations might be cited in the same domain. I shall, however, pass beyond this to some areas of substantive interpretation which appear to me to illustrate my theme.

2. The phase of our modern constitutional development that I conceive we can most confidently deem successful inheres in the broad reading of the commerce, taxing, and related powers of the Congress, achieved with so much difficulty little more than twenty years ago — against restrictions in the name of state autonomy to which the Court had for a time turned such a sympathetic ear.

Why is it that the Court failed so completely in the effort to contain the scope of national authority and that today one reads decisions like *Hammer* v. *Dagenhart*,[31] or *Carter Coal*,[32] or the invalidation of the Agricultural Adjustment Act[33] with eyes that disbelieve? No doubt the answer inheres partly in the simple facts of life and the consensus they have generated on the powers that a modern nation needs. But is it not a feature of the case as well — a feature that has real importance — that the Court could not articulate an adequate analysis of the restrictions it imposed on Congress in favor of the states, whose representatives — upon an equal footing in the Senate — controlled the legislative process and had broadly acquiesced in the enactments that were subject to review?

Is it not also true and of importance that some of the principles the Court affirmed were strikingly deficient in neutrality, sustaining, for example, national authority when it impinged adversely upon labor, as in the application of the Sherman Act, but not when it was sought to be employed in labor's aid? On this score, the contrast in today's position certainly is striking. The power that sustained the Wagner Act is the same power that sustains Taft-Hartley — with its even greater inroads upon state autonomy but with restraints on labor that the Wagner Act did not impose.

One of the speculations that I must confess I find intriguing is upon the question whether there are any neutral principles that might have been employed to mark the limits of the commerce power of the Congress in terms more circumscribed than the virtual abandonment of limits in the principle that has prevailed. Given the readiness of President Roosevelt to compromise on any basis that allowed achievement of the substance of his program, might not the formulae of coverage employed in the legislation of the thirties have quite readily embraced any such principles the Court had then been able to devise before the crisis became so intense — principles sustaining action fairly equal to the need? I do not say we would or should be happier if that had happened and the Court still played a larger part within this area of our federalism, given the attention to state interests that is so inherent in the Congress and the constitutional provisions governing the selection and the composition of the Houses, which make that attention very likely to endure.[34] I say only that I find such speculation interesting. You will recall that it was Holmes who deprecated argument of counsel the logic of which left "no part of the conduct of life with which on similar principles Congress might not interfere."[35]

3. The poverty of principled articulation of the limits put on Congress as against the states before the doctrinal reversal of the thirties was surely also true of the decisions, dealing with the very different problem of the relationship between the individual and government, which invoked due process to maintain laissez faire. Did not the power of the great dissents inhere precisely in their demonstrations that the Court could not present an adequate analysis, in terms of neutral principles, to support the value choices it decreed? Holmes, to be sure, saw limits beyond which "the contract and due process clauses are gone"; and his insistence on the need for compensation to sustain a Pennsylvania prohibition of the exploitation of subsurface coal, threatening subsidence of a dwelling belonging to the owner of the surface land, indicates the kind of limit he perceived.[36] Am I simply voicing my own sympathies in saying that his analysis of those limits has a thrust entirely lacking in the old and now forgotten judgments striking down minimum-wage and maximum-hour laws?

If I am right in this it helps to make a further point that has more bearing upon current issues, that I believe it misconceives the problem of the Court to state it as the question of the proper measure of judicial self-restraint, with the resulting issue whether such restraint is only proper in relation to protection of a purely economic interest or also in relation to an interest like freedom of speech or of religion, privacy, or discrimination (at least if it is based on race, origin, or creed). Of course, the courts ought to be cautious to impose a choice of values on the other branches or a state, based upon the Constitution, only when they are persuaded, on an adequate and principled analysis, that the choice is clear. That, I suggest, is all that self-restraint can mean, and in that sense it always is essential, whatever issue may be posed.

The real test inheres, as I have tried to argue, in the force of the analysis. Surely a stronger analysis may be advanced against a particular uncompensated taking as a violation of the Fifth Amendment than against a particular limitation of freedom of speech or press as a violation of the First.

In this view, the "preferred position" controversy hardly has a point — indeed, it never has been really clear what is asserted or denied to have a preference and over what.[37] Certainly the concept is pernicious if it implies that there is any simple, almost mechanistic, basis for determining priorities of values having constitutional dimension, as when there is an inescapable conflict between claims to free press and a fair trial. It has a virtue, on the other hand, insofar as it recognizes that some ordering of social values is essential; that all cannot be given equal weight if the Bill of Rights is to be maintained.

Did Holmes mean any less than this when he lamented the tendency "toward underrating or forgetting the safeguards in bills of rights that had to be fought for in their day and that still are worth fighting for"?[38] Only in that view could he have dissented in the *Abrams* and the *Gitlow* cases[39] and have struggled so intensely to develop a principled delineation of the freedom that he voted to sustain. Even if one thinks, as I confess I do, that his analysis does not succeed if it requires that an utterance designed to stimulate unlawful action must be accorded an immunity unless it is intended to achieve or creates substantial danger of *immediate* results,[40] can anyone deny it his respect? Is not the force of a position framed in terms of principles of the neutrality and generality that Holmes achieved entirely different from that of the main opinion, for example, in the *Sweezy* case,[41] resting at bottom, as it does, on principles of power separation among the branches of state government that never heretofore have been conceived to be a federal requirement and

that, we safely may predict, the Court will not apply to any other field?[42]

4. Finally, I turn to the decisions that for me provide the hardest test of my belief in principled adjudication, those in which the Court in recent years has vindicated claims that deprivations based on race deny the equality before the law that the Fourteenth Amendment guarantees. The crucial cases are, of course, those involving the white primary,[43] the enforcement of racially restrictive covenants,[44] and the segregated schools.[45]

The more I think about the past the more skeptical I find myself about predictions of the future. Would you not have thought that, viewed a priori, the invention of the cotton gin in 1792 should have reduced the need for slave labor and hence diminished the attractiveness of slavery? Brooks Adams tells us that its consequences were precisely the reverse; that the demand for slaves increased as cotton planting became highly lucrative, increased so greatly that Virginia turned from coal and iron, which George Washington envisaged as its future, into an enormous farm for breeding slaves — forty thousand of whom it exported annually to the rest of the South.[46] Only the other day I read that the Japanese evacuation, which I thought an abomination when it happened, though in the line of duty as a lawyer I participated in the effort to sustain it in the Court,[47] is now believed by many to have been a blessing to its victims, breaking down forever the ghettos in which they had previously lived.[48] But skeptical about predictions as I am, I still believe that the decisions I have mentioned — dealing with the primary, the covenant, and schools — have the best chance of making an enduring contribution to the quality of our society of any that I know in recent years. It is in this perspective that I ask how far they rest on neutral principles and are entitled to approval in the only terms that I acknowledge to be relevant to a decision of the courts.

The primary and covenant cases present two different aspects of a single problem — that it is a state alone that is forbidden by the Fourteenth Amendment to deny equal protection of the laws, as only a state or the United States is precluded by the Fifteenth Amendment from denying or abridging on the ground of race or color the right of citizens of the United States to vote. It has, of course, been held for years that the prohibition of action by the state reaches not only an explicit deprivation by a statute but also action of the courts or of subordinate officials, purporting to exert authority derived from public office. [49]

I deal first with the primary. So long as the Democratic Party in the South excluded Negroes from participation, in the exercise of an authority conferred by statutes regulating political parties, it was entirely clear that the amendment was infringed; the exclusion involved an application of the statute.[50] The problem became difficult only when the states, responding to these judgments, repealed the statutes, leaving parties free to define their membership as private associations, protected by the state but not directed or controlled or authorized by law. In this position the Court held in 1935 that an exclusion by the party was untouched by the amendment, being action of the individuals involved, not of the state or its officialdom.[51]

Then came the *Classic* case[52] in 1941, which I perhaps should say I argued for the government. *Classic* involved a prosecution of election officials for depriving a voter of a right secured by the Constitution in willfully failing to count his vote as it was cast in a Louisiana Democratic primary. In holding that the right of a qualified voter to participate in choosing representatives in Congress, a right conferred by Article I, section 2,[53] extended to participating in a primary which influenced the ultimate selection, the Court did not, of course, deal with the scope of party freedom to select its members. The victim of the fraud in *Classic* was a member of the Democratic Party, voting in a primary in which he was entitled to participate, and the only one in which he could.[54] Yet three years later *Classic* was declared in *Smith* v. *Allwright*[55] to have determined in effect that primaries are a part of the election, with the consequence that parties can no more defend racial exclusion from their primaries than can the state, a result reaffirmed in 1953.[56] This is no doubt a settled proposition in the Court. But what it means is not, as sometimes has been thought, that a state may not escape the limitations of the Constitution merely by transferring public functions into private hands. It means rather that the constitutional guarantee against deprivation of the franchise on the ground of race or color has become a prohibition of party organization upon racial lines, at least where the party has achieved political hegemony. I ask with all sincerity if you are able to discover in the opinions thus far written in support of this result — a result, I say again, that I approve — neutral principles that satisfy the mind. I should suppose that a denial of the franchise on religious grounds is certainly forbidden by the Constitution. Are religious parties, therefore, to be taken as proscribed? I should regard this result, too, as one plainly to be desired, but is there a constitutional analysis on which it can be validly decreed? Is it, indeed, not easier to project an analysis establishing that such a proscription would infringe rights protected by the First Amendment?

The case of the restrictive covenant presents for me an even harder problem. Assuming that the Constitution speaks to state discrimination on the ground of race but not to such discrimination by an individual even in the use or distribution of his property, although his freedom may no doubt be limited by common law or statute, why is the enforcement of the private covenant a state discrimination rather than a legal recognition of the freedom of the individual? That the action of the state court is action of the state, the point Mr. Chief Justice Vinson emphasizes in the Court's opinion,[57] is, of course, entirely obvious. What is not obvious, and is the crucial step, is that the state may properly be charged with the discrimination when it does no more than give effect to an agreement that the individual involved is, by hypothesis, entirely free to make. Again one is obliged to ask, What is the principle involved? Is the state forbidden to effectuate a will that draws a racial line, a will that can accomplish any disposition only through the aid of law, or is it a sufficient answer there that the discrimination was the testator's and not the state's?[58] May not the state employ its law to vindicate the privacy of property against a trespasser, regardless of the grounds of his exclusion, or does it embrace the owner's reasons for excluding if it buttresses his power by the law? Would a declaratory judgment that a fee is determinable if a racially restrictive limitation should be violated represent discrimination by the state upon the racial ground?[59] Would a judgment of ejectment?

None of these questions has been answered by the Court, nor are the problems faced in the opinions.[60] Philadelphia, to be sure, has been told that it may not continue to administer the school for "poor male white orphans," established by the city as trustee under the will of Stephen Girard, in accordance with that racial limitation.[61] All the Supreme Court said, however, was the following: "The Board which operates Girard College is an agency of the State of Pennsylvania. Therefore, even though the Board was acting as a trustee, its refusal to admit Foust and Felder to the college because they were Negroes was discrimination by the State. Such discrimination is forbidden by the Fourteenth Amendment." When the Orphans' Court thereafter dismissed the city as trustee, appointing individuals in substitution, its action was sustained in Pennsylvania.[62] Further review by certiorari was denied.[63]

One other case in the Supreme Court has afforded opportunity for reconsidering the basis and scope of the *Shelley* principle, *Black* v. *Cutter Labs.*[64] Here a collective-bargaining agreement was so construed that Communist Party membership was "just cause" for a discharge. In this view, California held that a worker was lawfully dismissed upon that ground. A Supreme Court majority concluded that this judgment involved nothing but interpretation of a contract, making irrelevant the standards that would govern the validity of a state statute that required the discharge. Only Mr. Chief Justice Warren and Justices Douglas and Black, dissenting, thought the principle of *Shelley* v. *Kraemer* was involved when the state court sustained the discharge.[65]

Many understandably would like to perceive in the primary and covenant decisions a principle susceptible of broad extension, applying to the other power aggregates in our society limitations of the kind the Constitution has imposed on government.[66] My colleague A. A. Berle, Jr., has, indeed, pointed to the large business corporation, which after all is chartered by the state and wields in many areas more power than the government, as uniquely suitable for choice as the next subject of such application.[67] I doubt that the courts will yield to such temptations; and I do not hesitate to say that I prefer to see the issues faced through legislation, where there is room for drawing lines that courts are not equipped to draw. If this is right the two decisions I have mentioned will remain, as they now are, *ad hoc* determinations of their narrow problems, yielding no neutral principles for their extension or support.

Lastly, I come to the school decision, which, for one of my persuasion, stirs the deepest conflict I experience in testing the thesis I propose. Yet I would surely be engaged in playing Hamlet without Hamlet if I did not try to state the problems that appear to me to be involved.

The problem for me, I hardly need to say, is not that the Court departed from its earlier decisions holding or implying that the equality of public educational facilities demanded by the Constitution could be met by separate schools. I stand with the long tradition of the Court that previous decisions must be subject to reexamination when a case against their reasoning is made. Nor is the problem that the Court disturbed the settled patterns of a portion of the country; even that must be accepted as a lesser evil than nullification of the Constitution. Nor is it that history does not confirm that an agreed purpose of the Fourteenth Amendment was to forbid separate schools or that there is important evidence that many thought the contrary;[68] the words are general and leave room for expanding content as time passes and conditions change. Nor is it that the Court may have miscalculated the extent to which its judgment would be honored or accepted; it is not a prophet of the strength of our national commitment to respect the judgments of the courts. Nor is it even that the Court did not remit the issue to the Congress, acting under the enforcement clause of the amendment. That was a possible solution, to be sure, but certainly Paul Freund is right[69] that it would merely have evaded the claims made.

The problem inheres strictly in the reasoning of the opinion, an opinion which is often read with less fidelity by those who praise it than by those by whom it is condemned. The Court did not declare, as many wish it had, that the Fourteenth Amendment forbids all racial lines in legislation, though subsequent per curiam decisions may, as I have said, now go that far. Rather, as Judge Hand observed,[70] the separate-but-equal formula was not overruled "in form,"but was held to have "no place" in public education on the ground that segregated schools are "inherently unequal," with deleterious effects upon the colored children in implying their inferiority, effects which retard their educational and mental development. So, indeed, the district court had found as a fact in the Kansas case, a finding which the Supreme Court embraced, citing some further "modern authority" in its support.[71]

Does the validity of the decision turn, then, on the sufficiency of evidence or of judicial notice to sustain a finding that the separation harms the Negro children who may be involved? There were, indeed, some witnesses who expressed that opinion in the Kansas case,[72] as there were also witnesses in the companion Virginia case, including Henry Garrett of Columbia,[73] whose view was to the contrary. Much depended on the question that the witness had in mind, which rarely was explicit. Was he comparing the position of the Negro child in a segregated school with his position in an integrated school, where he was happily accepted and regarded by the whites; or was he comparing his position under separation with that under integration where the whites were hostile to his presence and found ways to make their feelings known? And if the harm that segregation worked was relevant, what of the benefits that it entailed — a sense of security, the absence of hostility? Were they irrelevant? Moreover, was the finding in Topeka applicable without modification to Clarendon County, South Carolina, with 2,799 colored students and only 295 whites? Suppose that more Negroes in a community preferred separation than opposed it? Would that be relevant to whether they were hurt or aided by segregation as opposed to integration? Their fates would be governed by the change of system quite as fully as those of the students who complained.

I find it hard to think the judgment really turned upon the facts. Rather, it seems to me, it must have rested on the view that racial segregation is, in principle, a denial of equality to the minority against whom it is directed — that is, the group that is not dominant politically and therefore does not make the choice involved. For many who support the Court's decision this assuredly is the decisive ground. But this position also presents problems. Does it not involve an inquiry into the motive of the legislature, which is generally foreclosed to the courts?[74] Is it alternatively defensible to make the measure of validity of legislation the way it is interpreted by those who are affected by it? In the context of a charge that segregation *with equal facilities* is a denial of equality, is there not a point in *Plessy* in the statement that if "enforced separation stamps the colored race with a badge of inferiority" it is solely because its members choose "to put that construction upon it"?[75] Does enforced separation of the sexes discriminate against females merely because it may be the females who resent it and because it is imposed by judgments predominantly male? Is a prohibition of miscegenation a discrimination against the colored member of the couple who would like to marry?

For me, assuming equal facilities, the question posed by state-enforced segregation is not one of discrimination at all. Its human and its constitutional dimensions lie entirely elsewhere, in the denial by the state of freedom to associate, a denial that impinges in the same way on any groups or races that may be involved. I think, and I hope not without foundation, that the southern white also pays heavily for segregation, not only in the sense of guilt that he must carry but also in the benefits he is denied. In the days when I was joined with Charles H. Houston in a litigation in the Supreme Court, before the present building was constructed, he did not suffer more than I in knowing that we had to go to Union Station to lunch together during the recess. Does not the problem of miscegenation show most clearly that it is the freedom of association that at bottom is involved, the only case, I may add, where it is implicit

in the situation that association is desired by the only individuals involved? I take no pride in knowing that in 1956 the Supreme Court dismissed an appeal in a case in which Virginia nullified a marriage on this ground, a case in which the statute had been squarely challenged by the defendant, and the Court, after remanding once, dismissed per curiam on procedural grounds that I make bold to say are wholly without basis in the law.[76]

But if the freedom of association is denied by segregation, integration forces an association upon those for whom it is unpleasant or repugnant. Is this not the heart of the issue involved, a conflict in human claims of high dimension, not unlike many others that involve the highest freedoms — conflicts that Arthur Sutherland has recently described.[77] Given a situation where the state must practically choose between denying the association to those individuals who wish it or imposing it on those who would avoid it, is there a basis in neutral principles for holding that the Constitution demands that the claims for association should prevail? I should like to think there is, but I confess that I have not yet written the opinion. To write it is for me the challenge of the school-segregation cases.

Having said what I have said, I certainly should add that I offer no comfort to anyone who claims legitimacy in defiance of the courts. This is the ultimate negation of all neutral principles, to take the benefits accorded by the constitutional system, including the national market and common defense, while denying it allegiance when a special burden is imposed. That certainly is the antithesis of law.

34

David M. Potter

Social Cohesion and the Crisis of Law

When we attempt to appraise the place which law occupies in any given society, it is a good point of departure, I believe, to start by recognizing that the law is a uniform system of social control for the entire population living within a given jurisdiction. Its rules apply to everyone within the area of this jurisdiction. Other institutions may have rules which apply to parts of the population — churches, for instance, may do so, or labor unions — and they may impose penalties for violation of their rules. But these institutions do not apply uniformly to everyone, while, on the contrary, the law does. Since the law is uniform, it will, of course, operate most effectively when the population to which it applies is also uniform, or, as we might say, homogeneous. Or conversely, it may operate least effectively where the population is heterogeneous. In treating the relationship of law to society, legal thinkers commonly assume that the population, or society, to which the law applies *is* homogeneous — is a

holistic community. One finds this assumption, for instance, in the criterion that obscenity can be defined by "prevailing community standards." This is well and good if there is one community that coincides with the jurisdiction. But suppose there is no community; or suppose there are two or more separate and somewhat antagonistic communities, all within the same jurisdiction. Then there can be no holistic "prevailing community standards," and therefore no criterion for the law — perhaps no social "legitimacy" for it.

This is a point to which I must return later, but first I should observe that this problem does not arise in all systems of government. Historically, even the potentiality of such a dilemma could scarcely have arisen more than two hundred years ago, for up to that time legitimacy was regarded as residing in a single ruler rather than in a multiplicity of people — in a unitary authority rather than in a pluralistic one. Of course, as we all know, this theory had been modified in various ways, by making the ruler an institution ("the crown") rather than a man ("the king"), and by avoiding the enactment of laws that would arouse popular hostility. But still, authority, and also legitimacy,

Reprinted from *History and American Society: Essays of David M. Potter* (New York, Oxford University Press, 1973), pp. 390-418, by permission. This essay was óriginally presented at a symposium organized by The Bar of The City of New York, 1970.

were believed to come from above, and so long as this was true, the question of what happened to the legitimacy of law when it was vested in a society which might be deeply divided — that question did not arise. The kind of sanctions that would justify an authority as universal as that of the law seemed to be of so transcendent a nature that men tended to attribute a supernatural quality to them — the law was from the king and the king was from God. Such authority could hardly present problems of heterogeneity.

But the Americans of the late eighteenth century broke new ground by everlastingly rejecting the idea of authority from above and by repudiating the notions of rank which had buttressed such authority. America, they decided, was to be a society of men equal in formal rank. Without rank, there could be no hierarchical class of "natural" rulers, and government was specifically declared to derive its sanction ("its just powers") from the "consent of the governed."

Among the innumerable writers who have celebrated the advent two centuries ago of the principle of government by the consent of the governed, it is remarkable how few have ever recognized that this principle contained a built-in dilemma, and one which might have been seriously regarded as an insoluble dilemma: when the governed include the entire body of citizens (and even noncitizens), it is inevitable that they will disagree on many matters and that policies which win the consent of some will never gain the consent of others — perhaps of very numerous others. Therefore, at an operative level, government by the consent of the governed really means government according to the wishes of some of the governed and contrary to the wishes of some others of the governed. The phrase "consent of the governed," under the cover of a false assumption that the governed will always and inevitably be an integral body, concealed the imminent hazard that government by citizens might simply mean government by any combination of citizens strong enough to over-power any other combination or combinations of citizens. In this sense, the principle of "consent" might become an ironic fiction to cover the process by which a more powerful component in society would trample upon the deepest convictions of a less powerful component.

There was nothing inherent in the doctrine of consent itself — nothing in the logic of the idea — which would have prevented such a travesty. In terms of theory, one might say that the United States became exposed almost two centuries ago to the potentiality that conflicting popular factions might destroy the society by dividing it into irreconcilable opposing groups, for there was no authority higher than the people's own consent to restrain them. Once, of course, at the time of the Civil War, this potential hazard became a terrible reality. But it was only once; otherwise, for two centuries, the hazard remained potential only. Thus, by now, when divisiveness endangers our public policy as never before, we are so accustomed to the routines of government by consent and so in the habit of assuming that consent can always be attained at some kind of price that we have ceased to realize that our mechanism provides no recourse for society in situations where consent is really withheld. This lack of recourse constitutes a vulnerability in our system — an acute, distinctive, but largely unrecognized vulnerability — which renders the society almost helpless in the face of divisions which cannot be reconciled. This vulnerability is peculiar to the system of government by consent and is basic to the present crisis of law in a divided society.

Historically, the system of government by consent succeeded so well that we are now most inclined to take it for granted, at a time when we can least afford to take it for granted. At the beginning of the American experiment, there were men who felt acutely apprehensive about the cohesiveness of a system which gave a broad franchise to dissent and which sanctioned organized opposition to the policies of the

David M. Potter

government. Most of the founders were decidedly uneasy about the danger of political parties, because they felt that the creation of parties would deepen divisions in the society and would perpetuate strife. Strife was generally regarded as likely to tear the social fabric, and traditional governments had customarily sought to suppress it. Now the United States was about to incorporate political strife as a regular part of the system. Not unnaturally, some political sages viewed such a step with deep misgivings. Further, it was generally recognized that by sanctioning a high degree of freedom for individual citizens, the founders were releasing a force which might weaken the claims of the community as a whole — as an organism — vis-à-vis the claims of the unrestrained individual.

Thus, men recognized that democracy was a peculiarly fragile system, especially dependent upon the responsibility and self-restraint with which citizens exercised their freedom. Long after the Revolution, pundits continued to repeat these warnings and the public continued to nod approval of the repetitions. But the fact is that after a time, while still affirming these propositions ritualistically, we ceased to believe them. One may say that the system worked so well that it inspired faith in democracy, or one may say that America got along so well under the system (which is by no means the same thing) that people ceased to worry about it. Certainly the United States, under the Constitution of 1787, did grow with incredible rapidity in area and in population. It experienced a total economic transformation from a land of small farmers, producing food for their own use, to what some social analysts call a postindustrial society, with the immensely complex and interdependent economy which we have today. Democracy survived this transformation. It survived the transition from a horse-and-buggy technology based on the muscle of men and animals, the power of wind in a sail, and water in a waterwheel, and heat from fossilized

plants, to a technology which could put men on the moon and — what was even more remarkable — could bring them back. Naturally, we began to think that if democracy can flourish under such varied conditions and can contribute in a significant way to such remarkable achievements, it must be tough, adaptable, and resilient — not brittle or fragile after all.

Our confidence in the indestructibility of the democratic system was strengthened when we saw it survive crises which other, seemingly "stronger" systems might not have survived. To begin with, in the Civil War. more than a century ago, the nation faced a test of whether a democratic government can be, at the same time, strong enough to defeat its embattled adversaries and weak enough (or limited enough) to ensure that freedoms would not be sacrificed by the very severity of the measures required to protect them. Abraham Lincoln was deeply concerned with this problem, and he spoke very feelingly of "the necessity that is upon us of proving that popular government is not an absurdity." Before he was assassinated, he knew that the government of the Union — a democratic government — had vindicated itself, and that Old World critics could never again speak with their former confidence when they said that a republic might be all right in times of tranquillity but that it would fall apart at the first real test of strength.

Eight decades after the Civil War, the "inefficient" and hopelessly civilianized American democracy administered total defeat to the most "efficient" and powerful military machine that the world had ever seen up to that time. Meanwhile, on many fronts — industrial, and technological, and scientific — the country had passed from triumph to triumph in a way which further assured Americans of the invulnerability of their system.

Yet, all the while, we had been operating on a principle of government by consent, of which it might plausibly be said that the reason we trusted it so completely was that we had never taken the trouble to understand it. When we thought about it at all, it was usually in the simplistic terms of "majority rule." The consent of the governed, operationally, we thought was the will of the majority, and even while upholding individual rights and freedoms, we have been chronically oblivious to the contradiction between the principle of majority rule and the principle of individual rights, just as we have been uncritically susceptible to such unsophisticated corollaries of the majoritarian fallacy as the "one man, one vote" slogan. But as almost everyone would recognize, if he would only stop to reflect, the process of government in the United States has never been one of an omnipotent majority imposing its will upon a defenseless and unresisting minority. Rather, the process has been one by which the majority and the minority arrived at an understanding — not necessarily an amicable one, and indeed usually an arrangement by which the majority settled for less than it wanted to attain and the minority yielded more than it wanted to concede. Both accepted terms with which they were not entirely satisfied. While actual coercion was avoided, heavy pressure was frequently used, but even when pressure was heaviest a kind of understanding was involved, and this was what was meant by government by consent.

I doubt whether history or political science has ever done full justice to the subtlety and also to the pervasiveness of the arrangements by which the principle of consent — seldom totally voluntary, seldom entirely coercive — was woven into the fabric of our institutions. Politically, consent did not mean what we now sometimes mean when we speak of "consensus," and if my interpretation here should be damned as "consensus history," at least it is not consensus history of the orthodox kind. Consent did not mean either bland agreement on all questions or a decision to confine public dispute to nonessential or trivial questions. It did not mean that there would be no conflict.

On the contrary, many contests have been waged with heat and acrimony over issues that were felt to be fearfully urgent. For instance, in the struggles between Thomas Jefferson and Alexander Hamilton, Jefferson felt that he was saving the country, as he expressed it, from "monarchism and militarism." After Andrew Jackson's conflicts with the Bank of the United States and with the South Carolina nullificationists, Jackson is said to have expressed regret, when he left the White House, for two pieces of unfinished business — he had neither shot Henry Clay nor hanged John C. Calhoun. In 1884, when Grover Cleveland was being nominated for the presidency, one of his nominators declaimed, "We love him for the enemies he has made." So, we must certainly recognize, many of the contests were real, and many of the rivalries were intense. Also, as Richard Hofstadter asserted, many of the issues — the American Revolution, the Civil War, and many ethnic and immigrant divisions — represented conflict of the most genuine kind.

But if the principle of consent did not mean the elimination of conflict, what it did mean was that conflict should be limited. Adversaries might pit all their strength against one another, but they would not engage in remorseless attempts to destroy one another. There are many ways in which we have shown our purpose to avoid struggles leading to political extermination. The provisions in the Constitution against ex post facto laws and bills of attainder are pertinent examples. But far more telling, perhaps, is the habitual pattern of our political contests — notably our presidential elections. During these quadrennial episodes, the element of conflict has customarily been highly conspicuous. Almost every election was hotly contested, and if there were no important issues involved, the heat of the contest might be even more intense. Rhetoric, customarily, became very highly charged. Both parties talked big and denounced each other most abusively, and it was not unusual for one party to claim that if the rival party were elected it would be the end of republican government in the United States. Men made frenzied efforts to gain electoral victory, as if the future of mankind were at stake.

But after the election was over, what happened? We all know the scenario. The loser would send his congratulations to the winner; the newspapers which had supported the loser would begin to publish more flattering pictures of the winner than they had published during the campaign. One or two members of the losing party, after what we may call a decent interval, might agree to take positions in the new administration. When the Congress met, the majority party would assign a certain number of places on each committee to be filled by the minority party. They would do this as a matter of course, without even discussing whether or not to do so. Pretty soon they would be busily working out legislative compromises in the cloakroom while hurling rhetorical thunderbolts at one another on the floor.

In fact, the very structure of the parties themselves reflected this pattern of limited conflict, for the traditional two parties of American history — Federalists versus Jeffersonians, or Whigs versus Democrats, or Republicans versus Democrats — have been very unlike the ideologically "pure" splinter parties which have arisen so often in Central and Western Europe. The ideological parties have consisted of adherents from only one segment of the political spectrum, united in support of one particular doctrine, rather like small religious sects in this country. But the American political parties have been coalitions of conservative southern Democrats and reformist northern Democrats, or in the first half of the present century, of standpat Republicans from the East and progressive Republicans from the West, working together more or less reluctantly and with more or less internal friction.

Since both parties represented a coalition of men of diverse views, it followed that neither party was ideologically very different from its rival. Both tended to take what are called "moderate" positions and to avoid going very far to the right or very far to the left. This made it easier for them to reach accommodations with one another. So long as this relationship prevailed, it was always possible to evoke a spirit of unity between the parties as well as to rouse angry strife between them. In fact, this dualism became, as I have suggested, almost a ritual in which the parties were expected to assail each other vigorously in election campaigns, but never so vigorously that they could not be reminded, after the election was over, that what they shared as Americans far outweighed what they disagreed about as party members, and that the president, once elected, ceased to be merely a partisan leader and became president of all the people.

Thomas Jefferson was the first President to articulate this view of our political system, and no President has ever stated it better. At his first inaugural in 1801, Jefferson, addressing himself to both his supporters and his recent adversaries, stated a profound truth — a truth that was valid on several levels — when he declared, "Every difference of opinion is not a difference of principle. We have called by different names brethren of the same principle. We are all Republicans; we are all Federalists." At the lowest level this meant that each party constituted a kind of brokerage house, and that the brokerage houses can, as the phrase goes, "do business" with one another — a little opportunism along with the principle. At a higher level, it meant that once the contest was over, both parties would abide by the results of the contest, and the country would be spared the disruptive consequences of an endless feud. As Jefferson himself expressed it, since the "contest of opinion" had been "now decided by the voice of the nation . . . all will, of course, arrange themselves under the will of the law and unite in common efforts for the common good. All, too, will bear in mind this sacred principle, that, though the will of the majority is in all cases to prevail, that will, to be rightful must be reasonable; that the minority possess their equal rights, which equal law must protect, and to violate would be oppression." At the highest level of all, the principle of consent was based not only on a contract, but upon the recognition of a reality. The reality was that areas of agreement were always present among the American people — that these areas were more important than the areas of disagreement, which were also always present, and that therefore the factors of union and cohesion must take priority over the factors of dissension and disruption. This preponderance of factors shared in common was what made it possible for Americans to maintain a system of consent, even though limited conflicts over specific issues were always being waged.

It had been a quarter of a century earlier that Jefferson had coined his immortal phrase about governments deriving their just powers from the consent of the governed. I would suggest that in the passages I have just quoted he was at last defining what "consent of the governed" really meant. It meant, above all, that conflicting parties would constantly remember that they could be adversaries without being enemies, would observe the distinction between differences of opinion and differences of principle, and would work out more or less voluntary solutions to their differences of opinion, recognizing the obligation of the majority to respect the rights of the minority and the obligation of the minority to respect the popular mandate held up by the majority.

Such, as it appears to me, was government by consent — a system which prevailed in the United States for well over a century, and which is not yet terminated, though it is, I believe, badly impaired. As we look back at it, we are apt to romanticize it, and indeed I may have idealized it somewhat in my description here. Therefore, I must point out for the sake of verisimilitude, as Mark Twain used to say, that the system had some rather unlovely features. Sometimes, in the quest for accommodation, it reduced principles to such a negligible point that parties indulged in shameless bargaining, and thought more about how to win elections than about what to do with the elections they had won. "What are we here for," asked a delegate to the Republican convention of 1868, "except the offices?" Further, to mention a more serious flaw, the principle of consent exaggerated one of its own chief virtues into a vice. The virtue was the principle of compromise. The willingness to compromise was what enabled adversaries to get along with one another even when they disagreed. Compromise of all kinds — between large states and small states, between slavery and antislavery, between mercantile interests and planter interests, between advocates and opponents of national power — was what made "a more perfect union" possible in 1787. Great compromises again — in 1820, in 1832–1833, in 1850, and finally at the expense of the blacks, in 1877 — had either avoided or liquidated major crises in the republic. Partly because of this experience, compromise was almost sanctified, and men who rejected compromise were often written off as "fanatics" or "zealots" who refused the "tolerance" and the "give- and-take" of the American way. At times it seemed that there was no principle which could not be compromised if the parties to the transaction were sufficiently "reasonable."

The greatest flaw of all in the system of consent was one that was perhaps least recognized. The system had a fatal tendency to bring in those who could be conveniently included, but if there were groups whose voices would not harmonize, it practiced the brutally simple expedient of denying them a voice altogether. These excluded groups were just not regarded as, in the terminology of the sociologist, "significant others." Thus the American Indians were denied a voice. Negroes , both slave and free, were denied a voice, Also, occasional strong efforts were made to deny immigrants a voice. The denial of a voice to immigrants never succeeded in a formal sense, but, realistically, many immigrants were made to understand that they were on probation and that, if they behaved themselves, their children might be admitted to full membership in American society. Strange as it may now seem, for many of them this was enough, and they gave patient support to a system in which they occupied a very marginal position.

These major faults in the system of consent cannot and should not be extenuated, and indeed they were so serious that they might be regarded, in the eyes of some critics, as completely vitiating the entire structure. I certainly do not want to idealize it. I would not conceal the fact that compromise was often given a priority over principle, harmony over morality, and agreement over clarity of decision. I would not gloss over the fact that shameless bargaining and relentless arm-twisting were frequently employed to secure agreements in situations where direct coercion was taboo. But with all its faults, the system allowed for a measure of internal criticism and dissent such as few societies have known, and it reduced the factor of direct physical coercion to about as low a point as is possible in a complex and highly structured society. In fact this avoidance of coercion was the chief glory of the system, and the devices for obtaining consent were important primarily because they made the avoidance of coercion possible. To an astonishing degree in America, public affairs have been conducted on a basis that nothing could be done until it had been put into a form such that the opposition could be induced to agree to it. The use of the filibuster in the Senate, the copious devices for obstruction in both houses of Congress, the bicameral system itself, the arrangements for checks and balances, have all contributed to make it virtually impossible to enact a federal law if an opposition group of appreciable size is irreconcilably determined to prevent it.

But this emphasis upon more or less voluntary consent is by no means confined to the political sphere. Throughout the society, we regard the use of force in almost any situation as a confession of moral failure, whether it involves the use of a birch rod in the school or of militia in the streets. We even construct our buildings in a way which suggests our faith that people will accept the prevailing practices of the society without any duress to compel them to do so. In the past, tellers in banks sat guarded in little metal cages, but we have taken them out of these barricades and placed them behind low counters in rooms designed to look as little like a countinghouse as possible. In the past, honest burghers built their houses with heavy, solid shutters at the windows to repel marauders, but today we have turned to building and living in glass houses whose walls can be shattered with a small stone. Where loans were once granted only in return for formidable mortgages, we now flood the mails with unsolicited cards extending credit with a bounty so overflowing that it sometimes extends beyond adults to infants, deceased persons, and domestic animals. In place of compulsion we substitute agreement, but this substitution makes the necessity for agreement truly vital, so that when an important issue is in dispute, we are obsessively concerned that the negotiations that may lead to agreement shall never stop. The cessation of talk means crisis, and negotiations must go on, day and night. In a government by consent, the default of consent is the paralysis of authority.

Such was the system of government by the consent of the governed that prevailed in the United States for about two centuries. It never meant consent in the simple sense of spontaneous agreement by everyone. Sometimes the minority blackmailed the majority, and sometimes the majority put intolerable pressure upon the minority. Always certain disadvantaged groups were disregarded and left out. But withal the fact remained that the majority refrained from pushing the minority to the point of actual resistance, and the minority recognized an obligation, at a certain point, to abide by the terms of a settlement which they did not like — not an obligation to approve of it or even to agree to it, but at least to acquiesce in it, or as we say, "to go along" with it. Within this framework, men enjoyed remarkable opportunities to oppose the existing authority and to dissent from prevailing opinion. This system could operate without producing crises of social disorder because it was understood by all parties concerned that after the dissent had been heard and the issues had been canvassed, an arrangement would be worked out which the majority could accept as good enough and which the minority could tolerate as not utterly bad.

When the matter is viewed in this way, one might suppose the principle of consent succeeded simply because of the rationality or the tolerance of the American people — because men were logical enough to appreciate the philosophical elegance of this beautifully balanced political device and tolerant enough to cherish the mutual concessions by which the invocation of *force majeure* was avoided. But in fact human behavior is seldom this reasonable, and the ways and means by which society induces its members to do what is expected of them are never this voluntary. Government by consent may have succeeded partly because men recognized that submission to the majority is the price of democracy and that compliance with society's basic creed is the price of freedom within the context of that creed. But it succeeded less for these reasons than for two others: first, the American people were remarkably homogeneous and were well aware that the values which they shared were far more important to them than the values on which they disagreed; second, government by consent did not abolish the principle of authority — instead it substituted the equalitarian authority of the community as a whole for the hierarchical authority of a designated ruling class. It accomplished this transition by making conformity rather than obedience the device by which authority was enforced.

Social critics from Tocqueville to the present have, of course, given a great deal of attention to conformity in American life. They have pointed out how strong, and sometimes relentless, the pressure toward conformity has been. They have deplored its effects in stunting the growth of individualism and creativity, and even in making a travesty of freedom. Many of these criticisms are quite justified, and I would not gainsay them. But they have already been stated over and over again with skillful insight and with strong emphasis. At the same time, certain other aspects of social conformity have been relatively neglected, except by some sociologists.

To begin with, it has been poorly understood that conformity has an important constructive function, especially in a society which avoids the use of physical force or coercion. Every society has to have ways of coordinating the activities of its members, and this means that it has to have ways of inducing individuals to behave in ways in which they may not wish to behave and to do things which they would prefer not to do. This is almost what we mean when we speak of civilization. Some of the modes of inducing such behavior are quite formalized, and we have the law, the courts, the police, and the prisons. But on the whole, American society has relied less on formal authoritarian devices than almost any important society in history, and the force of law, for instance, has derived more from its claim to embody society's concept of justice than from its threat of penalties.

In this situation of minimal direct coercive control, conformity has imposed the coordinating arrangements in American society which authority has imposed in other societies. Our society demands "cooperation" with the community rather than "obedience" to the rulers, but both "socialize" the individual to behave as his society expects him to behave. Erich Fromm has expressed the essence of socialization in an elegant and subtle formulation: "In order that any society may function well, its members must acquire the kind of character which makes them *want* to act in the way they *have* to act . . . They have to *desire* what objectively is *necessary* for them to do.

David M. Potter

Outer force is to be replaced by *inner compulsion.*"

This is, I think, a perfect statement of what conformity is all about. But men in Jacksonian America anticipated Fromm by a century with a less learned but no less perceptive, formulation. With a kind of subtle crudity they asserted "this is a free country, and every man does as he pleases, and if he don't, we make him do so." This, too, was conformity, and, as I have suggested, I feel that scholars have not given enough attention to the social function of conformity in an antiauthoritarian society.

But if they have neglected the function of conformity, they have neglected even more the means by which conformity was enforced. It is, I believe, partly because we have never adequately recognized what these means were that we fail to understand today why values which, as recently as a decade ago, appeared to rest upon granite foundations have suddenly proved vulnerable to basic attack.

In brief, I would argue, conformity, and also the whole system of government by consent and law by consent, were based upon the sanction of community sentiment. But this statement can have no meaning until the term "community" has meaning, and the term "community" is one of the most loosely used words in the language. If the etymology is to count for anything, a community ought to mean an aggregate of people living in propinquity, who share the same basic values, attitudes, and outlook upon their social and physical environment. In brief, we might say that they share a common culture. But we all, apparently, have a tendency to believe that any aggregate of people living in propinquity *ought to* have these shared qualities, or wish that they did, and therefore we have gotten into the habit of speaking of any localized aggregate as a community, whether this aggregate has any shared values and attitudes or not. Thus we beg the question of whether it is a community, and we sometimes try to make it a community by

pretending that it is one. I recently heard a university administrator, in the midst of a campus crisis, state: "This disruption will end when the community decides that it must end, and no sooner." Of course, a public leader must assume the existence of a community, for, without one, there is nothing for him to lead. Also, sometimes, by a moving appeal, it is possible to invoke a spirit of community. But in realistic terms the question was not whether the community would decide; it was the question whether a community existed to decide — whether the aggregate of people in the situation was enough of a corporate group to be able to reach a collective decision.

Because of this practice of confusing actual community with mere physical propinquity or formal membership in a particular institution, it may be worth pausing to ask how the demographic, economic, and social circumstances of a earlier America contributed to the process of community formation. Briefly, let us consider the situation a century ago. At that time 34,427,000 Americans lived in rural areas, or in cities or towns of less than 100,000 population. Another 4,128,000 lived in cities of between 100,000 and 1,000,000 population. There were no cities with more than 1,000,000. This is to say that demographically about 88 percent of the population was distributed in a great multiplicity of small clusters of people. There were in fact 611 towns with between 2,500 and 25,000 population. There were only 14 cities of over 100,000, and only 2 over 500,000. These clusters of population were economically tied together by a network of railroads, rivers, and canals, and they were politically unified by national political parties, a strong but much limited national government, and a strong spirit of American nationalism. National church organizations and publishing houses, with a small but nationally distributed market, gave a limited degree of centralization to religious and cultural life—or at least the more elite and self-conscious aspects of cultural life. But by modern standards America's towns and villages were remarkably isolated from one another. America's system of roads and automobiles was still more than half a century in the future, and the only practicable way to make any journey of more than a hundred miles was to go by rail. Electronic communication was even more than half a century away and the chief medium of public communication was the local newspaper. Even the smaller towns had their own dailies or weeklies, with no national columnists and no syndicated news, and with a remarkable degree of self-sufficiency. The local editor, the local clergyman, the local political leader were not overshadowed by the quick accessibility and the technological dominance of the cities.

Population clusters of this kind tended to form strong cohesive communities. Their spatial isolation defined them as units. Their small size was conducive to a high degree of personal acquaintance and frequent contact among the people. The limitations of their technology intensified their cohesiveness, for the orbit of social interaction was effectively circumscribed by a circle whose radius was the distance that a person could conveniently walk (or, if a farmer, drive his wagon) to the corner grocery, to the neighborhood school — which really was a neighborhood school — or to the druggist a few blocks away. Their orientation to the physical environment gave them a good bit in common, for in a society which still relied primarily upon agriculture and did much of its work outdoors, they shared a common concern with the weather and a common adjustment to nature — to the phases of the moon, the rhythm of the seasons, the fatefulness of drought and flood and untimely freezes. The social institutions which flourished within a population cluster of this kind also greatly reinforced the cohesiveness of the cluster itself, for they were what the sociologists call primary institutions — family, church congregation, neigh-

borhood — which emphasize the personal bond of relationship among their members and the loyalties of one for all and all for one.

The strength and cohesiveness of the communities of this world we have lost are so well recognized that there is no need for me to dwell upon them. In fact they may have been too much sentimentalized and exaggerated. But there is a further point, quite crucial to the concept of consent, which I believe has not been sufficiently recognized. This is the fact that the traditional community was a preclusive community. As I have observed, it certainly did not lovingly embrace everyone and draw together all the human beings within its orbit. It restricted active participation to the "significant others" and it openly excluded Negroes, slighted immigrants, and made life difficult for any square pegs which did not fit into the round holes with which the society was equipped. But even for those who were excluded, the community exercised such a strong gravitational force that though they had been rejected, they usually displayed compulsive impulses to qualify as insiders by adopting the values and the behavior of the insiders. For instance, the few Negroes who had attained middle-class status rejected Negro mores and zealously imitated the follies as well as the values of white middle-class life. The outsiders were culturally assimilated though not accepted as insiders. To state this another way, they gave their allegiance to the *dominant* community, and this meant that there could be no competing community.

Of course there have always been dissenters — men who did not want to pay the price of community membership. It is possible to identify a few of these in almost any community, and American history is rich in its record of dissent. But in the traditional community which I have been trying to sketch out, the outlook for a consistent dissenter was bleak. The community frowned upon his deviance, and it had a whole arsenal of social weapons, ranging from social snubs to outright ostracism, with which to whip him into line. It could easily isolate him, and make him feel his isolation, because the population of the community was small and did not provide enough dissenters to form a socially self-sufficient group (or rival community) of their own. As for other dissenters in other communities, the dissenter might get some meager psychological support from reading what they had to say (Elbert Hubbard, H. L. Mencken, Brann the Iconoclast, Bob Ingersoll), but they were too remote to protect him from the dreadful anxieties of the socially isolated. He could not join them in the togetherness of sit-ins, be-ins, or marches on Washington. His lot was a lonely one, and indeed the brooding spirit of loneliness which pervades nineteenth-century American literature may be a reflex of this loneliness of the dissenter.

Thus the community was not only holistic in the positive sense of being strong, cohesive, and integrated, but it was monolithic in the negative sense of inhibiting the development of social units which might deviate from the patterns of the dominant community. The basic American social structure until nearly the middle of the present century was a world of tight and tiny local communities, heavily insulated against external influences, but strikingly resembling and strongly reinforcing one another because of their generally homogeneous character. Such communities exercised a monolithic cultural control over all who lived within their orbits. Men who marched to the beat of a different drummer paid a high price for their singularity and were therefore few.

It was the fundamental structuring of American society into such communities that formed the functional basis for an informal system of conformity, and it was the prevalence of the system of conformity that made possible the formal system of consent as the basis for

government and law. It is true, no doubt, that political philosophy encouraged both the forbearance of majorities and the acquiescence of minorities, both of which are essential to a consensual system. But the very notion of majorities and minorities is meaningless without the concept of a whole — a community — of which majority and minority are both parts. What, after, all, is a majority? It is a number greater than half, just as a minority is a number less than half. But this must mean more than or less than half of a whole. If a large number tries to control a smaller number, and they are not parts of a whole but are separate peoples, we regard the control as tyranny. If they are parts of a whole, and the whole is a community, then, under the doctrine of majority rule *and* consent of the governed, the control, if it does not violate basic individual rights, is legitimate. It is hard to say precisely why the fact of community makes such a vital difference. but it must be partly because of a recognition that the community is more or less homogeneous. Perhaps it is only a restatement of this same point in a more specific way to say that there is a recognition that the values on which the members of the community agree are more important to them than the matters on which they disagree, and therefore that the matters of disagreement must be subordinated to the matters of agreement, which means that conflict over the matters of disagreement must be limited.

Fundamentally, there are two ways of looking at the system of control by communities, whose outlines I have tried to sketch. From an adverse point of view, it can be regarded as a system of majoritarian control by a dominating group which demanded blind conformity and used the informal penalties of social disapproval and isolation to exercise a coercion just as forcible as the authoritarian control of an earlier time, which had used flogging, ear-cropping, and imprisonment to exercise a more naked coercion. This is a view with which all the most vociferous critics of conformity and the Establishment would agree. On the other hand, it can be regarded as a system which encouraged men to comply with accepted standards of decent behavior, to recognize the importance of the values they shared, to settle their disagreements with a minimum of strife, and to operate their society with a minimum use of force. It also encouraged them to base the legitimacy of law upon public consent. No matter which of these views one adopts, it is clear that the power of community sentiment was crucial, and that such sentiment was not generated by just any kind of community. It was generated by somewhat isolated and autonomous communities which were more or less homogeneous to begin with, and in which particular factors of size, technology, primary institutions, and general orientation strengthened the cohesive effect.

To say this is to say that if this particular kind of community disappeared, the means by which the consent or conformity of the reluctant was procured might disappear also, and with it the sanction for the kind of government and the kind of law which a system of consent makes possible. It is to say further that the unique vulnerability of a consent society, of which I spoke earlier, would be exposed, and that many of the institutions of the society would be revealed to have no defenses. They would be exposed to assault—both verbal and physical assault, since this country has largely renounced the kind of coercive legal controls with which most countries still defend their institutions. Being based upon the assumption that any opposition from within will always be limited opposition, and that any internal issues are always negotiable, the system of consent provides no mechanism for the contingency of unlimited opposition and nonnegotiable issues.

What I am contending here is that the system of consent succeeded historically because the American people lived in population aggregates of a certain kind.

These aggregates formed communities which were homogeneous with one another, strongly cohesive, and equipped with the means of inducing virtually everyone in the aggregate to accede to the decisions of the dominant elements—decisions which were in turn modulated by the right of those who were acceding to demand certain concessions. Most of all, communities of this kind were able to monopolize the field of social organization in such a way that no effective communities incompatible with the standard type of community could be created. The consent that followed was not really the consent of millions of individual persons; it was the consent of many hundreds of individual communities. But what I would contend further is that the traditional kind of community has deteriorated or even disappeared. As it has done so, it has left the field open for the emergence of a variety of different kinds of communities — each with something of the strength, cohesiveness, and self-sufficiency which result from personal association and shared values. But these new-style communities, far from being traditional or standard or homogeneous with one another, frequently hold values in conflict with one another's — even values antithetical to one another's. In a social structure of conflicting communities, there is no longer a sanction for consent, and the whole system of law and government based upon consent faces a supreme crisis.

It is almost too well known for me to go into any detail about what happened to the nineteenth-century constellation of more or less autonomous, small communities. The automobile multiplied manyfold the radius of men's mobility. This fact itself destroyed countless cherished community institutions. It also greatly increased the distance between men's work and their homes, and thus began to shatter the integration of both their personalities and their lives. Technological changes reared secondary environments—the office, the university, the ghetto—which stood between man and the primary environment. These secondary environments diminished the shared experience which exposure to the primary environment had offered. They also made possible the concentration of large populations in cities. By 1968, 63 percent of the population of the nation lived in places of more than 250,000 population. The impersonality of city life, in turn, gave men an anonymity which was sometimes welcome, sometimes unwelcome, but, in either case, which relieved them of the personal impact of social pressures and social expectations. At the same time, city life was more secular than the church-oriented life of the rural community, and this secularism encouraged a skepticism in the higher learning —a skepticism that began to strip away the mystique with which a religious society will always sanctify its civil institutions: the Constitution, the flag, the majesty of the law, the mandate of the people.

By the 1950s, the solidarity of communities was fractured, their cohesion was diluted, and their power over individuals was but a shadow of what it had been. As patterns became diffused, the processes of socialization for children became blurred. Boys who had identified fairly readily with fathers who plowed a furrow on the farm could not take their cues so readily from fathers, who were away most of the time, engaged in incomprehensible work at places which one had never seen. Boys and girls whose sex roles were no longer codified all too frequently wound up feeling uncertain about their identities. Communities were divided in voice, bewildered by the rapidity of social change, bullied by "experts" who told them what to believe, and silenced by the voices of the electronic media, which came from the metropolis and to which they could not talk back. As instruments of social control, communities became faint shadows of what they once had been. They could no longer speak to the dissenters in tones of authority, nor could they monitor the behavior of deviant individuals.

But these changes are well known, and what I would like to focus upon is a less recognized and perhaps more important aspect of this revolution in the patterns of social relatedness. This is a change in the scale of society, which has destroyed the power of traditional communities to control dissenters by isolating or ostracizing them, and has now given to those who reject or are rejected by the community a power to form communities of their own. This change is vital, because when the traditional community loses its power to deny the blessings of social relatedness to those who reject it, the principle of social control by communities is left with no effective means of enforcement.

The readiness with which alienated or nonconformist groups can now form communities of their own is cogently suggested by a comment of Daniel Bell's in the spring 1970 issue of The Public Interest. Bell asks how many constitute the "mass" of the radicals, and he cites Fortune surveys which indicate that as many as 30 percent "in the elite schools" may be significantly radical. But then he adds: "A more important consideration, however, and a crucial one for all our problems is less the percentage than the change of scale. In an arena of ten thousand students, five percent comes to 500, and these can form a powerful striking force."

No doubt this is true, but the power of the striking force which they can form is perhaps less important than the strength of the community that they can form. A community of five hundred is large enough to give the person who joins it a sense of belonging, large enough to protect him against the snubs and slights and disapproval of the larger society, large enough to isolate him from outgroups, as all communities do with their members. Five hundred strongly cohesive people can devise standards of dress, speech, and belief for their own group, and impose these as rigidly as if they were the most orthodox of conformists. David Riesman has touched this point rather effectively in his observation that "the Bohemians and the rebels are not usually autonomous; on the contrary, they are zealously tuned in to the signals of a defiant group that finds the meaning of life in a compulsive non-conformity to the majority group."

We still speak of the bohemians and the rebels as dissenters, which means that we are still held in the grip of the illusion that there is one "community" which includes everyone except those who opt out and float about as displaced persons on the margins of society. But the fact that large numbers of people, living in propinquity, on campuses, in communes, in bohemias, or whatever, may share common values and even impose standards of conformity upon their members means that these people are not dissenters at all. Rather, they are conforming members of new kinds of communities — not only new kinds of communities, but communities which are committed to a cultural separation from communities of the standard kind. To embark on an extended scrutiny of these new social organisms is beyond the scope of this paper, for all that we are immediately concerned with here is the impact of these changes upon a system of law based upon consent and uniformity. But the fact that they are communities, and communities of a special kind, is beginning to be recognized. J. Milton Yinger has already written about what he calls a "contraculture," and Theodore Roszak about a "counterculture." The "spirit of Woodstock" is a manifestation of an urge toward community in these new groups. This spirit in some ways is very different from the spirit of traditional communities. For instance, the traditional community was highly structured by a network of explicit commitments and loyalties binding individuals to one another in an intricate cohesive pattern. The spirit of the commune is much more an unstructured diffuse sense of "love" toward everyone in general and no one in particular. But in many respects we have new communities whose relation to the traditional community is as negative as their culture is negative toward the traditional culture, and if we are to speak of contracultures or countercultures, we might as well speak of contracommunities and countercommunities. It is such social entities as these which now withhold the consent which has been vital to our noncoercive society and which thus present a challenge to the legitimacy of law such as this basic institution has never before faced in America.

In sum, we have lived for some two centuries in a society which has minimized the use of physical compulsion at all levels and has used less compulsion than almost any society in history. Socially we have abandoned chastisement for children, both at home and in school. We have abolished, in law and almost in practice, the domination of husbands over wives. We have operated with a Congress in which it has remained almost impossible to enact a law to which a handful of senators are deeply and irrevocably opposed. We have operated with a court system in which there is no good way to induce the accused to let his trial proceed if he is not willing to let it proceed. The unanimity with which, in the past, accused persons accepted this system was so total that we were not even aware of the naked vulnerability of the courts until the Chicago Seven disclosed it to us.

Having rejected compulsion as a means of social control, except in the cases of punishment of palpable felons whose offenses were condemned by almost everyone, we became desperately dependent upon "agreement"—perhaps under pressure, perhaps reluctant, perhaps secured by bullying or bartering or bribery, but still with some measure of voluntarism or at least acquiescence in the result. Since agreement was the alternative to deadlock and paralysis, we became compulsively addicted to negotiation. I suppose that most legislation is negotiated before it is enacted, and that more legal disputes are negotiated than are ever brought to trial. In important disputes in the area of labor relations, we insist, above all, that the parties must never stop talking, and, if the matter is urgent, they must negotiate around the clock. Since our only truly instrumental device for resolving disputes is by talk, the prospect that the contestants might actually quit talking is too awful to contemplate. Agreement or what passes for agreement *must* be reached, because if agreement fails, our system offers no recourse.

For two centuries this system of government by consent operated, sometimes creaking loudly, sometimes brought to a dead halt, sometimes imposing injustice and hardship upon groups who were forced to the mockery of pretending to accept by agreement what they were compelled to accept by irresistible pressure. But on the whole the system worked reasonably well, not because it was intrinsically workable, but because the dominant communities wanted it to work. People truly regarded the points on which they agreed as more important than the points on which they disagreed. When they did disagree, it was as adversaries and not as enemies. We were "all Republicans and all Federalists," and for all its imperfections the operation of the system might well have gratified Thomas Jefferson.

But today we face confrontations with men who believe in revolution—believe in it, in a good many cases, with genuine conviction. They do not want to reach agreement. Their demands are, by stipulation, nonnegotiable. Their adversary may give in, but they will not let him agree. Often their terms are stated in a way carefully designed to make agreement impossible.

Thus we approach the answer to a question which most people never recognized as a question and to which those who did recognize it hoped never to have to learn the answer. What happens to law based upon the norms of the community if there is no prevailing community but only a multiplicity of conflicting communities? What happens to the principle of consent if the social structure has no center which can even speak the voice of consent?

The answers are far from clear. But perhaps it is important to remember that while consent requires what Richard Hofstadter has called an attitude of comity on the part of conflicting parties, and while even minimum comity seems unattainable in many confrontations today, still the principle of consent was never predicated upon the idea of bland agreement and readiness to avoid issues for the sake of superficial harmony. It was predicated upon the idea that adverse parties can limit their conflict, and can recognize the values they share, even while contesting the points on which they disagree. Whether the communities and countercommunities of America in the 1970s may be able to hold such a balanced view in the heat of the antagonisms and extremisms that now prevail is questionable indeed. But if it is possible to contest social issues without destroying essential institutions, it will have to be done by the difficult feat of combining tolerance with idealism. We need to look at people as individuals and not as types. We need to remember with Thomas Jefferson that "every difference of opinion is not a difference of principle," to recognize that a principle is not necessarily a moral absolute, and to remind ourselves frequently that an adversary need not be a mortal enemy.

NOTES

2. Notes Toward a History of American Justice

LAWRENCE M. FRIEDMAN

1. Leon de Valinger, Jr., ed., *Court Records of Kent County, Delaware 1680-1705* (Washington, 1959), 234-235, 270-271.

2. The trial of Joan Mills and Adam Latham did deviate somewhat from the norm in that a prison sentence was imposed. Colonial society did not, in general, make use of prisons in this way. Society needed workers; a man in jail was not a productive hand. The colonists used jails to detain people who did not pay their debts. Whipping, branding, fines, and the stocks were far more common. See David J. Rothman, *The Discovery of the Asylum: Social Order and Disorder in the New Republic* (Boston, 1971), 53.

3. Charles T. Libby, ed., *Province and Court Records of Maine* (Portland, Maine, 1931), II, 174.

4. Ibid., 224.

5. *Laws and Liberties of Massachusetts* (Cambridge, Mass., 1929), 4.

6. Kai T. Erikson, *Wayward Puritans: A Study in the Sociology of Deviance* (New York, 1966), 197.

7. James A. Henretta, "Economic Development and Social Structure in Colonial Boston," in Stanley N. Katz and Stanley I. Kutler, eds., *New Perspectives on the American Past*, 2d. ed. (Boston, 1972), I, 53, 62, table 1.

8. Lawrence W. Wylie and Armand Bégué, *Village in the Vaucluse*, rev. ed. (New York, 1969), 84-86.

9. See, e.g., John P. Reid, *A Law of Blood: The Primitive Law of the Cherokee Nation* (New York, 1970), 242-245; Geert Van den Steenhoven, *Leadership and Law Among the Eskimos of the Keewatin District* (Rijswijk, 1962), 91.

10. Joseph H. Smith, ed., *Colonial Justice in Western Massachusetts, 1639-1702* (Cambridge, Mass., 1961), 204.

11. Ibid., 209.

12. For a discussion of communist law as "parental" and "educational," see Harold I. Berman, *Justice in the U.S.S.R.: An Interpretation of Soviet Law* (New York, 1963), 277-284; Jesse Berman, "The Cuban Popular Tribunals," *Columbia Law Review* 69 (1969), 1317.

13. William E. Nelson, *Americanization of the Common Law* (Cambridge, Mass., 1974), 37. In every fornication case except one (and 95 percent of the sex cases were for fornication), the defendant was the mother of an illegitimate child. Yet Nelson rejects the argument that fornication was punished merely because it burdened towns with support of illegitimate children. He points out that prosecutions were brought even against mothers who had married their partners, and in cases where there was no economic motive at all.

14. Francis W. Laurent, *The Business of a Trial Court, 100 Years of Cases: A Census of Actions and Special Proceedings in Circuit Court for Chippewa County Wisconsin, 1855-1954* (Madison, 1959), 122.

15. Jack K. Williams, *Vogues in Villainy: Crime and Retribution in Ante-Bellum South Carolina* (Columbia, S.C., 1959), 55-58.

16. (James) Willard Hurst, *Law and the Conditions of Freedom in the Nineteenth Century United States* (Madison, 1956), 6.

17. Ibid.

18. Ibid.

19. Rothman, *The Discovery of the Asylum*, 71.

20. Williams, *Vogues in Villainy*, 101.

21. See Gustave de Beaumont and Alexis de Tocqueville, *On the Penitentiary System in the United States and Its Application in France* (Philadelphia, 1833).

22. Charles Dickens, *American Notes* (New York, 1900), 109; see Friedman, *A History of American Law*, 259-260.

23. Dickens, *American Notes*, 108.

24. Rothman, *The Discovery of the Asylum*, 242.

25. See Gerhard O. W. Mueller, "Inquiry into the State of a Divorceless Society," *University of Pittsburgh Law Review*, 18 (1957), 545.

26. See Nelson M. Blake, *The Road to Reno: A History of Divorce in the United States* (New York, 1962).

27. Ibid., 60-61.

28. Ibid., 130-151

29. See Steven Marcus, *The Other Victorians: A Study of Sexuality and Pornography in Mid-Nineteenth-Century England* (New York, 1966); Ronald Pearsall, *The Worm in the Bud: The World of Victorian Sexuality* (New York, 1969).

30. Joseph R. Gusfield, "Moral Passage: The Symbolic Process in Public Designations of Deviance," *Social Problems*, 15 (1967), 175.

31. Thomas F. O'Dea, *The Mormons* (Chicago, 1957), 41-75.

32. Roger Lane, *Policing the City: Boston, 1822-1885* (Cambridge, Mass., 1967); James F. Richardson, *The New York Police, Colonial Times to 1901* (New York, 1970), 23-51.

33. *Civil Judicial Statistics for the Year 1972* (London, 1973), 19. A study of litigation rates in Spain shows similar results for recent decades, a period of rapid economic growth in that country. José Juan Toharia, *Cambio social y vida jurídica en España* (Madrid, 1974).

34. Albert A. Ehrenzeig, "Reimbursement of Counsel Fees and the Great Society," *California Law Review*, 54 (1966), 792.

35. See, e.g., Jerome E. Carlin, Jan Howard, and Sheldon L. Messinger, *Civil Justice and the Poor: Issues for Sociological Research* (New York, 1967).

36. See, e.g., Stuart A. Schlegel, *Tiruray Justice; Traditional Tiruray Law and Morality* (Berkeley, 1970), 163.

37. On this point, see Nelson, above n. 13.

38. Lawrence M. Friedman, "Legal Rules and the Process of Social Change," *Stanford Law Review*, 19 (1967), 786, 806; see Marc Galanter, "Why the 'Haves' Come Out Ahead: Speculations on the Limits of Legal Change," *Law and Society Review*, 9 (1974), 95.

39. Lawrence M. Friedman, *A History of American Law* (New York, 1973), 295-299.

40. *Debates and Proceedings of the Constitutional Convention of the State of California*, 2 (1881), 700, 704.

41. John R. Commons, *Races and Immigrants in America* (New York, 1913), 133.

42. Ibid.

43. Ibid., 132.

44. Ibid., 133-134.

45. George M. Stephenson, *A History of American Immigration, 1820-1924* (Boston, 1916), 170-192.

46. Act of July 2, 1890, ch. 647, 26 Stat. 209 (codified at 15 U.S.C. § §107 [1973]).

47. See William Letwin, *Law and Economic Policy in America: The Evolution of the Sherman Antitrust Act* (New York, 1965), 54-71.

48. Act of June 1, 1908, *Laws of Ill.* 90.

49. Lawrence M. Friedman, "Freedom of Contract and Occupational Licensing 1890-1910: A Legal and Social Study," *California Law Review*, 53 (1965), 487.

50. Friedman, *A History of American Law*, 511-512; see, e.g., Act of May 25, 1897, ch. 188 [1897], Laws of Conn. 883. Of course, Sunday laws had been enforced off and on throughout the century. For some glimpse of this complex history, see Warren L. Johns, *Dateline Sunday, U.S.A.: The Story of Three and a Half Centuries of Sunday Law Battles in America* (Mountain View, Calif., 1967).

51. Act of March 2, 1895, ch. 191, 28 Stat. 963 (codified, *as amended*, at 18 U.S.C. §1301 (1970)). Lotteries, common in the early part of the century, were outlawed in many states. See John S. Ezell, *Fortune's Merry Wheel: The Lottery in America* (Cambridge, Mass., 1960).

52. Joseph R. Gusfield, *The Symbolic Crusade: Status Politics and the American Temperance Movement* (Urbana, 1963), 122. See generally, David J. Pivar, *Purity Crusade: Sexual Morality and Social Control, 1868-1900* (Westport, Conn., 1973).

53. Act of May 8, 1907, No. 280, [1907] Acts of Ark. 653.

54. Act of February 27, 1907, No. 55, [1907] Acts of Ark. 682.

55. Act of May 9, 1906, No. 287, [1907] Acts of Ark. 682.

56. Rufus King, *The Drug Hang-Up: America's Fifty-Year Folly* (New York, 1972), 17.

57. Troy S. Duster, *The Legislation of Morality: Law, Drugs and Moral Judgement* (New York, 1970), 3.

58. Act of June 25, 1910, ch. 395, 36 Stat. 825 (codified, *as amended*, at 18 U.S.C. 2421 [1966]).

59. Andrew Sinclair, *Era of Excess: A Social History of the Prohibition Movement* (New York, 1964), 178-219.

60. Doubleday and Co. v. New York, 335 U.S. 848 (1948) (per curiam), aff'g 297 N.Y. 687, 77 C.E.2d 6 (1947). The next obscenity case did not come before the Court until almost ten years later: Roth v. United States, 354 U.S. 476 (1957).

61. A Book Named *John Cleland's Memoirs of a Woman of Pleasure* v. Attorney General, 383 U.S. 413 (1966).

62. See Daniel Bell, *The End of Ideology: On the Exhaustion of Political Ideas in the Fifties* (New York, 1962), 151; Roger Lane, "Urbanization and Criminal Violence in the 19th Century: Massachusetts as a Test Case," in Hugh D. Graham and Ted R. Gurr, eds., *Violence in America* (New York, 1969), 468, 469.

63. See Charles L. Brace, *The Dangerous Classes of New York and Twenty Years' Work among Them*, 3rd ed. (New York, 1880).

64. Allan Silver, "The Demand for Order in Civil Society," in David L. Bordua, ed., *The Police: Six Sociological Essays* (New York, 1967), 1-24.

3. King's Law and Local Custom in Seventeenth-Century New England

JULIUS GOEBEL, JR.

1. It should here be pointed out that on the side of legal theory the problem of the transplantation of law during the colonial period presents three aspects, all of which underwent considerable change from 1600-1776. These are (1) the doctrine of the English Courts; (2) the doctrine of the Crown; (3) the doctrine of the Colonists. . .

In England the theory regarding the king's dominions in the Middle Ages remains to be completely studied, especially in respect to the extension of common law over conquered territory . . .

2. I do not wish to be understood as taking the position that everything done at Plymouth was imitated, because each colony seems to have had certain peculiar social characteristics which found individual expression. This was particularly true of Massachusetts Bay, where there were a greater number of persons of outstanding intellectual force in positions of authority who had designs utterly different from those of the Plymouth men. At the same time certain major achievements of Plymouth, such as the form of church organization and the device of codification, were very certainly borrowed.

3. Thus Roscoe Pound, "The Revival of Comparative Law," *Tulane Law Review*, 5 (1930), 3, 7, appears to lean toward this view. In his *Spirit of the Common Law* (Boston, 1921), 112, in a chapter headed "Pioneers and the Law," Pound says: "Administration of justice in America was at first executive and legislative, and these types of non-judicial justice persisted well into the last century" (113). "The colonies began with all manner of experiments in administering justice without law and it was not till the middle of the eighteenth century that the setting up of a system of courts and the rise of a custom of studying law in England began to make for a general administration of justice according to English law. Just prior to the Revolution the widespread study of Blackstone, whose first edition appeared in 1765, gave great impetus to the reception of the common law. But as late as 1791 the law was so completely at large in New Yrok that the genius of a Kent was needed to make the common law the law of that state" (115-116).

If Pound is talking about all the colonies, it may be said that the facts do not bear him out. If we take New York, with whose colonial legal records I am familiar, we start out with an elaborate code (1665). Beginning with the opening years of the eighteenth century the law rapidly becomes professionalized.

4. There can be no doubt from the terms of the royal charter to the New England Council that the legislative power conveyed by the Crown was not delegable. The charter reads to them and their successors. There is no mention of assigns. In the light of contemporary doctrines of corporations the legislative power over the lands granted conveyed by the charter was obviously conceived as a grant of bylaw powers.

5. There has never been a thoroughgoing study made of Separatism from the angle of corporate theory, and this is all the more remarkable because of the importance of the Congregational Church in New England and the close relation of state and church in that region. To comprehend the steps by which the Separatists reached their views we must remember that in England their churches were outside the pale of the law; that they rejected all ideas of hierarchical organization; that the protestant doctrines of the visible church made some form of organization essential. The central and most characteristic fact in Separatism was the covenant by which a church was organized. This was a dual act, a convenant with God—a solemn promise by the body of believers to God to do His will—and a second covenant, sometimes reduced to writing, made by the believers with one another, to work for the Lord, to avoid evil, to do good, and to stand together. Only in this way could a visible church be established.

The Separatists seem to have had English municipal institutions in mind, rather than ecclesiastical corporations like the dean and chapter. It was not until the Leyden Separatists had resided in Holland that the civil implications of their corporate theory developed, i.e., an identification of the church as a corporation for civil purpose.

6. To anyone familiar with the Separatist writings and not bemused by theories of democracy, or by hallucinations regarding the originality of the first settlers, it seems difficult to escape the conclusion that the civil order instituted at Plymouth was no more than the realization of the complete possibilities of their corporate theory of the church, and in this sense simply the consummation of their speculation regarding the church. Here is the result of growth, not an adaptation. At the outset the church in Plymouth was the state.

7. Certain superficial similarities between the 1636 preamble and those of the English custumals which may be mentioned are the following: The specification name of the committee coincides with the naming of authorities in some custumals; the prefacing or mention of the king's charter in the latter coincides with the recital of the compact and grant in the Plymouth document; finally, the express mention that the laws are made by consent both in the code of 1636 and in some of the custumals seems significant. This latter provision is not unusual in the guild ordinances.

The preambles of statutes and the long opening recitals of grants are not close enough in content and form for us to regard them as possible models. The statutes antedating the code of 1636 often have preambles, but these are concise statements of the facts motivating the statutes and do not resemble the code preamble.

The form of the preamble is interesting in giving some clue to the theory of legislative power. It states that the committee for the revision of the laws having read the compact and the letters patent (*sic*) of 1629 and "finding that as free borne subjects of the State of England we hither came endewed with all and singular the priviledges belong to such in the first place, we thinke good that it be established for an act."

"That according to the . . . due privilege of the subject aforesaid no imposicion law or ordinance be made or imposed upon or by ourselves or others at present or to come but such as shall be made or imposed by consent, according to the free liberties of the state and Kingdome of England and no otherwise."

It should be noted that the Committee goes behind both compact and grant to the intangible privileges of the Englishmen of which these documents are treated as mere evidence. No longer, as in the compact, is authority conferred by virtue of the fact of association. The preamble is a crudely phrased appeal to the rights of Englishmen. This statement anticipates to a degree the debates which occurred shortly thereafter in England over the distinction between fundamental laws and other legislation the basis for which had been laid in the discussions over the Petition of Right.

If anything in the nature of a constitutional foundation for the future existed in Plymouth, it was this preamble, with the important provision that the freemen must consent to all laws. There seems, moreover, to be an implicit rejection of royal authority in the reference to the "privileges" of the subject as the source of legislation. It is possible to regard this preamble as a retort to the King's Commission on Trade and Plantations of 1634 and to the projected royal government for New England.

8. The legislature and chief tribunal of Plymouth was known as the "General Court." The earliest records are missing, but the first ones indicate no clear distinction between the two functions . . .

9. What I have reference to is not only the concentration of jurisdiction in a single court, but also the failure to distinguish sharply between a prosecution publicly initiated and a private suit. As far as the records are concerned the Court Orders are very miscellaneous in character. They contain notices of presentments, criminal and civil trials, ordinances, admissions to the corporations, marriages, recordings of personalty, inquests on special matters, grants, and many other matters. The Judicial Acts are devoted chiefly to records of civil actions, but there are also military orders, trials of traversed presentments, testimony, etc.

10. In 1636 the grand jury was provided for by the code, and the trials by jury were to extend to all cases "as nearly as possible to English precidents." The grand jury was to present to the court persons they found guilty or probably suspect. After 1640 presentments had to be on oath.

11. The grand jury seems to have shared to some extent the power of the magistrate in determining what constituted an offense. In the case of the latter the statute directed that in "small offences" the magistrate shall "determine doe and execute as in widsom God shall dirct them." The power of the grand jury to determine misdemeanors was broadly laid down as misdemeanors tending to the hurt and detriment of "Society Civility peace and neighborhood." There is an English analogue in the power of the leet to present public nuisances, but this was rather the determination of whether certain facts constituted an offense over which its jurisdiction was recognized, rather than a specification of new offenses, particularly as the limits of the nuisance concept were well understood.

12. This conclusion is reached on the basis of rather unsatisfactory evidence. The records usually indicate the fact of presentment with a marginal notation of the fine, punishment, or discharge of the accused. Since no further notation of trial is made, this circumstance, taken in connection with the fact that where a jury was actually impaneled a record is made, seems to indicate that presentment was tantamount to conviction.

13. To anyone under illusions regarding the morality of the Pilgrim fathers, a perusal of the criminal records contained in the Court Orders will offer something of a shock. Between the years 1633-1641 offenses against morals (including sabbath breach, drunkenness, lewdness, fornication) outnumbered by three to one crimes having an element of breach of the peace and were double the number of offenses against the economic order (extortion, millers' frauds, vagrancy). In the period 1641-1651 crimes involving a breach of the peace increase, the ratio to offenses against morality being one to two, the infractions of economic regulations decrease, the ratio being one to three.

14. *Plymouth Laws*, 32 (1633); restated in the code, ibid., 74 . . .

4. The Legal Heritage of Plymouth Colony

GEORGE L. HASKINS

1. E.g., Julius Goebel, "King's Law and Local Custom in Seventeenth-Century New England," *Columbia Law Review*, 31 (1931), 448; George L. Haskins, "The Beginnings of the Recording System in Massachusetts,"

Boston University Law Review, 21 (1941), 281, 302.

2. Samuel E. Morison, *By Land and by Sea: Essays and Addresses* (New York, 1953), 234.

3. Ibid., 235.

4. Ibid., 234. Although he concedes that Plymouth instituted civil marriage, a registry of deeds, and the first Congregational church, Morison goes on to say that even the Pilgrim church at Plymouth was soon overshadowed by the Congregational churches that sprang up elsewhere in New England and by such learned clergymen as Hooker, Cotton, and Shepard, whose counterparts could not be found at Plymouth (ibid., 235). Since the publication of Morison's essay on Plymouth, *By Land and by Sea*, he has explicitly given the colony credit for instituting the first bill of rights. Samuel E. Morison, *The Story of the "Old Colony" of New Plymouth* (New York 1957), 152-153.

5. William Bradford, *History of Plymouth Plantation* 2 vols. (Boston, 1912), I, 28.

6. Cf. Morison, *By Land and by Sea*, 235.

7. Henry Adams, *History of the United States of America*, 9 vols. (New York, 1889), I, 133.

8. Mass. Const. Art. 30.

9. William Brigham, ed., *The Compact with the Charter and Laws of the Colony of New Plymouth Together with the Charter of the Council at Plymouth, and an Appendix, Containing the Articles of Confederation of the United Colonies of New England, and other Valuable Documents* (Boston, 1836), 35.

10. Ibid.

11. Ibid., 36.

12. William H. Whitmore, ed., *The Colonial Laws of Massachusetts* (Boston, 1889), 29-64.

13. Susan M. Kingsbury, ed., *The Records of the Virginia Company of London* (Washington, D.C., 1933), 12-29.

14. See generally George L. Haskins, "Codification of the Law in Colonial Massachusetts: A Study in Comparative Law," *Indiana Law Journal*, 30 (1954), 2-3.

15. Max Farrand, ed., *The Laws and Liberties of Massachusetts* (Cambridge, Mass., 1929). Further study of the 1636 Plymouth code has led me to revise an earlier opinion, expressed in my "Codification of the Law in Colonial Massachusetts: A Study in Comparative Law," 5, that because the traditional element in the code is strong it is difficult to classify the code as "modern."

16. Kingsbury, *The Records of the Virginia Company of London*, 164-168, 170-174.

17. Brigham, *The Compact with the Charter and Laws of the Colony of New Plymouth*, 105-121, 239-301.

18. George L. Haskins and Samuel E. Ewing, 3d, "The Spread of Massachusetts Law in the Seventeenth Century," *University of Pennsylvania Law Review*, 106 (1958), 413.

19. Although only a few copies of the collections of laws printed in 1671 and 1685 survive, these and earlier laws were published twice in the last century, in Brigham, *The Compact with the Charter and Laws of the Colony of New Plymouth*, and in Nathaniel B. Shurtleff and David Pulsifer, eds., *Records of the Colony of New Plymouth in New England* (Boston, 1861), XI, and are generally available in large libraries.

20. See George L. Haskins, "Law and Colonial Society," *American Quarterly*, 9 (1957), 357-358.

21. Brigham, *The Compact with the Charter and Law of the Colony of New Plymouth*, 45, 58.

22. Ibid., 47 (land to be forfeited when not occupied by grantee).

23. "And by drunkennesse is understood a person that either lisp or faulters in his speech by reason of over much drink, or that staggers in his going or that vomits by reason of excessive drinking, or cannot follow his calling" (ibid., 84).

24. See George L. Haskins, *Law and Authority in Early Massachusetts: A Study in Tradition and Design* (New York, 1960), 78-80.

25. See Haskins, "The Beginnings of the Recording System in Massachusetts," 289-291, where the land-registration system in force in Holland during the period of the Pilgrims' sojourn at Leyden is discussed.

26. Goebel, "King's Law and Local Custom in Seventeenth-Century New England," 435-438, also reprinted in this volume.

27. Ibid., 420.

28. Ibid., 435.

29. Ibid., 433-434.

30. Ibid., 420.

31. See Haskins and Ewing, "The Spread of Massachusetts Law in the Seventeenth Century," 18.

32. James K. Hosmer, ed., *Winthrop's Journal, "History of New England," 1630-1649* (New York 1908), I, 151.

33. Whitmore, *The Colonial Laws of Massachusetts*; see generally, Haskins, *Law and Authority in Early Massachusetts*, 124-126.

34. Brigham, *The Compact with the Charter and Laws of the Colony of New Plymouth*, 36.

35. Ibid.

36. Ibid., 42.

37. Ibid.

38. Ibid., 241-243.

39. Massachusetts Constitution, Arts. 4, 9, 11, 12, 15, 23.

40. Bradford, *History of Plymouth Plantation*, I, 218.

41. Haskins, *Law and Authority in Early Massachusetts*, 194-195.

42. Brigham, *The Compact with the Charter and Laws of the Colony of New Plymouth*, 43. The reference to equal descent is not implicit, but it may be inferred from the reference to "the comendable custome of Engl. and hold of Est. Greenwich" (ibid). At the manor of East Greenwich, the Kentish custom of gavelkind was believed to be in force. Lands held in gavelkind descended to all sons. On this question, see George L. Haskins, "Gavelkind and the Charter of Massachusetts Bay," *Transactions of the Colonial Society of Massachusetts*, 34 (1943), 483.

43. Letter from Isaak de Rasieres to Samuel Blommaert, *New York Historical Society Collection*, 2d ser. II (1849), 352.

44. See generally, George L. Haskins, "The Beginnings of Partible Inheritance in the American Colonies," *Yale Law Journal*, 51 (1942), 1280.

45. See Brigham, *The Compact with the Charter and Law of the Colony of New Plymouth*, 43.

46. Technically, dower at common law attached to all lands held in fee simple and fee tail of which the husband was solely and beneficially seised at any time during coverture and which issue of the marriage might inherit. The Plymouth provision merely specified "a third part of his lands during her life" and therefore seems to have included lands owned by the husband at his death rather than during the marriage. In 1646 it was enacted that a wife must consent to a sale of land, so that thereafter she received some protection in lands which the husband owned and conveyed during marriage (Brigham, *The Compact with the Charter and Law of the Colony of New Plymouth*, 86). See also George L. Haskins, "A Problem in the Reception of the Common Law in the Colonial Period," *University of Pennsylvania Law Review*, 97 (1949), 842.

47. Sir William S. Holdsworth, *A History of English Law* (London, 1936), III, 552.

48. 22 and 23 Car. 2, c. 10 (1670).

49. Brigham, *The Compact with the Charter and Laws of the Colony of New Plymouth*, 43.

50. See generally, Haskins, "The Beginnings of the Recording System in Massachusetts."

51. Mass. Ann. Laws ch. 183 (1955).

52. See generally, Note, "The Role of Law in Colonial Massachusetts, *University of Pennsylvania Law Review*, 108 (1960), 1001, dealing with the rule of law in the colony of Massachusetts Bay.

53. The foregoing is elaborated in George L. Haskins, "Executive Justice and the Rule of Law," *Speculum*, 30 (1955), 529.

54. Brigham, *The Compact with the Charter and Laws of the Colony of New Plymouth*, 19.

55. Ibid.

56. Ibid., 36.

57. Ibid., 241.

58. John N. Figgis, *The Divine Right of Kings* (Cambridge, Mass., 1914), 175.

59. Cicero, *Oratio pro cluentio*, c. 53: "Legum denique idcirco omnes servi sumus ut liberi esse possimus."

5. The Politics of Law in Colonial America: Controversies over Chancery Courts and Equity Law in the Eighteenth Century

STANLEY N. KATZ

1. Berthold Fernow, ed., *Calendar of Council Minutes, 1668-1783, Bulletin of the*

New York State Library, 58 (1902), 157-160, 202; *The Law Practice of Alexander Hamilton,* ed. Julius Goebel, Jr. (New York, 1964), I, 178-179.

2. Hunter to Board of Trade, May 7, 1711, in E. B. O'Callaghan and Berthold Fernow, eds., *Documents Relative to the Colonial History of the State of New York* (Albany, 1856-1887), V, 208 (hereafter *N.Y. Col. Docs.*).

3. Board of Trade to Hunter, June 29, 1711, ibid., V, 252.

4. See *Hamilton Law Practice,* I, 170-173, 180-181.

5. *Journal of the Votes and Proceedings of the General Assembly of the Colony of New York* (New York, 1764-1766), I, 308 (hereafter *Assemb. Jour.*); New York Council to Board of Trade, December 13, 1711, *N. Y. Col. Docs.,* V, 295-296.

6. Hunter to Board of Trade, January 1, 1712, *N. Y. Col. Docs.,* V, 298.

7. Hunter to Board of Trade, n.d. [1717], ibid, V, 499. On November 6, 1711, the Council sent to the Assembly a bill "for the better Recovery of her Majesty's Quit-Rents," *Assemb. Jour.,* I, 304.

8. William Smith, *The History of the Province of New York, Collections of the New York Historical Society,* (henceforth NYHS, *Colls.*), 1st ser. IV-V (1826) (New York, 1829) I, 237-238; *Assemb. Jour.,* I, 571-572. In an additional challenge to royal legal prerogatives, the Assembly passed a bill intended to prevent "Prosecutions by Informations" on November 10, 1727 (*Assemb. Jour.,* I, 586-570).

9. Report of the New York Council, December 5, 1727, in *New York Gazette,* no. 114 (January 1-8, 1727) and no. 115 (January 8-15, 1727).

10. Burnet to Board of Trade, December 21, 1727, *N.Y. Col. Docs.,* V, 847. See also Obadiah Palmer [et al.] . . . , *Complainants against Jacobus Van Cortland & Adolph Philipse, Defendants* [New York, n.d.], copy in NYHS.

11. See "A Word in Season," *New York Weekly Journal,* no. 200 (September 5, 1737).

12. Montgomerie to Board of Trade, November 30, 1728, *N. Y. Col. Docs.,* V, 874.

13. Lewis Morris, Jr., to Board of Trade, July 19, 1729, ibid., V, 883-885.

14. Board of Trade to Montgomerie, May 28, 1729, ibid., V, 876-877; Montgomerie to Board of Trade, October 20, 1729, ibid., V, 897; Board of Trade to Van Dam, December 18, 1732, ibid., V, 937.

15. Cosby to Board of Trade, December 18, 1732, ibid., V, 937.

16. Smith, *History,* II, 4. "Set-off" is a counterclaim by the defendant in an action for money damages which arises out of a transaction unconnected with the plaintiff's cause of action. The right of set-off was equitable rather than legal in origin, but the statute 2 George II c. 22 permitted the defendant to set his debt off against that of the plaintiff in a common-law court.

17. See, for instance, James Alexander to Alderman Perry, December 4, 1733, Rutherfurd Collection, I, 169, NYHS.

18. New York Council to Duke of Newcastle, December 17, 1733, *N. Y. Col. Docs.,* V, 980-981.

19. [Lewis Morris,] *The Opinion and Agrument of the Chief Justice of the Province of New York, concerning the Jurisdiction of the Supream Court of the said Province, to determine Causes in a Course of Equity, Proceedings of the New Jersey Historical Society,* 55 (1937), 89-116; *Mr. Murray's Opinion Relating to the Courts of Justice in the Colony of New York* . . . [New York, 1734]; *Mr. Smith's Opinion Humbly Offered in the General Assembly* . . . [New York, 1734]; Smith, *History, II,* 13-15. The arguments for and against the equitable jurisdiction of the Supreme Court were extremely formalistic and based almost entirely on archaic notions of English constitutional law. For a brief discussion of the literature, see Katz, Introduction to Alexander, *Brief Narrative,* p. 206, n. 8.

20. Matthew's speech of October 21, 1735, in NYHS Colls., (1934), 235; Minute Book, 1720-1748, N. Y. Chancery, Hall of Records, New York City, New York County Clerk's Office; Orders in Chancery, N. Y., December 1720-June 1735, Klapper Library, Queens College, C.U.N.Y.

21. James Alexander to [Philip Livingston], draft, September 29, 1735, Rutherfurd Collection, II, 131, NYHS.

22. For the petition, signed by William Smith and James Alexander among others, see *New York Weekly Journal*, no. 107 (November 24, 1735). See also *New York Gazette*, No. 525 (November 10-17, 1735); *Assemb. Jour.*, I, 682, 685, 686-687. For Lewis Morris's speech, see *New York Weekly Journal*, no. 122 (March 8, 1735/6). The Attorney General's complaint was filed on February 26, 1734, amended and refiled on March 10, 1739/40: New York Chancery, Decrees before 1800, B-58, Klapper Library, Queens College, C.U.N.Y.

23. "Reply to Arguments about Courts of Equity," n.d., NYHS, *Colls*, (1935), 262, 260-261.

24. *Assemb. Jour.*, I, 707-708.

6. Law and the Enforcement of Morals in Early America

DAVID FLAHERTY

1. Max Farrand, ed., Preamble to *The Laws and Liberties of Massachusetts* (Cambridge, 1929).

2. John Winthrop, *The History of New England from 1630 to 1649*, ed. James Savage (Boston, 1826), II, 289.

3. See the discussion by Julius Goebel, Jr., "King's Law and Local Custom in Seventeenth-Century New England," in David L. Flaherty, ed., *Essays in the History of Early American Law* (Chapel Hill, 1969), 92n; also George L. Haskins, "The Beginnings of Partible Inheritance in the American Colonies," ibid., 237n.

4. *Records of the Governor and Company of the Massachusetts Bay in New England*, ed. Nathaniel B. Shurtleff (Boston, 1853-1854), 87, 93.

5. The New Haven Colony did adopt Cott's draft until the authorities had an opportunity to shape the general stipulations from the Mosaic Code into particular statutes. See Isabel Calder, "John Cotton and the New Haven Colony," *New England Quarterly*, 3 (1930), 87, 93.

6. This identification of sin with crime was primarily a theoretical conception that legislators did not push to absurd lengths. It remained possible, for example, to sin without committing a crime. Increase Mather, in his famous sermon on drunkenness in 1673, made clear that "a man may be deeply and damnably guilty of this evil in the sight of God, though it should never proceed to those outrageous out-breakings, whereby men cannot but observe it" (Increase Mather, *Woe Unto Drunkards* [Cambridge, 1673], 40).

7. William H. Whitmore, ed., *The Colonial Laws of Massachusetts Reprinted from the Edition of 1660* . . . (Boston, 1889), 231; idem, *The Colonial Laws of Massachusetts, Reprinted from the Edition of 1672* . . . (Boston, 1887), 54-55.

8. Farrand, Preamble, *Laws and Liberties*; Williston Walker, ed., *The Creeds and Platforms of Congregationalism* (New York, 1893), 236. See also, on the separate roles of church and state, John Cotton, *A Discourse about Civil Government* (Cambridge, Mass., 1633), passim; also David Hall's comments on church and state in New England in the introduction to Perry Miller, *Orthodoxy in Massachusetts* (Harper Torchbooks: New York, 1970), xix.

9. See Roland A. Marchant, *The Church under the Law: Justice, Administration and Discipline in the Diocese of York, 1560-1640* (Cambridge, Eng., 1969), 223-224, and George L. Haskins, "Precedents in English Ecclesiastical Practices for Criminal Punishments in Early Massachusetts," Morris D. Forkosch, ed., *Essays in Legal History of Honor of Felix Frankfurter* (Indianapolis, 1966), 322.

10. In fact, given certain popular views concerning theocratic tendencies in New England, it is amusing to note that one of the few instances of a minister serving in public office occurred in Virginia. In 1694 the Reverend James Blair, the commissary of the Anglican Church in Virginia, was made a member of the Council, which constituted the upper house of the General Assembly and the General Court of the colony. This practice was followed with all succeeding commissaries. George M. Brydon, *Virginia's Mother Church* (Richmond, 1947), I, 310.

11. See Perry Miller, "Religion and Society in the Early Literature of Virginia," in Miller, *Errand into the Wilderness* (Cambridge, Mass., 1956), 129.

12. Solomon Stoddard, *The Way for a People* (Boston, 1703), 9. See also Cotton Mather, *Bonifacius: An Essay upon the Good* (1710), ed. David Levin (Cambridge, Mass., 1966), 133; also Joseph Moss, *An Election Sermon . . . at Hartford* (New London, 1715), 34.

13. Farrand, Preamble, *Laws and Liberties*.

14. Arthur P. Scott, *Criminal Law in Colonial Virginia* (Chicago, 1930), 291; see also 28.

15. See, for example, William W. Hening, comp., *The Statutes-at-Large: Being a Collection of All the Laws of Virginia, 1619-1792*, 13 vols. (1819-1823), facsimile reprint ed. (Charlottesville, 1969), II, 114-115 (1662); III, 73-74 (1691), 139-140 (1696), 361 (1705); also Thomas Bacon, ed., *Laws of Maryland at Large, 1637-1763* (Annapolis, Md., 1765), 1715, chap. 27.

16. Farrand, *Laws and Liberties*, pp. 5-6. Bestiality, sodomy, and rape were also capital offenses. The Duke's Laws of 1665 in New York made adultery a capital offense. See *The Colonial Laws of New York from the Year 1664 to the Revolution* (Albany, 1894), I, 21.

17. A man and woman were executed for adultery in Massachusetts in 1644 in a particularly flagrant case. See Winthrop, *History of New England*, II, 157-159. In a few other cases there is no real evidence that the death penalty was either imposed or carried out.

18. Emil Oberholzer, Jr., *Delinquent Saints: Disciplinary Action in the Early Congregational Churches of Massachusetts* (New York, 1956), 305.

19. Bradford, *Of Plymouth Plantation*, 319. Adultery was not a capital offense in Plymouth.

20. Farrand, *Laws and Liberties*, 23. The Duke's Laws of 1665 had a similar provision. See the *Colonial Laws of New York*, I, 35.

21. Thorp L. Wolford, "The Laws and Liberties of 1648," in Flaherty, *Essays in Early American Law*, 183. See the valuable article by Keith W. Thomas, "The Double Standard," *Journal of the History of Ideas*, 20 (1959), 195-216; and John Demos, *A Little Commonwealth: Family Life in Plymouth Colony* (New York, 1970), 97.

22. On this topic, see Herbert K. Fitzroy, "The Punishment of Crime in Provincial Pennsylvania," *Pennsylvania Magazine of History and Biography*, 60 (1936), 247-253.

23. Lawrence H. Gipson, *Crime and Punishment in Provincial Pennsylvania* (Bethlehem, Pa., 1935), 7.

24. Fitzroy, "Punishment of Crime," 262. See James T. Mitchell and Henry Flanders, eds., *The Statutes at Large of Pennsylvania from 1682 to 1801* (Harrisburg, Pa., 1896-1915), II, 5-7, 180-182.

25. Scott, *Criminal Law*, 25; on this general point, see the excellent discussion, ibid., 22-29.

26. Wolford, "Laws and Liberties of 1648," 184.

27. Blackstone, *Commentaries*, IV, 163.

28. WIlliam H. Seiler, "The Anglican Parish in Virginia," in James Morton Smith, ed., *Seventeenth-Century America* (Chapel Hill, 1959), 134.

29. George Webb, *The Office and Authority of a Justice of Peace* (Williamsburg, 1736), 165.

30. Scott, *Criminal Law*, 279.

31. Farrand, *Laws and Liberties*, 47.

32. Farrand, Preamble, *Laws and Liberties*.

33. For a few exceptional cases in secular courts, see Arthur Cleveland, "Indictments for Adultery and Incest before 1650," *Law Quarterly Review*, 29 (1913), 57-60. In defense of their property rights, medieval lords of the manor exercised some temporal jurisdiction over sexual offenses by their serfs. Some early-seventeenth-century justices of the peace also assumed an unauthorized jurisdiction over incontinence. In general, see Goeffrey May, *Social Control of Sex Expression* (New York, 1931), Chap. 8.

34. Marchant, *The Church under the Law*, 219; see also James Fitzjames Stephen, *History of the Criminal Law of England* (London, 1883), II, 404, 411.

35. Samuel R. Gardiner, ed., *The Constitutional Documents of the Puritan Revolution, 1625-1660*, 3d ed. rev. (Oxford, 1958), 142. As late as September 7, 1761, an article in the *Boston Gazette* attacked the idea of ecclesiastical courts in America, associating them with severity, persecution, and the absence of religious liberty (Carl Briden-

baugh, *Mitre and Sceptre: Transatlantic Faiths, Ideas, Personalities, and Politics, 1689-1775* [New York, 1962], 219).

36. The Bristol parish court established by the General Court of Virginia in December 1656 was not an ecclesiastical court. It was an unsuccessful effort to create a county court for a parish in a frontier area instead of immediately setting up a new county (Brydon, *Virginia's Mother Church*, I, 97).

37. Ibid., 282. This episode is treated at length on 278-289.

38. The Duke's Laws of New York in 1665 vested the whole duty of presenting offenses against morals in churchwardens (see *The Colonial Laws of New York*, I, 26). Maryland associated ministers and vestrymen with the churchwardens (Bacon, *Laws of Maryland*, 1715, chap. 27).

39. Webb, *Justice of Peace*, p. 71. For the basic legislation concerning churchwardens, see Hening, *Statutes-at-Large of Virginia*, I, 240 (1643), 310 (1646); III, 139-140 (1696), 361 (1705); XII, 28 (1785).

40. See G. E. Howard, *A History of Matrimonial Institutions* (Chicago, 1904), II, 185; James Truslow Adams, *Provincial Society, 1690-1763* (New York, 1927), 159; George E. Woodbine, "The Suffolk County Court, 1671-1680," in Flaherty, *Essays in Early American Law*, 192; Edmund S. Morgan, "Puritans and Sex," *New England Quarterly*, 15 (1942), 595-596; Oberholzer, *Delinquent Saints*, 128; Edwin Powers, *Crime and Punishment in Early Massachusetts, 1620-1692: A Documentary History* (Boston, 1966), 404-416.

41. Oberholzer, *Delinquent Saints*, 111, and chap. 5.

42. Fitzroy, "Punishment of Crime," 262, 259. On the prevalence of prosecutions for fornication and adultery in colonial New Jersey, see Harry B. and Grace M. Weiss, *An Introduction to Crime and Punishment in Colonial New Jersey* (Trenton, 1960), 82-88.

43. Scott, *Criminal Law*, 280-281.

44. Semmes, *Crime and Punishment in Maryland*, 188, and on the prevalence of adultery, fornication, and bastardy, chap. 8.

45. *Archives of Maryland*, ed. W. H. Browne et al. (Baltimore, 1883–), XIX, 497.

46. See May, "Experiments in the Legal Control of Sex Expression," *Yale Law Journal*, 39 (1929), 227n; Sumner C. Powell, *Puritan Village: The Formation of a New England Town* (Middletown, Conn., 1963), 69: Carl Bridenbaugh, *Vexed and Troubled Englishmen, 1590-1642* (New York, 1968), 40-41, 361-374.

47. See May, *Social Control of Sex Expression*, 194-199.

48. Leon Radzinowicz, *A History of English Criminal Law and Its Administration from 1750* (London, 1948–), II, 3-4.

49. Scott, *Criminal Law*, 254-255, 291-292; Hening, *Statutes-at-Large of Virginia*, I, 44 (1658); IV, 213 (1727).

50. Whitmore, *Laws of Massachusetts, 1660*, 231; *Laws of Massachusetts, 1672*, 54-55.

51. *The Diary of Samuel Sewall*, Collections of the Massachusetts Historical Society, 5th ser. V-VII (Boston, 1878-1882), II, 419-420.

52. Scott, *Criminal Law*, 281.

53. This statute in 1576 punished both the mother and reputed father of a bastard (Webb, *Justice of Peace*, 44-45.)

54. Scott, *Criminal Law*, 280. See in particular the major act against bastardy in 1769, in Hening, *Statutes-at-Large of Virginia*, VIII, 374.

55. Whitmore, *Laws of Massachusetts, 1672*, 55; for the similar situation in England, see Bridenbaugh, *Vexed and Troubled Englishmen*, 370. For the lack of impartiality in the remission of fines and infliction of whipping, see Jules Zanger, "Crime and Punishment in Early Massachusetts," *William and Mary Quarterly*, 3d ser. 22 (1965), 476-477.

56. Nicholas Trott, ed., *The Laws of the Province of South Carolina* (Charleston, S.C., 1736), 96.

57. Quoted in Brydon, *Virginia's Mother Church*, I, 404.

58. Writing about England in this same period, Keith Thomas has pointed out "the tradition of promiscuity" among the lower classes and the widespread practice of prostitution (Thomas, "Double Standard," 206, 198). For evidence of prostitution in the colonies, see Carl Bridenbaugh, *Cities in the Wilderness: The First Century of Urban Life in America, 1625-1742* (New York, 1938),

72-73, 226-227, 388-389; also *Cities in Revolt: Urban Life in America, 1743-1776* (New York, 1955), 121-122, 316-319.

59. Marquis de Chastellux, *Travels in North America in the Years 1780, 1781, and 1782*, ed. Howard C. Rice, Jr. (Chapel Hill, 1963), I, 120, 228, 288, 358.

60. Carl Van Doren, *Benjamin Franklin* (New York, 1938), 91, 290.

61. *The Secret Diary of William Byrd of Westover, 1709-1712*, ed. L. B. Wright and Marion Tinling (Richmond, Va., 1941), 101, 169, 337, 425.

62. In a letter late in his life to Judge Benjamin Lynde of Massachusetts, Byrd reminded his old friend of their activities with ladies of pleasure during student days at the Middle Temple in the 1690s ([Byrd,] *The London Diary [1717-172] and Other Writings*, ed. L. B. Wright and M. Tinling [New York, 1958], 9 and passim).

63. The widow Thomas's exploits can be followed in the records of the Suffolk County court; Samuel E. Morison, ed., *Records of the Suffolk County Court, 1671-1680 . . ., Publications of the Colonial Society of Massachusetts*, XXIX-XXX (Boston, 1933).

64. *Diary of Cotton Mather*, ed. Worthington C. Ford, *Collections of the Massachusetts Historical Society*, 7th ser. VII-VIII (Boston, 1911-1912), II, 160, 235, 229, 283.

65. Diary of Lt. John Peebles, Dec. 31, 1776, microfilm, Library of Congress, quoted in *William and Mary Quarterly*, 3d ser. 26 (1969), 441.

66. John Williams, *Warnings to the Unclean* (Boston, 1699), 22, 19-20, 8. Williams (1664-1729) was a Harvard graduate and the minister of Deerfield.

67. See H. B. Parkes, "New England in the 1730s," *New England Quarterly*, 3 (1930), 408.

68. Webb, *Justice of Peace*, p. 189.

69. See Stoddard, *Way for a People*, 21.

70. Suggestive evidence of Virginia appears in: *Baroness von Riedesel and the American Revolution: Journal and Correspondence of a Tour of Duty, 1776-1783*, ed. Marvin L. Brown, Jr., and Marta Huth (Chapel Hill, 1965), 86 (1779); *The Journal of John Woolman*, ed. Janet Whitney (Chicago,

1950), 52 (1757); John Davis, *Travels of Four Years and a Half in the United States of America during 1798, 1799, 1800, 1801 and 1802*, ed. A. J. Morrison (New York, 1909), 400, 413-424; *The Journal of Nicholas Cresswell, 1774-1777* (New York, 1924), 164-165; *Journal and Letters of Philip Vickers Fithian, 1773-1774: A Plantation Tutor of the Old Dominion*, ed. Hunter D. Farish (New York, 1957), 86, 185-188. See also Lorenzo J. Greene, *The Negro in Colonial New England* (New York, 1942), 204-210. The best treatment of interracial sexual activity is in Winthrop D. Jordan, *White Over Black: American Attitudes toward the Negro, 1550-1812* (Chapel Hill, 1968), 136-178.

71. Bacon, *Laws of Maryland*, 1715, chap. 44, secs. 26-28; Mitchell and Flanders, *Statutes of Pennsylvania*, IV, 63.

72. For a similar situation in eighteenth-century England, see Radzinowicz, *English Criminal Law*, II, 270-284; see the general discussion in David H. Flaherty, *Privacy in Colonial New England* (Charlottesville, 1971), chap. 7.

73. Henry Hartwell, James Blair, and Edward Chilton, *The Present State of Virginia, and the College*, ed. Hunter D. Farish (Williamsburg, 1940), 66-67. For a similar comment on the Congregational ministry in New England, see Cotton Mather, *A Faithful Monitor* (Boston, 1704), 38.

74. See Flaherty, *Privacy in Colonial New England*, chap. 7.

75. See the warnings of divine wrath conveyed in Samual Danforth, *The Cry of Sodom Enquired Into* (Cambridge, 1674), and Williams, *Warnings to the Unclean*.

7. Popular Uprisings and Civil Authority in Eighteenth-Century America

PAULINE MAIER

1. See the following by George Rudé: *The Crowd in the French Revolution* (Oxford, 1959); "The London 'Mob' of the Eighteenth Century," *Historical Journal*, 2 (1959), 1-18; *Wilkes and Liberty: A Social Study of 1763 to 1774* (Oxford, 1962); *The Crowd in His-*

tory: *A Study of Popular Disturbances in France and England, 1730-1848* (New York 1964), See also E. J. Hobsbawm, *Primitive Rebels: Studies in Archaic Forms of Social Movement in the 19th and 20th Centuries* (New York 1959), esp. "The City Mob," 108-125. For recent discussions of the colonial mob, see Bernard Bailyn, *Pamphlets of the American Revolution* (Cambridge, Mass., 1965), I, 581-584; Jesse Lemisch, "Jack Tar in the Street: Merchant Seamen in the Politics of Revolutionary America," *William and Mary Quarterly,* 3d ser. 25 (1968), 371-407; Gordon S. Wood, "A Note on Mobs in the American Revolution," *William and Mary Quarterly,* 3d ser. 23 (1966), 635-642, and more recently Wood's *Creation of the American Republic, 1776-1787* (Chapel Hill, 1969), passim, but esp. 319-328. Wood offers an excellent analysis of the place of mobs and extralegal assemblies in the development of American constitutionalism. Hugh D. Graham and Ted R. Gurr, *Violence in America: Historical and Comparative Perspectives* (New York, 1969), primarily discuss uprisings of the nineteenth and twentieth centuries, but see the chapters by Richard M. Brown, "Historical Patterns of Violence in America," 45-84, and "The American Vigilante Tradition," 154-226; reprinted in abridged form in this volume.

2. Carl Bridenbaugh, *Cities in the Wilderness: The First Century of Urban Life in America, 1625-1742* (New York 1964), 70-71, 223-224, 382-384; idem, *Cities in Revolt: Urban Life in America, 1743-1776* (New York 1964), 113-118; Charles J. Hoadly, ed., *The Public Records of the Colony of Connecticut* (Hartford, 1872), VI, 332-333, 341-348.

3. See particularly Richard M. Brown, *The South Carolina Regulators* (Cambridge, Mass., 1963). There is no published study of the New Jersey land riots, which lasted over a decade and resulted above all from the protracted inability of the royal government to settle land disputes stemming from conflicting proprietary grants made in the late seventeenth century. See, however, "A State of Facts concerning the Riots and Insurrections in New Jersey, and the Remedies Attempted to Restore the Peace of the Province," William A. Whitehead et al., eds., *Archives of the State of New Jersey* (Newark 1883), VII, 207-226. On other rural insurrections, see Irving Mark, *Agrarian Conflicts in Colonial New York 1711-1775* (New York 1940), chaps. 4 and 5; Staughton Lynd, "The Tenant Rising at Livingston Manor," *New York Historical Society Quarterly,* 48 (1964), 163-177; Matt Bushnell Jones, *Vermont in the Making, 1750-1777* (Cambridge, Mass., 1939), chaps. 12 and 13; John R. Dunbar, ed., *The Paxton Papers* (The Hague, 1957), esp. 3-51.

4. Richard L. Morton, *Colonial Virginia* (Chapel Hill, 1960), I, 303-304; Jonathan Smith, "The Depression of 1785 and Daniel Shays' Rebellion," *William and Mary Quarterly,* 3d ser. 5 (1948), 86-87, 91.

5. Bridenbaugh, *Cities in Revolt,* 114; idem, *Cities in the Wilderness,* 196, 383, 388-389; Edmund S. and Helen M. Morgan, *The Stamp Act Crisis,* rev. ed. (New York, 1963), 159; Anne Rowe Cunningham, ed., *Letters and Diary of John Rowe, Boston Merchant, 1759-1762, 1764-1779* (Boston, 1903), 218. On the marriage riots, see *New-York Gazette* (New York City), July 11, 1765 — and note that when the reporter speaks of persons "concern'd in such unlawful Enterprises" he clearly is referring to the husbands, not their "Disciplinarians." On the Rogerenes, see item in *Connecticut Gazette* (New Haven), April 5, 1766, reprinted in Lawrence H. Gipson, *Jared Ingersoll* (New Haven, 1920), 195, n. 1.

6. John Adams, "Novanglus," in Charles F. Adams, ed., *The Works of John Adams* (Boston, 1850-1856), IV, 76-77; Salem news of January 25 and February 1, 1774, in *Providence Gazette* (Rhode Island), February 5, and February 12, 1774.

7. Letter from "Friend to the Borough and County of Norfolk," in Purdie and Dixon's *Virginia Gazette Postscript* (Williamsburg), September 8, 1768, which gives the fullest account. This letter answered an earlier letter from Norfolk, August 6, 1768, available in Rind's *Virginia Gazette Supplement* (Williamsburg), August 25, 1768. See also letter of Cornelius Calvert in Purdie and Dixon's *Virginia Gazette* (Williamsburg), January 9, 1772. Divisions over the inoculation seemed to follow more general political lines. See

Patrick Henderson, "Smallpox and Patriotism: The Norfolk Riots, 1768-1769," *Virginia Magazine of History and Biography*, 73 (1965), 413-424.

8. James Madison to Thomas Jefferson, March 19, 1787, in Julian P. Boyd et al., eds., *The Papers of Thomas Jefferson* (Princeton, 1950-), XI, 223.

9. Bernard Knollenberg, *Origin of the American Revolution: 1759-1766* (New York, 1965), 126, 129. See also, Robert G. Albion, *Forests and Sea Power* (Cambridge, Mass., 1926), 262-263, 265. Joseph J. Malone, *Pine Trees and Politics* (Seattle, 1964), includes less detail on the forceful resistance to the acts.

10. Admiralty to Governor George Thomas, September 26, 1743, in Samuel Hazard et al., eds., *Pennsylvania Archives* (Philadelphia, 1852-1949), I, 639. For accounts of the Knowles riot, see Governor William Shirley to Josiah Willard, November 19, 1747, Shirley's Proclamation of November 21, 1747, and his letter to the Board of Trade, December 1, 1747, in Charles H. Lincoln, ed., *The Correspondence of William Shirley . . . 1731-1760* (New York 1912,) I, 406-419; see also Thomas Hutchinson, *History of the Province of Massachusetts Bay*, ed. Lawrence S. Mayo (Cambridge, Mass., 1936), II, 330-333; and *Reports of the Record Commissioners of Boston* (Boston, 1885), XIV, 127-130. David Lovejoy, *Rhode Island Politics and the American Revolution, 1760-1776* (Providence, 1958), 36-39; and, on the *Maidstone* in particular, see "O. G." in *Newport Mercury* (Rhode Island), June 10, 1765. Bridenbaugh, *Cities in Revolt*, 309-311; documents on the *St. John* episode in *Records of the Colony of Rhode Island and Providence Plantations* (Providence, 1856-1865), VI, 427-430. George G. Wolkins, "The Seizure of John Hancock's Sloop 'Liberty,'" *Proceedings of the Massachusetts Historical Society*, 55 (1921-1923), 239-284. See also Lemisch, "Jack Tar," 391-393; and Neil R. Stout, "Manning the Royal Navy in North America, 1763-1775," *American Neptune*, 23 (1963), 179-181.

11. Heathcote letter from Newport, September 7, 1719, *Records of the Colony of Rhode Island*, IV, 259-260; Lovejoy, *Rhode Island Politics*, 35-39. There is an excellent summary of the *Polly* incident in Morgan, *Stamp Act Crisis*, 59, 64-67; see also *Providence Gazette*, April 27, 1765. On the Falmouth incident, see the letter from the collector and comptroller of Falmouth, August 19, 1766, Treasury Group I (hereafter T. 1/) Class 453, Piece 182, Public Records Office (hereafter cited with numbers only). See also the account in Appendix I of Josiah Quincy, Jr., *Reports of the Cases Argued and Adjudged in the Superior Court of Judicature of the Province of Massachusetts Bay between 1761 and 1772* (Boston, 1865), 446-447. W. Noel Sainsbury et al., eds., *Calendar of State Papers, Colonial Series, America and the West Indies* (London, 1910,) 1701, no. 1042, xi, a. A summary of one of the New Haven informer attacks is in Willard M. Wallace, *Traitorous Hero: The Life and Fortunes of Benedict Arnold* (New York, 1954), 20-23. Arnold's statement on the affair which he led is in Malcolm Decker, *Benedict Arnold, Son of the Havens* (Terrytown, N. Y., 1932), 27-29. Gipson, in *Jared Ingersoll*, 277-278, relates the later incidents. For the New London informer attacks, see documents of July 1769 in T. 1/471. On the Saville affair, see Saville to collector and comptroller of customs in Newport, May 18, 1769, T. 1/471, and *New York Journal* (New York City), July 6, 1769. On later Rhode Island incidents, see Dudley and John Nicholl to governor of Rhode Island, August 1, 1770, T. 1/471. Dudley to commissioners of customs at Boston, Newport, April 11, 1771, T. 1/482. On the destruction of the *Liberty*, see documents in T. 1/471, esp. comptroller and collector to the governor, July 21, 1769.

12. On Philadelphia violence, see William Sheppard to commissioners of customs, April 21, 1769, T. 1/471; Deputy Collector at Philadelphia John Swift to commissioners of customs at Boston, October 13, 1769, ibid.; and on a particularly brutal attack on the son of customsman John Hatton, see Deputy Collector John Swift to Boston customs commissioners, November 15, 1770, and related documents in T. 1/476. See also Alfred S. Martin, "The King's Customs: Philadelphia, 1763-1774," *William and Mary Quarterly*, 3d ser. 5 (1948), 201-216. Documents on the

Maryland episode are in T. 1/513, including the following: Richard Reeve to Grey Cooper, April 19, 1775; extracts from a council meeting, March 16, 1775; deposition of Robert Stratford Byrne, Surveyor of his Majesty's Customs at Sassafras and Bohemia, and Byrne to customs commissioners, March 17, 1775. On the Virginia incident, see William Smith to Jeremiah Morgan, April 3, 1766, Colonial Office Group, Class 5, Piece 1331, 80, Public Record Office (hereafter cited as ·C.O. 5/1331, 80); W. W. Abbot, *The Royal Governors of Georgia, 1754-1775* (Chapel Hill, 1959), 174-175. These customs riots remained generally separate from the more central intercolonial opposition to Britain that emerged in 1765. Isolated individuals such as John Brown of Providence and Maximilian Calvert of Norfolk were involved in both the organized intercolonial Sons of Liberty and in leading mobs against customs functionaries or informers. These roles, however, for the most part were unconnected, that is, there was no radical program of customs obstruction per se. Outbreaks were above all local responses to random provocations and, at least before the Townshend duties, usually devoid of explicit ideological justifications.

13. Hobsbawm, *Primitive Rebels*, 111. For a different effort to see class division as relevant in eighteenth-century uprisings, see Lemisch, "Jack Tar," 25 387.

14. "Friends to the borough and county of Norfolk," Purdie and Dixon's *Virginia Gazette Postscript*, September 8, 1768. Wentworth quoted in Knollenberg, *Origin of American Revolution*, 124-125. Lemisch, "Jack Tar," 383-385. Shirley to Duke of Newcastle, December 31, 1747, in Lincoln, ed., *Shirley Correspondence*, I, 420-423. Dora Mae Clark, "The Impressment of Seamen in the American Colonies," *Essays in Colonial History Presented to Charles McLean Andrews* (New Haven, 1931), 199-200; John Swift to Boston customs commissioners, November 15, 1770, T. 1/476.

15. Malone, *White Pines*, 112. "Friends to the borough and County of Norfolk," Purdie and Dixon's *Virginia Gazette Postscript*, September 8, 1768; Calvert letter, ibid., January 9, 1772. Captain Jeremiah Morgan,

quoted in Lemisch, "Jack Tar," 25, 391; and William Smith to Morgan, April 3, 1766, C.O. 5/1331, 80. Decker, *Benedict Arnold*, 27-29; deposition of Capt. William Reid on the *Liberty* affair, July 21, 1769, T. 1/471; Ephraim Bowen's narrative on the Gaspée affair, *Records of the Colony of Rhode Island*, VII, 68-73; Charles Dudley to Boston customs commissioners, April 11, 1771, T. 1/482, and deposition by Byrne, T. 1/513. Edward Carrington to Jefferson, June 9, 1787, Boyd et al., eds., *Jefferson Papers*, XI, 408; see also Smith, "Depression of 1785," 88 — of the twenty-one men indicted for treason in Worcester during the court's April term in 1787, fifteen were "gentlemen" and only six "yeomen."

16. Gov. Samuel Ward's report to the Treasury lords, October 23, 1765, Ward Manuscripts, Box 1, fol. 58, Rhode Island Historical Society, Providence. See also deposition of Daniel Vaughn of Newport — Vaughn was the gunner at Fort George — July 8, 1764, Chalmers Papers, Rhode Island, fol. 41, New York Public Library, New York City. For British official accounts of the affair, see Lieut. Hill's version in James Munro, ed., *Acts of the Privy Council of England, Colonial Series* (London, 1912), VI, 374-376, and the report of John Robinson and John Nicholl to the customs commissioners, August 30, 1765, Privy Council Group, Class I, Piece 51, Bundle I (53a), Public Record Office. Hill, whose report was drawn up soon after the incident, does not contradict Ward's narrative, but seems oblivious of any warrant-granting process on shore; Robinson and Nicholl — whose report was drawn up over a year later and in the midst of the Stamp Act turmoil — claimed that a recent customs seizure had precipitated the attack upon the *St. John*.

17. On the Knowles and *Maidstone* incidents, see above, n. 10. On the *Liberty* affair, see documents in T. 1/471, esp. the deposition of Capt. William Reid, July 21, 1769, and that of John Carr, the second mate, who indicates the mob soon forgot its scheme of delivering the crew members to the magistrates.

18. Malone, *White Pines*, 8-9, and passim. *Records of the Colony of Rhode Island*, VIII,

60, 62-63, 174-175, including the deposition of Deputy Governor Darius Sessions, June 12, 1772, and Admiral Montagu to Governor Wanton, April 8, 1772. Also, Wanton to Hillsborough, June 16, 1772, and Ephraim Bowen's narrative, ibid., 63-73, 90-92, *Providence Gazette*, January 9, 1773.

19. Max Belloff, *Public Order and Popular Disturbances, 1660-1714* (London, 1938), passim; Albion, *Forests and Sea Power*, 263; J. H. Plumb, *England in the Eighteenth Century* (Baltimore, 1961; 1st ed., Oxford, 1950), 66.

20. See, for example, "A Pumpkin" in the *New London Gazette* (Connecticut), May 14, 18, 1773; "O. G." in *Newport Mercury*, June 10, 1765; *New London Gazette*, September 22, 1769; complaints of Marylander David Bevan, reprinted in Rind's *Virginia Gazette*, July 27, 1769, and *New London Gazette*, July 21, 1769. Stout, "Manning the Royal Navy," 174. For a similar accusation against a surveyor-general of the king's woods, see Albion, *Forests and Sea Power*, 262.

21. Joseph Reed to the president of Congress, October 21, 1779, in Hazard et al., eds., *Pennsylvania Archives*, VII, 762. Five years earlier Reed had tried to impress upon Lord Dartmouth the importance of constraining crown agents in the colonies if any reconciliation were to be made between Britain and the colonies. See his letter to Earl of Dartmouth, April 4, 1774, in William B. Reed, *Life and Correspondence of Joseph Reed* (Philadelphia, 1847), I, 56-57. For a similar plea, again from a man close to the American Revolutionary leadership, see Stephen Sayre to Lord Dartmouth, December 13, 1766, Dartmouth Papers, D 1778/2/258, William Salt Library, Stafford, England.

22. Rudé, *Crowd in History*, 60, 253-254. The restraint exercised by eighteenth-century mobs has often been commented upon. See, for example, Wood, "A Note on Mobs," 636-637.

23. Joseph Harrison's testimony in Wolkins, "Seizure of Hancock's Sloop 'Liberty,'" 254.

24. Jay to Jefferson, December 14, 1786, Boyd et al., eds., *Jefferson Papers,- X, 597; Beloff, Public Order*, 30. John Swift to Boston customs commissioners, November 15,

1770, Governor William Franklin's Proclamation, November 17, 1770, and John Hatton to Boston custom commissioners, November 20, 1770, T. 1/476. The last-mentioned riot occurred in November 1762. In October a cartel ship from Havana had stopped for repairs. On November 21 a rumor spread that the Spaniards were murdering the inhabitants, which drew seamen from His Majesty's Ship *Arundel*, also in the harbor, into town, where the seamen drove the Spaniards into a house, set fire to it, and apparently intended to blow it up. A dignitary of the Spanish colonial service, who had been a passenger on the cartel ship, was beaten and robbed of some money and valuables. Local men tried to quell the riot without success. It was eventually put down by militiamen from Norfolk. See "A Narrative of a Riot in Virginia in November 1762," T. 1/476.

25. Burke and others to the same effect, quoted in Jerome J. Nadelhaft, "The Revolutionary Era in South Carolina, 1775-1788" (Ph.D. diss., University of Wisconsin, 1965), 151-152. See also account of the "Ford Wilson" riot of October 1779 in J. Thomas Scharf and Thompson Westcott, *History of Philadelphia, 1609-1884* (Philadelphia, 1884), I, 401-403.

26. Rudé, *Crowd in History*, 255-257.

27. On the "hue and cry," see Frederick Pollock and Frederic W. Maitland, *The History of English Law before the Time of Edward I* (Cambridge, Eng., 1968; 1st ed., 1895), II, 578-580, and William Blackstone, *Commentaries on the Laws of England* (Philadelphia, 1771), IV, 290-291; John Shy, *Toward Lexington: The Role of the British Army in the Coming of the American Revolution* (Princeton, 1965), 40. The English militia underwent a period of decay after 1670, but it was revived in 1757. See J. R. Western, *The English Militia in the Eighteenth Century* (London, 1965).

28. Greenleaf's deposition, T. 1/446; *Providence Gazette*, August 24, 1765; Western, *English Militia*, 74.

29. Governor William Shirley explained the militia's failure to appear during the opening stages of the Knowles riot by citing the militiamen's opposition to impressment

and their consequent sympathy for the rioters. See his letter to the Lords of Trade, December 1, 1747, in Lincoln, ed., *Shirley Correspondence,* I, 417-418. The English militia was also unreliable. It worked well against invasions and unpopular rebellions, but it was less likely to support the government when official orders "clashed with the desires of the citizens" or when ordered to protect unpopular minorities. Sir Robert Walpole believed "that if called on to suppress smuggling, protect the turnpikes, or enforce the gin act, the militia would take the wrong side" (Western, *English Militia,* 72-73).

30. Shirley to Josiah Willard, November 19, 1747, Lincoln, ed., *Shirley Correspondence,* I, 407; Bernard's orders in *Providence Gazette,* April 27, 1765.

31. Shy, *Toward Lexington,* 39-40, 44, 47, 74; Amherst, quoted in J. C. Long, *Lord Jeffery Amherst* (New York, 1933), 124.

32. Shy, *Toward Lexington,* 44, Beloff, *Public Order,* 157-158; Bridenbaugh, *Cities in Revolt,* 297; C. F. Adams, ed., *Works of Adams,* IV, 74-75; V, 209.

33. The definition of the common law of riot most frequently cited — for example, by John Adams in the massacre trials — was from William Hawkins, *A Treatise of the Pleas of the Crown* (London, 1716), I, 155-159; see also, Blackstone, *Commentaries,* IV, 146-147, and Edward Coke, *The Third Part of the Institutes of the Laws of England* (London, 1797), 176.

34. Clark, "Impressment of Seamen," 198-224; Stout, "Manning the Royal Navy," 178-179; and Leonard W. Labaree, ed., *Royal Instructions to British Colonial Governors, 1670-1776* (New York, 1935), I, 442-443.

35. L. Kinvin Wroth and Hiller B. Zobel, eds., *Legal Papers of John Adams* (Cambridge, Mass., 1965), III, 253. Account of the Norfolk incident by George Abyvon, September 5, 1767, in Purdie and Dixon's *Virginia Gazette,* October 1, 1767. Capt. Morgan quoted in Lemisch, "Jack Tar," 391; Munro, ed., *Acts of the Privy Council, Colonial Series,* VI, 374; Gov. Samuel Ward to Treasury Lords, October 23, 1765, Ward MSS. Box I, fol. 58.

36. Knollenberg, *Origin of the Revolution,* 122-130; Albion, *Forests and Sea Power,* 255-258.

37. *New York Journal,* August 18, 1768 (the writer was allegedly drawing together arguments that had recently appeared in the British press); and *New York Journal Supplement* January 4, 1770. Note also that Jefferson accepted Shays's Rebellion as a sign of health in American institutions only after he had been assured by men like Jay that the insurgents had acted purposefully and moderately, and after he had concluded that the uprising represented no continuous threat to established government. "An insurrection in one of the 13. states in the course of 11. years that they have subsisted amounts to one in any particular state in 143 years, say a century and a half," he calculated. "This would not be near as many as has happened in every other government that has ever existed," and clearly posed no threat to the constitutional order as a whole (To David Hartley, July 2, 1787, Boyd et al., eds., *Jefferson Papers,* XI, 526).

38. John Locke, *The Second Treatise of Government,* paragraphs 223-225; "A State of Facts concerning the Riots ... in New Jersey," *New Jersey Archives,* VII, 217. *New York Journal Supplement, January 4, 1770. Johnson to William Pitkin, April 29, 1768, Collections of the Massachusetts Historical Society,* 5th ser. IX (1885), 275. Adams as "Determinus" in *Boston Gazette,* August 8, 1768; and Harry A. Cushing, ed., *The Writings of Samuel Adams* (New York, 1904-1908), I, 237; Jay to Jefferson, October 27, 1786, Boyd et al., eds., *Jefferson Papers,* X, 488.

39. Wroth and Zobel, eds., *Adams Legal Papers,* III, 249-250; *New York Journal Supplement,* August 18, 1768; Jefferson to Abigail Adams, February 22, 1787, Boyd et al., eds., *Jefferson Papers,* XI, 174. C. F. Adams, ed., *Works of Adams,* IV, 77, 80 (quoting Algernon Sydney).

40. Jefferson to Edward Carrington, January 16, 1787, Boyd et al., eds., *Jefferson Papers,* XI, 49, and Reverend James Madison to Jefferson, March 28, 1787, ibid., 252. Wroth and Zobel, eds., *Adams Legal Papers,* III, 250. Quincy's address to the jury

in the soldiers' trial after the Boston Massacre in Josiah Quincy, *Memoir of the Life of Josiah Quincy, Junior, of Massachusetts Bay, 1744-1775,* ed. Eliza Susan Quincy, 3d ed. (Boston, 1875), 46. See also Massachusetts Assembly's similar statement in its address to Gov. Hutchinson, April 24, 1770, Hutchinson, *History of Massachusetts Bay,* ed. Mayo, III, 365-366. This eighteenth-century devotion to political "jealousy" resembles the doctrine of "vigilance" that was defended by nineteenth-century vigilante groups; see Graham and Gurr, *Violence in America,* 179-183.

41. Jefferson to William Stephen Smith, November 13, 1787, Boyd et al., eds., *Jefferson Papers,* XII, 356, Jefferson to Carrington, January 16, 1787, ibid., XI, 49, Jefferson to James Madison, January 30, 1787, ibid., 92-93; Taylor's remarks in "History of Violence," *The Listener,* 129 (1968), 701. "Members of the House of Lords . . . said . . . if the people really don't like something then they wreck our carriages and tear off our wigs and throw stones through the windows of our town-houses. And this is an essential thing to have if you are going to have a free country." Hutchinson to [John or Robert] Grant, July 27, 1768, Massachusetts Archives, XXVI, 317, State House, Boston; see also the related story about John Selden, the famous seventeenth-century lawyer, told to the House of Commons in January 1775 by Lord Camden and recorded by Josiah Quincy, Jr., in the "Journal of Josiah Quincy, Jun., during his Voyage and Residence in England from September 28th, 1774, to March 3d, 1775," *Proceedings of the Massachusetts Historical Society,* 50 (1916-1917), 462-263. Selden was asked what lawbook contained the laws for resisting tyranny. He replied he did not know, "but I'll tell [you] what is most certain, that it has always been the custom of England — and the Custom of England is the Law of the Land."

42. On the developing distinction Americans drew between what was legal and constitutional, see Wood, *Creation of the American Republic,* 261-268.

43. *New York Journal Supplement,* January 4, 1770; Wroth and Zobel, eds., *Adams Legal Papers,* III, 250, and C. F. Adams, ed., *Works of Adams* VI, 151. Adams's views were altered in 1815, ibid., X, 181. It is noteworthy that the Boston town meeting condemned the Knowles rioters not simply for their method of opposing impressment but for insulting the governor and the legislature, and the Massachusetts Assembly acted against the uprising only after Governor Shirley had left Boston and events seemed to be "tending to the destruction of all government and order" (Hutchinson, *History of Massachusetts Bay,* ed. Mayo, II, 332-333. *Acts and Resolves of the Province of Massachusetts Bay,* III. 647, chap. 18 of the Province laws, 1752-1753, "An Act for Further Preventing all Riotous, Tumultuous and Disorderly Assemblies or Companies of Persons . . .)" This act, which was inspired particularly by Pope's Day violence, was renewed after the Boston Massacre in 1770 even though the legislature refused to renew its main Riot Act of 1751, ibid., IV, 87.

44. Arthur M. Schlesinger, "Political Mobs and the American Revolution, 1765-1776," *Proceedings of the American Philosophical Society,* 99 (1955), 246; Charles M. Andrews, *The Colonial Background of the American Revolution,* rev. ed. (New Haven, 1939), 176; Charles M. Andrews, "The Boston Merchants and the Non-Importation Movement," *Transactions of the Colonial Society of Massachusetts,* 19 (1916-1917), 241; Hobsbawm, *Primitive Rebels,* 111, 123-124.

45. Hutchinson to Thomas Pownall, [September or October 1765], *Mass. Archives,* XXVI, 157. Pauline Maier, "From Resistance to Revolution: American Radicals and the Development of Intercolonial Opposition to Britain, 1765-1776" (Ph.D. diss., Harvard University, 1968), I, 37-45, 72-215.

46. C. F. Adams, ed., *Works of Adams,* IV, 51; Reverend Samuel Langdon's election sermon to the Third Massachusetts Provincial Congress, May 31, 1775, quoted in Richard Frothingham, *Life and Times of Joseph Warren* (Boston, 1865), 499; Samuel Adams to Noah Webster, April 30, 1784, Cushing, ed., *Writings of Samuel Adams,* IV, 305-306. On Gadsden, see Richard

Walsh, *Charleston's Sons of Liberty* (Columbia, 1959), 87.

47. *New York Journal Supplement,* January 4, 1770; Jay to Jefferson, October 27, 1786, Boyd et al., eds., *Jefferson Papers,* X, 488; Johnson to William Pitkin, July 23, 1768, *Collections of The Massachusetts Historical Society,* 5th ser. IX, 294-295.

48. *The Statutes at Large* [of Great Britain] (London, 1786), V, 4-6; Hoadly, ed., *Public Records of Connecticut,* VI, 346-348 for the law, and see also 332-333, 341-348; *Acts and Resolves of Massachusetts Bay,* III, 544-546, for the Riot Act of 1751, and see also Hutchinson, *History of Massachusetts Bay,* ed. Mayo, III, 6-7; and *Acts and Laws of the Commonwealth of Massachusetts* (Boston, 1893), 87-88, for Act of 1786; "A State of Facts Concerning the Riots . . . in New Jersey," *New Jersey Archives,* VII, 211-212, 221-222; *The Statutes at Large of Pennsylvania* . . . (n.p., 1899), VI, 325-328; William A. Saunders, ed., *The Colonial Records of North Carolina* (Raleigh, 1890), VIII, 481-486; *Laws of the Colony of New York in the Years 1774 and 1775* (Albany, 1888), 38-43.

49. See additional instruction to Governor Josiah Martin, Saunders, ed., *Colonial Records of North Carolina,* VIII, 515-516; and *Laws of the State of New York* (Albany, 1886), I, 20.

50. *The Craftsman,* VI (London, 1731), 263-264. Connecticut and Massachusetts laws cited in n. 45; and *Laws of the State of New Jersey* (Trenton, 1821), 279-281.

51. Jefferson to Madison, January 30, 1787, Boyd, et al., eds., *Jefferson Papers,* XI, 93.

52. See Bradley Chapin, "Colonial and Revolutionary Origins of the American Law of Treason," *William and Mary Quarterly,* 3d Ser. 17 (1960), 3-21.

53. Elbridge Gerry in congressional debates, quoted in Irving Brant, *The Bill of Rights, Its Origin and Meaning* (Indianapolis, 1965), 486; Samuel Adams, quoting Blackstone, as "E. A." in *Boston Gazette, February 27, 1769,* and Cushing, ed., *Writings of Samuel Adams,* I, 317, Timothy Dwight, quoted in Daniel J. Boorstin, *The*

Americans: The Colonial Experience (New York, 1958), 353.

54. Wood, *Creation of the American Republic,* 410.

55. Judge Aedanus Burke's Charge to the Grand Jury at Charleston, July 9, 1783; and *South-Carolina Gazette and General Advertiser* (Charleston), June 10, "A Patriot, ibid., July 15, 1783; and to "Another Patriot," ibid., July 20, 1783; and on the relevance of jealousy of power, see a letter to Virginia in ibid., Aug. 9, 1783; "Democratic Gentle-Touch," *Gazette of the State of South Carolina* (Charleston), May 13, 1784.

56. Wood, *Creation of the American Republic,* 612-614.

57. J. H. Plumb, *The Origins of Political Stability, England 1675-1725* (Boston, 1967), xv, 187; John Adams on the leaders of Shays's Rebellion in a letter to Benjamin Hitchborn, January 27, 1787, in C. F. Adams, ed., *Works of Adams,* IX, 551; modern definitions of riot in "Riot Control and the Use of Federal Troops," *Harvard Law Review,* 81 (1968), 643.

8. Federalism and the Constitution: The Original Understanding

HARRY N. SCHEIBER

1. No. 85, *The Federalist,* ed. Jacob E. Cooke (Cleveland, 1961), 591. All subsequent references to *The Federalist* are to Cooke's edition.

2. Among the many studies of the Constitutional Convention, see especially Irving Brant, *James Madison: Father of the Constitution* (New York, 1950). Forrest McDonald's provocative study. *The Formation of the American Republic, 1776-1790* (Penguin ed., Baltimore, 1965; originally published as *E Pluribus Unum*) is useful for its insights into the national context of crisis in which the Convention deliberated. But valuable as it is, this work is based in some parts on ingenious but not always convincing speculations on circumstantial evidence (e.g., 180ff. and notes). Jackson T. Main, *The Antifederalists* (Chicago, 1965); and E. James Ferguson, *The Power of the Purse: A*

History of American Public Finance, 1776-1790 (Chapel Hill, 1961), both contain abundant data on the political and economic context of the convention issues. A brilliant interpretation by John P. Roche, "The Founding Fathers: A Reform Caucus in Action," American Political Science Review, 55 (1961), 799-816 goes too far, in my view, in contending that the Constitution was "makeshift" and a "patchwork" reflecting the founders' pragmatic concessions to realpolitik. See Leonard W. Levy's commentary In Essays on the Making of the Constitution, ed. L. W. Levy (New York, 1969), 175-178. The Levy volume is an excellent collection of essays on the founding. Other useful studies include Clinton Rossiter, 1787: The Grand Convention (New York, 1966); and William P. Murphy, The Triumph of Nationalism: State Sovereignty, the Founding Fathers, and the Making of the Constitution (Chicago, 1967).

3. McHenry's notes, May 31, in Max Farrand, ed., Records of the Federal Convention of 1787, 4 vols. (New Haven, reprinted 1966), I, 61 (hereafter cited as Farrand).

4. McDonald, Formation, 166.

5. The many achievements of the nation under the confederation, defined outside the context of what powers were essential to effective pursuit of national purposes, are the main theme of Merrill Jensen, The New Nation (New York, 1950).

6. Letters of Members of the Continental Congress, ed. Edmund C. Burnett, VIII (Washington, 1936), 300-301, 291.

7. The Federalist, No. 15, p. 91.

8. On the interplay of economic, sectional, and political groups in the convention, see McDonald, We the People (Chicago, 1958); McDonald, Formation, passim; Main, Antifederalists, passim.

9. Madison's notes, July 7, Farrand, I, 551-552.

10. Yates's notes, June 27, Farrand, I, 453. On the political thought of the Antifederalists generally, see Cecilia Kenyon's introduction to The Antifederalists, ed. Kenyon, The American Heritage Series (Indianapolis, 1966), xxi-cxvi; and Main, Antifederalists, chaps. 6-8.

11. Madison's notes, June 8, Farrand, I, 164.

12. Madison, his own notes, June 6, Farrand, I, 134. See also Hamilton's exegesis of the basic purposes of the Constitution in The Federalist, No. 85.

13. Read on June 29, Farrand, I, 463; Butler on June 6, I, 144, Hamilton on June 18, I, 287; Madison on June 21, I, 356-359.

14. Morris, on "compleat and compulsive operation," Madison's notes, May 30, Farrand, I, 34; Madison to N. P. Trist, December 1831, Farrand, III, 517.

15. Wilson in the Pennsylvania convention, November 1787, Farrand, III, 139. Martin Diamond, "What the Framers Meant by Federalism," Robert A. Goodwin, ed., A Nation of States (Chicago, 1961), 24-41, is the standard analysis of the pre-1787 understanding of such terms as confederation, consolidating government, and federalism.

16. Madison's notes, June 29, Farrand, I, 466. Madison's earlier intransigence was expressed in his speech of July 5, I, 527-528.

17. Johnson, in Madison's notes, June 29, Farrand, I, 461; Ellsworth, in Yates's notes, June 29, I, 474.

18. See McDonald's analysis, Formation, Chaps. 6-7. Also, Roche, "The Founding Fathers," above, n. 1, in Levy, Essays, 200-202.

19. In Pennsylvania's convention, November 1787, Farrand, III, 140.

20. Bernard Schwartz underlines the importance of restrictions and of the supremacy of the Constitution itself as a guarantee of liberties in The Reins of Power, American Century Series (New York, 1963), 40-41. See William M. Wiecek, The Guarantee Clause of the U.S. Constitution (Ithaca, 1972), for an analysis of Article IV and its impact on American federalism.

21. Vote of August 23, Farrand, II, 391. See also Robert A. Dahl's discussion of the convention debates, in Pluralistic Democracy in the United States (Chicago, 1967), 26-55; and McDonald, Formation, chap. 6.

22. Luther Martin in Yates's notes, June 27, Farrand, I, 439, Martin's reply to the landholder, Farrand, III, 392. Cf. Robert Allen Rutland, The Ordeal of the Constitution (Norman, Oklahoma, 1966), 151-153.

23. Martin on June 27, Farrand, I, 437; also, Patrick Henry in the Virginia convention, in Kenyon, ed., *The Antifederalists*, 249-250.

24. "Philadelphiensis," ibid., 70-87; "Address and Reasons of Dissent of the Minority . . . in Pennsylvania," ibid., 28-60; Mason, ibid., 191-195. Of course the Antifederalists were not alone in worrying about excessive centralization, in doubting the legitimacy of the convention's action in writing a new constitution, or in their other objections: many of those who became proponents of the 1787 Constitution harbored identical reservations about both the procedures and the results of the convention. See, for example, Robert A. East, "The Massachusetts Conservatives in the Critical Period," Richard B. Morris, ed., *Era of the American Revolution* (1939; Harper ed., New York, 1965), 349-391.

25. "Centinel," Kenyon, ed., *The Antifederalists*, 10-11; Richard H. Lee, ibid., 209ff.; Thomas Wait, quoted in Main, *Antifederalists*, 129.

26. Italics added. No. 39, 256.

27. No. 45, 311.

28. To Thomas Jefferson, October 24, 1787, Farrand, III, 134.

29. No. 46, 315, 320.

30. No. 15, 93.

31. No. 16, 102-103. See Alpheus T. Mason, "The Federalist: A Split Personality", "*American Historical Review*, 57 (1951), 625-643.

32. No. 23, 148; in the same essay (151) he wrote, "Let us not attempt to reconcile contradictions, but firmly embrace a rational alternative." Mason, in "A Split Personality," cited above n. 31, emphasizes the split between Madison and Hamilton, but fails to note that Hamilton spoke of "first principles" only by way of reference to a national government operating directly upon individuals instead of upon states. On this, Madison was in full agreement. Yet the very rhetorical differences in the two men's essays appear to me important, and I have so treated them in the text.

33. Italics added. No. 15, 89.

34. Ibid., 88; No. 23, 149.

35. No. 17, 107; No. 85, 593.

36. Italics added. No. 17, 105-106.

37. Farrand, I, 135-136; see also I, 284ff., I, 316ff.; and Madison in *The Federalist*, No. 46, 318-319.

38. Farrand, I, 136.

39. There are numerous excellent analyses of Madison's theory of factions, on all of which I have drawn here, esp. Benjamin F. Wright's excellent introduction to his edition of *The Federalist*, (Cambridge, Mass., 1961), 1-86, esp. 26ff., 77ff.; Douglass Adair, "The Tenth Federalist Revisited," *William and Mary Quarterly*, 3d ser. 8 (1951), 48-67; Adair, "That Politics May Be Reduced to a Science," *Huntington Quarterly*, 20 (1957), 343-360; and Adrienne Koch, *Power, Morals, and the Founding Fathers* (Ithaca, 1961). Alpheus T. Mason and John Roche, *In Quest of Freedom* (Englewood Cliffs, N.J., 1959), 79ff., treat Madison systematically as he differed from Adams and other contemporary thinkers.

40. Kenyon, *The Antifederalists*, xxxix-xli

41. No. 10, 64. Also, Madison on the role of the Senate, in the convention, June 7, Farrand, I, 151-152, and June 12, I, 218.

42. Koch, *Power, Morals*, 107-108; see also E. A. J. Johnson's excellent discussion of the contemporary view of "interests and factions" in 1787 and the Federalist era, in his "Federalism, Pluralism, and Public Policy," *Journal of Economic History*, 22 (1962), 427-444, esp. 431; also Richard Hofstadter, *The Idea of a Party System* (Berkeley, 1969), 53.

43. Quoted in Koch, *Power, Morals*, 107.

44. Quoted in John C. Miller, *Alexander Hamilton and the Growth of a New Nation* (New York, 1959), 212.

45. See Wright's introduction to *The Federalist*, 30-31. See, also, Hamilton on June 18 in the convention, Farrand, I, 284ff. In a sense Hamilton placed emphasis on the use of force as a remedy to internal disruption, Madison on its possibility as a deterrent (cf. Madison in No. 46, 320-322). For an entirely different interpretation, however, see Martin Diamond, "The Federalists' Views," *Essays in Federalism* (Claremont, Calif., 1961), 58-64.

456

46. No. 85, 592.

47. See text at n. 36, above. See also, *inter alia*, George Carey, "Federalism: Historic Questions and Contemporary Meanings — A defense of Political Processes," in Valerie Earle, ed., *Federalism: Infinite Variety in Theory and Practice* (Itasca, Ill., 1968), 42-61.

48. No. 45, 311.

49. See n. 24, above.

50. See Johnson, "Federalism, Pluralism," cited in n. 42; and Benjamin Franklin's statement in 1764 that the product of legislation was too often to produce "Advantages . . . not being *general* for the Commonwealth; but *particular*, to private Persons or Bodies in the State who procur'd them, and *at the Expense of the rest of the People*," as quoted by John Nef in Conyers Read, ed., *The Constitution Reconsidered* (New York, 1938), 101.

51. See Wright's introduction to *The Federalist*, 58, 75-76.

52. Hamilton in *The Federalist*, No. 78, 527.

53. Ibid., No. 44, 305; No. 46, 322.

54. No. 46, 315-316; No. 52, 353.

55. No. 39, 250.

56. Farrand, I, 133-134; see also ibid., I, 153.

57. Madison's notes, June 18, in the convention, Farrand, I, 285.

58. Wright's introduction to *The Federalist*, 53-54.

59. Madison, "Consolidation" (1791), in Madison, *Writings*, ed. Gaillard Hunt (New York, 1906), VI, 67-69; "Public Opinion" (1791), ibid., 70. Similarly Madison said in the Virginia ratification convention: "I go on this great republican principle, that the people will have virtue and intelligence to select men of virtue and wisdom . . . So that we do not depend . . . [on] our rules, but in the people who are to choose them." And also: "I hope the partiotism of the people will continue, and be a sufficient guard to their liberties" (quoted in Brant, *Madison: Father of the Constitution*, 221-223, 201).

60. Miller, *Alexander Hamilton*, 286.

61. Ibid., 289-290. These sentiments became the main theme, too, in Jacob E. Cooke, ed., *The Reports of Alexander Hamil-*ton (New York, 1964), in which see esp. 163ff., the nationalistic argument for positive governmental action that would obviate the effects of misplaced sectionalism and localism.

62. Alpheus T. Mason, "Our Federal Union Reconsidered," *Political Science Quarterly*, 65 (1950), 511-513. Both constitutional authority as derived from Supreme Court decisions and the problems of "real power" — sometimes consistent with judicially mandated doctrine, but often inconsistent with it — are considered in Harry N. Scheiber, "Federalism and the American Economic Order, 1789-1910," *Law and Society Review*, 10 (1975), 57-118.

63. See Arthur Selwyn Miller, *The Modern Corporate State: Private Governments and the American Constitution* (Westport, Conn., 1976); and Grant McConnell, *Private Power and American Democracy* (New York, 1966). Both of these works are highly critical of the performance of the federal system, especially in regard to the containment of private power. For a more benign view, see Morton Grodzins, *The American System: A New View of Government in the United States*, ed. Daniel Elazar (Chicago, 1966). Other works that provide historical surveys from different perspectives are Daniel Elazar, *The American Partnership* (Chicago, 1962); and Harry N. Scheiber, *The Condition of American Federalism: An Historian's View*, Senate Committee on Government Operations 89th Cong., 2d sess., 1966.

9. Liberty and the First Amendment: 1790-1800

LEONARD W. LEVY

1. Some reviewers of my book, *Legacy of Suppression: Freedom of Speech and Press in Early American History* (Cambridge, Mass., 1960), have criticized my failure to define the words, "libertarian" and "libertarianism." The words derive from a Latin root meaning "free" and, like "liberty" or "freedom," cannot be defined with precision. I use them to signify those persons and that school of thought advocating the widest measure of unrestricted freedom for speech

and press. The meanings of the terms are relative to time and place.

2. Most recently expressed by Justice Black in Communist Party of the U.S. v. Subversive Activities Control Board, 81 Sup. Ct. 1357, at 1443, n.46 (1961). Black quotes the statement by Holmes, Brandeis concurring, in Abrams v. U.S., 250 U.S. 616, at 630 (1919): "I wholly disagree with the argument of the Government that the First Amendment left the common law as to seditious libel in force. History seems to me against the notion." See also Beauharnais v. Ill., 343 U.S. 250, at 272 and 289 (1951). The leading scholarly statement of the accepted view is Zechariah Chafee, Jr., *Free Speech in the United States* (Cambridge, Mass., 1948), 21. The most recent restatements are James Morton Smith, *Freedom's Fetters: The Alien and Sedition Laws and American Civil Liberties* (Ithaca, N.Y., 1956), 427-431; C. Herman Pritchett, *The American Constitution* (New York, 1959), 430; and David Fellman, *The Limits of Freedom* (New Brunswick, N.J., 1959), 97.

3. Thomas Jefferson, *Notes on the State of Virginia,* ed. William Peden (Chapel Hill, N.C., 1955), 159.

4. "A Bill for new modelling the form of government and for establishing the Fundamental principles of our future Constitution," dated by Julian Boyd as "before 13 June 1776," in Julian P. Boyd et. al., eds., *The Papers of Thomas Jefferson,* 16 vols. (Princeton, N.J., 1950-), I, 353. Jefferson copied this provision from a similar one in an earlier draft, then bracketed it out, and finally omitted it from a third draft (ibid., 347).

5. "That the mere utterance of apolitical opinoin is being penalized in these cases becomes even clearer in a statute such as that in Virginia, which declared the utterance of the opinion, or action upon it, to be equally offensive, providing a fine not exceeding £20,000 and imprisonment not exceeding five years "if any person residing or being within this commonwealth shall . . . by any word, open deed, or act, advisedly and willingly maintain and defend thc authority, jurisdiction, or power, of the kind or parliament of Great Britain, heretofore claimed and exercised within this colony, or shall attribute any such authority, jurisdiction, or power, to the king or parliament of Great Britain' " (William Hurst, "Treason in the United States," *Harvard Law Review,* 58 [1944], 267, quoting *The Statutes at Large: Being a Collection of All the Laws of Virginia* [1619-1792], ed. William Waller Hening, 13 vols. [Richmond, Va., 1809-23], IX, 170.) For Jefferson's role, see Hurst, "Treason in the United States," 251, and *Boyd* et. al., eds., Jefferson Papers, I, 598.

6. The standard authority on the meaning of freedom of the press was William Blackstone, the oracle of the common law to the American framers, who summarized the law of criminal libels as follows: "Where blasphemous, immoral, treasonable, schismatical, seditious, or scandalous libels are punished by the English law . . . the liberty of the press, properly understood, is by no means infringed or violated. The *liberty of the press* is indeed essential to the nature of a free state; but this consists in laying no *previous* restraints upon publications, and not in freedom from censure for criminal matter when published. Every freeman has an undoubted right to lay what sentiments he pleases before the public; to forbid this is to destroy the freedom of the press: but if he publishes what is improper, mischievous, or illegal, he must take the consequences of his own temerity . . . But to punish (as the law does at present) any dangerous or offensive writings, which, when published, shall on a fair and impartial trial be adjudged of a pernicious tendency, is necessary for the preservation of peace and good order, a government and religion, the only solid foundations of civil liberty. Thus the will of individuals is still left free; the abuse only of that free will is the object of legal punishment. Neither is any restraint hereby laid upon freedom of thought or enquiry; liberty of private sentiment is still left; the disseminating, or making public, of bad sentiments, destructive to the ends of society, is the crime which society corrects" (Sir William Blackstone, *Commentaries on the Laws of England* 4 vols. [London, 1759-69], 4,

chap. 11, 151-152; or, in the 18th ed., which I used [2 vols., New York, 1836], II, 112-213.)

7. *A Complete Collection of State Trials to 1783,* comp. Thomas Bayly Howell, continued by T. J. Howell to 1820, 34 vols., (London, 1816-1828), XVII, 675; see also Livingston Rutherford, *John Peter Zenger: His Press, His Trial and a Bibliography of Zenger Imprints. Also a Reprint of the First Edition of the Trial* (New York, 1904). On the contemporary significance of the trial and its questionable influence in "freeing" the press, see Leonard W. Levy, "Did the Zenger Case Really Matter? Freedom of the Press in Colonial New York," *William and Mary Quarterly,* 3d ser. 17 (1960), 35-50.

8. "That the printing-presses shall be free to every person who undertakes to examine the proceedings of the legislature, or any branch of government, and no law shall ever be made to restrain the right thereof. The free communication of thoughts and opinions is one of the invaluable rights of man; and every citizen may freely speak, write, and print on any subject, *being responsible for the abuse of that liberty. In prosecutions for the publication of papers investigating the official conduct of officers or men in a public capacity, or where the matter published is proper for public information, the truth thereof may be given in evidence;* and in all indictments for libels the jury shall have a right to determine the law and the facts, under all direction of the court, as in other cases" (Pennsylvania Constitution of 1790 [Art. IX, sec. 7], in *The Federal and State Constitutions, Colonial Charters, and Other Organic Laws,* ed. Francis Newton Thorpe, 7 vols. [Washington, D.C., 1909], V, 3100; italics mine).

9. *Pennsylvania and the Federal Constitution, 1787-1788* ed. John Bach McMaster and Frederick D. Stone (Philadelphia, 1888), 308-309.

10. Respublica v. Oswald, 1 Dallas (Pa.) Reports 319 (1788); "Trial of William Cobbett," November 1797, in *State Trials of the United States during the Administrations of Washington and Adams,* ed. Francis Wharton (Philadelphia, 1849), 323-324; Respublica v. Dennie, 4 Yeates (Pa.) Reports 267 (1805).

11. Delaware Constitution of 1792 (Art, I, sec. 5), in *Constitutions,* ed. Thorpe, I, 569, and Kentucky Constitution of 1792 (Art, XII, sec. 7-8), ibid., III, 1274.

12. "Hitherto Unpublished Correspondence between Chief Justice Cushing and John Adams in 1789," ed. Frank W. Grinnell, *Massachusetts Law Quarterly,* 27 (1942), 12-16. Adams, of course, signed the Sedition Act into law and urged its enforcement; Cushing, as a Supreme Court judge, presided over some of the Sedition Act trials and charged juries on its constitutionality (see Smith, *Freedom's Fetters,* 97-98, 152, 242, 267, 268, 271, 284, 311, 363, and 371).

13. See cases cited above, 10. The judges in Oswald's case were Thomas McKean, then a Federalist but subsequently a Republican, and George Bryan, an Antifederalist and libertarian advocate of a national bill of rights.

14. Commonwealth v. Freeman, reported in the Boston *Independent Chronicle,* February 24, March 3, 10, 17, and 24, 1791.

15. "Draught of a Fundamental Constitution for the Commonwealth of Virginia," in Boyd et al., eds, *Jefferson Papers,* VI, 304: "PRINTING PRESS shall be subject to no other restraint than liableness to legal prosecution for false facts printed and published." Boyd dates this document between May 15 and June 17, 1783.

16. "A declaration that the federal government will never restrain the press from printing any thing they please, will not take away the liability of the printers for false facts printed" (Jefferson to Madison, July 31, 1788, in ibid., XIII, 442).

17. "Madison's Observations on Jefferson's Draft of a Constitution for Virginia," October 1788, in ibid., VI, 316.

18. Madison's original proposal was: "The people shall not be deprived or abridged of their right to speak, to write, or to publish their sentiments; and the freedom of the press, as one of the great bulwarks of liberty, shall be inviolable" (*Debates and Proceedings in the Congress of the United States* [hereinafter cited as *Annals of Congress*], 1st Cong., 1st sess., [June 8, 1789], I, 451).

19. Jefferson to Madison, August 28, 1789, Boyd et. al., eds., *Jefferson Papers*, XV, 367.

20. "The liberty of the Press is secured . . . In the time of King William, there passed an act for licensing the press. This was repealed. Since that time it has been looked upon as safe" (*Debates in the Several State Conventions on the Adoption of the Federal Constitution . . . and Other Illustrations of the Constitution*, ed. Jonathan Elliot, 2d. rev. ed., 5 vols. in 2 [Philadelphia, 1941], III, 247).

21. Ibid., 560.

22. Jefferson to Madison, July 31, 1788, in Boyd et al., eds., *Jefferson Papers*, XIII, 422-423.

23. Madison to Jefferson, October 17, 1788, in ibid., XIV, 20.

24. *Debates*, ed. Elliot, III, 656.

25. See above, note 18.

26. "There was a time in England when neither book, pamphlet, nor paper could be published without a license from government. That restraint was finally removed in the year 1694; and, by such removal, the press became perfectly free, for it is not under the restraint of any license. Certainly the new government can have no power to impose restraints" (Hugh Williamson, "Remarks on the New Plan of Government," in *Essays on the Constitution of the United States, Published during Its Discussion by the People*, ed. Paul Leicester Ford [Brooklyn, N.Y., 1892], 398).

27. Melancthon Smith, "An Address to the People of the State of New York" (1788), *Pamphlets on the Constitution*, ed. Ford (Brooklyn, 1888), 114.

28. The brief and vague statement by Eleazar Oswald in 1788 may be regarded by some as an exception to this proposition. Oswald, having been indicted for a criminal libel on a private party, published an address to the public in which he stated: "The doctrine of libel being a doctrine incompatible with law and liberty, and at once destructive of the privileges of a free country, in the communication of our thoughts, has not hitherto gained any footing in *Pennsylvania* . . ." (quoted in Respublica v. Oswald, 1 Dallas 319 at 320 [1788]).

29. Wilson's statement in the Pennsylvania ratifying convention, quoted in *Pennsylvania and the Federal Constitution*, ed. McMaster and Stone, 308; Hamilton in *The Federalist*, No. 84.

30. In my book, *Legacy of Suppression*, I missed the significance of the reference to Article III, section 2, and therefore misconstrued Wilson's statement to mean that criminal libels against the United States could be tried only in the *state* courts. I am indebted to John J. Cound for calling attention to my error in his review of my book in *New York University Law Review*, 36 (January 1961), 256-257. The corrected reading of Wilson's statement strengthens the thesis of the book regarding the restrictive views of the framers.

31. "Trial of Joseph Ravara" (1792), in *State Trials*, ed. Wharton, 90-92; "Trial of Gideon Henfield" (1793), in ibid., 49-92; U.S. v. Worrall, 2 Dallas 384 (1798), in ibid., 188-199; "Trial of the Northampton Insurgents" (1799), in ibid., 476; "Trial of Isaac Williams" (1799), in ibid., 652-654. See also U.S. v. Smith (1797), MSS Final Record of the United States Circuit Courts of Massachusetts, 1790-1799, I, 242 (Federal Records Center, Dorchester, Mass.). Smith's case is reported in 27 *Federal Cases*, No. 16323, where the date is erroneously given as 1792. Justice Samuel Chase, in Worrall's case mentioned above, disagreed with his associate, Judge Richard Peters, who supported the jurisdiction of the federal courts in cases of common-law crime. Chase, however, changed his opinion in U.S. v. Sylvester (1799), MSS Final Record, I, 303, an unreported case.

32. A federal grand jury in Richmond presented Congressman Samuel J. Cabell for seditious libel in 1797. Prosecutions for seditious libel were also begun against Benjamin F. Bache of the Philadelphia *Aurora* and John Daly Burk of the New York *Time Piece* in 1798, shortly before the enactment of the Sedition Act. See Smith, *Freedom's Fetters*, 95, 183-184, 188-220.

33. Supreme Court justices known to have accepted jurisdiction in cases of com-

mon-law crimes included James Wilson, Oliver Ellsworth, William Paterson, John Jay, James Iredell, and Samuel Chase. See cases mentioned above, note 31.

34. U.S. v. Hudson and Goodwin, 7 Cranch 32, at 34 (1812). Justice William Johnson, speaking for the "majority," gave an unreasoned opinion. The case had been decided without arguments of counsel. William W. Crosskey, *Politics and the Constitution*, 2 vols. (Chicago, 1953), II, 782, claims that Chief Justice Marshall and Justices Story and Washington dissented from Johnson's opinion without noting the fact of their dissent on the record.

35. On the English legislation of the 1790s, see Sir Thomas Erskine May, *Constitutional History of England since the Accession of George Third, 1760-1860*, 2 vols. (New York, 1880), II, 161-174. The parlimentary debates and the texts of the Treasonable Practices Act and of the Sedition Act of 1795, known together as "The Two Acts," were published in London in 1796 under the title *History of the Two Acts* and were imported into the United States and advertised under the title *History of the Treason and Sedition Bills Lately Passed in Great Britain*. For the influence of the English experience and legislation on Federalist thought, see Manning J. Dauer, *The Adams Federalists* (Baltimore, 1953), 157-159.

36. *Annals of Congress*, 5th Cong., 2d sess., 2152 (1798); see also ibid., Gallatin at 2163, Nicholas at 2142, and Livingston at 2153.

37. *Debates*, ed. Elliot, IV, 540-541.

38. *The Writings of James Madison*, ed. Gaillard Hunt, 9 vols. (New York, 1900-1910), VI, 333-334.

39. People v. Croswell, 3 Johnson's (N.Y.) Cases 336 (1804).

40. Chief Justice Morgan Lewis, joined by Judge Brockholst Livingston, whom Jefferson appointed to the United States Supreme Court in 1806, explicitly defined freedom of the press in common-law terms, relying on Blackstone and Mansfield for precedents. Ambrose Spencer, a Republican newly appointed to the New York Court of

Errors, disqualified himself because as attorney general he had represented the state in the Croswell case. Lewis's opinion was based on Spencer's argument. Hamilton defended Croswell, arguing Zengerian principles which were accepted by Judge James Kent, a Federalist, joined by Smith Thompson, a Republican who had studied law with Kent. In 1805 the state legislature enacted a bill allowing truth as a defense if published "with good motives and for justifiable ends," and allowing the jury to decide the whole issue. The statute is reported at 3 Johnson's (N.Y.) Cases 336, at 411-13, following the arguments of counsel and the opinions of Kent and Lewis.

41. Jefferson to Governor Thomas McKean, February 19, 1803, in *The Writings of Thomas Jefferson*, ed. Paul Leicester Ford, 10 vols. (New York, 1892-1899), VIII, 218-19.

42. Jefferson to Abigail Adams, September 4, 1804, in ibid., 311. In his eloquent first inaugural address, Jefferson declared, in a deservedly much-quoted passage: "If there be any among us who would wish to dissolve this Union or to change its republican form, let them stand undisturbed as monuments of the safety with which error of opinion may be tolerated where reason is left free to combat it." But in his second inaugural address, he spoke of the "licentiousness" with which the "artillery of the press has been levelled against us," alleged that the "abuses" of the press lessened its "usefulness," and stated, "they might, indeed, have been corrected by the wholesome punishments reserved and provided by the laws of the several States against falsehood and defamation . . ." He declared that the pressure of public duties prevent prosecution of the offenders and that his reelection demonstrated that the people could be trusted to choose truth in a conflict with falsehood. But he added, "No inference is here intended, that the laws, provided by the State against false and defamatory publications, should not be enforced; he who has time, renders a service to public morals and public tranquility, in reforming these abuses by the salutary coercions of the law . . ." (ibid., VIII, 346).

43. "Hampden," *A Letter to the President of the United States, Touching the Prosecutions under His Patronage, before the Circuit Court in the District of Connecticut* (New Haven, Conn., 1808), 28.

44. Ibid., 8-12.

45. Jefferson to Thomas Seymour, February 11, 1807, in *Writings to Jefferson*, ed. Ford IX, 30.

46. Sir James Fitzjames Stephen, *A History of the Criminal Law of England*, 3 vols. (London, 1883), II, 383; Frank Thayer, *Legal Control of the Press* (Brooklyn, N.Y., 1950), 17, 25, 178.

47. *Annals of Congress*, 5th Cong., 2d sess., 2103-11 (1798); 2139-43, 2153-54, 2160-66 (1798).

48. Boston *Independent Chronicle*, March 4-7, April 8-15, April 29-May 2, 1799, reporting the trial of Abijah Adams, editor of the *Chronicle*, for seditious libel against the state legislature of Massachusetts.

49. George Hay ["Hortensius"], *An Essay on the Liberty of the Press. Respectfully Inscribed to the Republican Printers throughout the United States* (reprint, Richmond, Va. 1803). In 1803 Hay also published a different tract with a similar title, *An Essay on the Liberty of the Press, Shewing, that the Requisition of Security for Good Behavior from Libellers, Is Perfectly Compatible with the Constitution and Laws of Virginia* (Richmond, Va., 1803). Hay, who was Monroe's son-in-law, served in the Virginia House of Delegates, was appointed United States attorney for Virginia by President Jefferson, conducted the prosecution of Burr for treason, and concluded his public career as a United States district judge.

50. The *Report* originally appeared as a tract of over eighty pages. The copy in the Langdell Treasure Room, Harvard Law Library, is bound together with the 1799 issue of Hay's *Essay*. Madison wrote the *Report* at the close of 1799; it was adopted by the Virginia legislature on January 11, 1800, which immediately published it. It is reproduced in *Debates*, ed. Elliot, IV, 546-580, under the title "Madison's Report on the Virginia Resolutions . . . Report of the Committee to whom were referred the Communications of various States, relative to the Resolutions of the last General Assembly of this State, concerning the Alien and Sedition Laws." The *Report* is also available in *Writings of Madison*, ed. Hunt, VI, 341-406. The edition cited here is *The Virginia Report of 1799-1800, Touching the Alien and Sedition Laws; Together with the Virginia Resolutions of December 21, 1798, the Debates and Proceedings thereon, in the House of Delegates in Virginia* (Richmond, 1850), 189-237, a book of great value for its inclusion of the Virginia debates on the Sedition Act (pp. 22-161). While those debates added little to the debates of the House of Representatives, the remarks of Republican speakers constitute another example of the new libertarianism.

51. Tunis Wortman, *A Treatise Concerning Political Enquiry, and the Liberty of the Press* (New York 1800). Wortman, one of the leading democratic theoreticians of his time, was a New York lawyer prominent in Tammany politics. From 1801 to 1807 he served as clerk of the city and county of New York. He was the author of several important tracts, one of which outlined a democratic philosophy of social reform, *An Oration on the Influence of Social Institutions upon Human Morals and Happiness* (New York 1796,) and another which was a leading defense of Jefferson against charges of atheism in the election of 1800. See *A Solemn Address, to Christians and Patriots, upon the Approaching Election of a President of the United States* (New York, 1800). Gallatin supported the publication of Wortman's *Enquiry* by undertaking to secure subscriptions to the book among Republican members of Congress (Wortman to Gallatin, December 24, 30, 1799, Albert Gallatin Papers, 1799, nos. 47, 49, New York Historical Society). In 1813–1814 Wortman published a newspaper in New York, the *Standard of Union*, to which Jefferson subscribed in the hope that it would counteract the "abandoned spirit of falsehood" of the newspapers of the country (Jefferson to Wortman, Aug. 15, 1813, Thomas Jefferson Papers, Henry E. Huntington Library).

52. John Thomson, *An Enquiry, concerning the Liberty, and Licentiousness of the Press* (New York, 1801). I have not been able to identify John Thomson.

53. Sir William Blackstone, *Commentaries on the Laws of England,* ed. St. George Tucker, 5 vols. (Philadelphia, 1803), I, pt. 2, 2. G, 11-30 of Appendix. Tucker, a professor of law at the College of William and Mary, was elected to the high court of Virginia in 1803. President Madison appointed him a United States district judge in 1813.

54. [Madison,] *Virginia Report of 1799–1800,* 220.

55. Hay, *Essay on the Liberty of the Press* (1803 ed. of the 1799 tract), 29; *Essay on the Liberty of the Press* (1803), 32. See above, note 49, for a distinction between the two tracts.

56. Thomson, *Enquiry, concerning the Liberty, and Licentiousness of the Press,* 6-7.

57. Wortman, *Treatise concerning Political Enquiry,* 173.

58. [Madison,] *Virginia Report of 1799-1800,* 226-227.

59. Wortman, *Treatise concerning Political Enquiry,* 253.

60. Hay, *Essay on the Liberty of the Press* (1803 ed. of 1799 tract), 28.

61. *Annals of Congress,* 5th Cong., 2d sess., 2162, [July 10, 1798].

62. Thomson, *Enquiry, concerning the Liberty, and Licentiousness of the Press,* 6-8.

63. [Madison,] *Virginia Report of 1799-1800,* 226.

64. Wortman, *Treatise concerning Political Enquiry,* 262.

65. Hay, *Essay on the Liberty of the Press* (1803 ed. of 1799 tract), 23-24.

66. Ibid., 25.

67. Hay, *Essay on the Liberty of the Press* (1803 tract), 29.

68. Wortman, *Treatise concerning Political Enquiry,* 140, 253; Thomson, *Enquiry, concerning the Liberty, and Licentiousness of the Press,* 79.

69. Ibid., 22.

70. [Madison,] *Virginia Report of 1799-1800,* 222.

71. Wortman, *Treatise concerning Political Enquiry,* 29.

72. Thomson, *Enquiry, concerning the Liberty, and Licentiousness of the Press,* 20, 22; Hay, *Essay on the Liberty of the Press* (1803 ed. of 1799 tract), 26.

73. "Originality" refers to the American scene. American libertarian thought lagged behind its British counterpart, which very likely provided a model for the Republicans in the same ways that British thought advocating suppression influenced Federalist opinion. For British precursors of the new American libertarianism, see "Father of Candor," *A Letter concerning Libels, Warrants, the Seizure of Papers, and Sureties for the Peace of Behaviour,* 7th ed. (London, 1771), 20, 34, 71, 161; Ebenezer Ratcliffe, *Two Letters Addressed to the Right Rev. Prelates* (London, 1773), 100; Andrew Kippis, *A Vindication of the Protestant Dissenting Ministers* (London, 1773), 98-99; Francis Maseres, *An Enquiry into the Extent of the Power of Juries* (1776) (Dublin, 1792), 6, 13, 18, 22, 24, 28; Jeremy Bentham, *A Fragment on Government* (London, 1776) 154; Capel Lofft, *An Essay on the Law of Libels* (London, 1785), 60-61; James Adair, *Discussions of the Law of Libels as at Present Received* (London, 1785), 27-28; Manasseh Dawes, *The Deformity of the Doctrine of Libels, and Informations Ex-Officio* (London, 1785), 11-24, 28; the celebrated argument of Thomas Erskine in defense of Tom Paine, in a trial for seditious libel, 1792, published as a contemporary tract and available in *Speeches of Thomas Lord Erskine, Reprinted from the Five Volume Octavo Edition of 1810,* ed. Edward Walford 2 vols. (London, 1870), I, 309-313; Robert Hall, *"An Apology for the Freedom of the Press and for General Liberty"* (1793) in *Miscellaneous Works and Remains of the Reverend Robert Hall,* ed. John Foster (London, 1846), 172-179.

10. The Release of Energy

JAMES WILLARD HURST

1. Lothrop's account of the Pike Creek history, including a copy of the Pike River Claimants Union, is contained in the *Journal of the Assembly, 8th Wisconsin Legislature,* Appendix, II (Madison, 1856), 472–275.

2. See generally, Edward S. Corwin, *Liberty Against Government* (Baton Rouge, 1948), and *Selected Essays on Constitutional Law* (Chicago, 1938), II, Chap. 1. Aspects of basic changes in property law are discussed in Paschal Larkin, *Property in the Eighteenth Century* (Dublin, 1930), 141, 148; John Scurlock, *Retroactive Legislation Affecting Interests in Land* (Ann Arbor, 1953), 210, 213; Lewis M. Simes, "Historical Background of the Law of Property," in *American Law of Property* (Boston, 1953), I, 58–60, 63–65.

3. Cf. Joseph Dorfman, *The Economic Mind in American Civilization* (New York, 1946), II, 630-634, 795, 958-960; Louis M. Hacker, *The Triumph of American Capitalism* (New York, 1940), 317–321, 339–345; David M. Wright, "The Modern Corporation — Twenty Years After," *University of Chicago Law Review*, 19 (1952), 662, 665, 667.

4. Fisher v. Horicon Iron & Manufacturing Co., 10 Wis. 351, 354 (1860); cf. Newcomb v. Smith, 2 Pinney 131, 140 (Wis. 1849).

5. Brandeis, J., in Louisville Joint Stock Land Bank v. Radford, 295 U.S. 555, 588 (1935), cf. Local Loan Co. v. Hunt, 292 U.S. 234, 244 (1934).

6. Waite, C. J., in Canada Southern Railway Co. v. Gebhard, 190 U.S. 527, 536 (1883).

7. Von Baumbach v. Bade, 9 Wis. 559, 583 (1859).

8. West River Bridge Co. v. Dix, 6 How. 507 (U.S. 1847).

9. Providence Bank v. Billings, 4 Pet. 514 (U.S. 1830); Stone v. Mississippi, 101 U.S. 815 (1880).

10. Legal Tender Cases, 12 Wall. 457 (U.S. 1871); cf. Norman v. Baltimore & Ohio Railroad Co., 294 U.S. 240 (1935).

11. Proprietors of the Charles River Bridge v. Proprietors of the Warren Bridge, 11 Pet. 420, 547-548, 552-553 (U.S. 1837).

12. Veto Message of Gov. Jeremiah Rusk, re Bill 100S, *Journal of the Senate, 35th Wisconsin Legislature* (Madison, 1882), 489. Compare the Veto Messages of Governor LaFollette, *Journal of the Assembly, 45th Wisconsin Legislature* (Madison, 1901), 723, re Bill 371 A ("The unqualified existence and continuance of the grant for the entire period might hamper and even stifle the growth of other great and paramount interests to the detriment of the public welfare."); *Journal of the Senate, 46th Wisconsin Legislature* (Madison, 1903), 1038-1039, re Bill 25S.

13. Cf. Zechariah Chafee, *Free Speech in the United States* (Cambridge Mass. 1942), 437; John C. Miller, *Crisis in Freedom* (Boston, 1951), 193, 221, 226-227, 230; C. Vann Woodward, *Reunion and Reaction* (Boston, 1951), 13, 15, 208, 211-212, 214-215.

14. See Joseph Spengler, "Laissez Faire and Intervention; a Potential Source of Historical Error," *Journal of Political Economy*, 57 (1949), 438, 440.

11. An Overview of American Land Policy

PAUL W. GATES

1. Merrill Jensen, *The New Nation: A History of the United States during the Confederation, 1781-1789* (New York 1965), 350-359; Henry Steele Commager, *Documents of American History* (New York, 1962), 144, Art. IV, sec. 3 of the Constituiton.

2. Thomas C. Donaldson, *The Public Domain: Its History, with Statistics* (Washington, 1883), 68-69.

3. Donaldson, *Public Domain*, 155-156.

4. Paul W. Gates, *History of Public Land Law Development* (Washington, 1968), 55-56.

5. Commager, *Documents*, 123-124.

6. Significant works on colonial land policies are listed in Frank Friedel, *Harvard Guide to American History*, 2 vols. (Cambridge, Mass., 1974), II, 717.

7. The population of Great Britain in 1791 was 9,747,000; that of the United States in 1790 was 3,929,214 (Phyllis Deane and W. A. Cole, *British Economic Growth* [New York and London, 1962], VI, 8; *World Almanac, 1975* [New York, 1975], 145).

8. Act of 4 August 1790, 1 Stat., 144.

9. For administrative restraint in not pressing lands into the market by President Pierce in the fifties and for the eighty-acre limitation upon the alienation of southern lands between 1866 and 1876, see Paul W. Gates, *Fifty Million Acres: Conflicts over Kansas Land Policy, 1854-1890* (Ithaca,

N.Y., 1954), 76-77; and Gates, "Federal Land Policy in the South, 1866-1868," *Journal of Southern History*, 6 (1940), 304-330.

10. Paul W. Gates, "Homestead Law in an Incongruous Land System" *American Historical Review*, 41 (1936), 652-681; idem, "The Homestead Act: Free Land Policy in Operation," Howard W. Ottoson, ed., *Land Use Policy and Problems in the United States* (Lincoln, 1963), 28-46; idem, "The Homestead Law in Iowa," *Agricultural History*, 38 (1964), 67-78.

11. I have discussed the terms laid down in the admission acts and the grants to the states in *History of Public Land Law Development*, 285-318.

12. Western feelings on the retention of the public lands by the United States in the later years are best seen in E. Louise Peffer, *The Closing of the Public Domain: Disposal and Reservation Policies, 1900-1950* (Stanford, 1951).

13. The classic treatment of the land-grant railroad as a promoter of settlement if James B. Hedges, "The Colonization Work of the Northern Pacific Railroad," *Mississippi Valley Historical Review*, 13 (1926), 312-342. Also excellent is Richard C. Overton, *Burlington West: A Colonization History of the Burlington Railroad* (Cambridge, Mass., 1941).

14. The latest attempt of the AAR is a flyer entitled *Railroad Land Grants: A Sharp Deal for Uncle Sam.*

15. The coal reserves in the alternate sections of the old Northern Pacific (now Burlington Northern) in North Dakota and Montana and the oil-bearing lands of the Southern Pacific in California have value almost beyond imagination.

16. The story of the various efforts of the original thirteen states and other non-public-land states to share in the proceeds from the sale or leasing of United States land is given in greater detail in *History of Public Land Law Development*, 11-28

17. Paul W. Gates, "Indian Allotments Preceding the Dawes Act," John G. Clark, ed., *The Frontier Challenge: Responses to the Trans-Mississippi West* (Lawrence, Kansas, 1971), 141-170.

18. *U.S. Indian Claims Commission, Annual Report, 1974*, Appendix 1.

19. Ray P. Teele, *The Economics of Land Reclamation in the United States* (Chicago, 1927), 261.

20. *Congressional Record*, 57th Cong. 1st sess., January 21, 1902, 830, June 13, 1902, 6733; compiled from *Agricultural Census of 1964*.

21. Returns from the sale, leasing, rentals, and licensing of the public lands that flowed into the reclamation fund were small in the early years, but with large increases in recent years they have averaged $19,124,000 over the entire period from 1901 to 1972 for a total of $1,372,952,847 (U.S. Department of the Interior, Bureau of Reclamation, *Federal Reclamation Projects: Water and Land Resource Accomplishments* [Washington, 1972], Appendix 2, p. 25).

22. A random sampling of the Senate and House committees on public lands in 1910 and 1930 shows the following:

	1910	
	House	Senate
From public-land states	17	15
From 19 non-public-land states	3	0

	1930	
	House	Senate
From public-land states	18	12
From 19 non-public-land states	4	2

The Public Land Law Review Commission was packed, 14 to 5, with appointees from the public-land states.

23. I have given in more detail the revenue-sharing features of federal policy in *History of Public Land Law Development*, 28-30, 582, 595, 603.

24. U. S. Public Land Law Commission, *One Third of the Nation's Land: A Report to the President and the Congess* (Washington, 1970), 237.

25. 67 Stat., 29.

26. An editorial in the *New York Times*, February 27, 1975, entitled "Whose Public Lands?" scores the Secretary of the Interior for ordering the transfer of three wildlife refuges from the Fish and Wildlife Service to the Bureau of land Management where they will presumably be subordinated to the welfare of livestock and mining interests.

27. In the extensive literature on this subject Joseph James Shomon, *Open Land for Urban America: Acquisition, Safekeeping, and Use* (Baltimore, 1971), well sumarizes the issues.

12. Property Law, Expropriation, and Resource Allocation by Government; 1789-1910

HARRY N. SCHEIBER

1. Harry N. Scheiber, "Government and the Economy: Studies of the 'Commonwealth' Policy in 19th Century America," *Journal of Interdisciplinary History*, 3 (1972), 135-151; (James) Willard Hurst, *Law and the Conditions of Freedom in the Nineteenth-Century United States* (Madison, 1964); James H. Soltow, "American Institutional Studies: Present Knowledge and Past Trends," *The Journal of Economic History*, 21 (1971), 87-105; Allan G. Bogue, "To Shape a Western State: Some Dimensions of the Kansas Search for Capital, 1865-1893," John G. Clark, ed., *The Frontier Challenge: Responses to the Trans-Mississippi West* (Lawrence, 1971), 203-234.

2. Edward S. Corwin, *American Constitutional History: Essays,* ed. A. T. Mason and G. Garvey (New York, 1964), 50.

3. Francis S. Philbrick, "Changing Conceptions of Property in Law," *University of Pennsylvania Law Review,* 86 (1938), 723; Edward S. Corwin, "The Basic Doctrine of American Constitutional Law," *Michigan Law Review,* 12 (1914), 247-276.

4. Lance E. Davis and Douglass C. North, *Institutional Change and American Economic Growth* (Cambridge, 1971), 75. The conventional interpretation of the Granger Cases and the doctrine of property "affected with a public interest" are considered at length and critically examined in Harry N. Scheiber, "The Road to *Munn:* Eminent Domain and the Concept of Public Purpose in the State Courts," *Perspectives in American History,* 5 (1971), 329-402. Extensive documentation is there available for some of the themes treated in this essay.

5. John R. Commons, *Legal Foundations of Capitalism* (Madison, 1959), 328. Two Massachusetts studies provide a more accurate perspective on the police power before 1861: Oscar and Mary F. Handlin, *Commonwealth: . . . Massachusetts, 1774-1861,* rev. ed. (Cambridge, Mass., 1969), *passim;* and Leonard W. Levy, *The Law of the Commonwealth and Chief Justice Shaw* (Cambridge, 1957), 229-281. The numerous valuable studies of Willard Hurst on this and related themes are considered in Scheiber, "At the Borderland of Law and Economic History: The Contributions of Willard Hurst," *American Historical Review,* 75 (1970), 744-756.

6. Simon Kuznets, *Economic Growth and Structure: Selected Essays* (New York, 1965), 108.

7. See text below, at notes 29-32.

8. Note, "Public Use Limitations on Eminent Domain," *Yale Law Journal,* 56 (1949), 605-606.

9. No single monograph, even in the literature of legal history, provides a dependable discussion of eminent-domain law, accurate and in a conceptual framework useful for analysis in economic history. Uniquely useful is Willard Hurst's case study of public economic policy, *Law and Economic Growth: The Legal History of the Lumber Industry in Wisconsin, 1836-1915* (Cambridge, Mass., 1964), 181ff, and *passim;* see also J.M. Cormack, "Legal Concepts in Cases of Eminent Domain," *Yale Law Journal,* 41, (1931), 221-261; and Levy, *Law of the Commonwealth,* 118-135.

10. Levy, *Law of the Commonwealth,* 255-258; Joseph K. Angell, *A Treatise on the Law of Watercourses,* 5th ed. (Boston, 1854), 547-565; Anon., "The Law of Water Privilege," *American Jurist and Law Magazine,* 2 (1829), 25-38.

11. Development of the limiting concepts in early jurisprudence is treated in J.A.C. Grant, "The 'Higher Law' Background of Eminent Domain," *Wisconsin Law Review,* 6, (1931), 67-85. See also Philip Nichols, Jr., "The Meaning of Public Use in the Law of Eminent Domain," *Boston University Law Review,* 20 (1940), 615-641. On the philosophical foundations of eminent domain, see Joseph L. Sax, "Takings and the Police Power," *Yale Law Journal* 74 (1964), 36-76; and Sax, "Takings, Private Property and

Public Rights," *Yale Law Journal,* 81 (1971), 149-186.

12. Rogers v. Bradshaw, 20 John R. 735 (N.Y. 1823) at 740.

13. Hurst, *Law and Economic Growth,* 181-182; Scheiber, "Road to Munn," 361. I am also indebted to Professor Morton Horwitz for useful suggestions and comments.

14. Parker, J. (per curiam), Callender v. Marsh, 1 Pick. 417 (Mass. 1823) at 430.

15. Monongahela Navig. Co. v. Coons, 6 Watts & S. 101 (Penn. 1843) at 115.

16. Smith v. Corp. of Washington, 20 How. 135 (U.S. 1857) at 147-149.

17. The bias of juries in favor of small-property owners suffering damages from takings can safely be assumed, I think. Corroborative evidence is in Wex S. Malone, "The Formative Era of Contributory Negligence," *Illinois Law Review,* 41 (1946), 155-160.

18. Apart from the staggering problem of evaluating the available data for damages awarded versus market value of property taken, there is the troublesome question of transaction costs: even if property owners arrived at negotiated settlement of damages, when did they do so because the offer made them was fair and when because the costs of litigation (the only alternative) and of time spent on it would be so dear?

19. For a brief period after 1840, New Hampshire suspended devolution policy. See Edward Chase Kirkland, *Men, Cities and Transportation: A Study in New England History, 1820-1900,* 2 vols, (Cambridge, Mass., 1948), I, 163-164.

20. Scheiber, *Ohio Canal Era: A Case Study of Government and the Economy, 1820-1861* (Athens, Ohio, 1969), 277-278. Frequent damage awards of one dollar, after offsetting had been figured, occurred in Illinois, as considered in a seminar paper (MS., 1972) by Mark Van Ausdal, University of Chicago Law School. Much later, awards of six cents, after offsetting, became a cause célèbre in New York. See New York, Constitutional Convention of 1894, *Revised Record* (Albany, 1900), 633-635, 651-653. "Oppression" of landowners through damage judgments is discussed in *American Jurist,* 2 (1829), 33; and, later in the railroad era, off-

setting of benefits was singled out as the source of great "loss and wrong" in a polemical pamphlet, *Eminent Domain and Rail Road Corporations: Some Thoughts on the Subject — By a Farmer* (Philadelphia, 1873), 9 (copy in Eleutherian Mills Historical Library). Cf. J. B. Thayer, "The Right of Eminent Domain," *Monthly Law Reporter,* n.s. 9 (1865), 307-312.

21. Newcomb v. Smith, 2 Pinn. 131 (Wisc. 1849) at 138; Angell, *Watercourses,* chap. 12.

22. Railroad Co. v. Wilson, 17 Illinois 123 at 127 (1856); Brainerd v. Clapp, 10 Cush. 6 (Mass. 1852) at 10-11; cf. Childs v. N. J. Centr. Railroad Co., 33 N. J. L. 323.

23. Beekman v. Railroad Co., 3 Paige 45 (N.Y. Ch., 1831) at 73; Boston etc. Mill Dam Co. v. Newman, 12 Pick, 467 (Mass., 1832) at 480.

24. On similar grounds, many states had permitted expropriation for building wharves and basins, establishing ferries, draining marshes and swamps, and conveying water to towns (see Scheiber, "Road to Munn," 367-368; and Thayer, "Right of Eminent Domain," passim).

25. Boston etc. v. Newman, 12 Pick. 467 (Mass., 1832); Murdock v. Stickney, 8 Cush. 113 (Mass. 1851); Glover v. Powell, 2 Stock. 211 (N. J. Ch., 1854).

26. Scudder v. Trenton Del. Falls Co., 1 N.J. Eq. 694 (1832). "The landholders adjacent to the Company's works held the key to its prosperity, and a perfect control over it" (Trenton Delaware Falls Co., *Second Annual Report* [1833], 12).

27. Boston etc. v. Newman, 12 Pick. 467 (Mass., 1832) at 481.

28. Cooley, C. J. (per curiam), Ryerson v. Brown, 35 Mich. 334 (1877) at 337.

29. West River Bridge v. Dix, 6 How. 507 (U.S. 1848), on which see Scheiber, "Road to Munn," 376-380.

30. Ibid.; the taking of a franchise was considered again in Richmond etc. Railroad v. Louisa Railroad, 13 How. 71 (U.S. 1852).

31. See sources cited above, note 20.

32. Mills v. St. Clair County, 8 How. 569 (1850) at 584.

33. Ohio State Constitutional Convention of 1850, *Reports and Debates,* 2 vols.

(Columbus, 1851), 883-893; Cormack, "Legal Concepts," 244-246 (on the Illinois convention of 1870 debate on consequential damages); Charles T. McCormick, "The Measure of Compensation in Eminent Domain," *Minnesota Law Review,* 17 (1933), 492-493 (on Iowa, etc.); *Proceedings of the New York Constitutional Convention of 1867-68* (Albany, 1868), 3247-56.

34. See, for example, Perry v. Wilson, 7 Mass. 393 (1811) on log-boom franchises; Anon., "Rights of the Public in Fresh Water Rivers," *American Law Magazine,* 5 (1845), 267-281, on Connecticut and Pennsylvania doctrines; Commonwealth v. Chapin, 5 Pick. 199 (Mass. 1827), on rights in fisheries; and Holyoke Co. v. Lyman, 15 wall. 500 (82 U.S. 133) (1873), retrospectively, on the same; State v. Tyre Glen, 7 Jones 321 (N.C. 1859); and Scheiber, "Road to Munn," 373-376.

35. See Charles Fairman, *Reconstruction and Reunion, 1864-88, Oliver Wendell Holmes Devise History of the Supreme Court,* vol. VI, pt. 1 (New York, 1971), 918-1116, an exhaustive analysis of railroad bond-aid litigation.

36. Penn. Coal Co. v. Sanderson, 113 Pa. 126 (1886) at 149; quotation from Hughes v. Anderson, 68 Ala. 280, in ibid., at 139. On railroad immunity from nuisance, compare Penn. Railroad Co. v. Marchant, 119 Pa. 541 (1888), and see generally Lewis Orgel, *Valuation under the Law of Eminent Domain,* 2d ed., 2 vols. (Charlottesville, 1953), I, 37-38.

37. On such Fourteenth Amendment applications, see John P. Roche, "Entrepreneurial Liberty and the Fourteenth Amendment," *Labor History,* 4 (1963), 3-31.

38. Talbot v. Hudson, 82 Mass. 417 (1860) at 425. Interestingly, the case involved a challenge to the state's condemnation of a dam originally built under the expropriation power by a private canal company.

39. 47 N.H. 444 (1867) at 471.

40. Colorado, 1876 Const., Art. II, sec.14 cf. D.W. Hensel, "History of the Colorado Constitution in the Nineteenth Century" (Ph.D. diss., University of Colorado, 1957), 167-174, esp. 169 on Colorado delegates' reference to drainage-works provisions for eminent-domain devolution in Missouri and Illinois constitutions.

41. John D. Hicks. *The Constitutions of the Northwest States, University of Nebraska Studies,* XXIII (Lincoln, 1923), 146, and passim. Gordon M. Bakken, "The Impact of the Colorado State Constitution on Rocky Mountain Constitution Making," *Colorado Magazine of History,* 47 (1970), 152-175 treats eminent-domain debates.

42. *Proceedings and Debates of the Constitutional Convention of Idaho, 1889* (Caldwell, 1912) 304.

43. Idaho Const. of 1889, Art. I, sec. 14.

44. Dayton Gold & Silv. Min. Co. v. Seawell, 11 Nev. 394 (1876) at 400-401, 411.

45. See, e.g., Highland Boy Gold Mining Co. v. Strickley, 78 Pac. 298 (Utah, 1904).

46. Butte, A. & P. Railroad Co. v. M.U. Railroad Co., 16 Mont. 504 (1895).

47. Stat. quoted in Potlatch Lumber Co. v. Peterson, 88 Pac. 430 (Idaho, 1906).

48. Ibid. at 431.

49. Oury v. Goodwin, 26 Pac, 376 (Ariz. 1891) at 382, and passim. This topic is a main theme of analysis in Samuel C. Wiel, *Water Rights in the Western States,* 3d ed., 2 vols. (San Francisco, 1911), esp. chap. 8.

50. Ibid., I, 148-157, and passim. Unlike western states which followed the Colorado-Idaho liberal line on private use, California and Oregon courts placed strict limitations upon expansion of the public-use doctrine to support strictly private interests. Cf. Gilmer v. Lime Point, 18 Cal. 229 (1861), and, *inter alia,* Weil, *Water Rights.* In 1894 the New York constitution was revised to include a provision declaring agricultural drainage to be a "public use," so as to permit construction of drainage lines across private property on payment of "just compensation." But the high court of New York State promptly declared the new provision to be in violation of the Constitution (New York, 1894 Constitutional Convention, *Revised Record,* 1061; Matter of Tuthill, 163 N.Y. 133, [1900, 79 Am. St. Rep. 574]).

51. Pumpelly versus Green Bay, 13 Wall. 166 (1872).

52. C.B. & Q. Railroad Co. v. Chicago, 166 U.S. 226 (1897).

53. Clark v. Nash, 198 U.S. 361 (1904); Fallbrook Irrigation District v. Bradley, 164 U.S. 112 (1896).

54. Clark v. Nash, 198 U.S. 367ff.

55. On this problem, cf. Hensel, "Colorado Constitution," 298-300.

56. Hairston v. Danville & W. Railroad Co., 208 U.S. 598 (1907) at 605. The Court also upheld statutes which specifically required offsetting of estimated benefits in appraising damages under eminent-domain takings; cf. Bauman v. Ross, 167 U.S. 548 (1897). On the other side of the coin, however, the Court reaffirmed and somewhat widened its requirement that consequential damages, when they utterly destroyed "the use and value" of property, must be compensated; cf. United States v. Lynah, 188 U.S. 445 (1903).

57. Orgel, Valuation, I, 35-38. Many of the same western states that adopted the broadest definitions of public use were also early in the movement to reform compensation law; hence it is all the more difficult to put a dollar value on the subsidy effects of expanded eminent-domain law in the West. What is indisputable is the strategic importance of the expanded doctrine of public use — enterprises were given powerful instruments to set themselves going, and without those instruments would probably have foundered altogether.

58. Robert E. Cushman, Excess Condemnation (New York, 1917) covers the subject thoroughly for that period. See also Flavel Shurtleff, Carrying Out the City Plan (New York, 1914.)

59. The best single source of analysis and documentation is Charles M. Haar, Land-Use Planning: A Casebook on the Use, Misuse, and Re-use of Urban Land, 2d. ed. (Boston, 1971).

60. Allison Dunham, "Giggs versus Allegheny County in Perspective," Supreme Court Review, 1962 (Chicago, 1963), 82.

61. Mimeographed, the White House, January 19, 1972.

62. See text at n. 26. The White House policy document discussed above is squarely within the tradition of imposing what are supposed to be American values and institutions "on less fortunate countries," but particularly when American investment interests are served, a topic discussed in Robert B. Zevin, "An Interpreta-

tion of American Imperialism," The Journal of Economic History, 32 (1972), 359-360.

63. Hurst, Law and the Conditions of Freedom, 24 (italics added).

13. The Transformation in the Conception of Property in American Law, 1780-1860

MORTON J. HORWITZ

1. For Blackstone, the right of property consisted of "that sole and despotic dominion which one man claims and exercises over the external things of the world, in total exclusion of the right of any other individual in the universe," Sir William Blackstone, Commentaries, II, 2.

2. Blackstone, Commentaries, II, 217-218.

3. See Francis H. Bohlen, "The Rule in Rylands versus Fletcher," University of Pennsylvania Law Review, 59 (1911), 298.

4. Use your own [property] so as not to harm another's.

5. Though there had been controversies involving diversion of water for irrigation or saw- and gristmills in the colonial period, the building of the large New England cotton mills after 1815 intensified the conflict.

6. Merritt v. Parker, 1 New Jersey L. 526, 530 (Sup. Ct. 1795). See also Beissell v. Sholl, 4 Dall. 211 (Pa. 1800); Livezay v. Gorgas (Pa. 1811), in Hugh H. Brackenridge, Law Miscellanies (Philadelphia, 1814), 454-456.

7. Perkins v. Dow, 1 Root 535 (1793), citing Howard v. Mason (1783). "If I can dispose of, and absorb upon my land, the whole of the stream excepting a sufficiency for necessary purposes," a legal commentator explained, "I have the prior right, because I am above him on the stream and have the first opportunity" (Zephaniah Swift, A System of the Laws of the State of Connecticut (Windham, Conn., 1796), II, 86.) This rule did not, of course, express a theory of prior appropriation since, regardless of who first occupied the stream, the upper proprietor was granted "that artificial advantage which the situation of his ground will admit" (ibid., 87). Indeed, it appears to be the only instance in American Law of adoption of the

pre–civil-code French rule. See James Kent, *Commentaries on American Law* 4th ed. (New York, 1840), III, 439.

8. Ingraham v. Hutchinson, 2 Conn. 584, 591 (1818). Interestingly, the judge whose opinion overruled these eighteenth-century decisions was Zephaniah Swift, whose *System of Laws* (1795) had justified them. See above note, 7.

9. W. Cushing, "Notes of Cases Decided in the Superior & Supreme Judicial Courts of Massachusetts from 1772 to 1789," Manuscript, Treasure Room, Harvard Law School.

10. Weston v. Alden, 8 Mass. 136 (1811); Bent v. Wheeler (Mass. 1800), in James Sullivan, *The History of Land Titles in Massachusetts* (Boston, 1801), 273-274.

11. Palmer v. Mulligan, 3 Cai R. 307, 312 (N. Y. Sup. Ct. 1805) (Spencer, J.); Ingraham v. Hutchinson, 2 Conn. 584, 595 (1818) Gould, J., dissenting). In Sherwood v. Burr, 4 Day 244 (1810), the Connecticut Supreme Court resorted to the doctrine of prescription to deal with the novel problem of downstream obstruction, thereby implying that without long use the upstream owner would have no right of action for obstruction.

12. 3 Cai. R. 307, 313-14 (1805).

13. Id. at 314.

14. 15 Johns. 213, 218 (N.Y. 1818).

15. Id. at 218.

16. Outside New York, I have found only one other case before 1825 that followed the principle that diversion or obstruction of water might be justified by a doctrine of reasonable use which took account of a right to equal exploitation of water; this is Runnels v. Bulle, 2 N. H. 532, 537 (1823). See also Merritt v. Brinkerhoff, 17 Johns. 306 (1820).

17. Joseph H. Angell, *A Treatise on the Common Law, in Relation to Watercourses* 1st ed. (Boston, 1824), 37.

18. Angell, *Watercourses*, 37.

19. 24 F. Cas. 472 (No. 14,312) (C.C.D.R.I. 1827).

20. Lauer correctly sees the "almost schizophrenic . . . nature" of these early transitional water cases, which wavered between "both the pre-existent law and the need for just apportionment of the water" (T.E. Lauer, "Reflections on Riparianism," *Missouri Law Review*, 35 (1970), 8).

21. Story continued: "The consequence of this principle is, that no proprietor has a right to use the water to the prejudice of another. It is wholly immaterial, whether the party be a proprietor above or below, in the course of the river; the right being common to all the proprietors on the river, no one has a right to diminish the quantity which will, according to the natural current, flow to the proprietor below, or to throw it back upon a proprietor above" (24 F. Cas. at 474).

22. Id.

23. Though Tyler v. Wilkinson has often mistakenly been understood to expound a doctrine of proportionate use, I have found no subsequent case in which Story upheld any interference with the flow, unless based on prescriptive right as in *Tyler* itself. See Lauer, cited above note 20, p. 8. Indeed, Story often seemed routinely to apply a "natural flow" rule in granting injunctive relief. Farnum v. Blackstone Canal Corp., 8 F. Cas. 1059 (No. 4675) (C.C.D.R.I. 1830); Mann v. Wilkinson, 2 Sumner 273 (C.C.D.R.I. 1835). More illuminating still, in Webb v. Portland Mfg. Co., 29 F. Cas. 506 (No. 17,332) (C.C.D. Me. 1838), he found against a defendant who had extracted a proportionate part of the water from a stream for mill purposes even though there was no proof of actual damage. In Whipple v. Cumberland Mfg. Co., 29 F. Cas. 934 (No. 17,516) (C.C.D. Me. 1843), he upheld an action against a downstream mill owner for flowing back water, again without proof of actual injury to the plaintiff's mills. There was no need to prove damage, he wrote, since: "the principle of law goes much further; for every riparian proprietor is entitled to have the stream flow in its natural channel, as it has been accustomed to flow, without any obstruction by any mill or riparian proprietor below on the same stream . . . And if any mill or riparian proprietor below on the same stream does . . . undertake to obstruct or change the natural stream, then, although the riparian proprietor above cannot establish in proof, that he has suffered any substantial damage thereby, still he is entitled to recover nominal damages, as it is an invasion of his rights." Id. at 934-36. By allowing a damage action — and presumably an

injunction — without proof of actual injury, Story went beyond the common law in restraining exploitation of water resources. It was one thing to hold that economic development could not take place at another's expense, and quite another to allow an existing riparian owner to prevent exploitation of surplus water [simply because] he might use it at some future time. Not only was Story's formulation contrary to any supposed right of equal use, but it also resulted in a rule still more monopolistic and exclusionary than anything the common law had required.

24. Contrast Story's views with those put forth by the Vermont court in the same year: "The common law of England seems to be that each land owner, through whose land a stream of water flows, has a right to the water in its natural course, and any diversion of the same to his injury, gives him a right of action . . . Should this principle be adopted here, its effect would be to let the man who should first erect mills upon a small river or brook, control the whole and defeat all the mill privileges from his mills to the source." In the absence of "wanton waste" or "obstruction," it allowed the upstream proprietor to build a milldam that would interfere with the natural flow of water (Martin v. Bigelow, 2 Aiken 184, 187 [Vt. 1827]).

25. See e.g., Omelvany v. Jaggers, 2 S.C. (Hill) 634 (1835); Buddington v. Bradley, 10 Conn. 213 (1834); Arnold v. Foot, 12 Wend. 330 (N.Y. Sup. Ct. 1834).

26. Elliot v. Fitchburg R.R., 64 Mass. (10 Cush.) 191, 195 (1852).

27. Snow v. Parsons, 28 Vt. 459, 462 (1858). For a much earlier recognition of this principle, see Hoy v. Sterrett, 2 Watts 327, 332 (Pa. 1834), in which the court, though citing Tyler v. Wilkinson for the purpose of rejecting the plaintiff's claim to a right derived from prior occupancy, nevertheless held that if "the water was no longer detained than was necessary for a proper enjoyment of it . . . for the use of [the defendant's] mill, it is damage to which the plaintiff must submit."

28. Robert W. Fogel, Railroads and American Economic Growth (Baltimore, 1964), 123.

29. Angell, Watercourses, 2d. ed. (1833), vii.

30. Damage without legal injury.

31. "The Law of Water Privileges," American Jurist, 2 (1829), 25, 27.

32. 49 Mass. (8 Met.) 466 (1844).

33. Id. at 476-477.

34. Id. at 477. In more conventional cases as well, Shaw's court often insisted that any use of water for manufacturing purposes was prima facie reasonable, regardless of proportionality. See, e.g., Pitts v. Lancaster Mills, 54 Mass. (13 Met.) 156 (1847), where a manufacturing company was held justified in obstructing a stream so long as "they detained the water no longer than was necessary to raise their own head of water and fill their own pond." Id. at 158. See also Hoy v. Sterrett, 2 Watts 327 (Pa. 1834).

35. 49 Mass. (8 Met.) at 477.

14. The Law of the Commonwealth and Chief Justice Shaw

LEONARD W. LEVY

1. Draper v. Worcester & Norwich RR., 11 Metc. 505, 508 (1846).

2. Alexis de Tocqueville, Democracy in America, trans. Henry Reeve, I, chap. 16. In the Bowen translation, the passage reads: "Scarcely any political question arises in the United States that is not resolved, sooner or later, into a judicial question" (ed. Phillips Bradley [New York, 1954]) I, 290.

3. Lemuel Shaw, "Profession of the Law in the United States," extract from an address delivered before the Suffolk Bar, May, 1827, American Jurist 7 (1832), 56, 65.

4. (James) Willard Hurst, The Growth of American Law (Boston, 1950), p. 18.

5. Oscar Handlin and Mary F. Handlin, Commonwealth: A Study of the Role of Government in the American Economy: Massachusetts, 1774-1861 (New York, 1947), 31.

6. Shaw, "Profession of the Law," American Jurist, 61; and see A Charge Delivered to the Grand Jury for the County of Essex . . . May Term, 1832 (Boston, 1832), 4.

7. "Public Interests," Boston Commerical Gazette, September 23, 1819, quoted by Handlin and Handlin, 54-55.

8. Ibid., 54. For the experience of other states, see Louis Hartz, Economic Policy

and *Democratic Thought: Pennsylvania, 1776-1860* (Cambridge, Mass., 1948), and James Neal Primm, *Economy Policy in the Development of a Western State: Missouri, 1820-1860 (Cambridge, Mass., 1854).* For the colonial period through the Revolution, see Richard B. Morris, *Government and Labor in Early America* (New York, 1946).

9. E. Merrick Dodd, *American Business Corporations until 1860* (Cambridge, 1954). 44.

10. See Palmer Co. v. Ferrill, 17 Pick. 58 (1835) and Hazen v. Essex Co., 12 Cush. 475 (1835).

11. Dodd, *American Business Corporations,* 161.

12. 7 Cush. 53 (1851).

13. See Henry Steele Commager, "Joseph Story," in A. N. Holcombe et al., *Gaspar G. Bacon Lectures on the Constitution of the United States* (Boston, 1953), 58, where the paraphrase omits "historians."

14. Commonwealth v. Alger, 7 Cush. 53, 83-84 (1851).

15. Roscoe Pound, *The Spirit of the Common Law* (Boston, 1921), 53-54.

16. Quotations are from Shaw's opinions in the Alger case and in Commonwealth v. Tewksbury, 11 Metc. 55 (1846).

17. Quoted by Pound, *Spirit of the Common Law,* 53.

18. Commonwealth v. Farmers & Mechanics Bank, 21 Pick. 542 (1839).

19. Crease v. Babcock, 23 Pick. 334 (1839).

20. Commonwealth v. Blackington, *24* Pick, 352 (1837); Fisher v. McGirr, 1 Gray 1 (1854); Brown v. Perkins, 12 Gray 89 (1858); Commonwealth v. Howe, 13 Gray 26 (1859). There are the leading cases among dozens.

21. Worcester v. Western R.R., 4 Metc. 564, 566 (1842).

22. Roxbury v. B. & P. RR., 6 Cush. 424, 431-432 (1850).

23. B. & W. RR. v. Western RR., 14 Gray 253 (1859), and L. & W. C. RR. v. Fitchburg RR., 14 Gray 266 (1859).

24. Davidson v. B. & M. RR., 3 Cush. 91 (1849). See also Baker v. Boston, 12 Pick. 183 (1831).

25. Wetherbee v. Johnson, 14 Mass. 412 (1817); Holden v. James, 11 Mass. 396

(1814). A third precedent of 1799 had been unreported and was "lost."

26. Sohier v. Mass. General Hospital, 3 Cush. 483 (1849).

27. Warren v. Mayor and Alderman of Charlestown, 3 Gray 84 (1854).

28. Commonwealth v. Coolidge, *Law Reporter,* V, 482ff. (1843).

29. Jones v. Robbins, 8 Gray 329 (1857).

30. Fisher v. McGirr, 1 Gray 1 (1854); Sullivan v. Adams, 3 Gray 476 (1855); and Robinson v. Richardson, 13 Gray 454 (1859).

31. Commonwealth v. New Bedford Bridge, 2 Gray 339 (1854).

32. Commonwealth v. Essex Co., 13 Gray 239 (1859); Central Bridge Corp. v. Lowell, 15 Gray 106 (1860).

33. Commonwealth v. Farmers & Mechanics Bank, 21 Pick, 542, 556 (1838).

34. Shaw, "Charge to the Grand Jury, 1832," 4; and idem, "Profession of the Law," 62.

35. See Pound, *Spirit of the Common Law,* 13-15, 18-20, 27-28 and 37.

36. Louis Hartz, *The Liberal Tradition in America* (New York, 1955), 89.

37. Pound, *Spirit of the Common Law,* 15.

38. Alger v. Thacher, 19 Pick. 51, 53 (1837) per Morton, J.

39. Ibid. at 54.

40. Ibid. italics added. This was a common-law case not involving any statute.

41. Pound, *Spirit of the Common Law,* 19.

42. Brown v. Kendall, 6 Cush. 292 (1850); Shaw v. B. & W. RR. 8 Gray 45 (1857).

15. Emerging Notions of Modern Criminal Law in the Revolutionary Era: An Historical Perspective

WILLIAM E. NELSON

1. See, e.g., George A. Billias, ed., *Law and Authority in Colonial America* (Barre, Mass., 1965); Julius Goebel, Jr., and T. Raymond Naughton, *Law Enforcement in Colonial New York* (New York, 1944); Arthur P. Scott, *Criminal Law in Colonial Virginia* (Chicago, 1930); Raphael Semmes, *Crime and Punishment in Early Maryland* (Baltimore, 1938).

2. See, e.g., George L. Haskins, *Law and Authority in Early Massachusetts* (New

York, 1960); Edwin Powers, *Crime and Punishment in Early Massachusetts, 1620-1692* (Boston, 1966). Seven of the ten articles in the Billias book cited above, deal with Massachusetts.

3. Haskins, *Law and Authority in Early Massachusetts,* 16.

4. Grand Jury Charge by Hutchinson, C. J., Suffolk Super. Ct., March 1768, in Josiah Quincy, Jr. *Reports of Cases Argued and Adjudged in the Superior Court of Judicature of the Province of Massachusetts Bay, between 1761 and 1772,* ed. Samuel M. Quincy (Boston, 1865), 258, 259.

5. Engel v. Vitale, 370 U.S. 421, 425 (1962).

6. The chief towns of Middlesex in the late 1700s were Charlestown, Cambridge, Concord, Lexington, Newton, Watertown, and Framingham.

7. L. H. Butterfield, Leonard C. Faber, and Wendell D. Garrett, eds., *Diary and Autobiography of John Adams,* 4 vols. (Cambridge, Mass., 1961), II, 27.

8. Blackstone, Table of Contents, *Commentaries,* IV.

9. See Scott, *Criminal Law in Colonial Virginia,* 280-281.

10. This interest is indicated by the requirement that a man found guilty of fornication give a bond to the town as a guarantee of his undertaking to support the child (see The King v. Mallet, Msex Gen. Sess., May 1760, at 582).

11. Ten women were prosecuted even though at the time of their prosecution they had married their partners. See, e.g., The King v. Patterson, Msex Gen. Sess., March 1761, at 618.

12. Between 1760 and 1775, there were thirty-one prosecutions for offenses against the persons of individuals, sixteen for offenses against public trade and health, fourteen for offenses against public justice, eleven for offenses against government, and four for homicide.

13. See Simeon Howard, "A Sermon Preached before the Honorable Council and Honorable House of Representatives of the State of Massachusetts-Bay," in John W. Thornton, *The Pulpit of the American Revolution* (Boston, 1860), 355, 382-383, 393-394.

14. Of sixteen accused between 1760 and 1774 of Sabbath breaking, there were eight farmers, four artisans, two laborers, and two gentlemen. The statistics given are not for total prosecutions, but only for cases in which the courts records give defendants' occupations.

15. The King v. How, Msex Super. Ct., Jan. 1762, f. 285 (twenty years of hard labor for counterfeiting).

16. An Act for the Punishment of Fornication, and for the Maintenance of Bastard Children, Mass. Acts and Laws 1785, ch. 66 (enacted March 15, 1786) [hereafter Fornication Act].

17. In 1786, there were at least eight cases, the same number as in 1785, one more than in 1780, and only one less than in 1764, while in 1787, there were at least twelve convictions.

18. There were twelve prosecutions during these three years. No reason for this sudden increase is apparent, although possibly it was related to the "Second Awakening" then occurring in New England. See Perry Miller, *The Life of the Mind in America from the Revolution to the Civil War* (New York, 1965), 6-7.

19. *Remarks on the Existing State of the Laws of Massachusetts Respecting Violations of the Sabbath* (1816), 3.

20. See Paul Goodman, *The Democratic-Republicans of Massachusetts* (Cambridge, Mass., 1964), 89.

21. Timothy Dwight, "A Discourse on Some Events of the Last Century," delivered January 7, 1801, quoted in V. Stauffer, *New England and the Bavarian Illuminati,* Columbia University Studies in History, Economics, and Public Law, 82 (1918), 25.

22. V. Stauffer, *The Bavarian Illuminati,* 24.

23. William Cushing, "Notes on Biennial Elections and Other Subjects under Debate in Massachusetts Ratifying Convention, Jan. 1788," in William Cushing Papers, New York Historical Society.

24. V. Stauffer, *The Bavarian Illuminati,* 26.

25. See, e.g., *Remarks on the Existing State of the Laws in Massachusetts Respect-*

ing Violations of the Sabbath (1816), 5, 12, for examples of the use of such terminology.

26. V. Stauffer, *The Bavarian Illuminati*, 26.

27. While there had been only two cases each in 1782 and 1783, there were eleven in 1784 and 1785.

28. Oscar Handlin and Mary F. Handlin, *Commonwealth: A Study of the Role of Government in the American Economy: Massachusetts 1774-1861* (New York, 1947), 35-36, 59-64; Samuel E. Morison, *The Maritime History of Massachusetts, 1783-1860* (Boston, 1961), 30-32, 35-36; William B. Weeden, *Economic and Social History of New England*, 2 vols. (Boston, 1890), II, 843.

29. See Morison, *Maritime History of Massachusetts*, 166-167.

30. The drop between 1790 and 1791 was dramatic. There were twelve cases in 1789, nineteen in 1790, three in 1791, and five in 1792.

31. There were seventeen cases in 1800 and twenty in 1801.

32. See Morison, *Maritime History of Massachusetts*, 191.

33. There were twenty-two cases in 1807, twenty-four in 1808, and eighteen in 1809.

34. Josiah Quincy, *Remarks on Some of the Provisions of the Laws of Massachusetts Affecting Poverty, Vice and Crime* (Cambridge, Mass., 1822.)

35. The twenty-seven were laborers. Six of the remaining cases were against artisans and five against farmers.

36. Of the fifty-three, forty-six were laborers and seven were "transient persons." The remaining defendants were fifteen farmers, two artisans, and two gentlemen.

37. Speech by His Excellency Caleb Strong, Esq., before the Senate and House of Representatives of the Commonwealth of Massachusetts, January 15, 1802, in *Patriotism and Piety: The Speeches of His Excellency Caleb Strong, Esq.* (Newburyport, 1808), 48, 50.

38. Act for the Punishing and the Preventing of Larcenies, Mass. Acts and Laws 1784, ch. 66 (enacted March 15, 1785); Act Providing a Place of Confinement for Thieves and Others to Hard Labor, Mass. Acts and Laws 1784, ch. 63 (enacted March 14, 1785).

39. Gamaliel Bradford, *Description and Historical Sketch of the Massachusetts State Prison* (Charlestown, 1816), 10.

40. The act authorizing the penalty in larceny cases so provided; Mass. Acts and Laws 1784, ch. 66, §3.

41. In three cases in the Supreme Judicial Court's November term of 1804, for example, the following penalties were imposed: (1) one hour on the gallows plus a whipping of thirty stripes plus six years at hard labor, Commonwealth v. Tuttle, Msex Sup. Jud. Ct., Nov. 1804, at 78; (2) payment of treble damages plus seven years at hard labor, Commonwealth v. Moore, Msex Sup. Jud. Ct., Nov. 1804, at 79; and (3) a whipping of thirty stripes plus either payment of treble damages or sale in service for three years, Commonwealth v. Moore, Msex Sup. Jud. Ct., Nov. 1804, at 80.

42. Harry E. Barnes, *The Evolution of Penology in Pennsylvania: A Study in American Social History* (Indianapolis, 1927).

43. See Act to Prevent Forgery, and for the Punishment of Those Who Are Guilty of the Same, Mass. Acts and Laws 1784, ch. 67.

44. Address by Governor John Hancock to a Joint Session of the Massachusetts Legislature, January 31, 1793, quoted in Edwin Powers, *Crime and Punishment in Early Massachusetts* (Boston, 1966), 192-193.

45. Powers, *Crime and Punishment*, 193.

46. Gamaliel Bradford, *State Prisons and the Penitentiary System Vindicated* (Charlestown, 1821), 5.

47. Bradford, *Description and Historical Sketch*, 15.

48. Bradford, *State Prisons*, 12.

49. Thomas B. Chandler, "A Friendly Address to All Reasonable Americans on the Subject of Our Political Confusions" (New York, 1774), 5, quoted in Bernard Bailyn, ed., *Pamphlets of the American Revolution, 1750-1776* (Cambridge, Mass., 1965), I, 198-199.

50. Grand Jury Charge by Hutchinson, C. J., Suffolk Super. Ct., August 1766, in Quincy, *Reports of Cases Argued and Adjudged in Massachusetts Bay*, 218, 220.

51. Grand Jury Charge by Hutchinson, C. J. Suffolk Super. Ct., March 1765, in Quincy,

Reports of Cases Argued and Adjudged in Massachusetts Bay, 110.

52. Diary and Autobiography of John Adams, I, 260.

53. Letter from Oliver Prescott, Town Clerk of Groton, Mass., to Town of Boston, Mass., 1774, quoted in Clifford K. Shipton, Sibley's Harvard Graduates, 1746-1750 (Boston, 1962), 570.

54. Diary and Autobiography of John Adams, I, 264.

55. Grand Jury Charge by Hutchinson, C. J., Suffolk Super. Ct., August 1776, in Quincy, Reports of Cases, Argued and Adjudged in Massachusetts Bay, 218, 219.

56. Bernard Bailyn, Introduction to Pamphlets of the American Revolution, 1750-1776, 190; Gordon S. Wood, "Rhetoric and Reality in the American Revolution," William and Mary Quarterly, 3rd ser. 23 (1966), 3, 5-6, 11.

57. Message from Governor Hancock to the General Court, quoted in Powers, Crime and Punishment, 193.

58. Gustav A. Koch, Republican Religion: The American Revolution and the Cult of Reason (New York, 1933), 295.

59. Commonwealth v. Waite, 5 Mass. 261, 264 (1809).

60. Bradford, State Prisons, 51.

16. Violence and Vigilantism in American History

RICHARD MAXWELL BROWN

1. Virgil C. Jones, The Hatfields and the McCoys (Chapel Hill, 1948).

2. Rufus L. Gardner, The Courthouse Tragedy, Hillsville, Va. (Mt. Airy, N.C., 1962).

3. One of the most spectacular of the family factional feuds in New Mexico was the Lincoln County War (1878) from which Billy the Kid emerged to fame. See Maurice G. Fulton, History of the Lincoln County War, ed. Robert N. Mullin (Tucson, 1968).

4. Earle R. Forrest, Arizona's Dark and Bloody Ground (Caldwell, Idaho, 1936); Zane Grey, To the Last Man (New York, 1922).

5. Mitford M. Mathews, ed., A Dictionary of Americanisms on Historical Principles, one-volume ed. (Chicago, 1956), 1010.

6. James E. Cutler, Lynch-Law: An Investigation into the History of Lynching in the United States (New York, 1905), 24-31.

7. In addition to Cutler, Lynch Law, see Walter White, Rope & Faggot: A Biography of Judge Lynch (New York, 1929), and Arthur F. Raper, The Tragedy of Lynching (Chapel Hill, 1938).

8. Cutler, Lynch-Law, 180-181, and passim. A total of 3,337 Americans were lynched from 1882 to 1903. Of the victims, 1,169 were whites, 2,060 were Negroes, and 108 were of other races.

9. Stanley F. Horn, Invisible Empire: The Story of the Ku Klux Klan, 1866-1871 (Boston, 1939).

10. Two outstanding recent studies of the second Ku Klux Klan are David M. Chalmers, Hooded Americanism: The First Century of the Ku Klux Klan, 1865-1965 (Garden City, N.Y., 1965); and Charles C. Alexander, The Ku Klux Klan in the Southwest (Lexington, Ky., 1965).

11. Ray A. Billington, The Protestant Crusade, 1800-1860: A Study of the Origins of American Nativism (New York, 1938.)

12. John E. Coxe, "The New Orleans Mafia Incident," Louisiana Historical Quarterly, 20 (1937), 1067-1110, and John S. Kendall, "Who Killa De Chief," ibid., 22 (1939), 492-530. The lynching of the Italians (which brought a threat of an Italo-American war) was the result of the vigilante action. Although there had been a recent criminal incident (the murder of the police chief) which to some seemed to justify vigilante action, the lynching was not merely a simple case of vigilante action. Ethnic prejudice against the Italians (who were allegedly members of a local Mafia organization) was crucial.

13. Donald L. Kinzer, An Episode in Anti-Catholicism: The American Protective Association (Seattle, 1964).

14. See, for example, Richard Walsh, Charleston's Sons of Liberty: A Study of the Artisans, 1763-1789 (Columbia, S.C., 1959), 3-55, and R.S. Longley, "Mob Activities in Revolutionary Massachusetts," New England Quarterly, 6 (1933), 108-111.

15. On the events of 1877, see one of the most important works on the history of

American violence: Robert V. Bruce, *1877: Year of Violence* (Indianapolis, 1959).

16. ... A seminal treatment is Arthur I. Waskow, *From Race Riot to Sit-In, 1919 and the 1960's: A Study in the Connections between Conflict and Violence* (Garden City, N.Y., 1966); two important case studies are Elliot M. Rudwick, *Race Riot at East St. Louis: July 2, 1917* (Carbondale, Ill., 1964), and Robert Shogan and Tom Craig, *The Detroit Race Riot: A Study in Violence* (Philadelphia, 1964), which covers the 1943 riot.

17. Walter Prescott Webb, *The Texas Rangers* (Boston, 1935).

18. Roger Lane, *Policing the City: Boston, 1822-1855* (Cambridge, Mass., 1967).

19. Martha Derthick, *The National Guard in Politics* (Cambridge, Mass., 1965), 16-17.

20. James D. Horan, *The Pinkertons: The Detective Dynasty that Made History* (New York, 1968).

21. See, for example, Anthony S. Nicolosi, "The Rise and Fall of the New Jersey Vigilant Societies," *New Jersey History*, 86 (1968), 29-32, and Hugh C. Gresham, *The Story of Major David McKee, Founder of the Anti Horse-Thief Association* (Cheney, Kans., 1937).

22. J[eremiah] P. Shalloo, *Private Police: With Special Reference to Pennsylvania* (Philadelphia, 1933), 58-134.

23. It will probably be impossible ever to obtain a definitive count of American vigilante movements; many small movements undoubtedly left no traces in historical sources, especially in the old Northwest and old Southwest in the first twenty or thirty years of the nineteenth century. Three hundred and twenty-six movements are presently known ...

24. There have been, indeed, urban as well as rural vigilante movements. The greatest of all American vigilante movements — the San Francisco Vigilance Committee of 1856 — was an urban one. Vigilantism has by no means been restricted to the frontier, although most typically it has been a frontier phenomenon.

25. Aside from the South Carolina regulators there was little vigilante activity in the original thirteen states of the Atlantic seaboard. The North Carolina regulators (1768-

1771) did not constitute a vigilante movement, but rather represented a violent agrarian protest against corrupt and galling local officials and indifferent provincial authorities.

26. The 96th meridian approximately coincides with both physiographic and state boundaries. Physiographically it roughly separates the prairies of the East from the semiarid Great Plains of the West. The states of Minnesota, Iowa, Missouri, Arkansas, and Louisiana fall into the province of eastern vigilantism. The states of North and South Dakota, Nebraska, Kansas, and Oklahoma mainly fall into the area of western vigilantism. In Texas the 96th meridian separates east Texas from central and west Texas, hence east Texas vigilantism was a part of eastern vigilantism, while central and west Texas properly belongs to the western variety. For the sake of convenience, however, all of Texas vigilantism (along with that of the Dakotas, Nebraska, Kansas, and Oklahoma) has been included in the tables under the heading of western vigilantism.

27. Lynn Glaser, *Counterfeiting in America* ... (New York, 1968), chap. 5. On the relationship between counterfeiting and the frontier money shortage, see Ruth A. Gallaher, "Money in Pioneer Iowa, 1838-1865," *Iowa Journal of History and Politics*, 31 (1934), 42-45.

28. The literature on this crucial organization is very large. The best and most complete account (although highly prejudiced in favor of the vigilantes) is the second volume of Bancroft's *Popular Tribunals*. See also, Richard Maxwell Brown, "Pivot of American Vigilantism: The San Francisco Vigilance Committee of 1856," *Reflections of Western Historians*, ed. John A. Carroll (Tucson, 1969), 105-119. The 1856 vigilance committee was preceded by that of 1851, which has been the subject of an outstanding scholarly study by Mary Floyd Williams, *History of the San Francisco Committee of Vigilance of 1851: A Study of Social Control on the California Frontier in the Days of the Gold Rush* (Berkeley, 1921). See also, Bancroft, *Popular Tribunals*, I, 201-428; and George R. Stewart, *Committee of Vigilance: Revolution in San Francisco, 1851* (Boston, 1964).

29. See, especially, Bancroft, *Popular Tribunals*, I, 441ff.

30. Thomas J. Dimsdale,*The Vigilantes of Montana* . . . (Virginia City, Mont. 1866); Nathaniel Pitt Langford, *Vigilante Days and Ways* . . ., 2 vols. (Boston, 1890); Hoffman Birney, *Vigilantes* (Philadelphia, 1929).

31. Granville Stuart, *Forty Years on the Frontier*, ed. Paul C. Phillips 2 vols (Cleveland, 1925), II, 195-210; Michael A. Leeson, *History of Montana: 1739-1885* (Chicago, 1885), 315-316.

32. Erna B. Fergusson, *Murder and Mystery in New Mexico* (Albuquerque, 1948), 15-32. Chester D. Potter, "Reminiscences of the Socorro Vigilantes," *New Mexico Historical Review*, 40 (1965), 23-54.

33. On the Butler County vigilantes, see A.T. Andreas, *History of the State of Kansas* . . . , 2 vols. (Chicago, 1883), 1431-1432, and the correspondence of Governor J.M. Harvey, File on County Affairs, 1869-1872 (MSS in Archives Department of Kansas State Historical Society, Topeka). Materials on Kansas vigilantism are also to be found in Nyle H. Miller and Joseph W. Snell, *Why the West Was Wild* . . . (Topeka, 1963), and Genevieve Yost, "History of Lynching in Kansas," *Kansas Historical Quarterly*, 2 (1933), 182-219; see also Robert R. Dykstra, *The Cattle Towns* (New York, 1968).

34. The classic (but far from flawless) contemporary account by the antiregulator Asa Shinn Mercer was *The Banditti of the Plains* . . . (Cheyenne, 1894). A very good recent study is Helena Huntington Smith, *The War on Powder River* (New York, 1966); general treatments of Western vigilantism are found in Bancroft, *Popular Tribunals*, I, 593-743; Wayne Gard, *Frontier Justice* (Norman, Okla., 1949), chap. 14 and Carl Coke Rister, "Outlaws and Vigilantes of the Southern Plains," *Mississippi Valley Historical Review*, 19 (1933), 537ff.

35. The figure of seventy-nine killings was gained from an analysis of Bancroft's narrative in *Popular Tribunals*, I, 515-576.

36. This distinction between "colonized" and "cumulative" new communities was formulated by Page Smith in *As a City upon a Hill: The Town in American History* (New York, 1966), 17-36.

37. The following sketch of the three-level American community structure is based upon my own research and recent studies on American society. Among the latter are Jackson Turner Main, *The Social Structure of Revolutionary America* (Princeton, 1965), and, for the nineteenth century Stephen Thernstrom, *Poverty and Progress: Social Mobility in a Nineteenth Century City* (Cambridge, 1964); Ray A. Billington, *America's Frontier Heritage* (New York, 1966), chap. 5, "The Structure of Frontier Society"; and Merle Curti, *The Making of an American Community* (Stanford, 1959), 56-63, 78, 107-111ff., 126, 417ff., 448.

38. On the marginal "lower people" of the South (where they are often called "poor whites" or "crackers") see Brown, *South Carolina Regulators*, 27-29, and Shields McIlwaine, *The Southern Poor White from Lubberland to Tobacco Road* (Norman, Okla., 1939), a literary study. For lower people in the North, see Bernard De Voto, *Mark Twain's America* (Boston, 1932), 54-58, and George F. Parker, *Iowa Pioneer Foundations*, 2 vols. (Iowa City, 1940), II, 37-48.

39. Kai Erikson, *Wayward Puritans: A Study in the Sociology of Deviance* (New York, 1966), chap. 1.

40. J. Milton Yinger, "Contraculture and Subculture," *American Sociological Review*, 25 (1960), 629, holds that a contraculture occurs "wherever the normative system of a group contains, as a primary element, a theme of conflict with the values of the total society . . ." See also, David M. Downes, *The Delinquent Solution: A Study in Subcultural Theory* (New York, 1966), 10-11.

41. See, for example, De Voto, *Mark Twain's America*, 58-62, and Parker, *Iowa Pioneer Foundations*, II, 37-48, 247-265.

42. David Donald, ed., "The Autobiography of James Hall, Western Literary Pioneer," *Ohio State Archaelogical and Historical Quarterly*, 56 (1947), 297-298.

43. Dimsdale, *Vigilantes of Montana*, p. 116.

44. Fred M. Mazzulla, "Undue Process of Law — Here and There," *Brand Book of Denver Westerners*, 20 (1964), 273-279. Dr. Osborne became governor of Wyoming in 1893.

45. Although at present I know of only 729 vigilante killings, it is surely possible that American vigilantism took as many as a thousand lives and perhaps more. In general, the statistics in this paper are tentative. Future findings might alter some of the figures, but it is not likely that the broad trends revealed by the statistics in this paper would be significantly changed.

46. On Coleman, see ... James A. B. Scherer, *The Lion of the Vigilantes: William T. Coleman and the Life of Old San Francisco* (Indianapolis, 1939).

47. See, for example, Anthony S. Nicolosi, "The Rise and Fall of the New Jersey Vigilant Societies," *New Jersey History*, 86 (1968), 29-32.

48. James Stuart, *Three Years in North America* 2 vols, (Edinburgh, 1933), II, 212-213. Jack K. Williams, "Crime and Punishment in Alabama," *Alabama Review*, 6 (1953), 26.

49. Jerome C. Smiley, *History of Denver* (Denver, 1901), 349 (emphasis mine).

50. M.H. Mott, *History of the Regulators of Northern Indiana* (Indianapolis, 1859), 15-18.

51. Alfred J. Mokler, *History of Natrona County, Wyoming 1888-1922* ... (Chicago, 1923).

52. Mott, *Regulators of Northern Indiana,* 17.

53. *Denver Tribune,* Dec. 20, 1879, cited in John W. Cook, *Hands Up ...,* 2d ed. (Denver, 1897), 103.

54. Robert B. David, *Malcolm Campbell, Sheriff* (Casper, Wyo., 1932), 18-32.

17. Urbanization and Criminal Violence in the Nineteenth Century: Massachusetts as a Test Case

ROGER LANE

1. See *The Challenge of Crime in a Free Society: A Report by the President's Commission on Law Enforcement and the Administration of Justice* (Washington, D.C., 1967), 29.

2. Four studies are especially germane: Harold A. Phelps, "Frequency of Crime and Punishment," *Journal of the American Institute of Criminal Law and Criminology,* 19 (1926), 165-180, which covers Rhode Island between 1897 and 1927; Sam Bass Warner, *Crime and Criminal Statistics in Boston* (Boston, 1934); Elwin H. Powell, "Crime as a Function of Anomie," *Journal of Criminal Law, Criminology, and Police Science* 57 (1966), 161, covering Buffalo from 1854 to 1956; and Theodore Ferdinand, "The Criminal Patterns of Boston since 1849," *American Journal of Sociology* 72 (1967), 84-89, which runs to 1951. These all differ in purpose and sophistication, and none are directly concerned with the long-term decline, which helps to make their results the more striking.

3. A survey of many of the official and criminal records of Boston and Massachusetts is contained in Roger Lane, *Policing the City: Boston, 1822-1885* (Cambridge, Mass., 1967), 225-229, 239-241.

4. See the Works by Ferdinand, Warner, and Lane, above, nn. 2 and 3. There is no attempt in them, or in this paper, to measure the extent of statutory or "white-collar" crime.

5. Thorstein Sellin and Marvin E. Wolfgang, *The Measurement of Delinquency* (New York, 1964), 31.

6. Ferdinand, "Criminal Patterns of Boston," 87. Together with roughly similar results in Powell's study of Buffalo, these figures suggest that the main conclusions of the present paper, which is largely confined to the nineteenth century, may be projected up to the founding of the Uniform Crime Reports and beyond.

7. Ferdinand, "Criminal Patterns of Boston," 99.

8. Statewide arrest figures were not compiled until very late in the nineteenth century, and comparing those for different cities involves many of the same problems as plague the students of the Uniform Crime Reports.

9. In this paper, except where specifically noted, no distinction is made between violent crimes — against the person — and other serious offenses. Such terms as "crime" and "disorder" are used to cover both.

10. Cf. *The Challenge of Crime,* 235, and Lane, *Policing the City,* passim, especially 112-113.

11. Alice Felt Tyler, *Freedom's Ferment: Phases of American Social History to 1860* (Minneapolis, 1944), chap. 13, especially p. 311.

12. Lane, *Policing the City*, 41, 71.

13. Unfortunately neither the federal nor the state census permits an accurate state-wide count of policemen during the nineteenth century.

14. Lane, *Policing the City*, pp. 230-232. The trend has continued. Modern police, despite the introduction of patrol cars and call wagons, make fewer arrests in general than did their predecessors, especially when the whole class of minor auto violations is eliminated.

15. Quoted in ibid., 25. For the other information in this paragraph see chap. 2, passim.

16. *Annual Report of the Commissioners of Police of the City of Boston for . . . 1885* (Boston, 1885), 28-30.

17. Lane, *Policing the City*, 173.

18. Population figures are from the *Census of Massachusetts . . . 1905* (Boston, 1909), I, xxxi. The urban definition based on a population of 8,000.

19. It should be noted that after the 1880s, when Boston already had nearly 2 policemen per 1,000 inhabitants, which is close to the present nationwide average for major cities, it was the smaller places only where the arrest rate continued to climb dramatically. Boston, because of its very small geographical area, was ahead of most American cities in this respect. It was still possible in other places to raise the arrest figures by extending patrol and demanding higher standards in previously neglected areas, such as outlying slums. This process and the reduction of the "dark figure" which results from better policing in general may account for many apparent "rises" in crime rates which are still occurring.

20. Oscar Handlin, *Boston's Immigrants: A Study in Acculturation*, rev. ed. (Cambridge, Mass., 1959), 244.

21. Lane, *Policing the City*, 72-74, 90-91 and 94-95.

22. First used by Josiah Quincy in his "Remarks on Some of the Provisions Affecting Poverty, Vice, and Crime" (Cambridge, Mass., 1822), these last four words became a stock phrase among the Commonwealth's reformers.

23. Lane, *Policing the City*, esp. pps. 122-125, 128-134, 142-156, and 213-219.

24. Lincoln Steffens, *Autobiography* (New York, 1931), 285-291.

25. In 1865, inspired by a fear of returning veterans much like that following World War II, the police made some 2,532 such arrests. See Lane, *Policing the City*, 149.

26. Ibid., 117.

18. Chattels Personal

KENNETH M. STAMPP

1. Extracts from the slave codes presented in this chapter were taken from the legal codes or revised statutes of the southern states. See also John C. Hurd, *The Law of Freedom and Bondage in the United States* (Boston, 1859-1862), and the various studies of slavery in individual states.

2. Helen T. Catterall, ed., *Judicial Cases concerning American Slavery and the Negro* (Washington, D.C., 1926-1937), I, 311.

3. Catterall, ed. *Judicial Cases*, I, 287; II, 76-77, 221.

4. Ibid., III, 68.

5. Wilmington (N.C.) *Journal*, July 12, 1853, quoting and commenting upon an editorial in the Anderson (S.C.) *Gazette*.

6. Catterall, ed., *Judicial Cases*, I, 149-150, 311; II, 112.

7. Ibid., II, 425-26, 561; James H. Easterby, ed., *The South Carolina Rice Plantation as Revealed in the Papers of Robert F. W. Allston* (Chicago, 1945), 69.

8. Catterall, ed., *Judicial Cases*, II, 440; III, 24.

9. Ibid., I, 390; II, 103, 541-542; III, 224.

10. *Richmond Enquirer*, December 8, 1831.

11. Catterall, ed., *Judicial Cases*, II, 168.

12. *Southern Presbyterian*, quoted in *De Bow's Review*, 18 (1855), 52; *Farmers' Register*, 4 (1836), 181.

13. Catterall, ed., *Judicial Cases*, II, 520-521.

14. Ibid., II, 240-241.

15. Ibid., II, 182; Howell M. Henry, *The Police Control of the Slave in South Carolina* (Emory, Va., 1914), 48; Joseph H. Ingraham, *The South-West by a Yankee* (Ann Arbor, Mich., 1966), II, 72-73; Ulrich B. Phillips, *American Negro Slavery* (New York, 1918), 497-498.

16. Henry, *Police Control*, 52; Charles S. Sydnor, *Slavery in Mississippi* (Gloucester, Mass., 1933), 83.

17. Undated petition from Chester District, South Carolina Slavery Manuscripts Collection; Clement Eaton, *Freedom of Thought in the Old South* (Durham, N.C., 1940), passim.

18. Austin, *Texas State Gazette*, February 19, 1859.

19. Wilmington (N.C.) *Journal*, August 24, 1849; Catterall, ed., *Judicial Cases*, III, 666.

20. Ulrich B. Phillips, *Plantation and Frontier Documents, 1649-1863, Illustrative of Industrial History in the Colonial and Antebellum South* (Cleveland, 1909), II, 113-114.

21. Austin, *Texas State Gazette*, July 22, 1854.

22. *Jackson Mississippian*, February 26, 1858; *Tallahassee Floridian and Journal*, April 11, 1857; *American Farmer*, II (1829), 167; Gwin G. Johnson, *Ante-Bellum North Carolina: A Social History* (Chapel Hill, 1937), 515-516.

23. Virginia Legislative Petitions (Mss., Virginia State Library, Richmond).

24. Austin, *Texas State Gazette*, September 12, 1857.

25. Catterall, ed., *Judicial Cases*, II, 530.

26. Ibid., II, 412-413.

27. Ibid., II, 107.

28. Ibid., II, 549-550; III, 35-36.

29. Ibid., II, 70-71, 132-34.

30. Henry, *Police Control*, 79; Thomas R.R. Cobb, *An Inquiry into the Law of Negro Slavery in the United States of America* (Philadelphia, 1858), 97-98.

31. Frederick Douglass, *My Bondage and My Freedom* (New York, 1855), 127.

32. Quoted in Sydnor, *Slavery in Mississippi*, 250–251.

33. Catterall, ed., *Judicial Cases*, III, 158–159.

34. Henry, *Police Control*, 58-61, 63-64; letter from Albert Rhett in Charleston *Courier*, January 27, 1842.

35. Alexandria (La.) *Red River Republican*, January 8, 1848; Harrison A. Trexler, *Slavery in Missouri, 1804-1865* (Baltimore, 1914), 79.

36. Catterall, ed., *Judicial Cases*, II, 161-62; John Hope Franklin, "Slaves Virtually Free in Ante Bellum North Carolina," *Journal of Negro History*, 18 (1943), 284-310; Richard B. Morris. "Labor Controls in Maryland in the Nineteenth Century; *Journal of Southern History*, 14 (1948), 385-387.

37. Catterall, ed., *Judicial Cases*, II, 442.

38. Ibid., III, 1-3, 61.

39. Ibid., II, 392; Charleston *Courier*, September 7, 1857.

40. Catteral, ed., *Judicial Cases*, III, 1-2.

41. Ibid., II, 49-50.

19. The American Civil War as a Constitutional Crisis

ARTHUR BESTOR

1. A contrary view is advanced by Sidney Hook: "The validity of the historian's findings will . . . depend upon his ability to discover a method of roughly measuring the relative strength of the various factors present" *Theory and Practice in Historical Study: A Report of the Committee on Historiography* (Social Science Research Council, Bulletin 54 [New York, 1946,] 113). Hook, writing as a philosopher, insists that his criterion is part of the "pattern of inquiry which makes a historical account scientific" (ibid., 112). But, as another philosopher, Ernest Nagel, points out, "the natural sciences do not appear to require the imputation of relative importance to the causal variables that occur in their explanations." On the contrary, "if a phenomenon occurs only where certain conditions are realized, all these conditions are equally essential, and no one of them can intelligibly be reguarded as more basic than the others" (Ernest Nagel, "Some Issues in the Logic of Historical Analysis," *Scientific Monthly*, 74 (March 1952), 162- 169, esp. 167).

2. Alexander H. Stephens, *A Constitutional View of the Late War between the States*, 2 vols. (Philadelphia, 1868-1870), I, 542.

3. Charles A. and Mary R. Beard, *The Rise of American Civilization*, 2 vols. (New York, 1927), II, 40, 42.

4. Ulrich B. Phillips, *The Course of the South to Secession*, ed. E. Merton Coulter (New York, 1939), 152.

5. William Blackstone, *Commentaries on the Laws of England*, 4 vols. (Oxford, 1765-1769), I, 49.

6. Joint Resolution to Amend the Constitution, March 2, 1861, 12 U.S. Statutes at Large 251. It passed the House by a vote of 133 to 65 on February 28, 1861, and the Senate by a vote of 24 to 12 on the night of March 3-4, 1861. Technically, the sitting of March 2, 1861, was still in progress in the Senate, hence the date attached to the joint resolution as officially published (*Congressional Globe*, 36th Cong., 2d sess., February 28, March 2, 1861, 1285, 1403).

7. First inaugural address, March 4, 1861, *Collected Works of Abraham Lincoln*, ed. Roy P. Basler et al., 9 vols. (New Brunswick, N. J., 1953-1955), IV, 270.

8. Ohio on May 13, 1861, Maryland on January 10, 1862, Illinois on February 14, 1862 (Herman V. Ames, *Proposed Amendments to the Constitution of the United States during the First Century of Its History*, *Annual Report, American Historical Association, 1896*, 2 vols. [Washington, D. C., 1897], II, 363.

9. Of the 3,953,760 slaves in the United States in 1860, 2,174,996 were held in the nine states of Kentucky, Tennessee, Florida, Alabama, Mississippi, Missouri, Arkansas, Louisiana, and Texas (U.S., Ninth Census [1870] I, *The Statistics of the Population* [Washington, D.C., 1872], 3-8 [a corrected recompilation of previous census figures].

10. U.S. Constitution, Art. I, sec. 8, clause 3.

11. The area of the so-called continental United States (exclusive of Alaska as well as of Hawaii) is officially put at 3,022,387 square miles. It attained this size in 1854. More than two-fifths of this area, that is, 1,234,381 square miles, is conventionally regarded as having been acquired through the annexation of Texas by joint resolution in 1845, the partition of the Oregon country by agreement with Great Britain in 1846, the cessions from Mexico by the treaty ending the Mexican War in 1848, and the additional territory acquired from the latter country by the Gadsden Purchase of 1853-1854. The conventional reckoning (which disregards all the complex questions created by prior American claims) is given in U. S. Bureau of the Census, *Historical Statistics of the United States, Colonial Times to 1957: A Statistical Abstract Supplement* (Washington, D. C., 1960), 236.

12. This was the form in which the proviso was adopted by the House on February 15, 1847 (*Congressional Globe*, 29th Cong., 2d sess., Feb. 15, 1847, 424-25). In its original form, as moved by David Wilmot of Pennsylvania on August 8, 1846, and adopted by the House the same day, it spoke only of "the acquisition of any territory from the Republic of Mexico" (ibid., 29th Cong., 1st sess., Aug. 8, 1846, 1217).

13. Ostend Manifesto (actually dated at Aix-la-Chapelle). October 18, 1854, *The Ostend Conference etc. (House Executive Documents)*, 33d Cong., 2d sess., X, no. 93), 131. Though Secretary of State William L. Marcy was forced by public opinion to repudiate the manifesto, James Buchanan was helped to the presidency in 1857 by the fact that his signature was on it.

14. *Collected Works of Lincoln*, ed. Basler et al., IV, 154, 155, 172. It should be noted that Stephen A. Douglas in his third debate with Lincoln, at Jonesboro, Illinois, on September 15, 1858, declared in forthright language that the doctrine of popular sovereignty ought to apply "when we get Cuba" and "when it becomes necessary to acquire any portion of Mexico or Canada, or of this continent or the adjoining islands" (ibid., III, 115). The word was "when," not "if."

15. Lincoln to Seward, February 1, 1861, ibid., IV, 183.

16. At the beginning of 1845 the United States comprised approximately 1,788,000 square miles (exclusive of its claims in the Oregon country). Of this total, 945,000

square miles were within the boundaries of the 26 full-fledged states of the Union; another 329,000 square miles belonged to organized territories; and the remaining 514,000 square miles were without organized civil governments. At the end of 1854 the total area had increased to approximately 3,022,000 square miles, of which 1,542,000 lay within the 31 states that were now members of the Union (Florida, Texas, Iowa, Wisconsin, and California having been admitted during the decade); another 1,410,000 square miles belonged to organized territories; and only 70,000 square miles remained in the unorganized Indian Territory. Boundaries are shown in Charles O. Paullin and John K. Wright, *Atlas of the Historical Geography of the United States* (Washington, D. C., 1932), plates 63A and 63B (for the situation in 1845), plates 63B, 64A, and 64C (for 1854).

17. In his first inaugural, Lincoln reiterated a statement he had made earlier in his debates with Douglas: "I have no purpose, directly or indirectly, to interfere with the institution of slavery in the States where it exists. I believe I have no lawful right to do so, and I have no inclination to do so" (*Collected Works of Lincoln*, ed. Basler et al., IV, 263). The statement was originally made in the debate at Ottawa, Illinois, August 21, 1858 (ibid., III, 16; see also the discussion of the proposed constitutional amendment of March 2, 1861, above, nn. 6-8).

18. U.S. Eighth Census (1860), *Preliminary Report on the Eighth Census, 1860* (Washington, D.C., 1862), 131; confirmed in the final report, *Population of the United States in 1860* (Washington, D.C. 1864), 598-599. Slaves were recorded in only three territories: fifteen in Nebraska, twenty-nine in Utah, and two in Kansas; a total of forty-six. Certain unofficial preliminary reports gave slightly higher figures: ten slaves in Nebraska, twenty-nine in Utah, twenty-four in New Mexico, and none in Kansas; a total of sixty-three (*American Annual Cyclopaedia, 1861* [New York, 1862], 696). It should be noted that the census figures for 1860 were tabulated in terms of civil divisions as they existed early in 1861. Thus Kansas was

listed as a state, though it was not admitted until January 29, 1861, and statistics were presented for the territories of Colorado, Dakota, and Nevada, though these were organized only in February and March 1861.

19. Census figures for the six states admitted from 1846 to 1861 inclusive (Iowa, Wisconsin, California, Minnesota, Oregon, and Kansas) and for the seven organized territories enumerated in the census of 1860 (Colorado, Dakota, Nebraska, Nevada, New Mexico, Utah, and Washington) showed an aggregate of 2,305,096 white persons, 7,641 free persons of color, and 46 slaves; making a total (including also "civilized Indians" and "Asiatics") of 2,382,677 persons (Eighth Census [1860], *Population*, 598-599). Ironically enough, the aborigines in the Indian Territory held in slavery almost as many Negroes as were to be found, slave or free, in the entire area just specified (Eighth Census [1860], *Preliminary Report*, 136. This special tabulation for the Indian Territory (not incorporated in the regular census tables) showed 65,680 Indians, 1,988 white persons, 404 free colored persons, and 7,369 slaves.

20. James G. Blaine, *Twenty Years of Congress*, 2 vols. (Norwich, Conn., 1884), I, 272, quoting an unnamed "representative from the South."

21. James G. Randall, *The Civil War and Reconstruction* (Boston, 1937), 114-115. In a later work, Randall described the issue of slavery in the territories, when debated by Lincoln and Douglas in 1858, as "a talking point rather than a matter for governmental action, a campaign appeal rather than a guide for legislation" (*Lincoln the President*, 4 vols. [New York, 1945-1955] I, 125).

22. As I have written elsewhere: "The fact that the controversy of 1846-1860 turned on the extension of slavery to the territories (and, to a lesser extent, on the fugitive-slave law) showed that antislavery leaders, far from flouting the Constitution, were showing it a punctilious respect. Had they been disposed, as their opponents alleged, to ride roughshod over constitutional limitations, they would hardly have bothered with the question of the territories or the question of fugitive slaves" (Arthur

Bestor, "State Sovereignty and Slavery," *Journal of the Illinois State Historical Society*, 44 [Summer 1961], 127).

23. The failure of the Republicans to mount a frontal attack upon slavery in the slaveholding states seemed to the Beards sufficient reason for treating the attack upon slavery as hardly more than a sham battle. Secession, they argued, was the southern planters' "response to the victory of a tariff and homestead party that proposed nothing more dangerous to slavery itself than the mere exclusion of the institution from the territories" (Beard, *Rise of American Civilization*, II, 37, see also 39-40.)

24. First debate with Douglas, Ottawa, Illinois, August 21, 1858, *Collected Works of Lincoln*, ed. Basler et al., III, 18 (italics of the original not reproduced here).

25. "Declaration of the Immediate Causes Which Induce and Justify the Secession of South Carolina from the Federal Union," December 24, 1860, *Journal of the Convention of the People of South Carolina, Held in 1860, 1861 and 1862* (Columbia, S. C., 1862), 465.

26. *Collected Works of Lincoln*, ed Basler et al., III, 18.

27. First inaugural, March 4, 1861, ibid., IV, 270; see also above, nn. 6-8.

28. In the U.S. Constitution the only reference to the slave trade is in a provision suspending until 1808 the power of Congress to prohibit "the Migration or Importation" of slaves (Art. I, sec. 9, clause 1). The power itself derives from the commerce clause (Art. I, sec. 8, clause 3), and Congress is not required to use it. By contrast, the Confederate Constitution not only announced that the foreign slave trade "is hereby forbidden," but also went on to require its Congress to pass the necessary enforcement laws. (Constitution of the Confederate States, Art. I, sec. 9, clause 1; text in Jefferson Davis, *The Rise and Fall of the Confederate Government*, 2 vols. (New York, 1881), I, 657).

29. U.S. Constitution, Art. I, sec. 8, clause 3.

30. In 1840 there were 448,743 slaves in Alabama and Mississippi, as against 448,987 in Virginia. In 1860 there were 871,711 slaves in the two Gulf states, as against only 490,865 in Virginia. During the same twenty years there was a net increase of 365,911 in the white population of the two Gulf states, and a net increase of 306,331 in the white population of Virginia, U.S., Ninth Census, (1870), I, *Population*, 3-8.

31. Last of the eight resolutions introduced in the Senate by Henry Clay, *Congressional Globe*, 31st Cong., 1st sess. Jan. 29, 1850, 246. According to Clay himself, the resolution proposed no new legislation, but merely asserted "a truth, established bv the highest authority of law in this country." He expected, he said "one universal acquiescence" (ibid.)

32. 9 Wheaton 1 (1824).

33. Champion v. Ames, 188 U.S. 321 (1903).

34. U.S. Constitution, Art. IV, sec. 2, clause 3.

35. Prigg v. Pennsylvania, 16 Peters 539 (1842).

36. South Carolina, "Declaration," Dec. 24, 1860, *Journal of the Convention*, 464.

37. In 1844, to be sure, the Liberty party solemnly repudiated this specific obligation: "We hereby give it to be distinctly understood, by this nation and the world, that, as abolitionists, . . . we owe it to the Sovereign Ruler of the Universe, as a proof of our allegiance to Him, in all our civil relations and offices, whether as private citizens, or as public functionaries sworn to support the Constitution of the United States, to regard and to treat the [fugitive slave clause] of that instrument . . . as utterly null and void, and consequently as forming no part of the Constitution of the United States, whenever we are called upon, or sworn, to support it" (*National Party Platforms, 1840-1956*, ed. Kirk H. Porter and Donald B. Johnson [Urbana, Ill., 1956], 8). Lincoln, on the other hand, solemnly reminded the nation in his first inaugural that public officials "swear their support to the whole Constitution — to this provision as much as to any other" (*Collected Works of Lincoln*, ed. Basler et al., IV, 263).

38. U.S. Constitution, Art. IV, sec. 3, clause 2.

39. *Congressional Globe,* 36th Cong., 2d sess., Dec. 18, 1860, 114.

40. *National Party Platforms,* ed. Porter and Johnson, 27. This argument from the due-process clause went back at least as far as the Liberty party platform of 1844 (ibid., 5). It was reiterated in every national platform of an antislavery party thereafter: in 1848 by the Free Soil party, in 1852 by the Free Democrats, and in 1856 and 1860 by the Republicans (ibid., 13, 18, 27, 32).

41. Ibid., 13. Repeated in the Free Democratic platform of 1852 (ibid., 18).

42. Stephen A. Douglas, "The Dividing Line between Federal and Local Authority: Popular Sovereignty in the Territories," *Harper's Magazine,* 19 (1859), 519-537, esp. 526.

43. Ibid., 520-521.

44. Douglas insisted that this clause referred "exclusively to property in contradistinction to persons and communities" (ibid., 528).

45. He likewise ignored all subsequent enactments of the same sort, save to register agreement with the dictum of the Supreme Court, announced in the Dred Scott opinion, that the Missouri Compromise had always been unconstitutional (ibid., 530).

46. Ibid., 525-526.

47. Report to Congress, March 1, 1784, and revised report, March 22, 1784, Julian P. Boyd et al., eds., *The Papers of Thomas Jefferson,* 16 vols. (Princeton, N.J., 1950-), VI, 604, 608.

48. Douglas, "Federal and Local Authority," 526. The antislavery provision came to a vote in the Continental Congress on April 19, 1784, under a rule requiring the favorable vote of the majority of the states for adoption. Six states voted in favor of the provision, only three against it. One state was divided. Another state could not be counted, because a quorum of the delegation was not present, but the single delegate on the floor voted "aye" (*Journals of the Continental Congress,* ed. Worthington C. Ford et al., 34 vols, [Washington, D.C., 1904-1937], XXVI, 247).

49. Ibid., XXXII, 343. This was the vote on July 13, 1787, adopting the Ordinance of 1787 with its antislavery article; only one member voted against the ordinance. There is no evidence of opposition to the antislavery article itself, which was added as an amendment in the course of the preceding debate.

50. Douglas, "Federal and Local Authority," 526.

51. *Journals of the Continental Congress,* ed. Ford et al., XXXII, 343. As if anticipating Douglas's contention that the earlier ordinance was "irrepealable," the Congress that had adopted it not only repealed it, but declared it "null and void."

52. These terms were suggested, and their propriety defended, in my article, "State Sovereignty and Slavery," 128-31, 147.

53. *Congressional Globe,* 29th Cong., 2d sess., Jan. 15, 1847, Appendix, 246.

54. Speech in Boston, reprinted in an appendix to Stephens, *Constitutional View,* I, 625-647, esp. 625.

20. The Reconstruction of Federal Judicial Power, 1863-1875

WILLIAM M. WIECEK

1. Only the original jurisdiction of the Supreme Court, accounting for a small portion of the Court's business, is beyond the power of Congress to enlarge or contract (U.S. Const. Art. III, sec. 2).

2. The president can veto a jurisdictional statute, or he can influence its contours before Congress passes it.

3. Among historians who have argued for judicial impotence during Reconstruction, see James F. Rhodes, *History of the United States from the Compromise of 1850,* 9 vols, (New York, 1900-1928), VI, 11, 12, 96; William A. Dunning, *Essays on the Civil War and Reconstruction and Related Topics* (New York, 1898), 121-122; William A. Dunning, *Reconstruction, Political and Economic 1865-1877* (New York, 1907), chap. 16; James G. Randall, *The Civil War and Reconstruction* (Boston, 1937), 802-806;

Claude Bowers, *The Tragic Era: The Revolution after Lincoln* (Cambridge, Mass., 1929), 153, 171, 215, to cite only some of the more influential. Specialists in constitutional development fell into the same errors, led by Charles Warren, *The Supreme Court in United States History*, 3 vols. (Boston, 1923), III, chaps. 27, 29, 30. See also, John W. Burgess, *Reconstruction and the Constitution, 1866-1876* (New York, 1903), 197; Robert H. Jackson, *The Struggle for Judicial Supremacy: A Study of a Crisis in American Power Politics* (New York, 1949), 326-327; Fred Rodell, *Nine Men: A Political History of the Supreme Court from 1790 to 1955* (New York, 1955), chap. 5; Walter F. Murphy, *Congress and the Court: A Case Study in the American Political Process* (Chicago, 1962), 35-43.

4. See Justice Robert Grier's oral remarks made when the Court announced its postponement of the decision on the merits in the McCardle case, quoted in Louis B. Boudin, *Government by Judiciary* (New York, 1932), II, 91-92; ex-President James Buchanan to Nahum Capen, June 11, 1867, in John B. Moore, ed., *Works of James Buchanan, Comprising His Speeches, State Papers and Private Correspondence* (Philadelphia, 1908-1911), XI, 446; Orville Browning, diary entry of April 9, 1868, in Theodore C. Pease and James G. Randall, eds., *Diary of Orville Hickman Browning* (Springfield, Ill., 1933), II, 191; ex-Attorney General Jeremiah S. Black to Howell Cobb, April (?), 1868, "The Correspondence of Robert Toombs, Alexander H. Stephens, and Howell Cobb," *American Historical Association Annual Report*, II (1911), 694; Gideon Welles, diary entry of March 20, 1868, Howard K. Beale, ed., *Diary of Gideon Welles*, 3 vols. (New York, 1960), III, 320. See also Stephen J. Field, "Personal Reminiscences," in Joseph A. Sullivan, ed., *California Alcalde* (Oakland, 1950). Even historians sympathetic to the accomplishments of the Reconstruction Congresses have misunderstood the effect of the McCardle repealer. See, e.g., Howard J. Graham, "Justice Field and the Fourteenth Amendment," *Yale Law Journal*, 52 (1943), 851, reprinted in Howard J. Graham, *Everyman's Constitution: Historical Essays on the Fourteenth Amendment, the "Conspiracy Theory" and American Constitutionalism* (Madison, 1968).

5. Reconstruction removal legislation has been recently examined in depth by Stanley I. Kutler, *Judicial Power and Reconstruction Politics* (Chicago, 1968), chap. 8.

6. U.S. Const. Art. III, sec. 2 defines the parties that may claim the Supreme Court's original jurisdiction and lists the types of subject matter which may form the grist for federal court mills.

7. 1 Wheat. 304 (U.S. 1816).

8. Ch. 20, 1 Stat. 79.

9. The jurisdiction that federal courts have over suits because the parties are residents of different states is known as "diversity jurisdiction"; the parties are said to be "diverse."

10. The "forum state" is the state in which the court where suit was brought is located.

11. Removal jurisdiction was so narrowly restricted because the Judiciary Act of 1789 was a compromise measure, trimmed down considerably from the original draft by Oliver Ellsworth to placate opponents of the lower federal courts. See Charles Warren, "New Light on the History of the Federal Judiciary Act of 1789," *Harvard Law Review*, 37 (1924), 49, 53. The short-lived Judiciary Act of 1801 (ch. 4, 2 Stat. 89, repealed by Act of 29 April, 1802, ch. 31, 2 Stat. 156) permitted removal of all federal question cases.

12. Ch. 21, 3 Stat. 195, reenacted by Act of 3 March 1815, ch. 94, 3 Stat. 231.

13. Act of 2 March 1833, ch. 57, 4 Stat. 632. In 1855 proslavery senators supported the Toucey removal bill (so called from the name of its sponsor, the Doughface Isaac Toucey of Connecticut) which would have extended similar protection to federal officials enforcing the federal fugitive-slave laws. Antislavery senators killed the bill in the Senate, condemning the "centralizing" tendencies of removal legislation. See debates in *Congressional Globe*, 33d Cong., 2d sess. App. 210ff. Both groups reversed their positions within a decade, *cui bono*.

14. Cf. Felix Frankfurter, "Distribution of Judicial Power Between United States and

State Courts," *Cornell Law Quarterly*, 13 (1928), 499-508.

15. Ch. 81, 12 Stat. 755. Similar provisions were contained in the Civil Rights Act of 1866, ch. 90, §§ 3, 10, 13 Stat. 507.

16. Act of 11 May 1866, ch. 80, 14 Stat. 46.

17. Ch. 99, 16 Stat. 433, rp. by Act of 8 Feb. 1894, ch. 25, 28 Stat. 36. For evidence of Congress's continuing concern for the safety of federal officers in southern state courts, see debates in *Congressional Globe*, 39th Cong., 2d sess., 1867, 729; 41st Cong., 3d sess., 1871, 1633ff.

18. Ch. 288, 14 Stat. 306.

19. 3 Cranch 267 (U.S., 1806).

20. For a discussion of the importance of this innovation, see Note, "Separation of Causes in Removal Proceedings," *Harvard Law Review*, 41 (1928), 1048.

21. Act of 2 March 1867, ch. 196, 14 Stat. 558.

22. See *Congressional Globe*, 39th Cong., 2d sess., 1867, p. 1865.

23. See Anthony Amsterdam, "Criminal Prosecutions Affecting Federally Guaranteed Civil Rights: Federal Removal and Habeas Corpus Jurisdiction to Abort State Court Trial," *University of Pennsylvania Law Review*, 113 (1965), 793, 818.

24. Felix Frankfurter and James M. Landis, *The Business of the Supreme Court: A Study in the Federal Judicial System* (New York, 1927), 65.

25. 18 Wall. 553 (U.S. 1874).

26. Jurisdiction and Removal Act of 1875, ch. 137, 18 Stat. 470.

27. 3 Cong. Rec. 2168 (1875).

28. U.S. Const., Art. I, sec. 9, clause 2.

29. Dallin H. Oaks, "The 'Original' Writ of Habeas Corpus in the Supreme Court," *Supreme Court Review*, 1962, 154.

30. See above, n. 8.

31. *Congressional Globe*, 39th Cong. 1st sess., 1866, p. 135.

32. *Congressional Globe*, 39th Cong. 1st sess., 1866, p. 4151.

33. Ex parte McCardle, 6 Wall. 318 (U.S., 1868).

34. See Kutler, *Judicial Power and Reconstruction Politics*, 99-100.

35. Act of 27 March 1868, ch. 34, § 2, 15 Stat. 44.

36. Debates are in *Congressional Globe*, 40th Cong. 2d sess., 1868, pp. 1860, 2096.

37. Ex parte McCardle, 7 Wall. 506, 515 (U.S., 1869).

38. Ex parte Yerger, 8 Wall. 85 (U.S. 1869).

39. Act of 3 March 1885, ch. 253, 23 Stat. 437.

40. See, e.g., "Abuses of the Writ of Habeas Corpus," *American Bar Association Reports*, 6 (1883), 243; "Federal Abuses of the Writ of Habeas Corpus," *American Law Review*, 25 (1891), 149.

41. 117 U.S. 241 (1886).

42. 140 U.S. 278 (1891).

43. Moore v. Dempsey, 261 U.S. 86 (1923). See Frank v. Mangum, 237 U.S. 309 (1915).

44. Waley v. Johnson, 316 U.S. 101 (1942); Brown v. Allen, 345 U.S. 946 (1953); Fay v. Noia, 372 U.S. 391 (1963); Townsend v. Sain, 372 U.S. 293 (1963).

45. Act of 2 Sept. 1789, ch. 12, 1 Stat. 65; Act of 8 May 1792, ch. 37, 1 Stat. 279; Act of 3 March 1817, ch. 45, secs. 1-4, 3 Stat. 366; Act of 19 April 1816, ch. 40, 3 Stat. 203.

46. See discussion in H.R. Rep. 730, 25 Cong. 2 sess. ser. 335.

47. Act of 24 Feb. 1855, ch. 122, 10 Stat. 612.

48. See *Congressional Globe*, 34th Cong. 1st sess., 1856, pp. 608-610, 970-972, 1241-1243.

49. James D. Richardson, comp., *A Compilation of the Messages and Papers of the Presidents*, 11 vols., (New York, 1911), VII, 3252.

50. See *Congressional Globe*, 37th Cong., 3d sess., 1863, 307-309, 426; Act of 12 March 1863, ch. 120, 12 Stat. 820.

51. The reporting of *Gordon v. United States* compounded the confusion. The official report, 2 Wall. 561, is not Chase's opinion, but rather a note drafted by the reporter, John A. Wallace, which was inaccurate. Chase's opinion appears only in 17 L.Ed. 921. A draft opinion in the case written by Chief Justice Taney just before his death was found and reprinted in 1886, 117 U.S. 697, App.

52. Act of 17 March 1866, ch. 19, 14 Stat. 9; *Congressional Globe*, 39th Cong., 1st sess., 1866, pp. 770-777.

53. Ch. 19, 2 Stat. 19. On the subject of bankruptcy, see generally, Charles Warren, *Bankruptcy in the United States* (Cambridge, Mass., 1935).

54. Act of 19 Dec. 1803, ch. 6, 2 Stat. 248.

55. Act of 19 Aug. 1841, ch. 9, 5 Stat. 440. Act of 13 March 1843, ch. 82, 5 Stat. 614.

56. Act of 2 March 1867, ch. 176, 14 Stat. 517.

57. Frankfurter and Landis, *The Business of the Supreme Court*, 63.

58. "Some New Aspects of the Right of Trial by Jury," *American Law Register*, n.s. 16 (1877) 705. See also, James Maclachlan, *Handbook of the Law of Bankruptcy* (St. Paul, 1956), 10; Leonard A. Jones, "Receivers of Railways," *Southern Law Review*, 4 (1879), 18, 20; "Suggestions of Amendments to the Bankruptcy Act," *American Law Register*, n.s. 12 (1873), 737.

59. See *American Law Review*, 1 (1867), 206. "The Bankrupt Law, Its Provisions and Objects," *Central Law Journal*, 6 (1878), 273; *Central Law Journal*, 13 (1881), 221; "A Permanent Bankrupt Law," *Western Jurist*, 6 (1872), 512; "Abuses of the Bankrupt Law," *American Law Review*, 7 (1873), 641; "Suggestions of Amendments to the Bankruptcy Act," *American Law Register*, 12 (1873), 737.

60. *Messages and Papers of the Presidents*, VII, 250; Act of 7 June 1878, ch. 160, 20 Stat. 99.

61. Patricia Acheson, *The Supreme Court: America's Judicial Heritage* (New York, 1961), 127.

21. Justice Field and the Jurisprudence of Government-Business Relations: Some Parameters of Laissez Faire Constitutionalism, 1863-1897

CHARLES W. MCCURDY

1. Robert A. Lively, "The American System: A Review Article," *Business History Review*, 29 (1955), 93. See also Harry N. Scheiber, "Government and the Economy: Studies of the Commonwealth Policy in Nineteenth-Century America," *Journal of Interdisciplinary History*, 3 (1972), 135-151.

2. Willard Hurst, *The Legitimacy of the Business Corporation* (Charlottesville, 1970), 13-30; Paul Gates, *History of Public Land Law Development* (Washingon, 1968), 341-386; John Ezell, *Fortune's Merry Wheel: The Lottery in America* (Cambridge, Mass., 1960); Harry N. Scheiber, "Property Law, Expropriation, and Resource Allocation by Government: The United States, 1789-1910," *Journal of Economic History*, 33 (1973), 232-251; John Cadman, *The Corporation in New Jersey: Business and Politics, 1789-1875* (Cambridge, Mass., 1949), 56-61.

3. Carter Goodrich, "Local Planning of Internal Improvements," *Political Science Quarterly*, 66 (1951), 411-445.

4. Harry Pierce, *The Railroads of New York: A Study of Government Aid, 1826-1875* (Cambridge, Mass., 1953), 84; Frederick Merk, "Eastern Antecedents of the Grangers," *Agricultural History*, 23 (1949), 1-8; Lee Benson, *Merchants, Farmers, and Railroads* (Cambridge, Mass., 1955); Harold D. Woodman, "Chicago Businessmen and the Granger Laws," *Agricultural History*, 23 (1962), 16-24; Dale E. Treleven, "Railroads, Elevators, and Grain Dealers: The Genesis of Anti-Monopolism in Milwaukee," *Wisconsin Magazine of History*, 52 (1969), 205-222; George Miller, *The Railroads and the Granger Laws* (Madison, 1971); Charles Fairman, *Reconstruction and Reunion, 1864-1888, Oliver Wendell Holmes Devise History of the Supreme Court*, vol. VI, pt. 1, (New York, 1971), 934-1010.

5. Stephen J. Field, "Centenary of the Supreme Court of the United States," *American Law Review*, 24 (1890), 365.

6. Stanley I. Kutler, *Judicial Power and Reconstruction Politics* (Chicago, 1968), 143-160.

7. Ex Parte Wall, 107 U.S. 265 (1883) at 302; Providence Tool Co. v. Norris, 2 Wall. 45 (1865) at 55-56; Mugler v. Kansas, 123 U.S. 623 (1887) at 678.

8. Edward S. Corwin, "The Supreme Court and the Fourteenth Amendment," *Michigan Law Review*, 7 (1909), 653.

9. Arthur S. Miller, *The Supreme Court*

and American Capitalism (New York, 1968), 50; Robert McCloskey, American Conservatism in the Age of Enterprise (Cambridge, Mass., 1951), 85, 74. See also Wallace Mendelson, "Mr. Justice Field and Laissez-Faire," Virginia Law Review, 36 (1950), 45-58; Howard J. Graham, Everyman's Constitution (Madison, 1968), 98-151; Carl Swisher, Stephen J. Field: Craftsman of the Law (Washington, 1930), 240-245.

10. Charles R. Burdick, "The Origin of the Peculiar Duties of Public Service Corporations," Columbia Law Review, 11 (1911), 514-531, 616-638, 743-764; Edwin Merrick Dodd, American Business Corporations until 1860 (Cambridge, Mass., 1954), 158-163; Leonard Levy, The Law of the Commonwealth and Chief Justice Shaw (Cambridge, Mass., 1957), 258; Harry N. Scheiber, "The Road to Munn: Eminent Domain and the Concept of Public Purpose in the State Courts," in Law in American History, ed. Donald Fleming and Bernard Bailyn (Boston, 1971), 342-402.

11. Charles Fairman, "What Makes a Great Justice? Justice Bradley and the Supreme Court, 1870-1892," Boston University Law Review, 30 (1950), 67.

12. C. Peter Magrath, Yazoo: The Case of Fletcher v. Peck (Providence, 1966), 109.

13. McCloskey, American Conservatism, 103; Mendelson, "Mr. Justice Field and Laissez-Faire," 55.

14. Slaughterhouse Cases, 16 Wall. 36 (1873) at 101, 90. See Howard M. Jones, The Pursuit of Happiness (Ithaca, 1953), 12; Richard Hofstadter, "William Leggett: Spokesman of Jacksonian Democracy," Political Science Quarterly, 58 (1943), 581-594; Louis Hartz, Economic Policy and Democratic Thought: Pennsylvania, 1776-1860 (Cambridge, Mass., 1948), 70-72; William E. Nelson, "The Impact of the Antislavery Movement upon Styles of Judicial Reasoning in Nineteenth-Century America," Harvard Law Review, 87 (1974), 513-566. See also David Dudley Field's laudatory 1841 review of Leggett's Political Writings, in Speeches, Arguments, and Miscellaneous Papers of David Dudley Field, ed. A.P. Sprague, 2 vols., (New York, 1884), II, 209-236.

15. Barbier v. Connolly, 113 U.S. 27 (1885) at 31.

16. Edward S. Corwin, "The Basic Doctrine of American Constitutional Law," Michigan Law Review, 12 (1914), 275; Charles G. Haines, The Revival of Natural Law Concepts (Cambridge, Mass., 1930), 154-165.

17. Scheiber, "The Road to Munn," 360.

18. Boom Co. v. Patterson, 98 U.S. 403 (1878) at 406.

19. West River Bridge v. Dix, 6 How. 507 (1848) at 546.

20. Olcott v. Supervisors of Fond Du Lac County, 16 Wall. 667 (1873) at 694.

21. Boom Co. v. Patterson, 98 U.S. 403 (1878) at 406.

22. See Philip Nichols, Jr., "The Meaning of Public Use in the Law of Eminent Domain," Boston University Law Review, 20 (1940), 615-624.

23. Pumpelly v. Green Bay Co., 13 Wall. 166 (1872).

24. Willard Hurst, Law and Economic Growth (Cambridge, Mass., 1965), 182. See, generally, Hurst, Law and the Conditions of Freedom in the Nineteenth-Century United States (Madison, 1956), 20-30; Morton Horwitz, "The Transformation in the Conception of Property in American Law, 1780-1860," University of Chicago Law Review, 40 (1973), 248-290, also reprinted in abridged form in this volume; Lawrence Friedman, A History of American Law (New York, 1973), 202-227, 261-264.

25. Joseph Cormack, "Legal Concepts in Cases of Eminent Domain," Yale Law Journal, 41 (1931), 221-261; Scheiber, "The Road to Munn," 362-73.

26. Monongahela Navigation Co. v. Coons, 6 Watts & Serg. 101 (Penn. 1843) at 114; see Stanley I. Kutler, "John Bannister Gibson: Judicial Restraint and the 'Positive State,'" Journal of Public Law, 14 (1965), 181-197.

27. Theodore Sedgwick, A Treatise on the Rules which Govern the Interpretation and Application of Statutory and Constitutional Law (New York, 1857), 525. On the impact of Pumpelly, see Cormack, "Legal Concepts in Cases of Eminent Domain," 233-261.

28. Pumpelly v. Green Bay Co., 13 Wall. 166 (1872) at 177-178.

29. Jack B. Scroggs, "Carpetbagger Constitutional Reform in the South-Atlantic States, 1867-1868," *Journal of Southern History*, 28 (1961), 493.

30. Carter Goodrich, "Public Aid to Railroads in the Reconstruction South," *Political Science Quarterly*, 71 (1956), 407-442.

31. Mitchell Franklin, "The Foundation and Meaning of the Slaughter-House Cases," *Tulane Law Review*, 18 (1943), 14.

32. Durbridge v. The Slaughter-House Co., 27 La. Ann. 676 (1875).

33. Slaughterhouse Cases, 16 Wall. 36 (1873) at 87, 89; see also Charles Fairman, *Mr. Justice Miller and the Supreme Court* (Cambridge, Mass., 1939), 180.

34. Slaughterhouse Cases, 16 Wall. 36 (1873) at 78.

35. Ibid. at 88.

36. Ibid.

37. Thomas Durant, "Brief of Counsel in Error, Paul Estaban and Others v. The State of Louisiana," 8-9.

38. Slaughterhouse Cases, 16 Wall. 36 (1873) at 88. Field was not innovating here. In the leading case of Boston & Lowell R.R. Co. v. Salem & Lowell R.R. Co., 2 Gray 1 (Mass. 1854), Chief Justice Shaw had emphasized the necessity for public consideration — governmental control of rates and services — before exclusive franchises might be granted. See Levy, *The Law of the Commonwealth and Chief Justice Shaw*, 124-126.

39. Slaughterhouse Cases, 16 Wall. 36 (1873) at 88; see also Field J. dissenting in Munn v. Illinois, 94 U.S. 113 (1877) at 148-149.

40. See the sources cited above, nn. 10, 18-20.

41. Slaughterhouse Cases, 16 Wall. 36 (1873) at 90. See also New Orleans Gas Co. v. Louisiana Light Co., 115 U.S. 650 (1885) at 658, where Justice Harlan, speaking for the Court, makes the identical distinction between "ordinary trades" and public utilities to determine when monopoly grants might subsequently be revoked by state legislatures.

42. Slaughterhouse Cases, 16 Wall. 36 (1873) at 88 (italics added).

43. Corwin, "The Supreme Court and the Fourteenth Amendment," 654.

44. *Messages and Papers of the Presidents, 1789-1897*, ed. James D. Richardson, 10 vols (Washington, 1897), VI, 30; see Eric Foner, *Free Soil, Free Labor, Free Men: The Ideology of the Republican Party before the Civil War* (New York, 1970), 11-39.

45. Dent v. West Virginia, 112 U.S. 114 (1889) at 121.

46. Slaughterhouse Cases, 16 Wall. 36 (1873) at 96; Bartmeyer v. Iowa, 18 Wall. 129 (1873) at 139.

47. Yick Wo v. Hopkins, 118 U.S. 356 (1886); see Howard J. Graham, *Everyman's Constitution*, 552-584. On the role of counsel in bringing Field's Fourteenth Amendment construction to fruition, see Walton Hamilton, "The Path of Due Process of Law," in *The Constitution Reconsidered*, ed. Conyers Read (New York, 1938), 167-190; Benjamin Twiss, *Lawyers and the Constitution* (Princeton, 1942), 42-62.

48. Bartemeyer v. Iowa, 18 Wall. 129 (1873) at 141; see also Missouri Pacific Ry. Co. v. Humes, 115 U.S. 512 (1885) at 520.

49. Bartemeyer v. Iowa, 18 Wall. 129 (1873) at 138.

50. Dent v. West Virginia, 112 U.S. 114 (1889); Crowley v. Christensen, 137 U.S. 86 (1890); Minneapolis Ry. Co. v. Beckwith, 129 U.S. 26 (1888); New York and New England Ry. Co. v. Bristol, 151 U.S. 556 (1894).

51. Soon Hing v. Crowley, 113 U.S. 703 (1885) at 710; Missouri Pacific Ry. Co. v. Mackey, 127 U.S. 205 (1887). Field was so antagonistic to the heavy-handed fellow-servant rule that he was simultaneously making doctrinal innovations in private law designed to enable injured workers to recover damages from intractable railroad corporations. See Chicago, Milwaukee & St. Paul Ry. Co. v. Ross, 112 U.S. 377 (1884). See also his vigorous lone dissent in Baltimore & Ohio Ry. Co. v. Baugh, 149 U.S. 368 (1893), where Justice Brewer persuaded the Court to abandon *Ross* and make the fellow-servant doctrine applicable throughout the nation.

52. Soon Hing v. Crowley, 113 U.S. 703 (1885) at 710.

53. Barbier v. Connolly, 113 U.S. 27 (1885) at 31; see also Pacific Ry. Co. v. Humes, 115 U.S. 512 (1885) at 523.

54. Field to Matthew Deady, October 29, 1884, Field Papers, Oregon Historical Society. Field told Judge Deady that he was fed up with "the multifariousness of lying from the inarticulate [Henry Ward] Beecher to Pecksniff [George William] Curtis. The Pharisees of old are the loudest proclaimers of their holier-than-thou virtues. The wealthy and the comfortable wonder as before at the grumblings of the needy and are measuring the eye of the needle, which the camels of old had some difficulty in squeezing through [Mark 10:17], to see what chance there is for the passage. They are not so confident of the 'good time' hereafter as they are of the condition of their bank account now. I am on the other side — and would given the under fellow a show in this life. It is a shame to put him off to the next world."

55. Lochner v. New York, 198 U.S. 45 (1905).

56. Corwin, "The Supreme Court and the Fourteenth Amendment," 653.

57. Roscoe Pound, "Liberty of Contract," *Yale Law Journal*, 18 (1909), 470.

58. Pacific Ry. Co. v. Humes, 115 U.S. 512 (1885) at 520.

59. Pumpelly v. Green Bay Co., 13 Wall. 166 (1872) at 181; cf. Transportation Co. v. Chicago, 99 U.S. 635 (1878).

60. Davidson v. New Orleans, 96 U.S. 97 (1877) at 107. Field's position on takings and the police power is best illustrated in cases involving governmental control of navigable waters. In Weber v. Harbor Commissioners, 18 Wall. 57 (1873), he refused to award compensation to a wharf owner whose landing had been summarily destroyed as an *impediment* to commerce. In Monongahela Navigation Co. v. United States, 148 U.S. 312 (1893), however, he joined a unanimous Court that required government to compensate stockholders of a company whose lock and dam were expropriated and incorporated into a larger publicly owned system of river improvements. On the one hand, property was destroyed as detrimental, on the other, government took it for the public's positive use. See also Ernst Freund, *The Police Power: Constitutional Rights and Public Policy* (Chicago, 1904), 546; Joseph Sax, "Takings and the Police Power," Yale *Law Journal*, 74 (1964), 36-76.

61. Barbier v. Connolly, 113 U.S. 27 (1885) at 31.

62. Baker v. Boston, 12 Pick. 183 (Mass. 1831) at 193; see Levy, *Law of the Commonwealth and Chief Justice Shaw*, 245-254. See also Field's opinion in Hagar v. Reclamation District, 111 U.S. 701 (1884).

63. In Re Tiburcio Parrot, 1 Fed. Rep. 481 (C.C.D. California 1880); Powell v. Pennsylvania, 127 U.S. 678 (1888). Field's circuit opinions on legislative discrimination against California's Chinese population are examined in Swisher, *Stephen J. Field*, 205-239; Graham, *Everyman's Constitution*, 142-149.

64. Soon Hing v. Crowley, 113 U.S. 703 (1885) at 710; Barbier v. Connolly, 113 U.S. 27 (1885) at 32.

65. Slaughterhouse Cases, 16 Wall. 36 (1873) at 88-89; see also the sources cited above, notes 20-21.

66. Barbier v. Connolly, 113 U.S. 27 (1885) at 32.

67. Ibid.

68. Pierce, *The Railroads of New York*, 82-83.

69. See the sources cited above, note 4.

70. See, for example, James A. Garfield, "The Future of the Republic: Its Dangers and Hopes," *Legal Gazette*, 5 (1873), 408.

71. Gene Gressley, *West by East: The American West in the Gilded Age* (Provo, 1972), 12. See also Leslie Decker, "The Great Speculation: An Interpretation of Mid-Continent Pioneering," in *The Frontier in American Development*, ed. David M. Ellis (Ithaca, 1969), 357-380; Allan Bogue, "Some Dimensions of the Kansas Search for Capital, 1865-1893," in *The Frontier Challenge: Responses to the Trans-Mississippi West*, ed. John G. Clark (Lawrence, 1971), 203-234.

72. Reporter's note to Citizen's Savings Assn. v. Topeka, 5 Fed. Cas. 737 (No. 2,734) (C.C.D. Kansas 1874) at 738.

73. George Miller, *The Railroads and the Granger Laws*, 140-160; Robert S. Hunt, *Law and Locomotives: The Impact of the Railroad on Wisconsin Law in the Nineteenth Century* (Madison, 1958), 85-87; Lewis Mills, "The Public Purpose Doctrine in Wisconsin, Part I," *Wisconsin Law Review*, 1957, 52.

74. Isaac Redfield, *A Practical Treatise on the Law of Railways*, 4th. ed., 2 vols. (Boston, 1869), II, 395-405; see Ellis Waldron, "Sharpless v. Philadelphia: Jeremiah Black and the Parent Case on the Public Purpose of Taxation," *Wisconsin Law Review*, 1953, 48-75.

75. People ex. rel. Detroit and Howell R.R. Co. v. Salem, 20 Mich. 452 (1870) at 477. See also Alan Jones, "Thomas M. Cooley and the Michigan Supreme Court, 1865-1885," *American Journal of Legal History*, 10 (1966), 97-121; Clyde E. Jacobs, *Law Writers and the Courts* (Berkeley, 1954), 106-121; Scheiber, "The Road to Munn," 389.

76. Whiting v. Sheboygan & Fond Du Lac R.R. Co., 25 Wis. 167 (1870).

77. [Charles F. Adams], "Summary of Events," *American Law Review*, 5 (1870), 148; see Mark De Wolfe Howe, *Oliver Wendell Holmes: The Proving Years, 1870-1882* (Cambridge, Mass., 1963), 55-57.

78. Pine Grove Township v. Talcot, 19 Wall. 666 (1874) at 667. On the development of "general jurisprudence," or a federal common law, see Mitchell Wendell, *Relations between State and Federal Courts* (New York, 1949), 113-180; Fairman, *Reconstruction and Reunion*, 935-940.

79. Pine Grove Township v. Talcot, 19 Wall. 666 (1874) at 676.

80. Olcott v. Supervisors of Fond Du Lac County, 16 Wall. 678 (1873) at 695-696.

81. Ibid. at 694.

82. Charles Warren suggested that the railroad-subsidy cases "probably had a more important effect upon the commercial development of the country than any other of the Court's extensions of National power" (*The Supreme Court in United States History*, 2d. ed., 2 vols. [Boston, 1926], II, 528). See also John F. Dillon, *The Law of Municipal Bonds* (St. Louis, 1876), 7.

83. Fairman, *Mr. Justice Miller*, 211-218.

84. Miller to William Ballinger, February 3, 1874, quoted in ibid., 232.

85. White v. Vermont & Massachusetts R.R. Co., 20 How. 575 (1858) at 578.

86. Field, J., dissenting in Rogers v. Burlington, 3 Wall. 654 (1866) at 671.

87. Ibid. Field, Grier, and Miller dissented on the ground that the city had only been authorized to borrow money, not to loan it; Town of Caloma v. Eaves, 92 U.S. 484 (1876): Miller, Field, and Davis dissented because the voters had authorized stock subscriptions in one road, while city officials conveyed the municipal funds to another; Town of Venice v. Murdock, 92 U.S. 502 (1876): Miller, Field, and Davis dissented because bonds were issued without voter approval; County of Moultrie v. Rockingham Savings Bank, 92 U.S. 631 (1876): Miller, Field, and Davis dissented on the ground that the bonds had been issued after a state constitutional amendment had prohibited local aid; Marcy v. Township of Oswego, 92 U.S. 637 (1876): Miller, Field, and Davis dissented because the voters had been duped into authorizing a debt exceeding the assessed valuation of the entire town, despite a statute restricting local aid to one percent of taxable property.

88. Loan Association v. Topeka, 20 Wall. 655 (1874).

89. Ibid. at 664.

90. Ibid.

91. See Miller's reiteration of his *Loan Association* position in Davidson v. New Orleans, 96 U.S. 97 (1877) at 105. Not until 1896 was the public-purpose maxim incorporated into the due-process clause. In the interim, however, the Court continued to invalidate local aid to manufacturing enterprises. See Parkersburg v. Brown, 106 U.S. 487 (1882); Cole v. La Grange, 113 U.S. 1 (1885); Edward S. Corwin, "Judicial Review in Action," *University of Pennsylvania Law Review*, 74 (May 1926), 669.

92. Loan Association v. Topeka, 20 Wall. 655 (1874) at 664.

93. Township of Burlington v. Beasely, 94 U.S. 310 (1877) at 313.

94. Fletcher v. Peck, 6 Cranch 87 (1810); New Jersey v. Wilson, 7 Cranch 164 (1812); Dartmouth College v. Woodward, 4 Wheat. 518 (1819).

95. Fletcher v. Peck, 6 Cranch 87 (1810) at 130.

96. Terrett v. Taylor, 9 Cranch 43 (1815) at 50.

97. Levy, *The Law of the Commonwealth and Chief Justice Shaw*, 280. See also Magrath, *Yazoo: The Case of Fletcher v.*

Peck, 101-109; Francis N. Stites, *Private Interest and Public Gain: The Dartmouth College Case* (Amherst, 1972), 99-113.

98. Dartmouth College v. Woodward, 4 Wheat. 518 (1819) at 712; Benjamin F. Wright, *The Contract Clause of the Constitution* (Cambridge, 1938), 58-61, 84-88.

99. Charles River Bridge v. Warren Bridge, 11 Pet. 420 (1837).

100. Ibid. at 552-553; see Stanley I. Kutler, *Privilege and Creative Destruction: The Charles River Bridge Case* (Philadelphia, 1971).

101. Wallace D. Farnham, "The Weakened Spring of Government: A Study in Nineteenth-Century American History," *American Historical Review,* 68 (1963), 666. See also Willard Hurst, *Law and Social Process in United States History* (Ann Arbor, 1960), 46; Hunt, *Law and Locomotives,* 33-34.

102. Ohio Life Insurance & Trust Co. v. Debolt, 16 How. 416 (1853) at 435-436.

103. Slidell v. Grandjean, 111 U.S. 412 (1884) at 438. See also Wheeling & Belmont Bridge Co. v. Wheeling Bridge Co., 138 U.S. 287 (1891), where Field restates Taney's concerns regarding the Charles River Bridge case.

104. Dodge v. Woolsey, 18 How. 331 (1855) at 371. For the persistent criticism of Fletcher v. Peck by Justices Campbell and Daniel during the Taney era, see Dodd, *American Business Corporations before 1860,* 130-132; John P. Frank, *Justice Daniel Dissenting: A Biography of Peter V. Daniel, 1784-1860* (Cambridge, 1964), 205-212.

105. Justice Field in Providence Tool Co. v. Norris, 2 Wall. 45 (1865) at 55-56, holding unenforceable contract for lobbying services whose performance was contingent on successful procurement of government contract.

106. West River Bridge Co. v. Dix, 6 How. 507 (1848) at 532.

107. See Field's equation of these inherent powers in The Delaware Tax Case, 18 Wall. 206 (1874) at 226.

108. Lawrence Friedman, *Contract Law in America* (Madison, 1965), 150; Oscar and Mary Handlin, *Commonwealth: A Study of the Role of Government in the American Economy, Massachusetts, 1774-1861,* 2d. ed. (Cambridge, Mass., 1969), 109; Cadman, *The Corporation in New Jersey,* 56-61.

109. Dodge v. Woolsey, 18 How. 331 (1855) at 370.

110. For the post-Civil War tax-reform movement generally, see Clifton K. Yearly, *The Money Machines: The Breakdown and Reform of Governmental and Party Finance in the North, 1860-1920* (Albany, 1970), 37-95.

111. Leslie Decker, *Railroads, Lands, and Politics: The Taxation of the Railroad Land Grants, 1864-1897* (Providence, 1964), 11.

112. New Jersey v. Wilson, 7 Cranch 164 (1812).

113. See, for example, Farrington v. Tennessee, 95 U.S. 679 (1878), where the majority (Field, Strong, and Clifford dissenting) refused to disturb *Wilson* because "contracts mark the progress of communities in civilization and prosperity. They guard, as far as possible, against fluctuations in human affairs . . . they seek to give stability to the present and certainty to the future . . . They are the springs of business, trade, and commerce; without them, society could not go on."

114. Home of the Friendless v. Rousse, 8 Wall. 430 (1869) at 443; see also Field's discussion in Tomlinson v. Jessup, 15 Wall. 454 (1873) at 458.

115. Pollock v. Farmers' Loan & Trust Co., 157 U.S. 429 (1895) at 586-608; see also Arnold M. Paul, *Conservative Crisis and the Rule of Law: Attitudes of Bar and Bench, 1887-1895* (Ithaca, 1960), 204.

116. Morgan v. Louisiana, 93 U.S. 217 (1876); Railroad Co. v. Maine, 96 U.S. 499 (1877). See also Ernest W. Huffcut, "Legislative Tax Exemptions," *American Law Review,* 24 (1890), 399-427.

117. See the long line of state court decisions cited in Thomas M. Cooley, *Constitutional Limitations,* 5th ed. (Boston, 1883), 340. See also James F. Colby, "Exemption from Taxation by Legislative Contract," *American Law Review,* 13 (1878), 26-39.

118. Harry N. Scheiber, *Ohio Canal Era: A Case Study of Government and the Economy, 1820-1861* (Athens, Ohio, 1969), 278, 296.

119. Friedman, *A History of American Law*, 312.

120. Ezell, *Fortune's Merry Wheel: The Lottery in America*, 233-270.

121. C. Vann Woodward, *The Origins of the New South, 1877-1913* (Baton Rouge, 1951), 14.

122. Boyd v. Alabama, 94 U.S. 645 (1877) at 650.

123. Stone v. Mississippi, 101 U.S. 814 (1880). See also Beer Co. v. Massachusetts, 97 U.S. 25 (1878); Fertilizing Co. v. Hyde Park, 97 U.S. 659 (1878).

124. Butcher's Union Slaughter-House Co. v. Crescent City Co., 111 U.S. 746 (1884) at 754.

125. Illinois Central R.R. Co. v. Illinois, 146 U.S. 387 (1892). Joseph Sax, an eminent legal scholar interested in protecting the "public trust" in such matters as wilderness areas and pesticide control, refers to Field's opinion as "the lodestar in American Public Trust Law" in "The Public Trust Doctrine in Natural Resource Law: Effective Judicial Intervention," *Michigan Law Review*, 68 (1970), 487.

126. This doctrine logically flowed from the Court's earlier commerce and admiralty opinions, where the Court had recognized navigable bodies of fresh water to be "public highways." See Field's opinion in The Daniel Ball, 10 Wall. 557 (1871); Milton Conover, "The Abandonment of the 'Tidewater' Concept in Admiralty Jurisdiction in the United States," *Oregon Law Review*, 38 (1958), 34-58.

127. Illinois Central R.R. Co. v. Illinois, 146 U.S. 387 (1892) at 452.

128. Ibid. at 451.

129. Ibid.

130. Providence Tool Co. v. Norris, 2 Wall. 45 (1865) at 55.

131. See the scathing editorial attack on Field's opinion, "The Police Power and the Lake Front Case," *Harvard Law Review*, 6 (1893), 444-445.

132. Munn v. Illinois, 94 U.S. 113 (1877).

133. Sinking-Fund Cases, 99 U.S. 700 (1878) at 747. See Scheiber, "The Road to Munn," 355-360; Charles Fairman, "The So-Called Granger Cases, Lord Hale, and Justice Bradley," *Stanford Law Review*, 5 (1953), 587-679.

134. Munn v. Illinois, 94 U.S. 113 (1877) at 132.

135. Ibid. at 139. If one takes Lord Hale's precepts literally, Field had the best of the argument. "[Those] things that are Juris publici," Hale wrote, "are [such] as . . . are common to all the King's Subjects, and are of [these] kinds, viz: (1) Common Highways, (2) Common Bridges, (3) Common Rivers, (4) Common Ports" (*Analysis of the Law* [Stratford, Eng., 1713], 63). For a detailed critique of Waite's use of Hale's tracts, see Van Buren Denslow, "Ira Y. Munn and George L. Scott v. The People of Illinois," *American Law Register*, 25 (1877), 539-545.

136. Slaughterhouse Cases, 16 Wall. 36 (1873) at 88.

137. Munn v. Illinois, 94 U.S. 113 (1877) at 149, 152.

138. Waite to J. Sheldon, March 30, 1877, quoted in C. Peter Magrath, *Morrison R. Waite: The Triumph of Character* (New York, 1963), 187.

139. See Morton Rothstein, "The International Market for Agricultural Commodities," in *Economic Change in the Civil War Era*, ed. David Gilchrist and W.D. Lewis (Greenville, Del., 1966), 62-72; Harold D. Woodman, "Chicago Businessmen and the Granger Laws," 16-24.

140. Munn v. Illinois, 94 U.S. 113 (1877) at 138, 140.

141. Ibid. at 141.

142. Corwin, "The Basic Doctrine of American Constitutional Law," 247.

143. In the "Granger" states, where the convergence of regulation and repudiation was most prominent, annual railroad construction declined from 3,086 miles added in 1872 to 550 miles added in 1876. Once the Court refused to condone repudiation and the rate laws were one by one repealed (the last in 1878), new construction rebounded to former levels. In 1880, 2,915 miles were added in the former "Granger" states. Although a financial panic and ensuing depression certainly played a major role in the decline of new construction between 1873 and 1878, contemporaries tended to attribute it to repudiation and regulation alone. See Andrew Allison, "The Rise and Probable Decline of Private Corporations in

America," *Report of the Seventh Annual Meeting of the American Bar Association* (Philadelphia, 1884), 241-256.

144. Harlan to Waite, not dated, quoted in Alan F. Westin, "Stephen J. Field and the Headnote to O'Neil v. Vermont," *Yale Law Journal,* 67 (1958), 376. See also Budd v. New York, 143 U.S. 517 (1892); Brass v. North Dakota, 153 U.S. 391 (1894).

145. Chicago, Burlington & Quincy R.R. v. Iowa, 94 U.S. 155 (1877); Peik v. Chicago & Northwestern R.R. Co., 94 U.S. 164 (1877); Chicago, Milwaukee & St. Paul Ry. v. Ackley, 94 U.S. 179 (1877); Winona & St. Peter R.R. v. Blake, 94 U.S. 180 (1877); Stone v. Wisconsin, 94 U.S. 181 (1877).

146. Munn v. Illinois, 94 U.S. 113 (1877) at 134.

147. Railroad Co. v. Maryland, 21 Wall. 456 (1875) at 471.

148. Justice Bradley dissenting in Chicago, Milwaukee & St. Paul Ry. v. Minnesota, 134 U.S. 418 (1890) at 461. See also Bradley's "Outline of My Views," in Fairman, "The So-Called Granger Cases," 670.

149. Balthasar H. Meyer, *Railway Legislation in the United States,* (New York, 1903); M.H. Hunter, "The Early Regulation of Public Service Corporations," *American Economic Review,* 7 (1917), 569-581.

150. As early as 1859, the fundamental principle of Field's jurisprudence was "security" for private landowners and investors, without which, he declared, "there would be little development, for the incentive to improvement would be wanting," Biddle Boggs v. Merced Mining Co., 14 Cal. 279 (1859) at 379.

151. Stone v. Wisconsin, 94 U.S. 181 (1877) at 184-185. Compare Swisher, *Stephen J. Field,* 372-385; Robert McCloskey's recent statement that, while Field "denied *all* legislative power to fix prices, a decade later he was willing to concede that some such regulation was permissible," in "Stephen J. Field," *The Justices of the United States Supreme Court, 1789-1969: Their Lives and Major Opinions,* ed. Leon Friedman and Fred L. Israel, 4 vols. (New York, 1969), II, 1085.

152. Lake Superior & Mississippi R.R. v. United States, 93 U.S. 442 (1876); Miller, Clifford, Swayne, and Davis dissented.

153. Ibid. at 455.

154. Stone v. Wisconsin, 94 U.S. 181 (1877) at 183. Virtually all the contemporary journalists and railroad "experts" asserted that what Field feared had, in fact, occurred. For a full analysis of the literature on rate regulation published between 1872 and 1878, see Charles R. Detrick, "The Effects of the Granger Laws," *Journal of Political Economy,* 11 (1903), 137-156.

155. Attorney General v. Railroad Companies, 35 Wis. 425 (1874) at 579.

156. See text at n. 28. Field quoted Miller's *Pumpelly* dictum in full in Munn v. Illinios, 94 U.S. 113 (1877) at 144.

157. Ibid. at 145-148; see discussion above, n. 60.

158. Ibid. at 141.

159. Tomlinson v. Jessup, 15 Wall. 454 (1873) at 459. See also William Maxwell Evarts's argument in the Wisconsin rate cases, partially reprinted in [Edward Abbott], "The Wisconsin Railroad Acts," *American Law Review,* 9 (October 1974), 50-73. Shortly after filing his brief, Evarts mailed a copy to Field, telling him that the "question of the scope of the reservation of a right to repeal, alter, or amend will have to be settled by your Court before long; if this opinion of mine had any value it is in that direction" (Evarts to Field, May 18, 1874, Field Papers, Bancroft Library, University of California at Berkeley).

160. Sinking Fund Cases, 99 U.S. 700 (1878) at 758.

161. See Miller v. State of New York, 15 Wall. 478 (1873); Holyoke v. Lyman, 15 Wall. 500 (1873). This doctrine was also assumed to be unquestionable in the several opinions delivered in the Sinking-Fund Cases, 90 U.S. 700 (1878) at 721 (per Waite, C.J. for the majority); at 742 (per Strong, J. dissenting); at 748 (per Bradley, J. dissenting).

162. Commonwealth v. Essex Co., 13 Gray 239 (Mass. 1859) at 253; see Levy, *The Law of the Commonwealth and Chief Justice Shaw,* 277-281.

163. Munn v. Illinois, 94 U.S. 113 (1877) at 143.

164. For a superb case study of Field's self-righteousness and indomitability (Justice Gray called him a "wild bull"), see

Westin, "Stephen J. Field and the Headnote to O'Neil v. Vermont," 363-383.

165. Ruggles v. Illinois, 108 U.S. 526 (1883).

166. In St. Louis and San Francisco Ry. Co. v. Gill, 156 U.S. 649 (1895), the Court unanimously held that when two companies consolidated, the new corporation had no defense against a rate that was confiscatory for only one line of the larger system. Instead, the proper test of reasonableness was the rate's effect upon the earnings of the consolidated system as a whole. On the difficulties the great-system managers had in producing the requisite proof, see Albro Martin, *Enterprise Denied: Origins of the Decline of American Railroads, 1897-1917* (New York, 1971), 225.

167. The Court did, however, later uphold Field's contention that rates could only be fixed by public officials if the state had reserved the power in the grant of incorporation. See Field's dissent in Schottler v. Spring Valley Water Works, 110 U.S. 347 (1884); Detroit v. Detroit City Ry. Co., 184 U.S. 367 (1902); Richard J. Smith, "The Judicial Interpretation of Public Utility Franchises," *Yale Law Journal*, 39 (1930), 957-979.

168. Railroad Commission Cases, 116 U.S. 307 (1886); see Magrath, *Morrison R. Waite*, 198-200.

169. Georgia R.R. & Banking Co. v. Smith, 128 U.S. 174 (1888) at 179.

170. Ibid. at 179.

171. Chicago, Milwaukee & St. Paul Ry. Co. v. Minnesota, 134 U.S. 418 (1890); Smythe v. Ames, 169 U.S. 466 (1898).

172. Oscar and Mary Handlin, *The Dimensions of Liberty* (Cambridge, Mass., 1961), 99.

173. John W. Cary, "Brief for Appellants in Error, Peik v. Chicago & Northwestern Ry. Co., " 64; see Twiss, *Lawyers and the Constitution*, 70-76; Fairman, "The So-Called Granger Cases," 634; Miller, *The Railroads and the Granger Laws*, 186.

174. People ex. rel. Detroit and Howell R.R. Co. v. Salem, 20 Mich. 252 (1870) at 477; Munn v. Illinois, 94 U.S. 113 (1877).

175. Missouri Pacific Ry. Co. v. Humes, 115 U.S. 512 (1885) at 521.

176. Field, "Centenary of the Supreme Court of the United States," 367.

177. Ibid., 363.

178. For a full analysis of the concerns that molded the "new judicialism" of the nineties, see Paul, *Conservative Crisis and the Rule of Law*.

179. Strickley v. Highboy Gold Mining Co., 200 U.S. 527 (1906); Green v. Frazier, 253 U.S. 238 (1920).

180. Nebbia v. New York, 291 U.S. 502 (1934) at 536.

22. Social Change and the Law of Industrial Accidents

LAWRENCE M. FRIEDMAN AND JACK LADINSKY

1. William Blackstone, *Commentaries on the Laws of England,* 4 vols. (1765-1769) has virtually no discussion of negligence. In early nineteenth-century America, tort law (and particularly the law of negligence) remained fairly obscure. Dane's *Abridgment* — a compendium of British and American law — has a short, miscellaneous chapter on negligence: cases "which cannot be brought conveniently under more particular heads" (Nathan Dane, *A General Abridgment and Digest of American Law,* 9 vols. [Boston, 1824] III, 31). These include some commercial and maritime instances ("If the owner of a ship, in the care of a pilot, through *negligence* and want of skill, sinks the ship of another, this owner is liable" [ibid., 35]) and some cases of negligence in the practice of a trade or profession ("If a register of deeds neglects to record a deed as he ought to do, this action lies against him for his negligence" [ibid., 32]). Under this latter heading comes one of the very few examples of personal injury — a doctor's negligent practice of his art (ibid., 32) Another example had to do with the negligent owner of a dog or other animal (ibid., 33). But, in general, personal-injury cases are rare in Dane, and the shadow of the industrial revolution has not yet fallen on this corner of the law.

2. Blackstone, *Commentaries*, I, 429-430.

3. 150 Eng. R. 1030 (Ex. 1837).

4. 45 Mass. (4 Met.) 49 (1842); Murray v. South Carolina R.R., 26 S.C.L. (1 McMul.) 385 (1841) was decided a year earlier and came to the same result. But *Farwell* is the better-known case, the one usually cited and quoted. In England, Baron Alderson extended *Priestley* to a railroad accident in Hutchinson v. York, N. & B. Ry., 155 Eng. R. 150 (Ex. 1849). The House of Lords, in Barton's Hill Coal Co. v. Reid, 111 Rev. R. 896 (1858), held the rule applicable in Scotland as well as in England. Lord Cranworth cited *Farwell* with great praise as a "very able and elaborate judgment" (id. at 906).

5. Farwell v. Boston & W.R.R., 45 Mass. (4 Met.) 49, 57 (1842) (emphasis added).

6. (James) Willard Hurst, *Law and the Conditions of Freedom in the Nineteenth-Century United States* (Madison, 1956), 5-6, and passim.

7. For a discussion of legal and political aspects of the short-lived national bankruptcy acts before 1898, see Charles Warren, *Bankruptcy in United States History* (Cambridge, Mass., 1935).

8. On the significance in American law of the doctrine of contributory negligence, see the important article by Wex Malone, "The Formative Era of Contributory Negligence," *Illinois Law Review*, 41 (1946), 151.

9. Wisconsin, in Chamberlain v. Milwaukee & M.R.R., 11 Wis. 248 (1860), rejected the fellow-servant rule, but one year later, in Moseley v. Chamberlain, 18 Wis. 700 (1861), the court reversed itself and adopted the rule which was "sustained by the almost unanimous judgments of all the courts both of England and this country . . . [an] unbroken current of judicial opinion" (id. at 736).

10. Ziegler v. Danbury & N.R.R., 52 Conn. 543, 556 (1885).

11. Parker v. Hannibal & St. J.R.R., 109 Mo. 362, 397 (1891) (Justice Thomas dissenting).

12. Unpublished survey and classification of all Wisconsin Supreme Court cases 1905-1915 by Robert Friebert and Lawrence M. Friedman.

13. Accidents were about 2.5 per 100 railway employees in 1889 and 5 per 100 in 1906. Calculated from ICC figures reported in [1909-1910] *Wisconsin Bureau of Labor and Industrial Statistics Fourteenth Biennial Report* (1911).

Railroads had been the earliest major source of industrial accidents, and most of the leading American and English fellow-servant cases arose out of railroad accidents. Railroads accounted for more serious industrial accidents than any other form of enterprise in the middle of the nineteenth-century. But in the late nineteenth-century, mining, manufacturing, and processing industries contributed their share to industrial injury and death. For example, close to 80 percent of the employer liability cases that reached the Wisconsin Supreme Court before 1890 related to railroad accidents; from 1890 to 1907 less than 30 percent were railroad cases [1907–1908] *Wisconsin Bureau of Labor and Industrial Statistics Thirteenth Biennial Report* (1909), 26. In 1907-1908, manufacturing injuries and deaths were more than double those of the railroads: [1909-1910] *Wisconsin Bureau of Labor and Industrial Statistics Fourteenth Biennial Report* (1911), 79.

14. [1907-1908] *Wisconsin Bureau of Labor and Industrial Statistics Thirteenth Biennial Report* (1909), 85-86.

15. Haley v. Case, 142 Mass. 316, 7 N. E. 877 (1886). In Priestley v. Fowler itself the same point was made.

16. Charles B. Labatt, *Master and Servant*, (Rochester, N. Y., 1913), IV, 4143.

17. 41 Wis. 478 (1887).

18. Dunn v. Southern Ry., 151 N. C. 313, 315, 66 S. E. 134-35 (1909); see Labatt, *Master and Servant*, III, 2476-84.

19. Theodore Sedgwick, Jr., "What Is a Monopoly?" (New York, 1835), quoted in Joseph L. Blau, ed., *Social Theories of Jacksonian Democracy* (Indianapolis, 1954), 220, 231.

20. No. 103 [1855] Ga. Acts 155.

21. Ch. 169, § 7 [1862], Iowa Laws 198.

22. Ch. 65 [1869], Wyo. Terr. Laws 433.

23. Ch. 93, § 1 [1874], Kan. Laws 143.

24. See Robert S. Hunt, *Law and Locomotives* (Madison, 1958).

25. Ch. 173 [1875], Wis. Laws 293 (*repealed*, ch. 232 [1880], Wis. Laws 270). A new act, somewhat narrower than that of

1875, was passed in 1889, ch. 348 [1889], Wis. Laws 487.

26. Arthur Larson, *Workmen's Compensation*, 3 vols. (Albany, 1965), I, 30.

27. Isaiah L. Sharfman, *The Interstate Commerce Commission: A Study in Administrative Law and Procedure* 4 vols. (New York, 1931), I, 246.

28. Safety Appliance Act, 27 Stat. 531-32 (1893) (now 45 U. S. C. § 7 [1964]).

29. 35 Stat. 65 (1908).

30. The 1908 act was limited to railroad employees injured while engaged in interstate commerce. A 1906 act [Act of June 22, 1906, ch. 3073, 34 Stat. 232] had been declared invalid by the Supreme Court in the Employers Liability Cases, 207 U.S. 463 (1908), because it applied to employees not engaged in interstate commerce. The 1908 act was liberalized in 1910 and in 1939; see 45 U.S.C. §§ 51-60 (1964). See generally Vernon X. Miller, "FELA Revisited," *Catholic University Law Review*, 6 (1957), 158.

31. Arguments by supporters and opponents of FELA are reviewed in Herman M. Somers and Anne R. Somers, *Workmen's Compensation* (New York, 1954), 320-325.

32. For a comparison of the cost efficiency of the two systems, see Walter F. Dodd, *Administration of Workmen's Compensation* (New York, 1936), 737-783.

33. *National Association of Manufacturers, Proceedings of the Fifteenth Annual Convention* (1910), 280.

34. *National Association of Manufacturers, Proceedings of the Sixteenth Annual Convention* (1911), 106 (remarks of Mr. Schwedtman).

35. For example, in 1907 Illinois required employers to report their employees' accidents to the state's Bureau of Labor Statistics, [1907] Ill. Laws 308.

36. See Dodd, *Administration of Workmen's Compensation*, 18.

37. For example, the Wisconsin Bureau of Labor and Industrial Statistics argued, on the basis of cost estimates in 1908, that: "Employers' liability insurance costs now in Wisconsin from 12 cents per $100 of wages in knitting mills to at least $9.00 in some building operations — an average of 50 or 60 cents. But it is very probable that this expense would be increased in the near future by weakening the defense of the employer in the courts ... The cost of the present system would be sufficient to inaugurate a general system of compensation if properly administered" [1907-1908] *Wisconsin Bureau of Labor and Industrial Statistics Thirteenth Biennial Report* [1909]).

38. Borgnis v. Falk Co., 147 Wis. 327, 133 N. W. 209 (1911).

39. Ch. 354 [1948], Miss. Laws 507.

40. Ives v. South Buffalo Ry., 201 N.Y. 271, 94 N.E. 431 (1911).

41. Ch. 50, § 1 [1911], Wis. Laws 43, 44.

42. Ch. 50, § 1 [1911], Wis. Laws 46.

43. Ch. 50, § 1 [1911], Wis. Laws 48.

44. See Arthur H. Reede, *Adequacy of Workmen's Compensation* (Cambridge, Mass., 1947), 231-238; Somers and Somers, *Workmen's Compensation*, 93-142.

45. (James) Willard Hurst, *Law and Social Process in United States History* (Ann Arbor, Mich., 1960), 69.

46. William F. Ogburn, *Social Change with Respect to Culture and Original Nature* (New York, 1950), 200, and more generally 199-280. In this book Ogburn offered cultural lag as a "hypothesis"; in later writing he referred to it as a "theory".

47. Stuart Chase, *The Proper Study of Mankind* (New York, 1948), 115-117.

48. Roscoe Pound, "The Economic Interpretation and the Law of Torts," *Harvard Law Review*, 53 (1940), 365-376.

49. N. Y. Const. Art. 1, sec. 19, was added in 1913; the new compensation law it authorized was enacted that same year; see ch. 816 [1913], N. Y. Laws 2277.

50. New York Cent. R.R. v. White, 243 U.S. 188 (1917); Hawkins v. Bleakly, 243 U.S. 210 (1917). In Mountain Timber Co. v. Washington, 243 U.S. 219 (1917), the Court also held an exclusive state insurance fund to be constitutional.

51. R. Warner, "Employers' Liability as an Industrial Problem," *Green Bag*, 18 (1906), 185, 192.

52. "Laying the personal injury burdens of production upon the things produced ... should have been efficiently recognized long ago, and would have been had the lawmaking power appreciated that it is its prov-

ince, not that of the courts, to cure infirmity in the law." Borgnis v. Falk Co., 147 Wis. 327, 370, 133 N. W. 209, 223 (1911) (Justice Marshall concurring).

53. Ch. 416, §§ 1, 4 [1905], Wis. Laws 680, 682.

54. Other instances of supposed cultural lag can be analyzed in similar terms. For example, Ogburn used exploitation of the forests and the tardy rise of conservation laws as another illustration of the lag. See Ogburn, *Social Change With Respect to Culture and Original Nature,* 203-210. Hurst's elaborate study of law and the Wisconsin lumber industry demonstrates that the legal system supported the exploitation of the forests of Wisconsin in the nineteenth century; the public did not and would not consider the ultimate social costs of destroying the forests. "Common opinion through the lumber era considered that the public interest *had no greater concern* than the increase of the productive capacity of the general economy" ([James] Willard Hurst, *Law and Economic Growth* (Cambridge, Mass., 1964), 261 [emphasis added]). "The dominant attention of nineteenth-century policy was upon promotional rather than regulative use of law" (ibid). The crucial problem was how to develop and settle the continent, not how to conserve or reforest it. Certainly no one was concerned with playgrounds for unborn urban masses. People backed demands arising out of immediate interests: the development of stable, economically prosperous communities. Courts reflected these attitudes. Blindness to future needs for natural resources did not result from evil intentions or from a yielding to the "pine barons"; the law reflected "prevailing community values," seeking concrete solutions to problems concretely and currently perceived (ibid.).

23. Legal Progressivism, the Courts, and the Crisis of the 1890s

ARNOLD M. PAUL

1. Attention has been focused on the intraprofessional pathways in the making of this revolution: Benjamin R. Twiss, *Lawyers and the Constitution* (Princeton, 1942);

Clyde E. Jacobs, *Law Writers and the Courts* (Berkeley, 1954).

2. The term "progressive" or "progressivism" is used here as descriptive of a political point of view favoring substantial use of government as a lever of change upon existing socioeconomic patterns, but stopping short of Socialist, Nationalist, Single-Tax, or purely inflationist programs.

3. The progressive criticism of judicial intervention in the 1890s, which was directed primarily at its social and economic implications, should be distinguished from an equally significant conservative criticism, which opposed on principle the radical innovations in judicial review inherent in the new role of the courts. Oliver W. Holmes, Jr., then on the Massachusetts Supreme Court, was only one — if today the most celebrated — of many such traditional legal conservatives. Though most scholars have overlooked or minimized the various professional cleavages of the period (e.g., Twiss, *Lawyers,* 141-142, 172; Sidney Fine, *Laissez Faire and the General-Welfare State, . . . 1865-1901* [Ann Arbor, 1956], 120-132), see Charles Warren, *The Supreme Court in United States History,* 3 vols. (Boston, 1923,) III, 421-426, for an early notice of legal dissidents in the 1890s.

4. Charles C. Bonney, "Impending Perils," *Reports of the Ohio State Bar Association,* IX (1888), 153-172; Seymour D. Thompson, "The Power of the People over Corporate and Individual Combinations and Monopolies," *Illinois State Bar Association, Proceedings of the Sixteenth Annual Meeting* (1893), 131-141; E. D. Shattuck, "Liberty Endangered," *Oregon Bar Association, Proceedings of the Fifth Annual Meeting* (1895), 126-131.

5. As source materials on legal progressivism, I have used the papers and addresses read at the annual meetings of the national and state bar associations and the articles and editorials printed in the law journals. The categories chosen offer the advantages of *manageability,* permitting examination of complete universes in order to estimate representativeness, and *professionalism,* significant for revealing opinion expressed "in church" as it were. It may be observed here that the sources examined, despite much

concern with social discontent, contain surprisingly few references to any specifically agrarian unrest; professional attention was apparently centered, until 1896 at any rate, on capital-labor issues and on the general problems of a corporation-dominated economy. Whether this has any bearing on the standard conceptualizations of the "Populist" and "Progressive" eras is an interesting question beyond the scope of this paper.

6. Richard T. Ely and L. S. Merriam, "Report on Social Legislation in the U.S. for 1889 and 1890," *Economic Review*, 1 (1891), 234-256; Fine, *Laissez-Faire*, 357-359. The most frequent types of labor laws in this period were "store order" acts, often called "scrip" or "truck" acts, providing for payment of wages in lawful money of the United States; coal-weighing laws, designed to prevent various types of fraud perpetrated on miners paid on a piecework basis; and weekly payment laws.

7. 94 U.S. 113 (1877). On *Munn* and other Granger Cases, including legislative background, see Charles Fairman, "The So-Called Granger Cases, Lord Hale, and Justice Bradley," *Stanford Law Review*, 5 (1953), 587-679.

8. Santa Clara County v. Southern Pacific Railroad, 118 U.S. 394. Howard J. Graham has contended that the significance of this case has been overemphasized: "An Innocent Abroad: The Constitutional Corporate 'Person,'" *U.C.L.A. Law Review*, 2 (1955), 160-165.

9. The principal cases were Beer Co. v. Massachusetts, 97 U.S. 25 (1878); Stone v. Mississippi, 101 U.S. 315 (1880); Butchers' Union v. Crescent City Co., 111 U. S. 746 (1884); Stone v. Farmers Loan and Trust Co., 116 U.S. 307 (1886); Mugler v. Kansas, 123 U.S. 623 (1887); and Powell v. Pennsylvania, 127 U.S. 673 (1888).

10. Ibid., 685. The legislature had labeled the act a bill to protect the public health, although it was well known that it was the dairy industry that the act sought to protect. The Court's opinion in *Powell*, as in some of the previous cases, did indicate that there were some limits to the police power, its exercise not extending to the impairment of fundamental rights under the "pretense" of

guarding the public health, morals, or safety; and in later years such provisos became pegs on which the Court hinged a reversal of its position.

11. "Impending Perils," 172.

12. "The Sovereign State," *American Law Register*, n.s. 27 (1889), 129-139.

13. 134 U.S. 418.

14. Ibid. at 458.

15. Ibid. at 461, 465. In 1894 the Court completed the outflanking of the *Munn* case by asserting its power to invalidate rate regulations een if set directly by the legislature (Reagan v. Farmers Loan and Trust Co., 154 U.S. 362), and in 1898 in Smythe v. Ames, 169 U.S. 466, the Court applied the new doctrine in overturning the rate schedules of the Nebraska legislature.

16. Thompson's many publications included such treatises as *Homestead and Exemption Laws* (St. Louis, 1878); *The Law of Negligence* (St. Louis, 1880); *The Law of Electricity* (St. Louis, 1891); and, in seven volumes, his masterwork, *Commentaries on the Law of Private Corporations* (San Francisco, 1895-1899). Thompson was editor, successively, of the *Central Law Journal*, the *Southern Law Review*, and the *American Law Review*. He was credited in 1897 with having "long exercised a continuous and virile influence upon legal thought." In 1904 President Theodore Roosevelt appointed him delegate to the international law congress held that year in St. Louis, but Thompson died before he could attend.

17. *American Law Review*, 24 (1890), 522.

18. *Chicago Legal News*, 24 (1892), 410. For other criticisms of the Supreme Court's decision in the *Chicago, Milwaukee* case (above, note 13), see the Minneapolis, *Advocate*, 2 (1890) 174-175; *American Law Register*, n.s. 31 (1892), 278-280.

19. The classic study is Roscoe Pound's article, "Liberty of Contract," *Yale Law Journal*, 18 (1909), 454-487. An excellent recent analysis is in Jacobs, *Law Writers*, 23-63.

20. Jones v. People, 110 Ill. 590. (1884); Millett v. People, 117 Ill. 294 (1886); and Godcharles v. Wigeman, 113 Pa. St. 431 (1886).

21. State v. Goodwill, 33 W. Va. 179, and State v. Coal Co., 33 W. Va. 188, rendered

simultaneously in 1889; Frorer v. People, 141 Ill. 171 (1892); State v. Loomis, 115 Mo. 307 (1893).

22. Ex parte Kubach, 85 Cal. 274 (1890). The ordinance also prohibited the employment of Chinese labor, but this was only incidentally referred to in the court's opinion.

23. Commonwealth v. Perry, 155 Mass. 117 (1891). The case featured a dissenting opinion by the already well-known Judge Holmes. Holmes maintained that the law should be sustained as a not unreasonable exercise of the legislative power to prevent fraud (ibid., 123-125).

24. Ramsey v. People, 142 Ill. 380 (1892).

25. San Antonio Railway Co. v. Wilson, 19 S.W. 910 (1892). Appearing in the court's opinion was this remarkable statement: "The employer and employee must always deal at arm's length. Their interest in making the contract is always adverse ... Unquestionably, so long as men must earn a living for their families and themselves by labor, there must be, as there always has been, oppression of the working classes" (ibid., 912).

26. Braceville Coal Co. v. People, 147 Ill. 66 (1893).

27. State v. Goodwill, 33 W. Va. 179, 184 (1889).

28. "Abuses of Corporate Privileges," *Ninth Annual Meeting of the Bar Association of the State of Kansas* (1892), 45. Thompson maintained a steady drumfire against freedom of contract in the editorial pages of the *American Law Review,* 1890-1894.

29. "Legislative Control over Contracts of Employment," *Harvard Law Review,* 6 (1892), 96.

30. Reno was active in the industrial arbitration and utilities regulation movements in Massachusetts in the 1890s and 1900s.

31. "Arbitration and the Wage Contract," *American Law Review,* 26 (1892), 849.

32. "State Regulation of the Contract of Employment," *American Law Review,* 27 (1893), 874-875. It is interesting to compare these early criticisms of a Spencerian reading of the Constitution with Justice Holmes's famous rebuke to the Supreme Court majority in the *Lochner* case of 1905: "The Four-

teenth Amendment does not enact Mr. Herbert Spencer's *Social Statics"* (198 U.S. 45).

33. Social conditions during the depression have recently been reexamined by Samuel Rezneck, "Unemployment, Unrest, and Relief in the United States during the Depression of 1893-1897," *Journal of Political Economy,* 61 (1953), 327.

34. *American Law Review,* 27 (1893), 409-410; see also U. M. Rose, "The Law of Trusts and Strikes," *American Bar Association, Report of the Sixteenth Annual Meeting* (1893), 314.

35. Farmers' Loan and Trust Co. v. Northern Pacific Railway Co., 60 Fed. 803 (E. D. Wis.), reversed in part by Circuit Justice Harlan in Arthur v. Oakes, 63 Fed. 310 (1894), for imposing a "condition of involuntary servitude."

36. *American Law Review,* 28 (1894), 268-272; *American Law Register,* n.s. 33 (1894), 81-82; Walter Murphy, "The Use of the Writ of Injunction to Prevent Strikes," *Territorial Bar Association of Utah, Report of the First Annual Meeting* (1894), 30-54.

37. *American Law Review,* 28 (1894), 591-592, 630-637.

38. *American Law Register,* n.s. 33 (1894), 609-622. See also *Pennsylvania Law Series,* 1 (1894), 4-18; and *Oregon Bar Association, Proceedings of the Fifth Annual Meeting* (1895), 129.

39. "Some Reflections on the Relations of Capital and Labor," *Texas Bar Association, Proceedings of the Thirteenth Annual Session* (1894), 51-66.

40. "Strikes," *Bar Association of Tennessee, Proceedings of the Thirteenth Annual Meeting* (1894), 67-71.

41. *American Law Review,* 29 (1895), 473-474. See also the comments of the prominent Judge Reuben M. Benjamin of Bloomington, Illinois, printed in the *Chicago Legal News,* 26 (1894), 406.

42. 156 U.S. 1 (1895).

43. Ibid., 43. For a survey of the extent of Harlan's dissidence from the conservative court of the 1890s, see Loren P. Beth, "Justice Harlan and the Uses of Dissent," *American Political Science Review,* 49 (1955), 1085-1104.

44. *American Law Register*, n.s. 34 (1895), 89-90.

45. *American Law Review*, 29 (1895), 288-289. See also Jackson Guy, "Trusts and Monopolies," *Virginia Law Register*, 1 (1896), 707-25.

46. Pollock v. Farmers' Loan and Trust Co., 157 U.S. 429, and Pollock v. Farmers' Loan and Trust Co. (rehearing), 158 U.S. 601.

47. Interesting material on the more sensational aspects of the *Pollock* case may be found in Robert T. Swaine, *The Cravath Firm and Its Predecessors, 1819-1947*, 2 vols (New York, 1946), I, 518-566; George Shiras III, *Justice George Shiras, Jr. of Pittsburgh* (Pittsburgh, 1958), 160-183; and David G. Farrelly's revealing "Harlan's Dissent in the Pollock Case," *Southern California Law Review*, 24 (1951), 175-182.

48. *American Law Review*, 29 (1895), 742-745; "Government and the Lawyers," *Texas Bar Association, Proceedings of the Fifteenth Annual Meeting* (1896), 64-85.

49. A former president of the Tennessee Bar Association as well as a Supreme Court judge, Ingersoll was also dean of the law faculty of the University of Tennessee from 1891 to 1914, and a vice president of the American Bar Association, 1907-13.

50. "The Revolution of 20th May, 1895," *Bar Association of Tennessee, Proceedings of the Fourteenth Annual Meeting* (1895), 180. For a similar comparison with the Dred Scott case, see the paper of David E. Bailey, "Stare Decisis," *Washington State Bar Association, Proceedings* (1895), 72-83, and the fascinating discussion it provoked reported from pp. 26 to 31, ibid.

51. Ritchie v. People, 155 Ill. 98.

52. S.S. Gregory, "Constitutional Limitations on the Police Power," *North Western Law Review*, 4 (1895), 50; Darius H. Pingree, "The Anti-Trust Cases, and Some Other Laws," *American Lawyer*, 3 (1895), 387.

53. In re Debs, 158 U.S. 564 (1895).

54. Percy L. Edwards, "The Federal Judiciary and Its Attitude towards the People," *Michigan Law Journal*, 15 (1896), 183-194.

55. *American Law Review*, 29 (1895), 550, 558; ibid., 856-63; ibid., 30 (1896), 188-202.

56. "Constitutional Changes Which Are Foreshadowed," *American Law Review*, 30 (1896), 702-709. Clark remained on the North Carolina bench until his death in 1924, always steadfast in his advocacy of advanced progressive reform and a radically democratized Constitution. Aubrey L. Brooks, *Walter Clark, Fighting Judge* (Chapel Hill, 1944).

57. Alan F. Westin, "The Supreme Court, the Populist Movement and the Campaign of 1896," *Journal of Politics*, 15 (1955), 3-41; Harvey Wish, "John P. Altgeld and the Background of the Campaign of 1896," *Mississippi Valley Historical Review*, 24 (1938), 503-518.

58. Thomas H. McKee, *The National Conventions and Platforms of All Political Parties, 1789 to 1904* (Baltimore, 1904), 294-295, 296, 297. The plan on life tenure would affect district and circuit-court judges.

59. See Westin, "The Supreme Court, the Populist Movement and the Campaign of 1896," for quotations from a number of conservative sources illustrating the excitement generated by the anticourt planks. The Cleveland wing of the Democracy, for example, which seceded from the regular organization and set up its own ticket, devoted several paragraphs of its National Democratic platform to pledging support to the Supreme Court. Seymour D. Thompson illustrates the dilemma that must have confronted many legal progessives: to begin with he approved of only part of the judicial plank, opposing the attack on the injunction; later he stated he was voting for McKinley because he disliked Bryan's monetary position. J. C. Rosenberger, mildly progressive editor of the *Kansas City Bar Monthly*, was outraged by the anticourt planks (I [1896], 1931).

60. Two of the more important decisions reflecting the new trend were Holden v. Hardy, 169 U.S. 366 (1898), sustaining a Utah eight-hour-day law for miners. and Knowlton v. Moore, 178 U.S. 41 (1900), affirming an inheritance tax with progressive-rate features.

26. Urban Crime and Criminal Justice: The Chicago Case

MARK H. HALLER

1. William F. Ogburn and Clark Tibbits, "A Memorandum on the Nativity of Certain

Criminal Classes . . .," July 30, 1930, Charles E. Merriam Papers, University of Chicago Library, 9, 11.

2. Ibid., 42-43, 47-48. For discussions of the background and recruitment of judges, see Albert Lepawsky, *The Judicial System of Metropolitan Chicago* (Chicago, 1932), 116-141. Interesting references about recruitment to the bench are also in Edward M. Martin, *The Role of the Bar in Electing the Bench in Chicago* (Chicago, 1936). For the social background of machine politicians, see Harold F. Gosnell, *Machine Politics: Chicago Model* (Chicago, 1937).

3. The classic study of the underworld of thieves in Chicago is Edwin H. Sutherland, ed., *The Professional Thief by a Professional Thief* (Chicago, 1937). John Landesco, "The Criminal Underworld of Chicago in the '80's and '90's," *Journal of Criminal Law and Criminology*, 25 (1934), 341-357; ibid., 25 (1935), 928-940; John Landesco, "Reformers? Why Not?" ibid., 28 (1937), 560-572. Joseph Weil, *"Yellow Kid" Weil* (Chicago, 1948). *Report of the Chicago, City Council Committee on Crime* (Chicago, 1915), 155-194; see also Boxes 87, 88, Merriam Papers.

4. For a discussion of relations between thieves and police in Boston during the 1860s and 1870s, see Robert Lane, *Policing the City: Boston, 1822-1885* (Cambridge, 1967), 142-156. For the relations between thieves and fences, see Jerome Hall, *Theft, Law and Society* (Indianapolis, 1955), 155-232.

5. John Landesco, *Organized Crime in Chicago* (Chicago, 1968), 245; David W. Mauter, *The Big Con* (Indianapolis, 1940), 170-215. For discussion of the gaps in our knowledge of the history of professional criminals, see the President's Commission on Law Enforcement and Administration of Justice, *Task Force Report: Crime and Its Impact — An Assessment* (Washington, D.C., 1967), 96-101.

6. There are a few scholarly and many journalistic accounts of racketeering in Chicago during the 1920s and early 1930s: Royal E. Montgomery, *Industrial Relations in the Chicago Building Trades* (Chicago, 1927), 19-21; Landesco, *Organized Crime in Chicago*, 149-167; Philip Hauser and Saul Alinsky, "Some Aspects of the Cleaning and Dyeing Industry in Chicago — A Racket," Ernest W. Burgess Papers, University of Chicago Library. See also Fred D. Pasley, *Muscling In* (New York, 1931); Edward D. Sullivan, *This Labor Union Racket* (New York, 1936); Gordon L. Hostetter and T. Q. Beesley, *It's a Racket!* (Chicago, 1929).

7. Roger Touhy, *The Stolen Years* (Cleveland, 1959).

8. The widespread opposition to prohibition and to enforcement of prohibition laws can best be followed in political histories of the period. Arthur W. Thurner, "The Impact of Ethnic Groups in the Democratic Party in Chicago" (Ph.D. diss., University of Chicago, 1966); Alex Gottfried, *Boss Cermak of Chicago* (Seattle, 1962).

9. Landesco, *Organized Crime in Chicago*, 45-83; Harold F. Gosnell, *Negro Politicians: The Rise of Negro Politics in Chicago* (Chicago, 1935), 124-125; Allan H. Spear, *Black Chicago: The Making of a Negro Ghetto, 1890-1920* (Chicago, 1967); St. Clair Drake and Horace R. Cayton, *Black Metropolis* (New York, 1945), 470-494.

10. Landesco, *Organized Crime in Chicago*, 169-221. For the situation in Chicago's black neighborhoods, see Gosnell, *Negro Politicians*, 115-135; Drake and Cayton, *Black Metropolis*, 470-494, 546-550. For the situation in Chicago's Italian neighborhoods before World War I, see Humbert S. Nelli, "Italians and Crime in Chicago: The Formative Years, 1890-1920," *American Journal of Sociology*, 74 (1969), 373-391.

11. Landesco, *Organized Crime in Chicago*, 169-205.

12. For a study of elite reformers and their beliefs, see David R. Johnson "Crime Fighting Reform in Chicago: An Analysis of Its Leadership, 1919-1927" (M.A. thesis, University of Chicago, 1966).

13. See Illinois Association for Criminal Justice, *The Illinois Crime Survey* (Chicago, 1929).

14. The best exemplification of the deterrent beliefs can be found in the publication of the Chicago Crime Commission, *Bulletin of the Chicago Crime Commission* (later called *Criminal Justice*), January 31, 1921. See also Chicago *Tribune*, January 11, 1925; September 21, 1929.

15. For expressions of the reformist views on criminal justice, see the *Annual Reports of the Juvenile Protective Association of Chicago*; see also Jane Addams, *A New Conscience and an Ancient Evil* (New York, 1912); Samuel P. Wilson, *Chicago and Its Cess-Pool of Infamy* (Chicago, n. d.). For analysis of the division between business leaders and social workers on law enforcement, see Graham Taylor, "Police Versus Crime," Chicago *Daily News*, January 20, 1923; Graham Taylor to Henry B. Chamberlin, January 20, 1923; File No. 600-9, Chicago Crime Commission, Chicago.

16. For founding of the Juvenile Court, see Robert M. Mennel, *Thorns and Thistles: Juvenile Delinquents in the United States, 1825-1940* (Hanover, N. H., 1973), chap. 5. Interesting but frequently misleading is Anthony Platt, *The Child Savers: The Invention of Delinquency* (Chicago, 1969), 129-152. Other studies include Grace Benjamin, "Constitutionality and Jurisdiction of the Juvenile Court of Cook County" (M.A. thesis, University of Chicago, 1932); T. D. Hurley, *Origin of the Illinois Juvenile Court Law* (Chicago, 1907); Helen Jeter, *The Chicago Juvenile Court* (Washington, 1922).

17. *Annual Reports of the Juvenile Protective Association of Chicago.* See also Louise de Koven Bowen, *Growing Up with a City* (New York, 1926), 103-118; Jane Addams, *My Friend, Julia Lathrop* (New York, 1935); Ray Ginger, *Altgeld's America* (New York, 1958), 221-230.

18. Elizabeth Parker, "Personnel and Organization in the Probation Department of the Juvenile Court of Cook County" (M.A. thesis, University of Chicago, 1934). William Healey's research findings were first published in his important *Individual Delinquent: A Text-Book of Diagnosis and Prognosis for All Concerned in Understanding Offenders* (Boston, 1915).

19. Quotations from Benjamin, "Constitutionality and Jurisdiction," 292; Jane Addams, *Twenty Years at Hull House* (New York, 1961), 227-229.

20. Perhaps the most extreme argument claiming that the founders of the juvenile court were insensitive to civil liberties is Platt, *Child Savers*, 143-163. For other points of view, see President's Commission on Law Enforcement, *Task Force Report: Juvenile Delinquency and Youth Crime* (Washington, 1967), 1-40; David Matza, *Delinquency and Drift* (New York, 1964), 101-151. See also A. P. Drucker, *On the Trial of the Juvenile-Adult Offender* (Chicago, 1912), 43; Louise de Koven Bowen, *Boys in the County Jail* (Chicago, 1913), 3-5.

21. Statistics from Clifford R. Shaw and Earl D. Myers, "The Juvenile Delinquent," *Illinois Crime Survey*, 647-648.

22. The activities of the Committee of Fifteen can be followed in its *Annual Reports.* See also Clifford G. Roe, *The Prodigal Daughter* (Chicago, 1911). For general studies of the progressive campaign against prostitution, see Roy Lubove, "The Progressive and the Prostitute," *The Historian*, 24 (1962), 308-330; Egal Feldman, "Prostitution, the Alien Woman and the Progressive Imagination, 1910-1915," *American Quarterly*, 19 (1967), 192-206.

23. Jerome H. Skolnick, *Justice without Trial* (New York, 1966); Wayne R. LaFave, *Arrest: The Decision to Take a Suspect into Custody* (Boston, 1965); James Q. Wilson, *Varieties of Police Behavior* (Cambridge, Mass., 1968).

24. Gosnell, *Negro Politicians*, 115-135; Chicago Commission on Race Relations, *The Negro in Chicago* (Chicago, 1922). An interesting comparison is a description of police attitudes in an Italian ghetto in Boston in the 1930s, in William Foote Whyte, *Street Corner Society: The Social Structure of an Italian Slum* (Chicago, 1943), 123-139. Wilson, *Varieties of Police Behavior*, 140-171, discusses the order-maintenance function of the police.

25. Quotations from Vice Commission of Chicago, *Social Evil in Chicago* (Chicago, 1911), 329-330. See also Carter H. Harrison, *Stormy Years* (Indianapolis, 1935), 308-309.

26. Quotation from *Annual Report of the Committee of Fifteen*, 1914.

27. Ibid., *Annual Reports*, for years 1912-1930; and special reports of the Committee of Fifteen for the 1920s, Ernest W. Burgess Papers, University of Chicago Library.

28. Walter C. Reckless, *Vice in Chicago* (Chicago, 1933); see also Lloyd Wendt and

Herman Kogan, *Big Bill of Chicago* (Indianapolis, 1953); William H. Stuart, *The Twenty Incredible Years* (Chicago, 1935).

29. *Bulletin of Chicago Crime Commission,* January 31, 1921.

30. *Illinois Crime Survey,* 204-209. Of the 276,000 persons arrested in Chicago in 1924 (including arrests for misdemeanors), more than 200,000 were discharged by the courts. Chicago *Daily News,* January 21, 1925. See also Donald J. Newman, *Conviction: The Determination of Guilt or Innocence without Trial* (Boston, 1966).

31. For background of the campaign, see Chicago Crime Commission File No. 11170, including its numerous newspaper clippings. For analysis of the judicial election of 1927, see Chicago Crime Commission File No. 9578; Martin, *Role of the Bar,* 75-85,

32. Newspaper clippings in Chicago Crime Commission File No. 11170. John J. Healy, the Crime Commission lawyer who presented the commission's case against the judges, had earlier blamed the state's attorney for felony waiver abuses. See John J. Healy, "The Prosecutor (in Chicago) in Felony Cases," *Illinois Crime Survey,* 285-331.

33. See Chicago Crime Commission File No. 11170; also newspaper clippings, Frank Loesch File, Chicago Crime Commission.

26. Negro Involuntary Servitude in the South, 1865-1940: A Preliminary Analysis

WILLIAM COHEN

1. *Editors' Note:* For full citation of statutes discussed in this article, the reader is referred to the original text in *The Journal of Southern History.*

2. "Report of Hon. Charles W. Russell," in *U. S. Attorney General's Annual Report, 1907* (Washington, 1908), 208.

3. The most recent and significant study is Pete Daniel, *The Shadow of Slavery: Peonage in the South, 1901-1969* (Urbana, Illinois, 1972). This excellent work restricts itself to the matter of peonage and does not discuss the larger system of involuntary servitude within which peonage existed.

4. For an able discussion of these state laws and their relationship to peonage and

involuntary servitude, see Howard Devon Hamilton, "The Legislative and Judicial History of the Thirteenth Amendment" (Ph.D. diss., University of Illinois, 1950), 210-229, 232-241.

5. Arney R. Childs, ed., *The Private Journal of Henry William Ravenel, 1859-1887* (Columbia, S. C., 1947), 256.

6. The best available monograph on the Black Codes is Theodore B. Wilson, *The Black Codes of the South* (University, Ala., 1965), especially 61-80, 96-115; see also William E. B. Du Bois, *Black Reconstruction, . . . 1860-1880* (New York, 1935), 166-179.

7. Richard B. Morris, *Government and Labor in Early America* (New York, 1946), 414-434; *American Digest,* Century ed. 50 vols. (St. Paul, Minn., 1897-1904), XXXIV, 2055-63.

8. State v. Hurdle, 113 Miss. 736, 739 (1917). Most of the reported higher-court cases involving enticement do not explicitly specify the race of the laborers involved, but inferential materials such as bits of dialogue leave little doubt that the laborers were almost always Negroes.

9. W. McKee Evans, *Ballots and Fence Rails* (CHapel Hill, 1967), 75; *North Carolina Public Laws* (1866), 100, 122-123; J. G. Mills to Herbert F. Seawell, August 11, 1911, appended to Seawell to the Attorney General, August 26, 1911, Doc. 150153-11, File 50-0, Materials Relating to Peonage, National Files, Classified Subject Files, Numerical Files, 1904-1937, General Records of the Department of Justice, Record Group 60, National Archives, cited hereafter as DJ Peonage Files; *Caswell Messenger,* quoted in Baltimore *Evening Sun,* December 6, 1939, sec. 2, p. 27.

10. Quoted in ibid.

11. Charleston *News and Courier,* December 27, 1908, p. 9. For other Mississippi incidents, see Jackson *Daily News,* November 29, 1911; Natchez *Democrat,* January 23, 24, 1920; St. Louis *Argus,* November 22, 1929. This last item was found in the Monroe N. Work Clipping File, Hollis-Burke-Frissell Library, Tuskegee Institute, Tuskegee, Ala. The item in the Jackson *Daily News* was located in Newspaper Clippings Relating to Cotton Boll Wee-

vil, Division of Southern Field-Crop Inspect Investigations, Records of the Bureau of Entomology and Plant Quarantine, Record Group 7, National Archives.

12. For Williams, see Atlanta *Constitution*, February 25, 1890; January 25, 1891; January 2, 1895; January 15, 17, 1900; Williams v. Fears, 179 U. S. 270 (1900). For Lane, see Lane v. Commissioners, 139 N. C. 443 (1905). Other higher-court cases involving the arrest of nonprofessional agents include: Braxton v. City of Selma, 16 Ala. App. 476 (1918); Rowe v. State, 19 Ala. App. 602 (1924); Theus v. State, 114 Ga. 53 (1901); State v. Lowe, 187 N. C. 524 (1924).

13. Often the records of the higher courts give little indication as to the race of those accused of recruiting labor without a license. In those cases which did have such inferential materials, about one-fourth appear to have involved blacks. This estimate is tentative and is not based on a systematic sampling of all the emigrant-agent cases that came before the higher courts. Moreover, even if the sample is representative, one would still be faced with the question of whether or not blacks accused of being agents came before the higher courts more often than whites.

14. 219 U. S. 219 (1911). The Federal Peonage Act was designed to end debt servitude in New Mexico, and, despite the date of its enactment, its sponsors did not intend it as a means of protecting southern blacks. This statute lay dormant until it was invoked in the Alabama Peonage Cases, 123 F. 671 (M.D. Ala. 1903). Two years later, in Clyatt v. United States, 197 U. S. 207 (1905), the Supreme Court opened the way for further use of this law in the South by holding that it applied to individuals as well as to state-sponsored systems of peonage. At the same time the Court restricted the use of the law to cases where forced labor was the result of a debt. Given the origins of this law, the Court's ruling was reasonable, but it also handed reluctant Justice Department officials a legitimate excuse for refusing to take action in many cases where blacks alleged they were being forced to labor against their wills. See Daniel, *Shadow of Slavery*, 12, 174, 191; and Hamilton, "History of the Thirteenth Amendment," 171-174, 178-179.

15. Thomas v. State, 13 Ala. App. 431 (1915); State v. Griffin, 154 N. C. 611 (1911). Compare *General Statutes of North Carolina of 1943* (Charlottesville, 1943), sec. 14-104, with W. H. Michie and C. W. Sublett, annotators, *North Carolina Code of 1939* (Charlottesville, 1939), sec. 4281. Unconstitutional laws which remained on the statute books could still be used to intimidate ignorant laborers. Wilson v. State, 138 Ga. 489 (1912); *Florida General Acts, 1913*, p. 417; ibid., *1919*, p. 286; Goode v. Nelson, 73 Fla. 29 (1917); Taylor v. Georgia, 315 U. S. 25 (1942); Pollock v. Williams, 322 U. S. 4 (1944).

16. These figures were compiled from cases given in the five decennial editions of the *American Digest System*, 164 vols. (St. Paul, 1908-1950), covering the period 1897-1946. The intervals used in this table were chosen to reflect the dichotomy between the periods before and after the Bailey decision (see above, n. 14) and to include the last Georgia Supreme Court decision on the contract law.

17. See Toney v. State, 141 Ala. 120 (1904); State v. Armstead, 103 Miss. 790 (1913); State v. Oliva, 144 La. 51 (1918); State v. Murray, 116 La. 655 (1906).

18. State v. Williams, 32 S.C. 123 (1890).

19. Ex parte Drayton, 153 F. 986, 996 (D. S.C. 1907); Ex parte Hollman, 79 S.C. 9 (1908). On South Carolina's system of involuntary servitude, see also George B. Tindall, *South Carolina Negroes, 1877-1900* (Columbia, S. C., 1952), 112-113.

20. Ex parte Drayton, 153 F. 986, 996.

21. Atlanta *Constitution*, September 2, 1904; Little Rock *Arkansas Gazette*, October 1, 1910; see also Carl V. Harris, "Reforms in Government Control of Negroes in Birmingham, Alabama, 1890-1920," *Journal of Southern History*, 38 (1972), 578-582.

22. Jacksonville *Florida Times Union*, October 12, 13, 1910.

23. Daniel, *Shadow of Slavery*, 25-26; Hamilton, "History of the Thirteenth Amendment," 225-229.

24. *Georgia Acts, 1874*, p. 29; Walton Co. v. Franklin, 95 Ga. 538 (1894); James J. Mayfield, annotator, *The Code of Alabama, 1907* (Nashville, 1907), secs. 6846 and 6847; Peonage Cases, 123 F. 671 (M. D. Ala. 1903).

25. Lee v. State, 75 Ala. 29 (1883). The figure of fifteen cases includes State v. Etowah Lumber Company, 153 Ala. 77 (1907); and the cases listed in the annotation for *Code of Alabama, 1907*, sec. 6846. The quotation in the text is from United States v. Reynolds, 235 U.S. 133, 139-140, 150 (1914).

26. Daniel, *Shadow of Slavery*, 110-131 (quotation from 116n.); *New York Times*, April 26, 1921.

27. For the background of southern penological developments after the Civil War, see Blake McKelvey, "Penal Slavery and Southern Reconstruction," *Journal of Negro History*, 20 (1935), 153-179; Dan T. Carter, "Prisons, Politics, and Business: The Convict Lease System in the Post–Civil War South" (M.A. thesis, University of Wisconsin, 1964), 35-60.

28. McKelvey, "Penal Slavery," 155-175; J. C. Powell, *The American Siberia, or, Fourteen Years' Experience in a Southern Convict Labor Camp* (Chicago, 1891).

29. Quoted in Carter, "Prisons, Politics, and Business," 91. For mortality figures, see ibid., 53, 91; and Tindall, *South Carolina Negros*, 271.

30. The ratios given above were calculated using 1880 census figures and combining them with figures cited in Fletcher M. Green, "Some Aspects of the Convict Lease System in the Southern States," in Green, ed., *Essays in Southern History* (Chapel Hill, 1949), 120; Francis B. Simkins and Robert H. Woody, *South Carolina during Reconstruction* (Chapel Hill, 1932), 335: Jesse C. Steiner and Roy M. Brown, *The North Carolina Chain Gang* (Chapel Hill, 1927), 15.

31. Quoted in Tindall, *South Carolina Negroes*, 267; Carter, "Prisons, Politics and Business," 42, 76, 79-83, 97.

32. Blake McKelvey, "A Half Century of Southern Penal Exploitation," *Social Forces*, 13 (1934), 113-119. Useful descriptions of the various forms of convict labor together with assessments of the status of the leasing system and compilations of state laws related to convict labor are to be found in U. S. Commissioner of Labor, *Second Annual Report, . . . 1886: Convict Labor* (Washington, D.C., 1906), 15-17, 615-787; *U. S. Bureau of Labor Statistics Bulletin*, no. 372: *Convict Labor in 1923* (Washington, D.C.,

1925), 3-4, 18, 169-265; ibid., no. 595 (Washington, D.C., 1933), 4, 20-24; ibid., no. 596 (Washington, D.C., 1933). Mortality rates were calculated on the basis of death lists in *Alabama Board of Administration Annual Report . . . 1932* (Montgomery, 1932), 62-63, 72-74. See also Frank Tannenbaum, *Darker Phases of the South* (New York, 1924), 84-89, 100-106.

33. *Alabama Board of Administration Annual Report . . . 1932*, 28, 63. As of 1938 the size of Alabama's all-black road force had increased to 1,720 men. U.S. Prison Industries Reorganization Administration, *The Prison Problem in Alabama* (Washington, D.C., 1939), 10. See also ibid., *The Prison Problem in Florida* (Washington, D.C., 1939), 33; ibid., *The Prison Problem in Virginia* (Washington, D.C., 1939), 35. The ratio of Georgia blacks to the total population of that state was calculated on the basis of figures given in U.S. Bureau of the Census, *Negroes in the United States, 1920-32* (Washington, D.C., 1935), 9. For the Georgia prisons, see *Prison Commission of Georgia Third (Fourth) Biennial Report* (Atlanta, 1933), 23-26.

34. The figures in this table have been calculated from ibid., 23-26.

35. Ibid.; U.S. Bureau of Labor Statistics, *Prison Labor, 1932*, p. 205. Felons and misdemeanants were treated separately in Georgia's statistical tables, but those felons who were assigned to the chain gang were not separated from the misdemeanants in actuality.

36. The percentages given above are based on calculations made from the tables given in U.S. Bureau of Labor Statistics, *Prison Labor, 1932*, 20-24, 205. Unlike other states, Georgia did not categorize her prisoners as "state" or "county" prisoners, but the terms "felons" and "misdemeanants" were roughly equivalent to the state-county dichotomy used elsewhere.

37. *New York Times*, September 16, 1937, p. 1. This incident or a similar one is described retrospectively by J. W. Whitely, a white Warren County pecan grower, in a letter to Secretary of Agriculture Henry A. Wallace, July 5, 1938, File 50-0, DJ Peonage Files.

38. On attempts to use force to stop Negro migration in 1916 and 1917, see for example Savannah *Tribune*, November 4, 1916; Atlanta *Constitution*, September 13, 1916; Cleveland *Gazette*, September 22, 1917.

39. Jonathan Daniels, *A Southerner Discovers the South* (New York, 1938), 170.

27. Moorfield Storey and the Struggle for Equality

WILLIAM B. HIXSON, JR.

1. Oswald Garrison Villard, *Fighting Years: Memoirs of a Liberal Editor* (New York, 1939); Mary White Ovington, *The Walls Came Tumbling Down* (New York, 1947).

2. Louis Ruchames, "Race, Marriage, and Abolition in Massachusetts," *Journal of Negro History*, 40 (1955), 250-273; idem, "Jim Crow Railroads in Massachusetts," *American Quarterly*, 8 (1956), 61-75.

3. Roberts v. City of Boston, 59 Mass. 158; Charles Sumner, *The Works of Charles Sumner*, 15 vols. (Boston, 1870-1883), II, 364. Charles Sumner's argument was rejected by the Supreme Judicial Court, but several years later the legislature abolished the remaining segregated schools in Massachusetts. In 1896, however, the Supreme Court cited *Roberts* to support its decision in the fundamental case upholding segregation, Plessy v. Ferguson, 163 U.S. 357 (1896). *Plessy*, of course, has been overturned in a number of Court decisions since 1954, and today Sumner's view has been upheld by all branches of the federal government.

4. Edward L. Pierce, *Memoir and Letters of Charles Sumner*, 4 vols. (Boston, 1877-1893), IV, 175-183, cites three such achievements during the Civil War: the inclusion of Negroes as inventors, mail carriers, and witnesses in federal courts; sponsorship of the first Negro attorney to practice before the Supreme Court (the attorney's acceptance by the Court implicitly revoked the *Dred Scott* doctrine that Negroes were not citizens); and the abolition of official segregation on Washington streetcars.

5. W. R. Brock, *An American Crisis: Congress and Reconstruction, 1865-1867* (London, 1962), 78-79.

6. Passed in greatly weakened form in 1875 (notably without the provisions for desegregated schools), it was this Civil Rights Act which the Supreme Court declared unconstitutional in the Civil Rights Cases, 109 U.S. 3 (1883).

7. Storey, unpublished autobiography, Storey Papers, Massachusetts Historical Society, hereafter cited as Storey Papers, MHS.

8. Storey to Mariana Storey, February 2, 1868, ibid.

9. See David Donald, *Charles Sumner and the Coming of the Civil War* (New York, 1960).

10. Storey, *To the Voters of Massachusetts* (1892), broadside issued by the Independent Cleveland Headquarters, Storey Papers, MHS. For the Mugwump role in helping defeat the Hoar-Lodge bill, see Stanley P. Hirschon, *Farewell to the Bloody Shirt* (Bloomington, 1962), 123-142.

11. "Ought the Negro to be Disfranchised?," *North American Review*, 78 (1879), 225-284; Thomas Wentworth Higginson, "Some War Scenes Revisited," *Atlantic Monthly*, 42 (1878), 1-9.

12. Carl Schurz to Storey, June 26, 1903, Storey Papers, MHS.

13. Frederic Bancroft, ed., *Speeches, Correspondence, and Political Papers of Carl Schurz*, 6 vols. (New York, 1913), VI, 343.

14. *Crisis*, I (February 1911), 5.

15. In particular, Storey championed the cause of the Japanese against intense discrimination. He also urged the resettlement of the oppressed Armenians in the United States and Canada.

16. See Christopher Lasch, "The Anti-Imperialists, the Philippines, and the Inequality of Man," *Journal of Southern History*, 24 (1958), 319-331.

17. *Boston Herald*, September 19, 1900.

18. Storey, *The Importance to America of Philippine Independence* (Boston, 1904), 9.

19. Storey, *Negro Suffrage Is Not a Failure* (Boston, 1903), 7.

20. Ibid., 16.

21. Charles Francis Adams, Jr., *The "Solid South" and the Afro-American Race*

Problem (Richmond, Va., 1908), 17.

22. James Ford Rhodes, *History of the United States from the Compromise of 1850 to the Final Restoration of Home Rule at the South*, 8 vols. (New York, 1893-1906), VI, vii; Robert Cruden, *James Ford Rhodes: The Man, The Historian, His Work* (Cleveland, 1961), 95.

23. Storey to Rhodes, May 12, 1906 (copy), Storey Papers, MHS.

24. Adams, *The "Solid South"*, 19.

25. Storey to Charles Francis Adams, Jr., February 4, 1914, in Mark A. DeWolfe Howe, *Portrait of an Independent: Moorfield Storey, 1845-1929* (Boston, 1932), 307.

26. Storey to Adams, February 11, 1914 (copy), Storey Papers. It is interesting to note, first, that Storey's library included a number of contemporary works challenging the Rhodes interpretation, including *The Facts of Reconstruction* (New York, 1913) by John R. Lynch, a Negro politician from Mississippi; and second, that Storey was one of the earliest white supporters of Carter G. Woodson's Association for the Study of Negro Life and History, whose *Journal of Negro History* has consistently defended the Negro against the hostile bias of earlier scholarship.

27. Storey's first exposure to Franz Boas, for example, seems to have occurred when he was already president of the NAACP. In a letter to W. E. B. Du Bois, he wrote, "There was a course of Lowell Lectures . . . on the so-called 'inferior races' in which the lecturer [probably Boas] reached conclusions most favorable to our cause" (Storey to Du Bois, November 22, 1910 [copy], Storey Papers, MHS.) Whether or not Storey ever actually read Boas, or any other "modern" anthropologist for that matter, remains an open question.

28. Charles W. Eliot's views either of immigrants in general or of Jews in particular should not be demeaned, but his defense—like that of Theodore Roosevelt, a very different man—seems to have been confined to the white race and its " assimilable" ethnic groups. Unlike Storey, Eliot accepted both the retention of the Philippines and the enforcement of segregation in the South (Henry James, *Charles W. Eliot, . . . 1869-*

1909, 2 vols. [Boston, 1930], II, 53-54, 118-119, 166-168, 210-211).

29. Springfield *Republican*, February 26, 1913.

30. Ibid., February 27, 1913.

31. Storey to Alexander Lawton, June 25, 1923 (copy), Storey Papers, MHS.

32. Draft of speech, possibly that presented before the Boston branch of the NAACP, December 1, 1913, Moorfield Storey Papers, Manuscript Division, Library of Congress, hereafter cited as Storey Papers, LC.

33. Storey to N. F. Lamb, February 16, 1913 (copy), Storey Papers, MHS.

34. Storey, letter to an unnamed newspaper, scrapbook 2, Storey Papers, LC.

35. Storey to A. Shuman, March 25, 1913; Storey to Marion Burton, October 14, 1913; Storey to Du Bois, June 1, 1917 (copies), Storey Papers, MHS.

36. Storey to Albert E. Pillsbury, March 4, 1912, ibid.,; Stephen S. Gregory to Storey, March 25, 1912; Storey, petition to members of the American Bar Association, Storey Papers, LC; Storey to E. Furness, April 30, 1913; Storey to Lucien H. Alexander, November 3, 1914; Storey to James C. Crosby, October 24, 1919 (copies), Storey Papers, MHS.

37. Storey to Julian Mack, June 6, 1922; Storey to Charles C. Jackson, June 20, 1922 (copies), Storey Papers, MHS; Lewis Gannett to Storey, June 2, July 26, August 2, 1922, Storey Papers, LC; Storey to John Jay Chapman, January 18, 22, 1923 (copies), Storey Papers, MHS.

38. Storey to Adams, November 19, 1908, Storey Papers. MHS.

39. Storey to Bolton Smith, February 24, 1921 (copy), ibid.

40. That private descimination could not be prohibited under the Fourteenth Amendment was the basis of the Court's decision in the Civil Rights Cases, 109 U.S. 3 (1883). Between 1875 and 1883 the Court also exempted the intimidation of Negroes from the prohibitions of the Amendment not only on the basis that the Amendment covered only "state action" but also on the basis that

the right to assemble preceded the Constitution thus was protected only by state law. U.S. v. Cruikshank, 92 U.S. 542 (1875); U.S. v. Harris, 106 U.S. 629 (1883).

41. Plessy v. Ferguson, 163 U.S. 537 (1896). The Court had already ruled, under the commerce clause, that although a state could not prohibit segregation in interstate transportation. (Hall v. DeCuir, 95 U.S. 485 [1877]), a state could require it (Louisville, etc. Railroad v. Mississippi, 133 U.S. 587 [1890]).

42. The NAACP was content to work within the "separate but equal" framework until the beginning of its final onslaught against school segregation after Sweatt v. Painter, 339 U.S. 629 (1950). A case within that framework, which distantly involved Storey, was McCabe v. Railway, 235 U.S. 151 (1914). The effect of the decision, which involved the constitutionality of an Oklahoma statute limiting Pullman accommodations to whites, was weakened, however, because the Negro plaintiffs had not actually sought accommodations and could not point to any denial of their rights. The NAACP participated in the case, but Storey did not because, as he put it, "it seemed to me that the petitioners did not state a case which would justify the Court in granting the relief and deciding the question." See Storey to William Monroe Trotter, December 2, 1914, copy, Storey Papers, MHS; also Charles S. Mangum, Jr., *The Legal Status of the Negro* (Chapel Hill, 1940), 203-207. The Court ruled that equal accommodations must be provided in all interstate Pullman facilities, Mitchell v. U.S., 313 U.S. 30 [1941]).

43. Strauder v. West Virginia, 100 U.S. 303 (1880).

44. Yick Wo v. Hopkins, 118 U.S. 356 (1886).

45. The exemptive clauses typically took two forms. The "understanding clause" permitted persons to vote who "understood" the state constitution when it was read to them (Alabama, Mississippi, South Carolina, Carolina, and Virginia) or who "understood the duties of a citizen under a republican form of government" (Georgia). The "grandfather clause," in contrast, restricted the vote to persons who were entitled to vote before 1867 and their descendants (Louisiana and North Carolina), or to persons who had fought in wars in which United States forces participated and their descendants, (Alabama, Georgia, and Virginia). Though the exemptive clauses expired shortly after they were passed (Arkansas, Florida, Tennessee, and Texas had no exemptive clauses), other restrictions on Negro suffrage were permanent. These included the institution of poll tax in every southern state and of statewide party rules barring Negroes from Democratic primaries (except in Florida, North Carolina, and Tennessee). See Gilbert T. Stephenson, *Race Distinctions in American Law* (New York, 1910), 299-310; V.O. Key, Jr., *Southern Politics in State and Nation* (New York, 1949), 617-620.

46. Williams v. Mississippi, 170 U.S. 213 (1898).

47. Mills v. Green, 159 U.S. 651 (1898); Giles v. Harris, 189 U.S. 475 (1903); Giles v. Teasley 193 U.S. 146 (1903); Jones v. Montague, 194 U.S. 147 (1904); Mangum, *Legal Status of the Negro*, 394-405.

48. Storey to Smith, March 11, 1921 (copy), Storey Papers, MHS.

49. Storey to Trotter, January 7, 1921 (copy), ibid.

50. Storey to May C. Nerney, August 6, 1915 (copy), ibid. Storey thought action to enforce the second section could be brought either by a suit "to ask the Supreme Court by mandamus to compel a statute making a new apportionment," or by a citizen's suit to ask "that the officers of a state be restrained from acting under the current apportionment." He acknowledged that the second section, if enforced, might also restrict the representation of those northern states with literacy tests. Storey to Turner M. Hackman, September 20, 1916 (copy), ibid.

51. *Brief for the N.A.A.C.P. in Frank Guinn and J. J. Beal v. the United States, in the Supreme Court, October Term, 1913* (Washington, D.C., 1913), 4.

52. Guinn and Beal v. U.S., 238 U.S. 347, 362, 365 (1915). The following year Oklahoma enacted a measure allowing all those who had voted under the old amendment to

reregister in a sixteen-day period; others — Negroes — could enroll only with the approval of registrars. This statute was finally declared unconstitutional. Lane v. Wilson et al., 307 U.S. 268 (1939).

53. Love et al. v. Griffith et al., 266 U.S. 32 (1924); Mangum, *Legal Status of the Negro*, 405-416.

54. Storey to Walter White, January 10, 1925 (copy), Storey Papers, MHS.

55. *Brief for Plantiff in Error, L. A. Nixon against C. C. Herndon and Charles Porres, in the Supreme Court, October Term,1925* (Washington, D.C. 1925).

56. Nixon v. Herndon, 273 U.S. 536, 540-541 (1927). Following the decision, the state legislature allowed each party to set its own qualifications. This, the Supreme Court held, was still "state action" and therefore unconstitutional (Nixon v. Condon et al., 286 U.S. 73 [1932]). Then, the state Democratic convention adopted an exclusionary policy; this, the Court ruled, could be permitted (Grovey v. Townsend, 295 U.S. 45 [1935]). A dacade later, using a decision that involved election frauds in Louisiana, U.S. v. Classic, 313 U.S. 299 (1941), which stated that primaries were an integral part of the election process, the Court ruled unconstitutional all primaries excluding any citizen because of his race. (Smith v. Allwright, 321 U.S. 649 [1944]).

57. In re Lee Sing et al., 43 Fed. 359 (C.C.N.D. Cal. 1890).

58. See Mangum, *Legal Status of the Negro*, 140-146; Roger L. Rice, "Residential Segregation by Law, 1910-1917," *Journal of Southern History*, 24 (1968), 179-199.

59. State v. Gurry, 121 Md. 534, 88 Atl. 228 (1913). A North Carolina court reached the same conclusion on the last point. State v. Darnell, 166 N.C. 300, 81 S.E. 338 (1914).

60. Hopkins et al. v. City of Richmond, 117 Va. 692, 86 S.E. 139 (1915); Harris v. City of Louisville, 165 Ky. 559, 177 S.W. 472 (1915); Harden v. Atlanta, 147 Ga. 248, 93 S.E. 401 (1917).

61. Harris v. Louisville, 165 Ky. 559.

62. *Brief for the Plaintiff in Error on Rehearing, in Charles H. Buchanan v. William Warley, in the Supreme Court, October Term, 1916* (Washington, D.C., 1916), 11-12.

63. Ibid., 22.

64. Ibid., 17.

65. Ibid., 33.

66. Ibid., 45.

67. Mangum, *Legal Status of the Negro*, 139; Jack Greenberg, *Race Relations and American Law* (New York, 1959), 277-278.

68. Buchanan v. Warley, 245 U.S. 60, 80-81 (1917).

69. Storey to Wells Blodgett, September 15, 1916 (copy), Storey Papers, MHS.

70. Storey to Oswald Garrison Villard, November 6, 1917 (copy), ibid. Villard had written him: "That the Supreme Court has stood by us on this is the most hopeful thing that has happened for some time in this dark period of our country's history"(Villard to Storey, November 5, 1917, ibid.).

71. Mangum, *Legal Status of the Negro*, 149-151.

72. Buchanan v. Warley, 245 U.S. 60, 82 (1917).

73. Storey to W. Hayes McKenney, November 23, 1922 (copy), Storey Papers, MHS.

74. This is an inference based upon two pieces of evidence. Marshall was hesitant about arguing that the Fourteenth Amendment applied to the District. Charles Reznikoff, ed., *Louis Marshall, Champion of Liberty: Selected Papers and Addresses*, 2 vols. (Philadelphia, 1957), I 461-462. But in the final brief nine pages were spent arguing this very point and placing heavy emphasis on the implication of the Court's decision in the Insular Cases of 1901, DeLima v. Bidwell, 182 U.S. 1 (1901), and Downes v. Bidwell, 182 U.S. 244 (1901). *Brief for appellants, Irene Hand Corrigan and Helen Curtis v. John J. Buckley in the Supreme Court, October Term, 1925* (Washington, 1925), 17-26.

75. Storey to Marshall, December 3, 1924 (copy), Storey Papers, MHS; Reznikoff, *Selected Papers*, I, 459-461.

76. Ibid., I, 461.

77. *Brief for Appellants, Corrigan v. Buckley*, 40.

78. Corrigan et al. v. Buckley, 271 U.S. 323 (1926).

79. Storey to James W. Johnson, May 26, 1926 (copy), Storey Papers, MHS.

80. Shelly v. Kraemer, 334 U.S. 1 (1948). Many commentators on this case have been misled by the court's assertion that it was not considering the "validity" of the covenants, as supposedly it had in *Corrigan*, but only the constitutionality of their judicial enforcement. However, it was precisely the issue of their enforcement in the courts that Storey and Marshall had emphasized in their *Corrigan* brief. It would be more accurate to say that a different Court, two decades later, reinterpreted the concept of "state action" to include such judicial enforcement. Five years later, in Barrows v. Jackson, 346 U.S. 349 (1953), the Court deprived convenants of whatever "validity" they still possessed by ruling that damage suits against the sellers were also unconstitutional. Clement E. Vose, *Caucasians Only: The Supreme Court, the NAACP, and the Restrictive Covenant Cases* (Berkeley, California, 1959).

81. Hurd v. Hodge, 334 U.S. 24 (1948).

82. Storey, statement in NAACP press release, December 20. 1926 (copy), Storey Papers, LC.

28. Earl Warren and the *Brown* Decision

S. SIDNEY ULMER

1. 347 U.S. 483 (1954).

2. 369 U.S. 186 (1962).

3. Ira M. Heyman, "The Chief Justice, Racial Segregation, and the Friendly Critics," *California Law Review*, 49 (1961), 104.

4. This is the manuscript collection of the late Justice Burton, now deposited in the Library of Congress.

5. Consideration is limited to the first *Brown* case decided on May 17, 1954.

6. 343 U.S. 989 (1952). The justices voted to "note jurisdiction" in conference on June 7, 1952. As recorded by Justice Burton, the vote was seven to "note" and one (Justice Jackson) to "hold." No vote is recorded for Chief Justice Vinson. Harold H. Burton Papers, Library of Congress (hereafter cited as Burton Papers).

7. Bolling v. Sharpe, 347 U.S. 497 (1954).

8. The following references to what was said in this conference are taken from notes made by Justice Burton (Burton Papers).

9. 163 U.S. 537 (1896).

10. Chief Justice Vinson died September 8, 1953. He was replaced by Warren, who took office on October 5, 1953.

11. Burton Diary (Burton Papers).[Editors' note: Subsequently Chief Justice Warren recalled that not until February did the members of the Court state their formal views on the constitutional issue. Until then, they restricted their discussions in conferences to analysis of the briefs and arguments, "and our own independent research." They did so because of hopes for unity and their sense that once individual justices' conclusions had been announced it would become more difficult to reconcile differences. *The Memoirs of Earl Warren*, excerpted in Warren, "Inside the Supreme Court: The Momentous School Desegregation Decision," *The Atlantic*, 239 (April 1977), 35-36.]

12. Burton Diary.

13. Frankfurter is on record elsewhere as being opposed to taking shortcuts to discriminate as partisans in favor of Negroes or of appearing to do so (Felix Frankfurter to Hugo Black, February 19, 1962, Frankfurter Papers, Library of Congress).

14. Burton Diary.

15. The role of Frankfurter in the Segregation Cases is somewhat mysterious. In the Vinson Court conference of 1952, he stated a willingness to vote that day that segregation in the District of Columbia was a violation of the due-process clause. But he excepted the states, arguing that the legislative history of the Fourteenth Amendment did not establish an intention to abolish segregation. He also disagreed at that point with Hugo Black's view that the states were more limited than the federal government — arguing instead the exact opposite. On December 3, 1953, he wrote to his colleagues: "The legislative history of the [14th] Amendment is, in a word, inconclusive, in the sense that the 39th Congress as an enacting body neither manifested that the Amendment outlawed segregation in the public schools or authorized legislation to that end, nor that it man-

ifested the opposite" (Burton Papers). In the 1953 conference he stated flatly that "as a pure matter of history — 1867 — XIV *did not* have as a purpose to abolish segregation" (as recorded by Burton, Burton Papers). On January 1, 1954, Frankfurter sent a memo to his colleagues suggesting that the Court appoint a Master and arguing that the inequalities deriving from segregated schools should be eliminated as soon as possible without disrupting school systems or substantially lowering standards for any sizable group (Burton Papers).

16. Burton Diary. I have considered the possibility that Burton intended "opinion" for "decree" but have rejected it since "decree" has such a specific meaning in the law.

17. On the day of Warren's first reported conference on the Segregation Cases, he lunched with Burton, Reed, Douglas, Clark, and Minton (four of whom supported him that day). On May 14, 1954, the day before the conference that approved the opinions in these cases, Warren had lunch with Burton, Reed, Clark, Douglas, and Minton — the same justices. Burton recorded that this luncheon group met frequently throughout the intervening period, that Frankfurter and Jackson never attended, and that Black joined the group only infrequently.

18. Burton Papers.

19. Burton Diary.

20. Ibid.

21. Burton Papers. This is an unsigned, undated note. After close comparison with known specimens of Frankfurter's handwriting, however, there is no doubt that it came from his pen.

22. Burton Diary.

23. Ibid.

24. Ibid.

25. Ibid.

26. Cf. Alexander M. Bickel, "The Original Understanding and the Segregation Decision," *Harvard Law Review*, 59 (1955), 1-65; and Albert Sacks, "Foreword to The Supreme Court, 1953 Term," ibid., 58 (1954), 96.

27. Burton Papers.

28. Ibid.

29. Ibid.

30. *New York Times*, July 6, 1968, p. 42.

29. Lawyers and Clients in the Twentieth Century

JEROLD S. AUERBACH

[Editors' Note: This essay was originally published as a review article of two works: *The Autobiographical Notes of Charles Evans Hughes*, ed. David J. Danelski and Joseph S. Tulchin (1973) and William H. Harbaugh, *Lawyer's Lawyer: The Life of John W. Davis* (1973). Quotations not otherwise cited are taken from one or the other of these works. Specific page references can be found in the original publication.]

1. These themes are explored in Lawrence M. Friedman, *A History of American Law* (New York, 1973), 525-566; J. Willard Hurst, *The Growth of American Law: The Law Makers* (Boston, 1950), 249-375; Robert Wiebe, *The Search for Order, 1877-1920* (*The Making of America*, ed. David Donald) (New York, 1967), 111-117; Robert Stevens, "Two Cheers for 1870: The American Law School," in Donald Fleming and Bernard Bailyn, eds., *Law in American History* (Boston, 1972), 416-441. For patterns of legal thought, a subject beyond the scope of this review, see Morton Horwitz, "The Emergence of an Instrumental Conception of American Law, 1780-1820," *Law in American History*, 287–326.

2. See O. Koegel, *Walter S. Carter, Collector of Young Masters* (New York, 1953), 68-80.

3. See William Miller, "American Lawyers in Business and in Politics," *Yale Law Journal*, 60 (1951), 66-76. Among those eligible by age to enter law school between 1905 and 1910, fewer than 4 percent had finished high school and college, a proportion higher than in Hughes's and Davis's student days. Christopher Jencks and David Riesman, *The Academic Revolution* (New York, 1968), 77.

4. Harlan B. Phillips, ed., *Felix Frankfurter Reminisces* (New York, 1960), 27.

5. See Moses Rischin, ed., *The American Gospel of Success* (Chicago, 1965), 8-9. For related developments in the legal profession, see Jerold S. Auerbach, "Enmity and

Amity: Law Teachers and Practitioners, 1900-1922," in *Law in American History*, 551-601.

6. Alexander Bickel, "Watergate and the Legal Order," *Commentary* (January 1974), 25.

7. Letter from Felix Frankfurter to Learned Hand, October 3, 1924, quoted in Sanford V. Levinson, "The Democratic Faith of Felix Frankfurter," *Stanford Law Review*, 25 (1973), 437.

30. American Jurisprudence between the Wars: Legal Realism and the Crisis of Democratic Theory

EDWARD A. PURCELL, JR.

1. Edward S. Robinson, *Law and the Lawyers* (New York, 1935), 49.

2. Wesley C. Mitchell, "The Prospects of Economics," in R. G. Tugwell, ed., *The Trend of Economics* (New York, 1935), 22.

3. For examples, see Charles Merriam, *New Aspects of Politics* (Chicago, 1925); Bronislaw Malinowski, Introduction to Robert I. Hogbin, *Law and Order in Polynesia*, 2d ed. (Hamden, Conn., 1961).

4. Charles A. Beard, *The Discussion of Human Affairs* (New York, 1936), 119-120. See also Beard, "Written History as an Act of Faith," *American Historical Review*, 39 (1934), 219-229; Carl L. Becker, "Everyman His Own Historian," ibid., 37 (1932), 221-236; Ruth Benedict, *Patterns of Culture* (New York, 1934).

5. See Roscoe Pound's original attack, "Mechanical Jurisprudence," *Columbia Law Review*, 8 (1908), 605-623; Edwin W. Patterson, *Jurisprudence: Men and Ideas of the Law* (Brooklyn, N.Y., 1953), 465-466; and Wilfred E. Rumble, Jr., *American Legal Realism: Skepticism, Reform, and the Judicial Process* (Ithaca, 1968), 49-51.

6. Oliver Wendell Holmes, Jr., "The Path of the Law," in Max Lerner, ed., *The Mind and Faith of Justice Holmes* (New York, 1943), 72, 76.

7. John Chipman Gray, *The Nature and Sources of the Law*, 2d ed. (Boston, 1963), 99-101, 168-73. For the "Brandeis brief," see the account in Robert E. Cushman and R. F.

Cushman, *Cases in Constitutional Law* (New York, 1958), 580.

8. Pound, "Mechanical Jurisprudence," 609.

9. Eighteen of the twenty-two were taken from Karl Llewellyn's initial identification of those whom he considered leading realists, in Llewellyn, "Some Realism about Realism," *Harvard Law Review*, 44 (1931), 1222-64. The eighteen are Underhill Moore, Herman Oliphant, Charles E. Clark, Llewellyn, Jerome Frank, Walter Wheeler Cook, Thomas Reed Powell, Leon Green, Max Radin, William O. Douglas, Hessel E. Yntema, Edwin W. Patterson, Arthur L. Corbin, Wesley A. Sturges, Leon Tulin, Joseph F. Francis, Joseph W. Bingham, and E. G. Lorenzen. Biographical information was unavailable for two of Llewellyn's original twenty (Joseph C. Hutcheson and Samuel Klaus). Four other scholars (Walter Nelles, Thurman Arnold, Robinson, and Felix S. Cohen) have impressed me as significant contributors to realism and have been added for that reason. The list does not include such younger realists as Myres McDougal or Fred Rodell. Brief biographical material on most of the realists is available in Association of American Law Schools, *Directory of Teachers in Member Schools* (St. Paul, Minn., 1922-1941).

10. Benjamin N. Cardozo, "Jurisprudence," in Margaret Hall, ed., *Selected Writings of . . . Cardozo* (New York, 1947), 8.

11. "Address of Elihu Root," *American Law Institute, Proceedings*, vol. I, pt 2 (1923), 48, cited in Rumble, *American Legal Realism*, 156. On the growth of case law, see also Benjamin N. Cardozo, *The Growth of the Law* (New Haven, 1924), 1, 3-5, 16.

12. Grant Gilmore, "Legal Realism: Its Cause and Cure," *Yale Law Journal*, 70 (1961), 1040-41.

13. Committee on the Establishment of a Permanent Organization for the Improvement of the Law, "The Law's Uncertainty and Complexity," *American Law Institute, Proceedings*, vol. I, pt 1 (1923), 66-76.

14. For a brief bibliography of the realist critique of the program of the American Law Institute, see Rumble, *American Legal Realism*, 156, n. 40.

15. Llewellyn, "A Realistic Jurisprudence — The Next Step," *Columbia Law Review,* 30 (1930), 443.

16. Ibid., 453.

17. Ibid., 439.

18. Ibid., 444.

19. Llewellyn, *The Bramble Bush* (New York, 1930), 12.

20. Idem, "Realistic Jurisprudence," 464.

21. Jerome Frank, *Law and the Modern Mind,* 2d. ed. (New York, 1963), 50.

22. Ibid., 109; see also ibid., 114-121.

23. Ibid., 159.

24. Ibid., 6.

25. Ibid., 19.

26. Ibid., 98.

27. Ibid., 65.

28. Roscoe Pound, "The Call for a Realist Jurisprudence," *Harvard Law Review,* 44 (1931), 697-711.

29. Llewellyn, "Some Realism about Realism," 1222-64. Although Llewellyn alone signed the article, he explained that it had been conceived and researched in cooperation with Frank. Because Llewellyn did the actual writing, Frank did not think he should receive credit as an author.

30. Patterson, *Jurisprudence,* 548-552.

31. Frank, *Law and the Modern Mind,* 125.

32. Joseph C. Hutcheson, Jr., "The Judgment Intuitive: The Function of the 'Hunch' in Judicial Decision," *Cornell Law Quarterly,* 14 (1929), 285.

33. Max Radin, "The Theory of Judicial Decision," *American Bar Association Journal,* 11 (1925), 359.

34. Hessel E. Yntema, "The Hornbook Method and the Conflict of Laws," *Yale Law Journal,* 37 (1928), 476.

35. Morris R. Cohen, "Positivism and the Limits of Idealism in the Law," *Columbia Law Review,* 27 (1927), 244.

36. Walter W. Cook, "Scientific Method and the Law," *American Bar Association Journal,* 13 (1927), 305.

37. Underhill Moore, "Rational Basis of Legal Institutions," *Columbia Law Review,* 23 (1923), 612.

38. Review of Cohen, *Ethical Systems,* in ibid., 33 (1933), 763, 766.

39. John Dickinson, "Legal Rules: Their Function in the Process of Decision," *University of Pennsylvania Law Review,* 79 (1931), 833-868; Hermann Kantorowicz, "Some Rationalism about Realism," *Yale Law Journal,* 43 (1934), 1240-53.

40. Hutchins's most famous attack on legal realism appeared as "The Autobiography of an Ex-Law Student," reprinted in *No Friendly Voice* (Chicago, 1936), 41-50; Mortimer Adler, "Legal Certainty," *Columbia Law Review,* 31 (1931), 82-115.

41. Review of Llewellyn, *Bramble Bush,* in *Yale Law Journal,* 40 (1931), 1121. For an example of the relationship between legal realism and political reform, see Jerome Frank, "Modern Trends in Jurisprudence," *American Law School Review,* 7 (1934), 1063-69.

42. Robinson, *Law and the Lawyers,* 225; see also review of H. E. Burtt, *Legal Psychology,* in *Yale Law Journal,* 41 (1932), 1106.

43. Thurman Arnold, *The Symbols of Government,* 2d ed. (New York, 1962), xiv; see also ibid., 10, 17, 34, 98.

44. Rufus C. Harris, "Idealism Emergent in Jurisprudence," *Tulane Law Review,* 10 (1936), 169-187; Philip Mecham, "The Jurisprudence of Despair," *Iowa Law Review,* 21 (1936), 669-672; review of Robinson, *Law and the Lawyers,* in *Cornell Law Quarterly,* 22 (1936), 171-178; and review of Arnold, *Symbols,* in *Illinois Law Review,* 21 (1936), 411-418.

45. Edgar Bodenheimer, *Jurisprudence* (New York, 1940), 316.

46. Roscoe Pound, *Contemporary Juristic Theory* (Claremont, Claifornia, 1940), 9; see also ibid., 1, 8-11.

47. Lon L. Fuller, *The Law in Quest of Itself,* 2d ed. (Boston, 1966), 89, 122; see also ibid., 4-6, 11, 64-65.

48. Clarence Manion, "The American Metaphysics in Law," *Proceedings of the American Catholic Philosophical Association,* 18 (1942), 133-134. For examples of the Catholic critique, see Miriam T. Rooney, "Law and the New Logic," ibid., 16 (1940), 192-222; Brendan F. Brown, "Natural Law and the Law-Making Function in American Jurisprudence," *Notre Dame Lawyer,* 15 (1939), 9-25; Frederick deSloovere, "Natural

Law and Current Sociological Jurisprudence," *Proceedings of the American Catholic Philosophical Association,* 17 (1941), 137-142; Dietrich von Hildebrand, "The Dethronement of Truth," ibid., 18 (1942), 3-16; and Paul L. Gregg, "The Pragmatism of Mr. Justice Holmes," *Georgetown Law Journal,* 31 (1943), 262-295.

49. Francis E. Lucey, "Natural Law and Americal Legal Realism," ibid., 30 (1942), 526, 533.

50. Walter Lippmann, *An Inquiry into the Principles of the Good Society* (Boston, 1937), 380.

51. Hans Kohn et al., *The City of Man: A Declaration on World Democracy* (New York, 1940), 19.

52. Raoul E. Desvernine, "Philosophy and Order in Law," *Proceedings of the American Catholic Philosophical Association,* 17 (1941), 135-136.

53. William Franklin Sands, "What Is an American?," *Commonweal,* 33 (February 21, 1941), 438.

54. See also Moorehouse F. X. Millar, "The Origins of Sound Democratic Principles in Catholic Tradition," *Catholic Historical Review,* 14 (1928), 104-126, and "Scholastic Philosophy and American Political Theory," *Thought,* 1 (1936), 112-136; Raoul E. Desvernine, "The Creed of Americanism," *Notre Dame Lawyer,* 17 (1942), 216-226; Robert I. Gannon, "What Are We Really Fighting?," *Fordham Law Review,* 11 (1942), 249-254; Goetz Briefs, "Philosophy of the Democratic State," *Proceedings of the American Catholic Philosophical Association,* 15 (1939), 36-50; and Patrick J. Roche, *Democracy in the Light of Four Current Educational Philosophies* (Washington, 1942).

55. Max Radin, "In Defense of an Unsystematic Science of Law," *Yale Law Journal,* 51 (1942), 1275.

56. Karl N. Llewellyn, "On Reading and Using the Newer Jurisprudence," *Columbia Law Review,* 40 (1940), 593, 603.

57. Yntema, "Jurisprudence on Parade," *Michigan Law Review,* 39 (1941), 1164-65; Patterson, Foreword to Edwin N. Garlan, *Legal Realism and Justice* (New York, 1941), viii; Cohen, "The Problems of a Functional Jurisprudence," *Modern Law Review,* 1

(1937), 24-25; Frank, *If Men Were Angels* (New York, 1942), Appendix V, esp. 297-300.

58. Frank, *Fate and Freedom* (New York, 1945), 295; see also ibid., 98-99. 259-260.

59. Idem, Preface to Sixth Printing of *Law and the Modern Mind,* xx.

60. Karl N. Llewellyn, "On the Good, the True, the Beautiful, in Law," *University of Chicago Law Review,* 9 (1942), 224, 247.

61. Idem, "One Realist's View of Natural Law for Judges," *Notre Dame Lawyer,* 15 (1939), 3, 8.

62. Idem, "On the Good, the True, the Beautiful," 264.

63. Max Radin, "The Education of a Lawyer," *California Law Review,* 25 (1937), 688.

64. Idem, *Law as Logic and Experience* (New Haven, 1940), 156-158.

65. "Walter Wheeler Cook," in *My Philosophy of Law: Credos of Sixteen American Scholars* (Boston, 1941), 64.

66. Yntema, "Jurisprudence on Parade," 1163.

67. Review of Lon L. Fuller, *The Law in Quest of Itself,* in *Iowa Law Review,* 26 (1940), 162-173.

68. Myres S. McDougal, "Fuller v. the Americal Legal Realists: An Intervention," *Yale Law Journal,* 50 (1941), 840.

69. Fred Rodell, *Woe unto You, Lawyers!,* 2d ed. (New York, 1957), 149.

70. "Walter B. Kennedy," in *My Philosophy of Law,* 151-152.

71. "Walter Wheeler Cook," in ibid., 64.

31. The New Property

CHARLES A. REICH

1. Stewart v. District of Columbia, 35 A.2d 247, 248 (D.C. Munic. Ct. App. 1943).

2. Wignall v.. Fletcher, 303 N.Y. 435, 441 (1952). See also Hecht v. Monaghan, 307 N.Y. 461 (1954).

3. CAB v. Delta Air Lines, Inc., 367 U.S. 316 (1961).

4. Thompson v. Gleason, 317 F. 2d 901, 906 (D.C. Cir. 1962).

5. Sherbert v. Verner, 374 U.S. 398 (1963).

6. Copper Plumbing & Heating Co. v. Campbell, 290 F.2d 368, 370-371 (D.C. Cir. 1961).

7. Green v. Silver, 207 F. Supp. 133 (D.D.C. 1962). The court held that the finding that the applicant lacked good moral character was not supported and ordered the issuance of a license.

8. Brown v. Tobriner, 218 F. Supp. 754 (D.D.C. 1963).

9. The dangers of contesting are shown by Nadiak v. CAB, 305 F.2d 588 (5th Cir. 1962). A pilot of twelve years' experience was suspended for sixty days because of a minor violation. He contested this order and appealed to the Civil Aeronautics Board. The Board commenced a full-scale investigation of his entire twelve-year career, an investigation which ended with revocation of all of his certificates for a minimum period of one year (ibid., 590-591).

10. Hecht v. Monaghan, 307 N.Y. 461 (1954).

11. See Nadiak v. CAB (above, note 9), which according to the Court "took over 8 months to complete, covering several thousand miles and brought in to review 12 years of [the pilot's] professional career."

12. Lawson v. Housing Authority, 270 Wis. 269, 287 (1955).

32. Judicial Review and Basic Liberties

JOHN P. FRANK

1. Charles Warren, *Congress, the Constitution, and the Supreme Court* (Boston, 1925), 301.

2. 261 U.S. 525 (1923).

3. Callan v. Wilson, 127 U.S. 540 (1888); United States v. Evans, 213 U.S. 297 (1909); United States v. Moreland, 258 U.S. 433 (1922).

4. Rassmussen v. United States, 197 U.S. 516 (1905).

5. 319 U.S. 463 (1943).

6. United States v. Cohen Grocery Co., 255 U.S. 81 (1921).

7. 116 U.S. 616 (1886).

8. 142 U.S. 547 (1892).

9. 4 Wall. 333 (U.S. 1867).

10. Wong Wing v. United States, 163 U.S. 228 (1896).

11. Carlson v. Landon, 342 U.S. 524 (1952).

12. United States v. Lovett, 328 U.S. 303 (1946).

13. Dred Scott v. Sandford, 19 How. 393 (U.S. 1857).

14. 92 U.S. 214 (1876).

15. 106 U.S. 629 (1883).

16. 109 U.S. 3 (1883).

17. This does not ignore, but rather puts aside, rare and minute utterances such as Joint Anti-Fascist Refugee Committee v. McGrath, 341 U.S. 123 (1951), and Lovett's case, cited above, n. 12.

18. Holmes, "Law and the Court," Harold Laski, ed., *Collected Legal Papers of Oliver Wendell Holmes* (New York, 1921).

19. Harold H. Burton, "The Cornerstone of Constitutional Law: The Extraordinary Case of Marbury v. Madison," *American Bar Association Journal*, 36 (1950), 805, 882.

20. Martin v. Hunter's Lessee, 1 Wheat. 304 (U.S. 1816); Cohens v. Virginia, 6 Wheat. 264 (U.S. 1821).

21. The form of this reaction is described in Charles Warren, *The Supreme Court in United States History* (Boston, 1924), 526ff.

22. 283 U.S. 697 (1931); 301 U.S. 242 (1937); 303 U.S. 444 (1938).

23. Youngstown Sheet & Tube Co. v. Sawyer, 343 U.S. 579 (1952).

24. 4 Wall. 2 (U.S. 1866).

25. 317 U.S. 1 (1942).

26. Duncan v. Kahanamoku, 327 U.S. 304 (1946).

27. Gitlow v. New York, 268 U.S. 652 (1925).

28. 4 Wall. 277 (U.S. 1867).

29. 250 U.S. 616 (1919).

30. 54 Stat. 670, 671 (1940), 18 U.S.C. sections 10, 11, 13 (1946); H.R. No. 9766, 76th Cong., 3d sess., 1940; 61 Stat. 146 (1947), 29 U.S.C., sec. 159h (Suppl., 1951); 64 Stat. 987 (1950), 50 U.S.C. sec. 781 (Suppl. 1952).

31. *Marbury* v. *Madison* and the *Dred Scott* decision are the sole instances of judicial review (in the sense used here) up to 1865.

32. Zechariah Chafee, book review, *Harvard Law Review*, 42 (1949), 894.

33. Minersville School District v. Gobitis, 310 U.S. 586 (1940).

34. The ex *cathedra* status of such memoranda is based on a composite of impres-

sions from the bills under discussion. The most striking example, however, is furnished by the McCarran Act debate, in which the brief of the American Bar Association "Standing Committee on Bill of Rights" played a leading role in upholding assertions of the act's constitutionality.

35. See, for example, the reception accorded the lengthy legal statements of a dozen witnesses appearing in opposition to the McCarran bill, in *Hearings before House Committee on Un-American Activities on H.R. 3903 and H.R. 7595*, 81st Cong., 2d sess., 1950. Most briefs received no countering constitutional argument at all; some, a few offhand remarks.

36. See, e.g., ibid., 2136.

37. See, e.g., *Congressional Record*, 96 (1950), 14299, 15254-58.

38. 277 U.S. 274 (1928).

39. Louisville Joint Stock Land Bank v. Radford, 295 U.S. 555 (1935).

40. The new Frazier-Lemke Act, drafted to overcome the objections of the Radford case, was upheld in Wright v. Vinton Branch of the Mountain Trust Bank, 300 U.S. 440 (1937).

41. The latest survey of content analysis repeatedly stresses that only a measurement of the content of verbal communication is ordinarily attempted with the new method and that it "is not normally done directly in terms of the latent intentions which the content may express nor the latent responses which it may elicit" (Bernard Berelson, *Content Analysis in Communications Research* [Glencoe, Ill., 1952], 16).

42. Senate Committee on Labor and Public Welfare, *Hearings on S. 55 and S. J. Res. 22*, 80th Cong., 1st sess., 1947, p. 1476.

43. *Congressional Record*, 93 (1947), 3626-29, 3633-34.

44. 54 Stat. 670, 671 (1940), 18 U.S.C. secs. 10, 11, 13 (1946).

45. *Congressional Record*, 84 (1939), 10359, 10452.

46. Ibid., 86 (1940), 3844-45.

47. Ibid., 84 (1939), 10452.

48. Ibid., 93 (1947), 4875-76.

49. "I cannot believe the Supreme Court would uphold such a law [she then reads entirely irrelevant excerpts from Jones &

Loughlin and J. I. Case.] No, Mr. Chairman, I do not believe the Supreme Court would uphold H.R. 3020" (ibid., 93 [1947], 3650).

50. Ibid., 86 (1940), 8213. Other examples of this approach are in hearings on the McCarran Act. Rep. Harrison: "Even if such legislation as this were struck down by a divided decision of the Court, wouldn't the enactment of it and subsequent decisions have a salutary effect on public opinion in directing the attention of the rank and file of the people to the Communist menace?" Or testimony of Omar B. Ketcham, witness for the Veterans of Foreign Wars: "No one can say such a law is unconstitutional until it has been interpreted by the Supreme Court of the United States" (House Committee on Un-American Activities, *Hearings* [cited above, n. 35], 2154, 2144.

51. *Congressional Record*, 86 (1940), 8205.

52. Ibid., 8345.

53. Ibid., 8183.

54. Ibid., 8200.

55. Ibid., 8201.

56. 76th Cong. 3d sess., 1940, *Senate Report*, no. 2031.

57. 81st Cong. 2d sess., 1950, *H.R. Report*, no. 2980, p. 5. This position was foreclosed for many Republicans since Governor Dewey had said in the 1948 campaign that he opposed outlawing the Communist Party "because it is a violation of the Constitution of the United States and of the Bill of Rights, and clearly so" (quoted in *Congressional Record*, 96 [1950], 15698).

58. 76th Cong., 1st sess., 1939, *H.R. Report*, no. 994, p. 5.

59. For discussion, see 81st Cong., 2d sess., 1950, *Sen. Report*, no. 2369, pt. 2, p. 7 (minority report).

60. 64 Stat. 1019 (1950), 50 U.S.C. secs. 811-826 (Suppl., 1952).

61. *Congressional Record*, 96 (1950), 14548. See also the statement of Senator Ferguson, ibid., 14585: "Mr. President, the substitute bill would wipe out . . . every known constitutional provision for the protection of the rights and liberties of the people of the United States, including the right to be tried by due process of law and by a jury of one's peers."

62. 64 Stat. 1021-8 (1950), 50 U.S.C. secs. 813-20 (Suppl. 1952).

63. *Congressional Record,* 96 (1950), 14548, 14551.

64. 64 Stat. 1022, 1023, 1025, 1026 (1950), 50 U.S.C. secs 814-d, f, secs. 819-c, g (Suppl. 1952).

65. *Congressional Record,* 96 (1950), 14548, 14578, 14593. Outrage over this threat to constitutional liberties evoked extremes of oratorical fury.

66. 64 Stat. 1022, 1023, 1025, 1026 (1950), cited above, n. 64.

67. See, for an outstanding example, impeachment proceedings in the Senate against Federal District Judge James H. Peck, reported fully in A. J. Stansbury, *Report of the Trial of James H. Peck* (1833). Peck had invoked the contempt power against editorial criticism of one of his decisions; the resulting trial treated Congress to a brilliant discussion of First Amendment limitations.

68. For a description of the sectional nature of the vote, see Henry Wilson, *History of the Rise and Fall of the Slave Power in America,* 3 vols. (Boston, 1872-1877), I, 432.

33. Toward Neutral Principles of Constitutional Law

HERBERT WECHSLER

1. See Henry B. Adams, *History of the United States of America during the Second Administration of Thomas Jefferson* (New York 1890), V, 267: "If Congress had the right to regulate commerce for such a purpose in 1808, South Carolina seemed to have no excuse for questioning, twenty years later, the constitutionality of a protective system."

2. Idem, *History of the United States of America during the First Administration of Thomas Jefferson* (New York, 1889), II, 90: "The Louisiana treaty gave a fatal wound to 'strict construction,' and the Jeffersonian theories never again received support. In thus giving them up, Jefferson did not lead the way, but he allowed his friends to drag him in the path they chose."

3. In his annual message of October 27, 1807, Jefferson said: "I shall think it my duty to lay before you the proceedings and the evidence publicly exhibited on the arraignment of the principal offenders before the curcuit court of Virginia. You will be enabled to judge whether the defect was in the testimony, in the law, or in the administration of the law; and wherever it shall be found, the Legislature alone can apply or originate the remedy. The framers of our Constitution certainly supposed that they had guarded as well their Government against destruction by treason as their citizens against oppression under pretense of it, and if these ends are not attained it is of importance to inquire by what means more effectual they may be secured." Quoted from James D. Richardson, *Messages and Papers of the Presidents, 1789-1897* (Washington, 1896-1899), I, 429.

4. See Yates v. United States, 354 U.S. 298, 318 (1957).

5. Oliver W. Holmes, "Law and the Court," in *Collected Legal Papers* (New York, 1920), 291, 292.

6. Learned Hand, *The Bill of Rights* (Cambridge, Mass., 1958), 65.

7. Ibid., 42.

8. Robert M. Jackson, *The Supreme Court in the American System of Government* (Cambridge, Mass., 1955), 76.

9. Felix Frankfurter, "Chief Justices I Have Known," in Philip Elman, ed., *Of Law and Men: Papers and Addresses, 1939-1956* (New York, 1956), 138.

10. Principality of Monaco v. Mississippi, 292 U.S. 313, 322 (1934).

11. Oliver W. Holmes, "Holdsworth's English Law," in *Collected Legal Papers* (New York, 1920), 285, 290.

12. Passenger Cases, 48 U.S. (7 How.) 83, 470 (1849).

13. Hand, *The Bill of Rights,* 30.

14. See Reid v. Covert, 354 U.S. 1 (1957), *reversing on hearing* 351 U.S. 487 (1956).

15. See Green v. United States, 355 U.S. 184 (1957).

16. "Throughout the eighteenth century counsel were allowed to speak in cases of treason and misdemeanour only" Sir James F. Stephen, *A History of the Criminal Law of England,* 3 vols. (London, 1883), I, 453.

17. See Johnson v. Zerbst, 304 U.S. 458 (1938).

18. Walker v. Johnston, 312 U.S. 275 (1941).

19. Benajmin F. Wright, *Consensus and Continuity, 1776-1787* (Boston, 1958), passim.

20. "Despite arguments to the contrary which had seemed to me persuasive, it is settled that the due process clause of the Fourteenth Amendment applies to matters of substantive law as well as to matters of procedure" (Whitney v. California, 274 U.S. 357, 373 [1927] [concurring opinion]).

21. Otis v. Parker, 187 U.S. 606, 609 (1903).

22. Joseph Burstyn, Inc. v. Wilson, 343 U.S. 495 (1952).

23. Id. at 506.

24. Gelling v. Texas, 343 U.S. 960, *reversing per curiam* 157 Tex. Crim. 516, 247 S.W.2d 95 (1952) (ordinance prohibited exhibition of picture deemed by censorship board "of such character as to be prejudicial to the best interests of the people" of Marshall, Texas, "if publicly shown").

25. Attention should be called to Kingsley Int'l Pictures Corp. v. Regents of the Univ. of N.Y., 360 U.S. 684 (1959). The Court was unanimous in holding invalid New York's refusal to license the exhibition of a film based on D. H. Lawrence's *Lady Chatterley's Lover*. The opinion of the Court by Mr. Justice Stewart, deeming the censorship order to rest solely on the ground that the picture portrays an adulterous relationship as an acceptable pattern of behavior, held the statute so construed an unconstitutional impairment of freedom to disseminate ideas. Justices Black and Douglas joined in the opinion, but in brief concurrences expressed their view that any prior restraint on motion pictures is as vulnerable as is the censorship of newspapers or books. Mr. Justice Frankfurter in one opinion and Mr. Justice Harlan in another, joined by Justices Frankfurter and Whittaker, conceived of the New York statute as demanding some showing of obscenity or of incitement. Hence the statute was invalid as applied.

26. Brown v. Board of Educ., 347 U.S. 483 (1954). See also Bolling v. Sharpe, 347 U.S. 497 (1954), dealing with segregation in the District of Columbia.

27. Brown v. Board of Educ., 349 U.S. 294 (1955).

28. Cooper v. Aaron, 358 U.S. 1 (1958).

29. New York City Park Improvement Ass'n v. Detiege, 358 U.S. 54, *affirming per curiam* 252 F.2d 122 (5th Cir. 1958); Gayle v. Browder, 352 U.S. 903, *affirming per curiam* 142 F. Supp. 707 (M.D. Ala. 1956); Holmes v. City of Atlanta, 350 U.S. 879, *reversing per curiam* 223 F.2d 93 (5th Cir. 1955); Mayor & City Council v. Dawson, 350 U.S. 877, *affirming per curiam* 220 F.2d 386 (4th Cir. 1955); Muir v. Louisville Park Theatrical Ass'n, 347 U.S. 971 (1954), *reversing per curiam* 202 F.2d 275 (6th Cir. 1953).

30. Ernest J. Brown, "Foreword: Process of Law, The Supreme Court, 1957 Term," *Harvard Law Review*, 72 (1958), 77.

31. 247 U.S. 251 (1918).

32. Carter v. Carter Coal Co., 298 U.S. 238 (1936).

33. United States v. Butler, 297 U.S. 1 (1936).

34. See Herbert Wechsler, "The Political Safeguards of Federalism: The Role of the States in the Composition and Selection of the National Government," *Columbia Law Review*, 54 (1954), reprinted in Arthur W. MacMahon, ed., *Federalism, Mature and Emergent* (Garden City, N.Y., 1955), 97.

35. Northern Sec. Co. v. United States, 193 U.S. 197, 403 (1904) (dissenting opinion).

36. Pennsylvania Coal Co. v. Mahon, 260 U.S. 393, 412 (1922).

37. See, e.g., Kovacs v. Cooper, 336 U.S. 77, 88 (1949).

38. Mark DeWolfe Howe, ed., *Holmes-Pollock Letters: The Correspondence of Mr. Justice Holmes and Sir Frederick Pollock, 1874-1932* (Cambridge, Mass., 1941), II, 25; see Mark DeWolfe Howe, ed., *Holmes-Laski Letters; The Correspondence of Mr. Justice Holmes and Harold J. Laski, 1916-1935* (Cambridge, Mass., 1953), I, 203, 529-30; cf. II, 888.

39. Abrams v. United States, 250 U.S. 616, 624 (1919); Gitlow v. New York, 268 U.S. 652, 672 (1925).

40. "I do not doubt for a moment that by the same reasoning that would justify punishing persuasion to murder, the United States constitutionally may punish speech that produces or is intended to produce a clear and imminent danger that it will bring about forthwith certain substantive evils that the United States constitutionally may seek to prevent" (Abrams v. United States, 250 U.S. 616, 627 [1919].

41. Sweezy v. New Hampshire, 354 U.S. 234 (1957).

42. See Uphaus v. Wyman, 360 U.S. 72, 77 (1959): "Since questions concerning the authority of the committee to act as it did are questions of state law, . . . we accept as controlling the New Hampshire Supreme Court's conclusion that 'the legislative history makes it clear beyond a reasonable doubt that it [the Legislature] did and does desire an answer to these questions.' "

43. Smith v. Allwright, 321 U.S. 649 (1944).

44. Shelley v. Kraemer, 334 U.S. 1 (1948), Barrows v. Jackson, 346 U.S. 249 (1953).

45. Brown v. Board of Education, 347 U.S. 483 (1954).

46. See Brooks Adams, "The Heritage of Henry Adams," in Henry Adams, *The Degradation of the Democratic Dogma* (New York, 1919), 22, 31.

47. Korematsu v. United States, 323 U.S. 214 (1944).

48. See *Newsweek*, December 29, 1958, 23.

49. See, e.g., Ex parte Virginia, 100 U.S. 339, 347 (1880); Robert L. Hale, *Freedom Through Law: Public Control of Private Governing Power* (New York, 1952), chap. 11.

50. See Nixon v. Condon, 286 U.S. 73 (1932); Nixon v. Herndon, 273 U.S. 536 (1927).

51. Grovey v. Townsend, 295 U.S. 45 (1935).

52. United States v. Classic, 313 U.S. 299 (1941).

53. "The House of Representatives shall be composed of Members chosen every second Year by the People of the several States, and the Electors in each State shall have the Qualifications requisite for Electors of the most numerous Branch of the State Legislature." The Seventeenth Amendment contains similar provisions for the choice of Senators.

54. The Government brief in *Classic* stated with respect to *Grovey*: "Moreover, what Article I, Section 2 secures is the right to choose. The implicit premise of the *Grovey* decision is that the negroes excluded from the Democratic primary were legally free to record their choice by joining an opposition party or by organizing themselves. In the present case the voters exercise the right to choose in accordance with the contemplated method; and the wrong alleged deprived them of an opportunity to express their choice in any other way" (Brief for the United States, 34-35, United States v. Classic, 313 U.S. 299 [1941].)

55. 321 U.S. 649 (1944). Mr. Justice Frankfurter concurred only in the result. Mr. Justice Roberts alone dissented.

56. Terry v. Adams, 345 U.S. 461 (1953). See also Rice v. Elmore, 165 F.2d 387 (4th Cir. 1947), *cert. denied*, 333 U.S. 875 (1948). There is no opinion of the Court in *Terry*. Justices Douglas and Burton joined in an opinion by Justice Black. Justice Frankfurter, saying that he found the case "by no means free of difficulty," wrote for himself. Chief Justice Vinson and Justices Reed and Jackson joined in an opinion by Justice Clark. Justice Minton dissented.

57. See Shelley v. Kraemer, 334 U.S. 1, 14-23 (1948).

58. Cf. Gordon v. Gordon, 332 Mass. 196, 210, 124 N.E. 2d 228, 236, *cert. denied*, 349 U.S. 947 (1955).

59. See Charlotte Park & Recreation Comm'n. v. Barringer, 242 N.C. 311, 88 S.E.2d 114 (1955), *cert. denied*, 350 U.S. 983 (1956).

60. Mr. Chief Justice Vinson, dissenting in Barrows v. Jackson, 346 U.S. 249, 260 (1953), urged a distinction between enforcement of the covenant by injunction, the problem in *Shelley*, and an action for damages against a defaulting covenantor by a co-covenantor. He was alone in his dissent.

61. Pennsylvania v. Board of Directors, 353 U.S. 230, 231 (1957).

62. Girard College Trusteeship, 391 Pa. 434, 441-442, 138 A.2d 844, 846 (1958).

63. Pennsylvania v. Board of Directors, 357 U.S. 570 (1958).

64. 351 U.S. 292 (1956).

65. Attention also should be called to Dorsey v. Stuyvesant Town Corp., 299 N.Y. 512, 87 N.E.2d 541 (1949), holding state action not involved in racial discrimination in the selection of tenants by the owner corporation, although the housing development involved had been constructed with the aid of New York City, which, pursuant to a contract authorized by statute, had condemned the land for the corporation and granted substantial tax exemptions. Certiorari was denied, 339 U.S. 981 (1950), Justices Black and Douglas noting their dissent.

66. See, e.g., William R. Ming, "Racial Restrictions and the Fourteenth Amendment: The Restrictive Covenant Cases," *University of Chicago Law Review*, 16 (1949), 203, 235-38.

67. See, e. g., Adolf A. Berle, Jr., "Constitutional Limitations on Corporate Activity — Protection of Personal Rights from Invasion through Economic Power," *University of Pennsylvania Law Review*, 100, (1952), 933, 948-951; Adolf A. Berle, Jr., *Economic Power and the Free Society* (New York, 1957), 17-18.

68. See Alexander M. Bickel, "The Original Understanding and the Segregation Decision," *Harvard Law Review*, 69 (1955), 1.

69. See Paul A. Freund, "Storm over the American Supreme Court," *Modern Law Review*, 21 (1958), 345, 351.

70. Hand, *Bill of Rights*, 54.

71. For a detailed account of the character and quality of research in this field, see note, "Grade School Segregation: The Latest Attack on Racial Discrimination," *Yale Law Journal*, 61 (1952), 730.

72. See Record, 125-26, 132 (Hugh W. Speer), Brown v. Board of Education, 347 U.S. 483 (1954); id. at 164-165 (Wilbur B. Brookover); id. at 170-171 (Louisa Holt); id. at 176-179 (John J. Kane).

73. See Record, 548-555, 568-572 (Henry E. Garrett), Davis v. County Board of Education, 347 U.S. 483 (1954).

74. Motive is open to examination when executive action is challenged as discriminatory, but there the purpose is to show that an admitted inequality of treatment was not inadvertent. See, e.g., Snowden v. Hughes, 321 U.S. 1 (1944). Even in such a case, invidious motivation alone has not been held to establish the inequality.

75. Plessy v. Ferguson, 163 U.S. 537, 551 (1896).

76. See Ham Say Naim v. Naim, 197 Va. 80, 87 S.E.2d 749, *vacated*, 350 U.S. 891 (1955), *on remand*, 197 Va. 734, 90 S.E.2d 849, *appeal dismissed*, 350 U.S. 985 (1956).

77. See Arthur E. Sutherland, *The Law and One Man among Many* (Madison, 1956), 35-62.

CONTRIBUTORS

JEROLD AUERBACH Associate Professor of History, Wellesley College

ARTHUR E. BESTOR Professor of History, University of Washington

RICHARD MAXWELL BROWN Beekman Professor of Northwest and Pacific History, University of Oregon

WILLIAM COHEN Associate Professor of History, Hope College

DAVID FLAHERTY Professor of History, University of Western Ontario

JOHN P. FRANK Attorney, Phoenix, Arizona

LAWRENCE M. FRIEDMAN Marion Rice Kirkwood Professor of Law, Stanford University

PAUL W. GATES Professor of American History, Emeritus, Cornell University

JULIUS GOEBEL, JR. Late Professor of Law, Columbia University

MARK H. HALLER Professor of History, Temple University

GEORGE L. HASKINS Algernon Sydney Biddle Professor of Law, University of Pennsylvania

WILLIAM B. HIXSON, JR. Associate Professor of History, Michigan State University

MORTON J. HORWITZ Professor of Law, Harvard University

WILLARD HURST Vilas Professor of Law, University of Wisconsin

STANLEY KATZ Professor of Legal History, University of Chicago School of Law

JACK LADINSKY Professor of Sociology, University of Wisconsin

ROGER LANE Associate Professor of History, Haverford College

LEONARD W. LEVY William W. Clary Professor of History, Claremont Graduate School

CHARLES W. MCCURDY Assistant Professor of History, University of Virginia

PAULINE MAIER Robinson Professor of History, University of Wisconsin

WILLIAM E. NELSON Associate Professor of Law, Yale University

ARNOLD M. PAUL Member of the California State Bar and Lecturer in Constitutional History, University of California, Santa Barbara

DAVID POTTER Late Coe Professor of American History, Stanford University

EDWARD A. PURCELL, JR. Associate Professor of History, University of Missouri, Columbia

CHARLES A. REICH Senior Fellow, Yale Law School

DAVID ROTHMAN Professor of History, Columbia University

HARRY N. SCHEIBER Professor of History, University of California, San Diego

KENNETH M. STAMPP Morrison Professor of American History, University of California, Berkeley

S. SIDNEY ULMER Professor of Political Science, University of Kentucky

HERBERT WECHSLER Harlan Fiske Stone Professor of Law, Columbia University

WILLIAM M. WIECEK Associate Professor of History, University of Missouri, Columbia